CW01669779

Pensions Law H

Ninth Edition

by the Pensions Department of Nabarro

JOINT EDITORS

Jennifer Bell BA (HONS)
Partner

and

Susan Jones LLB (HONS)
Solicitor

Bloomsbury Professional

Disclaimer

Detailed specialist advice should be obtained before taking or refraining from any action as a result of comments made in this publication. We are also not responsible for the content of external websites to which the reader is directed in the text.

Bloomsbury Professional Ltd, 41–43 Boltro Road, Haywards Heath, West Sussex, RH16 1BJ

Previously published by Tottel Publishing Ltd

A CIP Catalogue record for this book is available from the British Library.

ISBN 978 1 84766 382 5

Typeset by Phoenix Photosetting Ltd, Chatham, Kent
Printed and bound in Great Britain by CPI Antony Rowe, Chippenham, Wiltshire

TIM BENTLEY

Pensions Law Handbook

Ninth Edition

Preface

I am delighted to introduce this ninth edition of the immensely popular Pensions Law Handbook. As always, the book has been written and revised entirely by the pension lawyers who are members of the pensions team at Nabarro, together with support from other specialised practitioners around the firm. The detailed work of editing the book has been undertaken by myself and Susan Jones.

Nabarro is one of the largest independent law practices in the UK. Its pensions team has for many years been one of its strengths. Our pension lawyers have a deep technical knowledge of their subject and advise an impressive range of clients on the areas that the book covers.

I am sure that readers will find this new edition valuable. With the overwhelming volume of legislation that continues to swamp the pensions world and the constantly changing legal and economic environment within which trustees of pension schemes, sponsoring employers and their advisers operate, I hope this new edition will be helpful to all. Readers will note that we have removed the SSAS chapter and expanded the Personal Pension Scheme chapter to include details on the new Personal Accounts regime.

All members of the pensions team have contributed to the book. I am very grateful to all of them for their hard work and dedication. The contributors are (in alphabetical order) Lucinda Barker, Rachel Bassindale, Jennifer Bell, Alison Birkitt, Helen Butler, Judith Clixby, Michael Draper, Richard Gibson, Ian Greenstreet, Louise Howard, Susan Jones, Victoria Lee, Sharon Piert, Kate Richards, Michael Rooney, Nina Sharkey, Beth Sheehan, Anne-Marie Winton and, from other specialisms, Glen Flannery, Chris Stewart, Rob Moulton and Michal Stein.

Our aim has been to state the law as at the end of August 2009. Where there have been later developments that we have been able to take into account, this is clearly stated in the text.

Jennifer Bell
Editor
Nabarro LLP

Contents

Table of Cases

PARA

C

D

PARA

E

F

G

H

PARA

N

O

P

T

U

Table of Statutes

Table of Statutory Instruments

Draft statutory instruments

Table of European Legislation

Abbreviations and References

Abbreviations

A-Day	6 April 2006
Age Regulations	Employment Equality (Age) Regulations 2006 (SI 2006/1031) as amended
APPS	appropriate personal pension scheme
AVC	additional voluntary contribution
BIS	Department for Business, Innovation and Skills (previously BERR and DTI)
Business Order	Financial Services and Markets Act 2000 (Carrying on Regulated Activities By Way of Business) Order 2001 (SI 2001/1177)
CETV	cash equivalent transfer value
Contracting-Out Regulations	Occupational Pension Schemes (Contracting-out) Regulations 1996 (SI 1996/1172) as amended
CPR 1998	Civil Procedure Rules 1998 (SI 1998/3132)
DDA 1995	Disability Discrimination Act 1995
DDA 2005	Disability Discrimination Act 2005
Disclosure Regulations	Occupational Pension Schemes (Disclosure of Information) Regulations 1996 (SI 1996/1655) as amended
DWP	Department for Work and Pensions
EAT	Employment Appeal Tribunal
ECJ	Court of Justice of the European Communities
EFRBS	Employer-Financed Retirement Benefit Scheme
Employer Debt Regulations	Occupational Pension Schemes (Employer Debt) Regulations 2005 (SI 2005/678) as amended
Equal Treatment Framework Directive	Council Directive 2000/78/EC establishing a general framework for equal treatment in employment and occupation
Equal Treatment Regulations	Occupation Pension Schemes (Equal Treatment) Regulations 1995 (SI 1995/3183) as amended
EU	European Union
ERA 1996	Employment Rights Act 1996
FA 2003/2004/2006/2007/2008/2009	Finance Act 2003/2004/2006/2007/2008/2009

FAS	Financial Assistance Scheme
FAS Regulations	Financial Assistance Scheme Regulations 2005 (SI 2005/1986) as amended
Forfeiture Regulations	Occupational Pension Schemes (Assignment, Forfeiture, Bankruptcy etc) Regulations 1997 (SI 1997/785) as amended
FSA	Financial Services Authority
FSMA 2000	Financial Services and Markets Act 2000
GMP	guaranteed minimum pension
HMRC	Her Majesty's Revenue and Customs
IA 1986	Insolvency Act 1986
IA 2000	Insolvency Act 2000
ICE	initial cash equivalent
ICTA 1988	Income and Corporation Taxes Act 1988
Investment Regulations	Occupational Pension Schemes (Investment) Regulations 2005 (SI 2005/3378) as amended
IORP	Directive 2003/41/EC of the European Parliament and Council on the activities and supervision of institutions for occupational retirement provision
IP	Insolvency Practitioner
ITEPA 2003	Income Tax (Earnings and Pensions) Act 2003
LEL	lower earnings limit
LPI	limited price indexation
MCA 1973	Matrimonial Causes Act 1973
MND	member-nominated director
MNT	member-nominated trustee
MNT Regulations	Occupational Pension Schemes (Member-nominated Trustees and Directors) Regulations 2006 (SI 2006/714) as amended
Modification Regulations	Occupational Pension Schemes (Modification of Schemes) Regulations 2006 (SI 2006/759) as amended
NAPF	National Association of Pension Funds
NICO	National Insurance Contributions Office
NISPI	National Insurance Services to Pensions Industry
NRD	normal retirement date
Ombudsman Regulations	Personal and Occupational Pension Schemes (Pension Ombudsman) Regulations 1996 (SI 1996/2475) as amended
PA 1995/2004/2007/2008	Pensions Act 1995/2004/2007/2008
PMI	Pensions Management Institute

PPF	Pension Protection Fund
Preservation Regulations	Occupational Pension Schemes (Preservation of Benefit) Regulations 1991 (SI 1991/167) as amended
Protected Rights Regulations	Personal and Occupational Pension Schemes (Protected Rights) Regulations 1996 (SI 1996/1537) as amended
PSA 1993	Pension Schemes Act 1993
Regulated Activities Order	Financial Services and Markets Act 2000 (Regulated Activities) Order 2001 (SI 2001/544)
Regulator	Pensions Regulator (as established by PA 2004, s 1)
RPSM	Registered Pension Schemes Manual
S2P	State second pension
Scheme Administration Regulations	Occupational Pension Schemes (Scheme Administration) Regulations 1996 (SI 1996/1715) as amended
Scheme Funding Regulations	Occupational Pension Schemes (Scheme Funding) Regulations 2005 (SI 2005/3377)
SERPS	State Earnings-Related Pension Scheme
SFO	scheme funding objective
SIPP	self-invested personal pension
TA 1925	Trustee Act 1925
TA 2000	Trustee Act 2000
TCGA 1992	Taxation of Chargeable Gains Act 1992
TFEU	Treaty on the Functioning of the European Union
TPAS	The Pensions Advisory Service
Transfer Regulations	Occupational Pension Schemes (Transfer Values) Regulations 1996 (SI 1996/1847) as amended
TUPE	Transfer of Undertakings (Protection of Employment) Regulations 2006 (SI 2006/246)
UCTA 1977	Unfair Contract Terms Act 1977
Winding-up Regulations 2005	Occupational Pension Schemes (Winding-up) Regulations 2005 (SI 2005/706) as amended
WRPA 1999	Welfare Reform and Pensions Act 1999

References

AC	Appeal Cases (Law Reports)
All ER	All England Law Reports
Ch	Chancery (Law Reports)
E & E	Ellis & Ellis Queen's Bench Report

ECR	European Court Reports
ICR	Industrial Cases Reports
IRLR	Industrial Relations Law Reports
KB	King's Bench (Law Reports)
OPLR	Occupational Pensions Law Reports
PBLR	Pension Benefits Law Reports
PLR	Pensions Law Reports
TC	Tax Cases
TLR	Times Law Reports
WLR	Weekly Law Reports

Chapter 1

Pension provision in the UK – an introduction

Introduction

1.1 'Pension' is defined in the Oxford English Dictionary as 'an annuity or other periodical payment made, especially by a government, a company or an employer of labour in consideration of past services or of relinquishment of rights, claims or emoluments'.

A pension scheme is an arrangement for meeting these payments. As the definition suggests, pension schemes may be either State schemes or private arrangements. Where a scheme is established by the Government, it will often be a 'pay as you go' arrangement with no advance provision being made for funding of benefits. Private pension arrangements, whether established by an employer or arranged by an individual, will usually be funded; contributions will be made by the individual and/or his employer during his working life to ensure that, when he retires, sufficient money is available to provide his pension and any other benefits which are payable.

Private pension arrangements are governed by a mixture of trust, employment, fiscal, social security and family law, which together provide the framework within which such schemes must operate. Pension provision for the public sector tends to be governed more rigidly by legislation. Many public sector schemes, including the Local Government Pension Scheme and the National Health Service Pension Scheme, are governed and administered almost exclusively by statutory instruments and are, to a degree, unaffected by other legislation. Such schemes are generally outside the scope of this book. The law relating to personal pension schemes and stakeholder pensions schemes and the new personal accounts regime is considered in CHAPTER 13.

A brief history of pension provision in the UK

1.2 The first arrangement to contain features which are recognisable in modern pension schemes was established in 1671 by HM Customs and Excise.

Originally the arrangement provided for a retiring employee to be paid a pension by his successor. By 1686 employees were required to make advance provision for their own retirement by paying contributions towards a retirement fund.

Pension protection was gradually extended to a broader range of civil servants but it was not until the *Civil Service Superannuation Act 1834* (the first enactment devoted solely to pensions) that any formal legislative framework was established. During the early nineteenth century the concept of pension provision was extended so that other employees, both in the public and private sectors, became eligible for membership of pension schemes. Insurance and life assurance schemes became available and actuarial methods for assessing risk gradually developed.

The beginning of the twentieth century saw the introduction of the first State pension scheme. In 1908 the *Old Age Pension Act* was passed giving those over 70 a non-contributory, but means-tested, pension. General taxation paid for this early State scheme although that was changed following the passing of the *National Insurance Act 1911*. At the same time, there was a continuing increase in the establishment of pension funds by large private sector employers.

The growth in pension provision prompted pressure for change in the tax treatment of pension funds and in 1920 the Royal Commission on Income Tax recommended that investment income earned by pension funds should be tax-free. The *Finance Act 1921* provided a statutory right to tax relief on contributions made to pension funds by employers and employees and on the investment income of HMRC 'approved' pension funds. To gain HMRC approval, assets constituting pension funds had to be kept separate from an employer's other assets and consequently trust funds emerged as a natural vehicle for obtaining tax approved status.

The *Finance Act 1970* established a new system of approval for occupational pension schemes. Although this was consolidated and amended in the *Income and Corporation Taxes Act 1988*, the basic underlying taxation principles for UK occupational schemes remained the same until recently (see **1.3** below).

In addition to tax legislation, various pieces of social security legislation affecting pension schemes were passed during the 1970s. These included the *Social Security Act 1973* which introduced provisions to protect members who left service or opted out of the scheme before retirement (known as 'early leavers') and the *Social Security Pensions Act 1975*. The 1980s saw the introduction of further legislation; the *Social Security Acts 1985* and *1986* extended the protection offered to early leavers and, in particular, gave them the right to transfer their benefits to another pension scheme. The various Acts passed in the 1970s and 1980s, together with the relevant provisions of the *Social Security Act 1990*, are now consolidated in the *Pension Schemes Act 1993 (PSA 1993)*.

A major review of pension provision in the UK was undertaken in the early 1990s by the Pension Law Review Committee chaired by Professor Roy Goode following what has become known as 'the Maxwell scandal'. In its report, 'Pension Law Reform' (Cm 2342-1, September 1993), the Committee made many recommendations as to how the legislative framework for pension provision could be amended to provide greater protection for employees. Many of their recommendations were adopted in the *Pensions Act 1995 (PA 1995)* which came into force on 6 April 1997. Two further significant Acts followed, namely the *Welfare Reform and Pensions Act 1999 (WRPA 1999)* and the *Child Support, Pensions and Social Security Act 2000*. The most notable changes introduced by these Acts were the introduction of new pension sharing on divorce provisions, the stakeholder pension requirements and the State second pension.

More recently, a number of consultations and reviews have been undertaken which have led to two new Acts – the *Finance Act 2004* and the *Pensions Act 2004*.

Finance Act 2004 and Pensions Act 2004

(a) The Finance Act 2004 (FA 2004)

1.3 The pensions tax simplification regime introduced by *FA 2004* follows, broadly, the proposals outlined in a consultation paper published in December 2002, 'Simplifying the taxation of pensions: increasing choice and flexibility for all'. On 6 April 2006 (known as 'A-Day'), the eight then existing taxation regimes were replaced by a single set of rules, applicable to all 'registered schemes' (the equivalent of tax approved pension schemes under the previous regime), including defined benefit and defined contribution occupational pension schemes and personal pension schemes. The main features include:

- Removal of the pre-existing HMRC limits (including the earnings cap).
- Introduction of a single lifetime limit on the amount of pension saving that attracts favourable tax treatment (known as the 'lifetime allowance'). This was initially set at £1.5 million for the tax tear 2006/2007, rising to £1.8 million by the tax year 2010/2011.
- Introduction of an annual limit on the inflows of value to an individual's pension fund (both in the form of contributions and growth) that attract favourable tax treatment (known as the 'annual allowance'). This was initially set at £215,000 for the tax year 2006/2007, rising to £255,000 by the tax year 2010/2011.

- Subject to scheme rules, the possibility for members to draw pension benefits whilst continuing to work.
- Raising of the minimum age for taking early retirement benefits from 50 to 55 from 6 April 2010.
- Removal of the tax advantages for unapproved pension schemes.
- Increased flexibility in relation to the treatment of death benefits.

Transitional provisions give a level of protection to those who, as at 6 April 2006, had rights that were inconsistent with the new regime. *FA 2004* is considered further in CHAPTER 16.

(b) The Pensions Act 2004 (PA 2004)

The main provisions of *PA 2004* are as follows:

- **The Pensions Regulator**: On 6 April 2005, the Pensions Regulator ('the Regulator') became the regulator of occupational pensions in the UK under *PA 2004, Part 1*, replacing the Occupational Pensions Regulatory Authority (Opra). The Regulator's main objectives (as set out in *PA 2004, s 5*) are to protect the benefits of members of occupational and personal pension schemes; to reduce the risk of situations arising which may lead to compensation being payable by the Pension Protection Fund (see below); and to promote and improve understanding of the good administration of work-based occupational, personal and stakeholder schemes. The Regulator has a number of powers to enable it to achieve these objectives, in addition to those previously available to Opra, including power to collect data and demand information (in certain circumstances), to issue improvement notices where the security of members' benefits is under threat, and to issue contribution notices and financial support directions where it believes that an employer is attempting to avoid its pension obligations.
- **The Pension Protection Fund**: The Board of the Pension Protection Fund was introduced under *PA 2004, Part 2* and became operational on 6 April 2005. The Board is responsible for holding, managing and applying the Pension Protection Fund (PPF) (which became operational on 6 April 2005) and the Fraud Compensation Fund (which became operational on 1 September 2005). Since 10 July 2009 the Board of the PPF has also been responsible for managing the Financial Assistance Scheme (see CHAPTER 5).

  The PPF is designed to give members of defined benefit schemes a measure of protection where their employers are in financial difficulty. The Board will assume responsibility for eligible schemes where a 'qualifying insolvency event' has occurred in relation to the employer or where an employer of a prescribed description is unlikely to be able to continue as a going concern; the scheme is unable to secure its 'protected liabilities' and there is no possibility of a scheme rescue. Once the Board has assumed responsibility for a scheme, it must provide compensation to the scheme beneficiaries in the form of pension or lump sum payments. The assets from which such compensation payments are made derive from both the assets of the schemes for which it has assumed responsibility and the levy payable by eligible schemes. The 'pension protection levy' includes a risk-based and a scheme-based element meaning that schemes with poor funding positions and weak sponsoring employers are likely to be required to pay more.

- **Funding**: With effect from 30 December 2005, *PA 2004, Part 3* replaced the statutory minimum funding requirement for defined benefit schemes with a new scheme-specific funding standard, requiring each scheme to have sufficient and appropriate assets to cover its liabilities or have a recovery plan in place to achieve that within a stated period (see CHAPTER 11).
- **Member-nominated trustees**: Employers are no longer permitted to opt out of the requirement to have member-nominated trustees (or directors) governing their pension scheme following changes made by *PA 2004, ss 241, 243*. With effect from 6 April 2006, unless the scheme is exempt, at least one-third of trustees must be member-nominated, and all of the members and pensioners (or an organisation that adequately represents them) must be allowed to participate in the initial nomination stage of the process, and at least some of the members allowed to participate in the final selection. The legislation also confers a power on the Secretary of State to substitute the requirement that one-third of the trustees be member-nominated, with the requirement that at least half be so appointed (see CHAPTER 3).
- **Trustee knowledge and understanding**: *PA 2004, ss 247–249* also introduced, with effect from 6 April 2006, the legal requirement for all trustees to be conversant with their scheme documentation and to have knowledge and understanding of pensions and trust law and of the principles underpinning investment and funding (see CHAPTER 3).
- **Business transfers**: *PA 2004, ss 257 and 258* have, with effect from 6 April 2005, increased the protection of pension rights where there is a relevant transfer within the meaning of the *Transfer of Undertakings (Protection of Employment) Regulations 2006*. The protection applies to employees who are members of (or are, or would be, entitled to be members of) an occupational pension scheme to which the employer contributes (or would be required to contribute) before the transfer. In such situations the purchaser must ensure that, after the transfer, the employee becomes eligible to be a member of an occupational or a stakeholder pension scheme and that a minimum level of contributions

or benefits is provided, depending on the type of scheme from which and to which the member transferred (see CHAPTER 14).

- **Consultation requirements**: With effect from 6 April 2006, certain employers are required under *PA 2004, ss 259–261* to consult employees and/or their representatives before making certain prescribed changes to pension arrangements, including, for example, closing a scheme to future accrual, changing from a defined benefit scheme to a defined contribution scheme and reducing or removing the requirement for an employer to contribute to a defined contribution scheme (see CHAPTER 7).
- **Amendment power**: *PA 1995, s 67* was amended with effect from 6 April 2006, giving occupational pension schemes greater freedom to amend their rules in order to adapt to changing circumstances and to reduce administrative costs and complexity (see CHAPTER 12).
- **Early leavers**: *PA 2004* amends *PSA 1993* with effect from 6 April 2006, to provide protection for the pension benefits of early leavers with between three months and two years' pensionable service. Members falling within this category have the right to opt for either a cash transfer sum (cash equivalent) or a contribution refund on leaving the scheme (see CHAPTER 6).
- **Winding up priority**: A new statutory priority order was introduced by *PA 2004, s 270* for schemes that commenced winding up on or after 6 April 2005. The new priority order aligns the statutory winding-up priorities with the PPF provisions, the intention being to ensure that the benefits provided for members on the winding-up of a scheme are no less than would have been provided by the PPF had the Board assumed responsibility for the scheme (see CHAPTER 12).
- **Increases to pensions in payment**: The limited price indexation (LPI) requirement contained in *PA 1995, s 51* (which provides for statutory increases to be made to pensions in payment) is reduced from a revaluation percentage based on retail prices (RPI) capped at 5 per cent to RPI capped at 2.5 per cent in relation to defined benefits accrued after 6 April 2005. In relation to defined contribution benefits, the LPI requirement has been removed altogether for any pension that comes into payment on or after 6 April 2005 (other than pensions derived from protected rights); see **1.48** below.

Retirement provision by the State

Types of State pension

1.4 There are four categories of State retirement pensions, Category A, Category B, Category C and Category D. Entitlement to State retirement provision is principally governed by the *Social Security Contributions and Benefits Act 1992 (SSCBA 1992)* (as amended).

Category A and Category B pensions are contributory and are made up of the basic State pension and any additional element payable from the State Earnings Related Pension Scheme ('SERPS') or the State second pension ('S2P') (see **1.9** and **1.10** below). The Category A pension payable to an individual is derived from his National Insurance contribution record. The Category B pension is payable in certain circumstances by virtue of the contribution record of an individual's spouse or civil partner.

Category C and Category D pensions are non-contributory and are payable only in very restricted circumstances. Category C pensions are payable to men and women who were over State pension age on 5 July 1948 and to the spouses of those men who qualified. Certain individuals who are over age 80 may receive a Category D pension if they are not entitled to any other category of State pension or if the pension they are entitled to is less than the Category D pension.

Basic State pension

1.5 The basic State pension is payable to all individuals who have:

(*a*) reached State pension age;

(*b*) made sufficient National Insurance contributions; and

(*c*) made a claim for a State retirement pension.

The rate of the basic State pension is increased each year. From 9 April 2009, the full rate of the basic State pension is £95.25 per week for an individual (this is the basic Category A pension and the basic Category B pension payable to a person whose spouse or civil partner has died).

State pension age

1.6 The rules for determining State pension age, which are set out in *PA 1995, Sch 4, Part 1*, operate on the basis of a person's date of birth. As a rule of thumb, the more recently a person was born, the higher his State pension age will be. Following the amendments made by the *Pensions Act 2007* ('PA 2007') (which took effect from 26 September 2007), State pension age will range from 60 to 68 years of age.

A man born before 6 April 1959 reaches State pension age on his 65th birthday. A woman born before 6 April 1950 reaches State pension age on her 60th birthday and a woman born after 5 April 1955 but before 6 April 1959 reaches

State pension age on her 65th birthday. The State pension age for women born in the intervening period will be equalised to age 65 progressively over the ten years between 2010 and 2020.

People born on or after 6 April 1959 will be treated equally for the purposes of State pension age, regardless of their gender. However people within this group will be subject to a progressive increase in the State pension age to 68 over a period of 22 years beginning with 6 April 2024. The detail is set out in the tables in *PA 1995, Sch 4, Part 1.*

National Insurance contribution record

1.7 Generally, in order for an individual to qualify for a Category A or Category B State retirement pension, sufficient Class 1, Class 2 or Class 3 National Insurance contributions must have been paid or credited to him or sufficient earnings must have been credited to him (in accordance with *SSCBA 1992, Sch 3, Part 1*). From 26 September 2007 (the date on which *PA 2007* came into effect), where the contributor attains State pension age before 6 April 2010, in order to qualify for a full basic State pension those payments or credits must have been made for 44 years for a man and 39 years for a woman. Where the contributor attains State pension age on or after 6 April 2010, those payments or credits must have been made for not less than 30 years of his working life (which is a lesser requirement). Where the individual's National Insurance contribution record falls short of these requirements, a reduced basic State pension may still be payable.

An individual's 'working life' starts on 6 April immediately preceding his 16th birthday and ends on 5 April immediately preceding his attaining State pension age or his death. Usually, the working life of an individual born before 6 April 1959 will therefore be 49 years in the case of a man and between 44 and 49 years in the case of a woman depending on her State pension age. Individuals born on or after 6 April 1959 will usually have a working life of between 49 and 52 years depending on their State pension age (see **1.6** above).

The level of National Insurance contributions to be paid in respect of a person's earnings is set out in *SSCBA 1992, Part 1* and the *Social Security (Contributions) Regulations 2001*. The Class 1 National Insurance contributions payable depend on a person's earnings in relation to the primary and secondary thresholds and the lower and upper earnings limits. These are statutory measures which are prescribed each year. For the tax year 2009/2010, the primary and secondary thresholds are £5,715, the lower earnings limit (LEL) (or qualifying earnings factor) is £4,940 and the upper earnings limit (UEL) is £43,875. Class 1 National Insurance contributions are collected through the PAYE system.

Primary Class 1 National Insurance contributions are payable by employees in respect of earnings during their working lives (as described above). Employees are liable to pay Primary Class 1 contributions at the rate of 11 per cent on earnings in excess of the primary threshold but below the UEL. Additional contributions at the rate of 1 per cent are payable by employees on earnings in excess of the UEL. Employees earning between the LEL and the primary threshold do not pay primary Class 1 contributions but are treated as having done so for contributory benefit purposes.

Secondary Class 1 National Insurance contributions at the rate of 12.8 per cent are payable by employers in respect of those employees whose earnings are in excess of the secondary threshold. There is no upper limit on secondary Class 1 contributions.

Class 2 National Insurance contributions are flat rate contributions payable by the self-employed. Class 3 contributions are voluntary contributions. They can be made by an individual to boost his contribution record so as to ensure that he has sufficient contributions to entitle him to a particular benefit. Class 4 contributions are paid by the self-employed on profits in excess of the lower profit limit. For the tax year 2009/2010, Class 4 contributions are payable at 8 per cent on profits between the lower profit limit (£5,715) and upper profit limit (£43,875) and at 1 per cent on profits in excess of the upper profit limit.

The *State Pension Credit Act 2002*, which came into force over the course of 2002 and 2003, introduced a new social security benefit known as the State pension credit. It is calculated on the basis of a person's (or a couple's) existing income and consists of two main elements:

- a guarantee credit, to ensure a minimum level of income; and
- a savings credit which from age 65 (or State pension age from 6 April 2024) will provide an additional income for pensioners who have low or modest incomes on top of the basic rate pension.

Application for a State retirement pension

1.8 An individual must apply to receive the State retirement pension. The Department for Work and Pensions sends the appropriate forms to those who are eligible shortly before they reach State pension age.

Additional State pension scheme

1.9 The second element of a Category A or Category B pension is the additional earnings-related pension component. This was first brought into force in 1978 under the State Earnings-Related Pension Scheme (SERPS) which applied to certain earnings by employees from 6 April 1978 to 5 April 2002.

SERPS was replaced by the State second pension (S2P) from 6 April 2002 in order to provide a more generous additional State pension for certain categories of people (see **1.10** below). In order to receive an additional earnings-related pension the claimant must have reached State pension age. However if an individual chooses to contract out of this earnings-related pension component (see CHAPTER 4), HMRC will make an annual rebate into a contracted-out pension scheme of the individual's choice and he will not be entitled to an additional pension from the State for the period during which he is contracted out.

An individual may build up his entitlement to the additional earnings-related pension component in any tax year from 6 April 1978 that falls within his 'working life' (see **1.7** above). His entitlement will be based on the extent to which a proportion of his earnings exceeded the LEL in any tax year during that period. Consequently those individuals earning less than the LEL will not build up any entitlement to a pension under this earnings-related component.

The first step in calculating the additional earnings-related pension component is to calculate the individual's 'earnings factor' for each relevant tax year in accordance with *SSCBA 1992, s 44*. The calculation varies depending on the tax year in question and is dependent on the level of National Insurance contributions paid or treated as paid in respect of the individual (see **1.10** below in relation to the tax years from 6 April 2002). Once the earnings factor has been calculated, it will be compared to the LEL for that year and, where it exceeds the LEL, the difference between the two figures is counted as surplus. Any surplus for a particular year must be recalculated in accordance with the most recent Social Security Revaluation of Earnings Factors Order so that it maintains its value in line with the general level of earnings in Great Britain. The combined surpluses for each of the relevant tax years may then be used to calculate the annual rate of the individual's additional pension in accordance with *SSCBA 1992, s 45*.

State second pension

1.10 S2P was introduced by the *Child Support, Pensions and Social Security Act 2000* and is intended to provide a bigger pension than SERPS by boosting the second tier pension of low and moderate earners, carers and the long-term disabled.

In the tax years from 6 April 2002, the S2P regime operates automatically to provide a yearly earnings factor for people who fall within one of the prescribed categories described below. The factor is based on the LET, which is set at £13,900 for the tax year 2009/2010 (but varies each year in line with the general level of earnings in Great Britain). As described in **1.9** above, the earnings factor will be used as the basis on which to calculate the individual's annual rate of additional pension.

Individuals earning less than the LET, but equal to or in excess of the LEL for the year, will be treated for S2P calculation purposes as if they had earnings equal to the LET, as will carers in receipt of Carer's Allowance (or who would have been were it not for their receipt of other benefits). Certain other individuals will be treated as if their earnings are equal to the LET if they are entitled to Child Benefit for a child under six, to Income Support as a carer or are regularly engaged, for at least 35 hours per week, in caring for a long-term sick or disabled person. Those in the latter category may need to apply for Home Responsibilities Protection in order to build their entitlement to an additional pension.

Where a person is entitled to long-term incapacity benefit throughout a tax year he may also be treated as if his earnings were equal to the LET in that year provided that by the time he reaches State pension age he has either paid or is treated as having paid primary Class 1 National Insurance contributions on annual earnings of the LEL (or more) for at least one tenth of his working life (see **1.6** above).

From the tax year 2010 to 2011, *PA 2007* has modified the S2P regime by extending its scope and making it more flexible. Individuals will be granted an 'earnings factor credit' for each week in which they meet specified conditions as set out in *SSCBA 1992, ss 44B, 44C*. Those with 52 earnings factor credits at the end of the year, or who have sufficient earnings factor credits to make up their earnings factor to the LEL for the year will be treated for S2P calculation purposes as if they had earnings equal to LET. Broadly speaking, those earning less than the LET, but equal to or in excess of the LEL and carers in receipt of carer's allowance will continue to benefit, as will those entitled to long-term incapacity benefit. Entitlement will be extended to those receiving Child Benefit for a child under 12 and foster parents, as well as to anyone entitled to receive severe disablement allowance.

In the May 2006 White Paper, *Security in Retirement*, the Government announced its intention to make the S2P flat rate by 2030. The provisions enabling this are in *PA 2007*. The first stage in the process, whereby earnings above a new Upper Accrual Point will not be used to calculate S2P entitlements, was announced in the 2007 Pre-Budget Report and came into force in April 2009 by an amendment to *SSCBA 1992, s 44*.

Occupational pension schemes

What is an occupational pension scheme?

1.11 One definition of occupational pension scheme is set out in *PSA 1993, s 1*, which describes it as a pension scheme:

'(*a*) that—

(i) for the purpose of providing benefits to, or in respect of, people with service in employments of a description, or

(ii) for that purpose and also for the purpose of providing benefits to, or in respect of, other people, is established by, or by persons who include, a person to whom subsection (2) applies when the scheme is established or (as the case may be) to whom that subsection would have applied when the scheme was established had that subsection then been in force, and

(*b*) that has its main administration in the United Kingdom or outside the member States;

or a pension scheme that is prescribed or is of a prescribed description; …'

For the purposes of the definition, 'employment' means 'any trade, business, profession, office or vocation' and a person to whom *subsection (2)* applies means, broadly, the employer. 'Pension scheme' is defined in the same section as:

'a scheme or other arrangement, comprised in one or more instruments or agreements, having or capable of having effect so as to provide benefits to or in respect of people—

(*a*) on retirement,

(*b*) on having reached a particular age, or

(*c*) on termination of service in an employment.'

The *PSA 1993* definition of an occupational pension scheme is therefore wide: it can relate to an entire workforce, a specified group of employees or a single individual; it can be established and governed by a single clause in a contract of employment or by a complex trust deed.

The integrated tax regime established by *FA 2004* applies to all 'registered' schemes (which includes all pre A-Day approved pension schemes that did not opt out of registration). *FA 2004, s 150* separately defines 'occupational pension scheme' as meaning:

'… a pension scheme established by an employer or employers and having or capable of having effect so as to provide benefits to or in respect of any or all of the employees of—

(*a*) that employer or those employers, or

(*b*) any other employer,

(whether or not it also has or is capable of having effect so as to provide benefits to or in respect of other persons).'

Traditionally, most occupational pension schemes have been able to benefit from tax privileges if correctly structured. Prior to 6 April 2006 (A-Day), schemes were either approved by HMRC or unapproved. Those schemes approved by HMRC received considerably more tax privileges than unapproved schemes but were, as would be expected, more heavily regulated with detailed restrictions on the form and amount of benefits which could be paid.

On A-Day, these restrictions were simplified, so that all types of registered pension schemes may make any payment to a member. Where it is an 'authorised member payment' under *FA 2004* the usual tax privileges will apply. Unauthorised payments will have adverse tax consequences, usually for both the member and the scheme.

Most occupational pension schemes, whatever their nature, are required to comply with the provisions of the *PSA 1993* and the regulations made under that Act. In particular, all schemes are required to comply with the provisions dealing with protection for early leavers (see CHAPTER 6). Schemes which are contracted out of the SERPS/S2P component are also required to comply with the relevant provisions relating to contracting out (see CHAPTER 4).

Occupational pension schemes are also subject to *PA 1995* and *PA 2004* which aim to improve the administration of pension schemes and increase security for members. The effects of *PA 1995* and *PA 2004* are considered throughout this book. Certain types of occupational schemes have been exempted from many of the provisions of *PA 1995* and *PA 2004* by regulations. Most notably, unregistered schemes are exempt from many, but not all, of the requirements (see CHAPTER 5).

Why establish a pension scheme?

1.12 No occupational pension scheme is cheap to run. Understandably, employers have to think carefully about the costs involved before establishing an occupational pension scheme. The Office for National Statistics Occupational Pension Schemes Annual Report 2007 recorded average employer contributions of 6.4 per cent of payroll in defined contribution schemes and 15 per cent for defined benefit schemes (see **1.13** below). Contributions in the form of lump sum payments, life assurance premiums and the general day-to-day expenses of running the scheme can also add to the cost. Perhaps unsurprisingly, defined benefit schemes are generally perceived to be more expensive, and many have been closed in recent years.

According to the DWP's Employers' Pension Provision Survey 2007 the most common reason for an employer to provide a pension scheme (other than where there is a legal requirement to do so) is to look after its employees after retirement (the paternalistic approach). Other reasons given include recruitment and retention, maintaining parity with competitors, pressure from trades unions and building a reputation as a responsible employer. Sometimes, an employer may be required to establish a scheme as part of a commercial transaction or as a result of a public sector contracting-out exercise.

Registered pension schemes benefit from a number of tax advantages (see CHAPTER 16) and so, although costly, provision of an occupational pension scheme remains a relatively tax-efficient way of providing employee benefits.

From the employee's point of view, membership of an occupational scheme can be very attractive. The pension provided by the State is unlikely to be adequate for many people to maintain their standard of living during retirement; and although employees often have to contribute to an occupational pension scheme in order to build up their pension entitlement, they will also obtain the value of employer contributions made for their benefit and tax relief on their own contributions.

Types of benefits provided by occupational pension schemes

1.13 Occupational pension schemes are commonly described as either defined benefit (or final salary) schemes or defined contribution (or money purchase) schemes, depending on the type of benefits they provide. In a defined benefit scheme, the amount of pension which a member ultimately receives will be directly related to his remuneration, usually, at or around the date of his retirement (although schemes where benefits accrue on a 'career average' basis are becoming more popular). In a defined contribution scheme, the amount of pension a member receives will be related to the contributions made to the scheme by and in respect of him and the investment return on those contributions. The most important difference between the two types of scheme, other than the benefits they provide (see **1.36** to **1.47** below), is the way in which they are funded and the resulting implications, particularly in terms of burden of risk, for the employer and the member.

Defined benefit schemes

1.14 A member of a defined benefit scheme will generally be required to pay into the scheme a specific proportion of his remuneration by way of contributions (although in some schemes this can fluctuate and in others the member may not be required to contribute). The balance of the cost of providing scheme benefits will generally be met by the employer (hence these schemes are also known as 'balance of cost' schemes). The exact cost of providing the benefits will not be known until the last beneficiary under the scheme dies, so a defined benefit scheme represents a very open-ended risk to the employer. The way in which the contributions of the employer are calculated is considered further in CHAPTER 11.

Defined contribution schemes

1.15 As with a defined benefit scheme, the rules of a defined contribution scheme will usually specify the contributions a member is required to pay to the scheme and the contributions the member's employer is required to make in respect of him. Usually the rules will provide for the member to have a notional 'individual account' which is credited with his contributions, the contributions made by his employer in respect of him and the investment growth attributable to those contributions. When the member retires, assets equal to the value of his account will be realised and usually the proceeds are used to purchase an annuity to provide him with an income.

The amount of pension the member receives from a defined contribution scheme will be dependent on the contributions made, the investment growth achieved and the annuity rate obtained; it will not be directly related to the member's earnings before retirement. For many employers a defined contribution scheme represents an attractive proposition as the cost of financing the scheme can be predicted with some certainty. For an employee, such schemes are often less attractive because, if the investments perform poorly or annuity rates are high at the time of retirement, it is the employee upon whom this will impact, rather than the employer.

Hybrid schemes

1.16 It is possible to have a hybrid scheme that provides pensions accrued on both a defined contribution basis and a defined benefit basis, usually by operating a defined contribution and a defined benefit section. A member will accrue benefits under one or other section and may be able to switch between the two upon satisfying a specified condition. A hybrid scheme may alternatively provide defined contribution benefits but with a defined benefit underpin (or vice versa) so that the member will receive the greater of the benefits provided by his individual account and a pension calculated by reference to his salary before retirement.

As employers become more cost sensitive and wish to minimise the scope for fluctuations in contribution rates, other benefit structures are being introduced, often aimed at sharing the risk more evenly between employer and member.

KPMG case – the dividing line

1.17 Questions may arise as to whether a scheme is a defined benefit or a defined contribution arrangement, particularly where the benefit structure does not clearly fit into one category or another.

In *AON Trust Corpn Ltd v KPMG [2005] EWCA Civ 1004* the question arose, in relation to the obligation of the employer to fund a deficit, as to whether the scheme was a 'money purchase scheme' as defined in *PSA 1993*. The court looked in some detail at the meaning of 'money purchase scheme' and held that the scheme in question did not, as the employer was asserting, fall within this category. The direct relationship between contributions and benefits required in a money purchase scheme was broken by the introduction of actuarial factors in the calculation of benefits. This decision was distinguished in the case of *Bridge Trustees v Yates [2008] EWHC 964 (Ch)*, where it was held that the use of actuarial factors was not inevitably fatal to a benefit being money purchase.

Application of legislation to different types of occupational pension schemes

1.18 The legislation relating to occupational pension schemes generally applies equally to schemes which provide defined contribution benefits as to those which provide defined benefits. However, there are exemptions or modifications for defined contribution schemes from some of the requirements of the legislation, as referred to in the table below.

<table>
<tr><th rowspan="2">Legislation relating to:</th><th colspan="2">Applicability to occupational pension schemes:</th></tr>
<tr><th>Defined benefit schemes</th><th>Defined contribution schemes</th></tr>
<tr><td>Protection for early leavers, ie preservation, transfers and revaluation (see CHAPTER 6)</td><td colspan="2">All schemes are required to comply with the legislation relating to the protection of early leavers under PSA 1993, Part IV although the time limits for the payment of transfer values and ways in which benefits are calculated will vary as between defined benefit and defined contribution schemes.</td></tr>
<tr><td>Equal treatment (see CHAPTER 9)</td><td colspan="2">The equal treatment requirements set out in PA 1995, ss 62–66 apply to all schemes.</td></tr>
</table>

Legislation relating to:	**Applicability to occupational pension schemes:**	
	Defined benefit schemes	**Defined contribution schemes**
Independent trustees (see CHAPTER 3)	Where a scheme employer suffers an insolvency event, the Regulator may appoint an independent trustee under *PA 1995, ss 22–25*. The Regulator also has power to appoint an independent trustee if there is a Pension Protection Fund assessment period in relation to the scheme.	The independent trustee provisions also apply to defined contribution schemes but provisions relating to PPF assessment periods will not be relevant.
Employer debt (see CHAPTERS 12 AND 14)	Where a scheme is being wound up, a 'relevant event' occurs or an employer ceases to participate in the scheme (whilst at least one other continues) and the value of the assets of the scheme is less than the value of its liabilities, a debt may become due to the trustees of the scheme from the employer.	The employer debt provisions apply only in limited circumstances where the general scheme levy has not been paid or assets of the scheme have been reduced due to criminal action. In most circumstances the employer debt provisions do not apply to employers in hybrid schemes whose liabilities relate only to money purchase benefits, although they can be liable for orphan liabilities.
Disclosure (see CHAPTER 3 and APPENDIX II)	Trustees of all schemes are required to comply with the requirements of the *Occupational Pension Schemes (Disclosure of Information) Regulations 1996* (*SI 1996/1655*).	
Statutory pension increases (see **1.48** below)	Limited Price Indexation (LPI) applies where the pension is attributable to pensionable service accrued on or after 6 April 1997.	LPI does not apply to benefits coming into payment on or after 6 April 2005.

Legislation relating to:	**Applicability to occupational pension schemes:**	
	Defined benefit schemes	**Defined contribution schemes**
Investments (see CHAPTER 10)	All trustees must comply with the statutory requirements set out in *PA 1995, ss 33–36*. These requirements affect the choice of investments, the appointment of fund managers and the maintenance of a statement of investment principles amongst other things (unless the scheme has an appropriate exemption under the relevant regulations). Trustees should follow the Myners principles first set out in the March 2001 report: The Myners Review of Institutional Investment in the UK.	
Contracting out (see CHAPTER 4)	Contracting out is permissible under *PSA 1993, s 9(2)* on the basis of satisfying the reference scheme test or on a protected rights basis.	Contracting out is permitted on a protected rights basis.
Voluntary membership (see **1.21** below)	Membership of a scheme cannot be compulsory (*PSA 1993, s 160*) but see CHAPTER 13 for automatic enrolment requirements.	
Voluntary contributions (see **1.34** below)	The requirement for schemes to provide an AVC facility was removed from 6 April 2006 by *PA 2004, s 267*.	
Registration	All occupational pension schemes may register with HMRC under *FA 2004, s 153* and were deemed registered if exempt approved as at 6 April 2006. All schemes with more than one member must also register with the Pensions Regulator in accordance with *PA 2004, s 62*.	
Dispute resolution (see CHAPTER 3)	Trustees of all occupational pension schemes (other than those exempted by regulations) must put in place a dispute resolution procedure in accordance with *PA 1995, s 50*.	
Pensions Ombudsman (see CHAPTER 2)	The Pensions Ombudsman has jurisdiction to investigate a wide range of complaints in relation to all occupational pension schemes.	

Legislation relating to:	**Applicability to occupational pension schemes:**	
	Defined benefit schemes	**Defined contribution schemes**
Appointment of professional advisers (see CHAPTER 2)	Under *PA 1995, s 47*, trustees must appoint an individual as scheme actuary and an individual or firm as scheme auditor. Where the assets include 'investments', an individual or firm must be appointed as fund manager unless the scheme is wholly insured. Trustees should not rely on the advice of any professional adviser they did not appoint.	As for defined benefit schemes except there is no requirement to appoint a scheme actuary.
Member-nominated trustees (see CHAPTER 3)	Trustees must arrange for the appointment of member-nominated trustees (or directors in the case of a trustee company) unless the scheme is exempt under regulations.	
Pension Protection Fund (see CHAPTER 5)	Most defined benefit schemes are eligible for the PPF and required to pay the levy	Defined contribution schemes are not eligible for PPF entry.
Scheme Funding (see CHAPTER 11)	Must comply with the scheme funding requirements in *PA 2004, Part 3* (see **1.29** below).	Not required to comply with the statutory scheme funding requirements.
Winding up (see CHAPTER 12)	The order in which the liabilities of a tax approved defined benefit scheme must be secured in the event of a winding up is governed by *PA 1995, ss 73–76*.	The statutory winding-up priority order does not apply.
Payment of surplus (see CHAPTER 11)	*PA 1995, s 37* confers certain powers on trustees to make payments of surplus to an employer provided that conditions are satisfied.	

How are occupational pension schemes established?

1.19 Before 6 April 2006, tax relief for occupational pension schemes was only available to schemes approved by HMRC and established under irrevocable trusts in accordance with *ICTA 1988, s 592*. Consequently, the vast majority of such schemes were established by trust deed or a declaration of trust and were known as 'exempt approved schemes'.

An equivalent requirement was introduced with effect from 22 September 2005 by *PA 2004, s 252*, whereby if an occupational pension scheme has its main administration in the UK, the trustees or managers of the scheme are prohibited from accepting any payment to fund benefits unless the scheme is established under irrevocable trusts.

With effect from A-Day, newly established pension schemes must make an application to HMRC to be registered in accordance with *FA 2004, s 153*. The application must contain any information reasonably requested by HMRC and must be accompanied by a prescribed declaration by the scheme administrator and any other declarations reasonably required by HMRC (*FA 2004, ss 153(2), 270*); see CHAPTER 16. Schemes with exempt approved status immediately prior to A-Day were automatically treated as registered with the Inland Revenue on 6 April 2006 unless they opted out.

The documentation governing a scheme will usually consist of a definitive trust deed and one or more sets of rules. There is no particular agreed format as to what should be contained in the trust deed and what should be in the rules. It is quite common for the trust deed to contain the administrative provisions of the trust and for the rules to detail the benefits payable under the scheme, but there are many variations on this theme.

The first trust deed will generally appoint the first trustees of the scheme and set out the terms of the trust. In particular it will be necessary for the trust deed to include or make provision for a power of amendment so that the scheme can be amended to account for future changes in legislation and/or practice. The trustees will also need to be given sufficient powers in the trust deed to be able to administer the trust.

When a scheme's documentation is first drafted, consideration needs to be given to the 'balance of power' between the trustees and the employer. It is necessary to decide which powers should be vested in the trustees, which powers should be vested in the employer and which powers should be vested jointly. As a general rule, if the exercise of the power could have financial implications for the scheme, the employer will usually wish to be involved in exercising that power; the power could be vested in the employer or it could be vested in the trustees, subject to the consent of the employer. Legislation has, in some instances, overridden this 'balance of power' in the trust documentation. For example, under the statutory funding regime established by *PA 2004, s 222*, trustees in many schemes have been given more power in the process of determining the level of the employer's contribution.

The rules of a scheme will generally detail the benefits payable under the scheme. Usually, they will also set out conditions for membership and specify the contributions (if any) that the members are required to pay. The exact details of the rules will, of course, depend on the benefit structure of the scheme. However, *FA 2004, s 164* defines the authorised payments that a registered pension scheme can make in respect of scheme members. These include pensions permitted under *ss 165* and *167*, lump sums permitted under *ss 166* and *168* and 'recognised transfers' as defined in *s 169*. Generally, any unauthorised payments made are likely to have adverse tax consequences and many schemes will contain a rule restricting benefits to those which are authorised.

The taxation of pension schemes is considered further in CHAPTER 16.

Multi-employer schemes

1.20 It may be possible for an employer to participate in a 'centralised' or 'multi-employer' occupational pension scheme, rather than establish its own scheme, thus benefiting from lower administration costs. Such schemes generally have a principal employer, and a number of associated or participating employers on whose behalf the principal employer will generally act.

Before A-Day, the general rule was that a non-sectionalised occupational pension scheme had to restrict membership to employers of 'associated' employers to obtain and retain HMRC exempt approved status. However, under the *FA 2004* regime, a registered occupational pension scheme is now able to include employees of non-associated employers.

Participation is usually achieved by the trustees, the principal employer and the participating employer executing a deed of adherence or participation setting out the terms on which the employer can participate in the scheme.

Membership of occupational pension schemes

Non-compulsory membership

1.21 Membership of an occupational pension scheme cannot currently be made compulsory and any term in a contract of employment or any rule in an occupational pension scheme to the effect that an employee must be a member of a particular pension scheme is void. Legislation relating to non-compulsory membership was first introduced by the *Social Security Act 1986* and first became effective on 6 April 1988; it is now contained in *PSA 1993, s 160*. The only exception to this is that membership may be compulsory for a death in service only scheme if the benefit is provided on a non-contributory basis, as set out in *Pension Schemes (Voluntary Contributions Requirements and Voluntary and Compulsory Membership) Regulations 1987, reg 3*. In practice, it is, however, permissible (so long as the matter is correctly handled) for employees to be included automatically as members of their employer's scheme unless they specifically request to opt out.

PA 2007 sets out a new system of automatic enrolment. The provisions require all employers to automatically enrol their qualifying employees (those aged between 22 and State pension age earning a threshold amount) into a qualifying scheme provided by the employer, or into a centralised personal accounts scheme (see CHAPTER 13 for details).

HMRC requirements

1.22 Until 6 April 2006 (A-Day), membership of an occupational pension scheme was confined to the employees of employers participating in the scheme in order to obtain (and retain) exempt approved status. As from A-Day, an occupational pension scheme need not restrict membership to its own employees in order to remain registered, though it need not be open to all employees, or to any particular category of them. However, discriminatory entry conditions that cannot be objectively justified should be avoided (see CHAPTER 9).

In the past, save for limited exceptions, an employee could not be a member of an occupational pension scheme if he was also contributing to a personal pension scheme. This restriction was relaxed to a certain extent by the stakeholder legislation which allowed employees with P60 earnings of less than £30,000 in 2004/2005 to pay up to £3,600 to a personal pension or stakeholder pension, whilst at the same time continuing to be eligible for concurrent membership of their occupational pension scheme.

Under the *FA 2004* regime, members' contributions to registered pension schemes an individual may be a member of as many schemes or arrangements as he wishes. There is, however, a limit to the amount of tax privilege that will be allowed to an individual in respect of his pension savings in relation both to an annual and lifetime allowance (see **1.3** above).

The taxation of registered schemes is considered further in CHAPTER 16.

Sex discrimination

1.23 Sex discrimination claims relating to pensions tend to arise under two broad headings: equal benefits and equal access. Both are derived from *Article 157* of the *Treaty on the Functioning of the European Union* (*'TFEU'*) (formerly *Article 119* and then *Article 141* of the *EC Treaty*) which requires that Member States apply the principle of equal pay for equal work or work of equal value. The decision of the ECJ in *Bilka-Kaufhaus Gmbh v Weber (C-170/84)* established that pensions were 'pay' for the purposes of the *TFEU*.

Claims relating to unequal benefits cases originally tended to arise out of the fact that defined benefit schemes typically provided different retirement dates for men and women, meaning that men had to work longer in order to receive their full pension entitlement. The *Coloroll* decision *(C-200/91)*, which was given in September 1994, established that equal treatment claims could be brought in relation to benefits payable in respect of periods of service on and after 17 May 1990 (which was the date of the *Barber* judgment *(C-262/88)*). However, there was great uncertainty on how to equalise benefits, and recent claims have arisen out of failures to do this correctly.

The principle of equal access is set out in *PA 1995, s 62* which provides that the terms on which employees may become members of an occupational pension scheme must be the same for both men and women. Many disputes in this area tend to arise in the context of part-timer claims, due to the fact that historically, part-time workers were not given equal access to pension schemes. Since a greater proportion of women than men tended to work part-time, claims therefore arise on the grounds of indirect discrimination. A key case in this area is *Preston v Wolverhampton Healthcare NHS Trust [2001] UKHL 5*, in which the House of Lords decided that, subject to the employee making back-payments in respect of the membership period claimed, pension benefits could be calculated by reference to periods of service subsequent to 8 April 1976 (which was the date on which the ECJ decided in *Defrenne v Sabena (C-43/75)* that *Article 157* of the *TFEU* had direct effect).

It is worth noting in this context that the *Part Time Workers (Prevention of Less Favourable Treatment) Regulations 2000 (SI 2000/1551)* and the *Fixed Term Employees (Prevention of Less Favourable Treatment) Regulations 2002 (SI 2002/2034)* introduced measures to protect part-time and fixed term workers from unjustified exclusion from pension schemes (alongside more general employment protection).

The issue of sex discrimination in relation to occupational pension schemes is considered further in CHAPTER 9.

Disability discrimination

1.24 It is unlawful for an employer to discriminate, without justification, against disabled employees in terms of the benefits provided to those employees, including the access to and benefits provided from, an occupational pension scheme. *Disability Discrimination Act 1995, s 1* provides that a person has a disability 'if he has a physical or mental impairment which has a substantial and long term adverse effect on his ability to carry out normal day-to-day activities'. An employer discriminates against a disabled person if, for a reason which relates to the disabled person's disability, it treats that person less favourably than it treats, or would treat, a person who is not disabled and it cannot show that the treatment was justified.

Disability Discrimination Act 1995, s 4G incorporates an overriding 'non-discrimination rule' into the rules of every occupational pension scheme. Under the non-discrimination rule, trustees and managers may not, in relation to the scheme, discriminate against a disabled person in carrying out their functions (especially in relation to admission and treatment of members) and neither must they subject a disabled person to harassment. Trustees or managers must make 'reasonable adjustments', which may include altering scheme rules, to prevent any of their provisions, criterions or practices from putting a disabled person at a substantial disadvantage.

No obligation is placed on trustees to make reasonable adjustments if they do not know and could not reasonably be expected to know that a person is a disabled person for the purposes of the *Disability Discrimination Act 1995*, or that he has a disability and is likely to be disadvantaged.

Discrimination on the grounds of disability is considered further in CHAPTER 9.

Age discrimination

1.25 The *Employment Equality (Age) Regulations 2006* prohibit discrimination and harassment on the grounds of age, and also seek to protect those who take a stand (or are perceived to take a stand) against such discrimination. Under the Regulations, which are designed to implement the *Equal Treatment Directive (2000/78/EC)*, it is unlawful, in relation to rights accrued or benefits payable in respect of periods of service on or after 1 December 2006, for the trustees or employer in relation to an occupational pension scheme to discriminate on the grounds of age against a member or prospective member of the scheme in carrying out any of their functions (including in particular their functions relating to the admission of members to the scheme and the treatment of members of it).

Employment Equality (Age) Regulations 2006, Sch 2, para 2 incorporates an overriding 'non-discrimination rule' into the rules of every occupational pension scheme. Under the non-discrimination rule, trustees and managers must refrain from unlawfully discriminating on the grounds of age. *Paragraph* 2 also confers a power on the trustees or managers (sometimes with employer consent) to make alterations to the scheme in order to secure conformity with the non-discrimination rule.

Schedule 2 also introduces exemptions from the non-discrimination rule for occupational pension schemes which include:

- setting a minimum or maximum age for admission.
- using age criteria in actuarial calculations.
- making age-related contributions (subject to certain conditions).
- making reductions to pension levels where a dependant is a specified number of years younger than the member.
- setting a minimum age before which unreduced benefits cannot be taken.

Discrimination on the grounds of age is considered further in CHAPTER 9.

The Equality Bill 2009

1.26 The Equality Bill was introduced into Parliament on 27 April 2009, and has two main stated purposes:

- to harmonise discrimination law; and
- to strengthen the law to support progress on equality.

The majority of the provisions of the Bill which may impact on pension provision are covered by the first aim. Essentially, it is a consolidation of discrimination law, with the current statutes and regulations being repealed and a new statutory structure introduced.

The Bill contains key concepts:

- a list of 'protected characteristics'; and
- definitions of discrimination, harassment and victimisation.

These key concepts are then applied in specific areas, including pensions.

The protected characteristics are:

- age – by reference to a particular age or to a range of ages;

- disability (a physical or mental impairment having a substantial and long-term adverse affect on the ability to carry out normal day to day activities) – guidance may be issued on what can be taken into account when determining if someone is under a disability;
- gender reassignment – someone proposing to undergo, undergoing or who has undergone gender reassignment (no need for medical supervision);
- marriage and civil partnership;
- pregnancy and maternity;
- race;
- religion or belief;
- sex; and
- sexual orientation.

The Equality Bill is considered further in CHAPTER 9.

Procedure for becoming a member

1.27 The rules of a scheme will often set out the procedure which an employee must follow if he wishes to become a member of the scheme. The rules may provide for a minimum and maximum entry age, thus allowing an employer to exclude the very young (who may be likely to change jobs more frequently) and the very old (for whom the costs of benefits are particularly high). See **1.25** above and CHAPTER 9 in relation to age discrimination.

It is not uncommon for the rules of a scheme to impose a 'waiting period' where an employee has to be employed for a certain period of time before being eligible to become a member (although this is becoming less common). A waiting period may correspond to an employee's 'probationary period' under his contract of employment; some rules will provide that an employee is only eligible once he is a 'permanent' employee. However, the *Fixed-Term Employees (Prevention of Less Favourable Treatment) Regulations 2002 (SI 2002/2034)* now provide that fixed-term employees should be provided with benefits on a pro-rata basis equivalent to those provided to their permanent counterparts, unless their exclusion can be objectively justified (see CHAPTER 9). There may also be difficulties for trustees under the age discrimination legislation in imposing a waiting period in excess of five years unless it can be justified. Waiting periods in excess of 90 days will not be allowed under the new automatic enrolment requirements (see **1.21** above and CHAPTER 13).

An employee may be required to complete an application form for membership of an occupational pension scheme; in the case of a contributory scheme, this form will normally authorise the employer to deduct contributions from the employee's salary (see also **1.33** below). It is common for employers to ask employees who do not wish to join the scheme or who choose to opt out of the scheme to sign a waiver form confirming that they understand that they are giving up benefits.

From 2012, employers will be required to automatically enrol many of their employees into a qualifying pension scheme. The employee will then be given the option to opt out. This, and other details of the personal accounts regime established by the *PA 2008,* are dealt with in CHAPTER 13.

Making contributions to occupational pension schemes

Employer's contributions

1.28 Before *PA 1995* came into force, there was little in the way of statutory control over funding and the making of contributions (see CHAPTER 11). *PA 1995* introduced provisions requiring trustees to maintain, in the case of defined benefit schemes, schedules of contributions and, in the case of defined contribution schemes, schedules of payment. With effect from 30 December 2005, *PA 2004* superseded *PA 1995* in relation to defined benefit schemes.

Defined benefit schemes

1.29 The trustees of a defined benefit scheme which is subject to the statutory funding objective under *PA 2004, s 222* must produce, within 15 months after the effective date of the first actuarial valuation, a schedule of contributions which must be reviewed within 15 months after the effective date of subsequent valuations. In accordance with the *Occupational Pension Schemes (Scheme Funding) Regulations 2005*, the schedule must be signed by the trustees or managers of the scheme and must make provision for signature by the employer in order to signify its agreement to the matters included in it. The schedule must show:

(*a*) the rates and due dates of all contributions (other than voluntary contributions) payable towards the scheme by or on behalf of the employer and active members of the scheme during the period of five years after the date on which the schedule is certified;

(*b*) any contributions to cover expenses must be listed separately; and

(*c*) additional contributions under a recovery plan must be shown separately.

The schedule must be certified by the scheme actuary, ie the actuary appointed under *PA 1995, s 47(1)(b)*. The schedule will not come into force until it has been so certified.

Where employer or employee contributions are not made on time in accordance with the schedule, a report to the Regulator may be required where there is reasonable cause to believe that the failure is likely to be of material significance in the exercise by the Regulator of any of its functions (*PA 2004, s 228*). The Regulator has issued a Code of Practice on Funding defined benefits, which states that trustees should ensure that there is a robust procedure for monitoring the receipt of contributions and investigate any failure by the employer to adhere to the schedule of contributions. If the failure is likely to be of material significance to the Regulator, a report should be made within ten working days of the end of the period in which the payment should have been made (*PA 1995, s 49(9)*). Members of the scheme should be informed within one month.

If there has been 'fraudulent evasion' in failing to pass employee contributions to the trustees or managers, criminal penalties may apply (*PA 1995, s 49(11), (12)*).

The statutory requirements relating to scheme funding and to schedules of contributions are considered further in CHAPTER 11.

Defined contribution schemes

1.30 The trustees or managers of a defined contribution scheme must (unless the scheme is exempt) ensure that a payment schedule is periodically prepared, maintained and revised in relation to the scheme. Any trustee who fails to comply with the requirement to maintain a payment schedule may be fined (see also APPENDIX I). *PA 1995, s 87* and *Scheme Administration Regulations (SI 1996/1715), regs 18, 19* provide that the schedule must show, for the year to which it relates:

(*a*) the rates of contributions payable towards the scheme by or on behalf of the employer (or in the case of multi-employer schemes, each employer) and the active members of the scheme;

(*b*) the amounts payable towards the scheme by the (or each) employer in respect of expenses likely to be incurred during the year in question; and

(*c*) the dates on or before which these payments are to be made.

Where any amounts payable in accordance with a payment schedule by or on behalf of the employer have not been paid on or before the due date and the trustees and managers consider the failure to be material, then notice of the failure must be given to the Regulator and to the scheme members. The Regulator has issued a Code of Practice on Reporting Late Payment of Contributions to Occupational Money Purchase Schemes which sets out the Regulator's views on which late payments are likely to be material. A reasonable period for a report would usually be within ten working days of the trustees having identified the late payment as material.

Failure to put in place a payment schedule or to make the appropriate reports to the Regulator and the members amounts to a civil offence under *PA 1995*, punishable by fine. If there has been 'fraudulent evasion' in failing to pass employee contributions to the trustees or managers, criminal penalties may apply (*PA 1995, s 49(11), (12)*).

Scheme Administration Regulations, reg 17 provides that trustees of the following schemes do not have to maintain a payment schedule:

- public sector pension schemes;
- occupational pension schemes with fewer than two members;
- schemes with fewer than 12 members where all the members of the scheme are trustees or directors; and all decisions are made by the unanimous agreement of those trustees or directors or the scheme has an independent director or trustee;
- unregistered schemes with fewer than 100 members; and
- *s 615* schemes with fewer than 100 members.

HMRC requirements

1.31 Broadly speaking, employers can claim tax relief on the contributions they make to a pension scheme by deducting those contributions from their profits chargeable to UK tax. The tax treatment of contributions made by employers to registered occupational pension schemes is considered in CHAPTER 16.

Members' contributions

Ordinary contributions

1.32 The level of the contributions which members are required to make is a matter of scheme design. Contributory schemes typically require a contribution of between 4 and 7 per cent of salary. Contributions will generally be deducted from a member's salary by his employer through the payroll. The employee must specifically consent to contributions being deducted for this purpose (*Employment Rights Act 1996, s 13*) and consequently membership application forms will generally include provision for the necessary consent to be given.

Contributions deducted by a member's employer must be paid to the trustees of the scheme within 19 days (or 14 days in the case of minimum payments made by virtue of the member being contracted out of SERPS/S2P) of the end of the month within which the contribution is deducted in accordance with *PA 1995, s 49(8)* and *Occupational Pension Schemes (Scheme Administration) Regulations 1996, reg 16*. Failure to pay the contributions in this way may give rise to a civil penalty under *PA 1995, s 10* or, where there is fraudulent evasion, a criminal offence under *PA 1995, s 49(11)* and a prison sentence of up to seven years (see **1.29** and **1.30** above).

High earners

1.33 The Budget on 22 April 2009 announced a number of changes which will affect pension provision for high earners from 6 April 2011. The key change to pensions is the restriction of tax relief to the basic rate on pension contributions for individuals with income of £150,000 or more. This is dealt with in CHAPTER 16.

Voluntary contributions

1.34 A member may wish to enhance his pension benefits by making additional voluntary contributions ('AVCs') in addition to any contributions he is required to make under the rules of a scheme. Generally, the benefits deriving from AVCs are defined contribution benefits, irrespective of whether the scheme is defined contribution or defined benefit. Under the rules of a scheme, AVCs may sometimes be used to purchase added years of service which count toward the member's defined benefits, but this is unusual.

Prior to April 2006, under *PSA 1993, s 111*, the rules of a scheme had to allow members to pay voluntary contributions, except to the extent necessary to comply with HMRC requirements and as prescribed. However, the requirement for schemes to provide an AVC facility was removed by *PA 2004, s 267* from 6 April 2006, in the context of *Finance Act* changes allowing individuals to save as much as they like into pension schemes subject only to HMRC limits on tax relief. Trustees cannot, however, require members with existing AVCs to transfer out, so will still have to administer the AVC facility for existing members even if the rules are changed.

Instead of making voluntary contributions 'in-house' through an employer's scheme, individuals could choose to make contributions to their own personal pension arrangements. Prior to 6 April 2006 this was often through a 'free standing additional voluntary contributions' ('FSAVC') arrangement. Such arrangements have much in common with a personal pension scheme (see CHAPTER 13) and were established by a provider in exactly the same way. Usually the provider is an insurance company, friendly society, bank or building society. The main disadvantage with a personal pension or FSAVC arrangement is that the member is obliged to meet the fees associated with the administration and management of the arrangement whereas, if voluntary contributions are paid 'in-house', the employer will usually bear these costs (and, even if it does not, the members may benefit, as costs will be spread between them).

HMRC restrictions

1.35 Prior to A-Day, the total amount of contributions (ordinary and voluntary) that could be made to a scheme by a member in any tax year was restricted by HMRC to 15 per cent of the member's remuneration in that year. (*ICTA 1988, s 592*).

Under the *FA 2004* regime, contributions to registered pension schemes are not subject to any limits as such. Members are given tax relief on their annual pension contributions up to the greater of £3,600 or 100 per cent of their UK earnings chargeable to income tax (plus any contracted-out minimum payment sums received by the employer).

FA 2004, however, introduced an annual limit on the inflows of value to an individual's pension fund (both in the form of contributions and growth) that attract favourable tax treatment (known as the 'annual allowance'). The annual allowance is set by Treasury Order and will be reviewed every five years. It was set at £215,000 per individual for the tax year 2006/2007 and increases as follows:

- 2007/2008 – £225,000;
- 2008/2009 – £235,000;
- 2009/2010 – £245,000;
- 2010/2011 – £255,000.

Individuals will be taxed at 40 per cent on any 'pension input' above the annual allowance.

FA 2004 also introduced a single lifetime limit on the amount of pension saving that attracts favourable tax treatment (known as the 'lifetime allowance'). The lifetime allowance is set by Treasury Order and will also be reviewed every five years. It was set at £1.5 million per individual for the tax year 2006/2007 and increases as follows:

- 2007/2008 – £1.6 million;
- 2008/2009 – £1.65 million;

- 2009/2010 – £1.75 million;
- 2010/2011 – £1.8 million.

Individuals will be liable to pay a lifetime allowance charge of 55 per cent, or 25 per cent on crystallised amounts greater that the 'lifetime allowance', depending on whether a lump sum is paid or the monies are retained within the scheme. There are transitional provisions allowing individuals 'protection', giving them a lifetime allowance in excess of the standard figures listed above.

Benefits payable from occupational pension schemes

HMRC requirements

1.36 Prior to 6 April 2006 (A-Day), the benefits payable from an approved occupational pension scheme, whether defined contribution or defined benefit, were limited by HMRC. To obtain HMRC approval, the rules of the scheme had to reflect these limits.

The types of 'authorised payments' that can now be made from a registered pension scheme are set out in *FA 2004, Part 4*. If a registered pension scheme makes 'unauthorised member payments' or 'unauthorised employer payments', there may be adverse tax consequences for the employer, the member and for the scheme administrator (which will usually be the trustees).

When are benefits payable?

1.37 Benefits will usually become payable under a scheme either on the death of a member or on the member's retirement, whichever is the earlier (although *FA 2004* does enable benefits to be taken while the member remains in service if the scheme rules allow). Benefits in a defined benefit scheme are usually calculated on the basis of the member's 'normal retirement date' under the scheme, which will generally be between age 60 and 65. Under the Pension Rules set out in *FA 2004, s 165*, benefits may not be paid before a member reaches 'normal minimum pension age' (which will be increased from age 50 to age 55 from 6 April 2010), other than where the ill-health condition is met. Members who had a prospective right on 5 April 2006 (deriving from the scheme rules as at 10 December 2003) to draw any benefit before age 55 may retain those rights and have a protected pension age (*FA 2004, Sch 36*).

Normal retirement date may differ for different categories of members, for example, directors may have a normal retirement date of age 60 while all other members have a normal retirement date of age 65. In the past, it was common to find schemes with a different retirement age for men and women (usually reflecting the State pension age); but, following the decision in *Barber v GRE Insurance Group [1990] 1 ECR 1889*, this should no longer be the case (see CHAPTER 9 for a fuller consideration of the equalisation of normal retirement dates).

Benefits payable on early retirement are considered further in **1.39** below. Benefits payable on late retirement are considered in **1.40** below. Benefits coming into payment after age 75 will be unauthorised.

Final salary defined benefit schemes

Pension benefits at normal retirement

1.38 In the case of a final salary defined benefit scheme, a member's pension is calculated by reference to the remuneration he is receiving at or shortly before he retires or leaves service. The level of remuneration by which benefits are calculated is often referred to as 'final pensionable salary' or some similar expression. The definition of final pensionable salary is a matter of scheme design; the wider the definition, the higher a member's final pensionable salary is likely to be and, consequently, the greater his resulting pension will be. A member's final pensionable salary may be his earnings at the date on which he retires, his total earnings during the previous year or his earnings averaged over a certain period, such as the previous three years; it may include fluctuating emoluments such as commissions or bonuses or it may simply be basic salary. There may be offsets against final pensionable salary; for example, it is not uncommon for a deduction equal to the lower earnings limit to be made.

Typically, a scheme's rules will contain a formula for calculating the pension payable. This will generally be expressed as a fraction or percentage of final pensionable salary for each year of pensionable service (ie service whilst an active member and any service deemed, under the rules of the scheme, to be pensionable service); 1/60th or 1/80th are the most common annual accrual rates. A formula such as this gives the member some reassurance that, assuming that he has been a member of a scheme for much of his working life, his pension will be a reasonable proportion of the salary he was earning at the time he retired. For example, a person who has been a member of a scheme offering a 1/60th accrual rate for 30 years will receive a pension of 30/60ths, or one half of his final pensionable salary.

Pension benefits on early retirement

1.39 The rules of the scheme may allow members to retire on a pension at any time if retirement is due to incapacity, or at any time after age 50 for any other reason (this will rise to 55 in 2010). Generally the rules will specify that either employer or trustee consent is required for early retirement and, in the case of incapacity retirement, that satisfactory medical evidence is produced. Where a member receives his pension early he is effectively receiving benefits as an alternative to a preserved benefit and consequently the preservation legislation must be complied with. This is considered further in CHAPTER 6.

It is often the case that the level of benefits payable on early retirement will depend on whether or not the retirement is due to incapacity. A non incapacity-related early retirement pension will generally be calculated using the same formula as for normal retirement but taking account of actual pensionable service and final pensionable salary at the date of retirement. The resulting pension will often be reduced to take account of early receipt. This is usually done by applying a percentage reduction, for example, a member's pension may be reduced by 3 per cent for each year that actual retirement precedes normal retirement date.

Where the retirement is due to incapacity, the benefits provided will often be more generous. They may, for example, be calculated without reduction for early receipt or possibly on the basis of the pensionable service the member would have completed had he remained a member until his normal retirement date. Such pensions are obviously more expensive than non incapacity-related early retirement pensions and so the eligibility conditions are generally quite restrictive.

(a) Defining incapacity

Pre A-Day, incapacity was defined in HMRC's Practice Notes as 'physical or mental deterioration which is sufficiently serious to prevent the individual from following his or her normal employment, or which seriously impairs his or her earning capacity'. The definition added that incapacity does not mean 'simply a decline in energy or ability'. The rules of many schemes go further than that definition. For example, self-induced incapacity (eg self-inflicted injuries or drug addiction) may be excluded; employer and/or trustee consent will often be required before an individual can be said to fall within this category; and the member may have to be incapacitated to the extent that he is incapable of any full-time employment, not just of working for his current employer.

Under the Pension Rules set out in *FA 2004, s 165*, the 'ill-health condition' is similar, but not identical, to the pre A-Day definition of 'incapacity'.

The 'ill-health condition' will be met if:

(*a*) the scheme administrator has received evidence from a registered medical practitioner that the member is (and will continue to be) incapable of carrying on the member's occupation because of physical or medical impairment; and

(*b*) the member has in fact ceased to carry on the member's occupation (*FA 2004, Sch 28, Part 1, para 1*).

The ill-health condition is considered further in CHAPTER 16.

(b) Determining incapacity

The fact that there are often many conditions relating to the payment of an incapacity pension and that an incapacity pension is generally more generous than an ordinary early retirement pension has given rise to a number of disputes between members and trustees as to whether such a pension should be paid. The decisions, to an extent, turn on the particular wording of the incapacity rule in question but generally an employer must act in good faith when considering any medical evidence provided in relation to an application for an incapacity pension. Trustees may be required to exercise a discretion in relation to the payment of benefits such as an incapacity pension. When exercising such a discretion, trustees should ensure that they take into account all relevant, but no irrelevant, factors; ask themselves the proper questions; adopt a correct construction of the rules of the scheme; and do not arrive at a perverse decision (ie one which no reasonable body of trustees could arrive at in the light of the same circumstances and evidence) (*Lee v Showman's Guild [1952] 2 QB 329*; *Harris v Lord Shuttleworth [1994] PLR 47*; and *Edge v Pensions Ombudsman [1999] 49 PBLR (36)*).

(c) Early retirement or dismissal?

One area that has given rise to a number disputes is the question of whether a person can be said to have retired on grounds of incapacity when their employment has in fact been unilaterally terminated by their employer. Cases dealing with early retirement pensions in the context of dismissals have also turned on the rules of a particular scheme, but the courts have set out a number of principles that should assist trustees in deciding whether or not there has been a retirement for the purposes of the rules and consequently the relevant level of pension benefit. In *AGCO Ltd v Massey Ferguson Works Pension Trust Ltd [2003] EWCA Civ 1044, [2003] 57 PBLR*, the Court of Appeal considered the difference between retirement and dismissal in the context of redundancy. The rules provided more generous benefits on early retirement when an employee 'retire(d) from Service at the request of the Employer' and the question arose as to whether these words included voluntary and/or compulsory redundancy.

The Court held that in employment terms retirement is an entirely consensual event and comes about by 'effluxion of time and the expiry of the contract of employment'. 'Retire' therefore naturally covers situations distinct from dismissal and is different from the expression 'leaving Service' which covers broader circumstances. However, while both voluntary and compulsory redundancy involve an element of dismissal, voluntary redundancy (within the proper meaning of that term) occurs as a result of prior consent by the employee to such a dismissal. Consequently the words 'retires from Service at the request of the Employer and after his 50th birthday' did encompass voluntary redundancy as they were designed to enable the employer to offer early retirement to certain employees, subject to the employee's acceptance. Compulsory redundancy did not however fall within the wording of the rule.

The High Court in *Minter v Julius Bear Investment Management [2004] EWHC 2472 (Ch)* further considered the question of whether a person can be said to have retired with the consent of his employer. Rimer J stated that 'All the circumstances of the dismissal need to be examined in order to identify the true nature of the employee's departure'. The essence of 'retirement with the consent of the employer' is that 'the initiative to leave service comes from the employee and the employer (in effect) agrees to his premature release from the service agreement'. Although Mr Minter had negotiated the terms of his redundancy with the employer, the judge found on the facts that the decision that his employment was to come to an end was made by his employer.

Pension benefits on late retirement

1.40 The rules of a scheme may permit a member to remain in service after his normal retirement date.

Under the pre A-Day tax regime, where a member of an approved scheme postponed his retirement his pension did not become payable until he actually left service (except that all his benefits had to be taken on or before his 75th birthday, even if he had not retired). However, if the member had accrued (or was deemed to have accrued) benefits under the scheme before 1 June 1989, he was able to take his benefits at any time after attaining normal retirement date even though he was continuing in service.

Post A-Day there is nothing to prevent the member taking some or all of his benefits once he has reached 'normal minimum pension age', even if he remains in employment, as long as the scheme rules permit this. However, as under the pre A-Day regime, benefits must commence at age 75. There are age discrimination issues arising from such 'flexible retirement' arrangements, and DWP is considering issuing guidance on this (having decided not to legislate on the issue).

The benefits payable on late retirement will be greater than the benefits payable on normal retirement. Depending on the scheme rules, a member may continue to accrue pensionable service after his normal retirement date or alternatively his benefits may be calculated as at his normal retirement date and then increased by actuarial factors to take account of late receipt. The age discrimination provisions may effectively require schemes to offer continued accrual.

As with early retirement benefits, the provision of late retirement benefits is considered to be an alternative to a preserved benefit and so the legislation relating to preservation of benefits must be complied with (see CHAPTER 6).

Tax-free lump sum on retirement

1.41 A member may choose to take part of his retirement benefits in the form of a tax-free cash lump sum if the rules of the scheme allow. Under the pre A-Day regime, the maximum lump sum that could be taken was restricted by HMRC and, to an extent, depended on the circumstances of the retirement.

Under the *FA 2004* regime, there is more scope for a member to take tax-free cash. The general position is that up to 25 per cent of the value of an individual's fund or benefits crystallised on that date may be taken as tax-free cash.

If a higher amount is paid then it will be an unauthorised payment, and adverse tax consequences will arise unless the individual is entitled to benefit from the transitional protection provisions, under *FA 2004, Sch 36*, where the entitlement to maximum tax-free cash for service accrued up to 6 April 2006 exceeds the entitlement to tax-free cash under the new regime.

Full commutation of benefits may be permissible where the member is in serious ill-health (life expectancy of less than one year) or where the benefits payable are classed as trivial (see CHAPTER 16).

Lump sum death benefits

1.42 An occupational pension scheme will usually provide a life assurance benefit in the event of the death of an active member. This benefit is usually calculated by multiplying a member's salary (which can be pensionable salary, annual salary or final pensionable salary) by a specified figure, but occasionally it is a fixed sum. The maximum amount that may be paid from the scheme is the Lifetime Allowance (see CHAPTER 16).

In the event of a member's death, the life assurance benefit will usually be payable under 'discretionary trust' in order to mitigate any potential inheritance tax liability. If a payment is made through a discretionary trust, it will not form part of the member's estate and consequently will not be taken into account when assessing liability for inheritance tax. A scheme's governing rules will therefore usually contain an appropriate discretionary trust provision. When a member joins the scheme he may be asked to complete a 'statement of wishes' form to indicate to the trustees the person he would wish to receive a lump sum death benefit in the event of his death. This statement of wishes does not bind the trustees but simply acts as guidance for them. Irrespective of whether the member has completed a statement of wishes form, the trustees should make proper inquiries to establish whether or not they are paying the benefits to the most appropriate person. This is particularly true where there has been a change in the member's personal circumstances, such as a remarriage or death in the family. The trustees should tread carefully, as they will be exercising their discretion and so must take into account all relevant, but no irrelevant, factors; ask themselves the proper questions; adopt a correct construction of the rules of the scheme; and do not arrive at a perverse decision (ie one which no reasonable body of trustees could arrive at in the light of the same circumstances and evidence). (See **1.39** above; and *Wild v Smith [1996] PLR 275*.)

Lump sum death benefits are usually insured with a life assurance company. Only the largest occupational schemes are inclined to pay death benefits directly out of the fund as such benefits can be very costly.

Spouse's/dependant's pension

1.43 In addition to the lump sum life assurance benefit payable in the event of the death of a member, a pension is often payable to his surviving spouse or civil partner. The amount of the benefit payable will generally vary depending on whether the member died before or after retirement.

If a member dies whilst an active member, the amount payable will usually be a percentage (often 50 per cent) of the member's prospective pension. This will be calculated on the basis of either his actual pensionable service at the date of death or the pensionable service he would have completed had he remained an active member until his normal retirement date and had his pensionable salary remained static.

In the case of the death of a member following his retirement, the spouse's pension is often calculated as a percentage of the member's pension at the date of his death. A spouse's pension of 50 per cent of the pension the member was receiving at the date of his death is common.

The rules of the scheme may also permit a child or dependant's pension to be paid either where the member dies leaving no spouse (or a spouse who subsequently dies) or in addition to any spouse's pension which is payable. *FA 2004, s 167* sets out who may qualify for a dependant's pension and a child may fall within that category if he is under the age of 23 or has reached that age but, in the opinion of the scheme administrator, was dependent on the member at the date of the member's death because of physical or mental impairment (see CHAPTER 16 for further details).

Note that, in accordance with the *Civil Partnership Act 2005*, with effect from 5 December 2005, the surviving civil partner of a member of a pension scheme is entitled to a spouse's pension based on the pension rights accrued by the deceased civil partner in respect of service from that date. Schemes that are contracted out are also required to pay a civil partner a pension in respect of contracted out employment from 6 April 1988 (in the same way that they are required to pay a pension to a member's widower). As the contracting-out requirements are not overriding, rule amendments may need to be made to give effect to this, in which case *PA 1995, s 67* must be complied with by trustees. Alternatively, *Occupational Pension Schemes (Modification of Schemes) Regulations 2006, reg 7* allows trustees to make appropriate modifications under *PA 1995, s 68*.

Benefits on leaving service other than on retirement

1.44 A member is entitled to a preserved benefit within a scheme if his pensionable service under that scheme is terminated before his normal pension age and he has at least two years' qualifying service. Broadly speaking, qualifying service is pensionable service under the scheme, service in employment which was contracted out by reference to the scheme or service which is deemed to be qualifying service by virtue of a transfer payment received by the scheme in respect of the member. A member's normal pension age is the earliest date on which he has an unqualified right to retire on an unreduced pension, other than on special grounds, such as ill-health or redundancy.

PSA 1993, Part IV sets out the minimum requirements with which schemes must comply in the context of preservation. If a member has a preserved benefit under a scheme, he has a statutory right to have that benefit calculated on the same basis as if he had remained in the relevant employment and rendered service so as to qualify for benefits until normal pension age. Once calculated, the preserved amount must then be revalued in order to protect it from the impact of inflation.

Alternatively, the individual may choose to transfer the 'cash equivalent' of his benefits to a registered pension scheme, qualifying recognised overseas pension scheme or buy-out policy. Transfer values from defined benefit schemes are calculated by the trustees, who must determine the assumptions to be used on a 'best estimate' basis after obtaining actuarial advice.

Since 6 April 2006, members who leave a scheme having completed at least three months' qualifying service have had the right to elect for a 'cash transfer sum' which they may take as an alternative to a refund of their contributions. In contrast to a refund, a cash transfer sum includes the value of the employer's contributions as well as those of the member and therefore this represents an enhancement to the rights of early leavers.

The protection afforded to early leavers is considered in detail in CHAPTER 6.

Defined contribution schemes

Pension benefits

1.45 The benefits paid to a member of a defined contribution scheme are determined by two factors, namely:

(*a*) the amount of money held by the trustees on behalf of the member at retirement; and

(*b*) the annuity rates applicable at the time when the member's benefits become payable.

The amount of money held by the trustees under (*a*) will be determined by the level of contributions paid by the member's employer and the member himself, and the investment return realised in respect of those contributions. The total amount is generally referred to as the member's 'individual account' or, more colloquially, his 'pot'.

It is becoming increasingly common for members to be given some discretion over the way in which their individual account is invested. Often members will be given a choice of funds and are required to indicate to the trustees of the scheme what percentage of their individual account they wish to invest in each fund. The scheme must be carefully structured to ensure that the arrangements put in place, whilst offering the member choice, do not expose the trustees to potential claims from members whose investment choices do not perform as well as expected.

A member will not have any claim to any particular asset, even if he is given some power in relation to how his account is invested. All the assets of the scheme will be invested together so that, although the member's account will be credited with interest or investment growth, no specific scheme asset will be attributable to his account.

On the member's retirement, whether at, before or after normal retirement date, assets equal in value to his individual account will be realised and the proceeds will be used to provide the member with a pension. Some defined contribution schemes provide additional benefits on the retirement of a member due to incapacity, but this will almost certainly be at the discretion of the employer.

Under the *FA 2004* tax regime, defined contribution schemes can pay a 'scheme pension', a 'lifetime annuity' or an 'unsecured pension' to a member who has not yet reached age 75. However, a scheme pension can only be paid if the member has first been given the opportunity to select a lifetime annuity (*PA 2004, s 165*).

'Scheme pensions' are either pensions paid directly from the scheme out of its own resources, or by an insurance company selected by the scheme administrator (*FA 2004, Sch 28, para 2*). A 'lifetime annuity' is an annuity payable by an insurance company which meets certain specified requirements (*FA 2004, Sch 28, para 3*). An 'unsecured pension' is, broadly, either a short-term annuity or income withdrawal arrangement (*FA 2004, Sch 28, para 4*).

The pension rules in relation to defined contribution schemes are considered further in CHAPTER 16.

Death benefits

1.46 Most defined contribution schemes provide lump sum death-in-service benefits in much the same way as defined benefit schemes do (see **1.42** above).

The benefits provided to the spouse and/or dependants of a member of a defined contribution scheme may be a proportion of the member's salary or may be such level of pension as can be secured by the proceeds of the member's account. If the scheme provides a percentage of salary, there will usually be some form of insurance as it is possible (and in the case of young or new members, likely) that the member's account will be insufficient to provide the necessary funds to secure the benefit.

Benefits on leaving service

1.47 A member of a defined contribution scheme who terminates his pensionable service before his normal retirement date is entitled to benefits in much the same way as a member of a defined benefit scheme. The same statutory criteria determine whether the member has a right to preserved benefit or not, although the method of calculating the preserved benefit will, of course, be different.

A member of a defined contribution scheme who has at least three months' qualifying service under the scheme will also generally have a statutory right to require that the 'cash equivalent' of his benefits be transferred to a registered pension scheme, qualifying recognised overseas pension scheme or buy-out policy (see CHAPTER 6).

Increasing pensions in payment

1.48 *PA 1995, s 51* (which was amended with effect from 6 April 2005 by *PA 2004*) applies to any part of a pension under an occupational pension scheme that is:

(*a*) a defined benefit attributable to pensionable service on or after 6 April 1997; or

(*b*) a money purchase benefit in respect of employment carried out on or after 6 April 1997 but in payment before 6 April 2005.

Any payments in respect of the above benefits must be increased annually by a minimum amount. Pensions that were in payment before 6 April 2005 or that are wholly attributable to pensionable service before that date must be increased by the lesser of 5 per cent per annum and the increase in the RPI for that period (this is known as limited price indexation, or 'LPI'). Defined benefits pensions that are in payment on or after 6 April 2005 and that are attributable to pensionable service on or after that date must be increased by the lesser of 2.5 per cent and the increase in RPI. Where a pension comes into payment on or after 6 April 2005 and it is attributable to service both before and after that date, then increases will be payable at 5 per cent LPI on the pre-6 April 2005 portion and at 2.5 per cent LPI on the remainder.

As can be seen above, in relation to defined contribution schemes, *PA 2004* had the effect of removing altogether (other than in relation to contracted-out rights) the requirement to increase any pension coming into payment on or after 6 April 2005.

If an increase in excess of LPI is given in a particular tax year, the excess may be offset against the following year's LPI increase (*PA 1995, s 53*). LPI increases do not, however, have to be given in respect of pensions which derive from a member's voluntary contributions (*PA 1995, s 51(6)*). Nor do increases have to be given in respect of a pension paid to a member who has not attained the age of 55 at the time when the increase takes effect, unless he retired on account of incapacity (*PA 1995, s 52*).

LPI increases must be given in respect of benefits derived from transfer payments but only to the extent that they are attributable to pensionable service completed on or after 6 April 1997 (*Occupational Pension Schemes (Indexation) Regulations 1996, reg 2*). This requirement does not apply to transfer payments from a scheme which itself was not subject to the indexation requirement.

LPI increases do not have to be given in respect of benefits derived from a pension credit awarded as a result of a pension sharing order on the divorce of a member (*PA 1995, s 51(6)*).

Forfeiture and suspension of benefits

1.49 Generally, a member's entitlement or accrued right to a pension under an occupational pension scheme cannot be assigned, commuted, surrendered, charged or set-off (*PA 1995, s 91*). However, there are various exceptions to this general rule (see below). Where a pension is prevented from being assigned under *s 91*, a court is not able to make an order, other than an attachment of earnings order or an income payments order, that would restrain a member from receiving that pension (although unregistered schemes, apart from public service pension schemes and the Armed Forces Pension Scheme are excepted from this restriction).

Exceptions to inalienability

Commutation of pension

1.50 The rules of an occupational pension scheme may, and generally do, allow a member to commute part or, in some circumstances, all of his pension for a lump sum (see **1.41** above). The situations in which such commutation will fall within an exception to the inalienability rule are set out in *PA 1995, s 91(5)(c)* and *Occupational Pension Schemes (Assignment, Forfeiture, Bankruptcy etc) Regulations 1997 (the 'Forfeiture Regulations'), reg 2*.

Surrender in favour of a spouse and/or dependant

1.51 The rules of a scheme may allow a member to assign to, or surrender part of his pension to provide a pension for, his widow, widower, surviving civil partner and/or dependants. A person may also surrender part of his pension in order to acquire an entitlement to further benefits under the scheme (*PA 1995, s 91(5)(a), (b)*).

Charge, lien or set-off

1.52 *PA 1995, s 91(5)(d) and (e)* provide that the rules of a scheme may allow for a charge or lien on, or a set-off against, an individual's pension benefits to be made for the purposes of:

(*a*) enabling the individual's employer to discharge a monetary obligation due to the employer arising out of the individual's criminal, negligent or fraudulent act or omission (although only certain transfer credits may be used in this context); and

(*b*) discharging a monetary obligation due to the scheme arising out of:

(i) the individual's criminal, negligent or fraudulent act or omission; or

(ii) a breach of trust by the individual where he is a trustee (unless the court has relieved him, wholly or partly, from personal liability under *Trustee Act 1925, s 61*) (*Forfeiture Regulations, reg 4*).

A new *PA 1995, s 91(5)(f)* was inserted by *PA 2004, s 266* with effect from 6 April 2005, allowing trustees to reduce or suspend pensions in payment in order to recoup overpayments of benefits. There had previously been some debate as to whether *s 91* allowed trustees to do this. The Pensions Ombudsman had issued a number of determinations finding that the trustees could do so, and the amendment to *s 91* confirms this position.

The amount of any charge, lien or set-off (including a suspension or reduction under *s 91(5)(f)*) is restricted to the amount of the monetary obligation in question or, if less, the value of the member's entitlement (calculated on a cash equivalent basis (see CHAPTER 6)) or accrued right. The member must be given a certificate showing the amount of the charge, lien or set-off and its effect on his benefits under the scheme. If the member disputes the amount, the charge, lien or set-off cannot be effected unless the obligation becomes enforceable by a court order or an arbitrator's award. It is questionable whether silence on the part of the member concerned amounts to consent to the amount of the charge, lien or set-off, even if the certificate specifies that any dispute must be raised within a certain time limit. In effect, unless the member agrees to the charge, lien or set-off being exercised, the safest course of action is to obtain a court order or arbitrator's award.

A charge, lien or set-off cannot be exercised against a member's protected rights or accrued right to a guaranteed minimum pension. Neither can a charge, lien or set-off be exercised against a transfer payment received by the scheme in respect of a member (in the context of discharging a monetary obligation due to the employer) unless it is attributable to employment with the same or a financially associated employer, and the benefits transferred could have been subject to a charge, lien or set-off under the transferring scheme. (*Forfeiture Regulations, reg 3*).

Forfeiture

1.53 Forfeiture is defined under *PA 1995, s 92* to include any manner of deprivation or suspension of an entitlement, or accrued right, to a pension under an occupational pension scheme. Such an entitlement or right cannot be forfeited other than as a consequence of:

(*a*) an actual or purported assignment, commutation, surrender, charge, lien or set-off which under *s 91* is of no effect;

(*b*) the member being convicted of certain offences such as treason before the pension becomes payable;

(*c*) the failure of the member to make a claim within a limitation period or within six years of the benefit becoming due; or

(*d*) prescribed circumstances.

Where a member's benefits are forfeited under the circumstances in paragraph (*a*) above, the trustees have a discretion under *PA 1995, s 92(3)* to pay any pension or benefit which was, or would but for the forfeiture have become payable, to all or any of the following:

(i) the member of the scheme to, or in respect of whom the pension was, or would have become, payable;

(ii) the spouse, civil partner, widow, widower, surviving civil partner or any dependant of the member;

(iii) any other person to whom, under the rules of the scheme, the pension was or could have been paid.

The prescribed circumstances in paragraph (*d*) above include the situation where a pension is payable to a person nominated by the member and that person is convicted of the murder, manslaughter or an offence relating to the unlawful killing of the member; and where a potential beneficiary has caused a monetary loss to the scheme arising out of a breach of trust as trustee or as a result of a criminal, negligent or fraudulent act or omission. In each case an entitlement, or accrued right, to a pension under an occupational pension scheme may be forfeited. *PA 1995* also makes separate provision for public service pension schemes and the Armed Forces Pension Scheme.

A person's benefits may also be forfeited if he has incurred some monetary obligation due to the employer arising out of a criminal, negligent or fraudulent act or omission. The conditions are the same as those that apply when exercising a charge, lien or set-off, in respect of the amount of the monetary obligation and the requirements concerning disputes and certification. If a member's benefits are forfeited in these circumstances, the trustees have power to determine that the amount forfeited is paid to the employer (*PA 1995, s 93(5)*).

Pension rights following a member's bankruptcy

1.54 When an individual is declared bankrupt the general rule is that his estate automatically vests in the trustee in bankruptcy (*Insolvency Act 1986*

(IA 1986), s 306). The bankrupt's estate is defined as all property belonging to or vested in the bankrupt at the commencement of the bankruptcy, except for items for the bankrupt's personal use in his employment, and items for the basic domestic needs of the bankrupt and his family (*IA 1986, s 283*).

How does this affect an individual's pension rights? It was previously established that trustees in bankruptcy were entitled to claim the entire pension benefits of scheme members, not just pensions in payment (see *Re Landau [1997] 3 All ER 322*). In order to protect scheme members, many pension schemes included forfeiture clauses – these will all be slightly different but the purpose of them was automatically to forfeit the member's entitlement to scheme benefits on his bankruptcy and for the trustees to have a discretion to distribute payments, up to the value of those benefits, to the member or his family (commonly known as 'protective trusts').

As a result of the *Welfare Reform and Pensions Act 1999* (*WRPA 1999*), forfeiture clauses have become less significant. Indeed, for persons made bankrupt on or after 6 April 2002, forfeiture clauses are no longer effective (see **1.55** below).

However, while they still maintain some relevance in relation to bankruptcies prior to 6 April 2002, it is important to note that not all forfeiture clauses are automatically valid. The validity of forfeiture clauses has been scrutinised closely by the courts, most notably in *Kemble v Hicks [1998] 3 All ER 154*. This shows a difference between:

(*a*) clauses which purport to forfeit an absolute interest that is vested in possession, which are void;

(*b*) clauses which purport to forfeit determinable life interests that are vested in possession (ie interests that are valid until the happening of a certain event). These are only valid if the life interest is determinable in the same events that the forfeiture clause is expressed to operate; and

(*c*) clauses which forfeit a contingent interest that has not yet vested in possession, which are generally acceptable (ie an interest that will only become payable on the happening of a future specified event).

The relevance of a valid forfeiture clause to an individual, depending on the time that the bankruptcy order was made, is shown more clearly in the table in **1.55** below.

The Welfare Reform and Pensions Act 1999

1.55 The law concerning the effect of bankruptcy on an individual's pension rights changed dramatically under *WRPA 1999*. *WRPA 1999, Part*

II contains provisions on pensions and bankruptcy which apply to 'approved pension arrangements' which includes registered pension schemes together with certain occupational pension schemes set up by governments outside the UK and certain retirement annuity contracts.

The treatment of a member's scheme benefits on bankruptcy will now depend on the date the bankruptcy order was made. The position, as it applies to benefits under approved pension arrangements (see *WRPA 1999, ss 11, 14*), is summarised below.

Date of bankruptcy order	**Is there a valid forfeiture clause?**	**Treatment of bankrupt's benefit**
Before 29 May 2000	No	Benefits vest in trustee in bankruptcy on his appointment.
Before 29 May 2000	Yes	Benefits are forfeit and may be applied by scheme trustees under 'protective trusts'.
On or after 29 May 2000 and up to and including 5 April 2002	No	Benefits do not vest in trustee in bankruptcy on his appointment and are payable from scheme under the provisions of the trust deed and rules.
On or after 29 May 2000 and up to and including 5 April 2002	Yes	Benefits do not vest in trustee in bankruptcy on his appointment but forfeiture clause will operate provided the clause is valid and benefits may be applied by scheme trustees under 'protective trusts'.
On or after 6 April 2002	All forfeiture clauses are void	Benefits do not vest in trustee in bankruptcy on his appointment and are payable from scheme under the provisions of the trust deed and rules.

Pensions in payment

1.56 If a member is in receipt of a pension during the period of his bankruptcy (between the date of bankruptcy order and the date of discharge), it is open to the trustee in bankruptcy to apply to the court for an income payments order under *IA 1986, s 310* requiring the pension to be paid to the trustee in bankruptcy rather than the member. This would equally apply if a lump sum payment was made from the scheme during the period of bankruptcy. The court will only make such an order where it would not have the effect of reducing the income of the bankrupt (taking into account GMP and protected-rights payments) below what appears to the court to be necessary for meeting the reasonable domestic needs of the bankrupt and his family.

In most cases, income payments orders will be in force from the period of the commencement of the order until the bankrupt is discharged. It is important to remember that the trustee in bankruptcy can only exercise those rights under the pension scheme which the bankrupt himself can. Therefore, if there is a long period of time before a member reaches retirement age pension rights will be of little use to a trustee in bankruptcy.

The *Enterprise Act 2002* introduced an alternative to the income payments order, in the form of an 'income payments agreement' (as set out in *IA 1986, s 310A*). An income payments agreement is a written agreement between the bankrupt and his trustee in bankruptcy or official receiver. The agreement provides for the bankrupt or a third party (which can include the trustees of a pension scheme) to pay to the trustee in bankruptcy or official receiver an amount equal to a specified part or proportion of the bankrupt's income for a specified period.

Whilst, unlike an income payments order, an income payments agreement avoids the requirement of a court hearing, the terms of the income payments agreement can be enforced as if they were provisions of an income payments order. An income payments agreement must specify the period for which it is to have effect and it can continue in force past the date of the discharge of the bankrupt for up to a maximum period of three years from the date of the agreement.

The effect on unapproved schemes

1.57 The benefits provided by an unapproved pension scheme (within the meaning of *WRPA 1999, Part II*) will vest automatically in the trustee in bankruptcy. However, the Secretary of State is able to make regulations that define what constitutes an unapproved pension scheme and how that might, in prescribed circumstances, be excluded from his estate (see *WRPA 1999, s 12*). The member is now able to apply to the Court for an order excluding all or part of his entitlement under the scheme, or he may reach a formal agreement to that effect with the trustee in bankruptcy (see *Occupational and Personal Pension Schemes (Bankruptcy) (No 2) Regulations 2002, reg 4*).

Excessive contributions

1.58 *WRPA 1999, s 15* amends *IA 1986, ss 342A–342C*, so that the trustee in bankruptcy can seek an order from the court, where excessive contributions have been made to an approved pension scheme and the court is satisfied that the contributions:

(*a*) have unfairly prejudiced individual creditors; and

(*b*) have been made in an effort to keep them beyond the reach of creditors; and

(*c*) were excessive when looking at the individual's personal circumstances at the time.

Any order will restore the position to what it would have been, had the excessive contributions not been made (and the trustees of the scheme will be ordered to pay an amount to the trustee in bankruptcy).

Stakeholder pension schemes

Background

1.59 Stakeholder pensions were introduced by the Government as a new way for individuals to make provision for their retirement. The stakeholder pension scheme was designed to be a low cost, easy-to-understand, defined contribution pension plan targeted at individuals earning between £9,000 and £20,000 per annum who were not making pension provision at the time of introduction. Details of the original proposal were set out in the November 1997 consultation paper 'Stakeholder Pensions – A Consultation Document' and carried forward in the December 1998 Green Paper 'A new contract for welfare: Partnership in Pensions'. Several consultation papers seeking comment on the proposed workings of stakeholder pension schemes followed until finally, on 11 November 1999, with the publication of the *Welfare Reform and Pensions Act 1999,* the first statutory guidance on stakeholder pension schemes was published. The first stakeholder schemes became registrable from 1 October 2000 and were available to the public from 6 April 2001. The primary regulations governing the operation of stakeholder schemes are the *Stakeholder Pension Schemes Regulations 2000* (the *Stakeholder Regulations*).

The basic elements of stakeholder

1.60 The following outlines the basic aspects of a stakeholder pension scheme.

(a) Legal structure

Stakeholder schemes may be established either on the basis of a trust (ie similar to that of an occupational pension scheme) or on a contractual basis with a manager as prescribed in the *Stakeholder Regulations, reg 2*. The *Stakeholder Regulations* set out what must be included in the instruments establishing the scheme, and in particular that trust-based schemes must include the requirement that one-third of the trustees are independent. Typically the benefits provided by the scheme will be money purchase benefits and the scheme must be able to accept certain transfer payments in respect of members' rights. However, members must not be required to make choices as to how they invest their pension funds: options can be given, with a default available for those who do not wish to choose.

(b) Regulation

All stakeholder pension schemes must be registered with the Regulator which is responsible for enforcing the conditions that define a stakeholder pension. They must also be registered with HMRC and fall within the *FA 2004* taxation regime. The activities of establishing, operating and winding up a stakeholder pension scheme are regulated by the FSA and any person seeking to carry out one or more of those activities must be authorised to do so. Amongst other things, the FSA also regulates the marketing and promotion of stakeholder schemes, any financial advice given in relation to them and the investment of scheme assets. The Pensions Ombudsman has jurisdiction to hear complaints regarding maladministration.

(c) Charging

Stakeholder schemes are intended to have a simpler and more transparent charging structure than is sometimes seen with personal pension contracts. The *Stakeholder Regulations, reg 14* provides that an annual charge of 1 per cent per annum of the fund value (1.5 per cent for the first ten years) held by an individual is currently the maximum that a stakeholder scheme provider can levy. This may cover all costs associated with the administration of the scheme from expenses arising from the purchase or provision of an annuity to the charges incurred in connection with the sale or purchase of investments. All other additional services (and attaching costs) are optional to the scheme member.

(d) Minimum contributions

To ensure that those of modest means are not precluded from joining stakeholder schemes, the minimum permissible level of contributions is £20 (*Stakeholder Regulations, reg 17*), with members allowed to make contributions either on a regular or an infrequent basis, thereby catering for, amongst others, individuals who take a career break.

(e) The duty on employers

The duties of employers are set out in *WRPA 1999, s 3*. Subject to the exemptions below, all employers are required to designate at least one registered stakeholder scheme that all their employees (within the stated categories) can join. Employers are also required to supply details of that scheme to their employees and to provide a facility for the deduction of contributions from the pay of scheme members and the payment of those contributions to the scheme.

The requirement to provide access to stakeholder schemes applies to all employers, the current exemptions only applying to:

(*a*) employers with fewer than five employees;

(*b*) employers who offer a group personal pension to all employees over 18 to which they contribute at least 3 per cent per annum of their employees' earnings (deductible via payroll), and which levies no charges when an individual leaves the scheme to move to a new employer;

(*c*) employers who already offer occupational schemes where the employee may join within a year of starting work and where the qualifying age is no older than 18 and no younger than five years before the scheme's normal retirement date;

(*d*) employers whose employees all earn below the National Insurance lower earnings limit (*Stakeholder Regulations, regs 22, 23*).

On the introduction of personal accounts in 2012 (see CHAPTER 13), stakeholder pensions will continue to be one of the options for pension saving, but the designation requirement for employers will be removed. Further details relating to stakeholder pension schemes are set out in CHAPTER 13.

Chapter 2

People involved with pensions

Introduction

2.1 This chapter considers the roles of the individuals and organisations involved in the administration, management and regulation of pension schemes. The people involved in pensions fall within four main categories:

(*a*) those whose involvement is specific to the scheme in question; this group includes the trustees of the scheme and the professional advisers appointed by the trustees (ie the actuary, auditor and fund manager) to assist them in carrying out their functions;

(*b*) those which can broadly be termed the regulatory bodies; this group includes the Pensions Regulator ('the Regulator'), Her Majesty's Revenue and Customs ('HMRC'), National Insurance Services to Pensions Industry ('NISPI', which is a directorate within the National Insurance Contributions Office operated by HMRC), the Board of the Pension Protection Fund ('PPF') and the Personal Accounts Delivery Authority;

(*c*) The Pensions Advisory Service ('TPAS') (formerly OPAS) and the Pensions Ombudsman, both of whom may have a role to play when disputes arise; and

(*d*) the various professional bodies, the most important of which are the Pensions Management Institute and the National Association of Pension Funds.

Trustees

2.2 Where a pension scheme is established by an employer under trust, the role of the trustees is to hold the scheme's assets separately from the employer's assets and to apply them for the benefit of scheme members in accordance with the trust documents, general trust law and overriding legislation. If the scheme's liabilities are funded in advance over a period of time by employers' and employees' contributions, the use of a trust creates a degree of security for scheme members by placing the scheme's assets beyond the reach of the employers' creditors. With effect from 6 April 2006, any

UK-based occupational pension scheme wishing to accept payments to the scheme to fund benefits must be established under trust (*PA 2004, s 252*).

The role of a pension scheme trustee is evolving. In the past, there were few restrictions as to who could be a pension scheme trustee: for example, a trustee could be an individual, the scheme's principal employer, a company, an elected employee or a member representative. For practical reasons, however, a scheme's trustees would usually be either at least two individuals or a company, whose board of directors would take the relevant decisions. *PA 1995* imposed requirements as to who may and may not be a pension scheme trustee (see **3.2** below) and, in broad terms, entitled scheme members to nominate at least one third of the trustees (unless the scheme members accepted alternative arrangements proposed by the employer). The Government was concerned that many schemes did not have member-nominated trustees as a result of alternative employer arrangements and, as a consequence, *PA 2004* introduced new requirements for member-nominated trustees with effect from 6 April 2006. Schemes are no longer able to opt out of the requirement to allow members to nominate at least one third of the trustees. Opt-out arrangements already in place were allowed to continue for a limited period of time; however, since 31 October 2007 it has not been possible for a scheme to opt out of the member-nominated trustee requirements (see CHAPTER 3).

Trustees must act in the best interests of the beneficiaries (generally considered to mean their best financial interests) and in accordance with trust law and the scheme's trust deed and rules. CHAPTER 3 takes a more detailed look at trustees' duties and responsibilities in light of recent developments.

In 2001, Paul Myners published his review of institutional investment in the UK setting out the 'blueprint' for change and recommendations for pensions schemes. The Government published consultation papers focusing on three of the Myners' Report recommendations on which it intended to legislate. These included whether schemes should have independent custodians, encouraging shareholder activism, and the need for trustees to be familiar with the issues concerned when reaching investment decisions. This latter recommendation was provided for in *PA 2004* through the requirements for trustee knowledge and understanding (*PA 2004, ss 247–294*) which are considered in CHAPTER 3. The principles for investment recommended in the Myners' Review were adopted as a voluntary code in 2001 and revised in 2008. These are dealt with in more detail in CHAPTER 10.

PA 1995 introduced civil and criminal penalties for trustees in respect of breaches of certain sections of *PA 1995* (and *PSA 1993*, as amended) and the disqualification or suspension of trustees in certain circumstances. Certain breaches of *PA 2004* are also subject to penalties under *PA 1995*. Details of these appear throughout this book and are summarised in APPENDIX I.

Actuaries

The role of the actuary

2.3 Actuaries assess financial problems, using mathematical and statistical methods, specialising, in particular, in problems concerning uncertain future events. In the context of pension schemes this most often involves predicting movements in the scheme (deaths, retirements and withdrawals) and estimating the costs of providing the benefits due and accruing in the future.

Previously, the actuary to a scheme would have recommended the assumptions and methods to be used to value the scheme's assets and liabilities, would periodically value these (see CHAPTER 11) and, where the scheme promised defined benefits, would have recommended the rate of contribution which was necessary to provide those benefits. The actuary's role changed for all valuations with effect from 22 September 2005. The trustees (in most cases with the consent of the employer) must choose the assumptions to be used in the valuation, adopt a statement of funding principles and set the contribution rate. The trustees are required by *PA 2004* to take advice from the actuary before making any decisions on these matters.

The actuary will also advise on a day-to-day basis on benefit issues, such as the calculation of cash equivalents and early retirement factors (for example, the extent to which an early retirement pension should be discounted to take account of early payment). An actuary may also advise the trustees on strategic investment decisions.

The appointment of the actuary under PA 1995

2.4 Under *PA 1995, s 47* (subject to the exemptions listed below), the trustees of occupational pension schemes and stakeholder schemes (if registered in accordance with *Welfare Reform and Pensions Act 1999 (WRPA 1999), s 2*) must appoint an actuary. The actuary so appointed must be a named individual, even if working in an actuarial firm (*PA 1995, s 47(1)(b)*). The individual actuary appointed under this provision ('the scheme actuary') has specific functions to perform under *PA 1995* and *PA 2004*. In particular, it is the scheme actuary who is responsible for signing valuations (see CHAPTER 11).

Under the *Scheme Administration Regulations (SI 1996/1715, as amended), reg 3(2)*, the requirement for a scheme actuary does not apply to:

(*a*) money purchase schemes;

(*b*) statutory schemes, or schemes with a Crown guarantee;

(*c*) schemes with less than two members;

(*d*) unregistered schemes with fewer than 100 members;

(*e*) expatriate schemes under *ICTA 1988, s 615(6)* with fewer than 100 members;

(*f*) schemes with fewer than 12 members where all the members are trustees and either all decisions must be made unanimously by the trustees, or a statutory independent trustee has been appointed; and

(*g*) schemes with fewer than 12 members where all the members are directors of a company which is the sole trustee of the scheme and either the provisions of the scheme provide that any decisions made by the company in its capacity as trustee are made by the unanimous agreement of all the directors who are members of the scheme, or a statutory independent director has been appointed.

The *Scheme Administration Regulations (SI 1996/1715), reg 4(1)(b)* sets out the qualifications and experience or approval required for appointment as the scheme actuary. An actuary must be a Fellow of the Institute or Faculty of Actuaries or must be approved by the Secretary of State. Additionally, an actuary cannot be a trustee of the pension scheme nor must he be connected with or an associate of a trustee of that scheme (see **2.6** below).

Any actuary can perform functions which do not have to be performed by the scheme actuary, but if the trustees rely on the skill or judgement of an actuary not appointed by them, they will risk incurring civil penalties. Consequently, whenever trustees of a pension scheme (even one that is exempt from having to appoint a scheme actuary) seek advice from an actuary, they should ensure that the actuary has been properly appointed in accordance with the requirements of *PA 1995*.

There are specific requirements for trustees to observe in making the necessary appointments (see *Scheme Administration Regulations (SI 1996/1715), reg 5*. Appointments are also subject to the actuarial guidance note, GN29, issued by the Institute and Faculty of Actuaries). The notice must be in writing, must specify the date of the appointment, and must set out to whom he shall report and take instructions from (*Scheme Administration Regulations, reg 5(1)*). The actuary must acknowledge the notice in writing within one month of its receipt (*Scheme Administration Regulations, reg 5(2)(a)*). In addition, the actuary must confirm in writing that he will notify the trustees of any conflict of interest to which he is subject in relation to the scheme immediately on becoming aware of the existence of the conflict (*Scheme Administration Regulations, reg 5(2)(b)(ii)*). If the actuary resigns from the appointment or is removed by the trustees, he is required to certify whether the circumstances of the resignation or removal are likely to affect the members (*Scheme Administration Regulations, reg 5(4)*). Subject to these requirements, the trustees are free to determine the terms of the appointment and, where an actuary resigns or is removed from the appointment, the trustees are required to appoint a replacement within three months (*Scheme Administration Regulations, reg 5(8)*).

Whistleblowing

2.5 The scheme actuary is required by *PA 2004, s 70* to be a 'whistleblower' (see **2.14** below).

The actuary's professional obligations are set out in Guidance Note 29, 'Occupational Pension Schemes – Advisers to the Trustees' (GN 29). The Guidance Note is updated and the latest version (7.1) took effect on 31 March 2008. The purpose of the Guidance Note is to provide guidance for scheme actuaries on appointment, resignation or removal, absence, responsibilities and mentoring, on the responsibilities of trustees' advisers and on the responsibilities of mentors. Version 7.1 of the Guidance Note makes clear that the actuary is not required to police the trustees' compliance with the Regulator's Codes of Practice or Guidance, but must consider whether it is necessary to draw the trustees' attention to any obligations placed upon them or conduct expected of them.

If the actuary becomes aware that the trustees have, in his or her opinion:

- failed to comply with advising the actuary of specified events which could be of material significance to the financing or solvency of the scheme;
- failed to provide, or allow access to copies of any future reports to the Regulator;
- failed to provide, or allow access to copies of any order, notice, direction or statement which is relevant to the financing or solvency of the scheme issued by the Regulator (including copies of the scheme's books, accounts, supporting documentation, minutes of trustee meetings, trustee resolutions, documents recording decisions taken by trustees and copies of all documents constituting the scheme);
- shown inconsistency in decisions that the trustees have taken in areas relevant to the actuary's statutory responsibilities and those inconsistencies cast doubt on the trustees' proper management of the scheme; or
- failed to give appropriate consideration to any matter on which he or she is advising them in connection with his or her statutory responsibilities and this casts doubt on the trustees' proper management of the scheme;

then the actuary must discuss the underlying issues with the trustees and must then consider whether it would be appropriate to take further action. Depending on the circumstances, appropriate actions might include making a report to the Regulator under *PA 2004, s 70* and/or resigning his or her appointment (GN29 (version 7.1), para 5.3).

Ineligibility to act if a trustee

2.6 Under *PA 1995, s 27* a trustee of a pension scheme (including stakeholder schemes) (and any person 'connected' or 'associated' with such a trustee) may not be an actuary to the same scheme. (The terms 'connected' and 'associated' are defined in *PA 1995, s 123* by reference to *Insolvency Act 1986, ss 249, 435*.

However, a director, partner or employee of a firm of actuaries may act as a scheme's actuary even though another director, partner or employee of the firm is a trustee of that scheme (*PA 1995, s 27(2)*), or a company with which he is associated with is the trustee (*Scheme Administration Regulations (SI 1996/1715), reg 7*).

Breach of *PA 1995, s 27* is a criminal offence (*PA 1995, s 28*).

Auditors

2.7 Trustees of occupational pension schemes must appoint an individual or a firm as auditor under *PA 1995, s 47*. That individual or firm must be eligible for appointment as a statutory auditor under *Companies Act 2006, Part 42* or otherwise approved by the Secretary of State. Under the *Scheme Administration Regulations, reg 3(1)*, this requirement does not apply to:

(*a*) unregistered schemes;

(*b*) unfunded schemes;

(*c*) schemes with fewer than two members;

(*d*) overseas schemes under *ICTA 1988, s 615(6)*;

(*e*) schemes with fewer than 12 members where all the members are trustees and either all decisions must be made unanimously by the trustees, or a statutory independent trustee has been appointed;

(*f*) schemes with fewer than 12 members where all the members are directors of a company which is the sole trustee of the scheme and either the provisions of the scheme provide that any decisions made by the company in its capacity as trustee are made by the unanimous agreement of all the directors who are members of the scheme, or a statutory independent director has been appointed; and

(*g*) certain schemes established by statute.

Rules similar to those applying to the appointment of actuaries apply to the appointment of auditors under *PA 1995* (see **2.4** above). However, the bar on a trustee (or anyone 'connected' or 'associated' with a trustee) acting as auditor (see **2.6** above) is arguably wider, in that there is no specific provision enabling a director, partner or employee of a firm of auditors to act as auditor where another director, partner or employee of that firm is a trustee of the scheme. The same sanction as referred to in **2.6** above applies to any auditor who breaches the provisions of *PA 1995, s 27*. The auditor is also required to whistleblow in the circumstances set out in **2.5** above.

The *Occupational Pension Schemes (Requirement to obtain Audited Accounts and a Statement from the Auditor) Regulations 1996 (SI 1996/1975)*, as amended by the *Occupational Pension Schemes (Administration and Audited Accounts) (Amendment) Regulations 2005 (SI 2005/2426)*, which apply to all schemes which are required to appoint an auditor under *PA 1995, s 47*, except insured schemes which earmark insurance policies for each member, require:

(i) the trustees to obtain audited accounts and the auditor's statement regarding payment of contributions within seven months of the end of the scheme year;

(ii) the trustees to make provision as to the form and content of the accounts; and

(iii) the accounts to contain a statement that they have been prepared and audited in accordance with the regulations.

In addition, occupational pension schemes with 100 or more members which are unapproved or unregistered or overseas schemes under *ICTA 1988, s 615(6)* are required to produce audited accounts (despite the fact they are exempt from the requirements to appoint an auditor). This provision was introduced by the *Occupational Pension Schemes (Administration and Audited Accounts) (Amendment) Regulations 2005 (SI 2005/2426)* as a result of the European *Directive 2003/41/EC on the Activities and Supervision of Institutions for Occupational Retirement Provision*.

Further guidance for auditors can be found in the Auditing Practices Board's ('APB') Practice Note 15: 'The Audit of Occupational Pension Schemes in the United Kingdom' which was revised in March 2007.

Investment managers

2.8 A scheme's trust deed and rules will usually give the trustees wide investment powers to enable them to deal with trust assets as if they were the beneficial owners and to maximise their investment opportunities. In addition, *PA 1995, s 34* confers on occupational scheme trustees (including trust-based stakeholder scheme trustees registered in accordance with *WRPA 1999, s 2*) an investment power which is the same as if they were absolutely entitled to the scheme's assets themselves and which is subject only to any restrictions imposed by the scheme. *PA 2004* introduced amendments to *PA 1995, ss 34* and *36* which required trustees to exercise their powers of investment in accordance with regulations. The *Occupational Pension Schemes (Investment) Regulations 2005 (SI 2005/3378)* require trustees to exercise their powers of investment in a manner calculated to ensure the security, quality, liquidity and profitability of the portfolio as a whole and include some specific restrictions on investment and borrowing. These provisions are dealt with in more detail in CHAPTER 10.

The Financial Services and Markets Act 2000 (*FSMA 2000*) prohibits a person from carrying on a regulated activity unless they are authorised or exempt. Trustees will generally delegate their investment power to a fund manager who is authorised rather than seek authorisation themselves. This is usually achieved by way of an investment management agreement ('IMA'). The IMA must contain certain information as prescribed by *PA 1995*, which includes dealing with any conflicts of interest that may arise.

Trustees are required under *PA 1995, s 47(2)* to appoint a fund manager if their scheme has 'investments', which include 'any asset right or interest' as defined in *FSMA 2000, s 22*. The regulated activities are described more fully under *FSMA 2000, Sch 2* and separated into the following headings:

- dealing in investments;
- arranging deals in investments;
- deposit taking;
- safekeeping and administration of assets;
- managing investments;
- investment advice; and
- establishing collective investment schemes.

The *Scheme Administration Regulations (SI 1996/1715)* exempt (amongst others) unfunded schemes, schemes with fewer than two members, wholly insured schemes and schemes with no more than 12 members in which all members are trustees and all investment decisions are made by all or a majority of the trustees (further exemptions are provided for under the *Scheme Administration Regulations, reg 3(3)* and *Financial Services and Markets Act 2000 (Carrying on Regulated Activities by Way of Business) Order 2001 (SI 2001/1177), art 4(4)*, as amended by the *Financial Services and Markets Act 2000 (Carrying on Regulated Activities by Way of Business) (Amendment) Order 2005 (SI 2005/922)*).

Pension Schemes Services of Her Majesty's Revenue and Customs

2.9 In 2005 the Inland Revenue and Customs and Excise combined in a new department, Her Majesty's Revenue and Customs (HMRC). The pension scheme responsibility which was previously dealt with by the Inland Revenue Savings, Pensions, Share Schemes business stream of the Inland Revenue is now dealt with by Pension Schemes Services (PSS) of HMRC. PSS's main responsibility is to oversee the requirements placed on pension schemes claiming tax relief, as well as related implications for members, their employers and other parties.

The tax treatment of occupational pension schemes, including the 'simplified' tax regime which came into force on 6 April 2006, is dealt with further in CHAPTER 16 and of personal pension schemes in CHAPTER 13.

HMRC's guidelines (relevant until 6 April 2006) are set out in its Practice Notes, IR12 (2001) (as updated from time to time) for occupational schemes and IR76 (2000) (as updated from time to time) for personal pension schemes (including stakeholder schemes), and a general inquiry service is available. From 6 April 2006 the relevant guidance is the Registered Pension Schemes Manual. The PSS is located in Nottingham, and can be contacted at Pension Scheme Services, FitzRoy House, Castle Meadow Road, Nottingham NG2 1BD. Tel: 0845 600 2622; website: www.hmrc.gov.uk.

National Insurance Services to Pensions Industry

2.10 The National Insurance Services to Pensions Industry (NISPI) (formerly the Contracted-Out Employments Group (COEG)) is a Directorate within the HMRC National Insurance Contributions Office and is responsible for ensuring that the pension rights of employees contracted out of the State second pension (S2P) (which replaced the State Earnings Related Pension Scheme (SERPS) with effect from 6 April 2002) are maintained and safeguarded (see CHAPTER 4). In particular, NISPI is responsible for:

(*a*) dealing with the termination of contracted-out employment;

(*b*) approving and supervising schemes if they cease to be contracted out;

(*c*) withdrawing approval of arrangements or refusing to approve them;

(*d*) issuing certificates of non-approval and discharge of liabilities directives;

(*e*) communicating with scheme authorities about the facility for checking National Insurance numbers, dates of birth etc for funding purposes; and

(*f*) answering general queries regarding contracted-out arrangements (including personal pension arrangements).

NISPI can be contacted at the National Insurance Contributions Office, Benton Park View, Newcastle upon Tyne NE98 1ZZ. Contracting-out pensions helpline: 0845 915 0150.

Occupational Pensions Board (OPB)

2.11 The OPB was dissolved by *PA 1995, s 150* with effect from 5 April 1997. Some of the OPB's overseeing functions were, following the OPB's dissolution, taken over by Opra (see **2.12** below) and subsequently the Regulator. The OPB's responsibilities for contracting out have been taken over by NISPI (see **2.10** above).

To place these matters in context, it is worth mentioning the OPB's main functions before its dissolution on 5 April 1997, which were:

(*a*) running the Pensions Registry (see **2.31** below, now a function of the Regulator);

(*b*) making grants to approved bodies, for example, OPAS (see **2.45** below);

(*c*) making modification orders, now a function of the Regulator (see **12.10** below);

(*d*) monitoring and advising schemes on overriding legislation (for example, on preservation (see CHAPTER 6); responsibility now rests with the trustees);

(*e*) administering and dealing with the statutory disclosure requirements (see CHAPTER 3, now a function of the Regulator); and

(*f*) supervising schemes which have ceased to be contracted out (see CHAPTER 4, now a function of NISPI).

The Pensions Regulator

Objectives and functions

2.12 The Pensions Regulator ('the Regulator') is the body established under *PA 2004, Part 1*, which replaced the previous regulatory body, the

Occupational Pensions Regulatory Authority ('Opra'), from April 2005. The Chief Executive is Tony Hobman.

The role of the Regulator is defined by its objectives and functions as laid down by *PA 2004*. The objectives of the Regulator are wider than those of Opra and are not solely concerned with occupational pension schemes. The four main objectives are as follows:

- to protect the benefits of scheme members under occupational pension schemes;
- to protect the benefits of scheme members under personal pension schemes;
- to reduce the risk of situations arising which may lead to compensation being payable from the Pension Protection Fund; and
- to promote, and improve understanding of, the good administration of 'work-based' pension schemes.

The Regulator operates in part through the Non-Executive Committee and the Determinations Panel, both of which the Regulator is under a duty to establish and maintain.

The *Non-Executive Committee* is essentially an internal regulatory body, established pursuant to *PA 2004, s 8* to monitor, assess and report on the functions carried out by the Regulator. Its role includes:

- reviewing the strategic direction of the Regulator;
- scrutinising the performance of the Chief Executive;
- monitoring the extent to which objectives and targets are being met;
- reviewing internal financial controls and statutory reporting; and
- setting the remuneration of the Chief Executive.

The *Determinations Panel* is the body established pursuant to *PA 2004, s 9* to determine and exercise the 'reserved regulatory functions' on behalf of the Regulator (which can be extended or modified by regulations). These functions are listed in *PA 2004, Sch 2*. It is worth highlighting a few as follows:

Transferred from Opra (retained in relevant sections of *PA 1995*):

- trustee prohibition and suspension orders (*ss 3, 4*);
- appointment of trustee (*s 7*);
- imposition of penalties (*s 10*);
- direct a winding up (*s 11*);

- give directions to trustees (*s 15*);
- authorise modifications to schemes (*s 69*).

Some of the new powers (as established by the relevant sections of *PA 2004*) include:

- to issue and extend freezing orders (*s 23*);
- to issue contribution notices and financial support directions (*ss 38, 43*);
- to issue restoration orders where there has been a transaction at an undervalue (*s 52*);
- to issue notices requiring a report to be made to the Regulator (*s 71*); and
- to issue an order modifying a scheme, giving directions or imposing a schedule of contributions (*s 231*).

The Regulator may also delegate to the Determinations Panel other regulatory functions pursuant to *PA 2004, s 10*.

In addition to these and other specific functions the Regulator has supplementary powers under *PA 2004, s 6* to do anything, except borrow money, which '… is calculated to facilitate the exercise of its functions or which is incidental or conducive to their exercise'.

Codes of Practice (s 90)

2.13 The Regulator may issue practical guidance in relation to the exercise of its functions under pensions legislation and with regard to standards of conduct and practice in relation to the exercise of those functions.

The Regulator is also required to issue codes on a number of matters including what constitutes a 'reasonable period' for the purposes of any pensions legislation, the whistleblowing requirements under *PA 2004*, compliance with scheme specific funding requirements, member-nominated trustee requirements, knowledge and understanding requirements for trustees, requirements to report with regard to failure to pay contributions and other matters.

If any Code of Practice is not observed, this is not in itself a breach of a legal requirement. However, the Codes of Practice will be admissible in evidence in legal proceedings, including proceedings with the Pensions Ombudsman when, for example, consideration is given as to whether or not maladministration has occurred. *PA 2004* specifies a procedure to be followed for the issuing and publication of codes of guidance, including the publication of a draft and consultation on that draft. Before a Code of Practice can come into force, the draft must have been laid before Parliament for at least 40 sitting days (*PA 2004, s 91*).

Set out below is a list of the Code of Practices that have been issued by the Regulator.

Code of Practice	**Summary of scope**	**Date in force**
Code 1 Reporting breaches of the law	Reporting by statutory 'whistleblowers' of certain breaches of the law which affect pension schemes to the Regulator. (From April 2005 the requirement is extended to include trustees and their advisers and service providers, managers of schemes not set up under trust, and employers sponsoring or participating in work-based pension schemes.)	6 April 2005
Code 2 Notifiable events	Notifying the Regulator of prescribed events which occur in respect of pension schemes, and in respect of employers who sponsor pension schemes.	April 2005
Code 3 Funding defined benefits	Implementation of the funding arrangements that apply to most private sector occupational pension schemes that provide defined benefits.	February 2006
Code 4 Early leavers – reasonable periods	Trustees' or managers' duty to provide members who leave schemes after a short period of membership with a statement of their entitlements. Definition of reasonable period within which specified steps must be taken.	May 2006
Code 5 Reporting late payment of contributions to occupational defined contributions schemes	Trustees or managers of occupational defined contributions schemes to report late payments to the Regulator in certain circumstances.	May 2006

Code of Practice	Summary of scope	Date in force
Code 6 Reporting late payment of contributions to personal pension schemes	Managers of personal pension schemes to report late payments to the Regulator in certain circumstances.	May 2006
Code 7 Trustee knowledge and understanding	Trustees of relevant schemes to have an appropriate body of knowledge and understanding of the law relating to pensions and trusts and the principles relating to the funding of occupational pension schemes and investment of scheme assets.	May 2006 Revised version in force November 2009
Code 8 Member-nominated trustees and directors	Implementation of arrangements to ensure that at least one third of the trustees or trustee directors are member-nominated. Definition of reasonable period within which specified steps must be taken.	November 2006
Code 9 Internal controls	Implementation of the requirement for trustees and managers to have adequate internal controls to ensure that an occupational scheme is managed and administered correctly.	November 2006
Code 10 Modification of subsisting rights	Exercise of new power to make limited modifications to subsisting rights to benefits under occupational pension schemes whilst protecting the accrued rights of members.	January 2007
Code 11 IDR	Practical Guidance on what the Regulator expects would satisfy the 'reasonable time period' in relation to the period within which trustees and managers must make and communicate a decision via a scheme's internal dispute resolution procedure. The requirement for decisions to be made and communicated within a 'reasonable time period' was introduced in the *Pensions Act 2007*.	July 2008
Code 12 Material Detriment Test	Outlines the circumstances in which the Regulator would expect to issue a contribution notice under the 'material detriment' test introduced by the *Pensions Act 2008*.	June 2009

Reporting breaches of the law

Who has a duty to report?

2.14 *PA 2004, s 70* imposes on trustees, employers, advisers and anyone involved in the administration of a scheme a duty to report to the Regulator breaches of law in relation to the administration of the scheme which are likely to be of material significance to the Regulator.

A legal duty to report falls on:

- Trustees of trust-based pension schemes. The duty to report applies to each individually appointed trustee. If the trustee is a corporate body the requirement to report falls on the trustee company and not the individual directors.
- Managers of schemes not established under trust, ie managers of personal pension schemes, including stakeholder schemes.
- Persons otherwise involved in the administration of a scheme. This category covers all those who provide services for the trustees or managers that relate to the administration and management of occupational and personal pension schemes, including stakeholder schemes.
- Any employer participating in an occupational pension scheme.
- Professional advisers – scheme actuaries, scheme auditors, legal advisers, fund managers and custodians of scheme assets. However, *PA 2004, s 311* provides that legal advisers do not have to disclose anything which would be protected by legal professional privilege.
- Persons otherwise involved in advising a trustee (or manager of a scheme not established under trust) in relation to the scheme.

When does the duty to report arise?

2.15 The requirement to report breaches of the law arises when a duty which is:

- imposed by or by virtue of an enactment or rule of law; and
- relevant to the administration of a scheme

has not been or is not being complied with. Not every breach should be reported.

The decision to report

2.16 The decision to report requires two key judgments:

- Does the reporter have reasonable cause to believe there has been a breach of the law?
- If so, does the reporter believe the breach likely to be of material significance to the Regulator?

The Regulator has issued a Code of Practice and guidance on reporting breaches of law, and some of the principal themes from those documents are described below.

Reasonable cause to believe

2.17 A reasonable cause to believe means more than a suspicion that cannot be substantiated. The reporter is expected to make further inquiries if all the facts are not known. If, after further investigation, the reporter has reasonable cause to believe that a breach has occurred, it is not necessary for them to gather all the evidence which the Regulator would require before taking legal action.

Likely to be of material significance

2.18 The legal requirement is that breaches likely to be of material significance to the Regulator in carrying out any of its functions must be reported. What is of material significance will depend on:

- the cause of the breach;
- the effect of the breach;
- the reaction to the breach; and
- the wider implications of the breach.

The cause of the breach

2.19 Where a contributory cause of the breach is:

- dishonesty;
- poor governance or inadequate controls resulting in deficient administration or slow or inappropriate decision-making practices; or
- incomplete or inaccurate advice; or
- acting (or failing to act) in deliberate contravention of the law,

then the breach is likely to be of material significance to the Regulator.

The effect of the breach

2.20 The Regulator considers the following to be particularly important elements which are likely to be of material significance in the context of its objective to protect members' benefits:

- substantially the right money is paid into the scheme at the right time;
- assets are appropriately safeguarded;
- payments out of the scheme are legitimate and timely;
- defined benefit schemes are complying with legal requirements on scheme funding;
- trustees of occupational pension schemes are properly considering their investment policy and investing in accordance with it; and
- contributions in respect of defined contributions members are correctly allocated and invested.

In the context of reducing the risk of compensation being payable from the Pension Protection Fund (PPF):

- the Regulator is informed of notifiable events; and
- trustees comply with PPF requirements during an assessment period.

In the context of promoting a good administrator:

- schemes are administered properly and appropriate records are maintained; and
- members receive accurate, clear and impartial information without delay.

Making a report

2.21 All reporters should have effective arrangements in place to identify breaches that occur in areas relating to their functions. Reporters should establish a procedure for assessing a situation to determine whether a breach has occurred and whether it is likely to be of material significance to the Regulator. The Regulator considers that a satisfactory procedure would include the following:

- obtaining clarification of the law where it is unclear to the reporter, and clarifying the facts surrounding the breach where necessary;
- considering the material significance of the breach taking into account its cause, effect and wider implications, including dialogue with the trustees or managers where appropriate;

- an internal procedure and timeframe for assessing and recording breaches, citing the person or persons with the authority to make a decision on whether or not to report to the Regulator; and
- a process for promptly identifying any breaches which are so serious that a report must always be made to the Regulator.

Reports must be submitted in writing and wherever practicable use the standard format available on the Regulator's website at www.thepensionsregulator.gov.uk. Each report should be dated and include as a minimum: the name of the scheme; description of the breach; any relevant dates; name of the employer; name, position and contact details of the reporter; and the role of the reporter. Additional information is required, including the reason why the breach is thought to be of material significance and can be reviewed in full on the website provided above.

Failure to comply with the obligation to report a breach is a civil offence.

The Regulator's response to a breach

2.22 According to the Code of Practice, the Regulator has a wide range of measures it can use in reacting to a report of a breach, including:

- assisting or instructing trustees and others to achieve compliance;
- providing education or guidance;
- appointing trustees to help run the scheme;
- removing trustees from office;
- freezing the scheme;
- imposing special measures where the scheme funding requirements of *PA 2004* are not complied with;
- ordering that the scheme's funding position be restored to the level before a breach or other detrimental events occurred; and
- imposing fines where appropriate.

Reporting notifiable events

Notifiable events duty

2.23 Trustees and employers of schemes eligible for the PPF are required by *PA 2004, s 69* to notify certain events to the Regulator. The purpose of the notifiable events requirements is to reduce the risk of circumstances arising which may lead to compensation being payable from the PPF, as well as providing the Regulator with an early warning of problems which might give rise to a claim on the PPF. Details of events which are notifiable are set out in the *Pensions Regulator (Notifiable Events) Regulations 2005 (SI 2005/900)*, as amended by the *Occupational Pension Schemes (Miscellaneous Amendments) Regulations 2005 (SI 2005/2113)* and the *Occupational Pension Schemes (Miscellaneous Amendments) Regulations 2009 (SI 2009/617)*. The Regulator has issued a Code of Practice and Directions dealing with the notifiable events duty.

The duty to notify requires written notice to the Regulator of events:

- in respect of pension schemes (scheme-related events); and
- in respect of employers, in relation to their pension schemes (employer-related events).

The duty to notify falls on trustees (individually as well as collectively) and employers.

Timing of notification

2.24 An event must be notified in writing to the Regulator *as soon as reasonably practicable*. This will depend on the circumstances but in all cases it implies urgency. For example, where a trustee is made aware of a notifiable event on a Sunday, the Regulator should be notified on the Monday. It is not necessary to seek professional or expert advice on whether an event has occurred.

The requirement to notify *as soon as reasonably practicable* means that trustees and employers should consider putting in place notification procedures for situations requiring immediate action. For example, administrators working on behalf of trustees and employers should be required to alert them quickly, as soon as a notifiable event takes place.

How to notify

2.25 All notifications must be in writing and, where practicable, use the standard form available on the Regulator's website at www.thepensionsregulator.gov.uk. Reports may be sent by post, e-mail or fax. The minimum information that should be included in a notification is the:

- description of the notifiable event;
- date of the event;

- name of the pension scheme;
- name of the employer; and
- name, position and contact details of the notifier.

Further additional information that the Regulator would find useful is also set out in the Code.

Events to be reported

2.26 The *Pensions Regulator (Notifiable Events) Regulations 2005 (SI 2005/900)*, as amended, which came into force on 6 April 2005, confirm which events will need to be reported to the Regulator. The Directions (which also came into force on 6 April 2005) set down conditions excusing a report in certain circumstances.

Employer events

2.27 Employers must notify the following events:

- any decision by the employer to take action which will, or is intended to, result in a debt which is or may become due to the scheme not being paid in full;
- a decision by the employer to cease to carry on business in the UK, or cessation of business in the UK without a decision having been taken;
- receipt by the employer of advice that it is trading wrongfully or a director or former director of the company knows that there is no reasonable prospect that the company will avoid going into insolvent liquidation;
- any breach of a banking covenant by the employer, other than where the bank or other institution agrees with the employer not to enforce the covenant *unless* the conditions in A and B below are satisfied;
- a decision by a controlling company to relinquish control of the employer, or the controlling company relinquishing control without a decision to do so having been taken, *unless* the conditions in A and B below are satisfied; and
- the conviction of an individual for an offence involving dishonesty, if the offence was committed while the individual was a director or partner of the employer.

Trustee events

2.28 Trustees must report the following events:

- any decision by the trustees or managers to take action which will, or is intended to, result in any debt which is or may become due to the scheme not being paid in full *unless* the conditions in A, B and C below are satisfied;
- a decision by the trustees to make or accept a transfer value from another scheme, or making or accepting such a transfer where no decision is required, the value of which is more than the lower of 5 per cent of the value of the scheme assets or £1.5 million *unless* the conditions in A and B below are satisfied;
- a decision by the trustees to grant benefits on more favourable terms than those provided for by the scheme rules without either seeking advice from the actuary or securing additional funding where so advised; and
- a decision by the trustees to grant benefits or rights to benefits to a member, or granting such benefits where no decision is required, the cost of which is more than the lower of 5 per cent of the scheme assets and £1.5 million *unless* the conditions of A and B below are satisfied.

In addition, certain events occurring in relation to a guarantor of a withdrawal arrangement or an approved withdrawal arrangement have been prescribed as notifiable events and are set out in *Occupational Pension Schemes (Employer Debt) Regulations 2005 (SI 2005/678), Sch 1B*, as amended. More detail on employer debt can be found in CHAPTER 14.

The conditions

2.29 The conditions are set out in Directions issued by the Regulator on 6 April 2005 and updated in April 2009.

Condition A: Scheme funding must be at least at the PPF level at the most recent *s 179* valuation (see CHAPTER 5). If no PPF valuation has yet been conducted, the relevant basis will be determined in accordance with the last minimum funding requirement valuation.

Condition B: The trustees have not needed to report to the Regulator in the previous 12 months any failure of non-payment under the schedule of contributions.

Condition C: The debt not collected is less than 0.5 per cent of the scheme assets (as valued at the most recent valuation mentioned at condition A above).

Failure to notify

2.30 Trustees are required to take all reasonable steps to comply with the notifiable events requirements. This means considering whether, where a failure to notify a notifiable event occurs, an objective person would consider that the trustees nevertheless took all reasonable and expected steps in order to comply.

Employers must comply with the notifiable events regime unless they have a reasonable excuse for not doing so. Where a failure to comply occurs, it will be assessed on the basis of whether an objective person would consider that there was a reasonable basis for the failure.

A failure by itself will not lead to a transaction being void. However, the Regulator will seek an explanation for the failure and, where appropriate, a civil penalty may be imposed.

In practice, trustees and employers should ensure that they are aware of what the notifiable events are, who is required to notify and the exceptions to the requirement, and put in place an appropriate procedure for identifying and notifying.

The Registry

2.31 The office of the Registrar of Pension Schemes was established by the *Social Security Act 1990*. Opra took over the management of the Registry from the OPB on 6 April 1997. The office of Registrar was abolished on 6 April 2005 by *PA 2004* and the Regulator is now charged by *PA 2004, s 59* with maintaining a register of occupational and personal pension schemes.

The Regulator is required, in respect of each 'registrable scheme', to record in the register 'registrable information' and any notifications that a scheme has been wound up or transferred to the PPF.

Registrable schemes are prescribed in the *Register of Occupational and Personal Pension Schemes Regulations 2005 (SI 2005/597)* and include all pension schemes with more than one member, which have been registered in accordance with *Finance Act 2004, s 153*, have a superannuation fund as is mentioned in *ICTA 1988, s 615(6)*, and are schemes undertaking cross-border activities. Registrable information is defined in *PA 2004, s 60* and includes:

- the name and address of the scheme;
- the names and addresses of each trustee or manager;
- the status of the scheme (for example, is it admitting new members and are benefits accruing);
- the categories of benefits;

- the name and address of each relevant employer (occupational pension schemes only); and
- the number of members (occupational schemes only).

The *Register of Occupational and Personal Pension Schemes Regulations 2005* require further additional information, including the category of the scheme, the nature of the business of any relevant employer, and whether the scheme has commenced winding up.

The Regulator may obtain the information required for the register by issuing scheme return notices under *PA 2004, s 63*. Where a new registrable scheme is established or a scheme becomes registrable, the trustees or managers must notify the Regulator and provide the registrable information within three months. Where there is a change in registrable information or a scheme ceases to be registrable or is wound up, the trustees or managers must notify the Regulator as soon as reasonably practicable. Failure to do so could give rise to civil penalties under *PA 1995, s 10* (*PA 2004, s 62*).

The Department for Work and Pensions runs a pensions tracing service which allows individuals who think they are entitled to benefit under a scheme to make an application for information. The *Register of Occupational and Personal Pension Schemes Regulations 2005* allow the Secretary of State access to information from the register and the right to inspect the register for the purposes of operating the tracing service.

The Pensions Regulator Tribunal

2.32 The Pensions Regulator Tribunal was established with effect from 6 April 2005 by *PA 2004, s 102*. References may be made to the Tribunal by someone subject to or affected by a determination of the Regulator. Each tribunal is made up of individuals selected from a panel appointed by the Lord Chancellor. There are currently eight legally qualified members of the 'panel of chairmen' (including the President, Stephen Oliver QC) and 17 lay members. When considering a reference the tribunal may consider any evidence relating to the subject matter of the reference, whether it was before the Regulator or not, and regardless of whether it would be admissible in a court of law. On determining a reference the Tribunal must remit the matter to the Regulator with appropriate directions for giving effect to its determination. This may include directions to vary or revoke the Regulator's original determination or to substitute a different determination.

Matters should generally be referred to the Tribunal within 28 days of the determination or notice of the Regulator but an application to the Tribunal to make a late reference may be made (*Pensions Regulator Tribunal Rules 2005 (SI 2005/690), r 13*). The Rules set out the procedures to be adopted by the Tribunal. Matters should usually be decided following an oral hearing but this may be dispensed with in certain circumstances including where the parties agree in writing, the Regulator does not oppose the reference, the Regulator does not properly respond to the reference or the reference is for directions only (*rr 20, 21*). Appeals from the Tribunal may be made to the Court of Appeal (Court of Session in Scotland) on a point of law only, with the permission of the Tribunal. Permission may be requested at the end of the hearing or in writing within 14 days of notification of the decision (*r 28*).

A legal assistance scheme has been established (*Pensions Regulator Tribunal (Legal Assistance Scheme) Regulations 2005 (SI 2005/781)*) to provide funding for legal advice, assistance and representation for those referring matters to the Tribunal. Legal assistance may be granted where the Tribunal is satisfied that it is in the interests of justice to do so and that the applicant's financial resources are such that he requires assistance in meeting legal costs in relation to the proceedings before the Tribunal.

Cost of the Regulator

2.33 For the purposes of meeting the expenditure of the Regulator, regulations under *PSA 1993, s 175* (as amended by *PA 1995, s 165* and *PA 2004, s 174*) make provision for imposing a levy. The levy is payable to the Secretary of State by or on behalf of the administrator of public service schemes or the trustees or managers of occupational or personal pension schemes.

The Regulator can be contacted at The Pensions Regulator, Napier House, Trafalgar Place, Brighton BN1 4DW. Tel: 0870 6063636; e-mail: customersupport@thepensionsregulator.gov.uk; website www.thepensionsregulator.co.uk.

The Pension Protection Fund (PPF)

Establishment of the PPF

2.34

> 'The Pensions Act 2004 has established the Pension Protection Fund to protect members of private sector defined benefit schemes whose firms become insolvent with insufficient funds in their pension scheme.
>
> We will make sure that in future individuals in final salary schemes will never again face the injustice of saving throughout their lives only to have

their hard-earned pension slashed just before they retire. The Pension Protection Fund will allow individuals to save with confidence.'

Andrew Smith, the then Secretary of State for Work and Pensions, 12 February 2004.

The aim of the PPF

2.35 The main purpose of the PPF is to ensure that, where a company with a UK-based defined benefit scheme becomes insolvent and its pension fund is not sufficiently funded, members can be reassured that they will still receive the main benefits to which they are entitled. The PPF will, where it has assumed responsibility for the scheme, provide benefits in accordance with the '*pension compensation provisions*' which are:

- where a member has attained normal pension age at the date of insolvency, they will receive 100 per cent of their entitlement;
- for members who have yet to reach normal pension age at the date of insolvency, they will receive 90 per cent of their entitlement subject to an annual cap. From April 2009 the effective cap is £28,742.68 at age 65 (90% of £31,936.32), with a sliding scale lower cap for younger members;
- dependants' pensions payable on the future death of the member are limited to 50 per cent of the member's pension; and
- pensions in payment built up from April 1997 will increase in line with RPI capped at 2.5 per cent.

Eligibility for the PPF

2.36 Most private sector registered defined benefit or hybrid occupational pension schemes will be eligible for the PPF. Defined contributions schemes are not eligible (*PA 2004, s 126*). Any scheme which commenced winding up before 6 April 2005 will not be eligible (although some members of such schemes may be eligible for the Government's Financial Assistance Scheme). Schemes excluded from the PPF include those with fewer than two members and schemes with fewer than 12 members and all members are trustees and unanimous decisions are required or there is a statutory independent trustee, and schemes providing death benefits only. The *Pension Protection Fund (Entry Rules) Regulations 2005 (SI 2005/590), reg 2* (as amended) lists those schemes which are not eligible.

An otherwise eligible scheme may be rendered ineligible if the trustees compromise a *s 75* debt without actuarial advice or the consent of the Board (*reg 2(2)*).

When will the PPF get involved?

2.37 In broad terms, the PPF will become involved in a scheme if an insolvency event (as defined in *PA 2004, s 121*) occurs in relation to the employer after 5 April 2005 or, where the employer is a non-corporate organisation such as a trade union or charity, it appears to the trustees or the Regulator that the employer is likely to cease to continue as a going concern (*PA 2004, s 129*).

Where a qualifying insolvency event occurs, there then follows an 'assessment period' during which the Board will determine whether the PPF will take responsibility for the scheme, which it must do if:

- the value of the assets of the scheme were less than the amount of the *protected liabilities* immediately before the qualifying insolvency event occurs; and
- a 'scheme rescue' has been deemed impossible by the insolvency practitioner.

The protected liabilities are the liabilities for benefits up to the level of PPF compensation, plus scheme liabilities other than for benefits and the estimated winding-up expenses.

During this period of assessment, everything is frozen. No new members may be admitted to the scheme, contributions are suspended (other than those due to be paid before the beginning of the assessment period), no benefits accrue under the scheme in respect of the members and benefits in payment will be reduced to the PPF protection level. In addition, the Board may also give directions to ensure that the scheme's protected liabilities do not exceed its assets or keep the excess to a minimum.

In addition to the above, during an assessment period, the winding up of a scheme cannot begin, no transfers or transfer payments in respect of member's rights are to be made from the scheme and no other steps may be taken to discharge any liability to the scheme in respect of pensions or other benefits or such other liabilities as may be prescribed. For these purposes, the scheme, to a certain extent, ceases to function and civil penalties will apply to any trustee or manager who fails to take all reasonable steps to ensure compliance.

In order to assist with its assessment, the Board must obtain an actuarial valuation of the scheme. This is referred to as a *s 143* valuation. Regulations set out how the assets and protected liabilities are to be determined and the Board has issued guidance to assist actuaries undertaking *s 143* valuations.

If the valuation reveals a deficit of protected liabilities, the Board will issue to the trustees or the managers a 'transfer notice' and assume responsibility for the scheme. The effect of the Board assuming responsibility for a scheme is that:

- the property, rights and liabilities of the scheme are transferred to the Board without further assurance, with effect from the time the trustees or managers receive the transfer notice;
- the trustees or managers of the scheme are discharged from their pension obligations from that time;
- the Board assumes responsibility for securing that compensation is paid in accordance with the compensation provisions; and
- the scheme is to be treated as having been wound up immediately after that time.

If the Board determines that the valuation does not disclose a deficit, it must refuse responsibility for the scheme and issue a notice to that effect to the Regulator, the trustees/managers and to any insolvency practitioner (a 'determination notice'). The trustees or manager can make an application to the Board asking them to reconsider their decision. Where the Board refuses responsibility the trustees will be required to wind up the scheme, unless a 'scheme rescue' has occurred and the scheme has been taken over by another employer.

The PPF is dealt with in more detail in CHAPTER 5.

The Board of the PPF

2.38 The functions of the Board include paying compensation, calculating annual levies, and setting and overseeing the investment strategy of the Pension Protection Fund. Membership of the Board consists of a Chairman (Lawrence Churchill was appointed by the Secretary of State on 1 July 2004), the Chief Executive of the Board (Alan Rubenstein was appointed on 1 April 2009), and at least five other people, who are described as 'ordinary members'. To ensure independence, the Chairman cannot be appointed from the staff of the Board or be the chairman of the Regulator.

The Board has a Non-Executive Committee, consisting only of non-executive members of the Board. Its role is to keep under review the question of whether the Board's internal financial controls secure the proper conduct of its financial affairs; and it determines the terms and conditions as to remuneration of the Chief Executive and any member of staff who is also to be an executive member of the Board. As part of its functions, the Board must submit an annual report and accounts to the Secretary of State who, in turn, will present them to Parliament.

Funding the PPF

2.39 The PPF is funded by a pension protection levy, paid by eligible pension schemes on an annual basis. It comprises:

- a risk-based levy; and
- a scheme-based levy.

A *risk-based* levy is assessed by reference to the difference between the value of the scheme's assets and the amount of its protected liabilities, the likelihood of an insolvency event occurring in relation to an employer and other factors which the Board considers appropriate.

The *scheme-based* levy is assessed by reference to various scheme factors, which include the amount of a scheme's liabilities to or in respect of members, the number of members, or category of members, the total annual amount of pensionable earnings of active members of a scheme and such other factors as may be prescribed by regulations.

Before the beginning of each financial year, the Board must determine the factors with which to assess the levies, the timing of the assessments, the rate and when the levies will become payable. The levy imposed by the Board will be subject to a ceiling, which is set by the Secretary of State before the beginning of each financial year (to be increased annually in line with national average earnings), and the *risk-based* levy must amount to at least 80 per cent of the total pension protection levy – the aim being that costs are minimised for 'good' employers with well-funded schemes. The *scheme-based* levy must constitute no more than 20 per cent of the total pension protection levy.

The levy is payable by the trustees or managers of the scheme or such other person as prescribed in the regulations and is payable to the Board.

The Board has set a pension protection levy estimate for the financial year 2009/10 at £700 million, following its consultation in September 2008.

There is also an 'administration levy' which will be applied for the purpose of meeting the ongoing costs of the PPF. Schemes pay an amount per scheme member, which varies depending on the size of the scheme.

The Board published a consultation document on the pension protection fund levy in November 2008. The consultation proposals included allowing the Board to take into account several long-term factors in individual scheme calculations, including the probability that a scheme employer would become insolvent over a five-year period, and the risk a scheme's investment strategy posed to the PPF. The intention is to make the individual levy calculation fairer, with the intended result being that around half of all schemes will pay a smaller levy than at present.

Following the conclusion of its consultation on 13 February 2009, the Board announced in August 2009 that it would set up a steering group of senior business figures to come up with revised proposals for a new levy formula. In response to concerns expressed during the consultation period over the Board's proposals, particularly in regard to investment risk, the steering group's intention is to achieve a common consensus on these, assessing the options for measuring long-term insolvency risk and investment risk. The Board intends to consult on and finalise its revised levy policy in 2010; however, the new policy will not be implemented before the 2012/13 levy year.

All eligible schemes, as defined in *PA 2004, s 126* and the *Pension Protection Fund (Entry Rules) Regulations 2005*, must pay the scheme based element of the pension protection levy. All eligible schemes, except those whose *s 179* valuation certificates show them to be more than 140 per cent funded, are liable to be charged the risk-based element of the pension protection levy. 31 March 2010 is the deadline for the submission of *s 179* valuations for use in the 2010/11 levy.

The Board has engaged Dun and Bradstreet to provide insolvency risk scoring for employers, which will be ranked into one of ten grades. Each scheme's levy will be set based on a multiple of funding levels and insolvency risk. The 2009/10 cap on the risk-based levy is 1 per cent of the scheme's liabilities.

The Board supports the development of risk management products of various kinds, and recognises the following types of contingent assets:

- guarantees given by parent/group companies and undertakings (Type A);
- security over cash, securities or UK real estate (Type B); and
- letters of credit and bank guarantees (Type C).

In order to protect the Pension Protection Fund and levy payers against enforceability and valuation risks, there are certain acceptability criteria for each form of contingent asset which must be complied with. In particular, a standard certificate must be completed for each contingent asset arrangement for it to be recognised for levy purposes.

The Board's approach to contingent assets for the 2009/10 levy year can be found in its November 2008 contingent assets guidance, available on its website www.pensionprotectionfund.org.uk.

Information to be provided to the Board

2.40 The Board may issue a notice to persons including the trustees or manager of the scheme, the employer, a professional adviser to the scheme and an insolvency practitioner, amongst others. The notice may require the recipient to produce any document or provide any other information which is relevant to the exercise of the Board's functions in relation to an occupational pension scheme. When such a notice is received, the information must be provided in the form prescribed, at such a place and within timescales specified in the notice.

The Board's powers are such that it can enter premises at any reasonable time and whilst there, make inquiries as necessary, request any person on the premises to produce or secure the production of any relevant document, take copies of such documentation and may even remove them from the premises if it is necessary to prevent their interference.

Where a person (without reasonable excuse) neglects or refuses to provide information, he will be guilty of an offence and is liable on conviction to a fine not exceeding £5,000. If a person intentionally and without reasonable excuse alters, suppresses, conceals or destroys any document which is liable to be produced, a higher fine or a custodial sentence, not exceeding two years, could be imposed. The same penalties would be imposed on someone who knowingly or recklessly provides information which is false or misleading. (*PA 2004, Part 2, Chapter 5*).

The Fraud Compensation Fund

2.41 On 1 September 2005 the Board replaced the Pensions Compensation Board with the Fraud Compensation Fund as the body responsible for fraud compensation. It may pay compensation to occupational pension scheme members where there has been a misappropriation of assets/funds or cases of fraud. This also covers some schemes that are not covered by the PPF, including defined contributions schemes. Compensation may be payable where:

- the value of the assets of an eligible scheme has been reduced as a consequence of an act or omission which constitutes an offence of dishonesty, including an intention to defraud; and
- a qualifying insolvency event in relation to the employer has occurred and a scheme failure notice has been issued.

The Fraud Compensation Fund will be paid for by way of a fraud compensation levy. It will be determined by the Board, be payable at prescribed times, at a certain rate, and must be paid by the trustees or managers of a scheme. The Board will determine which schemes will be required to pay the levy, calculate the amount of the levy in relation to those schemes and notify any person liable to pay the levy in respect of the scheme as well as when it becomes payable. The levy is to cover all payments made from the Fraud Compensation Fund to ensure that the Fund's assets are sufficient to cover its liabilities.

The Board determines the amount of any fraud compensation payment to be made in accordance with the *Occupational Pension Schemes (Fraud Compensation Payments and Miscellaneous Amendments) Regulations 2005 (SI 2005/2184)*.

PPF Ombudsman

2.42 The office of PPF Ombudsman was established with effect from 6 April 2006 by *PA 2004, s 209*. The first PPF Ombudsman is Tony King, who is also the current Pensions Ombudsman. 'Reviewable matters' may be referred to the PPF Ombudsman following a reconsideration by the Board under *PA 2004, s 207*. 'Reviewable matters' include the issuing of a determination notice under *PA 2004, s 123*. Any person who is sent, or is required to be sent, a notice of the reconsideration decision is entitled to refer the matter to the PPF Ombudsman (*Pension Protection Fund (Reference of Reviewable Matters to the PPF Ombudsman) Regulations 2005 (SI 2005/2024), reg 2*). The referral must be made within 28 days from the date on which that person was sent a notice of the reconsideration decision.

The Board can be contacted at Pension Protection Fund, 17 Addiscombe Road, Croydon, Surrey CR0 6SR. Tel: 0845 600 2541; e-mail: information@ppf.gsi.gov.uk; website: www.pensionprotectionfund.org.uk.

The Personal Accounts Delivery Authority (the 'Authority')

2.43 Many people in the UK are not saving enough for their retirement. The Pensions Commission, in its 2005 report to the Government, called for fairer and wider pension coverage to address this problem. The report suggested that automatic enrolment into a workplace pension scheme with employer contributions should form the bedrock of any Government initiative to tackle the issue of under-saving for retirement.

It was with this in mind that the *Pensions Act 2007 (PA 2007)* established the Authority, which has been given responsibility for designing and introducing the infrastructure for the new personal accounts scheme. The new scheme is to be a trust-based occupational defined contribution scheme, and will be operational from October 2012. Broadly, employers will need to choose whether to enrol most of their employees into the Government's scheme, or into the employer's own 'qualifying scheme'. Under either option, employers will need to make contributions on the employees' behalf. Further details about the workings of the new personal accounts scheme can be found in CHAPTER 13.

Pensions Act 2008 (PA 2008), s 79 states the functions of the Authority, namely:

- giving assistance to the Secretary of State in establishing a statutory scheme; and
- giving assistance to the Secretary of State and the Regulator in connection with automatic enrolment arrangements.

The Authority's Corporate Plan 2009–2012 sets out its four key strategic goals. These are:

- establish an occupational pension scheme by 2012 which delivers the best possible scheme for its members, with low charges;
- set up a trustee corporation with an excellent governance framework, attracting high-calibre trustees, and manage a smooth and successful handover to the trustees;
- deliver valued advice and support to the Authority's strategic delivery partners; and
- build the Authority as an organisation that engenders confidence, and is an asset in launching the new scheme.

PA 2008, s 80 sets out principles for the carrying out of the Authority's functions, which include:

- participation in 'qualifying schemes' should be encouraged and facilitated by employers;
- burdens on employers when complying with the new system should be minimised;
- adverse effects on 'qualifying schemes' (eg levelling down) should be minimised;
- the cost of membership of a scheme established under *PA 2008* should be minimised;
- members' preferences on investment choice should be taken into account, so far as is practicable; and
- diversity among members and future members should be respected.

HMRC will be responsible for co-ordinating the reform programme, including agreeing policy with ministers and overseeing delivery of the new regime.

The Regulator will have responsibility for enforcement of, and compliance with, the employer duties set out in *PA 2004* regarding personal accounts. It will have the power to issue compliance notices (where the requirements are breached) and unpaid contribution notices. Where the employer continues to fail to comply with either of these notices, the Regulator will be able to take further action (including issuing a fixed penalty notice imposing a fine of up to £50,000). A wilful failure to comply with employer duties will be a criminal offence punishable by a fine or two-year prison sentence.

The Authority will cease to be operational once the personal accounts scheme goes live in 2012. At that point, it will hand over responsibility for the scheme to the personal accounts trustee board, which the Authority will have set up beforehand.

The Authority can be contacted at Personal Accounts Delivery Authority, St Dunstan's House, 201–211 Borough High Street, London SE1 1GZ. Tel: 020 7940 8519; e-mail: enquiries.padeliveryauthority@dwp.gsi.gov.uk; website: www.padeliveryauthority.org.uk.

Financial Assistance Scheme

2.44 The Financial Assistance Scheme (FAS) was introduced at a late stage of the *Pensions Bill 2004* as a result of sustained lobbying by and on behalf of members of defined benefit pension schemes who had lost some or all of their benefits when their schemes wound up in deficit but would not be able to qualify for the PPF (because the winding up had commenced before 6 April 2005). The provisions of *PA 2004, s 286* allowed for the establishment of the FAS but provided very little detail. The *Financial Assistance Scheme Regulations 2005 (SI 2005/1986)* came into force for most purposes on 1 September 2005. The Regulations set out which members of which schemes would qualify for assistance. Initially, schemes which qualified for the FAS included most occupational pension schemes (other than defined contributions or public sector schemes) which commenced winding up between 1 January 1997 and 5 April 2005 and where the employer had become insolvent by a specified date. The initial coverage of FAS was very narrow (limited to those members at or very near to retirement when their schemes wound up). Since the original Regulations, there have been a number of amendments, partly as a result of political pressure and the decision of the ECJ in *Carol Marilyn Robins and Others v Secretary of State for Work and Pensions* (C-278/05) which found that the UK Government had failed to properly protect pensions on the insolvency of an employer.

PA 2007, s 18 included amendments to *PA 2004, s 286* requiring the Secretary of State to make provision for all qualifying members to receive benefits totalling 80 per cent of their expected scheme pension subject to a cap of £26,000 and for initial payments of up to 80 per cent to be made during the winding up of a scheme. This benefit level has been modified by the *Financial Assistance Scheme (Miscellaneous Amendments) Regulations 2007 (SI 2007/3581)* which came into force on 19 December 2007, *PA 2008* and the *Financial Assistance Scheme (Miscellaneous Provisions) Regulations 2009 (SI 2009/1851)*.

The key changes include:

- All members of qualifying pension schemes will receive 90 per cent of their accrued pension entitlement at the date their scheme began to wind up, subject to a compensation cap of £29,386.00.
- Compensation payments deriving from service after 1997 will be index-linked, subject to an increase of 2.5 per cent per year.
- Compensation will be payable from each scheme's normal retirement age (subject to a minimum age of 60).
- Ill-health benefits are payable to those below normal retirement age.
- The FAS is further extended to cover members of schemes that began winding up between 1 January 1997 and 5 April 2005, where the employer is still trading but a compromise agreement is in place and there is evidence that enforcing the debt against the employer would have forced the employer into insolvency.
- The time period by which an employer must have an insolvency event in order for its scheme to be eligible for FAS assistance is extended indefinitely, provided that the scheme manager is of the opinion that the insolvency event of the employer and the winding-up of the scheme were linked.
- The description of small self-administered schemes is amended to enable some to be eligible for FAS assistance.
- Payments made to a person who is not a beneficiary may be suspended and overpayments may be recovered.

PA 2008, s 125(1) inserted *s 286A* into the *PA 2004*, with effect from 26 June 2008. This provides that the trustees of any qualifying pension scheme must not purchase or agree to purchase annuities without the permission of the FAS manager.

On 10 July 2009 the Board of the PPF became the manager of the FAS. The Government is currently consulting on draft regulations which will include provisions for the assets remaining in FAS qualifying schemes to be transferred to the PPF (to be held separately to main PPF assets). This will mean that all payments will in future come from FAS rather than it providing payments to top up the benefits paid by the pension scheme.

The *Financial Assistance Scheme (Internal Review) Regulations 2005 (SI 2005/1994)* allow for beneficiaries and potential beneficiaries under a scheme, or their representative, to apply for a review of a decision in relation to the FAS. The *Financial Assistance Scheme (Appeal) Regulations 2005 (SI 2005/3273)* came into force on 29 November 2005 and allow for the appeal to the PPF Ombudsman of a decision which had been subject to internal review (see **2.42** above).

FAS can be contacted at PO Box 702, York, YO32 9XR. Tel: 0845 6019941. Email: FAS-Operational-Unit@dwp.gsi.gov.uk.

FAS is dealt with in more detail in CHAPTER 5.

The Pensions Advisory Service

2.45 The Pensions Advisory Service ('TPAS') (formerly 'OPAS') is an independent, grant-aided, non-profit making company limited by guarantee with a network of local volunteer advisers, who are experienced pensions professionals. The aim of TPAS is to provide free assistance to members of the public with difficulties which they have failed to resolve with the trustees, administrators or pension provider of their pension scheme. The TPAS service is available to anyone who believes he has pension rights. This includes active members of pension schemes (including company, personal and stakeholder arrangements), pensioners, those with deferred pensions from previous employment, and dependants. TPAS can be contacted directly.

TPAS's remit is to explain pension scheme benefits to members and liaise directly with trustees or administrators to provide further information to members or to assist a member in obtaining his correct legal entitlement from a pension scheme.

If TPAS is unable to resolve the problem but believes that the complaint is valid, it may assist a member in making a formal complaint to the appropriate Ombudsman (the Pensions Ombudsman or the Financial Services Ombudsman). TPAS cannot:

(*a*) initiate legal action on a member's behalf;

(*b*) give financial advice;

(*c*) deal with complaints from a group or body of pension scheme members;

(*d*) act as a lobbying force for any improvement in pension scheme benefits;

(*e*) act through intermediaries;

(*f*) offer advice on State pension benefits; or

(*g*) assist if legal proceedings have been initiated or if the Pensions Ombudsman (see **2.46** below) has already investigated a complaint.

TPAS can be contacted at 11 Belgrave Road, London SW1V 1RB. National telephone helpline: 0845 601 2923; fax: 020 7233 8016; e-mail: enquiries@pensionsadvisoryservice.org.uk; website: www.pensionsadvisoryservice.org.uk.

The Pensions Ombudsman

The role of the Pensions Ombudsman

2.46 The Pensions Ombudsman's office was established on 1 October 1990. The Ombudsman is appointed by the Secretary of State under *PSA 1993, s 145* which also sets out his role. Tony King is the current Ombudsman.

Under *PA 1995* the Ombudsman has power to appoint his own staff (with the approval of the Secretary of State for Work and Pensions) and has taken advantage of this by seeking to appoint professional staff from the pensions industry and legally qualified pensions experts. The Ombudsman's budget is paid for out of the levy imposed on all occupational pension schemes.

The role of the Pensions Ombudsman is to investigate and decide complaints and disputes about the way that pension schemes are run. He is completely independent and acts as an impartial adjudicator.

PA 2004, s 274 inserted *s 145A* into *PSA 1993* which makes provision for the appointment of a Deputy Pensions Ombudsman. Charlie Gordon is the current Deputy Pensions Ombudsman who was appointed on 4 April 2005. The Deputy Pensions Ombudsman is appointed by the Secretary of State and may perform the functions of the Pensions Ombudsman where there is a vacancy in that office, where the Pensions Ombudsman is for any reason unable to perform his duties or otherwise as allowed by the Secretary of State.

Jurisdiction

2.47 The complaints and disputes which the Ombudsman may investigate are described in *PSA 1993, s 146* (as amended by the *Child Support, Pensions* *and Social Security Act 2000*) and are summarised in the following table:

Type of scheme	**Who may complain or refer a dispute to the Ombudsman**	**Parties against whom a complaint may be made or a dispute may be referred to the Ombudsman**	**Nature of complaint or dispute**
Complaints of maladministration			
Occupational or personal	By or on behalf of any actual or potential beneficiary.	Trustees, managers, employers and/or administrators.	Complaint of injustice in consequence of maladministration of the scheme.
Occupational	By or on behalf of any trustee or, manager of a scheme.	Trustees, employers.	Complaint of maladministration of that scheme.
Occupational	An employer in relation to a scheme.	Trustees or managers of that scheme.	Complaint of maladministration of that scheme.
Occupational	By or on behalf of any trustee or manager of a scheme.	Trustees or managers of another scheme.	Complaint of maladministration of the other scheme.
Trust scheme	By or on behalf of an independent trustee.	Trustees or former trustees who are/were not independent trustees of that scheme.	Complaint of maladministration of that scheme.
Disputes of fact or law			
Occupational or personal	By any actual or potential beneficiary.	Trustees, managers and/or employers.	Dispute of fact or law.

Occupational	By or on behalf of any trustee or manager of a scheme.	Trustees, managers or employers of that scheme. (Note that trustees/ managers cannot refer disputes with managers; and employers cannot refer disputes with other employers.)	Dispute of fact or law.
Occupational	An employer in relation to a scheme.	Trustees or managers of that scheme.	Dispute of fact or law.
Occupational	By or on behalf of any party to the dispute.	Trustees or managers of another scheme.	Dispute of fact or law in relation to the other scheme.
Complaints or disputes			
Occupational	By or on behalf of at least half the trustees of the scheme.	Different trustees of the same scheme.	Dispute of fact or law or maladministration of that scheme.
Occupational subject to insolvency procedures	By or on behalf of the independent trustee who is a party to the dispute.	Trustees or former trustees of the scheme who are not independent.	Any dispute (in relation to a time when *PA 1995, s 22* applies).
Occupational	By or on behalf of the sole trustee.		Any question relating to the carrying out of functions of that trustee.

The word 'maladministration' is not defined in the legislation, although the Pensions Ombudsman's booklet describes it as including bias, neglect, inattention, delay, incompetence and arbitrariness. The complaint must include behaviour which constitutes maladministration which in turn has lead to 'injustice'. Again, this is not defined but is described by the Pensions Ombudsman as not only including a financial loss, but incorporating distress, delay or inconvenience. In November 2005 the Pensions Ombudsman issued a guide 'How to Avoid the Pensions Ombudsman'. It contains guidance for those running pension schemes, based on actual cases which have been determined by the

Pensions Ombudsman, on how they might operate schemes and manage disputes in order to avoid complaints being made. It is available on www.pensions-ombudsman.org.uk.

The *Personal and Occupational Pension Schemes (Pensions Ombudsman) Regulations 1996 (SI 1996/2475)* ('the *Ombudsman Regulations*'), introduced under *PA 1995*, provide that the Ombudsman may not investigate or determine a complaint unless the internal dispute resolution procedure has first been followed (*Ombudsman Regulations, reg 3*). (The internal dispute resolution procedure is discussed in CHAPTER 3.) The only exception to this is where a complaint has been referred to the internal dispute procedure and the Ombudsman is satisfied that there is no prospect of a decision being reached within a reasonable period (*Ombudsman Regulations, reg 3(2)*).

Ombudsman Regulations, reg 5 covers the time limits for referring a dispute to the Ombudsman's office. The Ombudsman is not permitted to investigate a complaint if it is received by him more than three years after the date on which the act or omission complained of occurred, or three years after the date on which the complainant knew or ought to have known of its occurrence. However, this period can be extended where the Ombudsman believes it was reasonable for a complaint not to be made before the end of this period, in which case the time limit may be extended to such further period as he considers reasonable (*Ombudsman Regulations, reg 5(3)*).

Ombudsman Regulations, reg 2 also confirms the extension of the Ombudsman's jurisdiction to administrators of pension schemes. The definition of 'administrator' includes 'any person concerned with the administration' of a scheme. *PA 2004, s 275* has clarified the jurisdiction in relation to administrators by inserting *s 146(4A)* into *PSA 1993* which provides that a person is concerned with the administration of a scheme where he is responsible for carrying out 'an act' of administration concerned with the scheme. This means that the Ombudsman can investigate one-off administrative acts.

It has been held that the jurisdiction of the Ombudsman extends to situations where an insurance company manages a scheme from day to day (*Century Life v The Pensions Ombudsman [1995] PLR 135*) even where there are separate trustees and that, in these circumstances, the insurance company can fall within the definition of a 'manager'. It may also extend to other advisers in some circumstances, as shown in the Pension Ombudsman's determination in the 2003 case of *McMann Interiors Limited (L00552)*, when the incorrect actuarial guidance produced by the insurance company's actuary was held to be maladministration.

Pensions managers have also fallen foul of the definition (see the Ombudsman's determination in *Bennett July 1998 G00016*).

In *Ewing v Arthur Cox [2000] 22 PBLR (7)*, the Court of Appeal of Northern Ireland, although rejecting the Ombudsman's determination that a firm of solicitors were 'administrators' in this instance, left open the possibility that solicitors could potentially be seen as administrators if sufficiently involved in the running of the scheme. What would constitute sufficient involvement would be a matter of fact and degree, depending on the circumstances of the case.

Investigating a complaint

2.48 The procedure which the Ombudsman follows during his investigations is set out in the *Personal and Occupational Pension Schemes (Pensions Ombudsman) (Procedure) Rules 1995 (SI 1995/1053)* ('the *Procedure Rules*' (as amended)); it is summarised in the booklet accompanying the complaint form, which is sent out, on request, to those wishing to bring a complaint. Upon receipt of the complaint form a caseworker at the Ombudsman's office will make an initial review of the case to decide whether it should be accepted for formal investigation. Then the complaint form and accompanying papers, if any, are copied to the respondent (ie the employer, trustees, managers or administrators) and any other person against whom allegations are made in order to allow them an opportunity to respond in writing to the allegations (*Procedure Rules, r 5(2)*).

The Ombudsman has powers to demand papers from parties (*PSA 1993, Part X, s 150(1)*) who may hold them and can also hold oral hearings if he considers this necessary (although to date, these have been rare (*Procedure Rules, r 10(1)*)). Both the complainant and the respondent have an opportunity, with leave of the Ombudsman, to submit a supplementary statement and/or amend details of their original complaint/response (*Procedure Rules, rr 3, 7*).

In conducting the investigation, the Ombudsman must comply with the statutory rules to ensure fairness and must also comply with the principles of natural justice (*Duffield v Pensions Ombudsman [1996] PLR 285*). In particular, he must:

(*a*) make clear to the respondent the specific allegation(s) to be investigated;

(*b*) express the substance of the allegation(s) in plain and simple language; and

(*c*) disclose to the respondent all potentially relevant information obtained by him (particularly all evidence and representations made by the complainant).

The Court of Appeal's 1999 decision in *Edge v Pensions Ombudsman [1999] PLR 215* emphasised this need for the Ombudsman to observe the principles of natural justice. In particular, it was decided that he could not consider complaints which could only be remedied by steps which would adversely affect someone who was not a party to the investigation. Turning this the other way, in the case of *Marsh Mercer Pension Scheme v Pensions Ombudsman [2001] 16 PBLR (28)* (the *Williamson Case*) heard in the High Court, the Ombudsman's decision that a pension scheme should equalise all GMP's between men and women was set aside. Principally, it was held that the Pension Ombudsman had affected all members of the scheme, not only the complainant. Accordingly, he should have either declined jurisdiction or made a decision which would only affect the complainant.

After receiving a copy of the complaint the respondent has 21 days within which to produce a written reply (*Procedure Rules, r 6(3)*), although time extensions can be requested (*Procedure Rules, r 16(1)*). The reply can include a reference to any other person (such as a manager or administrator of the scheme) who, in his opinion, has a direct interest in the subject matter of the complaint (*Procedure Rules, r 6(2)*). It is not, however, possible for the respondent to join a third party as a second respondent. The Ombudsman will then issue a written determination of his decision, which will initially be sent out to both the respondent and the complainant in draft form for their comments. At this stage, changes to the determination can still be made.

Although not stated in the *Procedure Rules*, in practice the Ombudsman operates a 'fast-track' procedure for those complaints which he thinks have no merit. In these instances, the investigator will inform the complainant who will then have 14 days in which to make a further submission which would make the Ombudsman change his mind. Equally, the Ombudsman can fast track to success those complaints where he considers the complainant to have a winning case.

After investigating the complaint, and examining the comments of both parties, the Ombudsman will issue a final written determination. This determination will direct any person responsible for the management of the scheme concerned 'to take or refrain from taking' such action as the Ombudsman considers appropriate (*PSA 1993, Part X, s 151(2)*). Following a number of conflicting authorities, it is now thought that the Pensions Ombudsman can award compensation for distress and inconvenience to a complainant, although this is not beyond doubt. In *Westminster City Council v Haywood [1996] PLR 161* the court considered that the Ombudsman's powers under *s 151(2)* included the payment of reasonable compensation for distress and inconvenience. However, the court ruled in *City and County of Swansea v Johnson [1999] PLR 187* that such compensation must be modest, not exceeding £1,000. The courts have made clear that, if the Ombudsman does have power to award compensation, he should consider not only the amount of compensation but also upon whom the ultimate liability for this will fall (for example, it may not be appropriate for a liability to fall on a scheme which is in deficit).

The Ombudsman's determination is final and binding on the parties, subject only to an appeal to the High Court on a point of law, and can be enforced through the county court. Costs cannot be awarded against a complainant, even if the complaint is not upheld.

It is becoming increasingly common for the Ombudsman's determinations to be appealed to the High Court under the High Court's general jurisdiction to hear appeals from any court, tribunal or person. This is referred to in *Civil Procedure Rules 1998, Part 52.*

Notice of the appeal must be served and the appeal entered within 21 days after the date of the Ombudsman's determination. The appeal may only be made on a point of law and, in addition to the original complainant, the Ombudsman himself will be a respondent to the Appeal (although in practice he will only appear where the appeal raises an issue of jurisdictional importance for his role). A High Court judge has discretion to remit matters on appeal to the Ombudsman for further consideration.

The Pensions Ombudsman website can be found at www.pensions-ombudsman.org.uk, and determinations issued from 1 April 2001 (and frequently requested determinations issued before 1 April 2000) are available for review. The Pensions Ombudsman can be contacted at 11 Belgrave Road, London SW1V 1RB. Tel: 020 7630 2200; fax: 020 7821 0065; e-mail: enquiries@pensions-ombudsman.org.uk.

Other bodies

Pensions Management Institute (PMI)

2.49 The PMI was established in 1976 to promote professionalism amongst those working in the field of pensions. It is an independent non-political organisation which establishes, maintains and improves professional standards in every aspect of pension scheme management and consultancy. There are four grades of membership: the first is student membership, which is the introductory level for those wishing to study the Institute's examinations. After student membership, there are a further three grades of qualified membership; Ordinary Member (someone who has passed one of the Institute's examinations), Associate Member (someone who has passed the Institute's examinations and has three years' experience in pensions management or administration) and Fellowship (an individual who was an Associate and has eight years' experience, five of which must have been spent in a position with 'substantial pensions accountability and responsibility'). The PMI is directed by a Council of 16 elected fellows, who are actively involved in pension schemes.

The PMI also offers examinations for trustees in basic pensions knowledge, a qualification in administration, a Diploma in international employee benefits and the retirement provision certificate to name a few.

The PMI can be contacted at PMI House, 4–10 Artillery Lane, London E1 7LS. Tel: 020 7247 1452; fax: 020 7375 0603; e-mail: enquiries@pension-pmi.org.uk; website: www.pensions-pmi.org.uk.

The National Association of Pension Funds (NAPF)

2.50 The NAPF describes itself as the 'leading UK body providing representation and other services for those involved in designing, operating, advising and investing in all aspects of pensions and other retirement provision.' Among its members are large and small companies, local authority and public sector bodies which provide pension benefits for some 15 million members, accounting for around £800 billion of pension funds. NAPF members also include corporate trustees and other organisations providing professional advice to schemes. The NAPF also allows individual trustees, trustee directors and chairmen of trustee boards of NAPF member funds to join. The NAPF's principle aim is to encourage pension provision by employers by representing the interests of members to the UK Government, Europe, regulators and other professional bodies (including the media). It seeks to achieve this by:

(*a*) influencing public opinion;

(*b*) consulting Government bodies;

(*c*) collecting and disseminating information on best practice and trends involving schemes;

(*d*) publishing guidelines and information; and

(*e*) providing education in the form of seminars and conferences.

The NAPF can be contacted at NAPF Ltd, Cheapside House, 138 Cheapside, London EC2V 6AE. Tel: 020 7601 1700; fax: 020 7601 1799; e-mail: napf@napf.co.uk; website: www.napf.co.uk.

Information Commissioner

2.51 Although not a pensions body as such, the Information Commissioner's Office regulates the holding, use and protection of personal information relating to living individuals by data controllers. The Information Commissioner enforces and oversees the *Data Protection Act 1998* and the

Freedom of Information Act 2000. The Commissioner is a UK independent supervisory authority.

The Information Commissioner maintains a public register of data controllers. Each register entry contains the name and address of the data controller and a general description of the processing of personal data by a data controller. The public register is updated weekly, but new notifications, renewal and amendments may take several weeks to appear during busy periods. Under the *Data Protection Act 1998* the Information Commissioner can, in certain circumstances, serve an information notice and assess compliance with the Act and, where there has been a breach, serve an enforcement notice ordering compliance. The impact of the data protection legislation and in particular, the *Data Protection Act 1998* is considered further in CHAPTER 3.

The Information Commissioner's Office can be contacted at Wycliffe House, Water Lane, Wilmslow, Cheshire SK9 5AF. ICO Helpline: 0845 630 6060 or 01625 545 745; fax: 01625 524 510; website: www.ico.gov.uk.

The Department for Work and Pensions

2.52 The Department for Work and Pensions (DWP) is responsible for employment, equality, benefits, pensions and child support. It was formed in June 2001 from parts of the former Department of Social Security and the Department for Education and Employment.

The DWP's priorities include (amongst others) delivering the Government's pension reform agenda. The Secretary of State for Work and Pensions is currently Rt Hon Yvette Cooper MP and she has overall responsibility for all work and pension matters. Angela Eagle MP is the Minister for Pensions and the Ageing Society whose responsibilities include (but are not limited to): pensions reform and legislation, the Pensions Service, personal accounts and regulatory reform.

To contact the DWP or any minister write to Caxton House, Tothill Street, London SW1H 9DA or via their website: www.dwp.gov.uk.

The Thornton Review of Pension Institutions

2.53 We reported in our last edition of this book that the Thornton Review of Pension Institutions (the 'Review') was published in June 2007. The review made a number of recommendations, including a closer working relationship between the Regulator and the PPF rather than a full merger. Other recommendations included appointing common non-executives to each board and establishing a Pensions Institutions Forum to discuss key issues.

Following the Review, an updated version of the Memorandum of Understanding between the DWP, the Regulator and the PPF was published in February 2008. The Memorandum establishes a framework for co-operation between the three institutions and sets out how they will work together towards a common goal of pensions security. The guiding principles to be used to achieve this goal are transparency, accountability, no duplication of roles, and regular and appropriate information exchange between them.

The Review recommended that the Financial Services Authority and the Regulator work more closely on the regulation of defined contribution schemes. In November 2007, the two institutions published a joint guide on the regulation of workplace contract-based pensions, setting out the respective roles of the two bodies.

The headline recommendation of the Review was that the Office of the Pensions Ombudsman should be transferred to the Financial Ombudsman Service. It was intended that there would be a separate section within the Financial Ombudsman Service to manage cases currently dealt with by the Pensions Ombudsman. The Review considered that this would lead to improved workflow and case management, clarity, customer focus and cost savings.

However, the DWP announced in February 2009 that the proposed merger would not be going ahead. Rather, the two entities would aim for closer working ties, to be achieved via a 'closer working initiative'. It was felt that the respective roles of the two Ombudsmen were simply too different to be reconciled meaningfully within a unified body. For example, the Pension Ombudsman's jurisdiction is much wider than the Financial Ombudsman Service, and the Pension Ombudsman's determinations are as binding on all parties as a county court judgment (see **2.47** and **2.48** above), whereas decisions of the Financial Ombudsman are only binding if accepted by the complainant, and they may be subject to judicial review.

The 'closer working initiative' will include changes to streamline processes between the two institutions. However, no detailed proposals about the initiative are available as yet.

Chapter 3

Trustees

Introduction

3.1 The role of a pension scheme trustee is to apply the scheme assets for the benefit of scheme members and other beneficiaries in accordance with the scheme's trust documents and relevant legislation, such as *PA 1995*. *PA 2004* has subsequently made further changes to the role of trustees, such as altering the requirements and procedure for member-nominated trustees, making changes to scheme funding negotiations, and introducing a statutory knowledge and understanding requirement.

PA 1995 introduced civil penalties (of up to £5,000 for individuals and £50,000 for companies) and criminal penalties (ie fines and/or imprisonment) for breaches of certain legislative provisions. The Regulator was given expanded enforcement powers under *PA 2004*. APPENDIX I summarises the penalties which may be imposed by the Regulator under *PA 1995* and *PA 2004*.

Who can be a trustee?

3.2 Anyone who is legally capable of holding property can act as a trustee. In effect, this means that anyone aged 18 or over, whether based in the UK or overseas, can be appointed as a trustee. There are, however, circumstances where an individual may be disqualified from being a trustee. Under *PA 1995, s 29*, a person is disqualified from acting as a trustee if, for example:

(*a*) he has been or is convicted of an offence involving dishonesty or deception;

(*b*) he is an undischarged bankrupt;

(*c*) in the case of a trustee which is a company, any director of the company is disqualified for any of the reasons set out in *s 29*;

(*d*) he has made an arrangement with his creditors and has not been discharged in respect of it; or

(*e*) he is disqualified as a company director.

Further, the Regulator may prohibit any person from being a trustee if it is satisfied that they are not a fit and proper person to be a trustee (*PA 1995, s 3*). The Regulator also has the power to suspend a trustee from acting as a trustee (*PA 1995, s 4*). Anyone who tries to act as a trustee while disqualified or prohibited or suspended from doing so is liable to a fine and/or imprisonment (*PA 1995, s 6*).

A trustee, and any person connected or associated with them, is not allowed to be the actuary or auditor for the scheme of which he is trustee. This will not, however, prevent another person in the same firm of actuaries from being the scheme actuary where their colleague is a trustee (*PA 1995, s 27* and *Scheme Administration Regulations (SI 1996/1715), reg 7*).

Type of trustee

Individual trustees and corporate trustees

3.3 A trustee will either be an individual, acting in a personal capacity, or a corporate body such as a limited company (a 'corporate trustee'). A company will often be specifically formed to act as a trustee, but any company may act as a trustee if its memorandum and articles of association allow this. Although it is the company (not the directors) which is the trustee, in practical terms, the directors will take all the relevant trustee decisions. Whilst the exposure to liability of a director of a corporate trustee is reduced (as compared with the position of an individual trustee) because of the 'corporate veil', the director concerned may not escape all liability to the beneficiaries. For further discussion of this topic, see **3.50** onwards below.

A director (or other officer of a trustee company) is also subject to the same civil penalties as individual trustees under *PA 1995* where it can be shown that a breach took place with his consent or connivance or was attributable to neglect on his part (*PA 1995, s 10(5)*).

Trust corporations

3.4 A trust corporation is either the Public Trustee, or a corporation:

(*a*) appointed by the court to be a trustee; or

(*b*) entitled by rules made under the Public Trustee Act 1906 to act as a custodian trustee (a special type of trustee with a role limited to holding trust assets) (*TA 1925, s 68*).

The main advantage of a trust corporation over individual trustees or a trustee company is that a trust corporation can give a valid receipt for the proceeds of a sale of land on its own. Otherwise, two trustees are needed to give a valid receipt (*TA 1925, s 14*).

Independent trustees

Non-statutory appointments

3.5 A scheme may have a trustee who is independent of the employer, either as the sole trustee or as a director of the trustee company or one of the individual trustees, even though there is no statutory requirement to make such an appointment. The reason for having an independent trustee may be to manage conflicts of interest within the trustee body and/or between the employer and the trustees, or to have a professional independent trustee with particular skills or experience. Such an appointment would be made by exercising the scheme's power of appointment, as modified by *PA 2004* requirements in relation to member-nominated trustees (see **3.32** onwards below).

Statutory appointments

3.6 Where an insolvency practitioner or official receiver has been appointed in relation to the scheme employer, or during a PPF assessment period, an independent trustee may be appointed by the Regulator. This legislation was first introduced by the *Social Security Act 1990* but, since 6 April 1997, such appointments have been governed by *PA 1995, ss 22–26* (as amended by *PA 2004* with effect from 6 April 2005) and the *Occupational Pension Schemes (Independent Trustee) Regulations 2005 (SI 2005/703)* (the '*Independent Trustee Regulations 2005*').

While there is an independent trustee of the scheme appointed under *PA 1995, s 23*, any discretionary power vested in the trustees of the scheme may be exercised only by the independent trustee, and any discretionary power which the scheme confers on the employer as trustee of the power may also be exercised only by the independent trustee.

The Regulator must maintain a register of trustees and must only appoint an independent trustee from that register. Detailed requirements for the register are set out in the *Independent Trustee Regulations 2005*. The Regulator must compile and maintain a register of persons who satisfy various conditions set out in *reg 3*. That regulation includes the requirements that the applicant must not be subject to a prohibition order or suspension order or be disqualified from being a trustee. The Regulator must be satisfied that the applicant has sufficient relevant experience of occupational pension schemes, is a fit and proper person to act as a trustee of an occupational pension scheme, operates sound administrative and accounting procedures, and has adequate indemnity insurance cover. Further, the applicant must have premises in the UK from which he conducts his business as a trustee and he must disclose the address to the Regulator. The applicant must agree to have his fees and costs scrutinised by an independent adjudicator, must agree to the Regulator disclosing his name, address and area of trustee work on the version of the trustee register which is to be publicly available, must comply with the reasonable requests of the Regulator to provide information to the Regulator, and must inform the Regulator as soon as is reasonably practicable if he becomes disqualified under *PA 1995, s 29*.

The *Independent Trustee Regulations 2005* also contain provisions regarding the refusal by the Regulator to register an applicant in the trustee register and the removal from the trustee register.

PA 1995, s 25 provides that an order appointing an independent trustee may make provision for their fees and expenses to be paid either by the employer or out of the scheme's resources, or by a combination of both. Where an appointed trustee's fees are to be met out of a scheme's resources, such fees will take priority over all other claims to be met by the scheme's resources.

Where a trustee has been appointed by the Regulator under *PA 1995, s 7(1) or (3)* (to replace a prohibited or disqualified trustee) or *PA 1995, s 22* ('the appointed trustee'), it is the responsibility of such appointed trustee to supply in writing its name and address to every member (excluding deferred members whose address is not known to the trustees) or relevant trade union within a reasonable period following his appointment.

- The appointed trustee must also provide on request:
  - (i) the scale of fees that would be chargeable by the appointed trustee and payable by the scheme; and
  - (ii) details of the amounts charged to the scheme by the appointed trustee in the past 12 months.

PA 1995, s 25 (as amended) provides that, where an independent trustee having been appointed ceases to be an independent person, he must, as soon as reasonably practical, notify the Regulator in writing and step down (or, if he is the only trustee, be replaced as trustee). Any failure to give such notice will result in civil penalties under *PA 1995, s 10*.

Member-nominated trustees

3.7 *PA 1995* provided for the appointment of member-nominated trustees and directors. Revised statutory requirements are now found in *PA 2004, ss 241–243*. This is dealt with in **3.32** onwards below.

Constructive trustees

3.8 In certain circumstances, a person (although not formally appointed as such) may find that he is treated in law as being a trustee of a scheme. This will usually happen because the person has, by his conduct, assumed trustee-like responsibilities. For example, where a person has never validly been appointed as a trustee but has nevertheless acted as one, he could at law be regarded as a constructive trustee. Another example is where a scheme has a pensions committee whose role includes exercising discretionary functions which relate directly to members' interests.

Employment protection for trustees under the Employment Rights Act 1996

3.9 The *Employment Rights Act 1996 (ERA 1996)* offers protection for employees who are trustees of their employer's occupational pension scheme, whether as individuals or directors of a trustee company (see also CHAPTER 7). In particular *ERA 1996*:

(*a*) gives an employee the right not to be subjected to any detriment by any act, or any deliberate failure to act, done by his employer on the ground that, being a trustee of an occupational pension scheme which relates to his employment, the employee performed (or proposed to perform) any functions as a trustee (*ERA 1996, s 46*).

(*b*) entitles employee trustees to reasonable time off during working hours to perform their trustee duties or undergo trustee training (*ERA 1996, s 58*);

(*c*) entitles employee trustees to payment for time taken off due to his trustee role (*ERA 1996, s 59*);

(*d*) permits employee trustees to complain to an employment tribunal if the employee has suffered any detriment under (*a*) above *(ERA 1996, s 48)* or the employer has failed to comply with (*b*) or (*c*) above (*ERA 1996, s 60*) (generally, such a complaint must be made within three months); and

(*e*) provides that employee trustees are to be regarded as unfairly dismissed if the reason, or the principal reason, for the dismissal is that they performed any functions as a trustee (*ERA 1996, s 102*).

Appointment, removal and discharge of trustees

3.10 Generally, a scheme's documentation will contain a specific provision setting out the power to appoint and remove trustees, such power most frequently being vested in the principal employer. An employer's power to remove or appoint trustees is generally regarded as a fiduciary power and so must be exercised in the interests of the scheme's beneficiaries. If an employer disregards those interests, his position will be similar to that of a trustee who has committed a breach of trust. There are, in addition, statutory provisions governing the appointment and removal of trustees contained in *TA 1925* and, in relation to member-nominated trustees, in *PA 2004* (see **3.32** to **3.45** below). The Regulator must be informed of changes of individual trustees and corporate trustees (but not changes to the directors of a trustee company) as soon as reasonably practicable after the change taking place (*PA 2004, s 62(4)*). In the majority of schemes, the power of appointment should be sufficiently widely drawn that reliance need not be placed on *TA 1925*.

TA 1925, s 36 deals with the power of appointing new or additional trustees where a trustee:

(*a*) is dead;

(*b*) remains out of the UK for more than 12 months;

(*c*) desires to be discharged;

(*d*) refuses or is unfit to act;

(*e*) is incapable of acting; or

(*f*) is an infant.

In such a situation, the power of appointment is exercisable by the person specified in the governing documentation as having the power of appointment. If there is no-one in whom such a power is vested (for example, because the employer has been liquidated) or no-one who is able and willing to act, then the surviving or continuing trustee or trustees or the personal representatives of the last surviving or continuing trustee may make the appointment. The court also has power to appoint trustees, either in addition to or in substitution for existing trustees, where it is otherwise difficult or impracticable to do so.

TA 1925, s 39 allows the retirement of an individual trustee without a new appointment being made, provided that, after the trustee's retirement, there remains either a trust corporation (see **3.4** above) or at least two remaining individual trustees. In such circumstances, the retiring trustee is discharged from the trust, provided a deed is executed by the retiring trustee, the remaining trustees and the person who has the power to appoint trustees.

Whenever there is a change in the trustees of a pension scheme, it is important to ensure that the ownership of the assets of the pension fund is transferred accordingly. Land and chattels (but not stocks and shares) vest automatically in a new trustee if the appointment is by way of a deed (*TA 1925, s 40*). A change of sole corporate trustee may also require agreements to be novated or assigned.

In addition to the powers to disqualify, prohibit and suspend trustees referred to in **3.2** above, the Regulator also has power to appoint a trustee or trustees to a scheme (*PA 1995, s 7*) in circumstances other than those set out in **3.6** above. Such an appointment may be made following the prohibition or disqualification of a former trustee or where the Regulator is satisfied that it is reasonable to make an appointment:

(*a*) to secure that the trustees as a whole have, or exercise, the necessary knowledge and skill for the proper administration of the scheme;

(*b*) to secure that the number of trustees is sufficient for the proper administration of the scheme;

(*c*) to secure the proper use or application of the assets of the scheme; or

(*d*) otherwise to protect the interests of the generality of the scheme members.

The employer, existing trustees and scheme members can all apply to the Regulator for the appointment of a trustee under grounds (*a*) or (*c*) above.

When making an order, the Regulator may also: determine the appropriate number of trustees for the proper administration of the scheme; require a trustee appointed by them to be paid fees and expenses by the employer, out of the scheme's resources, or a combination of both; and provide for the removal or replacement of such a trustee (*PA 1995, s 7(5)*). Finally, in most cases, unlike a statutory independent trustee, a trustee appointed by the Regulator under *s 7* shall have the same powers and duties as the other trustees of the scheme, unless the order appointing the trustee restricts those powers and duties or provides that those powers and duties are to be exercised by the trustee so appointed to the exclusion of the other trustees (*PA 1995, s 8(3), (4)*).

The Regulator's actions in the *Telent* case are an interesting example of the use of these powers. In October 2007 the Regulator used its special procedure to appoint three independent trustees to the GEC 1972 Plan (the Telent pension scheme) under *s 7*, as it was 'satisfied that it is necessary to do so in order to ... secure the proper use or application of the assets of the scheme'. That decision was subsequently confirmed by the Determinations Panel in November 2007 at a compulsory review hearing, following a complete reconsideration of the initial decision.

The facts in brief were that Pension Corporation made a bid for Telent (the principal employer of the GEC 1972 Plan) and the scheme trustees were concerned that it would appoint a majority of its own nominees as trustees in order to determine the scheme's investment strategy, and possibly release monies held in an escrow account, with the ultimate intention of achieving profit for its investors. Pension Corporation argued before the Determinations Panel that the appointment of the independent trustees was not appropriate and should be overturned.

The main issue was one of conflict of interests between the stated business aims of Pensions Corporation and the interests of scheme members. The main concern was that the proposed trustees (who it was suggested would also be shareholders of Pension Corporation and have a personal interest in the funding of the scheme) would operate an excessively risky investment policy. The factors considered by the Regulator included:

- Pension Corporation's business model of seeking to 'gain control' of pension funds;
- Pension Corporation's executives were amongst its shareholders and had a personal interest;
- those who would be appointed as trustees would be Pension Corporation executives;
- the level of conflict/potential conflict created a danger that scheme assets and the interests of the members were at risk; and
- in order to achieve Pension Corporation's aimed investment return, the scheme would have to adopt a highly risky investment strategy.

The Determinations Panel found that the *s 7* power was not constrained to situations in which a breach of trust had either occurred or was about to occur. It was a question of fact and degree as to whether the appointment power should be used when there was no realistic prospect of a threat to assets occurring in the reasonably foreseeable future. In this case the transaction was still at bid stage, Pension Corporation did not yet have control of Telent and no steps had been made actually to appoint the nominee trustees. However, the Determinations Panel concluded that Pension Corporation had shown no real recognition of the potential conflicts and there was a realistic prospect that conflicts might occur and insufficient arrangements had been proposed to manage them. On this basis the appointment of the independent trustees under *s 7* was confirmed since, on the balance of probabilities, the requirements of *s 7* had been met and the threat to the scheme's assets was sufficiently proximate to justify the use of the power.

Trustees' duties

3.11 The following are some of the general duties with which trustees must comply. Except where those duties are stated as arising under a particular piece of legislation, they are general trust law duties and may, to some extent, overlap. Trust law duties are fiduciary. This means that they must be exercised in the best interests of the scheme's beneficiaries.

Whilst there is argument as to what may or may not be in the best interests of the members, it is an established principle that the best interests of the beneficiaries of a scheme are usually the best financial interests of those beneficiaries. In *Cowan v Scargill [1984] 2 All ER 750*, Megarry V-C stated: '… under a trust for the provision of financial benefits, the paramount duty of the trustees is to provide the greatest financial benefits for the present and future beneficiaries.'

'Beneficiaries' has a wide meaning. It can include active, deferred and pensioner members, recipients of death benefits (such as spouses, civil partners, dependants and children) and, in some circumstances, the employers participating in the scheme.

Trustees have to take care to identify, monitor and manage potential and actual conflicts of interest. A conflict of interest, or duty, can arise when a fiduciary is obliged to act in the best interests of a beneficiary but has a competing personal interest or other fiduciary duty. The Regulator has issued specific guidance dealing with conflicts of interest, with suggestions on how to manage or avoid conflicts. It is good practice, although not a legal obligation, for trustees to put in place a conflicts of interest policy, which sets out how conflicts will be dealt with.

Duty not to profit from position as a trustee

3.12 As a general principle, a trustee may not receive any benefit from the scheme or exercise his powers in a way which creates a conflict between his personal interest and his duties to the scheme's beneficiaries. However, *PA 1995, s 39* provides that this principle does not apply to a trustee who is also a member of the scheme if, on exercising his powers in any manner, he benefits merely because the exercise of a power in that manner benefits (or may benefit) him as a scheme member. Despite this provision of *PA 1995*, a trustee may still not profit in other ways: for example, a trustee cannot buy assets from or sell assets to the scheme.

A trustee may, if the trust documents expressly permit it, be paid for acting as a trustee out of the trust fund. An independent trustee appointed under *PA 1995* (see **3.6** above) may be paid his reasonable fees and expenses out of the trust fund regardless of whether this is permitted by the trust instrument (*PA 1995, s 25(6)*). Under *PA 1995, s 7(5)(b)*, the Regulator has the power to order that the fees and expenses of a trustee appointed by it are paid out of the scheme's resources.

Duty of prudence

3.13 Each trustee has an obligation to act as a prudent person would, not only in the conduct of his own affairs, but also in looking after the affairs of third parties. In doing so, trustees must also use any skills or expertise which they possess (so a higher standard will be required of professional trustees). (*Bartlett v Barclays Bank Trust Company Limited [1980] Ch 515* illustrates this point.)

The Government adopted Paul Myners' proposal in his report dated 6 March 2001 entitled 'Institutional investment in the United Kingdom: a review' that trustees' duty of care in investment decision-making must be raised. The Government said that it would legislate to enforce the new standard, and *PA 2004* is an example of this intention. It has stated that where trustees are taking a decision, they should be able to take it with the care and skill of someone familiar with the issues concerned and that they should have appropriate training. See **3.22** below for an outline of what issues trustees will have to be conversant with under *PA 2004*.

Duty to act in accordance with the trust deed and rules

3.14 Decisions and actions of trustees must be taken in accordance with the scheme's trust documents, and will be open to challenge if they are not. Trustees must therefore familiarise themselves and be conversant with the scheme's documentation and, if they are unsure as to the interpretation of any trust documentation (which may not be written in a particularly user-friendly manner) and any announcement which has not been incorporated into the trust documentation, suitable professional advice should be sought. Trustees should bear in mind that the effect of the trust deed and rules may be qualified or even contradicted by overriding legislation and decisions of the UK courts and the European Court of Justice and should, therefore, ensure that scheme documents are kept up to date.

Duties relating to investment decisions

3.15 All trustees should familiarise themselves and be conversant with their investment powers. This is one of the most fundamental duties of a trustee and must be exercised within the parameters of the trust deed, legislation and case law. *PA 1995, s 34(1)* reflects the general legal principle that trustees of occupational pension schemes have the power 'to make an investment of any kind as if they were absolutely entitled to the assets of the scheme', subject only to any specific restrictions imposed by their scheme documents. If trustees disregard any such restrictions, they may find themselves liable for any resulting loss to the value of the fund as a breach of trust.

If trustees do not wish to, or do not have the skills to, take investment decisions, they may delegate responsibility for these decisions to someone who does have the skills and knowledge to take them effectively, whether a sub-committee of the trustees or a fund manager appointed in accordance with *PA 1995, s 34*.

The fact that trustees have power to make a particular investment does not necessarily mean that it is an appropriate investment for them to make; for instance, a high proportion of investment in property would be inappropriate in a fund where liquidity was required to pay pensions. Similarly, trustees would generally diversify their investments so as to maintain a balance between achieving good returns and protecting the fund against unnecessary risk.

PA 1995 contains specific provisions relating to the delegation by trustees of their investment discretions. In particular, for every occupational pension scheme whose assets include 'investments', the trustees must appoint a fund manager (*PA 1995, s 47(2)*). The *Occupational Pension Schemes (Investment) Regulations 2005* (*SI 2005/3378*) make provision as to how trustees must exercise their power of investment (see further in CHAPTER 10).

Duty to act impartially between the different classes of beneficiaries

3.16 A trustee must act fairly between different classes of beneficiary (such as pensioners, active members, deferred members, contingent beneficiaries and, in some cases, prospective members) and must also act fairly as between individuals and other beneficiaries. In some cases the employer may also be regarded as a beneficiary. This issue could arise where trustees are considering the allocation of surplus on the winding-up of a scheme.

That is not to say that all classes of beneficiary must be treated in an identical manner. In the case of *Edge v Pensions Ombudsman [1999] 49 PBLR (37)*, Chadwick LJ confirmed that the duty to act impartially:

> '… is no more than the ordinary duty which the law imposes on a person who is entrusted with the exercise of a discretionary power: that he exercises the power for the purpose for which it is given, giving proper consideration to the matters which are relevant and excluding from consideration matters which are irrelevant. If pension fund trustees do that, they cannot be criticised if they reach a decision which appears to prefer the claims of one interest – whether that of employers, current

employees or pensioners – over others. The preference will be the result of a proper exercise of the discretionary power.' (paragraph 50)

The *Edge* case also sets out the duty, when taking decisions, for trustees to take into account relevant factors and ignore irrelevant factors.

Duty to seek appropriate professional advice on matters which a trustee does not understand

3.17 This duty is self-explanatory and should be complied with in areas where a trustee is not an expert. A trustee's decisions will generally be harder to challenge if it can be shown to have been based on appropriate professional advice. Specific requirements as to the use and appointment of professional advisers were introduced by *PA 1995* (see CHAPTER 2).

Delegation

3.18 Trustees must not generally delegate their powers or discretions unless they are authorised to do so by the trust deed and rules (although there are some statutory powers of delegation, most notably the limited general power to delegate under *TA 1925, s 25*, the narrow default powers contained in *TA 2000* and the power to delegate investment discretions under *PA 1995, s 34* – see CHAPTER 10).

It may be appropriate for the trustees (provided there is power under the scheme's documentation), to appoint a person (whether one of the trustees or an external person) as pensions manager with delegated authority to administer the scheme and deal with member enquiries on a day-to-day basis. The person so appointed should be fully informed of the duties and responsibilities which the trustees have delegated to him. This person will often be in the employment of the sponsoring company. The trustees may also appoint an outside party to provide other administration services such as payment of pensions, retention of their membership records and other services. There should be a written agreement between the trustees and the administrator not least because the trustees are required to ensure that the external administrator has appropriate systems in place to ensure the security and proper processing of members' personal data (see **3.57** below) and the trustees should receive undertakings to that effect in the agreement. Some schemes use the employer's in-house staff to provide these services. The trustees are required to act prudently in choosing any person to whom they delegate any of their duties or responsibilities.

Note that the exercise of discretions by the trustees cannot be delegated unless the trust deed and rules and relevant legislation specifically permit this.

Duty to collect contributions

3.19 *PA 1995* introduced the requirement for trustees to arrange for a schedule of contributions (in the case of a final salary scheme – *s 58*, now replaced by *PA 2004, s 227*) or schedule of payments (in the case of a money purchase scheme – see *PA 1995, s 87*) to be prepared. In either case the schedule must show the rates of contributions payable and the dates on or before which such payments are due. Failure by the employer or members to make payments due may be reportable by the trustees to the Regulator (see **3.64** below). Trustees' duties generally in relation to scheme funding have increased very significantly with the introduction of the new overriding statutory funding requirement as set out in *PA 2004, ss 221–233* (see CHAPTER 11).

Duty to keep receipts, payments and records

3.20 *PA 1995, s 49* requires trustees to keep any money received by them in a separate bank account kept at an authorised deposit-taking institution. Trustees may instead arrange to keep money in an account operated by a third party and separate from the employer's bank account if they have entered into a suitable arrangement or contract with them. Any such arrangement or contract must ensure that records (including details of the amount paid, date of payment, and from whom it was paid, the amount paid out, the date of withdrawal and to whom, and the interest earned) are kept for at least six years and that all interest is credited to the scheme (*Scheme Administration Regulations, reg 7*).

Trustees are required by *PA 1995, s 49* and *Scheme Administration Regulations, reg 13* to keep written records of their meetings (including meetings of any of their number, for example, sub-committees of the trustees) for at least six years from the end of the scheme year to which they relate, stating:

(*a*) the date, time and place of the meeting;

(*b*) the names of all the trustees invited to the meeting;

(*c*) the names of the trustees who attended the meeting and those who did not attend;

(*d*) the names of any professional advisers or other persons who attended the meeting;

(*e*) any decisions made at the meeting; and

(*f*) whether since the previous meeting there has been any occasion when a decision has been made by the trustees and if so the time, place and date of such a decision, and the names of the trustees who participated in the decision.

In addition, trustees are required by *PA 1995, s 49* and *Scheme Administration Regulations, reg 12* to keep, for at least six years from the end of the scheme year to which they relate, books and records relating to certain transactions including records of:

(i) any amount received in respect of any contribution payable in respect of an active member of the scheme;

(ii) the date on which a member joins the scheme;

(iii) payments of pensions and benefits;

(iv) payments made by or on behalf of the trustees to any person including a professional adviser, including the name and address of the person to whom the payment was made and the reason for that payment;

(v) any movement or transfer of assets from the trustees to any person including a professional adviser, including the name and address of the person to whom the assets were moved or transferred and the reason for that transaction;

(vi) the receipt or payment of money or assets in respect of the transfer of members into or out of the scheme along with certain prescribed details about the transfer;

(vii) payments made to a member who leaves the scheme including the name of that member, the date of leaving, the member's entitlement at that date, the method used for calculating any entitlement under the scheme and how that entitlement was discharged;

(viii) payments made to the employer;

(ix) other payments to, and withdrawals from, the scheme, including the name and address of the person the payment was made to or from whom it was received; and

(x) generally where a scheme is wound up, details as to how protected rights were discharged by the taking out of an insurance policy (see CHAPTER 4).

In addition, *Registered Pension Schemes (Provision of Information) Regulations 2006 (SI 2006/567), reg 18* requires the scheme administrator for HMRC purposes (which will usually be the trustees) and the trustees to retain certain records for a period of six years from the end of the relevant tax year.

Disclosure of information to members

3.21 Trustees are obliged to disclose certain documents and information to scheme members, prospective members (provided that the employer has told the trustees that the person is a member or prospective member), spouses and civil partners, other beneficiaries and recognised trade unions (but only if the employer has told the trustees that the union is recognised) under *PA 1995, s 41*, *PSA 1993, s 113* and the *Disclosure Regulations*. The requirements do not apply to schemes with only one member nor to schemes which only provide death benefits.

In practice, the issue of a scheme booklet and individual benefit statements satisfies many of the disclosure of information requirements. Amending regulations have put in place an obligation on trustees to provide members of defined contribution schemes with information about the open market option to select an annuity on retirement.

Currently, there are other regulations which also require disclosure of information to members in certain situations, for example, on pension sharing or earmarking on divorce. These are referred to in the context of the relevant chapter in this book, and a general summary of the information which must be disclosed is given at APPENDIX II.

Under the legislation, trustees are obliged to disclose, amongst other things, details of the scheme's governing documentation, basic scheme information (which is usually contained in the scheme's explanatory booklet), an annual report commenting on the accounts and funding of the scheme and details of benefits payable.

Most information need only be disclosed at the request of the member, prospective member, spouse, civil partner, other beneficiary or trade union, although some information – most notably the basic scheme information – must be provided as a matter of course, regardless of whether or not a request is made. The legislation does not entitle a person to receive information which is not relevant to his own rights or entitlements under the scheme.

Case law has established that beneficiaries of a trust may have the right to compel trustees to disclose certain information where it is being challenged that they have not performed their duties. The general trust law principle, however, is that trustees are entitled to exercise their discretionary powers in a confidential manner.

The right of a beneficiary to have access to certain trust documents was considered in the case of *Re Londonderry's Settlement; Peat v Walsh [1964] 3 All ER 855*. The Court of Appeal held that, whilst a beneficiary is entitled to see trust documents, this rule did not extend to requiring trustees to disclose documents (such as minutes of a meeting) recording the reasons behind the exercise of a discretion.

The later case of *Wilson v Law Debenture Trust Corporation plc [1995] 2 All ER 337* applied the position in *Londonderry* more directly to a pensions context. It showed that it is only in exceptional circumstances that trustees should be compelled to give reasons for the exercise of a discretion, for example, where there was evidence that the trustees had failed to take into account a relevant consideration when exercising that discretion. However, the general presumption was that 'in the absence of evidence to the contrary a trustee has exercised his discretion properly' (paragraph 29).

However, this long-held position has come under attack more recently both in the courts and in front of the Pensions Ombudsman. First, in the decision in *Allen v TKM Group Pension Trust Ltd (L00370 – 25 April 2002) [2002] PLR 333*, the Pensions Ombudsman took a different view from the established position at law as concerns the disclosure of trustees' reasons. He decided in this case that it was maladministration (but not a breach of the law) for the trustees not to provide reasons for their decisions, not to have disclosed in full the minutes of their meetings, and not to provide copies of the material they considered in taking their decision to those with a legitimate interest in the matter. This case illustrates the importance of trustees keeping clear records of decisions and it would appear that, when making decisions, trustees could be expected by the Pensions Ombudsman to give their reasons or be at risk of a finding of maladministration, in particular where a decision adverse to the interests of a member is taken.

Further, in *Schmidt v Rosewood Trust [2003] 2 WLR 1442, [2003] 3 All ER 76*, a case before the Privy Council, the belief that a beneficiary's right to view trust documents was based on the sort of proprietary interest put forward in *Londonderry* (ie a right to access documents that are your own) was dismissed. Instead, a beneficiary's right to see trust documents was viewed as a part of the court's inherent powers of supervision over trusts. This is a difficult concept for a trustee to consider in practice, as it would seem to be at the court's discretion which documents ought to be disclosed to a beneficiary where there is no statutory duty to disclose information. Especially where there are issues of personal or commercial confidentiality, the court may have to balance the competing interests of different beneficiaries, the trustees and third parties when considering what ought to be disclosed.

The Pensions Act 2004

Trustee knowledge and understanding ('TKU')

3.22 *PA 2004* created a new statutory requirement for knowledge and understanding for trustees of occupational pension schemes (whether individuals or directors of a corporate trustee). Trustees must be 'conversant' with key documents including the trust deed and rules, the statement of investment principles, the most recent statement of funding principles (where appropriate), and any other document regarding the policy of the scheme's administration.

Trustees must also have knowledge and understanding of the law relating to pensions and trusts, the principles relating to the funding of occupational pension schemes, the principles relating to the investment of assets and such other matters as are prescribed. The degree of knowledge and understanding is that appropriate for enabling the person properly to exercise their functions as trustee (including as a member of any sub-committee of the trustees, such as one dealing with investment or death benefit cases).

PA 2004, ss 247 to 249

3.23 The requirements for trustee knowledge and understanding are contained in *PA 2004, ss 247–249* and are stated to apply to 'every individual who is a trustee of an occupational pension scheme' and 'any company which is a trustee of an occupational pension scheme'. A trustee company has a duty to ensure that any individual who exercises any function which the company has, as trustee, satisfies the knowledge and understanding requirements.

PA 2004, s 247 deals with individual trustees, and *s 248* deals with corporate trustees. *Section 249* provides supplementary provisions in relation to both corporate and individual trustees.

Requirements

3.24 *Sections 247* and *248* state that trustees must be 'conversant' with the following scheme documents:

- The trust deed and rules.
- Any statement of investment principles (SIP).
- Any statement of funding principles (SFP).
- Any other document recording the policy adopted in relation to scheme administration. This would include the scheme booklet, announcements, member communications, trustee minutes and the annual report.

The Regulator has stated that 'to be "conversant with" scheme documents is taken to mean to be familiar with and able to make use of them to carry out trustee functions'. A working knowledge of the documents is expected.

In addition to being 'conversant' with the above, trustees must have 'knowledge and understanding' of the following:

- the law relating to pensions and trusts;
- the principles relating to the funding of occupational pension schemes;
- the principles relating to the investment of assets; and
- such other matters as are prescribed.

Level of knowledge and understanding

3.25 In relation to individual trustees, *s 247(5)* states that the degree of knowledge and understanding is that appropriate for the purposes of enabling the individual properly to exercise his functions as a trustee.

In relation to corporate trustees, *s 248(6)* states that the degree of knowledge and understanding is that appropriate for the purposes of enabling the individual director properly to exercise his functions in relation to the trustee company.

The Regulator

3.26 The Regulator recommends that trustees regularly (at least annually) review their own knowledge and understanding against the published Scope documents (see **3.28** below) and carry out learning or training to fill any gaps. Trustees may need to acquire new knowledge in relation to specific scheme changes or events (such as a buy-in or buy-out of liabilities).

Under *PA 2004, s 13* the Regulator has the power to issue an improvement notice where it is of the opinion that a person is contravening pensions legislation or has contravened pensions legislation in circumstances that make it likely that the contravention will be continued or repeated. Therefore, it is within the Regulator's power to issue an improvement notice where trustees have not complied with the knowledge and understanding requirements. Under *s 13*, where a trustee has failed to comply with an improvement notice, civil penalties may be applied.

Code of Practice

3.27 The Regulator has issued and revised Code of Practice No 7 on the trustee knowledge and understanding requirements.

The Code sets out the broad subject areas of knowledge and understanding that trustees must have to enable them to meet the legal requirements. These areas are set out under the following nine headings:

- The law relating to trusts.
- The law relating to pensions.
- Investment: defined benefit ('DB') and defined contribution ('DC') occupational arrangements (including AVCs).
- Funding: DB.
- Contributions: DB.
- Strategic asset allocation: DB.
- Funding: DC (including AVCs).
- Investment choices: DC (including AVCs).
- Fund management: DB and DC (including AVCs).

In addition, the Code is accompanied by Scope Guidance issued by the Regulator, available on the Regulator's website (www.pensionsregulator.gov.uk). The guidance consists of two 'scope' documents – one for trustees of DB schemes with associated DC arrangements, and the other for trustees of DC schemes with no link to DB arrangements, intended as a checklist for identifying gaps in knowledge and understanding, and planning further learning.

In both Scope documents, the areas upon which trustees are required to have knowledge are divided into 'Units'. To give an idea of the breadth of the requirements, summarised below are some of the areas covered:

Scope Guidance – defined benefit schemes (with associated defined contribution arrangements)

3.28 **Unit 1 – The law relating to trusts.** This unit includes the definition and nature of a pension trust, fiduciary duties, professional advice and decision-making, conflicts of interest, fitness and properness to act as trustees.

Unit 2 – The law relating to pensions. This unit includes key provisions of *PA 1995*, *PA 2004*, the role of the Regulator, Codes of Practice, dispute resolution, the Pensions Ombudsman, tax privileges and requirements for occupational pension schemes, and the relationship between an occupational pension scheme and the State pension scheme.

Unit 3 – Investment (DB and DC occupational arrangements, including AVCs). This unit includes the different types of assets available for investment, the major asset classes and their characteristics, valuation of assets (actuarial valuations and company balance sheets), and the implications of overseas investment.

Unit 4 – Funding (DB occupational arrangements). This unit includes how liabilities are valued, the nature and strength of the employer covenant, potential risks to the scheme, transfers and bulk transfers and the impact of trustee powers.

Unit 5 – Contributions (DB occupational arrangements). This unit includes the assumptions underlying contribution calculations, professional advice and funding deficits.

Unit 6 – Strategic asset allocation (DB occupational arrangements). This unit includes how to fund particular future benefits, reviewing asset allocation decisions and the process of strategic asset allocation.

Unit 7 – Funding (DC occupational arrangements). This unit includes how the funding for occupational DC arrangements works, the risks borne by members and the implications of contracting out.

Unit 8 – Investment choices (DC occupational arrangements). This unit includes investment strategy and member investment choices, administration procedures specific to DC arrangements.

Unit 9 – Fund management (DB and DC arrangements, including AVCs). This unit includes the statement of investment principles, measuring performance including the use of indices, the ownership of assets, the selection of fund managers and the structure of investment portfolios.

Unit 10 – Trust deed and rules. This unit includes the duties, powers and discretions of trustees, the balance of powers, benefits offered and classes of members in the scheme.

Unit 11 – Statement of investment principles. This unit includes responsibilities for investment decisions, investment objectives, socially responsible investment and corporate governance and the types of investments undertaken.

Unit 12 – Statement of funding principles. This unit includes responsibilities for preparing the SFP, contents of the SFP and review of the SFP.

Unit 13 – Other scheme documents. This unit includes the scheme booklet, announcements, actuarial valuations, annual reports and accounts, insurance policies, significant contracts, the internal dispute resolution procedure, memorandum and articles of association of a trustee company and minutes of meetings. Trustees should also know where their original documents are kept.

Formal qualifications

3.29 The Regulator has developed a free online modular course called the Trustee Toolkit, which it hopes will help trustees to meet the required standards of knowledge and understanding. It is available at www.trusteetoolkit.com. In addition, the Pensions Management Institute has developed the Awards in Pension Trusteeship providing formal recognition of TKU. There are no current plans for a mandatory qualification.

The Occupational Pension Scheme (Trustees' Knowledge and Understanding) Regulations 2006 (SI 2006/686)

3.30 These Regulations disapply the knowledge and understanding requirements for individual trustees and directors of corporate trustees for six months from the date on which they are appointed. However, this six-month period of grace does not apply to independent trustees, or to trustees or directors who hold themselves out as having expertise in the law relating to pensions and trusts and the principles of funding and investment.

The Regulator states in its Code of Practice that, although the legislative requirements do not apply immediately to newly appointed trustees, these new trustees remain responsible in law for any trustee decisions that are taken during this period.

Trustees' meetings

3.31 Specific provisions relating to the conduct of trustees' meetings are sometimes specified in the trust documents (or, in the case of a corporate trustee, its articles of association) and will typically cover such matters as how and when notice of meetings is to be given, the number of trustees that will constitute a quorum (so that decisions can validly be made), how/if a chairman of the trustees is to be appointed and, if so, whether he has a casting vote. If not set out in the trust documents (or articles), there should be some written record of these details, for example in a minute or resolution passed at a trustees' meeting.

It is important to comply with these requirements. If, for example, notice has not been given to all of the trustees of a forthcoming meeting, then the validity of the decisions made at that meeting may subsequently be open to challenge.

Under *PA 1995, s 32*, unless the scheme provides otherwise, decisions of trustees may be made on the basis of a majority vote and trustees may set their own quorum for meetings at which majority decisions may be taken. However, in certain situations, specific decision-making requirements apply (see *PA 1995, s 32(4)*). For example the removal of a member-nominated trustee requires the agreement of all the other trustees (*PA 2004, s 241*). Notice of occasions where decisions may be taken by majority must be given to each trustee to whom it is reasonably practicable to give such notice, and must, unless the trustees agree otherwise, state the date, time and place of the meeting and be sent at least ten business days before the meeting to the last known address of each trustee (*Scheme Administration Regulations, reg 10*). However, notice of such a meeting does not have to be given in the manner described above where it is necessary, as a matter of urgency, for the trustees to make a decision (*Scheme Administration Regulations, reg 9*).

Member-nominated trustees

The Pensions Act 1995: the old regime

3.32 Under *PA 1995* and the *Occupational Pension Schemes (Member-nominated Trustees and Directors) Regulations 1996 (SI 1996/1216)* (the '*MNT Regulations 1996*' – revoked from 6 April 2006) the trustees of occupational pension schemes were under a duty to secure arrangements for the selection of member-nominated trustees ('MNTs') and the implementation of the arrangements (*PA 1995, s 16(1)*) unless the employer 'opted out' of the MNT requirements or the scheme in question was exempt.

There was a parallel duty upon the directors of a corporate trustee to appoint member-nominated directors ('MNDs'), unless an employer opt-out was in place.

The Pensions Act 2004

3.33 The Government set out its long-term intention to simplify the member-nominated trustee regime in its Green Paper published in December 2003 (Cm 5677 'Simplicity, Security and Choice: Working and Saving for Retirement'), much of which was subsequently carried through into *PA 2004*. The Government wanted schemes to have greater flexibility to manage themselves in a more efficient and effective way that reflects and supports the business of the sponsoring employer. It reduced the level of prescription on nomination and selection processes for MNTs and MNDs so that the legislation focuses upon the outcome to be achieved – at least one-third of trustees should be member-nominated – and not on the detailed processes that schemes must follow to achieve that outcome.

Main change under PA 2004: the new regime

3.34 The principal change under *PA 2004* is the removal of the employer opt-out, thereby making it mandatory for all affected schemes to have one-third of the trustee body as MNTs/MNDs. Enabling legislation allows for the proportion of MNTs/MNDs to be increased from one-third to one-half, but regulations have not yet made this change.

Who has to comply with the new MNT/MND provisions?

3.35 *PA 2004, s 241(1)* provides that the trustees of an occupational trust scheme (other than those schemes exempted by regulations) must secure that the MNT requirements are complied with. For MNDs, *PA 2004, s 242(1)* provides that it is the trustee company which is responsible for securing compliance.

PA 2004, s 241(8) provides the following exceptions in relation to MNTs:

- where every member of the scheme is a trustee of the scheme and no other person is a trustee;
- where every trustee of the scheme is a company; or
- where the scheme is of a 'prescribed description'.

The prescribed scheme exemptions in the *MNT Regulations* include:

- a scheme with fewer than two members;
- a scheme to which *PA 1995, s 22* applies (conditions for a statutory independent trustee);
- a scheme which is not registered;
- a relevant small occupational pension scheme (fewer than 12 members and decisions must usually be unanimous);
- a relevant centralised scheme (non-associated employers);
- a stakeholder scheme; and
- a small insured scheme (fewer than 12 members).

One important new exemption is for schemes where the sole trustee or all the trustees are independent of the employer (but not necessarily a statutory independent trustee). It has been suggested that for some schemes this will effectively still allow the employer to opt out of the MNT requirements by appointing a sole professional trustee.

Time limit for compliance

3.36 *PA 2004, s 241(1)* states that the new provisions must be implemented 'within a reasonable period of commencement date' which was 6 April 2006 or any later date on which a scheme becomes subject to the MNT requirements. The Regulator issued a Code of Practice No 8 which proposed six months as the maximum 'reasonable period', but what is reasonable will depend on the circumstances of each scheme.

The *MNT Regulations 2006* provide that, where an existing opt-out was in force on 6 April 2006, the arrangements were permitted to continue until its approval expired in accordance with the previous law, subject to an overall cut-off date of 31 October 2007. MNTs appointed under previous arrangements could remain until their term of office expired but, if appointed under an opt-out, would not count towards the new one-third MNT requirement.

What are the requirements?

Number of member-nominated trustees

3.37 Under *ss 241(1)* (MNTs) and *242(1)* (MNDs), trustees must secure that arrangements are in place and implemented which provide for at least one-third of the total number of trustees to be member nominated. Note that the scheme rules may require a higher proportion of trustees to be member nominated, in which case that higher proportion will apply.

Nomination and selection

Who nominates and selects?

3.38 Under *ss 241(2)* (MNTs) and *242(2)* (MNDs), the nomination process has to include all the active members of the scheme (or an organisation which adequately represents them) and all the pensioners of the scheme (or an organisation which adequately represents them). The representative organisations might be trades unions, staff committees, pensioner groups or any other organisation considered by the trustees adequately to represent the relevant members. Deferred and pension credit members can, but do not have to, be included in the process. Where a scheme has no active or pensioner members, the nomination process must include such deferred members as the trustees determine are eligible to participate.

MNTs are to be selected as a result of a 'process which involves some or all of the members of the scheme'. This could be a selection panel or ballot.

Neither *PA 2004* nor the Code of Practice specifies any particular process which must be adopted for nomination or selection. However, the Regulator does expect the process to be 'proportionate, fair and transparent'.

Sections 241(5)(c) and *242(5)(c)* provide that a person who is not a member of the scheme must have the employer's approval to qualify for selection as a MNT or MND.

The appointment process

3.39 Generally, scheme rules provide for the appointment of a new trustee to be by deed. The appointment of a new trustee director will simply require the appropriate formalities under the corporate trustee's articles of association (and completion of the relevant Companies House form). However, under *PA 2004, s 306(2),* where any arrangements made under *s 241* and *242* conflict with the provisions of the scheme, the statutory arrangements override. So, if a member is selected in accordance with the MNT/MND arrangements, it would appear that they are automatically appointed as a trustee. It would be preferable, though, to still have a confirmatory deed or trustee company resolution.

Other provisions

Vacancies

3.40 *Sections 241(5)(b)* and *242(5)(b)* require that the MNT/MND arrangements must provide that, where a vacancy is not filled because insufficient nominations are received, the nomination and selection process is to be repeated at reasonable intervals until the vacancy is filled. The Code of Practice suggests this period should be no longer than three years.

Removal of MNTs/MNDs

3.41 *Sections 241(6)* and *242(6)* state that the MNT/MND arrangements must provide that the removal of the member-nominated trustee requires the agreement of all the other trustees or directors.

Larger number of MNTs/MNDs

3.42 *Sections 241(4)* and *242(4)* state that the MNT/MND arrangements may provide for a greater number of MNTs/MNDs than is required to satisfy the one-third minimum, but only if the employer approves the greater number or where the scheme rules require a higher number (*MNT Regulations 2006, reg 5(2)*).

Functions of MNTs

3.43 *Sections 241(7)* and *242(7)* provide that the arrangements must not exclude MNTs/MNDs from the exercise of any of the functions exercisable by the other trustees by reason only of the fact that they are member nominated. The principle is that all trustees are equal and have the same duties (unless otherwise ordered by the Regulator).

Penalties for failure to comply

3.44 *Sections 241(9)* and *242(11)* provide for the imposition of civil penalties where the MNT/MND requirements have not been complied with.

Scope for change

3.45 *Section 243* provides that the Secretary of State may, by order, amend *ss 241* and *242* to provide for a minimum of one-half MNTs/MNDs.

Internal dispute resolution ('IDR')

Introduction

3.46 *PA 1995, s 50* (subsequently amended by *PA 2004, s 273,* itself amended by *PA 2007*) established the requirement for trustees of occupational pension schemes to secure that arrangements are made and implemented for the resolution of disagreements about matters in relation to the scheme between 'any person with an interest in the scheme' (defined in *s 50A*) or their estate or representative.

Schemes of which all the members are trustees, or which have only one member, or of which there is a sole corporate trustee and every member is a director of that company, are exempt from the requirements (*s 50(8)*).

The aim is to provide a flexible, low-cost way to resolve disputes about an occupational pension scheme. Note that not every member or beneficiary query necessarily needs to be treated as an IDR dispute.

The IDR procedure can be either two-stage (involving a specified decision-maker and then the trustees) or single-stage (involving the trustees alone).

The time limits involved are flexible, but the decision must be both taken and notified to the applicant within a reasonable period. See the guidance in the Regulator's Code of Practice No 11 'Dispute Resolution – reasonable periods'.

The process is also flexible, but when an application under IDR is received the trustees must 'as soon as reasonably practicable' provide the applicant with details of The Pensions Advisory Service; and, when a decision is made, the trustees must notify the applicant that the Pensions Ombudsman can investigate and determine any complaint or dispute of fact or law in relation to a scheme.

Details of the IDR procedure, including the address and job title of who to contact, must be set out in writing and given as part of the 'basic information about the scheme' under the *Disclosure Regulations*.

Ideally, the IDR procedure should be in addition to other efforts to resolve the matter and should be operated to provide an opportunity to resolve misunderstandings before they escalate to the Pensions Ombudsman. Bearing this in mind, it is useful to provide a simple form to assist individuals who have a complaint. Failing to help individuals with a grievance may, in some situations, amount to 'maladministration' and lead to criticism of the trustees. An IDR complaint can be compromised by the parties, possibly with a payment by the trustees in full and final settlement of the dispute.

The Government's Green Paper, 'Simplicity, Security and Choice: Working and Saving for Retirement' published in December 2002 included proposals to improve the procedures for dealing with internal disputes, in particular by giving scheme trustees more flexibility to adopt a procedure which best suits the scheme and its members and setting a shorter timescale for the process to be completed (paragraph 61). These proposals then formed the basis for changes to the IDR legislation made under *PA 2004*.

Who can make a complaint?

3.47 Under *PA 1995, s 50* (as amended by *PA 2004, s 273*) the IDR procedure must cover disagreements between the trustees and any 'person with an interest in the scheme' as set out in *PA 2005, s 50A*. These are:

(*a*) members (ie active members, deferred pensioners, pensioners and pension credit members);

(*b*) the widow, widower, surviving civil partner or dependant of a deceased member;

(*c*) someone other than in (*b*) who is entitled to benefits on the death of a member;

(*d*) prospective members of the scheme. A 'prospective member' means any person who, under the terms of his contract or the scheme rules, is:

   (i) able at his own option to become a member;

   (ii) will be able at his own option to become a member providing he remains in the same employment for long enough;

   (iii) will automatically become a member unless he elects otherwise; or

   (iv) may become a member if his employer consents;

(*e*) someone who has ceased to be in one of the above categories;

(*f*) someone claiming to be within one of the above categories.

Any claim by someone in category (*e*), or someone in category (*f*) claiming to be in category (*e*) must be made within a period of six months beginning immediately after the date on which he ceased to be, or claims he ceased to be, a person with an interest in the scheme (*PA 1995, s 50B(3)* and the Regulator's Code of Practice No 11). The trustees may include a reasonable time limit of their choosing for claimants in any of the other categories (*PA 1995, s 50B(3)(b)*).

A claimant can nominate a representative to make or continue the complaint on his behalf. If the claimant is incapable of acting for himself or is a minor, a family member or other suitable person can bring or continue a claim. In the case of a deceased member, his personal representatives can bring or continue a claim (*PA 1995, s 50B*).

IDR procedures

3.48 Originally, there was a requirement for a two-stage IDR procedure: the first stage providing for a nominated decision-maker to reach a decision about the complaint, and a second stage under which the trustees, on the application of a complaint, would reconsider the stage one decision and decide whether to confirm or replace it.

PA 2004, s 273, as amended by *PA 2007*, replaced the existing *PA 1995, s 50* on 6 April 2008 and greatly simplified the statutory IDR requirements. There is no longer a requirement for a two-stage IDR procedure (although trustees can retain one if they wish, provided that it is consistent with the legislation), and a single-stage approach can be adopted.

Relevant time limits as to the periods within which decisions must be made and notified are set out in the Regulator's Code of Practice No 11. The Regulator expects that a decision on a dispute will be made within four months of receiving the application, and complainants should be notified within 15 working days of a decision being made. The same time periods apply to each stage if a two-stage IDR procedure is in place. If it is likely that any specified deadlines are not going to be met, it would be good practice to let the complainant know.

Whether the IDR procedure is one-stage or two-stage, the (initial) decision-maker must inform the complainant as soon as reasonably practicable on receipt of an IDR complaint of the availability of the Pensions Advisory Service ('TPAS') to assist with any difficulty with the scheme, and its contact details. The notification of a final decision must include a statement that the Pensions Ombudsman may investigate and determine any complaint or dispute of fact or law in relation to a scheme, and provide his contact details.

Exempted disagreements

3.49 Under *PA 1995, s 50(9)* the IDR procedure cannot be used where proceedings have begun in a court or tribunal, or where the *Ombudsman Regulations* provide that the Pensions Ombudsman will generally refuse to investigate a complaint unless the complainant has first made full use of the IDR procedure and has received a final decision, unless he is satisfied that:

(*a*) there is no real prospect of notice of a decision under the IDR procedure being issued within a reasonable period from the date on which he received a complaint; and

(*b*) it is reasonable, in the circumstances, that he should investigate and determine the complaint.

Protection from liability

General

3.50 Trustees who act outside of their powers, or who act in a way which is in breach of their trust law duties to scheme beneficiaries, may find themselves personally liable to the beneficiaries for breach of trust. Alternatively, where they are in breach of a statutory duty, they will usually be liable as stated in the relevant Act (see APPENDIX I for examples). In practice, directors of a trustee company may have more protection than they would if they were individual trustees through the 'corporate veil', although the position is not straightforward. The extent to which directors of a trustee company can be held directly liable to scheme beneficiaries (ie where the corporate veil is pierced) was considered in the case of *HR v JAPT [1997] PLR 99* where the court found that directors of a trustee company do not normally owe a direct fiduciary duty to beneficiaries of a trust. The exception to this principle is where a director is found guilty of 'accessory liability'. In order to be found liable as an 'accessory' to a breach of trust, the director must have acted dishonestly in the sense described in the case of *Royal Brunei Airlines v Tan [1995] 2 AC 378* and referred to in the case of *JAPT* as follows:

> 'It is (*Royal Brunei*) dishonest for a person, unless there is a very good and compelling reason, to participate in a transaction if he knows it involves a misapplication of trust assets to the detriment of the beneficiaries or if he deliberately closes his eyes and ears or chooses deliberately not to ask questions so as to avoid his learning something he would rather not know and for him then to proceed regardless.' (paragraph 61)

JAPT was followed more recently in the High Court case of *Gregson v HAE Trustees and Others [2008] EWHC 1006 (Ch)* which confirmed that trustee directors do not owe a duty directly to the scheme's beneficiaries.

There are, however, some protections from liability available to trustees. These are considered below.

Exoneration clause in the trust deed

3.51 Most pension schemes' trust deeds will contain a provision under which the trustees (or directors of a trustee company) will not be liable except in limited circumstances. This is known as an exoneration (or exclusion) clause. These circumstances will typically be conduct which involves some degree of bad faith or negligence on the part of the person sought to be made liable. 'Wilful neglect or default' is a phrase commonly used in exoneration clauses; 'deliberate and knowing breach of trust' is another. Clauses of this nature have been upheld by the courts in relation to trustees' liabilities to beneficiaries (for example, Walton J in *Re Imperial Foods Ltd Pension Scheme [1986] 2 All ER 802* and in *Armitage v Nurse [1998] Ch 24*), although such wording in a trust deed would not be sufficient to exclude liabilities to third parties (ie liabilities to persons with whom the trustees deal who are not beneficiaries or parties to the trust deed; such liability will most usually arise under the terms of a contract with that third party, rather than under the terms of the trust deed), or penalties imposed by statute, most particularly, those imposed under *PA 1995* (see APPENDIX I) which cannot be met from the assets of the scheme.

UCTA 1977, s 2(2) restricts the validity of certain clauses which seek to exclude liability for negligence. However, this restriction applies only to business liability, and so (in the context of actions brought by beneficiaries) is likely only to apply to professional trustees who charge for acting as such; it is for this reason that some exoneration clauses in trust deeds specify that liability for the negligence of a professional trustee is not excluded.

PA 1995, s 33(1) prohibits the exclusion or restriction of any liability for breach of an obligation under any rule of law to take care or exercise skill in the performance of any investment functions (where that function is exercisable by a trustee of the scheme or by a person to whom that function has been delegated under *PA 1995, s 34*). However, where the trustees have delegated discretion to make investment decisions to a fund manager under *s 34*, *s 34(4)* relieves them of responsibility for any act or default of that fund manager in the exercise of any discretion delegated to him, so long as they (or anybody else making the delegation on their behalf) have taken all reasonable steps to satisfy themselves as to the fund manager's appropriate knowledge and experience for managing the investments of the scheme and that he is carrying out his work competently and complying with the requirements of *PA 1995, s 36* (see CHAPTER 10).

It should be noted that, in January 2003, the Law Commission issued a consultation paper (CP171) on exemption clauses, entitled 'Trustee Exemption Clauses'. The Law Commission's view was that increased regulation of trustee exemption clauses was necessary because their increased use in recent years had reduced the protection afforded to beneficiaries in the event of breach of trust. The Law Commission proposed to draw a distinction between the professional and the lay trustee; the consultation paper suggested that professional trustees should no longer be able to rely on clauses which excluded their liability for breach of trust arising from negligence nor would professional trustees be able to be indemnified from the trust fund in respect of breaches of trust arising from negligence. Professional (and lay) trustees would however have the right to use trust assets to buy indemnity cover. Lay trustees would still be able to benefit from exemption/indemnity clauses.

The Law Commission received a total of 118 written consultation responses and concluded that there were a number of obstacles to statutory intervention of the sort provisionally proposed in the Consultation Paper and that there was a significant risk that any such legislation could lead to adverse consequences more damaging than they had anticipated. They suggested that a practice-based approach, rather than legislation, is the better means to bring about reform. Its recommendations were published in a July 2006 report which proposed the adoption of a non-statutory rule of practice that 'any paid trustee who causes a settlor to include a clause in a trust instrument which has the effect of excluding or limiting liability for negligence must before the creation of the trust take such steps as are reasonable to ensure that the settlor is aware of the meaning and effect of the clause'. But importantly, the Report recognised that the rule should be of no application to pension trusts.

Indemnity clause in the trust deed

3.52 A scheme's trust deed will often provide for the trustees to be indemnified against liability. The clause may entitle them to be indemnified by the sponsoring employer or from the trust fund in the event of default on the indemnity by the employer. In any case, any kind of liability which is not covered by the trust deed's exoneration clause will typically also not be covered by the indemnity clause. *PA 2004, s 256* prevents trustees from being indemnified out of the fund in respect of fines or certain civil penalties (see APPENDIX I).

Care needs to be taken with corporate trustees as some statutory restrictions apply on indemnities given from one company to directors of another in the group (assuming here that the shareholder of the corporate trustee is a company in the employer or the employer's group).

Employer indemnity – position before 1 October 2007

3.53 Previously, under *Companies Act 1985, s 310*, any indemnity given by a company to its directors was void to the extent that it was in connection with any breach *in relation to the company*. This meant that individual trustees and directors of a corporate trustee (assuming the corporate trustee to be associated with the employer) who were also directors of the employer could not benefit from any indemnity in respect of liabilities in relation to the company. However, it was strongly arguable that this would not prevent such individuals from being indemnified against liability *in relation to the pension scheme*. These provisions did not impact on individual trustees or trustee directors who were not also directors of the employer and they could benefit from a full employer indemnity.

Then came *Companies Act 1985, ss 309A–309C* (introduced with effect from 6 April 2005 and repealed on 1 October 2007). These provided that any attempt by a company to indemnify a director of the company *or an associated company* in respect of any liability in relation to the company of which he was director was void, unless it was a 'qualifying third party indemnity provision', under which indemnity for liability incurred by the director to a person other than the company or associated company was given.

Qualifying third party indemnity provisions (QTPIP) must not allow indemnity against:

- liability by the director to the company or associated company;
- liabilities for criminal or regulatory fines or penalties; and/or
- the cost of defending criminal or civil proceedings.

Individual trustees who were also directors of the employer could not be indemnified in respect of liabilities in relation to the company, unless the indemnity was a QTPIP. Similarly, trustee directors who were also directors of the employer could not benefit from an indemnity in relation to the trustee company or the employer unless it was a QTPIP. Crucially, this meant that (even where a QTPIP was in place) they could not be indemnified in respect of liabilities to the trustee company (previously they could). This opened up the possibility of claims in relation to pension scheme liabilities (as, potentially, the trustee company could be found liable for losses to the scheme and then itself seek to recover that from individual directors).

Transitional provisions provided that *s 309A* had no effect on indemnities which were in place before 29 October 2004 and were valid under the old *s 310*. So, directors with indemnities in place before that date could keep them. However, for certainty, incoming directors wishing to take advantage of an existing indemnity (eg one in a trust deed executed before 29 October 2004) could have been given a QTPIP which was only operative if they were found to be unable to rely on the existing indemnity.

Employer indemnity – position from 1 October 2007

3.54 The provisions of the 1985 Act are repealed and restated in the *Companies Act 2006*. In addition to restating the requirements in relation to QTPIPs, the *Companies Act 2006* also introduced new provisions (*s 235*) in relation to 'qualifying pension scheme indemnity provisions' (QPSIPs). The new provisions apply to any indemnity given on or after 1 October 2007 (to both new and existing directors).

A QPSIP allows a director of a corporate trustee of an occupational pension scheme to be indemnified by an associated company against liability incurred in connection with the company's activities as a trustee of the scheme. A QPSIP must not provide any indemnity against:

- liabilities for criminal or regulatory fines or penalties; or
- the cost of defending criminal proceedings in which he is convicted.

The QPSIP permits a much wider indemnity than the QTPIP provisions as it allows for an indemnity against liabilities to the trustee company itself. This represents a relaxation of the position imposed by *Companies Act 1985, s 309A*.

The new QPSIP provisions do not apply to indemnities given to individual trustees.

QTPIPs continue to be allowed under *Companies Act 2006, s 234*.

Employer indemnity – transitional provisions

3.55 *Companies Act 2006 (Commencement No 3, Consequential Amendments, Transitional Provisions and Savings) Order 2007 (SI 2007/2194)*,

Sch 3, para 15 provides transitional protection for existing indemnities. It provides that the new sections apply to 'any provision made on or after 1 October 2007'. It also provides that *Companies Act 1985, ss 309A* and *309B* will continue to apply 'in relation to any provision to which they applied immediately before that date'.

This means that existing indemnities and QTPIPs made under *s 309A* before 1 October 2007 remain valid (although consideration should be given to replacing them with a QPSIP where appropriate). The transitional provisions also appear to save pre-October 2004 indemnities which were previously expressly protected and exempt from *s 309A,* as the new statutory provisions only apply to indemnities made after 1 October 2007 (although the safest approach would be to put in place a QPSIP which is operative only if the previous indemnity is found not to be saved by the transitional provisions). It is not entirely clear whether newly appointed directors can take advantage of existing indemnities under the transitional provisions (in particular, new directors may wish to seek the protection of a pre-October 2004 indemnity). The safest course again might be to put in place a new indemnity (with a QPSIP if appropriate) which is operative only if the director is found not to be able to rely on the existing indemnity.

Court's discretion

3.56 Under *TA 1925, s 61*:

> 'If it appears to the court that a trustee … is or may be personally liable for breach of trust...but has acted honestly and reasonably, and ought fairly to be excused for the breach of trust … the court may relieve him either wholly or partly from personal liability for the same.'

This is only a discretion of the court, and trustees should be reluctant to place too much reliance on it. In most situations the trustees are likely to rely on any exoneration and/or indemnity in the trust deed and rules, and only where none exists would the trustees seek an order under the provisions of this section.

Insurance

3.57 Trustees may wish to take out insurance against liability, but should be mindful as to how far the terms of the policy restrict the circumstances in which they could make a claim. If it is intended that the premiums be paid from the trust fund, advice should be sought as to whether the circumstances and the terms of the scheme will permit this (for example, see *Kemble v Hicks [1999] PLR 287* on whether trustees can use scheme funds to pay for winding-up insurance). In any event, *PA 2004, s 256* (formerly *PA 1995, s 31(2)*) prohibits the payment of premiums from a scheme's assets to insure against the imposition of fines or civil penalties (see APPENDIX I). More commonly, insurance tends to be used to protect the trustees against claims by 'missing beneficiaries' on the winding up of a scheme, rather than liabilities generally in relation to their actions (for example, see *NBPF Pension Trustees Ltd [2008] EWHC 455 (Ch)*).

Data Protection Act 1998

3.58 Pension fund trustees must comply with the *Data Protection Act 1998* (*DPA 1998*) which, despite its title, came into force on 1 March 2000. In most cases, trustees will be 'data controllers' since they determine the purpose for which and the manner in which personal data is held and processed. The emphasis of *DPA 1998* is on compliance with the data protection principles and the rights of individuals (the data subjects) in respect of whom personal data is held.

Personal data is, broadly, data from which a living person can be identified, and which relates to that person in a way that might affect their privacy. Sensitive personal data includes information relating to health and can only be processed with the data subject's consent.

The eight data protection principles have been modified from previous legislation. In summary, the data protection principles require that information relating to individuals must be:

(i) processed fairly and lawfully – in certain circumstances it will be necessary to obtain the consent of the data subject and provide certain information to him;

(ii) obtained and processed only for specified and lawful purposes;

(iii) adequate, relevant and not excessive;

(iv) accurate and, where necessary, kept up to date;

(v) kept for no longer than necessary;

(vi) processed in accordance with the rights of data subjects;

(vii) kept secure, by ensuring appropriate technical and organisational measures are in place; and

(viii) not transferred outside the European Economic Area unless adequate data protection safeguards are in place.

The law enhances the rights of data subjects by giving them:

(*a*) rights of access to information;

(*b*) express rights to prevent direct marketing;

(*c*) rights to rectify and erase inaccurate data;

(*d*) rights relating to decisions taken by computer;

(*e*) certain rights to prevent processing of data; and

(*f*) rights to compensation.

Paper records

3.59 Paper records as well as computerised data are covered by *DPA 1998*. Paper records will be covered if they are part of a 'relevant filing system' where specific information relating to a particular individual can be readily accessed. Manual files organised by reference to individual policy holders will, therefore, be caught.

Registration of pension fund trustees

3.60 Information about registration can be sought from the Information Commissioner's Office (www.ico.gov.uk). Every data controller must register, unless exempt (for example where the processing is only of manually held personal data). Failure to register when required to do so is a criminal offence.

Data processors

3.61 Under *DPA 1998*, data processors (ie third parties who process personal data on behalf of a data controller) do not need to register in that capacity. This means that pension fund administrators (who often act as agents on behalf of pension fund trustees in terms of processing data), advisers and annuity providers will not need to register in that capacity.

A data controller will, however, need to ensure that its data processors comply with data protection legislation. For example, a data controller will need to have a contract in writing with its data processors under which they agree only to act on the instructions of the data controller and to put in place sufficient technical and organisational measures to keep data secure. This is to comply with the seventh data protection principle referred to above. Processing is defined extremely widely and includes merely holding data on behalf of another and so would encompass data held by the likes of administrators and actuaries.

Practical steps to ensure compliance

3.62 Pension fund trustees can take a number of practical steps to show that they are complying with the legislation and data protection principles:

(*a*) appoint one person to take overall responsibility for data protection;

(*b*) periodically carry out an audit of personal data activity;

(*c*) regularly update the forms used to collect personal and sensitive personal data;

(*d*) ensure that suitable agreements are in place with all data processors;

(*e*) address security issues both technical and organisational;

(*f*) have procedures in place to deal with data subjects' requests; and

(*g*) review how necessary it is to collect data, especially 'sensitive' data as defined under *DPA 1998*.

Of particular impact on pension fund trustees will be:

(i) data protection notices which need to be given to scheme members;

(ii) the requirement to obtain express member consent for the processing of sensitive personal data;

(iii) the security obligations, particularly with regard to data held by third parties; and

(iv) restrictions on transferring data outside Europe.

Trustees' duties to the employer

3.63 Whilst it is true that trustees must act in the best interests (and that usually means best financial interests) of their members and other beneficiaries, case law requires trustees in certain circumstances to take into consideration the interests of the sponsoring employer. This follows on from the trustees' fundamental duty to give effect to the trust deed and rules, which in turn is a reflection of the employer's promise (contractual or otherwise) to its employees to provide pension benefits. The trust deed and rules will confer a variety of powers, duties and discretions on the trustees to enable them to give effect to the promise of the employer to the employees. How the trustees exercise their powers, duties and discretions can have a significant impact on the ultimate costs borne by the employer.

An employer's interests in the occupational pension scheme which it sponsors are varied. One particular example of a trustee power which can significantly affect the interests of the employer is the trustee's power of investment. In a balance of cost scheme (such as a final salary or career average scheme), any failure by the trustees to obtain reasonable returns on the investment of the pension fund will result in the employer having to make greater contributions to the scheme to fund the promised benefits. In support of this are *PA 1995, s 35* and the *Investment Regulations, reg 2*, which oblige trustees to consult the employer when preparing or revising the statement of investment principles. Whilst the consultation process does not require the consent of the employer (indeed, this is prohibited by *s 35(5)*), the employer nevertheless may have rights against the trustees, should they cause loss to the employer by exercising their powers in an imprudent manner.

Another example where the employer's interests are evident is in the case of the distribution of any surplus (less common more recently), especially upon the winding up of a scheme. There is a significant body of case law on this subject, the most useful of which is the case of *Thrells Limited v Lomas [1993] 1 WLR 456*. In *Thrells* the scheme was winding up and was in surplus with an insolvent employer. The ultimate beneficiaries of any refund of surplus to the employer would be its creditors. The case set out factors that trustees should take into account in deciding how to exercise their discretion on allocation of surplus monies. The principal factors to consider are the scope of the discretion and its purpose, the source and size of the surplus, the financial position of the employer and the needs of members of the scheme. The usual duties of trustees will also apply when exercising their powers and they should, therefore, give proper consideration to all matters relevant to the exercise of the discretion.

This duty to the employer was noted by the court in *Edge v Pensions Ombudsman [1998] Ch 512* where it stated:

> '... the proposition that the trustees were not entitled, when deciding how to reduce the £29.9 million surplus, to take any account of the position of the employers is one with which I emphatically disagree. The Employers play a critical part in this Pension Scheme. They have to pay contributions sufficient to keep the Scheme solvent.'

It is clear from the above that it would be wrong for the trustees blindly to ignore the interests of the employer when exercising their powers. On those occasions where trustees enter into negotiations with the employer about benefit changes or cessation of accrual, the trustees should be mindful that any extra financial burden which is placed (or continues to be placed) on the employer could ultimately jeopardise the ability of the employer to continue sponsoring the scheme. The circumstances of each exercise of the trustees' powers should be carefully examined and the interests of the employer taken into consideration.

Reporting breaches of the law

3.64 From 6 April 2005, *PA 2004* imposed on trustees, employers, advisers and anyone involved in the administration of a scheme a duty to report to the Regulator breaches of law in relation to the administration of the scheme which are likely to be of material significance to the Regulator (*PA 2004, s 70*). The Regulator issued Code of Practice No 1 'Reporting breaches of the law' setting out the requirements.

Who has a duty to report?

3.65 A legal duty to report falls on:

- Trustees of trust-based pension schemes. The duty to report applies to each individually appointed trustee. If the trustee is a corporate body, the requirement to report falls on the trustee company.
- Managers of schemes not established under trust, ie managers of personal pension schemes, including stakeholder schemes.
- Persons otherwise involved in the administration of a scheme. This category includes insurance companies and third party (as well as in-house) administrators.
- Any employer participating in an occupational pension scheme.
- Professional advisers – scheme actuaries, scheme auditors, legal advisers, fund managers and custodians of scheme assets; where the appointment is of a firm rather than an individual, the firm must put in place suitable systems to ensure that it meets this duty.
- Persons otherwise involved in advising a trustee (or manager of a scheme not established under trust) in relation to the scheme. This could include IFAs, pensions consultants, investment consultants and auditors.

Whistleblowing protection and confidentiality

3.66 *PA 2004* makes clear that the duty to report overrides any other duties a reporter may have such as confidentiality and that any such duty is not breached by making a report. The Regulator expects reporters to act conscientiously and honestly and to take account of expert or professional advice where appropriate.

The duty to report does not, however, override legal privilege. The Regulator will, if asked, try to keep the identity of the reporter confidential.

When does the duty to report arise?

3.67 The requirement to report breaches of the law arises when a duty which is:

- imposed by or by virtue of an enactment (ie an Act of Parliament) or rule of law (ie decisions of the courts and general trust law); and
- relevant to the administration of a scheme (ie anything which could potentially affect members' benefits or their ability to access information to which they are entitled);

has not been or is not being complied with. Not every breach should be reported. In particular, the Regulator does not normally regard a breach as materially significant where prompt action is taken to remedy the breach and its cause, and to notify any affected members.

The decision to report

3.68 The decision to report requires two key judgements:

(i) Does the reporter have reasonable cause to believe there has been a breach of the law relevant to the administration of the scheme?

(ii) If so, does the reporter believe the breach likely to be of material significance to the Regulator?

Reasonable cause to believe

3.69 A reasonable cause to believe means more than a suspicion that cannot be substantiated. The reporter is expected to make further inquiries if all the facts are not known. If, after further investigation, the reporter has reasonable cause to believe that a breach has occurred it is not necessary for them to gather all the evidence which the Regulator would require before taking legal action.

Likely to be of material significance

3.70 The legal requirement is that breaches likely to be of material significance to the Regulator in carrying out any of its functions must be reported. What is of material significance will depend on:

- the cause of the breach;
- the effect of the breach;
- the reaction to the breach; and
- the wider implications of the breach.

The cause of the breach

3.71 Where a contributory cause of the breach is:

- dishonesty;
- poor governance or inadequate controls resulting in deficient administration or slow or inappropriate decision-making practices;
- incomplete or inaccurate advice; or
- acting (or failing to act) in deliberate contravention of the law,

then the breach is likely to be of material significance to the Regulator. However, the Regulator will not consider as materially significant a breach arising from an isolated incident.

The effect of the breach

3.72 The Regulator considers the following to be particularly important elements which, if breached, are likely to be of material significance to the Regulator in the context of its statutory objective to protect members' benefits:

- substantially the right money is paid into the scheme at the right time;
- assets are appropriately safeguarded;
- payments out of the scheme are legitimate and timely;
- defined benefit schemes are complying with the legal requirements on scheme funding;
- trustees of occupational pension schemes are properly considering their investment policy and investing in accordance with it; and
- contributions in respect of money purchase members are correctly allocated and invested.

The Regulator also has a statutory duty to reduce the risk of compensation being payable from the PPF, and so is concerned that notifiable events (see **3.75** below) are reported to it and that PPF requirements are complied with during an assessment period.

Finally, the Regulator has a statutory duty to promote good administration of pension schemes, and so is concerned to hear that schemes are administered properly, appropriate records are maintained and members receive accurate, clear and impartial information without delay.

Making a report

3.73 All reporters should have effective arrangements in place to identify and report breaches that occur in areas relating to their functions. Reports must be submitted as soon as reasonably practicable (depending on the circumstances). There is a standard format available on the Pensions Regulator's website at www.thepensionsregulator.gov.uk. Each report should be dated and include as a minimum: the name of the scheme; description of the breach; any relevant dates; name of the employer; name, position and contact details of the reporter; and the role of the reporter. Joint reports are possible. Additional information is available on the website and in the Code of Practice.

Failure to comply with the obligation to report a breach, without a reasonable excuse, is a civil offence.

The Regulator's response

3.74 The Regulator has a wide range of measures it can use in reacting to a report of a breach, including:

- assisting or instructing trustees and others to achieve compliance;
- providing education or guidance;
- appointing trustees to help run the scheme;
- removing trustees from office;
- freezing the scheme;
- imposing special measures where the scheme funding requirements of *PA 2004* are not complied with;
- ordering that the scheme's funding position be restored to the level before a breach or other detrimental event occurred; and
- imposing fines where appropriate.

Trustees must be aware of these reporting requirements and should put in place a formal policy for identifying, investigating and reporting breaches. Any policy should include arrangements for liaising with other 'reporters' and ensuring that systems are in place to identify and, where appropriate, investigate suspected breaches at an early stage so that timely reports may be made where judged to be of material significance to the Regulator.

Reporting notifiable events

3.75 *PA 2004* introduced, with effect from 6 April 2005, a new duty on the employer and the trustees to notify the Regulator of certain events (*PA 2004, s 69*). The notifiable events are laid out in the *Pensions Regulator (Notifiable Events) Regulations 2005 (SI 2005/900)* (the '*Notifiable Events Regulations*'), as amended. The purpose of these new provisions is to give the Regulator an early warning of problems which might give rise to a claim on the PPF. In addition, the Regulator issued Code of Practice No 2 – Notifiable Events, in June 2005, and Directions which provide exceptions to the duty to notify (broadly, fewer events need be notified if the scheme is funded above a certain level (see below)). The notifiable events regime does not apply to money purchase schemes as they are not eligible for PPF protection. Further notifiable events have also been introduced as part of the employer debt regime (see CHAPTER 14).

Notifiable events duty

3.76 There are two main types of notifiable events:

- scheme-related events (*s 69(2)(a)*) notifiable by trustees (individually and collectively); and
- employer-related events (*s 69(2)(b)*) notifiable by employers.

Timing of notification

3.77 An event must be notified in writing to the Regulator as soon as reasonably practicable after the person becomes aware of the notifiable event. The events themselves are deliberately worded to make clear when they should be notified. This will depend on the circumstances. For example, where a trustee is made aware of a notifiable event on a Sunday, the Regulator expects to be notified on the Monday. It is not necessary to seek professional or expert advice on whether an event has occurred, but ideally a system should be put in place by trustees and employers to identify and report notifiable events.

Trustees should seek to enter into a dialogue with the employer with a view to agreeing a process for exchanging relevant information about potential notifiable events (on a confidential basis, if required by the employer).

How to notify

3.78 All notifications must be in writing and, where practicable, use the standard form available on the Regulator's website at www.thepensionsregulator.gov.uk. Reports may be sent by post, e-mail or fax. The minimum information that should be included in a notification is the:

- description of the notifiable event;
- date of the event;

- name of the pension scheme;
- name of the employer; and
- name, position and contact details of the notifier.

Further additional information that the Regulator would find useful is also set out in the Code of Practice. The duty on trustees and employers to notify overrides any other duty of confidentiality.

Failure to notify

3.79 Trustees must take all reasonable steps to comply with the notifiable events duty and employers must comply unless they have a reasonable excuse for not doing so. In the event of a failure to notify, the Regulator will in the first instance seek an explanation. Following this it will have a range of actions it can take including requiring training or other assistance – although the Regulator does not have the power to unwind any particular transaction. Where appropriate, however, civil penalties can be imposed, and failure to notify will be taken into account by the Regulator in deciding whether or not to impose a contribution notice.

Events to be reported

3.80 The *Notifiable Events Regulations* confirm which events will need to be reported to the Regulator. The Directions (see **3.75** above) set down Conditions in which no report is required in certain circumstances.

Trustee events

3.81 Subject to the Conditions, trustees must notify the following events:

(*a*) any decision by the trustees to take action which will, or is intended to, result in any debt which is or may become due to the scheme not being paid in full *unless* the Conditions in A, B and C (set out below) are satisfied;

(*b*) a decision by the trustees to make or accept a transfer payment to or from another scheme, or the making or acceptance of such a transfer payment where a decision is not required, the value of which is more than the lower of five per cent of the value of the scheme assets and £1.5 million *unless* the Conditions in A and B are satisfied;

(*c*) a decision by the trustees to grant benefits, or a right to benefits, on more favourable terms than those provided for by the scheme rules, without either seeking advice from the scheme actuary or securing additional funding where such funding was advised by the actuary;

(*d*) a decision by the trustees to grant benefits or rights to benefits to a member, or the granting of such benefits or rights where a decision is not required, the cost of which is more than the lower of five per cent of the scheme assets and £1.5 million *unless* the Conditions in A and B are satisfied.

The requirement for trustees to notify two or more changes in the holders of any key scheme post within the previous 12 months was repealed from 6 April 2009.

Employer events

3.82 Subject to the Conditions, employers must notify the following events:

(*a*) any decision by the employer to take action which will or is intended to result in a debt which is or may become due to the scheme not being paid in full;

(*b*) a decision by the employer to cease to carry on business in the UK or, where the employer ceases to carry on business in the UK without such a decision being taken, the cessation of business by that employer;

(*c*) receipt by the employer of advice that it is trading wrongfully or circumstances being reached where a director or former director of the company knows that there is no reasonable prospect that the company will avoid going into insolvent liquidation;

(*d*) any breach of a banking covenant by the employer, other than where the bank agrees with the employer not to enforce the covenant, *unless* the Conditions in A and B are satisfied;

(*e*) a decision by a controlling company to relinquish control of the employer or, where the controlling company relinquishes such control without a decision to do so having been taken, the relinquishing of control of the employer company by the controlling company, *unless* the Conditions in A and B are satisfied;

(*f*) the conviction of an individual, in any jurisdiction, for an offence involving dishonesty if the offence was committed while the individual was a director or partner of the employer.

Changes to or ceasing to have a credit rating and two or more changes to holders of key employer posts within the previous 12 months ceased being notifiable events on 6 April 2009.

The Directions

3.83 **Condition A:** The value of the scheme's assets is equal to or greater than the value of the scheme's liabilities calculated on the 'relevant basis'. The relevant basis is the most recent PPF risk-based levy valuation ('*s 179* valuation') or, where no *s 179* valuation has been carried out, the MFR valuation.

Condition B: The trustees have not incurred a duty to make a report in the previous 12 months for:

- the employer's failure to make a payment to the scheme of material significance to the Regulator in accordance with the most recently agreed schedule of contributions under *PA 2004*; or
- the employer's failure to pay contributions due under a schedule of contributions in force under *PA 1995* on or before the due date.

Condition C: The decision by the trustees to compromise a debt where the full amount is less than 0.5 per cent of the scheme's assets calculated on the relevant basis (see Condition A).

Internal controls

Requirement for internal controls

3.84 *Article 14* of the EC *Directive on Institutions for Occupational Retirement Provision* requires that occupational pension schemes have adequate internal control mechanisms. The *Occupational Pension Schemes (Internal Controls) Regulations 2005 (SI 2005/3379)* came into force on 30 December 2005. These Regulations inserted a new *s 249A* into *PA 2004* which requires trustees or managers of occupational pension schemes to establish and operate internal controls which are adequate for the scheme to be administered and managed in accordance with the scheme rules and in accordance with pensions and other relevant legislation. Internal controls are defined as arrangements and procedures for administering and managing the scheme, systems and arrangements for monitoring that administration and management, and arrangements and procedures to be followed for the safe custody and security of the scheme's assets.

Code of Practice

3.85 The Regulator issued Code of Practice No 9 – Internal Controls, and Guidance relating to the requirement for internal controls. The Code and

Guidance set out the Regulator's expectations of how occupational pension schemes should comply with the requirement to have adequate internal controls, in particular as to the implementation of a risk management process by the trustees to identify, assess and manage risk in a proportionate manner. Specific types of risk identified by the Regulator are operational, financial, funding, regulatory and compliance risk.

Chapter 4

Contracting out

Introduction

4.1 The HMRC website (www.hmrc.gov.uk) states:

> 'Contracting-out is when employees leave the additional State Pension (currently the State Second Pension; prior to April 2002 the State Earnings Related Pension Scheme (SERPS)) and join a contracted-out occupational pension or personal/stakeholder pension instead. They receive a pension from the scheme rather than the additional State Pension. To reflect this, they receive a rebate of National Insurance contributions.'

Occupational pension schemes may be contracted-out of the additional State pension on either a salary related (defined benefit) and/or a money purchase (defined contribution) basis. Individuals in such schemes will continue to receive their basic State pension, but payments representing their additional State pension will be made from the scheme.

A person who contracted out under a contracted-out salary related (COSR) scheme would have become entitled to a Guaranteed Minimum Pension (GMP) for contracted-out employment between 6 April 1978 and 5 April 1997, and would become entitled to post-1997 COSR rights (also known as '*s 9(2B)* rights') for contracted-out employment on and from 6 April 1997.

A person who contracts out under a contracted-out money purchase (COMP) scheme would become entitled to protected rights for contracted-out employment on and from 6 April 1988. A person who contracts out under a contracted-out mixed benefit (COMB) scheme will accrue contracted-out rights on either a salary related or a money purchase basis, depending on the section of the scheme in which he participates.

In order to contract out of the additional State pension, an occupational pension scheme must hold a contracting-out certificate and satisfy, amongst other things, the requirements set out in *PSA 1993, Part III* (as amended), the *Occupational Pension Schemes (Contracting-out) Regulations 1996 (SI*

1996/1172) (as amended) ('the *Contracting-out Regulations*') and, in the case of a COMP scheme, the *Personal and Occupational Pension Schemes (Protected Rights) Regulations 1996 (SI 1996/1537)* ('the *Protected Rights Regulations*'). These are modified in relation to a COMB scheme by the *Occupational Pension Schemes (Mixed Benefit Contracted-out Schemes) Regulations 1996 (SI 1996/1977) ('the Mixed Benefits Regulations*') and are examined in more detail below.

Contracting out by way of a personal pension scheme is dealt with in CHAPTER 13.

A brief history of contracting out

Background

4.2 On 6 April 1978, the State Earnings Related Pension Scheme (SERPS) was created, which introduced a mandatory, earnings-related top up to the basic flat-rate State pension to supplement individuals' retirement pensions.

From the outset, it was possible for occupational pension schemes to contract out of SERPS, giving members the choice as to how their additional State pension provision would be made. Contracted-out schemes were required to satisfy certain statutory requirements and hold a contracting-out certificate. Members benefitted from National Insurance rebates, and the intention was that they would receive pensions from their scheme that were at least equal to what they would have received from SERPS. Meanwhile, the State received a lower immediate NIC income but would no longer be required to pay for additional State pension out of future tax or National Insurance contributions.

Initially, it was only possible for schemes to contract out of SERPS on a salary related basis and members were able to accrue rights to a GMP. From 6 April 1988, schemes could instead choose to contract out on a money purchase basis, and members were able to accrue protected rights.

The legislation changed on 6 April 1997 (under *PA 1995*) when GMPs could no longer accrue but the scheme could still contract out on a final salary basis provided that it met an overall scheme quality test. The legislation also made it possible for schemes to contract out on both a salary related and a money purchase basis. From 6 April 1997, this was possible for schemes contracted out on a final salary basis and schemes that were newly contracted out. From 6 April 1988, it became possible for schemes contracted out on a money purchase basis to allow members to contract out on either basis.

On 6 April 2002, SERPS was replaced by the State second pension (S2P). S2P is designed to boost the additional State pension of low and moderate earners and also to extend the category of people who would qualify. These changes were not, however, intended to have a significant impact on the way in which occupational pension schemes were contracted out. Certain other simplification measures, such as increasing the options available for discharging contracted-out rights and increasing members' transfer options, were also introduced (*Child Support, Pensions and Social Security Act 2000*).

The whole concept of contracting out has been subject to Government review as part of 'the Government's wider agenda to promote better regulation and reduce the administrative burden on schemes' (see the Government's White Paper, *Security in retirement: towards a new pensions system*, published in May 2006). Recent changes, which took effect from 6 April 2009 (under *PA 2007*), have included a fixed cap on the earnings used to calculate S2P and the ability for schemes to convert GMPs into main scheme benefits. Contracting out on a money purchase basis is due to be abolished from 2012, ie from the date the basic State pension is due to be linked to earnings, and it is likely that contracting out on a salary related basis will be further reviewed in future.

Defined benefits schemes

4.3 Initially, defined benefits schemes could only contract out if they satisfied two tests:

(*a*) a qualitative test, namely the requisite benefit test, which in simple terms meant providing 1/80th of pensionable salary for each year of pensionable service; and

(*b*) a quantitative test, namely the provision of a GMP broadly equivalent to the SERPS entitlement being given up (*Social Security Pensions Act 1975, ss 33–41*).

The requisite benefit test was abolished in November 1986. As from 6 April 1997, salary related schemes wishing to contract out were once again required to pass a scheme quality test. The reference scheme test, introduced by *PA 1995*, is based loosely on the requisite benefit test and aims to ensure that a certain overall level of benefits will be provided for members of the scheme. Although members of COSR schemes ceased accruing GMPs on 5 April 1997, GMPs are retained in respect of service completed before that date and so, in order to continue to be contracted out, schemes must continue to comply with the requirements relating to GMPs.

Defined contribution schemes

4.4 In April 1988 it became possible for members of money purchase arrangements, including personal pension schemes and freestanding additional voluntary contribution schemes, to contract out of SERPS. In the case of an employer-sponsored arrangement, generally a COMP scheme, each member has to be provided with benefits based on contributions actually made and the investment return on those contributions. The employer's contributions must be at least equal to the contracted-out rebate.

In order to promote contracting out for new arrangements, the Department of Social Security (now DWP) paid an 'incentive' of 2 per cent of earnings between the upper and lower earnings limit. This payment ceased in April 1993. From 6 April 1997, age-related rebates are payable in addition to the flat-rate contracted-out rebate (see **4.38** below).

Mixed benefit schemes

4.5 Prior to 6 April 1997, a scheme could only be contracted out on either a salary related or a money purchase basis. A scheme could not contract out by both methods simultaneously, nor could it elect to convert from one to the other, unless it first ceased to contract out on the original basis and discharged its liability to pay contracted-out benefits on that basis.

From 6 April 1997, it became possible for schemes to contract out via both the money purchase and salary related routes at the same time. Initially, only schemes which were contracting out for the first time, and COSR schemes which re-elected to contract out on or after 6 April 1997, were able to become COMB schemes. However, this flexibility was extended to COMP schemes from 6 April 1998.

The contracted-out rebate

4.6 As explained in CHAPTER 1, an individual's entitlement to a State pension will generally depend on the National Insurance contributions that have been paid or credited to him. Primary Class 1 National Insurance contributions are payable by employees, and secondary Class 1 National Insurance contributions are payable by employers. When a person is in contracted-out employment, those Class 1 contributions are reduced and the reduction is known as the 'contracted-out rebate'. See **4.27** and **4.37** below for further detail about the rebate in the context of post-1997 COSR rights and protected rights.

The contracted-out rebate was originally intended to be equivalent to the cost of providing the additional State pension benefit being given up (which increases with the age of the person in respect of whom the benefit is provided). The contracted-out rebate has historically been based on the cost of providing the benefit for a person of 'average' age. It was financially advantageous for those younger than the average age to contract out of, and for those older than the average age to contract in to, S2P.

PA 1995 changed the way in which the contracted-out rebate applies to COMP schemes by introducing age-related rebates. As from 6 April 1997 an age-related top-up became payable under *PSA 1993* in addition to a flat-rate rebate (see **4.38** below).

The contracting-out certificate

4.7 Contracting-out certificates are issued to employers and state that the employment of earners (or a category or description of earners) in a particular trade, business, profession, office or vocation is contracted-out employment by reference to a named occupational pension scheme. An employer must have a valid contracting-out certificate in order to deduct and pay National Insurance contributions at the reduced rate.

A person will be in contracted-out employment during any period that he is under State pension age, there is a contracting-out certificate in force in relation to his employment, and either his service qualifies him for a pension provided by a COSR scheme or his employer makes minimum payments in respect of his employment to a COMP scheme.

An occupational pension scheme will be a contracted-out scheme in relation to an earner's employment if it is for the time being specified in a contracting-out certificate in relation to that employment. Certain conditions must be satisfied by the scheme in order for it to be contracted out (see **4.16** and **4.34** below).

As a consequence of the changes introduced by *PA 1995*, all occupational pension schemes which were contracted out on a salary related basis prior to 6 April 1997 were required to re-elect to contract out by 31 January 1998, at the latest, if they wished to continue to be contracted out on and after 6 April 1997. There was no similar requirement to re-elect for schemes contracted out on a money purchase basis (*PSA 1993, s 70*).

Schemes contracting out for the first time after 6 April 1997 are required to comply with the election procedure set out in the *Contracting-out Regulations, regs 2–16* (see **4.8** to **4.15** below).

A contracting-out certificate will include the name and address of the employer and the date from which the certificate is to have effect. It will also show both the employer's contracting-out number (ECON) and the scheme's contracted-out number (SCON). COMB schemes will be issued with two SCONs: one for the salary related part of the scheme, and one for the money purchase part. ECONs and SCONs are used by NICO to monitor National Insurance contributions and pension liability.

Electing for the issue, variation or surrender of a contracting-out certificate

4.8 An employer may elect to issue, vary or surrender a contracting-out certificate, and the Pension Schemes Services division of HMRC has power to give effect to such an election or refuse to do so and to cancel any contracting-out certificate already held.

Full details of the election procedures for obtaining, varying or surrendering a contracting-out certificate are given in the manuals 'Contracted-out Guidance for Salary Related Pension Schemes and Salary Related Overseas Schemes' (CA14C), 'Contracted-out Guidance for Money Purchase Pension Schemes and Money Purchase Overseas Schemes' (CA14D) and 'Contracted-out Guidance for Mixed Benefit Pension Schemes and Mixed Benefit Overseas Schemes' (CA14E), all of which are available from the HMRC website (the 'Contracting-out Manuals').

The procedure for electing to become a COMB scheme is not covered in detail below but it is very similar to the procedure for electing to become a COSR or a COMP scheme. Additional information must be included in the notices of the election and in the election itself, as described in the *Mixed Benefits Regulations, reg 3* and Contracting-out Manual CA14E.

Notices of intention and notices of explanation

4.9 Before making an election for the issue, variation or surrender of a contracting-out certificate, the employer must usually give either a notice of intention or a notice of explanation (*Contracting-out Regulations, regs 2, 3, 9 and 10*). However, no such notice will be required if the proposed variation:

(*a*) is a change in the name or address of the employer or in the name of the scheme; or

(*b*) would not alter (i) the categories or descriptions of the earners affected by the certificate, (ii) the protected rights under a COMP scheme or the benefits provided by any other scheme, or (iii) the contributions (if any) payable by those earners to the scheme.

Notice of intention and consultation requirements

4.10 Subject to the exceptions mentioned in **4.9** above, upon electing to issue, vary or surrender a contracting-out certificate, a notice of intention must be given unless a notice of explanation may be given in the circumstances described in **4.11** below.

Notices of intention must be in writing and must contain the information specified in *Contracting-out Regulations, reg 3* or *9* (as applicable). Specimen notices of intention are given in the Contracting-out Manuals.

A notice of intention must be given to all the earners in the employments which are to be covered by the certificate, whether or not they are members of the scheme or will be otherwise be excluded from the scope of the certificate. The notice must also be given to any independent trade unions recognised for the purpose of collective bargaining, the trustees of the scheme, the scheme administrator and, if the contracted-out rights are secured by a policy of insurance or annuity contract, the insurance company. Notices can be given by sending or delivering them to all relevant parties or, in the case of employees, by exhibiting them conspicuously at the employees' place of work or employment and by drawing the employees' attention to it in writing.

In the case of an election for the issue of a contracting-out certificate, the notice of intention must specify a date of expiry, which generally must be at least three months after the date on which the notice is given. If there are no independent trade unions in relation to the affected employees or if all unions involved agree in writing, the notice period can be shortened but it must not be less than one month after the date on which the notice is given.

In the case of an election for the variation or surrender of a contracting-out certificate, a notice of intention must specify a date of expiry, which must generally be within three months of the event to which the election relates.

During the notice period, employees must be permitted to make representations to a named contact and to the HMRC Commissioners. In the case of an election for the issue or variation of a contracting-out certificate, the employer must also undertake consultations (if he has not already done so) about the matters covered by the notice with all independent trade unions recognised in relation to the earners concerned.

An employer may amend his election at any time before the issue, variation or surrender of a contracting-out certificate, but only if the amendment does not alter the categories or descriptions of the earners to which the election relates, or the date from which it is intended that the certificate, variation or surrender is to have effect. However, if incorrect information is shown in the original notice of intention, the employer must issue fresh notices, and the notice period will start to run again (see the Contracting-out Manuals).

Notice of explanation

4.11 *Contracting-out Regulations, reg 10* permits a notice of explanation to be given (instead of a notice of intention) if:

(*a*) the earners covered by the election will continue to qualify for either GMPs and post-1997 COSR rights or protected rights, as the case may be, under the scheme when the election takes effect;

(*b*) the accrued rights of those earners under that scheme to GMPs and post-1997 COSR rights or protected rights, as the case may be, will be unaffected; and

(*c*) the employment of those earners will continue to be contracted out by reference to that same scheme.

Where a notice of explanation is used, no notice period need be given and no consultation with trade unions is required. The employees need not be allowed the opportunity to make representations about the election.

Notices of explanation must be given to the earners to whose employment the election relates and, in the same circumstances as for a notice of intention, to any independent trade unions, the trustees of the scheme, the scheme administrator and any insurance company. The notice must include the name of the scheme, the reason for the election, the date from which the change is to have effect, and the reasons that it is appropriate to give a notice in this form.

A notice of explanation will generally be used where changes occur within a group of companies (see the Contracting-out Manuals). For example, if all the employees of a company are transferred to another company within the same group which is also named on the contracting-out certificate, it would be appropriate to use a notice of explanation, as the election would not result in any change of contracted-out status for any of the employees involved.

One notice of explanation can cover more than one election (see the Contracting-out Manuals). For example, in the scenario referred to above, the notice would explain both the surrender of the certificate held by the original employer (or its removal from a holding company certificate) and the election for a contracting-out certificate by the new employer (or for its inclusion on a holding company certificate). A notice of explanation will have to be tailored to the exact requirements of the elections to be made, but specimen notices of explanation are given in the Contracting-out Manuals.

Making an election to contract out or to vary or surrender a contracting-out certificate

Timing of elections

4.12 An election to contract out must be made to HMRC within three months of the expiry of any notice of intention or, where no notice is required, within three months of the event to which the election relates (*Contracting-out Regulations, regs 5, 9* and *10*). Elections made outside this period may be accepted at the discretion of the HMRC Commissioners but must be accompanied by an explanation for the delay. Where possible, an election to contract out should be submitted before the date from which the contracting-out certificate is to have effect, but back-dating may be permitted in exceptional circumstances at the discretion of the HMRC Commissioners (see the Contracting-out Manuals).

The election

4.13 The election must contain the information specified in *Contracting-out Regulations, reg 6*. In particular, in the election to contract out, the employer must confirm that:

(*a*) unless exempt, the scheme is complying with the employer related investment requirements of *PA 1995, s 40*;

(*b*) where applicable, the scheme funding requirements of *PA 2004, Part 3* are being complied with; and

(*c*) a notice of intention or explanation has been given.

If a scheme is contracting out on a money purchase basis, the employer must also confirm that it will comply with obligations concerning minimum payments, as set out in *PSA 1993* and the *Contracting-out Regulations*.

An election to contract out will generally be made by completing Form APSS101, and an election to vary a contracting-out certificate will generally be made by completing Form APSS155. Both are available from the HMRC website. The forms must be signed by the scheme administrator, the employer or a trustee and, in the case of an occupational pension scheme, any trustee signing must also declare that the contents of the form have been approved by the employer and that the employer has authorised the trustee to submit the form.

Supporting documents and information

4.14 Employers who elect for the issue of a contracting-out certificate must provide HMRC with such reports, accounts, other documents and information relating to the scheme as HMRC requires. HMRC may also require the employer to notify any changes affecting the scheme as soon as possible after their occurrence (*Contracting-out Regulations, reg 15*) and to provide written confirmation and other evidence in accordance with *Contracting-out Regulations, reg 16*.

When making any election in relation to a COSR scheme, the employer must provide written confirmation or evidence either that the actuary is satisfied that the resources of the scheme are sufficient to meet the statutory funding objective or that the actuary has certified that, in his opinion, it can be expected to be met by the end of the period specified in the recovery plan (*Contracting-out Regulations, reg 18*). The employer must also submit a certificate signed by the scheme actuary confirming that the scheme satisfies the reference scheme test. These requirements differ slightly for cross-border schemes.

Multi-employer schemes

4.15 In the case of a multi-employer scheme where all of the employers are either part of the same corporate group or associated by a common interest, a holding company may give notices of intention or explanation on behalf of its subsidiaries (*Contracting-out Regulations, reg 12*). A corporate entity will be a holding company if it is:

(*a*) a holding company within the meaning of *CA 2006, s 1159*; or

(*b*) an employer who is the principal employer in accordance with the rules of a scheme or who has power in relation to the scheme rules to act on behalf of all employers in the scheme.

If the holding company does give such notices, it shall be treated as an employer of earners for the purposes of the contracting-out legislation. It may therefore elect for and be issued with a contracting-out certificate (which will also cover its associated or subsidiary companies) and it will be subject to the regulations governing the cancellation, variation, surrender and refusal of such certificates (*Contracting-out Regulations, reg 12*).

Notwithstanding the status conferred on the holding company by *reg 12*, the subsidiary companies will still be required to undertake any consultations in connection with a notice in respect of their employees, unless all the recognised trade unions agree in writing that the holding company may carry out such consultations on the subsidiaries' behalf.

Previously, details of changes to holding company certificates had to be supplied to the Pension Schemes Service on an annual basis under the periodic return system. This system was abolished with effect from 1 August 2007, and changes now need to be notified as and when they occur using Form APSS155 (see the Contracting-out Manuals).

Defined benefits schemes

Requirements for contracting out

4.16 A salary related scheme can be contracted out in relation to an earner's employment only if:

(*a*) in relation to service completed before 6 April 1997 (*PSA 1993, s 9(2A)*):

  (i) the scheme complies with the requirements of *PSA 1993* relating to the provision of GMPs (as set out in *PSA 1993, ss 13* to *24E* and the *Contracting-out Regulations*); and

  (ii) the rules of the scheme applying to GMPs are framed so as to comply with any requirements relating to the form and content of contracted-out schemes as may be prescribed in regulations or imposed by HMRC; and

(*b*) in relation to service completed on or after 6 April 1997 (*PSA 1993, s 9(2B)*), HMRC is satisfied that:

  (i) the scheme satisfies the reference scheme test (see **4.28** to **4.32** below);

  (ii) unless the scheme is a public service pension scheme, it is subject to, and complies with, the provisions of *PA 1995* relating to employer-related investments (as set out in *PA 1995, s 40*, see CHAPTER 10);

  (iii) all parts of the scheme meet the statutory funding objective or the actuary has certified that, in his opinion, the statutory funding objective can be expected to be met by the end of the period specified in the recovery plan (see CHAPTER 11);

  (iv) the scheme does not permit the payment of a lump sum instead of a pension unless the payment is an authorised lump sum under *FA 2004* and satisfies certain other conditions (see CHAPTER 5);

  (v) any post-1997 COSR rights will not be forfeited in circumstances where the person entitled to payments is, in the opinion of the trustees, unable to act by reason of mental disorder and the scheme rules satisfy the requirements set out in *Contracting-out Regulations, reg 20A*;

  (vi) the scheme provides for benefits to be payable by reference to an age which is equal for men and women and is permitted by *FA 2004* (see CHAPTER 5); and

  (vii) the rules of the scheme are framed so as to comply with any requirements relating to the form and content of contracted-out rules as may be prescribed in regulations or specified by HMRC.

(*PSA 1993, s 9* and *Contracting-out Regulations, Part III*).

Generally, schemes which are not registered (see CHAPTER 16) are not permitted to contract out on a salary related basis (*Contracting-out Regulations, reg 29*).

Pre 6 April 1997 – guaranteed minimum pensions

4.17 Guaranteed minimum pensions could only be accrued in respect of service from 6 April 1978 to 5 April 1997 and do not include any 'equivalent pension benefits' for the purposes of the *National Insurance Act 1965* or any previous corresponding enactments.

Although it is no longer possible to accrue GMPs (and therefore no further contracted-out rebate will be granted in respect of them), if a scheme was contracted out of SERPS on a salary related basis prior to 6 April 1997, or if a scheme wishes to be able to accept transfers of GMPs from a COSR scheme, it must comply with the requirements of *PSA 1993* relating to the provision of GMPs. The relevant requirements are contained in *PSA 1993, ss 13–24H* and *Contracting-out Regulations, regs 55–69B*.

Conditions relating to members' GMPs

4.18 A member will be entitled to a GMP under a scheme if, in any tax week in the period from 6 April 1978 to 5 April 1997, earnings in excess of the lower earnings limit were paid to or in respect of him while he was in contracted-out employment by reference to that scheme (*PSA 1993, s 14*).

In order to satisfy the requirements of *PSA 1993* in relation to GMPs, the rules of the scheme must provide for the member to be entitled to a pension of not less than the guaranteed minimum (*Contracting-out Regulations, reg 55*) unless the scheme has become exempt from these requirements by satisfying the conversion conditions (see **4.25** below).

The rules must also provide that a GMP will commence no later than the date on which the member attains State pension age (unless it is postponed as described below) and be payable for life. Although State pension age is being equalised progressively (see CHAPTER 1), GMPs will continue to be payable when the member reaches the State pension age in force when the benefits accrued, ie 60 for women and 65 for men (*PSA 1993, s 13*).

A scheme can provide for the commencement of the GMP to be postponed for any period during which a member continues in employment after attaining State pension age. However, the consent of the member must be obtained if the period of postponement exceeds five years from State pension age, or if the postponement relates to employment which is not contracted out by reference to the scheme (*PSA 1993, s 13*). Where payment of a GMP is postponed until after State pension age, it must be increased to take account of late receipt (*PSA 1993, s 15*).

All GMPs in payment which are attributable to service in the period from 6 April 1988 to 5 April 1997 must be increased each year by at least the lesser of increase in the retail prices index and 3 per cent per annum (*PSA 1993, s 109*).

Certain schemes rules are also required to provide that GMPs (amongst other benefits) are to be accorded priority over other liabilities on a winding up (*PSA 1993, s 23*), although this provision is currently effectively for those schemes subject to *PA 1995, s 73,* which sets out statutory priorities on winding up (see CHAPTER 12).

Conditions relating to survivors' GMPs

4.19 If a member who is entitled to a GMP dies, leaving a widow, widower or surviving civil partner (whether before or after attaining State pension age), the scheme must provide that the widow, widower or surviving civil partner will be entitled to a GMP under the scheme (*PSA 1993, s 17).* However, this requirement will not apply if the scheme has become exempt by satisfying the conversion conditions (see **4.25** below).

The scheme rules must set out the minimum rates of pension payable to any widow, widower or surviving civil partner (*Contracting-out Regulations, reg 55*). The GMP payable to a widow must be one half of the GMP payable to the member. The GMP payable to a widower or surviving civil partner must be one half of that part of the member's GMP which is attributable to earnings in the period 6 April 1988 to 5 April 1997.

The scheme must also provide for the widow, widower or civil partner's pension to be payable for the periods and in the circumstances set out in the legislation (see *PSA 1993, s 17* and *Contracting-out Regulations, regs 57* and *58*).

Calculating the GMP

4.20 The GMP payable to a member is based on the level of his earnings in excess of the lower earnings limit while in contracted-out employment on which primary Class 1 National Insurance contributions have been paid or treated as paid. It is calculated according to the appropriate percentage of the member's 'earnings factors' derived from those earnings during the tax years from 6 April 1978 to 5 April 1997 (*PSA 1993, s 14*).

A member's earnings factors are derived from his earnings up to the upper earnings limit each year and are revalued in line with the retail prices index. The basis on which earnings factors were calculated changed in April 1987, so separate calculations must be made in respect of pre- and post-April 1987 service.

The appropriate percentage also depends on the age of the member at 6 April 1978. Essentially, the calculation is:

(*a*) for a person within 20 years of State pension age on 6 April 1978 (ie a man born before 6 April 1933 and a woman born before 6 April 1938), 1.25 per cent of his revalued earnings factors for each year between 6 April 1978 and 5 April 1988 *plus* 1 per cent of his revalued earnings factors for each year between 6 April 1988 and 5 April 1997;

(*b*) for any other person (ie a man born on or after 6 April 1933 and a woman born on or after 6 April 1938), 25 per cent of his revalued earnings factors for each tax year between 6 April 1978 and 5 April 1988 divided by the number of complete tax years after 5 April 1978 (or the start of working life) up to State pension age *plus* 20 per cent of his revalued earnings factors for each tax year between 6 April 1988 to 5 April 1997 divided by the number of complete tax years after 5 April 1978 (or the start of working life) up to State pension age.

Different methods of revaluing a member's earnings factors may also be used by a scheme according to whether or not the member is an early leaver and whether or not a transfer of the member's accrued rights is taking place (see *Contracting-out Regulations, regs 65* and *66*).

A member's GMP must be reduced by the appropriate percentage where it becomes subject to a pension debit (*PSA 1993, s 15A*).

Revaluing GMPs

4.21 To counter some of the effects of inflation and to allow for the fact that a GMP will be based on band earnings during the tax years from 6 April 1978 to 5 April 1997, *PSA 1993, s 16* provides that GMPs of early leavers must be revalued from the date of leaving up to State pension age. The two methods currently available to revalue GMPs are:

(*a*) *s 148* orders – this involves increasing the earnings factors used for calculating the GMP by the percentage prescribed by the last earnings factor order to come into force in the final tax year of the member's working life (in the same way as for active members); and

(*b*) fixed rate revaluation – this involves:

  (i) increasing the earnings factors used for calculating the GMP by the percentage prescribed by the last earnings factor order in force before the end of tax year in which the member's contracted-out service ends; then once the guaranteed minimum has been calculated,

(ii) for each subsequent tax year in the member's working life, revaluing the guaranteed minimum by a fixed percentage as prescribed by *Contracting-out Regulations, reg 62*. The rate ranges from 4.0 to 8.5 per cent compound according to when the member's period of contracted-out service ended.

To a limited extent, it is possible to revalue GMPs for those leaving before 6 April 1997 by what is known as limited rate revaluation (*PSA 1993, s 16(3)*, as preserved by *Pensions Act 1995 (Commencement No 10) Order 1997, art 3*). Using this method, GMPs must be increased by the lesser of:

(i) five per cent compound for each complete tax year in the earner's working life after that in which contracted-out service terminated; and

(ii) the increase which would apply using the last order made under *s 148* in the tax year before the member reaches State pension age.

If limited rate revaluation is used, a Limited Revaluation Premium has to be paid to Services to Pensions Industry.

Discharge of liability in respect of GMPs

4.22 If a member's GMPs are not paid from the scheme, they may be discharged by taking out a policy or policies of insurance, entering into an annuity contract or contracts, or transferring the benefit of such a policy or policies to such contract or contracts (*PSA 1993, s 19*). The transaction must take place after the member's pensionable service has terminated, the GMPs must be appropriately secured, and the requirements of *PSA 1993, s 19* must be satisfied. Further provision about the discharge of such liability is made in the *Occupational Pension Schemes (Discharge of Liability) Regulations 1997 (SI 1997/784)*.

It is also possible to transfer the rights to and liability for GMPs to another occupational pension scheme, personal pension scheme or overseas arrangement (*PSA 1993, s 20*). Further provision about such transfers is made in the *Contracting-out Transfer Regulations 1996* (see **4.50** to **4.56** below).

Commutation, suspension and forfeiture

4.23 A member's or survivor's GMP may generally be commuted for a lump sum once it has become payable, provided that the payment would be authorised for the purposes of *FA 2004* and the payment would be permitted either as a trivial commutation lump sum or trivial commutation lump sum death benefit, or as a winding-up lump sum or winding-up lump sum death benefit. It is also possible to commute GMPs in certain other circumstances including ill-health (*PSA 1993, s 21* and *Contracting-out Regulations, reg 60*), in which case a survivor's pension must continue to be payable if provided under the rules.

A scheme may provide for a member's or survivor's GMP to be suspended where the person entitled to the payments is, in the opinion of the trustees, unable to act by reason of mental disorder, is in prison or detained in legal custody, or the earner is re-employed in contracted-out employment by reference to the scheme. In each case, the scheme rules must be in line with *Contracting-out Regulations, reg 61(1)* to permit the suspension.

A scheme may provide for a member's or survivor's GMP to be forfeited where the person entitled to the payments has committed a serious offence such as treason, or where no claim has been made for payment and at least six years have elapsed since payment was due (see *Contracting-out Regulations, reg 61(2)*).

Equalisation of GMPs

4.24 In January 2000, the then Ombudsman concluded (in *Mr I B Williamson [H00177]*) that GMPs for men and women should be equalised (ie based on the same retirement age), on the basis that *PA 1995, s 62(1)* is overriding and requires occupational pension schemes to be treated as including an equal treatment rule. He ruled that the scheme in question should therefore ensure that GMPs were equalised. On 23 February 2001, in *Marsh Mercer Pension Scheme v Pensions Ombudsman [2001] 16 PBLR*, Rimer J decided that the Ombudsman did not have jurisdiction to make that ruling but left open the question of whether legislation requires GMPs to be equalised and, if so, how.

The issue of GMP equalisation thus remains unresolved and members could still bring claims on this point. Trustees and employers should consider reserving costs to cover the issue if it is raised in the future and should also think about who is to bear the risk on a transfer-in and in the context of share acquisitions and transfers of past service rights. Trustees may also wish to consider whether, and if so how, GMPs could be equalised in the context of a scheme wind-up. The PPF consulted on the topic of GMP equalisation in 2008, but its proposal has not yet been published.

Sex equality of scheme benefits is dealt with in CHAPTER 9.

Conversion of GMPs

4.25 From 6 April 2009, it has been possible for a scheme to become exempt from the requirement to guarantee a minimum pension. In order to become exempt, the scheme must satisfy the five conditions set out in *PSA 1993, s 24B*, which are as follows:

- the post-conversion benefits must be actuarially at least equivalent to the pre-conversion benefits. The trustees are responsible for determining actuarial equivalence, having considered the advice of the actuary (*Contracting-out Regulations, reg 69A*);
- there must be no reduction in pension for those entitled to payment of a pension immediately before the conversion;
- the post-conversion benefits must not include money purchase benefits (other than money purchase benefits provided under the scheme immediately before the conversion), ie no GMPs can be converted to money purchase benefits;
- the scheme must provide survivors' benefits in the circumstances and during the periods prescribed by *Contracting-out Regulations, reg 69B*. Widows' benefits must be at least 50 per cent of the pension to which the member would have been entitled for the period from 6 April 1978 to 5 April 1997. Widowers' and surviving civil partners' benefits must be at least 50 per cent of the pension to which the member would have been entitled for the period from 6 April 1988 to 5 April 1997 (*PSA 1993, s 24D*); and
- the procedural requirements of *s 24E* must have been met.

The procedural requirements are:

- the employer must consent to the GMP conversion in advance;
- the trustees must take all reasonable steps to consult the earner in advance and to notify all affected members and survivors before or as soon as is reasonably practicable after the conversion date; and
- HMRC must be notified on or before the conversion date that the conversion will occur or has occurred and that it affects the earner.

In future, regulations may impose conditions or restrictions on transfers out of benefits from a converted scheme (*PSA 1993, s 24F*). Meanwhile, where a member applies to take his cash equivalent, the trustees may, with his consent, adjust any guaranteed cash equivalent so as to reflect rights that would have accrued if the scheme had been converted.

Section 24G gives trustees the power to amend their scheme by resolution to give effect to GMP conversion in accordance with the *s 24B* conditions. Furthermore, if the trustees choose to effect the conversion using the existing scheme amendment power, *PA 1995, s 67* will not apply insofar as the power enables the conversion in accordance with the *s 24B* conditions. Trustees may also include other amendments which they think are necessary or desirable as a consequence of, or to facilitate, the GMP conversion.

Where a scheme is winding up, the trustees may adjust rights under the scheme so as to reflect what would have happened if the scheme had been subject to GMP conversion.

The Regulator has certain powers in relation to the conversion process which may be exercised where it thinks that the *s 24B* conditions have not been satisfied in relation to any guaranteed cash equivalent or scheme amendment. The Regulator may make an order declaring the amendment, modification or adjustment void (*PSA 1993, s 24H*) and may require the trustees to take specified steps and declare that other steps are permissible. The Regulator may also intervene during the conversion process and give specific directions to trustees.

Under *PA 1995, s 10*, civil penalties will apply to trustees who fail to take all reasonable steps to secure compliance with the conditions for conversion. Doubts have, however, been expressed as to the likely update of the GMP conversion process, not least due to the requirement to provide survivor benefits after the conversion and the fact that many schemes have not equalised GMPs.

Post 6 April 1997 – the reference scheme test

4.26 If a COSR scheme wishes to continue to contract out of SERPS on a salary related basis from 6 April 1997, to contract out of S2P from 6 April 2002, or to be able to accept transfers of post-1997 COSR scheme rights from another COSR scheme, it must comply with the requirements of *PSA 1993* relating to the reference scheme test and provide at least a minimum level of pensions. The relevant requirements are contained in *PSA 1993, ss 12A–12D* and *Contracting-out Regulations, regs 17–29*. Contracted-out employers and employees will also benefit from a rebate on their National Insurance contributions.

Contracted-out rebate

4.27 The total contracted-out rebate on Class 1 National Insurance contributions for COSR schemes in 2009/10 is 5.3 per cent of band earnings (ie earnings between the lower earnings limit and the upper accrual point). The employee currently benefits from a reduction in his Class 1 National Insurance contributions equal to 1.6 per cent of his band earnings, and the employer from a reduction equal to 3.7 per cent of his band earnings. These percentages may be altered in future by order on the recommendation of the Secretary of State (*PSA 1993, s 42*).

The lower earnings limit for the tax year 2009/10 is £95 per week (*Social Security (Contributions) Regulations 2001, reg 10*) and the upper accrual point is £770 per week (*SSCBA 1992, s 122*). The lower earnings limit is revised each year but the upper accrual point is a fixed amount. Disregarding any salary increases, the effect of inflation is therefore likely to mean that band earnings will reduce over time. Prior to 6 April 2009, band earnings were measured in each tax year as the earnings between the lower and upper earnings limits, which were both revised each year.

The reference scheme

4.28 The reference scheme test aims to ensure that the pensions to be provided for most members (which includes active members and any other members still in employment) and their widows, widowers or surviving civil partners satisfy the statutory standard. In other words, they must be broadly equivalent to, or better than, the pensions which would be provided to them under the 'reference scheme'.

Details of the reference scheme are set out in *PSA 1993, s 12B* and *Contracting-out Regulations, regs 25* and *26*. Essentially, the reference scheme is an occupational pension scheme which:

(*a*) has a normal pension age of 65 for both men and women;

(*b*) provides a pension for life at normal pension age based on 1/80th (per year of pensionable service) of average qualifying earnings in the last three tax years preceding the end of service, subject to a maximum of 40 years;

(*c*) provides that, the day following the death of a member, a pension is payable to the member's widow, widower or surviving civil partner unless:

- the member married or formed a civil partnership after having received benefits under the scheme; or
- the widow, widower or surviving civil partner marries, forms a civil partnership or cohabits with another person after having received benefits under the scheme; or
- the widow, widower or surviving civil partner is cohabiting with a person other than the member at the time of the member's death;

(*d*) provides that on the death of a member before normal pension age, any pension payable to a widow, widower or surviving civil partner is equal to 50 per cent of the pension the reference scheme would have provided to the member if his pension had become payable on the date of his death;

(*e*) provides that on the death of a member on or after normal pension age, any pension payable to a widow, widower or surviving civil partner is equal to 50 per cent of the pension the reference scheme was required to provide to the member immediately before his death;

(*f*) provides annual pension increases in accordance with *PA 1995, s 51* (see CHAPTER 1); and

(*g*) revalues deferred pensions between the date of leaving and normal pension age in accordance with *PSA 1993* (see CHAPTER 6).

For the purposes of the reference scheme test, qualifying earnings in any tax year before 2009/10 means 90 per cent of earnings between the lower and upper earnings limits for National Insurance contributions and, in any tax years including and after 2009/10, means 90 per cent of earnings between the lower earnings limit and the upper accrual point.

The test – actuarial certification

4.29 A scheme meets the reference scheme test only if the scheme actuary (or, if the trustees are not required to appoint a scheme actuary, an actuary appointed for the purpose) certifies that pensions to be provided to the members and their widows, widowers or surviving civil partners are to be treated as broadly equivalent to, or better than, those payable under the reference scheme.

In order to provide the necessary certification, the actuary must follow the actuarial guidance note, 'Retirement Benefit Schemes – Adequacy of Benefits for Contracting-out' (GN 28) and comply with *Contracting-out Regulations, reg 23*.

GN 28 states that, if a scheme provides pensions equal to or better than the reference scheme in every respect, including the earnings definition and widow, widowers' and surviving civil partners' pensions, the actuary can in most circumstances provide a certificate without further investigation (GN 28, para 4.1).

GN 28 also states that a scheme does not have to match the benefit structure of the reference scheme in order to contract out, provided that broad equivalence can be certified. In order to certify broad equivalence, it is necessary to compare the scheme benefits with those under the reference scheme.

The *Contracting-out Regulations* provide that at least 90 per cent of the pensions to be provided to the members and their widows, widowers or surviving civil partners in the scheme at the effective date of the certificate must be broadly equivalent to those provided under the reference scheme. Money purchase benefits (such as additional voluntary contributions) and the pensions to be provided under the scheme in respect of members who are not in contracted-out employment must be ignored. The actuary may have regard to the payment of a lump sum, but must take no account of any provision made by the scheme for the suspension of any post-1997 COSR rights.

When carrying out the comparison between the scheme in question and the reference scheme, it will in certain circumstances be necessary for the actuary to make four separate comparisons between the value of the respective benefits (GN 28, para 4.8). The benefits to be compared are usually those that the members are expected to accrue in the three years following the effective date of certification, assuming that they were to leave service at the end of that period or on reaching normal pension age, if earlier (GN 28, paras 4.9 and 4.10). Pensions for widows, widowers and surviving civil partners must be compared separately in respect of death in service during the three-year period, death in deferment and death in retirement (GN 28, para 4.12). GN 28 also sets out further detailed provisions about how the comparison should be carried out.

Schemes with more than one benefit structure

4.30 If a scheme has different sections which apply to different categories of employment or which offer different benefit structures for earners in the same category of employment, each section which is to be contracted out must satisfy the reference scheme test independently (*Contracting-out Regulations, reg 22* and GN 28, para 4.3.1). If a scheme with multiple sections has one section which does not satisfy the reference scheme test, that section cannot be contracted out, even if, overall, the scheme would satisfy the reference scheme test.

Schemes with more than one employer

4.31 Where there is more than one employer participating in a scheme, each employer must either have its own contracting-out certificate or be included in a holding company certificate (see **4.15** above). If an employer wishes to have its own certificate in respect of its own employees, the reference scheme test must be complied with separately in respect of those employees. Where a holding company certificate is used, separate tests are not required unless different employers operate different benefit structures (GN 28, para 4.3.2).

How stringent is the reference scheme test?

4.32 There are a number of reasons why a scheme may not satisfy the reference scheme test. The most obvious example is a scheme which has an accrual rate of less than 80ths, but the relationship between pensionable earnings and band earnings is equally significant, as illustrated below.

In **4.28** above, we saw that the reference scheme uses an average of 'qualifying earnings' in the last three tax years for calculating benefits. Qualifying earnings are defined as 90 per cent of earnings between the lower earnings limit and either the upper earnings limit or upper accrual point, depending on the tax year in question. If a scheme's benefits are based on a pensionable salary which is lower than a member's actual salary (for example, because it excludes commission, bonuses, overtime and other fluctuating emoluments or because there is an offset for the lower earnings limit), there is a possibility that the benefits provided will not better those provided under the reference scheme. This is best illustrated by way of an example:

> A member's actual earnings during the tax year 2009/10 are £24,500 comprising of £12,000 basic salary, £10,000 commission and bonuses and £2,500 overtime. The scheme's definition of pensionable salary for the purpose of calculating benefits is basic salary plus overtime (but excluding commission and bonuses). The member's pensionable salary is therefore £14,500. The average of 90 per cent of his band earnings (which will take into account commission and bonuses) over the last three years (ie 2007/08, 2008/09 and 2009/10) is £17,807. For the purposes of the reference scheme test, the member's scheme benefits, calculated on a salary of £14,500, will be tested against benefits based on a salary of £17,807.

If a significant proportion of a scheme's membership receive much of their earnings in fluctuating emoluments which do not form part of pensionable salary, it is possible that the scheme will not satisfy the reference scheme test even if the accrual rate is greater than 80ths.

The reference scheme benefits do not form any kind of underpin; they are simply a benchmark against which a scheme's benefits are measured. A scheme could be designed to incorporate an underpin based on the reference scheme, with the rules being drafted to ensure that those benefits are provided as a minimum. Such a scheme would clearly be more complicated to administer and more costly to provide than a scheme based on a single benefit structure, as additional records would have to be maintained and checks made whenever a benefit became payable. However, an underpin might be attractive to employers, particularly in circumstances where a scheme generally provides benefits greater than the reference scheme but has difficulty demonstrating that it meets the reference scheme test.

Defined contribution schemes

4.33 Since April 1988, when the relevant provisions of the *Social Security Act 1986* first came into force, it has been possible for employers and individuals to contract out of the additional State pension by way of money purchase arrangements. Such arrangements are now governed by *PSA 1993, ss 10* and *26–33* (as amended by *PA 1995*), the *Contracting-out Regulations* and the *Protected Rights Regulations*. Employers and employees will receive a rebate on their Class 1 National Insurance contributions based on the flat-rate rebate and the age-related rebate.

Requirements for contracting out

4.34 *PSA 1993, s 9(3)* and *Contracting-out Regulations, reg 30* provide that an occupational pension scheme can contract out of S2P on a money purchase basis only if:

(*a*) it complies with the requirements of *PSA 1993* regarding the provision of protected rights;

(*b*) unless the scheme is a public service pension scheme, it is subject to, and complies with, the provisions of *PA 1995* relating to employer-related investments (as set out in *PA 1995, s 40*), see CHAPTER 10);

(*c*) its rules provide that any contributions made by members in addition to the minimum payments are invested so as to provide money purchase benefits (unless the rules provide that those additional payments will entitle the member to additional benefits which are not money purchase benefits);

(*d*) in the case of an insured scheme, its rules require the insurance company to be notified of any alteration in the membership of the scheme and the amount of earnings of any member;

(*e*) its rules require 'minimum payments' to be invested on behalf of the member within one month of the end of the income tax month to which they relate and age-related payments to be invested on behalf of the member within one month of the date of payment by HMRC; and

(*f*) its rules (insofar as they apply to protected rights) are framed so as to comply with any requirements relating to the form and content of contracted-out rules as may be prescribed in regulations or specified by HMRC.

A scheme which is not registered (see CHAPTER 16) is not permitted to contract out on a money purchase basis (*Contracting-out Regulations, reg 40*).

Minimum payments and protected rights

4.35 An occupational pension scheme contracts out of S2P on a money purchase basis by providing 'protected rights'. These are the rights derived from the 'minimum payments' made to the scheme in respect of a member and certain other payments, including age-related rebates and transfers to the scheme of rights accrued in another contracted-out arrangement (*PSA 1993, s 10*).

Identification and valuation of protected rights

4.36 Unless the scheme rules otherwise provide, a member's protected rights are all his rights to money purchase benefits under the scheme. Under *PSA 1993, s 10* the rules of an occupational pension scheme may instead provide that a member's protected rights are:

(*a*) the rights derived from the payment of minimum payments (see **4.37** below) and age-related rebates (see **4.38** below) and incentive payments made in respect of the member; and

(*b*) money purchase benefits derived from protected rights which have been transferred to the scheme from another arrangement; and

(*c*) money purchase benefits derived from a GMP or post-1997 COSR rights which have been transferred to the scheme from another arrangement.

If the rules of a scheme limit a member's protected rights as outlined above, they must also make provision for their identification. The value of such protected rights must be calculated in a manner which is no less favourable than that in which the value of any other money purchase rights are calculated and in such manner as is prescribed under *Protected Rights Regulations, reg 2* (*PSA 1993, s 27*).

A member's protected rights must be reduced by the appropriate percentage where they become subject to a pension debit (*PSA 1993, s 10(4)*) (see CHAPTER 8).

Minimum payments and the flat-rate rebate

4.37 The flat-rate rebate, known in the legislation as the appropriate flat-rate percentage, is based on a percentage of band earnings (see **4.27** above for further discussion of band earnings). The employee currently benefits from a reduction in his Class 1 National Insurance contributions equal to 1.6 per cent of his band earnings, and the employer from a reduction equal to 1.4 per cent of his band earnings. These percentages may be altered by order on the recommendation of the Secretary of State (*PSA 1993, s 42B*).

In certain circumstances, HMRC may pay certain sums back to the employer provided that the employer makes an application for this purpose (*PSA 1993, s 42A*).

The employer may recover an employee's share of the flat-rate rebate from him by deducting it from his earnings (*Contracting-out Regulations, reg 31*). If the member's share of the rebate is to be recovered in this way, the scheme effectively becomes contributory for the members, even if no other contributions are payable, and the rules of the scheme should be framed accordingly so that the members receive tax relief on the contributions.

The employer is required to make a 'minimum payment' equal to the value of the total flat-rate rebate to the trustees of the scheme within 14 days of the end of the income tax month to which the rebate applies, ie on or before the 19th of the following month (*Contracting-out Regulations, regs 32* and *33*). Such payments may be calculated by reference to the scale prepared by the Secretary of State. Minimum payments must be invested on behalf of the member within one month of the end of the income tax month to which they relate (*Contracting-out Regulations, reg 30*).

Age-related rebate

4.38 The age-related rebate, known in the legislation as the appropriate age-related percentage, is based on the age of the earner immediately before any tax year. For the tax year 2009/10, age-related rebates range from 3.0 per cent to 7.4 per cent (see the *Social Security (Reduced Rates of Class 1 Contributions, Rebates and Minimum Contributions) Order 2006 (SI 2006/1009)*).

Age-related payments equal to the amount by which the age-related rebate exceeds the flat-rate rebate are payable by HMRC to the scheme bank account (*Contracting-out Regulations, reg 35*) at the end of each tax year and must be invested by the trustees within one month of payment (*Contracting-out Regulations, reg 30*). A member may be required by HMRC to provide documentary evidence of his date of birth, and information about the member's age may be disclosed by the authorities to the trustees or any person responsible for administering the scheme (*PSA 1993, s 45B* and *Contracting-out Regulations, reg 36*).

As the age-related payment is effectively paid a year in arrears on submission of the end-of-year return, the amount due will have to be taken into account on transfers and on the death or retirement of a member (see below). The employer may choose to make arrangements to 'credit' the member with the payment on a month-by-month basis, but the additional costs and cash flow implications will then fall on the employer who would recover the expenditure at the end of the tax year.

There are some circumstances in which age-related payments are not payable.

Age-related payments are not payable in respect of a member for the tax year in which he reaches State pension age (or would have done but for his death), although the flat-rate rebate is still available (*Contracting-out Regulations, reg 37*).

Once effect has been given to a member's protected rights by means of a pension from the scheme, a transfer payment, a lump sum or purchasing an annuity (see **4.39** below), no age-related payment for previous tax years will be paid in respect of the member unless one of the exceptions in *Contracting-out Regulations, reg 37* applies. The exceptions apply where effect has been given to a member's protected rights:

- by means of an annuity purchase or scheme pension and the amount due is at least ten times the weekly lower earnings limit in the tax year in which HMRC first becomes aware that the amount is payable. In such a case, the payment will be made to the insurance company in the case of an annuity purchase, or to the trustees in the case of a scheme pension.
- by means of an annuity purchase or scheme pension and the amount due is less than ten times the weekly lower earnings limit in the tax year in which HMRC first becomes aware that the amount is payable or by means of a lump sum. In such a case, the payment will be made to the member, the member's widow, widower or surviving civil partner or, if the member dies unmarried, to any person at the discretion of the Secretary of State.
- by means of a transfer payment, for example, in circumstances where the whole or part of a contributions equivalent premium has not been paid (see **4.60** below). In such a case, the payments will be made to the trustees of the receiving scheme and will be payable up to the date on which the transfer payment was made.

Once effect has been given to a member's protected rights by means of an appropriate policy of insurance in the context of a winding-up, the age-related payments in respect of all or part of the tax year prior to the tax year in which he reaches State pension age (or would have done but for his death) will be payable to the insurer.

Giving effect to protected rights

4.39 Protected rights may only be discharged under a scheme's rules by providing a pension from the scheme, a transfer payment, a lump sum or purchasing an annuity. Where the scheme rules do not provide for a pension or in circumstances where the member (or, where he has died, his widow, widower or surviving civil partner) so elects, the rules must provide for the protected rights to be used to purchase an annuity in line with PSA 1993, s 28. The scheme rules may also provide for effect to be given to a member's protected rights by means of a pension, transfer payment or lump sum or, in circumstances where the member has died without giving effect to his protected rights, as prescribed by *Protected Rights Regulations, regs 12* and *13*.

Member's pension and annuity purchase

4.40 Where protected rights are to be discharged by means of a pension, the pension must comply with the pension requirements set out in *PSA 1993, s 29*. In order to do this, the pension must commence no later than the member's 65th birthday, unless he agrees to a later date, and must continue for life. On the death of the member while the pension is payable, provision must also be made for his widow, widower or surviving civil partner, as described in **4.41** below.

In addition to satisfying the pension requirements, the pension must also be offered and its rate calculated on a basis which does not discriminate on the basis of sex or (unless the member was neither married nor in a civil partnership and agreed to his pension rate being determined on his life only) marital or civil partnership status (*Protected Rights Regulations, reg 15*).

When protected rights are to be discharged by means of an annuity purchase, the annuity must comply with the annuity requirements set out in *PSA 1993, s 29*. In order to do this, the annuity must satisfy the same conditions as a pension would, under the pension requirements described above.

In addition to satisfying the annuity requirements, the member must be given the opportunity to choose the insurance company which is to provide the annuity. This is commonly known as the 'open market option'. The member must generally notify the trustees of his choice, in writing, at least one month, and not more than six months, before his normal pension age (unless the scheme rules allow a longer notice period) (*Protected Rights Regulations, reg 10*). If the member does not notify the trustees of his choice, the trustees can decide from which insurer to purchase an annuity. Any such insurer must have the appropriate permissions to effect and carry out contracts of long-term insurance and must offer annuities on the non-discriminatory basis described above (*Protected Rights Regulations, reg 11*).

Any pension or annuity purchase must also comply with the conditions set out in *Protected Rights Regulations, reg 4*. *Regulation 4* makes provision about the rate and frequency with which the pension or annuity should be paid and the persons to whom it might continue to be paid after the member's death.

Benefits payable on death after retirement

4.41 As indicated in **4.40** above, when discharging a member's protected rights by means of a pension or annuity, the rules of a scheme must provide for a pension or annuity to become payable to the member's widow, widower or surviving civil partner (or commuted for a lump sum if it is a trivial amount) on the member's death after retirement (*PSA 1993, s 29* and *Protected Rights Regulations, reg 5*). No such provision is required, however, if the member was not married or in a civil partnership at the date of his retirement and specifically elected not to make provision for a spouse or surviving civil partner.

The pension payable to a member's widow, widower or surviving civil partner must be equal to 50 per cent of the pension that would have been payable to the member if he had survived. However, during the five years beginning with the commencement of the member's pension, any pension that becomes payable to a widow, widower or surviving civil partner may be paid at the full rate that would have been payable to the member.

The rules of the scheme must provide for the pension or annuity to be payable for the life of the survivor or until he or she remarries or forms a civil partnership while under State pension age. However, where the member died before 5 December 2005, the pension or annuity must not cease on the formation of a civil partnership by the survivor. Notwithstanding these provisions, the rules of the scheme may provide for any such pension or annuity to be payable for a longer period. They may, for example, provide for the benefit to be payable for life, irrespective of whether or not the survivor remarries.

Benefits payable on death before retirement

4.42 The rules of a scheme that is contracted out on a money purchase basis must provide for the situation where a member dies before the benefits deriving from his protected rights have been given effect by means of a pension from the scheme, a transfer payment, a lump sum or an annuity purchase (*PSA 1993, s 28(5)*).

Where the member is survived by a widow, widower or civil partner, his protected rights will be used to provide that person with a pension, an annuity, or, where the amount is trivial, a lump sum (*Protected Rights Regulations, reg 12*). Any such pension or annuity must be paid at a maximum of half the rate that would have been paid to the member (unless it is being paid during a five-year guarantee period) (*Protected Rights Regulations, reg 4(7)*) and begin to be paid as soon as practicable after the member's death for the life of the survivor or until he marries or forms a civil partnership before State pension age. However, where the member died before 5 December 2005, the pension or annuity must not cease on the formation of a civil partnership by the survivor.

On the remarriage or formation of a civil partnership by the survivor, his pension or annuity may continue to be paid to him and, where he dies whilst in receipt of such payments, it may be paid at the same rate for the benefit of any qualifying children until they reach the age of 18.

Where the trustees of the scheme conclude in good faith after making reasonable inquiries that the member was not survived by a widow, widower or civil partner (or that such person died before a survivor's pension could be paid to him), they must make provision for the value of the member's protected rights to be paid to the member's estate or to or for the benefit of any persons nominated, in writing, by the member.

Transfer payment

4.43 In certain circumstances, effect may be given to protected rights in an occupational pension scheme by the making of a transfer payment from that scheme to another occupational pension scheme, a personal pension scheme or an overseas arrangement (*PSA 1993, s 28(2)*). The scheme to which the payment is made must satisfy the prescribed requirements (see **4.50** to **4.56** below).

Lump sum

4.44 In certain circumstances, effect may be given to protected rights by the provision of a lump sum that is equal to the value on that date of those protected rights (*PSA 1993, s 28(4)*). Any such lump sum must be an authorised member payment (*Protected Rights Regulations, reg 8*).

Where the lump sum payment qualifies as a pension commencement lump sum or a serious ill-health lump sum, the scheme rules must also satisfy the applicable requirements of *Protected Rights Regulations, reg 8*. In the case of a pension commencement lump sum, those requirements limit the amount of protected rights funds that can be taken in this form. In the case of a serious ill-health lump sum, where the member has a spouse or civil partner on the date he qualifies for the payment and the scheme rules provide for the payment of a pension to surviving spouses or civil partners, then at least one-half of the value of the member's protected rights must be retained in the scheme.

The lump sum payment may also be payable as a trivial commutation lump sum (or trivial commutation lump sum death benefit) or as a winding-up lump sum (or winding-up lump sum death benefit). In such cases, the scheme rules need satisfy no particular requirements. No other lump sum payments are permissible.

Suspension and forfeiture

4.45 Generally, the rules of a scheme must not permit the suspension of a member's protected rights or of payments giving effect to them (*PSA 1993, s 32*).

The rules may, however, permit such benefits to be suspended where the person entitled to the payments is, in the opinion of the trustees, unable to act by reason of mental disorder and the scheme rules are in line with *Protected Rights Regulations, reg 9(1)*. In such a situation, the trustees must comply with the scheme rules by (a) paying to another person such part of the benefit as is in the trustees' opinion required for the maintenance of the incapacitated person and/or his dependants, and (b) retaining the remainder for the pensioner until he should be again able to act or, if he dies, for his estate. The rules may also permit such benefits to be suspended where the member is in prison or detained in legal custody, in which case the benefit can be paid or applied for the maintenance of such of his dependants as the trustees may in their discretion determine.

Generally, the rules of a scheme must not permit forfeiture of a member's protected rights or of payments giving effect to them (*PSA 1993, s 32*). The rules may, however, permit forfeiture where the trustees of the scheme do not know the address of the person to whom the payment should be made and at least six years have elapsed since payment was due (*Protected Rights Regulations, reg 9(2)*).

Mixed benefit schemes

4.46 Since 6 April 1997, it has been possible for a COSR scheme to contract out of the additional State pension on a money purchase basis under *PA 1995, s 149* and the *Mixed Benefit Regulations*. This could be done by opening up a COMP section.

Since 6 April 1998, it has been possible for a COMP scheme to contract out of the additional State pension on a salary related basis under *PA 1995, s 149* and the *Mixed Benefit Regulations*. This could be done by opening up a COSR section.

Schemes contracting out for the first time on or after 6 April 1997 can elect to be a COMB scheme from the outset.

Requirements for contracting out and ceasing to be a COMB

4.47 COMB schemes are essentially treated as two different schemes, so that the requirements of *PA 1993* relating to a COSR scheme apply to the salary related part, and those relating to a COMP scheme apply to the money purchase part (*Mixed Benefit Regulations, regs 1* and *2*). The scheme will be given two scheme contracting-out numbers (see **4.7** above). However, while members may move from one section to another in accordance with the scheme rules, a member's service in a single employment at any given time may be qualifying service by reference only to one of the separate parts.

A COMB scheme can elect to become a pure money purchase or salary related scheme by closing the salary related or money purchase part, as appropriate, without discharging its liabilities in respect of existing contracted-out rights (*Mixed Benefit Regulations, reg 3*). In such cases, the scheme is no longer a true COMB scheme. The inactive part of the scheme will be treated as if it were a scheme which has ceased to contract out, and a contracting-out certificate will be issued for the active part of the scheme.

During the period 6 April 1997 to 31 January 1998, it was possible for an existing COSR scheme to switch to being a COMP scheme for future service without first having to discharge its liability for GMPs (*Contracting-out Regulations, reg 76B*). Again, the accrued GMPs are treated as if they were provided under a separate scheme which had ceased to contract out immediately before 6 April 1997, and a new contracting-out certificate would have been issued for the active part of the scheme.

Amendment of contracted-out schemes

4.48 *PSA 1993, s 37* prohibits changes to the rules of contracted-out schemes unless the change is permitted by *Contracting-out Regulations, reg 42*. In summary:

- the rules of a COSR scheme cannot be altered in relation to any post-1997 COSR rights unless the scheme will continue to satisfy the conditions of *PSA 1993, s 9(2B)* (see **4.16** above) and the actuary confirms in writing that the scheme will continue to satisfy the reference scheme test after the change;
- the rules of a COMP scheme cannot be altered in relation to any protected rights if the alteration would prevent the scheme from satisfying the requirements of *PSA 1993, s 9(3)* (see **4.34** above) or would affect any of the matters subject to the legislative requirements relating to protected rights in a manner which would or might adversely affect any entitlement or accrued rights of any member acquired before the alteration takes effect; and
- the rules of a scheme cannot be altered in relation to any GMPs if the alteration would prevent the scheme from satisfying the requirements of *PSA 1993, s 9(2)* (see **4.16** above), would affect the increases payable on GMPs, or would affect any of the matters subject to the legislative requirements relating to GMPs in a manner which would or might adversely affect any entitlement or accrued rights of any member, acquired before the alteration takes effect.

Note that, where a scheme was subject to *PSA 1993, s 37* immediately prior to 6 April 1997, any requirements under its rules for the consent of the Occupational Pensions Board to such change will no longer have effect (*Contracting-out Regulations, reg 76B*).

Transfers between contracted-out arrangements

4.49 Broadly speaking, a member who terminates pensionable service at least one year before his normal retirement date has a statutory right to require the trustees of the scheme to transfer the cash equivalent of his benefits to another pension arrangement. In certain circumstances, such as the sale of a business, a group or bulk transfer of the accrued rights of a group of members may be made to another scheme.

In either case, where the transfer would include the accrued rights to which a member is entitled by virtue of his contracted-out employment, additional restrictions may apply in accordance with the *Contracting-out (Transfer and Transfer Payment) Regulations 1996 (SI 1996/1462)* (the '*Contracting-out Transfer Regulations*') or the *Protected Rights (Transfer Payment) Regulations 1996 (SI 1996/1461)* (the '*Protected Rights Transfer Regulations*').

While this chapter focuses on transfers to UK-based pension arrangements, it is also possible for transfer payments to be made to an overseas scheme or arrangement (see, in particular, *Contracting-out Transfer Regulations, regs 6* and *11* and *Protected Rights Transfer Regulations, reg 5*).

A tabulated summary of **4.50** to **4.55** below is included at **4.56** below.

Transfers from a contracted-out salary related scheme to a contracted-in salary related scheme

4.50 A transfer can be made from a COSR scheme to a contracted-in salary related scheme, but only in respect of the member's accrued rights in excess of his GMP and his post-1997 COSR rights (*PSA 1993, s 96*).

Transfers from a contracted-out salary related scheme to another contracted-out salary related scheme

4.51 A transfer in respect of a member's GMP and post-1997 COSR rights can be made from a COSR scheme to another COSR scheme if:

(*a*) the member consents in writing;

(*b*) the member is either employed by an employer who contributes to the receiving scheme or has previously been a member of the receiving scheme;

(*c*) in the case of a member's GMPs, the member does not enter contracted-out employment under the receiving scheme, the receiving scheme satisfies the conditions set out in *Contracting-out Transfer Regulations, Sch 1, paras 1–4* (see below);

(*d*) the transfer includes liability for the payment of a GMP to or in respect of a person who has become entitled to it, the pension must, in the case of the member, commence from the date on which the receiving scheme assumes liability for the GMP and, in the case of any survivor, commence from the same date as it would have under the transferring scheme; and

(*e*) in the case of a member's post-1997 COSR rights, the transfer payment is applied to provide rights for the member, in accordance with the rules of the receiving scheme relating to contracted-out employment, as if those rights had accrued in the receiving scheme (*Contracting-out Transfer Regulations, regs 3* and *8*).

For the purposes of condition (*c*) above, under *Sch 1*, the receiving scheme must provide for a GMP to be payable of at least the amount which would have been payable by the transferring scheme had the transfer not taken place. The receiving scheme must contain the same provisions as the transferring scheme for commencement and continuation of the GMP and (if any) for commutation, suspension and forfeiture. It must also revalue GMPs for such members at the same rate by which they would have been revalued under the transferring scheme, although it may allow for alternative methods of revaluation.

Where (i) the transferring scheme and the receiving scheme apply to employment with the same employer, or (ii) the transfer is a bulk transfer as a consequence of a financial transaction between the employers, or (iii) the employers are part of the same corporate group (consisting of a holding company and one or more subsidiaries, within the meaning of *CA 2006, s 1159*), then neither of conditions (*a*) or (*b*) above applies (*Contracting-out Transfer Regulations, regs 4* and *9*). However, in the case of any post-1997 COSR rights, the transfer must be made in accordance with conditions set out in *Occupational Pension Schemes (Preservation of Benefit) Regulations 1991 (SI 1991/167), reg 12(3)* (the '*Preservation Regulations*') (see CHAPTER 6).

Transfers from a contracted-out salary related scheme to a contracted-out money purchase scheme or a contracted-out personal pension scheme

4.52 A transfer in respect of a member's GMP and post-1997 COSR rights can be made from a COSR scheme to a COMP scheme if:

(*a*) the member consents in writing;

(*b*) in the case of a contracted-out occupational scheme, the member is either employed by an employer who contributes to the receiving scheme or has previously been a member of the receiving scheme;

(*c*) the transfer payment is applied so as to provide money purchase benefits under the receiving scheme for or in respect of the member; and

(*d*) if the transfer includes a GMP, the amount of the transfer payment is at least equal to the cash equivalent of the GMP (*Contracting-out Transfer Regulations, regs 5* and *10*).

It may also be possible to transfer a member's rights to another occupational or personal pension scheme without consent, provided that the requirements of *Preservation Regulations, reg 12* are satisfied (see CHAPTER 6).

Transfers from a contracted-out money purchase scheme to a contracted-in money purchase scheme or a contracted-in personal pension scheme

4.53 A transfer can be made from a COMP scheme to a contracted-in salary related scheme, but only in respect of the member's accrued rights in excess of his protected rights (*PSA 1993, s 96*). However, in certain circumstances, transfer payments including protected rights may be made to occupational pension schemes which were formerly contracted-out schemes and which continue to be under HMRC supervision (*Protected Rights Transfer Regulations, reg 4A*).

Transfers from a contracted-out money purchase scheme to another contracted-out money purchase scheme or a contracted-out personal pension scheme

4.54 A transfer in respect of a member's protected rights can be made from a COMP scheme to another COMP scheme (or the money purchase part of a COMB scheme) or contracted-out personal pension scheme (*PSA 1993, s 28*) if:

(*a*) the member consents in writing (or without member consent where the transfer payment is made from a stakeholder scheme which has commenced winding-up to another stakeholder scheme and *Stakeholder Pension Schemes Regulations 2000 (SI 2000/1403), reg 6* is complied with);

(*b*) the part of the transfer payment representing protected rights is of an amount which is at least equal to the cash equivalent of those rights, as calculated and verified in accordance with the requirements of *PSA 1993, s 97* (see CHAPTER 6);

(*c*) the transfer payment is applied to provide money purchase benefits for or in respect of the member; and

(*d*) in the case of a contracted-out occupational scheme, the member is either employed by an employer who contributes to the receiving scheme or has previously been a member of the receiving scheme (*Protected Rights Transfer Regulations, reg 3B*).

It is also possible to make such a transfer payment to a contracted-out occupational pension scheme without the member's consent, if:

(i) conditions (*b*) and (*c*) are satisfied;

(ii) the transferring scheme is or was previously a COMP scheme (or the money purchase part of a COMB scheme);

(iii) the trustees have given three months' written notice to the member's last known postal or e-mail address and have not received any written objections; and

(iv) the transferring scheme and the receiving scheme (a) apply to employment with the same employer, or (b) apply to employment with different employers, the transfer is a bulk transfer and either is a consequence of a financial transaction between the employers or the employers are connected as described in *Preservation Regulations, reg 12(2)*.

Alternatively, the requirement in (iii) can be dispensed with and replaced with just one month's notification (and no opportunity to object) if the actuary certifies to the trustees of the transferring scheme that the transfer credits for the members' protected rights in the receiving scheme are, broadly, no less favourable than the rights to be transferred (*Protected Rights Transfer Regulations, reg 3C*).

Transfers from a contracted-out money purchase scheme to a contracted-out salary related scheme

4.55 A transfer in respect of a member's protected rights can be made from a COMP scheme to a COSR scheme if:

(*a*) the member consents in writing;

(*b*) the part of the transfer payment representing protected rights is of an amount which is at least equal to the cash equivalent of those rights, as calculated and verified in accordance with the requirements of *PSA 1993, s 97* (see CHAPTER 6);

(*c*) the member is either employed by an employer who contributes to the receiving scheme or has previously been a member of the receiving scheme;

(*d*) any part of the transfer payment representing pre-1997 protected rights must be used to provide a GMP in accordance with the *Protected Rights Transfer Regulations*; and

(*e*) any part of the transfer payment representing post-1997 protected rights must be used to provide the member with contracted-out rights under the rules of the receiving scheme (*Protected Rights Transfer Regulations, reg 4*).

Transfers between contracted-out arrangements: tabulated summary

4.56

	Type of transfer	**Is transfer permitted?**		**Conditions**
		GMP	Post-1997 rights	
1.	*Contracted-out salary related* to *contracted-in salary related*	Rights over GMP may not be transferred	Rights over post-1997 COSR rights may be transferred	**Not applicable**
2.	*Contracted-out salary related* to *contracted-out salary related*	Yes – subject to conditions	Yes – subject to conditions	Except in the case of employments with the same employer, connected employers and bulk transfers (where (*a*) and (*b*) below will not apply, but conditions set out in the *Preservation Regulations* will): (*a*) member consents (*b*) member employed by employer who contributes to or has previously been member of, receiving scheme (*c*) receiving scheme's rules apply required conditions to transferred GMPs (*d*) part of transfer representing post-1997 rights applied to provide rights as if accrued in receiving scheme
3.	*Contracted-out salary related* to *contracted-out money purchase*	Yes – subject to conditions	Yes – subject to conditions	Except in certain cases (where member consent is not required and *Preservation Regulations* will apply): (*a*) member consents (*b*) member employed by employer who contributes to or has previously been member of, receiving scheme (*c*) transfer payment applied to provide money purchase benefits under receiving scheme (*d*) if transfer includes GMP, transfer payment is at least equal to cash equivalent of GMP

4.	*Contracted-out salary related* to *contracted-out personal pension*	Yes – subject to conditions	Yes – subject to conditions	See 3 above but condition (*b*) does not apply
5.	*Contracted-out money purchase* to *contracted-in money purchase*	Protected right cannot generally be transferred. If protected rights are separately identifiable, excess rights can be transferred.		Not applicable
6.	*Contracted-out money purchase* to *contracted-in personal pension*	Protected right cannot be transferred. If protected rights are separately identifiable, excess rights can be transferred.		Not applicable
7.	*Contracted-out money purchase* to *contracted-out money purchase*	Yes – subject to conditions		(*a*) Either: (i) member consents, and member employed by employer who contributes to or has previously been member of, receiving scheme; or (ii) the notice and/or actuarial requirements in the *Protected Rights Transfer Regulations* are satisfied and the employers are connected (*b*) member employed by employer who contributes to or has previously been member of, receiving scheme (*c*) transfer payment representing protected rights is at least equal to cash equivalent of those rights (*d*) transfer payment is applied to provide money purchase benefits

8.	*Contracted-out money purchase to contracted-out personal pension*	Yes – subject to conditions	See 7 above but condition (*b*) does not apply
9.	*Contracted-out* *defined contributions to contracted-out salary related*	Yes – subject to conditions	(*a*) member consents (*b*) transfer payment representing protected rights is at least equal to cash equivalent of those rights (*c*) member employed by employer who contributes to/or has previously been member of, receiving scheme (*d*) transfer payment representing pre-1997 protected rights used to provide a GMP (*e*) transfer payment representing post-1997 protected rights used to provide contracted-out rights

Termination of contracted-out employment

4.57 Full details of the procedures which must be adopted following the cessation of contracted-out employment are given in the manuals entitled 'Termination of Contracted-out Employment'. There is a manual for Salary Related Pension Schemes and Salary Related Parts of Mixed Benefit Schemes (CA14), and one for Money Purchase Pension Schemes and Money Purchase Parts of Mixed Benefits Schemes (CA14A). There is also a manual entitled 'Cessation of Contracted-out Pension Schemes' (CA15). All are available from the HMRC website.

When does contracted-out employment cease?

4.58 A member will be treated as having ceased to be in contracted-out employment if:

(*a*) his contract of service expires or is terminated;

(*b*) in the absence of a contract of service, the service itself has ended;

(*c*) the contracting-out certificate by virtue of which his employment was contracted out has been surrendered or cancelled;

(*d*) the contracting-out certificate by virtue of which his employment was contracted out has been varied in such a way that the certificate no longer applies to his employment;

(*e*) he has ceased to be within the description of earners covered by the contracting-out certificate or he has ceased to be a member of a contracted-out scheme; or

(*f*) his employer dies or disposes of the whole or part of his business so that the member ceases to be employed by that employer and the contracted-out employment is not, or cannot be, treated as continuing with any new employer (*Contracting-out Regulations, reg 43*).

In such circumstances, a notification will usually have to be made to HRMC (*Contracting-out Regulations, reg 44*).

When is a member's contracted-out employment treated as not having ceased?

4.59 A member's contracted-out employment will not be treated as having ceased if:

(*a*) where his service or contract of service had ended, within six months he resumes membership of the same scheme either as a result of employment with the same employer or employment with a new employer. Certain other conditions must also be satisfied in order for the member to continue in contracted-out employment for example, his accrued rights to GMP, post-1997 COSR rights and/or protected rights must not have been secured outside the scheme. Furthermore, the total period of contracted-out employment will not include any intervals between employments;

(*b*) where the contracting-out certificate had been varied, surrendered or cancelled, within six months he becomes a member in contracted-out employment of another contracted-out scheme under the same employer to which his accrued rights to GMP, post-1997 COSR rights and/or protected rights are transferred;

(*c*) where he had ceased to fall within the scope of the contracting-out certificate or to be a member of the scheme, within six months he again falls within the scope, or he becomes a member in contracted-out employment, of another contracted-out scheme under the same employer to which his accrued rights to GMP, post-1997 COSR rights and/or protected rights are transferred;

(*d*) where his employer had died or otherwise ceased to be the employer and the business is taken over by a new employer, he continues to be treated as being in contracted-out employment, the new employer accepts all the responsibilities of the former employer for any outstanding contributions or premiums, and the new employer notifies HMRC of the change within one month of it taking place (*Contracting-out Regulations, reg 43*).

The Regulations also make provision about the treatment of women returning to work after pregnancy or confinement, earners employed outside Great Britain, and concurrent employment in two or more contracted-out employments by reference to the same scheme and with the same employer.

Securing contracted-out rights when a member leaves a scheme

4.60 Where a member's pensionable service terminates after he has completed two years of qualifying service, he is entitled to a preserved benefit under the scheme (see CHAPTER 6). In the case of a contracted-out scheme, the member's protected rights or GMP and post-1997 COSR rights, as appropriate, will form part of the preserved benefit and, as such, must be appropriately revalued and secured. In each case, a member's rights may be secured by means of a scheme pension, transfer payment, lump sum or annuity purchase (see, in particular, **4.22** and **4.23** above in relation to GMPs, and **4.39** onwards in relation to protected rights).

A member who leaves pensionable service with more than three months but less than two years of qualifying service will be entitled to a refund of his contributions or a transfer payment to another scheme. Anyone leaving with less than three months' pensionable service would usually be entitled only to a refund of contributions (see CHAPTER 6).

In circumstances where the member has less than two years of contracted-out service in a COSR scheme, it may be possible to reinstate his rights into the State scheme by the trustees of the scheme paying to HMRC a 'contributions equivalent premium' (*PSA 1993, ss 55–58* and *Contracting-out Regulations, regs 51* and *52*). The consequence of paying such a premium is that the member is treated as if he had not contracted out for the period in respect of which the premium was paid. The member's protected rights or accrued GMP and post-1997 COSR rights, as appropriate, are extinguished (*PSA 1993, s 60*).

Anti-franking

4.61 The GMPs of early leavers are protected by the principle of 'anti-franking', and the legislation relating to anti-franking is contained in *PSA 1993, ss 87–92*.

The purpose of this legislation is to prevent the relevant pension benefits, broadly those in excess of GMP, from being eroded by financing the cost of providing for the revaluation of GMP rights out of that excess (ie by 'franking' that cost).

The legislation principally applies where the member ceases to be in contracted-out employment (on a salary related basis) before the date on which his GMP under that scheme commences. It will be relevant where, immediately after ceasing to be a member of the scheme, the value of his pension in payment or his revalued deferred pension exceeds the value of his GMP rights at that time and the GMP, when it comes into payment, is greater than it was when contracted-out employment ceased (which it generally will be).

PSA 1993, s 87(3) prescribes a minimum level of benefits which must be provided when the pension is required to be paid:

(*a*) where the pension has been provided as a substitute for short service benefit, the value of the deferred pension; and

(*b*) in any other case, the aggregate of:

- the value of his pension in payment or his revalued deferred pension;
- the amount by which the value of his pension in payment or his revalued deferred pension exceeded the value of his GMP rights immediately after he ceased to be in the scheme;

- an additional amount comprising the member's pension, if any, accrued after he ceased to be contracted out on a salary related basis, together with any increases due to postponement on the non-GMP part of his pension accrued before that time; and
- a further additional amount in respect of any pension accrued after the member ceased to be contracted out on a salary related basis, based on the amount by which the non-GMP element of his pension would have increased from the date he ceased to be contracted out on a salary related basis to the earlier of the date he took his pension or left the scheme.

The legislation provides equivalent protection in relation to GMPs for surviving spouses and civil partners.

Supervision of formerly contracted-out schemes

4.62 When a scheme ceases to be contracted out, members' protected rights or accrued GMPs and post-1997 COSR rights, as appropriate, may be preserved in the scheme or transferred out in accordance with arrangements approved by HMRC (*PSA 1993, s 50* and *Contracting-out Regulations, reg 45*).

HMRC has a duty to continue to supervise schemes which have lost their contracted-out status in circumstances where the scheme still holds accrued rights to GMPs, post-1997 COSR rights and/or protected rights (*PSA 1993, ss 52* and *53*). The trustees of such a scheme can be directed to take (or refrain from) such action as HMRC may, in writing, specify (*PSA 1993, s 53(1)*). This will usually take the form of monitoring the funding of the scheme, by requiring actuarial certification, so as to ensure that the scheme has sufficient assets to meet its liabilities for protected rights or accrued GMPs and post-1997 salary related contracted-out rights, as appropriate.

Stakeholder schemes

4.63 It is possible to contract out of the additional State pension through a contracted-out money purchase stakeholder pension. If this occurs, minimum payments equal to the employer and employees' contracted-out rebates must be paid to the scheme, and members will be provided with a pension based on those amounts, together with any investment return. Contracting out via an appropriate personal pension stakeholder pension scheme has also been possible since April 2001.

HMRC explains the procedures to be used where a stakeholder pension is used to contract out of S2P in 'Stakeholder Pension Scheme Manual' (CA84), which is available from the HMRC website.

Proposed legislative changes

4.64 The key change which is expected in the area of contracting out is the abolition of contracting out for defined contribution pension schemes. As was explained in the Government's White Paper, *Security in retirement: towards a new pensions system*, published in May 2006, the abolition is part of the Government's proposals to 'streamline the regulatory environment' and 'reduce administrative complexity': factors which also influenced the decision to allow the conversion of GMPs (see **4.25** above).

The legislation that will govern the abolition of contracting-out for DC schemes was included in *PA 2007* (*s 15* and *Sch 4* (which principally amend *PSA 1993*)) and will apply to both occupational and personal pension schemes. The legislation has not yet been brought into force, but it is anticipated that this will happen in 2012, at the same time that the up-rating of the basic State pension is linked back in to average earnings.

The effect of the legislation will be that any contracting-out certificates for COMP schemes will cease to have effect immediately before the abolition date, and no further COMP certificates will be able to be issued. Schemes continuing to hold protected rights going forward will still be required to meet the existing requirements for the certification of COMP schemes (*PSA 1993, s 25A* (not yet in force)). They will also have to satisfy the prescribed conditions when they give effect to protected rights by means of a scheme pension, annuity purchase or lump sum (*PSA 1993, s 27A* (not yet in force)) or by means of an insurance policy in the context of a winding up (*PSA 1993, s 32A* (not yet in force)). In particular, this will include requirements to provide survivors' benefits on the death of the member.

All protected rights will ultimately be abolished, as *PA 2008, s 106* (not yet in force) will repeal most of the provisions of *PSA 1993* dealing with protected rights. The Government's intention is that, by removing all remaining conditions applying to protected rights, scheme members' entire money purchase pension funds can be treated in the same way (see the September 2006 consultation paper, *Abolition of defined contribution (DC) contracting out: treatment of protected rights accrued in the past and proposed operational arrangements*). As yet, no date has been appointed for these changes to come into force.

It is expected that contracting out on a salary related basis will be reviewed in the future.

Chapter 5

Insolvency and the Pension Protection Fund

Introduction

5.1 There are various types of corporate insolvency regimes ('regimes') under the *Insolvency Act 1986* (*IA 1986*) (as amended) supplemented by the *Insolvency Rules 1986 (SI 1986/1925)* (*IR 1986*) (as amended) that may affect pension schemes. This chapter aims to be a general introduction to those regimes, and the relevant persons appointed under them to protect the interests of creditors. This chapter also details the effect of such regimes on pension schemes and discusses the operation of the Pension Protection Fund and the Financial Assistance Scheme.

We have restricted our commentary in this chapter to the application of the regimes on and in relation to English formed and registered companies. However, it should be noted that entities that are not English formed and registered companies may also be able to become subject to a regime if they have a connection with England and Wales.

Consequences of corporate insolvency under English law – the regimes

Company voluntary arrangements ('CVAs')

5.2 Company voluntary arrangements ('CVAs'), under *IA 1986, ss 1–7, Sch A1* and *IR 1986, Part 1*, are where a company enters into what is effectively a contract with its creditors for either a composition in satisfaction of its debts (an agreement that a debt is to be discharged by payment of a proportion of it), or a scheme of arrangement of its affairs (*IA 1986, s 1*). They are typically initiated by the directors of the company, but can also be initiated by a liquidator or administrator.

CVAs are initiated by the circulation of a proposal which is voted upon by creditors and shareholders of the company. If approved (with or without modifications) the proposal (as modified) becomes the CVA; that is, the contract between the company and its creditors.

There are presently two broad types of CVA available. The original type of CVA is one where a proposal is put together without the benefit of any moratorium against creditor claims/actions. The provisions regulating this type of CVA are found in the main body of *IA 1986, ss 1–7*. The new type of CVA is one that does provide for a moratorium against creditor claims/actions while the proposal is being formulated and put out for approval. It is, however, only available to a 'small company' within the meaning of that term in *Companies Act 2006, ss 382–465* (*CA 2006*), provided certain other prescribed criteria are also satisfied. This type of CVA was introduced into *IA 1986* by the *Insolvency Act 2000* (*IA 2000*). The provisions regulating it are to be found in *IA 1986, s 1A, Sch A1*.

The primary difference between the types of CVAs is that, under the original, the company has no protection from its creditors when formulating the proposal, but under the small company type, it does. That is, there is no bar on creditor action under the original type, until and unless (typically) the proposal is approved.

The provisions regulating the content and procedure for approval and implementation of both types of CVA are broadly the same, despite the fact that they are separately provided for in *IA 1986*.

Terms

5.3 The terms of either type of CVA will depend entirely on what is proposed and accepted (creditors can propose modifications to the proposal put to them) by at least 75 per cent in value of the company's unsecured creditors. Certain votes will not be taken into account, and/or may render invalid a resolution passed (*IR 1986, rr 1.19, 1.54*). For example, a resolution will be invalid if without taking into account the votes of connected creditors, the unconnected unsecured creditors have voted against the proposal. For the definition of 'connected' in this context, see *IA 1986, ss 249* and *435*. The terms will also depend on who are entitled to, and do, vote on the proposal, provided that (in general terms) a secured creditor (a creditor who has a valid right of recourse to the assets of the company, as opposed to only a right of action against the company – the latter is an unsecured creditor) or preferential creditor (a creditor whose claim is preferential as defined in *IA 1986, s 386, Sch 6*) cannot be affected by what is proposed without its express consent. This means that the general order of priority of payment of creditors on insolvency will typically not be affected by the CVA. That is, holders of fixed charge security are entitled to the net (less costs of/in connection with the sale) proceeds of sale of the fixed charge asset. Other assets are to be used to pay (in the following order): costs; preferential creditors; floating charge holders; and, only then, unsecured creditors. Except for secured creditors (where priority issues will be governed either by law, or if negotiated, by contract – typically, if there is more than one secured creditor, a deed of priority will have been entered into governing not only which creditor has priority to the assets, but also enforcement rights), creditors in each category will rank *pari passu* (equally) with each other if there are insufficient funds to pay them all in full.

Shareholders of the company are also required to vote (approval is by more than one half in value of those voting, in person or by proxy, subject only to any express provision in the company's articles) on the proposal (and any proposed modifications).That said, the decision taken by the creditors will prevail, although an aggrieved shareholder can challenge that decision by application to court within 28 days of the last meeting held.

If approved, the CVA binds all persons who:

(*a*) were entitled to vote on the proposal whether or not they did so; or

(*b*) would have been entitled to vote on it if they had had notice of the meeting at which the proposal was voted upon.

There is a right for creditors to challenge a decision taken in the meetings held to approve the proposal by application to court within a 28-day period, the starting date of which period depends on the circumstances. There are two grounds for such a challenge:

- the CVA unfairly prejudices the interests of a creditor; and/or
- there has been some material irregularity at or in relation to the meeting at which the proposal was voted upon.

The proposal will nominate a person to be the supervisor of the CVA. A licensed insolvency practitioner ('IP') is typically nominated. To be qualified to act as an IP, an individual must be authorised by a specified competent authority or by virtue of his membership of a specified professional body (*IA 1986, s 390*) and properly insured. If an individual purports to act as an IP without being so qualified, he commits a criminal offence (*IA 1986, ss 388, 389*). Authorisation and membership requires the individual to be generally fit and proper, to meet acceptable levels of education and to have sufficient practical experience in the field. An undischarged bankrupt or a person who has been subject to a disqualification order under the *Company Directors Disqualification Act 1986* is not qualified to act as an IP (*IA 1986, s 390(4)*). That said, since *IA 2000*, a supervisor can now (subject to certain restrictions) also be any individual who, although not an IP, is a member of a body recognised by the Secretary of State (*IA 1986, s 389A(1)*) and is satisfactorily insured.

The extent of the supervisor's powers and obligations will be as prescribed in the CVA. In a CVA initiated by the directors of the company, it is typical for the company to continue trading as normal (with its own management), its obligations being simply to make contributions into the CVA from its trading ultimately to satisfy (or part satisfy) creditors' claims. In such a CVA, the supervisor's powers and obligations will typically be limited to monitoring the company's compliance with the CVA terms, agreeing creditors' claims and making distributions in accordance with the CVA. It is rare for a supervisor's powers and obligations to extend to 'running' the company. This means the directors remain in office, although subject to any restriction imposed on them by the CVA. This can lead to some confusion for those dealing with the continuing company.

Typically, the terms of the CVA will prohibit action being taken against the company in connection with debt and liabilities bound by the CVA. However, action in respect of debt and liabilities outside the CVA will not be prohibited. This means that if the company is continuing to trade, a creditor incurred by the company after the approval of the CVA will be entitled to take such steps as it deems appropriate against the company for that post-CVA debt, including steps to wind up the company.

What effect such steps (and indeed, any actions taken by the company post CVA) will have on the CVA and the funds realised in it will depend on the terms of the CVA. For instance, presentation of a winding-up petition could default the CVA, resulting in it being brought to an end. Typically, CVAs will provide that funds realised in the CVA are held on trust for the CVA creditors meaning that even if it fails, the funds already realised can be paid to the CVA creditors and do not need to be shared with all of the company's creditors. The CVA creditors are not in principle prevented from also claiming in any liquidation of the company for the full amount of their debts, less the amount received in the CVA. The interrelationship between CVAs and liquidation has been the subject of a number of cases and is a difficult area. Presently, the leading case is *Re NT Gallagher & Son Ltd, Shierson v Thompson [2002] 1 WLR 2380, [2002] 3 All ER 374*. Among other things, it confirms the basic principle that the terms of the CVA are key and should be respected. Even if the CVA terms do not expressly refer to a trust being created in respect of CVA funds, wording that implies that to be the intention should be effected.

What happens to the contracts of employees will depend upon the circumstances. It may be that the company seeks to terminate some employment contracts, leaving the employees with claims bound by the CVA. Alternatively, the company may decide that as it is continuing to trade, it wishes to retain its employees. How it does this will depend on circumstances.

The CVA will end when it states it will. A well-drawn CVA will contain clear and specific terms about how it will come to an end and in what circumstances, including what happens if the CVA terms are breached.

Liquidation

5.4 This is a regime that can either be initiated by the company voluntarily, or against the company by, among others, its creditors. It provides for the appointment of an IP to the company as a 'liquidator', who takes control of the company's assets, replacing, in effect, the directors, whose powers cease. It represents the beginning of the end for a company and, except in exceptional circumstances, its business, because once the liquidation ends, the company will be automatically dissolved (unless an appeal against dissolution is lodged). It will therefore cease to be a legal entity after the liquidation is completed.

Solvent liquidations

5.5 Solvent liquidations (members' voluntary liquidations ('MVL')) are used where, for example, a company was incorporated for a particular purpose which it has achieved and it is, therefore, no longer required. The aim of an MVL is to realise all remaining assets in the company and to settle all outstanding claims against it (with interest), with a view to realising whatever surplus there is in the company so that it can be distributed to the company's members.

The MVL process is initiated by the company's directors swearing a statutory declaration of solvency (under the threat of criminal liability if they do not do so reasonably) to the effect that they have made a full inquiry into the company's affairs and that having done so, they have formed the view that the company can pay all of its debts and liabilities, including contingent and prospective liabilities, in full within a period not exceeding 12 months. Once they have done this, they then call a meeting of the company's members (shareholders) to pass a special resolution (21 days' notice and a majority of 75 per cent in value of those voting, in person or by proxy) (*CA 2006, s 283*) to put the company into liquidation. The MVL takes effect from the time of the passing of this resolution. If the company is later found, by the liquidator appointed, to be insolvent, he has a duty to convert it into a creditors' voluntary liquidation ('CVL'), which is an insolvent liquidation. Unless the company turns out to be insolvent, creditors of companies that go into MVL should be paid in full for their debts.

Insolvent liquidations

5.6 Insolvent liquidations can be either voluntary (CVLs) or compulsory, the latter initiated through the court. These will usually occur where there is no prospect of the company being able to continue trading or of its business surviving in any form, and there is no option but to appoint a liquidator to collect in all the company's assets to distribute them fairly among the company's creditors in the order prescribed in *IA 1986*.

The general order of priority of payment of creditors on insolvency is that holders of fixed charge security are entitled to the net (less costs of/in connection with the sale) proceeds of sale of the fixed charge asset. Other assets are to be utilised to pay (in the following order): costs; preferential creditors; floating charge holders; and, only then, unsecured creditors, except in regards to secured creditors (where priority issues will be governed either by law, or if negotiated, by contract). Creditors in each category will rank equally with each other if there are insufficient funds to pay them all in full. The aim of an insolvent liquidation is to ensure a fair distribution to creditors of the company's remaining assets.

Like an MVL, a CVL commences when the shareholders of the company resolve, by special resolution (75 per cent in value of those voting, in person or by proxy (*CA 2006, s 282* and *IR 1986, r 4.67* contain detailed provisions about entitlement to vote)), to put it into liquidation. The liquidator will be the IP nominated by either the creditors or shareholders.

A compulsory liquidation actually begins on the making of a winding-up order against the company the liquidation is deemed to have commenced at the time of the presentation of the petition pursuant to which it is wound up (*IA 1986, s 129*).This, among other things, makes vulnerable actions taken by the company between presentation of the petition and the making of an order on that petition (*IA 1986, s 127*). If the company disposes of any of its property in that period, that disposition will be void unless it is authorised or ratified by the court. Even a payment by the company to a creditor during that period could be void on this basis. Generally, such a disposition will only be authorised or ratified if the disposition is likely to benefit all of the company's creditors, or at least not disadvantage them (*Re Gray's Inn Construction Co Ltd [1980] 1 WLR 711, [1980] 1 All ER 814*).

The first liquidator appointed to a company in a compulsory liquidation is typically the 'Official Receiver'. The Official Receiver is a person appointed to the office by the Secretary of State to carry out functions conferred upon him by *IA 1986*. The Official Receiver then has 12 weeks within which to investigate the company's affairs (*IA 1986, s 132* explains his duties) and to call meetings of, amongst others, the creditors of the company for the purpose of their choosing an IP to become the liquidator of the company in his place, or to give them notice that he will not be doing so, in which case he will continue as the liquidator (*IA 1986, s 136*). He will typically only call such meetings if there are assets in the company.

The company's business will typically cease on the company going into any form of liquidation. It will only ever continue after liquidation in exceptional circumstances (where it would be beneficial to the winding up). The liquidator's powers are very wide (*IA 1986, Sch 4*), albeit not all of them can be actioned without the prior sanction of the creditors or the court.

Actions against the company and its property are prohibited without court leave in a compulsory liquidation (*IA 1986, s 130*).This means that no actions already commenced against it can be proceeded with, and no new actions can be commenced, unless the court gives leave. The court will typically only give leave in cases where the normal process of making a claim in the liquidation is not seen as sufficient. The proving process (the process of making a claim in a liquidation is called 'proving' and the claim is called a 'proof' – the rules as to proofs can be found in *IR 1986, rr 4.73–4.85, Chapter 9*) enables unsecured creditors to make their claim in the liquidation as fully as they wish (providing such supporting evidence as they deem appropriate), which the liquidator considers in a quasi-judicial capacity. If the liquidator needs more information in order to reach a decision on the claim, he can ask for it. If the creditor is ultimately unhappy with the liquidator's decision on their proof (the liquidator can reject all or part of it), the creditor has a right to appeal by making an application to court within 21 days of receiving the liquidator's notice of the rejection. An unsecured creditor with a simple unsecured claim (for example, a simple debt claim) is unlikely to ever get leave to continue or commence proceedings, or indeed, for there to be any benefit to it seeking leave.

There is no such automatic prohibition on proceedings in a voluntary liquidation. That said, the liquidator may apply to court for a stay of any proceedings commenced for the same reasons as outlined above. A liquidator is likely to do so if proceedings for recovery of a simple debt claim are commenced.

The effect of liquidation on employment contracts is not prescribed in *IA 1986* (as it is in administration and receivership). As a consequence, there is some uncertainty as to what that effect is. It is generally accepted, although there is little firm authority on the point, that in a CVL and MVL, the employees' contracts typically terminate on liquidation, but not because of the liquidation, rather because the company's business has ceased and so their contracts are effectively repudiated. In a compulsory liquidation, on the other hand, it is thought that the employees' contracts automatically terminate because of the making of the winding-up order against the company.

Receivership

5.7 The method typically used by secured creditors to enforce their security is by appointing a receiver or manager over the assets secured in their favour.

In an enforcement context, a receiver is a person who is appointed by a creditor who holds security over a company's assets. The receiver's primary function is to use the powers given to him to deal with those assets, with the aim of satisfying the debt owed to that secured creditor. A receivership appointment is not for the benefit of the company and its creditors as a whole, but rather for the benefit of the secured creditor alone. This means that the receiver owes only limited duties to the company and its creditors. The exact extent of those duties is not clear (there have been a number of cases on this point which have called the extent into question). At the very least, it is clear that if the receiver realises any assets, he must get the best price reasonably obtainable for those assets in all the circumstances. (See, for instance, *Standard Chartered Bank v Walker [1982] 1 WLR 1410, [1982] 3 All ER 938*).

The receiver will not typically deal at all with the claims of the company's unsecured creditors. He would only do so if necessary, such as where the unsecured creditor is a crucial supplier to the company's business and so, to ensure continued supply, the receiver has to agree to pay some or all of the unsecured creditor's pre-receivership debt, as well as its new debt. This is what is typically referred to as a 'ransom payment'.

The types of receivership in this context are an administrative receivership and an ordinary receivership, often also referred to as 'fixed charge' or *Law of Property Act 1925* (*LPA 1925*) receiverships (the *IA 1986* provisions which regulate these appointments are found in *IA 1986, ss 28–49, 72, 72A–72H*); the provisions which regulate *LPA 1925* receiverships are found in *LPA 1925, ss 99–109*).

(*a*) *Administrative receivers*: appointed by floating charge holders over all or substantially all of the assets of the company, which typically means that they are appointed over businesses. The *IA 1986* does not contain a right to appoint an administrative receiver. The floating charge must contain that right. The appointee must be an IP.

(*b*) *Ordinary or 'fixed charge' receivers*: appointed over fixed charge assets – *LPA 1925* receivers being the type of receiver typically appointed by secured creditors where the only asset is land. *LPA 1925* receivers are the only type of receiver appointee that does not need to be an IP. *LPA 1925* contains a right to appoint a receiver where the security is a mortgage created by deed. Otherwise, a receiver can only be appointed if the security contains a right to appoint. (Most security these days contains a provision that provides that after the security becomes enforceable, the secured creditor can appoint a receiver over the secured assets.)

The ability to appoint an ordinary/*LPA 1925* receiver has not been affected by the legislative changes to *IA 1986* as introduced by the *Enterprise Act 2002*; only the ability to appoint an administrative receiver is affected (*IA 1986, s 72A*). Those changes mean that, unless the floating charge was created before 15 September 2003 or otherwise falls into the list of exceptions (*IA 1986, ss 72B–72H*), a floating charge holder, who prior to these changes would have had an unrestricted right to appoint an administrative receiver, no longer has that right. Consequently, the appointment of an administrative receiver has become increasingly rare.

Once a receiver is appointed, it is up to him to exercise his powers over the secured property as he deems appropriate to achieve the purpose for which the appointment has been made (i.e. to satisfy the debt for the person who appointed him). This is because the receiver is not the secured creditor's agent, even though the secured creditor appoints him. Under *IA 1986* and, to a limited extent, under *LPA 1925*, and in any event almost always also provided for in the security, the receiver is made the agent of the company over whose assets he is appointed. This agency lasts until the company goes into liquidation. So the company is liable in the normal course for the receiver's actions as the receiver's principal. Even after liquidation, the receiver does not become the secured creditor's agent, although his exact status after liquidation is not clear. What is clear, however, is that the secured creditor does not become liable for the receiver's actions simply because of the liquidation.

Following appointment, the secured creditor is not involved in the enforcement process (although in practice, the receiver will typically report to the secured creditor along the way). The secured assets are usually managed and sold by the receiver in the company's name. The directors of the company remain in office notwithstanding the appointment, but they cannot exercise any powers over the assets over which the receiver is appointed.

What deductions must be made from any receivership realisations depends upon the nature of those realisations. Secured creditors are entitled to fixed charge realisations without any further deductions following deduction of the costs and expenses of the receivership where it is an *LPA 1925* receivership, or the costs and expenses incurred in connection with those fixed charge assets in an administrative receivership. Floating charge realisations are also available to meet preferential creditor claims, and for floating charges created after 15 September 2003, for payment of the 'prescribed part'. The 'prescribed part' is a concept introduced by the *Enterprise Act 2002*. It is a sum (presently up to a maximum of £600,000) of net (after deduction of the costs and preferential creditors) floating charge realisations that must be made available for unsecured creditors save in limited circumstances (mainly, in general terms, where the amount would be small and not cost-effective to distribute).

The receiver is given powers to deal with the assets over which he is appointed. The powers given and where they can be found depend upon the type of appointment. They will often include a power to sell the assets. There are some restrictions to the exercise of that power, prohibiting a sale to the receiver and qualifying the right to sell to associated parties. An *LPA 1925* receiver will not have the power to sell, or indeed any powers other than to receive rent, and possibly insure, issue and accept lease surrenders, unless other powers are given to him in the security. The assets do not vest in the receiver, nor do they vest in the secured creditor, but the receiver is able to exercise those powers using the company's name, enabling him to pass title to the assets where necessary.

The receivership process does not prevent action being taken against the company by an aggrieved creditor. Indeed, such a creditor could issue a petition to wind up the company and it could go into liquidation, while still being in receivership. A liquidation will affect the capacity in which the receiver acts (he will no longer act as the company's agent) but it will not affect his powers over the secured assets.

If the secured assets are the only assets of the company and they are insufficient to pay in full the secured creditor's debt, then there will be nothing left for the unsecured creditors. The unsecured creditors will then be reliant for some recovery on either:

(*a*) the prescribed part (see above), if applicable; or

(*b*) successful proceedings within the liquidation, in actions that do not form part of the company's assets.

There are certain actions that only a liquidator can bring, which if successful will mean the recoveries go into the 'pot' available for unsecured creditors, and do not fall into the assets secured by the secured creditor's security.

Ultimately, the level of any recovery will depend on the level of costs incurred, and of any unpaid preferential creditors.

Contracts of employment do not automatically terminate when a receiver is appointed. The receiver has 14 days' grace after appointment (*IA 1986, ss 37, 44*) to decide whether or not to adopt any contract of employment. If he fails to take any steps in connection with any contract of employment within that period, he will (on the basis of current case law) be taken to have adopted it (see *Re Paramount Airways Ltd (No 3) [1994] BCC 172*). The liability that the receiver becomes subject to under the adopted contracts of employment depends on the nature of the receivership. If the receiver decides not to adopt a contract of employment, the contract will be terminated and the employee will be an unsecured creditor of the company (albeit some parts of his claim may be a preferential debt). See **5.16** below for further discussion of this issue.

Administration

5.8 Administration (see *IA 1986, ss 8–27* for pre-15 September 2003 style administrations and *IA 1986, Sch B1* for post-15 September 2003 style administrations) was introduced into *IA 1986*, as an alternative process to liquidation, where there is a chance of the company or its business surviving. It was based very loosely on *Chapter 11* of the *US Bankruptcy Code* and is presently the primary formal rescue process available in England. Some of the changes introduced on 15 September 2003 following the *Enterprise Act 2002* are outlined below.

Administration involves the appointment of an IP to the company (called an administrator), whose purpose is to manage the company (effectively replacing the directors, who remain in office but neither they nor the company can exercise a management power without the administrator's consent) while putting together a proposal for the creditors to vote on which achieves the objectives for which the administrator is appointed. In both pre- and post-15 September 2003 style administrations, the proposals will be approved if they are approved by a majority in value of those persons voting, in person or by proxy, and entitled to vote. Certain votes will not be taken into account, and/or may render invalid a resolution passed (see *IR 1986, Part 2*). For example, a resolution will be invalid if, without taking into account the votes of connected creditors, the unconnected unsecured creditors have voted against the proposal. For the definition of 'connected' in this context, see *IA 1986, ss 249* and *435*. What that proposal is will depend entirely on the facts and circumstances. In both styles of administration, the proposal should be put to creditors within a short period after the administration is commenced (three months on the pre-15 September 2003 style administrations (*IA 1986, s 23*), and ten weeks in the post-15 September 2003 style administrations (*IA 1986, Sch B1, para 51*) – both periods can be extended), the intent being that the administration process should be creditor driven. That is, the ultimate fate of the company should be in the creditors' hands. The administrator may, however, before the proposals are put to the creditors, do such things as he thinks necessary and appropriate (including sell the company's business) if he is of the view that it is in the best interests of the company and its creditors to do so.

Until the legislative changes introduced by the *Enterprise Act 2002*, administration was, in effect, an intermediate process in the sense that an administrator had virtually no powers to pay any of the company's creditors within the process. This meant that (unless the court's leave could be obtained to do otherwise, which was becoming increasingly common practice but recently disallowed in a 'typical' administration case) to pay realisations to creditors, administration would have to be exited into another formal insolvency process, such as liquidation. Administrators can now make distributions to secured and preferential creditors within the process, and with court leave, may also be able to make distributions to the company's unsecured creditors, effectively making it possible for administration to be a 'one stop shop'. The general order of priority of payment of creditors in an insolvency applies. See **5.6** above and the following in this section.

Until the legislative changes introduced by the *Enterprise Act 2002*, there were also four aims the administrator could have been appointed to achieve, being (in summary):

(*a*) the survival of the company; or

(*b*) the entering into by the company of a company voluntary arrangement; or

(*c*) the entering into by the company of a scheme of arrangement with its creditors; or

(*d*) getting a better realisation of the company's assets than would happen if the company is wound up immediately.

Administrations which commenced before 15 September 2003 will have as their purpose(s) one or more of the above points. For administrations which commenced on or after 15 September 2003, there is a sliding scale of objectives. The administrator must try to rescue the company as a going concern. There is no definition of 'rescue', making it extremely flexible as to what it might encompass. If the administrator concludes that the company cannot be rescued as a going concern or that the following objective would achieve a better result for all the creditors, his next objective is to get a better realisation of the company's assets than would be the case if the company had been immediately wound up instead of going into administration. Only if he concludes that this cannot be done and achieving the following objective will not 'unnecessarily harm' the interests of all creditors, the administrator's third objective is simply to sell the company's assets and distribute the realisations to the secured creditors and the creditors of the company who are preferential under *IA 1986*.

A key feature of the administration process under both the pre- and post-15 September 2003 style administrations is that from initiation (except in one limited circumstance for post-15 September 2003 style administrations, when the moratorium will not commence until later) until either the application for administration is dismissed or the administration ends, there is a ring-fencing of the company from its creditors' claims and actions (including enforcement by secured creditors). This moratorium even prevents, in certain circumstances, a creditor trying to recover its own property from the company. Such claims can only be pursued with either the leave of the court, or (after the company is in administration) the administrator's consent. Consent/leave will only typically be given when there is some good reason to, such as because the prejudice being suffered by the creditor whose rights have been restricted by the moratorium outweighs the benefit the company/administration is getting. It is unlikely that a simple unsecured creditor would ever get consent/leave.

There are some limited exceptions to this ring-fencing in the initial period of the moratorium, which include that a secured creditor who can appoint an administrative receiver is still able to appoint one. If the secured creditor does so, administration cannot happen. This gives floating charge holders some power, although this power has been severely curtailed by restrictions on when such a receiver can be appointed. The intention of the moratorium is to give a company a breathing space and to give it time to enable something to be done.

Once the company goes into administration, the secured creditors' position as regards a fixed charge is, in very general terms, protected because the net proceeds of disposal must be paid to the secured creditor. The position of a floating charge creditor is less satisfactory. Floating charge realisations are first made available to meet the administration costs, expenses and liabilities and preferential creditors. In addition, for charges created after 15 September 2003, the prescribed part (see **5.7** above) needs to be considered.

Administrators have very wide powers (principally set out in *IA 1986, Sch 1*), which include power to manage the business and to sell the company's assets. Administrators take control of the company. They act as agent of the company, however, so all actions are in the company's name.

Like administrative receivers, administrators have 14 days after appointment within which to decide what employment contracts, if any, they want to adopt, with the same consequences (*IA 1986, s 19* for pre-15 September 2003 style administrations, and *Sch B1, para 99* for post-15 September 2003 style administrations).

In addition to those changes, other significant changes are that:

- Administration is now available as an out-of-court process (previously, it was only available via an application to court). An administrator can be appointed by the company or its directors or by the holder of a qualifying floating charge.
- The time limits for steps within the administration, and the administration process as a whole, have been shortened/prescribed. For example, a post-15 September 2003 style administration will, however, end automatically after a year, unless extended by the creditors or the court.

Notifying trustees of a pension scheme of the appointment of an insolvency practitioner

5.9 The IP must inform the trustees of a pension scheme that he has been appointed within one month of his appointment. Failure to do so may be subject to a civil penalty under *PA 1995*. This is because every employer in relation to a pension scheme is under a duty to notify the pension scheme trustees within one month of the occurrence of an event relating to the employer which will be of material significance to the trustees or their advisors in the exercise of any of their functions under *PA 1995, s 47(9)(a)* and *Occupational Pension Schemes (Scheme Administration) Regulations 1996 (SI 1996/1715), reg 6(1)(b)*. Under *PA 1995, s 10*, the Regulator can levy a civil penalty if there is failure by an employer to comply with the above information requirements. The maximum penalty is £50,000 for a company and £5,000 for an individual.

This obligation is in addition to the obligation on the IP to give the trustees notice of a qualifying insolvency event occurring in relation to an employer (see **5.23** below).

Where an IP is acting in relation to a scheme or the Official Receiver becomes (i) the liquidator or provisional liquidator of a company which is the employer in relation to the scheme, or (ii) the interim receiver of the property of a person who is the employer in relation to the scheme, the IP or Official Receiver must provide the trustees of the scheme, as soon as practicable after the receipt of the request, with any information the trustees may reasonably require for the purpose of the scheme (*PA 1995, s 26(1)*). Any expenses incurred by the IP or Official Receiver in complying with a request for information are recoverable by him as part of the expenses incurred by him in the discharge of his duties (*PA 1995, s 26(2)*). The IP or Official Receiver is not required to take any action which involves expenses which cannot be recovered, unless the trustees of the scheme undertake to meet them (*PA 1995, s 26(3)*).

If an IP is appointed, the employer-nominated and member-nominated trustees of the pension scheme may want to resign as trustees of the pension scheme if they are no longer in employment. Those individual trustees that remain may be unwilling to act despite their continuing fiduciary duties to the pension scheme and its members. Under the provisions of *TA 1925, s 39*, a resignation will be effective where it leaves the pension scheme with at least two persons to act as trustees or a trust corporation, although the trust deed and rules governing the pension scheme may allow the scheme to have only one trustee. In the case of a corporate trustee, the directors may resign their directorships, leaving no directors of the corporate trustee in place. The consequences of leaving no directors should be set out in the articles of association of the corporate trustee company.

Possible claims against the pension scheme by the insolvency practitioner

5.10 Administrators and liquidators have the power to make applications to the court for certain transactions, that the company has entered into prior to administration or liquidation, to be set aside. In the context of a pension scheme the most obvious vulnerability is under *IA 1986, s 239*, dealing with preferences. A preference is given if a company's actions at a time when it is unable to pay its debts (or as a consequence of which it becomes unable to pay its debts) puts a creditor into a better position in an insolvent liquidation than he would have been if that action had not taken place and the administrator/liquidator can show that the company was influenced by a desire to put the creditor into such a better position.

This means that, at least in theory, an administrator/liquidator could make a claim in respect of contributions made into the scheme by the employer if he can show that the employer was influenced by a desire to prefer the scheme. For example, the administrator/liquidator may argue that a preference occurred where benefit enhancements occurred or substantial contributions were made into the scheme when the company was in financial difficulties.

Independent trustee requirements

5.11 The statutory obligation on IPs to consider appointing independent trustees transferred to the Regulator with effect from 6 April 2005. After that date, IPs appointed to employers with relevant defined benefit pension schemes are obliged to report their appointment to the Regulator (as well as to the Pension Protection Fund ('PPF') and the trustees). It is for the Regulator to consider whether the appointment of a statutory independent trustee is appropriate (*PA 1995, s 23*). Where any appointment is made, it must be a trustee taken from the register maintained by the Regulator (*PA 1995, s 23(1)(b)*).

An order made by the Regulator to appoint an independent trustee may provide for any fees and expenses of the independent trustee to be paid (a) by the employer, (b) out of the resources of the scheme, or (c) partly by the employer and partly out of the resources of the scheme (*PA 1995, s 25(6)*). Such an order may also provide that an amount equal to the amount paid out of the resources of the scheme is to be treated as a debt due from the employer to the trustees of the scheme (*PA 1995, s 25(7)*). Where an order makes provision for any fees or expenses of the trustee to be paid out of the resources of the scheme, the trustee is entitled to be paid in priority to all other claims falling to be met out of the scheme's resources (*PA 1995, s 25(8)*).

While *PA 1995, s 22* applies to the scheme and there is an independent trustee appointed by the Regulator, all discretionary powers of the trustees and all powers of the employer of a fiduciary nature are exercisable by the independent trustee (*PA 1995, s 25(2)*). While *PA 1995, s 22* applies in relation to a scheme and there is an independent trustee of the scheme appointed under *s 23(1)*, the independent trustee may not be removed from being a trustee by virtue only of any provision of the scheme (*PA 1995, s 25(3)*).

Insolvency of the employer and the winding up of a pension scheme

5.12 When an employer becomes subject to a regime, the following are the typical considerations for the pension scheme trustees:

(*a*) Does the pension scheme have to go into winding up?

(*b*) Are there unpaid contributions? If so, how do they rate in the insolvency? Can they be claimed from elsewhere?

(*c*) Is there a deficit? How is that deficit calculated and where does it rank in the insolvency?

(*d*) What happens if there is a surplus in the pension scheme?

(*e*) Can the IP have a claim against the pension scheme arising purely as a consequence of the insolvency?

It is common for occupational pension schemes to include provisions that require the scheme to be wound up (see CHAPTER 12) in certain circumstances involving the 'insolvency' of the employer or principal employer. Triggering events often include:

- the appointment of an IP to the principal employer;
- the principal employer ceasing to trade;
- the winding up or liquidation of the principal employer; and
- a company going from administration to winding up by way of a notice from the administrator.

In the case of a CVL (see **5.6** above), the liquidation will be from the date of the passing of the shareholders' resolution. In the case of a compulsory liquidation, it will be from the date of the passing of the order for the winding up of the company (*IA 1986, s 247(2)*). This date is also relevant as the 'applicable time' for the purposes of the debt calculation under *PA 1995, s 75* (see CHAPTER 12).

Some schemes may simply refer to the company going into 'insolvency'. Unless the context of the pension scheme would infer a meaning otherwise, 'insolvency' can probably be read wide enough to include all of the regimes, particularly given *IA 1986, s 247*. 'Liquidation', on the other hand, has a specific and narrower meaning and so would probably only be capable of being read as when the employer goes into formal liquidation (see **5.4** to **5.6** above).

Under *IA 1986, s 247*, 'insolvency', in relation to a company, includes the approval of a voluntary arrangement, or the appointment of an administrator or administrative receiver. A company 'goes into liquidation' if it passes a resolution for voluntary winding up or an order for its winding up is made by the court at a time when it has not already gone into liquidation by passing such a resolution.

Even the winding up of the scheme has not been triggered by the appointment of an IP, the appointment of the IP may result in the termination of the contracts of employment of all or most of the employees which may again trigger the winding up of the scheme. The failure on the part of the principal employer to pay contributions may also be a triggering event. However, where the triggering of the winding up has not occurred even as a result of these events, the trustees may wish to use any powers in the scheme rules to wind the scheme up or continue the scheme as a closed scheme for the future.

The trustees' powers to wind up a scheme, or take any steps to secure liabilities once the winding up of the scheme has commenced, may be affected if all or part of the scheme has entered a PPF assessment period. Broadly, during a PPF assessment period the winding up of a scheme cannot commence (*PA 2004, s 135(2)*). Also, whether or not the winding up has commenced prior to a PPF assessment period, generally no steps can be taken to transfer members' benefits or secure members' benefits during a PPF assessment period (*PA 2004, s 135(4)*). If a scheme enters a PPF assessment period, and then comes out of it by virtue of the fact that it has sufficient assets to meet the PPF protected liabilities, and a scheme rescue is not possible, the trustees are then generally required to wind up the scheme or to continue the winding up if it has commenced (*PA 2004, s 154*).

A trustee claiming a debt under *PA 1995, s 75* against the employer in a liquidation will be claiming as an unsecured creditor. In the event of the compulsory liquidation of the employer, the trustees as unsecured creditors must lodge, with the liquidator, a claim for the deficit debt called 'proof of debt' (unless otherwise ordered by the court) in order for the trustees to seek recovery of the deficit or at least a share in what is available from the fund for distribution to the creditors.

The trustees of a pension scheme can in certain circumstances enforce any debt or deficit in the pension scheme against the company (*PA 1995, s 75*). However, the liquidator, whether appointed by the creditors or the shareholders, can make an application to the court for an order to stay all actions against the company while it remains in voluntary liquidation. In view of the size of most pension scheme deficits, the liquidator is likely to proceed with such an application to prevent the trustees of a pension scheme from taking such action or proceeding with such claims.

Administrators can also generally exercise the company's non fiduciary powers in relation to the scheme using their general powers (to do all things necessary to manage the affairs of the company) (*Polly Peck International plc (in administration) v Henry [1998] All ER (D) 647*).

There are also a number of cases which suggest that administrative receivers can exercise the company's powers in relation to the pension scheme on the basis that it forms part of the affairs of the company (*Simpson Curtis Pension Trustees Ltd v Readson Limited and others [1994] PLR 289, [1994] OPLR 231*).

The decision in *Simpson Curtis* should be contrasted with another case, *Buckley v Hudson Forge [1999] OPLR 249*, where the employer was in receivership and then liquidation and was also a trustee of the scheme. A surplus arose and the court had to consider whether the receiver would exercise a discretion to augment benefits. The court held that the company could not exercise a fiduciary power of an employer. Even if a receiver had such powers, he could not exercise them because of the potential for conflict.

In cases where an IP begins to act in relation to an employer and an independent trustee is appointed, all fiduciary powers will in any event now vest in the independent trustee, so this should no longer be an issue in most cases (see *PA 1995, s 25(2)*).

Recovery of contributions to a pension scheme on the insolvency of an employer

5.13 It is unlikely that on the insolvency of an employer there will be significant unpaid employee and employer contributions. Under the *PSA 1993*, employee contributions that had been deducted from salary generally have to be paid over to the trustees within 19 days of the end of the calendar month in which they were deducted. Employer contributions have to be paid over within the time limits specified in the schedule of contributions.

If there are arrears of contributions on the insolvency of an employer an element of those contributions may count as preferential debts (*IA 1986, Sch 6, paras 8, 9*; *PSA 1993, s 128, Sch 4*):

(*a*) employee contributions deducted from earnings of the employee and not yet paid over to the scheme in the four months before the insolvency of the employer (*PSA 1993, Sch 4, para 1*);

(*b*) certain unpaid employer contributions to a defined benefit contracted out scheme that were payable in the 12 months before the insolvency event.

The amount of employer contributions that count as preferential is 3 per cent for a contributory scheme and 4.6 per cent for a non-contributory scheme (ie one where the employees are not required to contribute) (*PSA 1993, Sch 4, para 2* and the *Social Security (Reduced Rates of Class 1 Contributions) (Salary Related Contracted-out Schemes) Order 1996 (SI 1996/1054)*);

(*c*) unpaid minimum payment contributions for contracting-out purposes in a defined contribution contracted-out scheme in the 12 months before the insolvency of the employer. The amount of contributions which counts as preferential is the actual amount, if identifiable, or if not will be equal to:

(i) in a contributory scheme, the appropriate flat rate percentage for secondary Class 1 contributions; and

(ii) in a non-contributory scheme the appropriate flat rate percentage for primary and secondary Class 1 contributions (*PSA 1993, Sch 4, para* 2).

To the extent that any unpaid contributions are not preferential they will count as an unsecured debt.

Recovering arrears of contributions from the National Insurance Fund

5.14 An application can be made to the Secretary of State to recover 'relevant contributions' where the employer has become insolvent and there are unpaid 'relevant contributions' falling to be paid by the employer to the scheme (*PSA 1993, ss 123–125*).

'Relevant contributions' include both contributions payable by the employer on its own account and contributions payable on behalf of the employee which have been deducted from salary but not paid over by the employer to the scheme (*PSA 1993, s 124(2)*).

The maximum amount of employer contributions recoverable from the National Insurance Fund in relation to an occupational pension scheme or personal pension scheme is limited to the smallest of the following amounts:

(*a*) the amount unpaid in the previous 12 months on the date the employer became insolvent (*PSA 1993, s 124(3)(a)*);

(*b*) in the case of a scheme which is not a money purchase scheme, the amount certified by an actuary as necessary to meet the scheme liabilities on dissolution to or in respect of employees of the employer (*PSA 1993, s 124(3)(b)*); and (*c*) 10 per cent of the total amount of remuneration paid or payable to employees in the 12 months preceding the date of insolvency (*PSA 1993, s 124(3)(c)*).

The maximum amount recoverable in relation to a defined contribution scheme is the smaller of amounts (a) and (c) (*PSA 1993, s 124(3A)*).

The maximum amount recoverable in relation to employee contributions that have been deducted but not paid over is limited to the amounts deducted during the 12 months preceding the date of insolvency (*PSA 1993, s 124(5)*).

Any application for recovery of 'relevant contributions' is made by the person competent to act on behalf of the scheme, ie generally the trustees (*PSA 1993, s 124(1)*).

A statement will generally be required by the Secretary of State from the IP of the amount relevant contributions (*PSA 1993, s 125*).

If the Secretary of State makes a payment out of the National Insurance Fund, it has subrogated rights against the employer in relation to these amounts, and stands in the shoes of the employee or pension scheme in relation to the recovery of these amounts in any insolvency proceedings.

The pension scheme as creditor in insolvency proceedings

5.15 If a relevant insolvency event occurs in relation to an employer participating in a single employer defined benefit pension scheme this may trigger a contingent employer debt under *PA 1995, s 75(4)* which will be payable unless there is a scheme rescue.

In relation to multi-employer schemes, again a contingent *s 75* debt may be triggered by virtue of a relevant insolvency event occurring in relation to an employer. Again generally unless there is a scheme rescue this debt will be payable.

Following a relevant insolvency event the scheme will generally enter into a PPF assessment period (see **5.27** below). During a PPF assessment period, the rights and powers of the trustees of the scheme, in relation to any debt (including any contingent debt) due to them by the employer, are exercisable by the PPF to the exclusion of the trustees (*PA 2004, s 137*).

A debt due solely by virtue of *s 75* is not preferential (*PA 1995, s 75(8)*). Generally, *s 75* debts are now calculated on an annuity buy-out basis (see CHAPTER 12) and can be very large. Accordingly, the PPF may have a significant influence in whether any proposals put forward as part of an administration (see **5.8** above) are approved and whether the required 75 per cent majority of unsecured creditors can be obtained to approve any proposals under a CVA (see **5.2** and **5.3** above). The PPF exercising the powers of the trustees during the PPF assessment period will generally be able to prove for voting purposes on the basis of the estimate of the contingent *s 75* debt payable.

For the purposes of any dividend due to unsecured creditors in a liquidation or under an administration where a dividend is paid out without first appointing a liquidator, the PPF/trustees will be able to prove for dividend purposes the amount of any certified *s 75* debt due to the scheme. The trustees will need to put in a proof of debt (see **5.6** above).

As part of any negotiations for clearance or over a recovery plan to make good a deficit, the trustees of an occupational pension scheme may have negotiated security over an employer's assets. Accordingly the trustees may have security for some of the debt.

Payment of employer and employee contributions to an occupational pension scheme during pre- and post-15 September 2003 style administration, administrative receivership or receivership

5.16 If a company goes into liquidation then it is generally considered that this will automatically bring to an end the contracts of employment of the employees. The liquidation will also often be a trigger event giving rise to the winding up (or the potential winding-up) of the occupational pension scheme or, in a multi-employer occupational pension scheme, the partial wind-up of the scheme. Accordingly in liquidations active members will invariably be treated as having ceased to be in pensionable service and no further benefits will accrue and no ongoing employer and employee contributions will be due.

Contracts of employment do not automatically come to an end in an administration or administrative receivership or receivership (see **5.7** above). The administrator, administrative receiver or receiver, as the case may be, has 14 days from his appointment to decide whether or not to adopt the contracts of employment.

The statutory provisions relating to the payment of employer and employee contributions differ slightly depending on the type of insolvency procedure. The relevant statutory provisions are as follows:

(*a*) pre-15 September 2003 style administrations – where employment contracts adopted by an administrator on or after 15 March 1994 but before 15 September 2003 (pre-15 March 1994 administrations are still governed by the old law as interpreted by the House of Lords in *Powdrill v Watson [1995] 2 AC 394*) – *IA 1986, s 19(4)–(8)*;

(*b*) post-15 September 2003 style administrations under *IA 1986, Sch B1* – *Sch B1, para 99*, which applies to employment contracts that have been adopted;

(*c*) administrative receiverships – *IA 1986, s 44*;

(*d*) receiverships – *IA 1986, s 37*.

If a contract of employment is adopted by a pre-15 September 2003 style administrator, any liability to pay a sum by way of wages or salary or contribution to an occupational pension scheme in respect of services rendered wholly or partly after the adoption of the contract has to be paid in priority to the administrator's own remuneration and expenses (*IA 1986, s 19*). It will also rank ahead of any floating charge.

If a contract of employment is adopted by a post-15 September 2003 style administrator, any liability to pay wages or salary or a contribution to an occupational pension scheme (except insofar as it arises by reference to anything done or which occurs before the adoption of the contract of employment) is also paid in priority to the administrator's own remuneration and expenses (*IA 1986, Sch B1, para 99*).

In an administrative receivership, the administrative receiver is personally liable on any contract or contract of employment adopted by him in carrying out his functions. The administrative receiver is obliged to pay any wages and salary and contributions due to an occupational pension scheme to the extent that the contributions relate to services rendered after the adoption of the employment contract (*IA 1986, s 44*).

In the case of an ordinary receiver appointed under powers contained in a charge (ie not by the court), he is personally liable on any contract or employment contract adopted by him in carrying out his functions (*IA 1986, s 37*). Unlike the position in relation to an administrative receiver, there is no specific provision expressly limiting the obligation make contributions that relate to services rendered after the adoption of the employment contract. However, it would appear that, as a result of the House of Lords' decision in *Powdrill v Watson*, any obligation to make contributions relates to benefits accrued before the contracts were adopted; these contributions do not have preferential status. So, it would appear to be difficult to argue that a receiver who adopts a contract of employment is then personally liable to meet any debt on the employer under *PA 1995, s 75* or any employer contribution needed to meet enhanced early retirement/redundancy benefits due as a matter of right under the scheme.

In most situations, it is unlikely that there will be any further ongoing employer and employee contributions due, following the commencement of an administration or the appointment of an administrative receiver. The commencement of an administration or the appointment of an administrative receiver are both 'insolvency events' (see above) which will generally lead to the commencement of a PPF assessment period. During a PPF assessment period, generally no further benefits accrue or contributions (other than those due to be paid before the beginning of the assessment period) may be paid (*PA 2004, s 133(3), (4)*).

If the PPF does not accept responsibility for the occupational pension scheme either because:

(*a*) it has assets that are more than sufficient to provide PPF compensation; or

(*b*) a scheme rescue occurs and a withdrawal notice is served;

broadly, as long as back employee contributions are paid, the employer is then under an obligation to pay back employer contributions (*PA 2004, s 150(6)*; *PPF (Entry Rules) Regulations 2005, reg 20(3), (4)* (the '*PPF Entry Rules*')) and the members will be granted the benefits they would have accrued if the scheme had not entered the PPF (subject to any scaling down under *PA 1995, s 73* if the scheme is wound up).

IPs who adopt contracts of employment may therefore need to reserve for any potential arrears of employer and employee contributions that may become due if the scheme or section of the scheme does not enter the PPF. This is only relevant, however, if employees are not automatically treated as early leavers on the insolvency event occurring under the rules of the scheme with the consequence that employee and employer contributions cease to be payable.

Entering into 'Bradstock agreements' – impact on eligibility for the PPF

5.17 Before 6 April 2005 it was common for companies that were unable to continue to fund their pension liabilities on an ongoing basis to enter into an agreement with trustees to compromise a debt due from an employer under *PA 1995, s 75* in return for a payment to make good part of any funding shortfall. This enabled the company to emerge free of its pension liabilities without going through any insolvency process. These types of compromise were commonly referred to as 'Bradstock agreements', named after the first case where it was held it was legally possible to enter into such an arrangement (*Bradstock Group Pension Scheme [2002] PLR 327*). The case established that it was possible to compromise a debt once it was triggered. From a trust law perspective the trustees would need to be satisfied that the potential recovery to the scheme was greater than the amount that could be recovered if the employer went into an insolvency process.

Under *PPF Entry Rules, reg 2(2)*, if the trustees enter into a legally enforceable agreement the effect of which is to reduce the amount of any debt due to the scheme under *PA 1995, s 75* this will generally now prevent the scheme being an eligible scheme for PPF entry purposes.

This requirement was introduced to prevent trustees entering into an agreement to compromise a *s 75* debt before the commencement of a PPF assessment period where the scheme is funded below PPF funding levels.

The PPF can however compromise a *s 75* debt after the commencement of a PPF assessment period without preventing the scheme entering the PPF (*PPF Entry Rules, reg 2(3)(c)*). Following the beginning of a PPF assessment period, the trustees' powers to compromise a debt are exercisable by the PPF (*PA 1995, s 137*). There have been a number of cases since April 2005 where the PPF has entered into pre-pack type solutions where a viable business has been separated from the pension liabilities with prior clearance from the Regulator, the most widely publicised case being *Heath Lambert*.

It is understood that the Regulator/PPF will consider solutions involving the PPF ending up with an equity stake of up to one-third the equity where the sponsoring employer's business is sold to a new company connected with the existing shareholders/management. Accordingly, the PPF could for example compromise a debt as part of a CVA which will result in the pension scheme entering the PPF and a company emerging free of its pension liabilities. The PPF is only likely to agree to this (but could be outvoted in a CVA if more than 75 per cent of the creditors in the CVA approve the compromise) if it will produce greater recovery to the PPF than the alternatives. The IP should not generally be exposed to contribution notice risk if it enters into a Bradstock agreement with the PPF, as a contribution notice can only be issued if the Regulator is of the opinion that the person, in being a party to the act or failure, was not acting in accordance with his functions as an IP in relation to another person (*PA 2004, s 38(3)(c)*, and see CHAPTER 14 for more on contribution notices).

Trustees can also compromise a *s 75* debt without preventing PPF entry if the scheme's assets before the beginning of the assessment period are sufficient to meet the level of compensation that would be provided by the PPF (see **5.32** below). The scheme actuary has to provide the PPF with a written estimate of the current assets and PPF compensation liabilities of the scheme together with the effect the compromise agreement will have on the value of the assets (*PPF Entry Rules, reg 2(3)*). The PPF then has to validate the estimate and the statement provided. The trustees are only likely to agree to this, however, if potentially the compromise will result in greater recovery than the alternatives (insolvency of the employer), given that the trustees are likely to be a contingent creditor for the full annuity buy-out costs under *PA 1995, s 75*. If a debt is compromised other than by an IP, the directors of the company compromising the debt are likely to want to obtain clearance of the compromise of the debt to confirm that they are not exposed to contribution notice liability, and any purchaser will want clearance to confirm that a financial support direction will not be made (see CHAPTER 14 for more on clearance, contribution notices and financial support directions).

It is also possible (without jeopardising PPF entry) for a *s 75* debt to be compromised before the beginning of a PPF assessment period, as part of an arrangement under *Companies Act 2006, Part 26* (formerly *Companies Act 1985, s 425*), the effect of which is to reduce the amount of the debt due to the scheme under *PA 1995, s 75* which may be recovered by, or on behalf of, those trustees or managers.

As a result of the risk that a compromise in other circumstances could jeopardise PPF entry if the scheme was funded below PPF compensation levels, properly advised trustees would not agree to compromise a debt without the company going into insolvency or as part of a company scheme of arrangement under *Companies Act 2006, Part 26*. In a restructuring situation it can be damaging to the business to put a company through an insolvency process.

Under the current version of the *Occupational Pension Schemes (Employer Debt) Regulations 2005* it is now possible to enter into a 'regulated apportionment arrangement', enabling a reduced debt to be paid by an exiting employer that previously participated in a multi-employer scheme without the employer going through an insolvency process. A regulated apportionment arrangement is designed to be used in restructuring situations where the trustees consider that there is a reasonable likelihood that their scheme will enter a PPF assessment period in the next 12 months or where an assessment period has already started but not ended (*Employer Debt Regulations, reg 7A*).

Broadly, a regulated apportionment arrangement is an arrangement under the scheme rules which:

(*a*) provides for the employer to pay a 'regulated apportionment arrangement share' instead of the full amount of the employer's share of the liability;

(*b*) apportions the difference to one or more of the remaining employers;

(*c*) may provide for when the remainder is to be paid;

(*d*) is entered into before, on or after the applicable time;

(*e*) sets out the amount of an employer's regulated apportionment arrangement share;

(*f*) if a PPF assessment period has not already begun, satisfies the following conditions:

   (i) the trustees and the employer (or any employer to whom all or part of the employer's liability has been apportioned) consent to the arrangement;

   (ii) the arrangement and any amendments to it are approved by the Regulator in a notice of approval (which the Regulator will only issue if it considers the arrangement reasonable); and

   (iii) the PPF does not object.

This arrangement allows a smaller amount of the employer debt to be apportioned in order to avoid employer insolvency, enabling the employer to continue to trade free of its pension liabilities. It will be used only where the potential recovery to the PPF is greater than putting the employer through an insolvency process. In practice, trustees should not agree to the arrangement unless it is structured so that PPF entry can still be achieved on the insolvency of the remaining employer or employers.

One issue that has emerged from this is that pre-April 2005 Bradstock agreements may still invalidate entry into the PPF. This is, of course, balanced by the fact that compromise agreements occur in relation to actual *s 75* debts which will most often have emerged from a scheme actually entering wind up. If wind up occurred pre-April 2005, the scheme will be ineligible for PPF protection in any event but may still be eligible for assistance under the Financial Assistance Scheme (see **5.40** below).

The Pension Protection Fund

5.18 The PPF is a statutory fund that is designed to give members of eligible defined benefit pension schemes a measure of protection where their sponsoring employer suffers a qualifying event and there are insufficient assets in the pension scheme to cover PPF levels of compensation. It is funded by a charge levied on all eligible schemes and provides a guaranteed minimum level of payment, known as compensation, to beneficiaries of schemes for which it has assumed responsibility.

To enter the PPF:

(*a*) the scheme must be 'eligible';

(*b*) a 'qualifying insolvency event' must occur in relation to the employer; and

(*c*) the assets of the scheme must be less than the protected liabilities.

Each of these concepts is discussed in more detail below.

Eligible schemes

5.19 *PA 2004* itself, at *s 126*, does not specify many eligibility conditions. It merely comments that an eligible scheme is one which is not a defined contributions scheme and is not a scheme of a 'prescribed description'. However, these have since been supplemented by the voluminous *Pension Protection Fund (Entry Rules) Regulations 2005 (SI 2005/590)* (the '*PPF Entry Rules*'). These set out a number of specific circumstances where a scheme will not be eligible.

Excluded schemes

5.20 The list of excluded schemes is fairly predictable and can be found in *PPF Entry Rules, reg 2*. Local government schemes and many other public sector schemes are excluded, often because they are backed up with a Crown guarantee. Unregistered schemes that are not statutory schemes also fall outside the PPF's remit, along with schemes that are administered outside the UK or are for employees outside the UK. Schemes which only provide death benefits or, in the case of a contracted-out centralised scheme, provide only lump sum benefits, are also excluded.

The number of members in a scheme can also be grounds for its exclusion from the PPF. A scheme with fewer than two members, or where there are less than 12 members and all are trustees making unanimous decisions (or it has a registered independent trustee), will not be able to enter the PPF.

A scheme which does not have an employer as at 6 April 2005 will also be ineligible.

However, after the beginning of a PPF assessment period, if a scheme becomes unregistered, or as a result of members dying it ceases to have a sufficient number of members, it will still be eligible for the PPF as a result of the *PPF Entry Rules*.

Date of winding up

5.21 If the scheme was being wound up prior to 6 April 2005 it will not be an eligible scheme for the PPF (*PA 2004, s 126(2)*; *Pension Protection Fund (Eligible Schemes) Appointed Day Order 2005 (SI 2005/599)*).

Previous status of the scheme

5.22 If a scheme has not been eligible for the past three years from the date on which a PPF assessment period begins (see **5.27** below), or was not eligible since the date of its inception, the PPF need not assume responsibility for it. Likewise, if the scheme was established to replace an existing non-eligible scheme within the last three years, it will not be taken into the PPF (*PA 2004, s 146*; *PPF Entry Rules, regs 21, 22*).

Qualifying insolvency events

Insolvency events

5.23 There are two separate tests when determining whether a qualifying insolvency event has occurred in relation to an employer. First, the employer must suffer an 'insolvency event', and second it must be considered to be a 'qualifying insolvency event'. *PA 2004, s 121* lists the insolvency events. It sets out the particular events that must occur in relation to different types of corporate entity. In relation to companies, which will arguably be of most relevance, it is a fairly wide-ranging list and essentially seeks to catch most insolvency events except those that are solvent liquidations such as a members' voluntary liquidation. For the sake of completeness, in relation to a company, these are:

- the nominee in relation to a proposal for a voluntary arrangement under *IA 1986, Part I* submits a report to the court under *IA 1986, s 2* (procedure where nominee is not the liquidator or administrator) which states that, in his opinion, meetings of the company and its creditors should be summoned to consider the proposal;
- the directors of the company file with the court documents and statements in accordance with *IA 1986, Sch A1, para 7(1)* (moratorium where directors propose voluntary arrangement);
- an administrative receiver within the meaning of *IA 1986, s 251* is appointed in relation to the company;
- the company enters administration within the meaning of *IA 1986, Sch B1, para 1(2)(b)*;
- a resolution is passed for a voluntary winding up of the company without a declaration of solvency under *IA 1986, s 89*;
- a meeting of creditors is held in relation to the company under *IA 1986, s 95* (creditors' meeting which has the effect of converting a members' voluntary winding up into a creditors' voluntary winding up); and
- an order for the winding up of the company is made by the court under *IA 1986, Part IV or V* (*PA 2004, s 121(3)*).

The *PPF Entry Rules* set out further events that will constitute an insolvency event in respect of a company:

- an administration order is made by the court in respect of the company by virtue of any enactment which applies *IA 1986, Part II* (administration orders) (with or without modification);
- a notice from an administrator under *IA 1986, Sch B1, para 83(3)* (moving from administration to creditors' voluntary liquidation) in relation to the company is registered by the registrar of companies;
- the company moves from administration to winding up pursuant to an order of the court under *IR 1986, r 2.132* (conversion of administration to winding up – power of court); or
- an administrator or liquidator of the company, being the nominee in relation to a proposal for a voluntary arrangement under *IA 1986, Part I* (company voluntary arrangements), summons meetings of the company and of its creditors, to consider the proposal, in accordance with *IA 1986, s 3(2)* (summoning of meetings) (*PPF Entry Rules, reg 5*).

The *PPF Entry Rules* also assist in dealing with entities other than partnerships, companies and individuals, for example, building societies and friendly societies (*PPF Entry Rules, reg 5*). Likewise, entities that cannot suffer an insolvency event, such as certain public bodies and charities that are not a body corporate, are dealt with in *PPF Entry Rules, reg 7*.

The mechanism for those entities allows the trustees to make an application to the PPF to assume responsibility for the scheme, even though the employer cannot suffer the relevant insolvency event, by stating that the employer will not continue as a going concern. This is not a route for trustees generally to choose. It is specifically for those schemes which cannot suffer a relevant insolvency event, and generally only schemes with public bodies or charities as an employer can take advantage of this (see **5.29** below).

Becoming a qualifying insolvency event

5.24 Any of these insolvency events in isolation will not trigger a PPF assessment period (see **5.27** below), as the 'insolvency event' must be a 'qualifying insolvency event'. To be a 'qualifying' event, in accordance with *PA 2004, s 127(3)*, it must occur on or after the day appointed under *s 127(3)* (that date being 6 April 2005), and be the first insolvency event to occur in relation to the employer on or after that date.

Insolvency practitioner

5.25 An IP has a duty to give a notice to the Board of the PPF, the Regulator and the trustees or manager of an affected scheme if a qualifying insolvency event occurs in relation to that employer. It must give that notice within the 'notification period', which the *PPF Entry Rules* set as being within 14 days of the IP becoming aware of the qualifying insolvency event (*PA 2004, s 120*; *PPF Entry Rules, reg 4*).

The IP will then make a decision as to whether a 'scheme rescue' is possible. Where he believes it is not possible, he must confirm this with a 'scheme failure notice' or, alternatively, if a scheme rescue has occurred he must issue a 'withdrawal notice'. In looking at whether a scheme rescue is possible, the IP should turn to the *PPF Entry Rules*. These provide that a rescue occurs where the employer will continue as a going concern or where another company has taken on the pension liabilities. The *PPF Entry Rules* also set out the required contents of these notices (*PA 2004, s 122*; *PPF Entry Rules, regs 4, 9*).

In order to become binding, the Board of the PPF must issue a determination notice. This determines whether the IP was required to give the notice and whether it complies with the requirements of the *PPF Entry Rules*. The Board of the PPF can issue the notice itself where the IP has failed to do so (*PA 2004, ss 123, 125*; *PPF Entry Rules, reg 13*).

Protected liabilities

5.26 *PA 2004, Sch 7* highlights how compensation will be paid, and is set out later in this chapter (see **5.32** below). However, the amount of compensation payable needs to be separated from the concept of protected liabilities, of which compensation only forms a part. The PPF will look at the assets of the scheme in question to determine whether they will meet the 'protected liabilities' of the scheme (*PA 2004, s 131*). It will be this that goes towards ascertaining whether the PPF will assume responsibility of the scheme under *PA 2004, s 127* or *128* (see **5.27** below). The protected liabilities are made up of the cost of securing the PPF level of compensation together with the liabilities of the scheme which are not liabilities in respect of a member (ie third party debts) and the cost of winding up the scheme.

PPF assessment periods and entry into the PPF – single employer schemes

5.27 A scheme can only enter the PPF once it has been through an assessment period (*PA 2004, s 132*). Where a 'qualifying insolvency event' (see **5.24** above) occurs in relation to the employer of an eligible scheme (see **5.19** above), the PPF assessment period will begin. It is during this period that the PPF will decide whether or not to assume responsibility for the scheme. The PPF assessment period begins with the occurrence of the qualifying insolvency event and ends:

(*a*) when the Board of the PPF ceases to be involved with the scheme (*PA 2004, s 149*); or

(*b*) when the trustees of managers receive a transfer notice under *PA 2004, s 160*; or

(*c*) where, although no scheme rescue has occurred, there are sufficient assets to meet the protected liabilities of the scheme and the other conditions of *PA 2004, s 154(2)* have been met.

During the assessment period, the PPF will try to assess whether the value of the scheme's assets are less than the scheme's protected liabilities (see **5.26** above), which will be through an actuarial valuation (*PA 2004, s 143*). They will also be looking at whether a scheme rescue can be effected, which the *PPF Entry Rules* show to be the employer continuing as a going concern or another entity becoming responsible for the pension liabilities. During the assessment period, a number of restrictions will apply to the scheme and these are dealt with in **5.30** below.

The sequence of events during the PPF assessment period in relation to a single employer scheme under *PA 2004, s 127* is as follows.

(1) The sponsoring employer undergoes a qualifying insolvency event. This marks the beginning of the PPF assessment period (*PA 2004, s 132(2)(a)*).

(2) The IP issues a *s 120* notice. The *s 120* notice is given to the Board, the Regulator and the trustees to the effect that the insolvency event has occurred in relation to the employer. Notification must be given within 14 days beginning on the later of the insolvency date and the date on which the IP becomes aware of the existence of the scheme (*PPF Entry Rules, reg 4*).

(3) The PPF confirms the assessment period has begun (*Registered Pension Schemes (Provision of Information) Regulations 2006*).

(4) The IP issues a *s 122* notice (a 'scheme failure notice'). The *s 122* notice is given to the PPF, the Regulator and the trustees to the effect that a scheme rescue is not possible (*PA 2004, s 122(2)(a)*). In relation to a company, the notice would need to state, for the purposes of *s 122(5)(b)*, that:

   (*a*) after the beginning of an assessment period, the PPF has entered into a legally enforceable agreement on behalf of the trustees the effect of which is to reduce the amount of the debt due to the scheme under *PA 1995, s 75* which may be recovered by, or on behalf of, those trustees; or

   (*b*) the employer is not continuing as a going concern and no other person has assumed responsibility for meeting the employer's pension liabilities under the scheme and the IP is of the opinion that this will not take place (*PPF Entry Rules, reg 9(2)*).

Notices may also be given under *PA 2004, s 122* that a scheme rescue has occurred (a 'withdrawal notice') (*PA 2004, s 122(2)(b)*) or that it is not possible to confirm that a scheme rescue either is not possible or has occurred (*PA 2004, s 122(4)*).

(5) The PPF issues a determination notice. A determination notice is given upon the PPF determining to approve the *s 122* notice. This will only happen if the PPF is satisfied that the IP was required to issue the notice and that it complies with the statutory requirements (*PA 2004, s 123*).

(6) The PPF issues a notice confirming the status of the scheme. Once any period for reviewing the determination notice has expired (after 28 days (*PPF (Reviewable Matters) Regulations 2005 (SI 2005/600), reg 3*), then the *s 122* notice will become binding and the PPF will give notice of this fact to the Regulator, trustees and IP(s) (*PA 2004, s 125*). The PPF assessment period will then continue.

(7) The PPF obtains an actuarial valuation of the scheme as at the relevant time (the time immediately before the qualifying insolvency event). The purpose of the valuation is to establish whether the value of the assets of the scheme at the relevant time was less than the amount of the protected liabilities at that time (*PA 2004, s 143(2)*). The scheme actuary will carry out the actuarial valuation for the PPF, but he may require assistance from the scheme's legal advisers in determining how to split the asset value of the scheme into the relevant 'segregated parts' where there is more than one employer.

(8) The PPF approves the valuation. A copy is given to the Regulator, the trustees and any IP (*PA 2004, s 144*). If the PPF is not satisfied, it will obtain another valuation under *PA 2004, s 143*.

(9) The PPF gives notice that the valuation is binding. Once any period for reviewing the approval of the valuation has expired (two months after the date of the valuation summaries issued to members (*PA 2004, Sch 9, para 9*; *PPF (Reviewable Matters) Regulations 2005, Sch*), the *s 143* valuation will become binding. The PPF will give notice of this fact, together with a copy of the binding valuation, to the Regulator, trustees and IP(s). A binding valuation is conclusive in determining whether or not the scheme assets are less than the protected liabilities (*PA 2004, s 145*).

(10) The PPF gives a transfer notice. The notice must be given to the trustees, the Regulator and any IP (*PA 2004, s 160*). Where a transfer notice is given to the trustees of an eligible scheme, the PPF assumes responsibility for the scheme (*PA 2004, s 161*). The effect of this is that:

(*a*) the property, rights and liabilities are transferred to the PPF with effect from the time the trustees receive the transfer notice,

(*b*) the trustees are discharged from their pension obligations from that time, and

(*c*) from that time, the PPF is responsible for securing that compensation is (and has been) paid in accordance with the pension compensation provisions.

The scheme is treated as having been wound up immediately after that time (*PA 2004, s 161(2)*).

Appeals

5.28 There are provisions within *PA 2004* and the *PPF Entry Rules* that allow trustees or managers to appeal against the PPF's refusal to take on a scheme. For example, where the PPF does not take responsibility for a scheme under *PA 2004, s 127* or *128* because the value of the assets was greater than the protected liabilities, the trustees or manager may apply for the PPF to reconsider and for the scheme to be taken on by the PPF after all (*PA 2004, s 151*). This application must be made in a form set out in *PPF Entry Rules, reg 24* and within six months (*PA 2004, s 151(6)*; *PPF Entry Rules, reg 24*). The intent is that the trustees get quotations from insurers to provide benefits at the level that the PPF would provide compensation at. If this is greater than the assets, together with third party debts and winding-up costs, the PPF must assume responsibility after all (*PA 2004, s 151*).

Regulations also compel the PPF to review certain 'reviewable matters' on which it has made a decision (*PA 2004, s 206, Sch 9*). Reviewable matters include things such as making a determination, or issuing a notice under this part of *PA 2004*. Any determination made may be suspended while that matter is reviewed (*PA 2004, Sch 9*). The Regulations dealing with this are the *Pension Protection Fund (Reviewable Matters) Regulations 2005 (SI 2005/600)*.

There is also a PPF Ombudsman (*PA 2004, s 213*). The PPF Ombudsman may review decisions reconsidered by the PPF, and then determine what action the PPF should take. Regulations set out the mechanics of this (*Pension Protection Fund (Multi-employer Schemes) (Modification) Regulations 2005 (SI 2005/441)*). He has many of the powers of the Pension Ombudsman, such as being able to hold oral hearings and compel the disclosure of documents. The current PPF Ombudsman is Tony King, who is also the Pensions Ombudsman.

Entry into PPF with no insolvency event

5.29 As mentioned at **5.23** above, a mechanism is included in *PA 2004, ss 128* and *129* and *PPF Entry Rules, reg 7* to allow the trustees of a scheme or the Regulator to apply to the PPF where the employer is unlikely to continue as a going concern and certain prescribed requirements are met. This is designed to catch employers who cannot suffer insolvency events, and will therefore not have an IP appointed who can make the application. The prescribed requirements are that the employer is a 'public body' or charity, or an EEA credit institution or EEA insurer. The *PPF Entry Rules* provide that the trustees should give such a notice within 28 days of becoming aware that the employer is unlikely to continue as a going concern (*PPF Entry Rules, reg 8*).

It should be noted that this mechanism does not include overseas employers, which can create practical problems achieving PPF entry for pension liabilities in UK occupational pension schemes relating to employment with non-UK registered companies (see **5.40** below for a discussion of this issue).

Restrictions during the PPF assessment period

5.30 During the PPF assessment period, *PA 2004* allows for a number of restrictions to be imposed on the scheme and further powers made available to the PPF, which include:

(*a*) no new members of any class may be admitted to the scheme (*PA 2004, s 133(2)*);

(*b*) no further contributions, other than those due to be paid before the beginning of the assessment period or contributions from the employer relating to a *PA 1995, s 75* debt, will be paid towards the scheme during the assessment period (*PA 2004, s 133(2)*; *PPF Entry Rules, reg 14*);

(*c*) benefits will not accrue during the PPF assessment period (though this does not prevent any statutory increases in benefit or the accrual of defined contributions benefits to the extent that they are derived from income or capital gains arising from the investment of payments made in respect of the member) (*PA 2004, s 133(5)–(7)*);

(*d*) no transfers are to be made from the scheme or any discharge of other liabilities (other than pension credits), except in prescribed circumstances (*PA 2004, s 135(4)*; *PPF Entry Rules, reg 16*);

(*e*) only the Regulator can begin winding up a scheme during the PPF assessment period (*PA 2004, s 135(2), (3)*);

(*f*) benefits payable to a member during the PPF assessment period will reduce to the amount that would be paid by the PPF compensation. *Section 138* also contains a number of other restrictions available to the trustee, including the ability to curtail early leaver payments.

The PPF may also make certain directions in relation to the scheme, given to any relevant person (including the employer, the trustees or anyone else prescribed by regulation). The idea behind this would be to ensure that the scheme's protected liabilities do not exceed its assets (or, if they do exceed the assets, then any excess is kept to a minimum). This is so that the cost to the PPF is kept manageable. Such directions may concern:

- the investment of the scheme's assets (*PA 2004, s 134(2)*);
- the incurring of expenditure by the scheme (*PA 2004, s 134(2)*);
- the instigation or conduct of legal proceedings (*PA 2004, s 134(2)*);
- the right to any debt owed to the trustees transfers to the Board of the PPF, though this must be subsequently paid to the trustees (*PA 2004, s 137*); and
- the amendment of scheme rules (*PPF Entry Rules, reg 15*).

The PPF may make a loan to the trustees if they are not able to pay benefits as they fall due, though this will have to be repaid with interest at specified times (*PA 2004, s 139(2)*). This is not a personal liability on the trustees.

Paying benefits during a PPF assessment period

5.31 This will be one of the key issues for trustees to consider during a PPF assessment period. They (or their advisers) will need to undertake a review of the scheme rules to see where benefit adjustment should take place. The trustees will be asked to produce a project plan by the PPF to show how they will deal with this and other issues, which they will have to prepare in consultation with the Board of the PPF.

Payments made during a PPF assessment period will be based on the scheme's 'admissible rules' (*PA 2004, Sch 7, para 35* and see also the *Pension Protection Fund (Compensation) Regulations 2005 (SI 2005/670)*). The PPF will ask the trustees to review their scheme rules and determine which parts are admissible. For example, changes made three years before the assessment date, and discretionary increases granted three years before the assessment date, will be disregarded, along with any rule that operates by virtue of an insolvency event, if they increase the scheme's overall liabilities.

The PPF may also review ill-health awards made under the scheme prior to the beginning of the assessment period (*PA 2004, s 140* and also the *Pension Protection Fund (Reviewable Ill Health Pensions) Regulations 2005 (SI 2005/652)*).

PPF Compensation

5.32 The compensation that will be paid will depend on the status of the member and the admissible rules (see **5.31** above) of the scheme (*PA 2004, Sch 7*):

(*a*) individuals who have already reached the scheme's normal retirement date, or are already in receipt of a survivor's pension or ill-health pension, will be paid 100 per cent of their entitlement;

(*b*) individuals who have not reached normal retirement date will be paid 90 per cent of their entitlement accrued up to immediately before the assessment period began. This will include those members who are still below the scheme's normal retirement date having taken early retirement.

For those limited to 90 per cent, there is a compensation cap which varies with age (from 1 April 2009 it is £31,956.32 for a 65 year old, giving an effective cap of £28,742.69)(*Pension Protection Fund (Pension Compensation Cap) Order 2009 (SI 2009/795)*). If entitled to receive 100 per cent under (*a*) above, the member will not be subject to a cap. Pension increases will be at RPI, limited to 2.5 per cent, on pensions attributable to service after 6 April 1997 (*PA 2004, Sch 7, para 28*).

Compensation will be applied differently in respect of dependants where the member has died after the assessment period has begun. In many cases the dependant will only be able to receive 50 per cent of the member's compensation under the PPF (*PA 2004, Sch 7* and see also the *Pension Protection Fund (Compensation) Regulations 2005 (SI 2005/670)*).

Levies

5.33 One of the most controversial issues that emerged from the PPF was how it would be funded. The Government is not, despite public perception to the contrary, intending to guarantee the solvency of the PPF and, by extension, the solvency of the schemes it seeks to support. Instead, it is funded in part by compulsory levies on all eligible schemes, with the balance of funding coming from the remaining assets of the schemes that the PPF takes on. Details are contained in CHAPTER 2.

Application of PPF entry requirements to multi-employer schemes

Meaning of multi-employer schemes

5.34 The PPF entry requirements relating to single employer schemes (see **5.27** above) are modified in relation to multi-employer schemes.

A 'multi-employer scheme' is defined as 'an occupational pension scheme in relation to which there is more than one employer' (*PA 2004, s 307(4)*). As a consequence, when analysing the legislation relating to the PPF it will always be necessary to establish who is an employer within the meaning of *PA 2004*. The definition of employer is considered in **5.36** below. First, it is helpful to understand the structure of the *PPF (Multi-employer Schemes) (Modification) Regulations 2005 (SI 2005/441)* (the '*PPF Multi-employer Regulations*') and how they categorise different schemes. This too affects who is an employer for the purposes of the legislation.

PPF Multi-employer Regulations

5.35 The *PPF Multi-employer Regulations* are divided into a number of different parts, and we have set out the relevant ones below for ease of reference:

Part 2	Segregated schemes: single employer sections
Part 3	Segregated schemes: multi-employer sections without requirement for partial wind up on withdrawal of a participating employer
Part 4	Segregated schemes: non-segregated multi-employer sections of segregated schemes with requirement for partial wind up on withdrawal of participating employer
Part 5	Non-segregated schemes: schemes with a requirement for partial wind up on the withdrawal of a participating employer
Part 6	Non-segregated schemes: schemes without provision for partial wind up on withdrawal of a participating employer
Part 7	Non-segregated scheme with an option to segregate on the withdrawal of a participating employer
Part 8	Segregated schemes: multi-employer sections of segregated schemes with an option to segregate on the withdrawal of a participating employer

As is clear from the headings of the different parts, these can be divided into those relating to:

(1) Segregated schemes (*Parts 2, 3, 4* and *8*); and

(2) Non-segregated schemes (*Parts 5, 6* and *7*).

A segregated scheme is:

> 'a multi-employer scheme which is divided into two or more sections where—
>
> (*a*) any contributions payable to the scheme by an employer in relation to the scheme or by a member are allocated to that employer's or that member's section; and

(*b*) a specified proportion of the assets of the scheme is attributable to each section of the scheme and cannot be used for the purposes of any other section.' (*PPF Multi-employer Regulations, reg 1*)

Each section is regarded as a separate scheme for the purposes of the *PPF Entry Rules*.

As discussed in **5.18** above, the key factors for achieving PPF entry in relation to a single employer scheme are that the scheme is eligible, the employer has suffered a qualifying insolvency event (or can no longer continue as a going concern), and the value of the assets is less than the protected liabilities. The same principles apply to a section of a multi-employer scheme.

In practice, the schemes most commonly encountered are the non-segregated *Part 5, Part 6* and *Part 7* schemes, and these are the ones discussed below. When considering entry to the PPF, the same principles apply as in **5.18** above, but with the key difference that there is more than one employer in relation to which an insolvency event may occur.

The *PPF Entry Rules* deal with the existence of multiple employers in different ways according to the provisions of their scheme's partial wind-up rule, and it is on this basis that schemes are categorised into different parts. Broadly speaking, upon the occurrence of an insolvency event in relation to a participating employer:

- *Part 5* schemes will segregate, and the part relating to the insolvent employer will enter a PPF assessment period;
- *Part 7* schemes will segregate, and the part relating to the insolvent employer will enter a PPF assessment period unless and until the trustees of the scheme decide to retain the segregated part; and
- *Part 6* schemes will not segregate and will not enter a PPF assessment period until an insolvency event occurs in relation to the last employer (or the *Rover* exemption applies – see **5.39** below).

When assessing into which *Part* of the *PPF Entry Rules* a scheme falls, it is necessary to establish whether it has multiple employers (within the meaning of the legislation), whether it is segregated (see above), and what the rules of the scheme require the trustees to do in circumstances where an employer ceases to participate in the scheme.

What is an employer for the purposes of PPF entry?

5.36 *PA 2004, s 318* defines 'employer', in relation to an occupational pension scheme, as 'the employer of persons in the description of employment to which the scheme in question relates'. This is subject to any regulations extending the meaning of 'employer' to include 'persons who have been the employer in relation to the scheme'.

The meaning of employer is extended, in an almost identical way, by both the *PPF Multi-employer Regulations* and the *PPF Entry Rules*. In summary:

(*a*) In relation to a single employer section of a segregated scheme which has no active members, 'employer' includes the person who was the employer of persons in the description of employment to which the scheme or section relates immediately before the scheme or section ceased to have any active members (*PPF Multi-employer Regulations, reg 1(2)*). Note that the *PPF Entry Rules* apply the same definition of 'employer' to an occupational pension scheme which is not a multi-employer scheme and does not have active members (*PPF Entry Rules, reg 1(4)*).

(*b*) In relation to a multi-employer scheme that is not a segregated scheme or a multi-employer section of a segregated scheme, 'employer' includes any person who before the assessment date has ceased to be the employer of persons in the description of employment to which the scheme or section relates unless one of a number of alternative conditions is satisfied (*PPF Multi-employer Regulations, reg 1(3)*). The *PPF Entry Rules* adopt a virtually identical definition save that, when a scheme is not in an assessment period, that person must have ceased to be an employer before the PPF assessment date.

In summary, the conditions provide that a person will not be deemed to be an employer if, before the assessment date:

A a *s 75* debt became due and has been paid in full;

B a *s 75* debt became due but was reduced by means of a legally enforceable agreement and the reduced amount has been paid in full;

C a *s 75* debt became due but was excluded from the value of the assets because it is unlikely to be recovered without disproportionate costs or within a reasonable time; or

D at the time the person ceased to be an employer (of persons in the description of employment to which the scheme or section relates), the value of the assets was such that no *s 75* debt was treated as becoming due.

The *PPF Entry Rules* adopt the same conditions save that, when determining who is an employer when a scheme is not in an assessment period, there is no requirement that these conditions should have been satisfied before the assessment date.

It is not entirely clear from the legislation exactly when a debt should be treated as becoming due, and this point, although discussed, was not decided in the case of *L v M Ltd [2007] 01 PBLR*. Sir Andrew Morritt VC had expressed the view in *Phoenix Venture Holdings Ltd [2005] 38 PBLR* (at paragraph 26) that, for the purposes of *PA 1995, s 75(2)*:

> 'There cannot be a debt until a sum certain has been ascertained. The designation of the time is so that the Actuary may know as of what date his calculations should be made. But until those calculations have been made in the prescribed manner the difference between the value of the assets and the amount of the liabilities cannot be ascertained and an amount equal to that difference remains uncertain.'

However, Warren J commented (at paragraph 98 of *L v M*):

> 'Whether a debt is due before it is quantified is not a question I need to answer, nor therefore do I need to say whether the decision in *Phoenix* governs the meaning of Regulation 2(2) (PPF Entry Rules).'

Our view is that it is possible to have a debt falling due even if it has not been certified. However, we recognise that it is an open point.

The definition of employer for the purposes of the *PPF Entry Rules* is not the same as the definition used for the purposes of the employer debt legislation. The key point to note is that an employer may have ceased to be an employer for *s 75* debt purposes but still be an employer for PPF entry purposes. This may create issues achieving entry regardless of the part of the *PPF Entry Rules* the scheme falls into.

Partial wind up rules – general

5.37 Having established that a scheme has multiple employers, it is then necessary to look at the rule governing the situation when an employer in relation to the scheme ceases to participate in the scheme (the 'partial wind up rule'). In this way, it can be determined whether the scheme falls into *Part 5, 6* or *7* of the *PPF Multi-employer Regulations*.

Many schemes will have a partial wind up rule requiring a segregation of assets when an employer ceases to participate and indeed, it used to be a requirement for Inland Revenue Approval that a scheme provided for a partial wind up in these circumstances. In recent years such a requirement was not always considered appropriate and therefore provisions permitting retention of liabilities with the consent of the trustees or the principal employer were inserted. Despite the old Revenue requirement, even before 6 April 2006, some scheme rules were drafted on the basis that there would be no partial wind up upon cessation of participation, just retention of the liabilities relating to former employees of the exiting employer as deferred liabilities.

For *PPF Entry Rules* purposes, the categorisation of a non-segregated scheme will depend on whether, upon an employer ceasing to participate, the trustees have a requirement to segregate the scheme, an option to segregate the scheme, or there is no provision to partially wind up the scheme. These are set out as follows:

> 'the requirement in the scheme rules for the trustees or managers of the scheme to segregate such part of the assets of the scheme as is attributable to the scheme's liabilities to provide pensions or other benefits to or in respect of the pensionable service of some or all of the members by reference to an employer in relation to the scheme … would be triggered when an employer in relation to the scheme ceases to participate in the scheme' (*reg 45* (*Part 5*))
>
> 'the rules ... do not provide for the partial winding up of the scheme when an employer in relation to the scheme ceases to participate in the scheme' (*reg 61* (*Part 6*))
>
> 'under the rules of the scheme, the trustees or managers have an option, in circumstances where an employer in relation to the scheme ceases to participate in the scheme, to segregate such part of the assets of the scheme as is attributable to the scheme's liabilities to provide pensions or other benefits to or in respect of the pensionable service of some or all of the members by reference to that employer'. (*reg 71* (*Part 7*))

Many scheme rules do not fit easily within the categories available.

Partial wind up rules – practical difficulties

5.38 If a non exhaustive interpretation of the above classification is taken, it would mean that certain schemes may never be able to obtain PPF entry. For example, there are schemes with partial wind up rules where the principal employer alone has a right to determine when a partial wind up has been triggered. Arguably, this type of scheme is not a *Part 5* or a *Part 7* scheme, as there is no requirement on the trustees to segregate part of the scheme assets, but it is also not a *Part 6* scheme as there is a requirement for a partial winding up.

The author's view is that, in interpreting the entry requirements, a purposive approach to the legislation should be taken to fit all schemes, if at all possible, into the classification to ensure that entry can be achieved.

There is a more detailed discussion of the above issues in a paper entitled 'No

Room at the Orphanage: Some Issues Relating to PPF Entry' by Ian Greenstreet and Helen Butler of Nabarro LLP, to be published in *Pension Lawyer*.

Impact of categorisation

5.39 Having classified a scheme into the relevant *Part*, the *PPF Entry Rules* then determine what happens next. In this section, we consider the impact of that categorisation on orphan liabilities. Orphan liabilities comprise any liabilities (other than those which have already entered the PPF) which relate to entities that are no longer employers at the commencement of the PPF assessment period in relation to the last remaining employer.

Part 5 Schemes: Requirement to segregate

As indicated above, *PPF Multi-employer Regulations, Part 5* applies where there is a requirement to segregate such part of the assets of the scheme as is attributable to the scheme's liabilities to provide pensions or other benefits to or in respect of the pensionable service of some or all of the members by reference to an employer in relation to the scheme (the 'segregation requirement'). When an insolvency event occurs, the segregation requirement is deemed to have been triggered immediately and a segregated part created, whether or not the relevant triggering event in the partial wind up rule has in fact occurred *(PPF Multi-employer Regulations, reg 45(2)(b))*.

The 'segregated part' is defined as the section of the scheme which is created when a segregation requirement in the scheme rules has been triggered. The segregated part is then treated as a separate eligible scheme for the purposes of the *PPF Entry Rules* under *PA 2004*, and all references to the employer are treated as references to the employer in relation to the segregated part (*PPF Multi-employer Regulations, regs 45(4)(b), 47*).

Our understanding of PPF practice is that, in a *Part 5* scheme, the orphan liabilities cannot enter a PPF assessment period until there is only one employer remaining for *PPF Entry Rules* purposes, and a qualifying insolvency event occurs in relation to that employer. The scheme will then no longer be treated as a multi-employer scheme, and the orphan liabilities will be able to enter the PPF when the remaining employer enters the PPF under the procedure for a single employer scheme.

Part 7 Schemes: Option to segregate

PPF Multi-employer Regulations, Part 7 applies where there is an option to segregate such part of the assets of the scheme as is attributable to the scheme's liabilities to provide pensions or other benefits to or in respect of the pensionable service of some or all of the members by reference to that employer. When an insolvency event occurs, the trustees are deemed to have exercised the option to segregate under the scheme rules so as to create a segregated part of the scheme unless and until they decide not to exercise that option and have given the PPF a notice to this effect (*PPF Multi-employer Regulations, reg 71(2)(a)*).

Consequently, if the trustees do nothing, the scheme will broadly be treated in the same way as a *Part 5* scheme. If, however, the trustees decide not to exercise the option and give the PPF a non-segregation notice under *PA 2004, s 120(3A)*, the IP must issue a withdrawal notice as soon as practicable (*PA 2004, s 122(2A)* as inserted by *PPF Multi-employer Regulations, reg 71(3)(b)*). Once the withdrawal notice has become binding, the PPF will cease to be involved with the segregated part and, amongst other things, the assessment period will come to an end (*PA 2004, ss 149, 150*). In certain circumstances, benefits will accrue to members under the scheme rules in respect of any period of service for which they would have accrued but for the PPF assessment period (*PPF Entry Rules, reg 20*).

Our understanding of PPF practice is that, in a *Part 7* scheme, the orphan liabilities cannot enter a PPF assessment period until there is only one employer remaining for the purposes of the *PPF Entry Rules* and a qualifying insolvency event occurs in relation to that employer.

Part 6 Schemes: No partial wind-up

Part 6 applies where the rules do not provide for the partial winding up of the scheme. Take, for example, the following rule:

> 'An Employer may cease to participate in the Fund at any time by written notice to the Trustee, and will cease to participate if required to do so by the Principal Employer, or if its continued participation would prejudice Revenue Approval of the Fund.
>
> When an employer ceases to participate in the Fund, any Members who are then in employment with that employer will become entitled to benefits as if they had then left Service.'

This rule does not provide for the partial winding-up of the scheme when an employer in relation to the scheme ceases to participate in the scheme, but provides for its employees to be treated as deferred members.

In a *Part 6* scheme, an insolvency event will not be a 'qualifying insolvency event' and the scheme will not therefore be able to enter a PPF assessment period, unless:

(*a*) insolvency events have occurred simultaneously in relation to all the other employers; or (*b*) it occurs in relation to the last remaining employer at a time when insolvency events have occurred (and IPs are still required) or *s 129* notices have been given in relation to all the other employers;

and it occurs on or after 6 April 2005 and is either the first insolvency event to occur in relation to that employer or does not occur within an earlier assessment period (*PA 2004, s 127* as modified by *PPF Multi-employer Regulations, reg 64*).

Similar provision is made in relation to entities that cannot continue as going concerns (*PA 2004, ss 128, 129* as modified by *PPF Multi-employer Regulations, reg 64, 65*). However, there is also a specific exemption (the '*Rover* exemption') which was inserted in *Part 6* following the *Rover* litigation.

The *Rover* exemption provides for circumstances where the trustees become aware that a person is (or persons are) no longer employer(s) in relation to a scheme at a time when all the other employers have suffered insolvency events (and an IP is still required by law to be appointed to act in relation to them) or *s 129* notices have been given in respect of them. In practice, this situation could arise if a solvent employer paid its debt in full after such insolvency events had taken place in relation to all the other employers. In such cases, except where a PPF assessment period has already begun in relation to that scheme, the trustees can make an application to the PPF to assume responsibility for the scheme.

The existence of this exemption avoids many, but not all, of the existing problems with PPF entry for orphans for *Part 6* schemes. However, there is no comparable provision in place for *Part 5* or *Part 7* schemes.

Technical bars to PPF entry

5.40 There are a number of technical problems to achieving PPF entry under the existing *PPF Entry Rules*.

Non-UK insolvency proceedings are not generally insolvency events for the purposes of the *PPF Entry Rules*. This can create issues in achieving PPF entry where there are non-UK registered employers who employ or have employed UK employees participating in a UK occupational pension scheme. It has been suggested that the lack of an insolvency event in relation to an employer for PPF entry purposes can be overcome by instituting secondary insolvency proceedings in the UK.

Secondary insolvency proceedings are, however, not always going to be a solution, as a court will not necessarily consent to a parallel insolvency proceeding.

If what is proposed would be prejudicial to the interests of the main body of creditors (for example, if they want to save the business and they need to sell the UK operations as a going concern), the court may not be willing to make a winding up order in relation to the UK branch. In other cases there may not be sufficient nexus in the UK to justify a parallel proceeding. If the court does not consent, this will mean that, in the case of a *Part 5* or *Part 7* scheme, the liabilities relating to the foreign company and the orphans cannot enter the PPF and, in relation to a *Part 6* scheme or a single employer scheme, the whole scheme cannot enter.

There can also be problems in multi-employer schemes achieving PPF entry if Conditions A to D cannot be satisfied in relation to all the employers (see **5.36** above). In a *Part 5* or *Part 7* scheme, this will mean that the liabilities relating to the employers in respect of whom Conditions A to D cannot be met and any orphan liabilities cannot enter the PPF. In the case of a *Part 6* scheme (unless the *Rover* exemption applies (see **5.39** above), the whole scheme may not be able to achieve PPF entry. There is a detailed discussion of these issues in 'No Room at the Orphanage: Some Issues Relating to PPF Entry' by Ian Greenstreet and Helen Butler of Nabarro LLP, to be published in *Pension Lawyer*.

Financial assistance scheme

Changing nature of Financial Assistance Scheme over time

5.41 The Financial Assistance Scheme ('FAS') was established under *PA 2004, Part 6* to assist members of certain pension schemes which commenced winding up before 6 April 2005 and thus could not benefit from compensation under the PPF. The circumstances in which applications for entry into FAS can be made by scheme trustees has been widened, and the compensation to be provided under FAS has been improved a number of times since FAS was first established. At the date of writing, the fine detail of how FAS will operate is still being finalised.

The main statutory provisions relating to FAS can be found in *PA 2004, ss 286, 286A* and the *Financial Assistance Scheme Regulations 2005 (SI 2005/1986)* (as amended) (the '*FAS Regulations*'). A further set of draft regulations, the *Financial Assistance Scheme (Miscellaneous Amendments) Regulations 2010*, has been issued with an accompanying detailed consultation paper.

FAS started life as a top-up arrangement, with FAS topping up benefits provided by pension schemes being wound up with an insolvent employer to FAS assistance levels. FAS has since evolved. The Government will now take over the residual scheme assets of the scheme being wound up, and FAS will take over responsibility for making all payments. Schemes applying for FAS entry are prevented from buying out their benefits by purchasing annuities (see below). This ensures that whatever remaining assets are available will transfer to Government to help fund the FAS benefits.

The PPF has taken over as manager of FAS (*FAS Regulations, reg 5*).

Under the revised FAS, benefits to be provided may be different in form from the benefits which would previously have been paid under the pension scheme. The Government does accept, however, as a matter of policy, that, if the 'asset share' attributable to a member from the pension scheme exceeds the FAS benefits, the member will still receive benefits equivalent in value to that asset share. In its latest consultation paper, it states that:

> 'In order to establish whether members are entitled to payments above normal assistance levels, the Government proposes that the approximate amount of annuity which could have been purchased for the member if it is wound up. The amount of notional pension can then be compared with the amount of Assistance under normal rules and the higher amount paid.'

The original FAS terms were reviewed following litigation about whether the Government had complied with the European Insolvency Directive (*Robins v Secretary of State for Work and Pensions [2007] 02 PBLR*) and investigations by the Parliamentary Ombudsman into whether the Government had misled people as to the security of their pension schemes.

There have been various improvements to the assistance levels provided under FAS over time. Broadly, at the date of writing, the benefits/compensation to be provided are as follows:

- all qualifying members of FAS qualifying pension schemes will receive 90 per cent of their accrued pension at the start of the wind up, revalued and indexed in accordance with the FAS rules and subject to the FAS cap (see *FAS Regulations, Sch 2*);
- this pension will be subject to a FAS cap of £29,386 a year for anyone whose entitlement begins between 1 April 2009 and 31 March 2010 (see *FAS Regulations, Sch 2, para 7*). A different cap applies where the pension commences from an earlier or later date. The amount of the cap is indexed each year;
- payments derived from post-1997 service are increased in line with inflation, subject to a 2.5 per cent limit (see *FAS Regulations, Sch 2*);
- assistance is generally paid from the scheme's normal retirement age (NRA), subject to a lower limit of age 60 and upper age of 65, but not before 14 May 2004 (*FAS Regulations, reg 17(2)*);

- those who are unable to work due to ill-health are able to apply for earlier access from a date which falls five years before NRA subject to actuarial reduction (*FAS Regulations, reg 17A*). Severe ill-health payments are also payable in certain circumstances from age 55 without reduction (*FAS Regulations, reg 17C*);
- the Government has indicated that members who have not started taking a scheme pension nor reached NRA will be able to take 25 per cent of their FAS payment or their share of scheme assets, whichever is lower, as a tax-free lump sum (see consultation paper accompanying the *draft Financial Assistance Scheme (Miscellaneous Amendments) Regulations 2010*);
- a surviving spouse or civil partner (and, in certain circumstances, a surviving partner) of a qualifying member may be eligible for a payment (FAS *Regulations, reg 16*). A survivor becomes eligible for payments from the day after the date the qualifying member dies, but not before 14 May 2004. Broadly, the assistance is equal to one half of 90 per cent of the member's expected pension (see *FAS Regulations, Sch 2*);
- a surviving child of a deceased member can also qualify for assistance where, broadly, they were financially dependent on the deceased member and are less than 18, or are less than 23 and attending a qualifying course, or are disabled (*FAS Regulations, reg 16B*);
- payments may be made to members whose asset share would have produced more than 90 per cent of the expected pension, had their scheme continued to wind up in the normal manner (see consultation paper accompanying the *draft Financial Assistance Scheme (Miscellaneous Amendments) Regulations 2010*).

The original scope of FAS has been extended so that, broadly, FAS qualifying schemes now include single employer defined benefit schemes that:

- began winding up between 1 January 1997 and 5 April 2005 and an insolvency event has occurred in relation to the employer (*FAS Regulations, regs 9(c)(i), 11*);
- began winding up between 1 January 1997 and 5 April 2005 and the employer paid the debt due under *PSA 1993, s 144* or *PA 1995, s 75* or no debt was due when the scheme began to wind up (*FAS Regulations, regs 9(1)(c)(iii), 12A*);
- as above, but the PPF, as scheme manager, is satisfied that an appropriate proportion of the debt was discharged or is likely to be discharged and, in its opinion, it was reasonable that the debt due has not been discharged (*FAS Regulations, regs 9(1)(c)(iii), 12A(3)*);
- commenced winding up on or after 6 April 1997 and before 11 June 2003 and the employer discharged the debt under *PA 1995, s 75* or no

debt was due under that section when the scheme began to wind up (*FAS Regulations, regs 9(1)(c)(vi), 12(A)(2)*);

- began winding up between 1 January 1997 and 5 April 2005, where a compromise agreement is in place and there is evidence that enforcing the debt against the employer would have forced the employer into insolvency (*FAS Regulations, regs 9(1)(c), 11*);
- started winding up after 6 April 2005 and before 22 December 2008 but is ineligible for assistance from the PPF due to the employer becoming insolvent before 6 April 2005 (*FAS Regulations, reg 9(1)(b), (1B)*).

There are more complicated eligibility provisions relating to multi-employer schemes (see *FAS Regulations, regs 9(1)(b), 12* and *12A*).

The key stages of the process under which the assets of the Scheme will be transferred to the Government on FAS entry, and the payment of benefits before FAS entry is achieved, are not discussed in this chapter, as they have not yet been finalised.

Surplus of scheme on employer insolvency

5.42 Although unlikely in the light of current financial circumstances, if a surplus becomes available on the winding up of a pension scheme, the IP may seek to return it to the employer (if the rules permit this) for distribution to creditors. Many rules require, or give trustees discretion as to, the use of surplus to augment members' benefits on wind up. The case of *Thrells Limited (1974) Pension Scheme v Lomas [1993] 2 All ER 546* gives guidance on some of the factors trustees may wish to consider when deciding how to allocate surplus where the trustees have discretion.

PA 1995, s 76 provides that members must be notified prior to any repayment of surplus being made to an employer. Under *Occupational Pension Schemes (Payments to Employers) Regulations 2006 (SI 2006/802), reg 7*, notices must be given to the members of the proposal to return the surplus to the employer. Any member dissatisfied with the proposal can make representations to the trustees or the employer or, ultimately, the Regulator on whether the correct procedure has been followed. The surplus in the scheme can be returned to the employer, subject to a 35 per cent tax charge, provided that all the scheme liabilities have been discharged in full, and the trust deed and rules which govern the pension scheme permit the return of surplus. In addition, if there is a power under the scheme to distribute any surplus assets to persons other than the employer, that power must be exercised or a decision taken not to exercise it.

Chapter 6

Protection for early leavers

Introduction

General

6.1 Historically, one of the main sources of dissatisfaction with occupational pension schemes has been the treatment of members who leave such schemes (usually because they have left employment) before normal pension age. (The meaning of 'normal pension age' is discussed in **6.23** below.)

Consequently, legislation was been introduced to provide the following protections for early leavers relating to preservation (see **6.2** below), revaluation (see **6.3** to **6.5** below) and transfer values (see **6.6** below).

Preservation requirements

6.2 The preservation requirements set out the benefits which occupational pension schemes are required to provide for early leavers. These requirements are summarised in **6.10** to **6.29** below.

The preservation requirements were first introduced by the *Social Security Act 1973* with effect from 6 April 1975, but have since been amended to give increased protection to leavers. They are now consolidated in *PSA 1993, Part IV, Chapter I (ss 69–82)* (as amended by *PA 1995*, *WRPA 1999* and *PA 2004*) and the *Occupational Pension Schemes (Preservation of Benefit) Regulations 1991 (SI 1991/167)* (the '*Preservation Regulations*') (as amended).

Revaluation

6.3 An early leaver's scheme entitlement under the preservation requirements (see **6.2** above) will most typically take the form of a deferred pension from the scheme (commonly referred to as vested rights), prospectively payable from his normal pension age.

Legislation requires the calculation of any such pension to be revalued in respect of the period of deferment. Two separate types of revaluation apply, depending on whether or not the benefit concerned is a guaranteed minimum pension earned in relation to pre-6 April 1997 contracted-out employment (see CHAPTER 4).

Revaluation of benefits other than guaranteed minimum pensions

6.4 This is governed by *PSA 1993, Part IV, Chapter II (ss 83–86)*. These requirements were first introduced by the *Social Security Act 1985*, but have since been revised; they are discussed in **6.30** to **6.40** below.

Revaluation of guaranteed minimum pensions

6.5 This is governed by *PSA 1993, Part IV, Chapter III (ss 87–92)*. These requirements (which were originally introduced by the *Health and Social Security Act 1984*) are summarised in CHAPTER 4.

Transfer values

6.6 *PSA 1993, Part IV, Chapter IV (ss 93–101)* sets out certain statutory entitlements for an early leaver with vested rights to require a sum of money representing the value of his rights under the scheme to be used in one of a number of ways (for example, transferred to another scheme or used to buy an annuity). This right (first introduced by the *Social Security Act 1985*) is covered further in **6.42** below.

PSA 1993, Part IV, Chapter IV (ss 101AA–101AI) was inserted by *PA 2004, s 264* with effect from 6 April 2006. These provisions give those leaving service with at least three months' pensionable service, but without any vested rights, the opportunity to take a cash transfer sum as an alternative to a refund of contributions. This is covered further in **6.58** below.

Scope of early leaver legislation

Schemes affected

6.7 The legislation referred to in **6.1** to **6.6** above applies to occupational pension schemes (as now defined in *PSA 1993*). The High Court, in the case of *Royal Masonic Hospital v Pensions Ombudsman [2001] 1 PBLR (9)* held that *PSA 1993, s 69* did not cover unfunded private sector schemes (now known as employer-financed retirement benefit schemes under *FA 2004, s 245*) as the pension promise was merely a contractual one that would be met in the future from the general assets of the employer rather than from an accrued fund.

Relationship of early leaver legislation to scheme rules

6.8 *PSA 1993, Part IV, Chapter I* (which relates to preservation) requires scheme rules to contain provisions which comply with the preservation requirements (summarised in **6.10** to **6.29** below). However, *Chapter I* does not actually go so far as to override the scheme rules if they do not comply (*PSA 1993, s 131*). Nevertheless, employers and trustees can still be challenged by members and beneficiaries for operating a scheme whose rules do not comply with the preservation requirements (see **6.9** below). In particular, it should be noted that *PSA 1993, s 132* requires trustees, where their scheme's rules do not meet the preservation requirements, to take such steps as are open to them for rectifying this.

By contrast, *PSA 1993, Part IV, Chapters II, III, IV* and *V* (which relate to revaluation and transfer values) do override the scheme rules (subject to limited exceptions) (*PSA 1993, s 129*).

The legislation prescribes the minimum protections to be given to early leavers. A scheme's rules may apply the protection on a more generous basis.

Enforcement of preservation legislation

6.9 Until 6 April 1997 the Occupational Pensions Board ('OPB') had certain functions which included powers to ensure that schemes complied with preservation.

The OPB was dissolved on 5 April 1997, and its functions in relation to preservation were not transferred to any other regulatory body. Since 6 April 2005 the Regulator has had power to issue improvement notices where it is of the opinion that a provision of pensions legislation (including *PSA 1993*) is not being complied with. A trustee or employer not complying with an improvement notice could be subject to penalties under *PA 1995, s 10*. Alternatively, a member who is not satisfied that his scheme complies with preservation could instead seek recourse against the employer and/or the trustees through an application to the Pensions Ombudsman (see CHAPTER 16) or through the courts.

Preservation

Defined terms

6.10 *PSA 1993* uses a number of defined terms in relation to the preservation requirements. These are broadly summarised below.

'Two years' qualifying service'

6.11 This is defined in *PSA 1993, s 71(7)*. It means two years (whether a single period of that duration or two or more periods, continuous or discontinuous, totalling two years) in which the member was at all times employed either:

(*a*) in 'pensionable service' (see **6.12** below) under the scheme; or

(*b*) in service in employment which was contracted out by reference to the scheme; or

(*c*) in 'linked qualifying service' (see **6.13** below) under another scheme.

There are special provisions in relation to periods of service previously terminated (*PSA 1993, s 71(9)* and *Preservation Regulations, reg 21*).

'Pensionable service'

6.12 This is defined in *PSA 1993, s 70(2)*. In effect, pensionable service means actual service in employment to which the scheme relates which qualifies the member (assuming it continues for long enough) for retirement benefits at normal pension age.

There are detailed regulations regarding breaks in pensionable service (*Preservation Regulations, reg 21*). In particular, the service before and after the break must be added together (in ascertaining whether there are two years' qualifying service – see **6.11** above) where one or more of the following conditions are satisfied:

(*a*) the break does not exceed one month; or

(*b*) the break corresponds to the member's absence from work wholly or partly because of pregnancy or confinement and the member returns to pensionable service no later than one month after returning to work in exercise of her statutory rights to return to work; or

(*c*) the break corresponds to the member's absence from work in furtherance of a 'trade dispute' as defined in the *Social Security Act 1975*.

Whether or not the break counts towards pension benefits is determined not only by the rules of the scheme, but also by any relevant employment and pensions legislation – particularly where the period is a period of maternity, adoption, paternity or family leave (see CHAPTER 9).

'Linked qualifying service'

6.13 Linked qualifying service is relevant where the scheme has accepted a transfer payment from another occupational pension scheme or a buy-out policy. The qualifying service under the transferring scheme or secured by an insurance policy or annuity, is added to qualifying service in the scheme receiving the transfer payment. The trustees will be given certified details of the qualifying service as part of the conditions for accepting the transfer payment. The detailed definition of linked qualifying service is contained in *PSA 1993, s 179*. This includes restrictions on what can and cannot count as linked qualifying service. For example, regard can only be had to 'actual service'.

'Normal pension age'

6.14 Normal pension age is defined in *PSA 1993, s 180* and is discussed in detail in **6.23** below. The term is relevant to the questions as to whether a member is an early leaver and when a preserved pension for him becomes payable.

'Long service benefit'

6.15 Long service benefit is defined in *PSA 1993, s 70(1)*. Broadly, it is:

(*a*) retirement benefits for a member at normal pension age; and

(*b*) benefits for his spouse, civil partner, dependants or others on his attaining normal pension age or, if later, death,

which would have been payable under the scheme had the member remained in pensionable service until normal pension age.

'Short service benefit'

6.16 Short service benefit is the benefit which a scheme may be required to provide in respect of an early leaver unless one of the prescribed 'alternatives to short service benefit' (see **6.24** to **6.29** below) applies instead. The definition is contained in *PSA 1993, s 71*. Short service benefit must be paid directly from scheme resources or assured to the member in accordance with the requirements of *Preservation Regulations, reg 6 (PSA 1993, s 73(1))*.

Qualifying for short service benefit

6.17 Under *PSA 1993, s 71(1)* a scheme must provide short service benefit (consisting of benefit of any description which would otherwise have been payable as long service benefit) where a member's pensionable service is terminated before normal pension age and:

(*a*) he has at least two years' qualifying service; or

(*b*) a transfer payment in respect of his rights under a personal pension scheme has been made to the scheme.

The short service benefit is generally payable from the member's normal pension age or age 65 if later (see **6.23** below).

Calculating the short service benefit – an overview

6.18 The method of calculating short service benefit is set out in *PSA 1993, s 74*.

Same basis as long service benefit

6.19 *PSA 1993, s 74(1)* requires that, except where the principle of 'uniform accrual' applies (see **6.20** below), 'a scheme must provide for short service benefit to be computed on the same basis as long service benefit'.

The application of this requirement to defined contribution benefits is relatively simple. If a scheme provides long service benefit on a defined contribution basis, the corresponding short service benefit should also be computed on the same basis (ie on a defined contributions basis). Further details regarding defined contribution benefits are contained in *Preservation Regulations, regs 9, 14* and *14A*.

Where long service benefits are calculated by reference to a member's salary at normal pension age, short service benefits must also be calculated in a corresponding manner by reference to the member's salary at the date of termination of pensionable service. Similarly, if the member's salary is averaged over a specified period before normal pension age when calculating his long service benefits, a period of the same duration must be used to average the member's salary for the purpose of calculating short service benefits (*PSA 1993, s 74(7)*).

The calculation of short service benefit in relation to defined benefits can be illustrated by the following example:

A member's pension, calculated at normal pension age, is 1/60th of final pensionable salary for each year of pensionable service. Final pensionable salary is defined as the average of the member's salary over the three years immediately preceding normal pension age. The member joins the scheme at age 30 and his normal pension age is 65. The calculation of his pension will be as follows:

(*a*) if the member stays to normal pension age, and so completes 35 years of pensionable service, his long service benefit will be a pension of 35/60th of final pensionable salary, calculated by averaging his salary over the three years immediately preceding normal pension age; but (*b*) if the member leaves pensionable service, say, at age 40, having completed ten years of pensionable service, his short service benefit will be a pension of 10/60th of final pensionable salary, calculated by averaging his salary over the three years immediately preceding the date of leaving pensionable service. This pension will be payable from the scheme at the normal pension age of 65.

Uniform accrual

6.20 There are a number of circumstances where the legislation requires that short service benefits be computed on the basis of 'uniform accrual' rather than as set out in **6.19** above (*PSA 1993, s 74(6)*). In particular, uniform accrual must be applied where the following situations arise:

(*a*) the long service benefit formula is not related to the length of pensionable service or the number or amount of contributions paid (*PSA 1993, s 74(4)*); or

(*b*) the long service benefit accrues at a higher rate or otherwise more favourably if the member's pensionable service is of some specified minimum length or if he remains in pensionable service up to a specified minimum age (*PSA 1993, s 74(3)*).

In effect, uniform accrual is required where there is no obvious accrual rate in the scheme rules or the only accrual rate available would give an anomalous result. The principle of uniform accrual is that benefits accrue evenly over the period of pensionable service (thus creating a notional accrual rate). This is best illustrated by way of an example:

A member joins a scheme at age 30 and is promised a pension of two-thirds of his salary on retirement at age 60. This formula is not related to his length of pensionable service and so, under *PSA 1993, s 74(4), (6)*, uniform accrual applies. The principle of uniform accrual treats the 'two-thirds' pension, which he will receive at age 60 if he remains in pensionable service, as accruing uniformly throughout the 30 years of his pensionable service (ie from age 30 to age 60). If the member leaves at age 45, he will have completed one half of this 30 year period (ie 15 years), so his short service benefit will be one half of the 'two-thirds' pension which he would have received had he stayed to age 60 (ie one-third of his salary at the date of termination of pensionable service).

Uniform accrual also applies (in a slightly different way) to any part of a member's long service benefit which derives from a benefit improvement granted in relation to previous pensionable service. In these circumstances, the benefit improvement is treated as accruing uniformly over the period from the date when the improvement was granted to the attainment of normal pension age (*PSA 1993, s 75(5)*).

Lump sum death benefits before normal pension age

6.21 It should be noted that the definition of 'long service benefit' contained in *PSA 1993, s 70* does not cover benefits payable on the death of an early leaver before his normal pension age. Consequently, a scheme is not required by the preservation laws to provide death benefits where an early leaver subsequently dies before normal pension age (although many schemes do provide some level of benefit in these circumstances).

Discretionary benefits

6.22 A further question which arises is how far discretionary benefits must be preserved. *PSA 1993, s 72(1)* provides that a scheme must not contain any rule which could result in an early leaver being treated less favourably for any purpose relating to short service benefit than he would have been treated for the same purpose relating to long service benefit if he had stayed in service. However, this does not apply to a rule which merely confers discretion on the trustees or some other person, so long as the rule does not specifically require the discretion to be exercised in any discriminatory manner against members in respect of the short service benefit (*PSA 1993, s 72(3)*). It is arguable that a scheme rule relating to discretionary augmentation which provides that the trustees cannot consider deferred members is discriminatory.

Date of payment of preserved benefits

6.23 Short service benefits are payable from an age no greater than 65, or 'normal pension age' if greater than 65 (*PSA 1993, s 71(3)* as amended by *PA 2004, s 263(1)*).

A member's 'normal pension age' is defined in *PSA 1993, s 180* as the earliest age at which the member is entitled to receive benefits (other than guaranteed minimum pension) on his retirement from any employment to which the scheme applies. Where the scheme only provides a guaranteed minimum pension, the normal pension age is the earliest age at which the member is entitled to receive the guaranteed minimum pension on retirement from such employment. An entitlement would arise where the member can call for his benefit without employer or trustee consent.

For the purposes of determining a member's normal pension age, any special provision as to early retirement on grounds of ill-health or otherwise must be disregarded (*PSA 1993, s 180(2)*).

Alternatives to short service benefit

6.24 *PSA 1993, s 73(2)* permits the rules of a scheme to provide one or more of a number of alternatives to short service benefit. The alternatives may be provided as a complete or partial substitute for the early leaver's short service benefit (*Preservation Regulations, reg 7(2)*).

Transfer payments

6.25 A member's accrued rights may be transferred to another occupational pension scheme, or to a personal pension scheme, with a view to acquiring rights for the member under the receiving scheme (*PSA 1993, s 73(2)(a)*). Furthermore, a scheme may provide for the member's accrued rights to be transferred, if the member consents, to an overseas arrangement. 'Overseas arrangement' means a scheme or arrangement, other than an occupational pension scheme, which:

(*a*) has effect, or is capable of having effect, so as to provide benefits on termination of employment or on death or retirement to or in respect of earners;

(*b*) is not an appropriate scheme; and

(*c*) is administered wholly or primarily outside the UK (*Preservation Regulations, reg 11A*).

Except in limited circumstances (see **12.28** below), the consent of the member must be obtained if a transfer is to be made as an alternative to providing short service benefits within the scheme (*PSA 1993, s 73(4)*).

Early retirement

6.26 The rules of a scheme may permit payment of benefits to commence before normal pension age. In such a situation, the benefits payable may be of different amounts, and be payable to different recipients (but must include the member), than applies in relation to short service benefit (*Preservation Regulations, reg 8(1)*).

However, where a scheme provides an early retirement pension as an alternative to short service benefits, the following requirements will apply:

(*a*) the benefits must include a benefit payable to the member (*Preservation Regulations, reg 8(1)*);

(*b*) it must be the case that either:

- the member meets the ill-health condition in *FA 2004, Sch 28, para 1*; or

- the member has attained normal minimum pension as defined in *FA 2004, s 279*;

(*c*) the member's consent must be obtained unless:

- his earning capacity is destroyed or seriously impaired because of physical or mental infirmity; and
- in the opinion of the scheme's trustees, he is incapable of deciding whether it is in his interests to consent (*Preservation Regulations, regs 7(2), 8(3)*); and

(*d*) the relevant scheme rule must require the trustees to be reasonably satisfied that the total value of the benefits when they become payable is at least equal to the value of the accrued benefits which they replace (*Preservation Regulations, regs 8(4), 11*).

Late retirement

6.27 The rules of a scheme may also permit payment of benefits to commence after normal pension age as an alternative to short service benefit. The benefits payable may be of different amounts, and be payable to different recipients, than applies in relation to short service benefit (*Preservation Regulations, reg 8(1)*).

In this situation, the following requirements will apply:

(*a*) the benefits must include a benefit payable to the member (*Preservation Regulations, reg 8(1)*);

(*b*) the member's consent to this alternative must be obtained (*Preservation Regulations, reg 7(2)*); and

(*c*) the relevant scheme rule must require the trustees to be reasonably satisfied that the total value of the benefits when they become payable is at least equal to the value of the accrued benefits which they replace (*Preservation Regulations, regs 8(4), 11*).

Bought-out benefits

6.28 A scheme may provide for a member's benefits to be appropriately secured or 'bought out' by the purchase of an annuity contract or insurance policy from an insurance company. The benefits provided may be different from those required to constitute short service benefit. If this option is to be exercised the trustees must be reasonably satisfied that the payment made to the insurance company is at least equal to the value of the benefits that have accrued to or in respect of the member under the rules (*Preservation Regulations, regs 9 and 11*).

Generally the consent of the member is required before benefits can be bought out (*Preservation Regulations, reg 7(2)*). However, consent is not required if the insurance policy or annuity contract to be purchased satisfies certain prescribed conditions (set out in the *Preservation Regulations, reg 9(4)(a)*) and:

(*a*) the scheme is being wound up; or

(*b*) the member has less than 'five years qualifying service' (as defined in *Social Security Act 1973, Sch 16, para 7* immediately before the coming into force of *Social Security Act 1986, s 10* (changes to preservation requirements); or

(*c*) the trustees consider that, in the circumstances, it is reasonable for the benefits to be bought out without member consent (*Preservation Regulations, reg 9(4)(b), (5)*).

In the case of (*b*) and (*c*) above, the following further requirements must be satisfied:

(i) the member's rights under the scheme must not include protected rights (see CHAPTER 4);

(ii) at least 12 months must have elapsed between the termination of the member's pensionable service and the purchase of the insurance policy or annuity contract;

(iii) the trustees give the member at least 30 days' written notice of their intention to take out the policy or enter into the annuity contract unless the member exercises the right to a cash equivalent (see **6.54** below); and

(iv) when the trustees actually take out the policy or enter into the annuity contract there must be no outstanding application by the member for a cash equivalent (see **6.54** below) (*Preservation Regulations, reg 9(6)*).

Defined contributions benefits

6.29 A scheme may provide defined contributions benefits as an alternative to short service benefit. The relevant scheme rule must require the trustees to be reasonably satisfied that the total value of the benefits when they become payable is at least equal to the value of the accrued benefits which they replace (*Preservation Regulations, regs 10, 11*). The member's consent is required if this alternative is to be provided (*Preservation Regulations, reg 7(2)*). In practice, this alternative is not widely used.

The alternatives to short service benefit discussed above may not include a return of contributions except in limited circumstances relating to service completed before 6 April 1975 (*PSA 1993, s 73(5)*).

Revaluation

Background

6.30 *PSA 1993, Part IV, Chapters II* and *III* provide for an element of revaluation to protect members' preserved pensions from the impact of inflation in respect of the period from leaving pensionable service to normal pension age. Effectively, two separate systems of revaluation apply:

(*a*) guaranteed minimum pensions accrued by reference to contracted-out employment before 6 April 1997 are subject to revaluation under *Part IV, Chapter III* (this is summarised in CHAPTER 4);

(*b*) revaluation of other benefits is as set out in PSA 1993, *Part IV, Chapter III and Sch 3*. It is these provisions which are summarised in **6.31** to **6.41** below.

General application of the revaluation requirements

6.31 Under *PSA 1993, s 83(1)(a)* the revaluation requirements of *Chapter II* apply where benefits are payable to or in respect of a member of an occupational pension scheme and:

(*a*) his pensionable service ends on or after 1 January 1986;

(*b*) when his pensionable service ends, he has accrued rights to benefits under the scheme;

(*c*) there is a period from his date of leaving to his normal pension age of at least a year (see **6.23** above for meaning of 'normal pension age'); and

(*d*) in the case of benefits payable to any other person in respect of the member, the member dies after normal pension age.

However, revaluation is not required to be applied in respect of any pension or other benefit (*PSA 1993, s 85*; *Preservation Regulations, regs 8–10*; *Pension Sharing (Pensions Credit Benefit) Regulations 2000 (SI 2000/1054), regs 7–9*) provided in accordance with the alternatives to short service benefit (*PSA 1993, s 73(2)(b)*) or pension credit benefit (*PSA 1993, s 101D(2)*).

For the purposes of the revaluation requirements, where 'normal pension age' is before the age of 60, it is taken to mean the age at which short service benefit is made payable under the scheme rules (see **6.23** above) (*Occupational Pensions Schemes (Revaluation) Regulations 1991 (SI 1991/168)*, reg *3*).

Determining which method of revaluation applies

6.32 There are four methods of revaluation:

(*a*) the 'average salary method';

(*b*) the 'flat rate method';

(*c*) the 'money purchase method'; and

(*d*) the 'final salary method' (*PSA 1993, s 84* and *Sch 3*).

The first step in revaluing a particular benefit is to decide which method is to apply.

The average salary method

6.33 The average salary method applies where the benefit is an average salary benefit (ie one whose rate or amount is calculated by reference to a member's average salary over the period of service on which the benefit is based, such as a career average scheme) and the trustees consider it appropriate to use the average salary method (*PSA 1993, s 84(2)*).

The average salary method itself is set out in *PSA 1993, Sch 3, para 3*.

The flat rate method

6.34 The flat rate method applies where the benefit is a flat rate benefit (ie one whose rate or amount is calculated by reference solely to the member's length of service) and the trustees consider it appropriate to use the flat rate method (*PSA 1993, s 84(2)*).

The flat rate method will rarely apply in practice. The method itself is set out in *PSA 1993, Sch 3, para 4*.

The money purchase method

6.35 Where the benefit is a defined contribution benefit, the money purchase method must be used.

The money purchase method is set out in *PSA 1993, Sch 3, para 5*. Effectively, the money purchase method requires the trustees to apply investment yield and bonuses arising from contributions paid by and on behalf of the member towards the provision of benefits, in the same way which would have applied had the member not left pensionable service.

The final salary method

6.36 In all other cases, the final salary method applies. This is described in **6.37** to **6.41** below (*PSA 1993, s 84(1)*).

The final salary method

General

6.37 The final salary method is set out in *PSA 1993, Sch 3, paras 1, 2*. This method introduces the concept widely known as limited price indexation or 'LPI'. The effect of applying LPI to a benefit is to increase it in line with cost of living increases over a given period, subject to a maximum of 5 per cent or 2.5 per cent per annum, depending on when the member left pensionable service and whether the scheme has or is able to take advantage of the lower revaluation cap introduced by *PA 2008* (see **6.41** below). Precisely how LPI applies in this context is dealt with in the following paragraphs.

The 'revaluation percentage'

6.38 *PSA 1993, Sch 3, para 2* requires the Secretary of State to specify by order, in each calendar year, a 'higher revaluation percentage' and a 'lower revaluation percentage' for each period which is a 'revaluation period' in relation to that order.

A 'revaluation period' is a period which:

(*a*) begins with 1 January 1986 or with an anniversary of that date falling before the making of the order; and

(*b*) ends with the next day after the making of the order which is 31 December.

The 'higher revaluation percentage' in relation to a given revaluation period is the lesser of:

(i) the percentage which appears to the Secretary of State to be the percentage increase in the general level of prices in Great Britain during that revaluation period; and

(ii) 5 per cent per annum.

The 'lower revaluation percentage' in relation to a given revaluation period is the lesser of:

(i) the percentage which appears to the Secretary of State to be the percentage increase in the general level of prices in Great Britain during that revaluation period; and

(ii) 2.5 per cent compound per annum.

Calculating the appropriate revaluation percentage

6.39 The 'appropriate higher revaluation percentage' is the higher revaluation percentage (see **6.38** above) specified in the last calendar year before the date on which the member reaches normal pension age for a period of the same length as the number of complete years from the member's leaving pensionable service to his reaching normal pension age. Conversely, the 'appropriate lower revaluation percentage' is the lower revaluation percentage (see **6.38** above) specified in the last calendar year before the date on which the member reaches normal pension age for a period of the same length as the number of complete years from the member's leaving pensionable service to his reaching normal pension age (*PSA 1993, Sch 3, para 2(7)*).

Applying the appropriate revaluation percentage

6.40 The final salary method of revaluation is to add to the amount that would otherwise be payable an amount equal to the whole or part of the appropriate revaluation percentage (see **6.39** above) of the benefit which has accrued on the date when pensionable service ends (*PSA 1993, Sch 3, para 1*).

Where pensionable service ends on or after 1 January 1991 or all pensionable service falls on or after 1 January 1985 the whole amount is added (*PSA 1993, Sch 3, para 1(1)(a)*). In any other case, a proportionate amount is added. The proportion is calculated by reference to the proportion which the member's post-31 December 1984 pensionable service bears to his total pensionable service (*PSA 1993, Sch 3, para 1(1)(b)*).

The higher revaluation percentage will apply to benefits accrued in relation to service prior to 6 April 2009 and may continue to apply after that date unless the scheme provisions allow the lower revaluation percentage introduced by *PA 2008* to be used (see **6.41** below).

Guaranteed minimum pensions are excluded from the benefit for the purpose of this calculation. These are revalued separately (see CHAPTER 4).

Revaluation in accordance with PA 2008

6.41 *PA 2008, s 101* introduced the lower revaluation percentage, meaning that the cap on LPI revaluation may be reduced from 5 per cent to 2.5 per cent with effect from 6 April 2009. The lower cap can only apply to benefits accrued in respect of pensionable service on or after 6 April 2009 (*PA 2009, s 101(2)* and *Sch 2, Part 1*).

The lower rate of revaluation is not obligatory. Schemes may continue (if the rules so permit) providing revaluation by reference to LPI capped at 5 per cent. Depending on how the scheme's rules are written, it may well be that the new lower cap will apply automatically or that the old cap will continue to apply unless specific amendment is made.

Where the scheme's rules incorporate the revaluation requirements by reference to the applicable statutory requirements, the lower cap of 2.5 per cent on LPI will apply automatically. On the other hand, if the revaluation rule specifically provided for LPI with an express reference to 5 per cent, revaluation would continue at the rate of LPI capped at 5 per cent unless and until action was taken to change it.

The table below summarises the statutory revaluation requirements applying to different periods of service.

Date of leaving service	**Period of accrual**	**Statutory revaluation**
Before 1 January 1985	Before 1 January 1985	None
1 January 1985 to 31 December 1990	Some before 1 January 1985, some after	5% LPI on accrual from 1 January 1985
1 January 1985 to 31 December 1990	On or after 1 January 1985	5% LPI
1 January 1991 to 5 April 2009	Any	5% LPI
On or after 6 April 2009	Any	5% LPI on pre-6 April 2009 accrual 2.5% LPI on post-5 April 2009 accrual

Transfer values – introduction

6.42 Occupational pension schemes have always been able to offer a transfer payment as an alternative to providing benefits from the scheme. However, the *Social Security Act 1985* introduced legislation giving early leavers a statutory right to have the 'cash equivalent' of their benefits transferred to another pension arrangement. This statutory right overrides any inconsistent provisions in the scheme's governing documentation (other than those relating to the winding up of the scheme), but this does not prevent a scheme from being more generous.

A scheme-specific approach to the calculation of cash equivalent transfer values, and a shift in the responsibility from the actuary to the trustees for the calculation and verification of cash equivalent transfer values, was introduced with effect from 1 October 2008.

The legislation is now consolidated in *PSA 1993, ss 93–101* (as amended by *PA 1995, ss 152–154* and *PA 2004, s 319*) and the *Occupational Pension Schemes (Transfer Values) Regulations 1996 (SI 1996/1847)* (the '*Transfer Regulations*'), as amended, in particular by the *Occupational Pension Schemes (Transfer Values) (Amendment) Regulations 2008 (SI 2008/1050)* (the '*2008 Transfer Regulations*').

A flow chart summarising the cash equivalent process can be found at **6.69** below.

The right to a cash equivalent

When does a member acquire a right to a cash equivalent?

6.43 Broadly speaking, before 6 April 1997 a member of an occupational pension scheme acquired a statutory right to a cash equivalent if he terminated pensionable service on or after 1 January 1986 and at least one year before normal pension age (see **6.23** above). The ambit of the legislation was extended by *PA 1995* to include members who terminated pensionable service before 1 January 1986 (*PA 1995, s 152*). However, the legislation does not apply to a member of a defined benefits scheme who terminated his membership before 1 January 1986, if all his pension benefits have been revalued by at least the rate of inflation (*Transfer Regulations, reg 2(b)*).

PA 1995 introduced the concept of a 'guaranteed cash equivalent'. As from 6 April 1997, the 'cash equivalent' of the benefits to which a member of a defined benefits occupational pension scheme is entitled must be guaranteed for a certain period. As a consequence of this change, the time at which a member acquires a right to a cash equivalent now differs depending on whether the scheme is defined contribution or defined benefit.

A member of a defined contribution occupational pension scheme acquires a right, when his pensionable service terminates, to the cash equivalent of any benefits which have accrued to or in respect of him under the rules of the scheme or any overriding legislation (*PSA 1993, s 94(1)(a)*).

A member of a defined benefits scheme acquires the right to a guaranteed cash equivalent if he has received a statement of entitlement (see **6.44** below) and has made a relevant application (see **6.54** below) within three months of the 'guarantee date' (*PSA 1993, s 94(1)(aa)*).

A further change was introduced from 1 October 2008, with the introduction of the concept of an 'initial cash equivalent' or 'ICE' (*Transfer Regulations, reg 7* (as amended)).

Guaranteed statement of entitlement

6.44 On the application of a member of a defined benefits scheme, the trustees must provide him with a written statement, as at a 'guarantee date', of the amount of the cash equivalent of any benefits which have accrued to or in respect of him under the rules of the scheme or any overriding legislation. This statement is referred to in the legislation as a 'statement of entitlement' (*PSA 1993, s 93A(1)*).

The guarantee date specified in the statement of entitlement must generally be within three months of the date of the member's application. However, this period can be extended (to a period which may not exceed six months) if the trustees are unable to provide the statement of entitlement for reasons beyond their control within the three-month period (*Transfer Regulations, reg 6(1)*). If the scheme is or becomes subject to a freezing order under *PA 2004, s 23*, the guarantee date must be within three months (or, if applicable, up to six months) of the member's application for the statement of entitlement or, if later, within three months of the date on which the direction prohibiting the issue of statements of entitlement no longer applies (*Transfer Regulations, reg 6(1A)*).

The statement of entitlement must be given to the member within ten days (excluding weekends, Christmas Day, New Year's Day and Good Friday) of the guarantee date (*Transfer Regulations, reg 6(2)*).

A member cannot make more than one request for a statement of entitlement within any 12-month period unless the rules of the scheme specifically provide for this or the trustees otherwise allow it (*Transfer Regulations, reg 6(3)*). Any trustee who fails to take all reasonable steps to provide a statement of entitlement to any member who requests it can be fined up to £1,000 in the case of an individual or £10,000 in any other case (*PSA 1993, s 93A(4)*; *Transfer Regulations, reg 20*). See APPENDIX I regarding penalties generally.

Partial cash equivalents

6.45 If a member leaves pensionable service but does not leave service (ie he ceases to be a member of his employer's scheme but remains an employee), he only acquires a right to that part of his cash equivalent which is attributable to his post-6 April 1988 pensionable service; it is only when he ceases to be an employee that he has a statutory right to the remaining part of his cash equivalent (assuming employment terminates at least one year earlier than the member's normal pension age) (*PSA 1993, s 98*; *Transfer Regulations, regs 3, 4*).

In practice, many schemes do not restrict a member's cash equivalent, preferring to avoid the unnecessary administration costs associated with providing two cash equivalent calculations; instead of relying on the statutory provision, the scheme's governing documentation will specifically allow a member to take a transfer in respect of all of his pensionable service, even if he remains in service.

Losing the right to a cash equivalent

6.46 *PSA 1993, s 98* provides that the right to a cash equivalent is lost if:

(*a*) it is not exercised before the 'last option date', ie at least one year before the date on which the member attains normal pension age, or within six months of terminating pensionable service, whichever is the later; or

(*b*) the scheme is wound up (ie the completion of the winding-up process).

Calculating the cash equivalent from 1 October 2008

6.47 In June 2006, the DWP published a consultation document 'Approaches to the Calculation of Pensions Transfer Values'. Following that consultation, the *2008 Transfer Regulations* came into force on 1 October 2008. The *2008 Transfer Regulations* amend the *Transfer Regulations* by inserting new *regs 7–7E*, removing the former *reg 8*, and adding *Schs 1A* and *1B*.

The *2008 Transfer Regulations* introduce a new minimum transfer value, although trustees have the option to calculate and verify a cash equivalent 'in such manner' as they determine, provided that it is higher than the cash equivalent that would otherwise be calculated under the *Transfer Regulations* (*Transfer Regulations, reg 7E(3)*).

Calculating the initial cash equivalent transfer value

Defined benefits

6.48 The trustees must calculate and verify the initial cash equivalent (or ICE) in accordance with the requirements of *Transfer Regulations, regs 7, 7A* and *7B*. The initial cash equivalent should be the trustees' best estimate of the amount 'at the guarantee date which is required to make provision within the scheme for a member's accrued benefits, options and discretionary benefits' (*Transfer Regulations, reg 7A(2)*).

Only those options which would increase the value of the member's ICE may be taken into account, and the trustees may take account of the proportion of members likely to exercise the various options. The trustees must have regard to any established custom or consent requirements when deciding which discretionary benefits, if any, should be taken into account (*Transfer Regulations, reg 7A(3)*).

The Regulator has published guidance (primarily intended for trustees) on calculating transfer values in defined benefit schemes.

The trustees calculate the ICE on the basis of various assumptions which are chosen with a view to making the best estimate of the ICE. *Transfer Regulations, reg 7B* requires the trustees to determine:

(*a*) the financial, economic and demographic assumptions used to calculate the initial cash equivalent (after taking actuarial advice on the assumptions from the scheme actuary (ie the actuary appointed in accordance with *PA 1995, s 47(1)(b)*);

(*b*) when the trustees determine the demographic assumptions, they must have regard to the main characteristics of the scheme members or, if the scheme members are not a large enough group, then the characteristics of a wider population sharing similar characteristics to the members;

(*c*) the scheme's investment strategy must be taken into account when setting the discount rate.

The Regulator in its guidance suggests that the trustees should review the assumptions from time to time (for example, following a scheme valuation) and take account of changes, if any, to the policy on discretionary benefits, the scheme's investment strategy and the impact of external changes, such as increases in longevity.

Alternative calculation of the initial cash equivalent

6.49 The trustees may choose an alternative manner to calculate and verify the initial cash equivalent. The alternative must result in an amount that is greater than the ICE calculation based on the trustees' best estimate of the cost of providing the same benefits in the scheme (*Transfer Regulations, reg 7E*).

Reducing the initial cash equivalent

6.50 The ICE may be reduced if the trustees have an insufficiency report and the insufficiency conditions are met. Also, the trustees may reduce it to reflect reasonable administration costs, but these must be offset by any reasonable administrative savings (*Transfer Regulations, reg 7D, Sch 1A*).

The insufficiency report must be prepared by the scheme actuary in accordance with the detailed requirements of *Transfer Regulations, Sch 1B*.

The insufficiency conditions are described in *Transfer Regulations, Sch 1A, para 3* and, in order to be satisfied, the insufficiency report must show (at the effective date of the report) that the scheme's assets were less than its liabilities, in respect of all of the members and any category of member. The scheme's assets are measured by reference to the market value of those assets, and the liabilities are measured by reference to the ICE value calculated in accordance with the requirements of the *Transfer Regulations* (as varied by *Transfer Regulations, Sch 1B*).

There is no requirement for the trustees to reduce ICEs, and the Regulator has suggested that trustees should not rely on the insufficiency report itself as a reason to reduce. However, trustees need to be cautious about deciding not to reduce ICEs where there is a deficiency report because they could, for example, be criticised for continuing to pay full transfer values if the deficit increased significantly (which could partly be attributable to the payment of full cash equivalents) or the scheme went into winding up. In addition to the insufficiency report, the Regulator suggests that the trustees should take other factors into account, such as:

(*a*) the level of underfunding in the scheme;

(*b*) the strength of the employer covenant;

(*c*) length and structure of any recovery plan;

(*d*) any contingent assets that might be in place.

(Pensions Regulator Guidance, Transfer Values, paras 34–37)

The insufficiency report will include a statement as to the maximum percentage by which a member's ICE may be reduced, known as the deficiency percentage.

Defined contribution benefits

6.51 The ICE of any defined contribution benefits is the realisable value at the date of the calculation of the member's benefits. The realisable value is calculated by the trustees, in accordance with the scheme rules, and will also include any interest payments which are payable under the scheme's rules (*Transfer Regulations, reg 7C*). Generally, the ICE transfer value available in respect of defined contributions benefits will simply be the accumulated value of the contributions made by and in respect of the member plus the investment growth of those contributions.

Taking account of customary discretionary benefits

6.52 As already mentioned (see **6.48** above), the trustees of defined benefit occupational pension schemes must, after 1 October 2008, take into consideration those discretionary benefits in respect of which there is an established custom for the purposes of calculating a member's ICE.

A common discretionary benefit for which allowance should be made is where early retirement is permitted without actuarial reduction but subject to employer consent. If it would be usual for the employer to consent to any such retirement after, say, age 62, there would be an established custom of granting the additional benefits. The calculation of any cash equivalent should therefore reflect this, unless the trustees determine otherwise.

Reduction of guaranteed cash equivalents

6.53 It is only possible to reduce the guaranteed cash equivalent of members of defined benefit schemes. A guaranteed cash equivalent generally cannot be reduced unless either the scheme begins to be wound up or benefits have been surrendered, commuted or forfeited. A guaranteed cash equivalent can be recalculated and either increased or reduced, as appropriate, if it transpires that it was not originally calculated in accordance with the statutory requirements (*Transfer Regulations, reg 9*).

Exercising the right to a cash equivalent

Making a relevant application

6.54 The right to a cash equivalent can be exercised at any time after termination of pensionable service (but before the last option date (see **6.46** above)); it does not have to be exercised coincident with, for example, the date on which the member leaves service. A member exercises his right to a cash equivalent by making a relevant application, ie an application, in writing, to the trustees requiring them to use the cash equivalent by transferring it to a specified arrangement (*PSA 1993, s 95*; *Transfer Regulations, reg 12*). The legislation provides that an application is taken to have been made if it is delivered to the trustees personally or sent by post in a registered letter or by recorded delivery (*PSA 1993, s 95(9)*). However, in practice this requirement is often waived.

Broadly speaking, in the case of a registered pension scheme, a member can ask for his cash equivalent to be paid to any other suitable registered arrangement or a qualifying recognised overseas pension scheme which is able and willing to accept a transfer. However, some restrictions apply, particularly in relation to transfers from a contracted-out scheme (see CHAPTER 4) (*PSA 1993, s 95*; *Transfer Regulations, reg 12*). Generally, a transfer will be used to:

(*a*) acquire transfer credits under the rules of a registered occupational pension scheme;

(*b*) acquire rights under the rules of a registered personal pension scheme;

(*c*) purchase an annuity from an insurance company chosen by the member; or

(*d*) acquire rights under a qualifying recognised overseas pension scheme.

The application must specifically identify the receiving arrangement. An application which does not do this will simply be treated as an enquiry (or possibly a request for a statement of entitlement) and not a relevant application.

In the case of a defined benefits scheme, a member must make a relevant application within three months of the guarantee date (*PSA 1993, s 94(1)(aa)*). As not more than one request for a statement of entitlement can be made within any 12-month period unless the rules of the scheme specifically provide for this (or the trustees otherwise allow it (see **6.44** above)), a member who fails to make a relevant application within the three-month period could find that he cannot require the trustees to take any action for another nine months.

A member may withdraw an application for a cash equivalent at any time before the trustees are committed to complying with the member's request (*PSA 1993, s 100*). A member could not, therefore, withdraw his application if the trustees have already made a transfer or entered into a binding agreement with a third party, such as an insurance company. A member who withdraws an application is not prevented from making another application at some future date.

'Splitting' a cash equivalent

6.55 A cash equivalent can be 'split' between a number of arrangements. For example, a member can transfer part of his cash equivalent to an occupational pension scheme and part to a personal pension scheme (*PSA 1993, s 96(1)*). This is most commonly done where the transfer is from a contracted-out scheme to a contracted-in scheme which cannot accept assets representing the member's contracted-out rights (but, due to changes in the contracting-out system (see CHAPTER 4), this is likely to become less common in the future).

Although a cash equivalent can be split between different arrangements, a member must generally take his whole cash equivalent at one time (*PSA 1993, s 96*). There are, however, two exceptions to this: first, where the member's cash equivalent is restricted because he terminated pensionable service without terminating service (see **6.45** above); and, second, where his cash equivalent includes contracted-out rights which the receiving arrangement (not being contracted out) is unable or unwilling to accept (*PSA 1993, s 96(1)(b), (2)*). This does not prevent a member taking a partial transfer value in other circumstances if the scheme rules allow, but this will be outside the cash equivalent regime and the trustees will not benefit from the statutory discharge (see **6.62** below).

Benefits to be provided by the receiving arrangement

6.56 The benefit which the receiving arrangement provides in respect of a cash equivalent will depend on the rules of that arrangement. A defined benefits scheme may provide a fixed amount of pension, similar to a revalued preserved pension. Alternatively the money may be invested in the same way as a member's additional voluntary contributions, or it may be translated into 'added years'. In the case of a defined contributions scheme, a transfer value will usually simply be invested along with other contributions.

The *2008 Transfer Regulations* do not regulate how the receiving arrangement treats the transfer payment. The Regulator has issued Transfer Value Guidance, which sets out a number of principles that the Regulator expects trustees to follow when calculating the transfer credit, and recommends that the trustees should take account of the following principles:

(*a*) the assumptions applied to transfers in should be consistent with the assumptions used for calculating transfers values out of the scheme;

(*b*) the transfer credit, from the member's perspective, should give fair value for the amount of the transfer payment;

(*c*) the transfer credit should not prejudice the security of existing members' benefits; and

(*d*) the transfer credit should not require additional funding from the employer unless the employer has agreed to such funding in advance.

Trustees' duties after member exercises his right

Complying with the member's request

6.57 The trustees must do what is necessary to carry out the member's request, in the case of a defined benefits scheme, within six months of the guarantee date or (if earlier) the date on which the member reaches normal pension age (*PSA 1993, s 99(2)*). As the six-month period is from the guarantee date the trustees will have a minimum period of three months and a maximum period of six months in which to make the transfer payment (depending on how quickly the member requests the guaranteed cash equivalent).

In any other case, the necessary action must be taken within six months of the date on which the trustees received the application, or (if earlier) the date on which the member reaches normal pension age.

HMRC requirements

6.58 Broadly speaking, in the case of a registered pension scheme, a member can ask for his cash equivalent to be paid to any other suitable registered arrangement or a qualifying recognised overseas pension scheme which is able and willing to accept a transfer. However some restrictions apply, particularly in relation to transfers from a contracted-out scheme (see CHAPTER 4) (*PSA 1993, s 95*; *Transfer Regulations, reg 12*).

From 6 April 2006, in addition to the detailed rules governing transfer payments found in the *PSA 1993* and the *Transfer Regulations*, the trustees (in their capacity as scheme administrator) must also have regard to various provisions of the Registered Pension Schemes Manual.

Before making the transfer, the 'scheme administrator should make sure that the person to whom they are transferring monies is someone with a position of responsibility in the receiving scheme' (Registered Pension Schemes Manual, RPSM14107010). In addition, where the receiving scheme is an insured scheme the scheme administrator will be liable to a penalty of up to £3,000 if the transfer payment is not made directly to the scheme administrator or an insurance company issuing policies under the receiving scheme. Only transfers made to other registered schemes or qualifying recognised overseas schemes will be 'recognised transfers', a transfer to any other arrangement will incur a tax penalty. See CHAPTER 16.

Pension liberation

6.59 New provisions dealing with pensions liberation were introduced with effect from 6 April 2005 by *PA 2004, ss 18–21*. Where money has been transferred out of a pension scheme on the basis that it would be used in an 'authorised way' and it has not or is not likely to be used in that way, the Regulator may apply to the court for an order of restitution to recover the money, or assets of an equivalent value, from the recipient (*PA 2004, s 19*). An 'authorised way' means, where it is a statutory transfer such as the exercise of the right to take a cash equivalent, a way authorised under the relevant statutory provisions. Where the transfer is made pursuant to the scheme rules or by exercising a statutory right to a transfer value, then an 'authorised way' is as allowed under the scheme rules or in accordance with the relevant statutory provision.

As an alternative to applying to the court for a restitution order, the Regulator has power to take action itself. *PA 2004, s 20* allows the Regulator to make a restraining order over any account which it is satisfied contains money which has been liberated, pending consideration of a repatriation order. *PA 2004, s 21* provides that, where a restraining order is in place and the Regulator is satisfied that the restrained account contains money liberated from a pension scheme, it may direct the person holding the account to pay the money to another pension scheme, towards an annuity or to the scheme member affected.

Where a transfer has been made to an occupational or personal pension scheme, trustees will not obtain a statutory discharge under *PSA 2003, s 99* (see **6.57** above) unless they have taken all reasonable steps to ensure that the trustees or managers of the receiving scheme are acting in good faith (*PSA 1993, s 99(1)* as amended by *Occupational and Personal Pension Schemes (Pensions Liberation) Regulations 2005 (SI 2005/992), reg 3*).

Variations and extensions of time limits

6.60 Under *PSA 1993, s 99(4)* and *Transfer Regulations, reg 13*, the Regulator may grant an extension of the time limits for making the transfer payment in certain circumstances, including where:

(*a*) the scheme is being wound up or is about to be wound up;

(*b*) the scheme is ceasing to be a contracted-out scheme;

(*c*) the interests of the members of the scheme generally would be prejudiced if the trustees acted on a member's request within the statutory time limit;

(*d*) the trustees have not been provided with the information they reasonably require to carry out properly what the member requires;

(*e*) the guaranteed cash equivalent has been increased or reduced in accordance with *Transfer Regulations, reg 9*; and

(*f*) the member has disputed the amount of the cash equivalent.

An application for an extension must be made during the period within which the trustees should have complied with the member's request.

The time limits may also be extended where the scheme is or has, within 3 months of the end of the guarantee period, become subject to a freezing order under *PA 2004, s 23*, which includes a direction that no transfers may be made or if the scheme is a former contracted-out scheme and HMRC have made a direction in relation to the scheme under *PSA 1993, s 53*.

If disciplinary or court proceedings are brought against a member within 12 months of the termination of his pensionable service and there is a likelihood that his benefits may be forfeited as a result, the period within which the trustees are required to comply with the member's request is extended to three months after conclusion of the disciplinary or court proceedings (*PSA 1993, s 99(3)*).

Consequences of delay

6.61 If the trustees fail to do what is needed to carry out the member's request within the appropriate time frame, and cannot establish grounds for an extension, they must notify the Regulator of the failure to comply. In making their notification to the Regulator the trustees should give an explanation. The Regulator has power to impose a financial penalty (of up to £1,000 in the case of an individual or £10,000 in any other case) if the trustees have failed to take reasonable steps to ensure compliance (*PSA 1993, s 99(7)*; *Transfer Regulations, reg 20*).

A member's cash equivalent must be increased if the trustees delay implementing the member's request for more than six months. If there is a reasonable excuse for the delay, the cash equivalent must be recalculated, and increased as appropriate, as if the date on which the trustees carry out the member's request had been the guarantee date (in the case of a defined benefits scheme) or the date on which the trustees received the member's application for a cash equivalent (in any other case).

If there is no reasonable excuse for the delay, either the cash equivalent must be recalculated as above, or interest must be added to the original cash equivalent at one per cent above base rate if this would produce a greater amount (*Transfer Regulations, reg 10*).

Discharge of trustees

6.62 Once the trustees have done what is needed to carry out the member's request, they are discharged from any obligation to provide benefits to which the cash equivalent relates (*PSA 1993, s 99(1)*).

Cash transfer sums

6.63 Employees leaving service on or after 6 April 2006 before normal retirement age with at least three months' pensionable service and linked qualifying service but no vested rights (usually less than two years' pensionable service) may choose a 'cash transfer sum' as an alternative to a refund of their contributions. The provisions were introduced by *PA 2004, s 264*, which inserts new *ss 101AA–101AI* into *PSA 1993*.

The cash transfer sum is defined in *PSA 1993, s 101AB* as being the cash equivalent value of the benefits that would have accrued for the member had there not been a rule requiring a minimum period of service before vesting of those rights. The *Occupational Pension Schemes (Early Leavers: Cash Transfer Sums and Contribution Refunds) Regulations 2006 (SI 2006/33)* (the '*Early Leaver Regulations*') provide for the cash equivalent to be reduced in certain circumstances including scheme underfunding based on an insufficiency report (see **6.50** above).

If the member wishes to exercise his right to a cash transfer sum, he must, by the reply date, make a written application to the trustees (*PSA 1993, s 101(AD)*). The reply date is not fixed in *PSA 1993* and trustees have a discretion to accept a response from the member after the reply date. The Regulator's *Code of Practice No 4, Early leavers – reasonable periods* suggests that three months is a reasonable period. A member loses his right to a cash transfer sum if he does not exercise his rights on or before the reply date or the scheme is wound up.

A member may use a cash transfer sum to acquire rights under another occupational pension scheme or a personal pension scheme or for purchasing one or more appropriate annuities (*PSA 1993, s 101AE*).

PSA 1993, s 101AC requires trustees to provide relevant departing members with information regarding the nature and amount of the rights acquired and details of what he must do to exercise those rights. *Early Leaver Regulations, reg 7* requires other information to be given to relevant members including the details and reasons for any reduction, details of any tax liability and the possibility of any reduction if the scheme were to commence winding up before payment is made.

The Regulator's Code of Practice includes suggested time limits for the various stages of the process:

(*a*) the trustees should notify a member of his rights as soon as reasonably possible, normally within three months of leaving service;

(*b*) the member should usually be given at least three months from the date the statement is given to him in which to make his election;

(*c*) the trustees should complete the transfer or refund without unjustifiable delay and usually within three months of receiving the election.

A summary of the application of the cash transfer sum provisions can be found at **6.70** below.

Calculating the cash transfer sum

Defined benefits

6.64 The trustees must calculate and verify the initial cash transfer sum in accordance with *Early Leaver Regulations, regs 2A* and *2B* or, alternatively, in accordance with *reg 2D*, which reflect the provisions contained in the *Transfer Regulations* (see **6.48** above).

The initial cash transfer sum should be the trustees' best estimate of the initial cash transfer sum which is the amount 'required to make provision within the scheme for a member's accrued benefits, options and discretionary benefits' (*Early Leaver Regulations, reg 2A(2)*). Only those options which would increase the value of the member's initial cash transfer sum may be taken into account, and the trustees may take account of the proportion of members likely to exercise the various options. The trustees must have regard to any established custom or consent requirements when deciding which discretionary benefits, if any, should be taken into account (*Early Leaver Regulations, reg 2A(3)*).

Early Leaver Regulations, reg 2B requires the trustees:

(*a*) to determine the financial, economic and demographic assumptions used to calculate the initial cash equivalent (after taking actuarial advice on the assumptions from the scheme actuary (ie the actuary appointed in accordance with *PA 1995, s 47(1)(b)*);

(*b*) when determining the demographic assumptions, to have regard to the main characteristics of the scheme members or, if the scheme members are not a large enough group, then the characteristics of a wider population sharing similar characteristics to the members; and

(*c*) to take into account the scheme's investment strategy when setting the discount rate.

The trustees have the option of choosing an alternative manner of calculating and verifying the initial cash transfer sum. The alternative must result in an amount that is greater than the initial cash transfer sum calculation based on the trustees' best estimate of the cost of providing the same benefits in the scheme (*Early Leaver Regulations, reg 2D*).

The Regulator's guidance on transfer values states that the trustees should use the same basis for calculating initial cash transfer sums as they use for calculating ICEs (Pensions Regulator Guidance, Transfer Values, para 53).

Reducing the initial cash transfer sum

6.65 The initial cash transfer sum may be reduced if the trustees have an insufficiency report and the insufficiency conditions are met. Also, the trustees may reduce it to reflect reasonable administration costs but these must be offset by reasonable administrative savings (*Early Leaver Regulations, reg 4(12)*).

The insufficiency conditions and insufficiency report for the purposes of the initial cash transfer sum are the same conditions and the report prepared in accordance with the requirements of the *Transfer Regulations* (see **6.50** above) (*Early Leaver Regulations, regs 1(2), 4(2)*).

The trustees may reduce the initial cash transfer sum by no more than the deficiency percentage (*Early Leaver Regulations, reg 4(3)*).

Defined contribution benefits

6.66 The initial cash transfer sum in respect of any defined contribution benefits is the realisable value at the date of the calculation of the member's benefits. The realisable value is calculated by the trustees, in accordance with the scheme rules and which also includes any interest payments which are payable under the scheme's rules (*Early Leaver Regulations, reg 2C*). Generally, the initial cash transfer sum in respect of defined contributions benefits will be the accumulated value of the contributions made by and in respect of the member plus the investment growth of those contributions.

Disclosure requirements

6.67 Active members of any scheme and deferred members of defined contributions schemes are entitled to certain information regarding cash equivalents and transfer values (*Transfer Regulations, reg 11, Sch 1*). In particular, a statement of whether or not a cash equivalent or other transfer value is available, or would be available if the member terminated pensionable service, must be provided. Members must also be given information about:

(*a*) help available from the FSA, the Regulator and TPAS on transfers;

(*b*) if the scheme is eligible to enter the PPF;

(*c*) the need to consider taking financial advice before transferring.

(*Transfer Regulations, Sch 1*)

Trustees must also supply the following information as soon as practicable, and in any event within three months of the request being made:

(*a*) an estimate of the amount of the cash equivalent (calculated on the basis that the member's service terminated or will terminate on a particular date);

(*b*) details of the accrued rights to which the cash equivalent relates;

(*c*) details of any additional discretionary benefits that have been taken into account when giving the estimate of the cash equivalent (or any part of it); and

(*d*) if the initial cash equivalent was reduced in accordance with *Transfer Regulations, Sch 1A,* the fact of the reduction must be disclosed, together with information about why there has been a reduction and the amount of the reduction. The member must also be given an estimate of when an unreduced payment would be available and a statement of his right to obtain further estimates.

A member is only entitled to request this information once in every 12-month period. Similar information must be given in respect of any non-statutory transfer value that may be available to the member (*Transfer Regulations, reg 11*).

When a member is given a statement of entitlement to a guaranteed cash equivalent transfer value, certain additional information must also be given. In particular, the member must be given a statement explaining:

(*a*) that the member can only request a statement of entitlement once in every 12-month period unless the trustees allow otherwise or the scheme rules permit more frequent requests;

(*b*) that if the member wishes to exercise his right to take the guaranteed cash equivalent he must submit a written application to that effect within three months of the guarantee date; and

(*c*) in exceptional circumstances the guaranteed cash equivalent may be reduced and the member will be informed if his cash equivalent is reduced.

Any trustee who fails to take all reasonable steps to comply with these disclosure requirements can be fined up to £1,000 in the case of an individual or £10,000 in any other case (*PSA 1993, s 93A*; *Transfer Regulations, reg 20*). See APPENDIX I regarding penalties generally and APPENDIX II regarding disclosure.

Hybrid schemes

6.68 The *Transfer Regulations* (at *reg 19*) make special provisions for 'hybrid schemes', ie schemes which are defined benefits but under which some of the benefits which may be provided are defined contributions benefits, or vice versa. In relation to such schemes, a member has a right to:

(*a*) a guaranteed cash equivalent in respect of his defined benefits; and

(*b*) a cash equivalent in respect of his defined contributions benefits.

In exercising his rights, the member must take the whole of his cash equivalent, ie both the guaranteed and non-guaranteed element.

Summary of guaranteed cash equivalent procedure

6.69

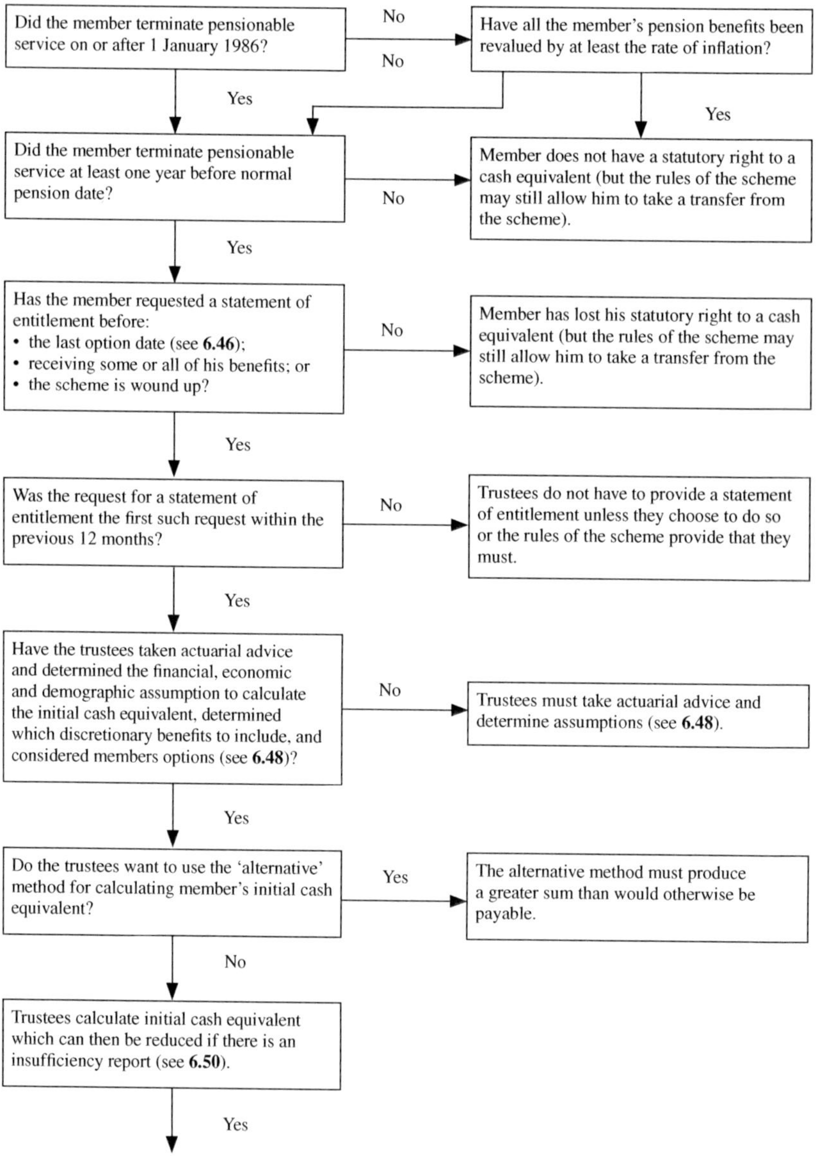

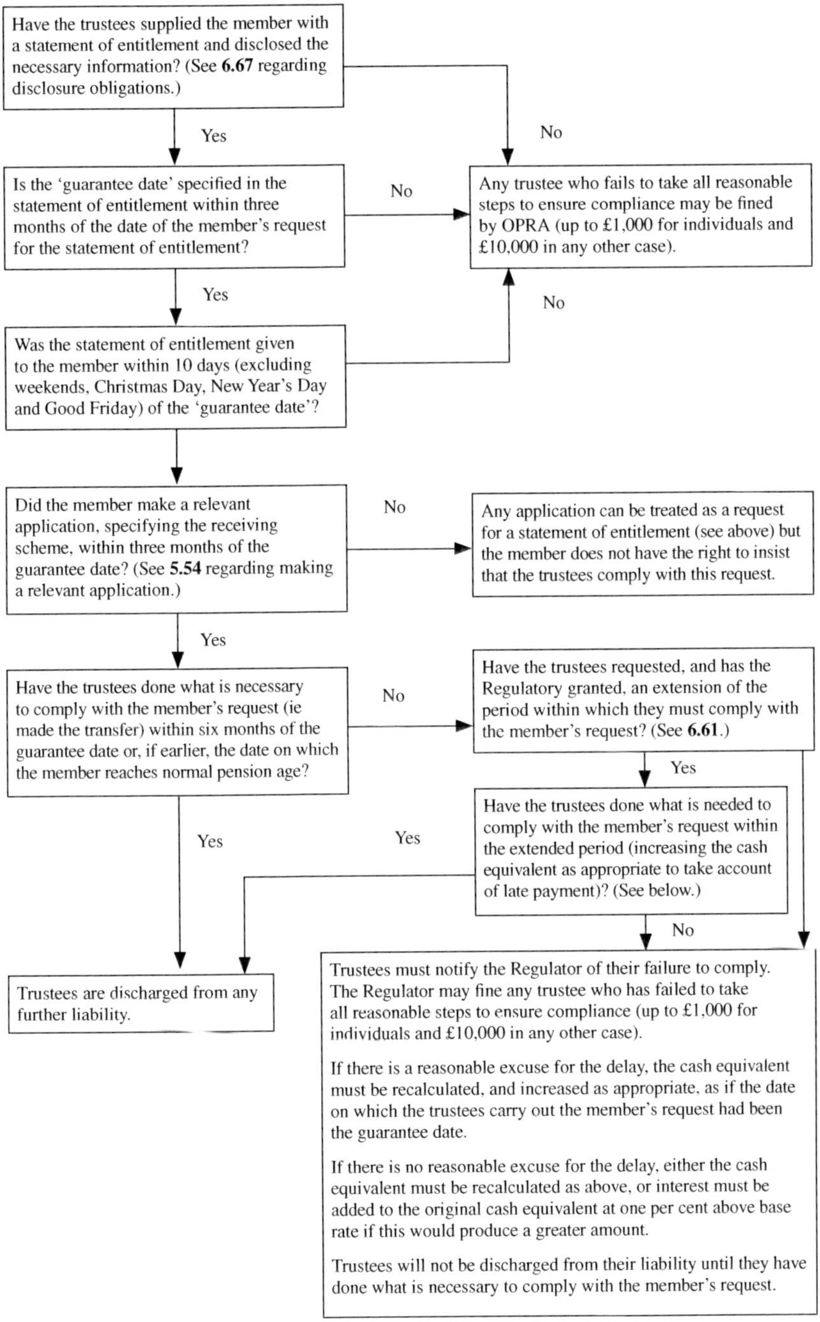
Have the trustees supplied the member with a statement of entitlement and disclosed the necessary information? (See **6.67** regarding disclosure obligations.)
Yes
No
Is the 'guarantee date' specified in the statement of entitlement within three months of the date of the member's request for the statement of entitlement?
No
Any trustee who fails to take all reasonable steps to ensure compliance may be fined by OPRA (up to £1,000 for individuals and £10,000 in any other case).
Yes
No
Was the statement of entitlement given to the member within 10 days (excluding weekends, Christmas Day, New Year's Day and Good Friday) of the 'guarantee date'?
Did the member make a relevant application, specifying the receiving scheme, within three months of the guarantee date? (See **5.54** regarding making a relevant application.)
No
Any application can be treated as a request for a statement of entitlement (see above) but the member does not have the right to insist that the trustees comply with this request.
Yes
Have the trustees done what is necessary to comply with the member's request (ie made the transfer) within six months of the guarantee date or, if earlier, the date on which the member reaches normal pension age?
No
Have the trustees requested, and has the Regulatory granted, an extension of the period within which they must comply with the member's request? (See **6.61**.)
Yes
Yes
Yes
Have the trustees done what is needed to comply with the member's request within the extended period (increasing the cash equivalent as appropriate to take account of late payment)? (See below.)
No
Trustees are discharged from any further liability.
Trustees must notify the Regulator of their failure to comply. The Regulator may fine any trustee who has failed to take all reasonable steps to ensure compliance (up to £1,000 for individuals and £10,000 in any other case).
If there is a reasonable excuse for the delay, the cash equivalent must be recalculated, and increased as appropriate, as if the date on which the trustees carry out the member's request had been the guarantee date.
If there is no reasonable excuse for the delay, either the cash equivalent must be recalculated as above, or interest must be added to the original cash equivalent at one per cent above base rate if this would produce a greater amount.
Trustees will not be discharged from their liability until they have done what is necessary to comply with the member's request.

Rights of early leaver to cash transfer lump sum

6.70

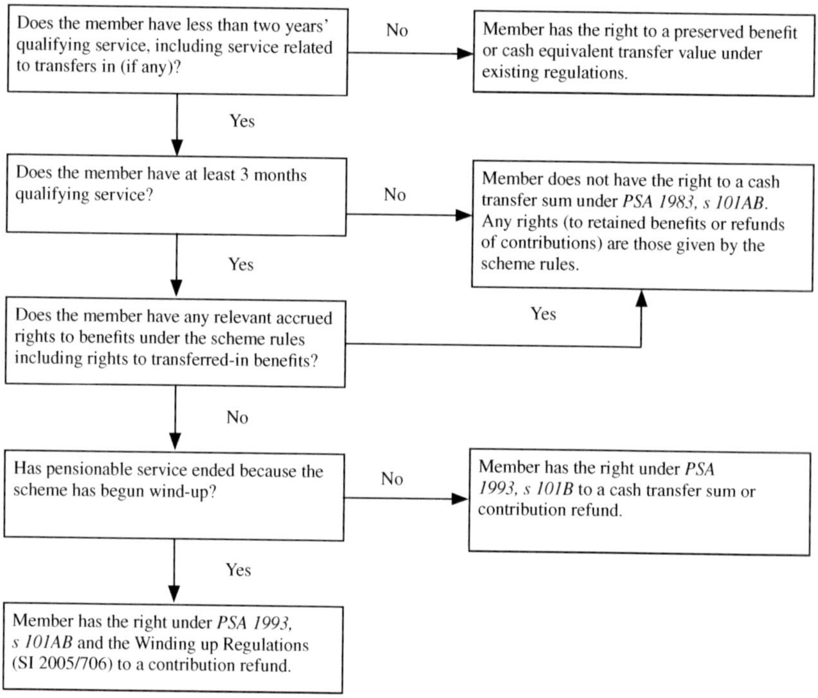

Source: Pensions Regulator, Code of Practice no. 4, Early leavers' – reasonable periods

Chapter 7

Employment issues

Introduction

7.1 Traditionally, lawyers attempted to keep pension schemes and employment issues entirely separate, but the distinction between pension rights deriving from a trust and contractual employment rights is becoming more blurred. In the past, pensions were seen as being provided by employers out of gratitude for the employee's long and dutiful service. The employer, as settlor, had absolute discretion as to what level or type of benefits were to be provided to the employee.

Pension schemes are now an integral part of the total remuneration package offered by employers (pension provision is often a key recruitment and retention issue) and the provision of pension benefits is heavily regulated by statute and secondary legislation.

Historically there has been no legislation requiring an employer to run a pension scheme (except in limited circumstances for ex-public sector employees, although such rights are statutory and not the norm). However, there has been some gradual erosion of the position: since 8 October 2001, employers of five or more employees have been required to designate a stakeholder pension scheme which their employees may elect to join, and to arrange for salary deductions to be made and contributions paid directly to the provider on behalf of employees (*Welfare Reform and Pensions Act 1999, s 1* (as amended by *PA 2004*)). From 6 April 2005, if an employer buys the business of another employer which has an occupational pension scheme, the transferee employer must offer, to transferring employees who are either scheme members or eligible to join, (broadly) membership of the transferee employer's occupational pension scheme or of a stakeholder scheme and either provide benefits of a specified minimum level or make matching contributions of up to 6 per cent of an employee's basic pay. For details, see **7.24** below.

As a consequence of the *Social Security Act 1986* (now *Pension Schemes Act 1993, s 160* ('*PSA 1993*'), an employer can no longer make membership of a pension scheme compulsory. However, from 2012 employers will be required to arrange for the automatic enrolment of their employees aged between 22 and State pension age into the Government's default scheme (a trust-based defined contribution occupational pension scheme, originally referred to as the 'personal accounts system') or into the employer's own qualifying scheme. The requirements can be found in the *Pensions Act 2007* ('*PA 2007*') and the *Pensions Act 2008*, and regulations will set out the detail. Employees outside these age bands will be able to opt into the scheme, with access to an employer contribution if they fall within the earnings bands. The maximum annual contribution level will be £3,600 (in 2005 earnings terms, rising in line with earnings). Contributions will be based on gross earnings between £5,035 and £33,540 pa, with employers contributing a minimum of 3 per cent and total contributions being at least 8 per cent. These contributions will be phased in over three years. Employers' defined benefit occupational qualifying schemes must give at least 1/120th accrual. The contribution levels will be phased in over three years.

Once the automatic enrolment regime is in place, the stakeholder designation requirement will be removed. For further details of automatic enrolment, see CHAPTER 13.

There is currently no minimum or maximum level of benefits that may or should by law be provided under a pension scheme, except that a contracted-out scheme must provide certain minimum benefits required by statute (see CHAPTER 4); before 6 April 2006 an exempt approved scheme was not permitted to provide benefits which exceeded HMRC limits, but this was changed by *FA 2004* to a restriction on the amount of tax-advantaged pension saving which may be made in a registered pension scheme (see CHAPTER 16) and final salary schemes must meet the scheme-specific funding requirements (see CHAPTER 11). None of the tax, preservation, revaluation or contracting-out legislation states that the contract of employment should contain any rights for the employee as against the employer; the employee's rights are ostensibly against the trustees of the pension scheme alone.

An employee does have specific rights against his employer in the areas of equal pay, sex, race, religion or belief, sexual orientation, disability and age discrimination (covered in CHAPTER 9), maternity absence and, as of 6 April 2003, paternity and adoption absence and parental leave, though these rights are statutory rather than contractual. It is true that *Barber v Guardian Royal Exchange [1990] 2 All ER 660* (as subsequently clarified by *Coloroll Pension Trustees Ltd v Russell [1995] All ER (EC) 23*) confirmed that pensions are pay, but that is only in the context of the equality provisions of *Article 157* of the *Treaty on the Functioning of the European Union* (formerly *Article 119* and then *Article 141* of the *EC Treaty* – see **9.2** below), as regards access to pension schemes and the benefits to be provided for men and women. In addition, although defined pension contributions and benefits were also recognised as pay by the Central Arbitration Committee, this was only in respect of trade union recognition for collective bargaining purposes (*UNIFI v Union Bank of Nigeria plc [2001] IRLR 712*). Neither *Barber* nor *UNIFI* answers the more fundamental question of whether (and if so, to what extent) pensions are an employment right, and neither does *PA 1995*. *PA 2004*, however, does so to a limited extent, in that it includes provisions regarding pension protection on transfer of employment, expressly providing that, on a TUPE transfer, it is a condition of the employee's contract of employment with the transferee that the requirements of *PA 2004* are complied with (see **7.24** below).

What is the employee promised?

Wording of the employment contract

7.2 The wording of an employment contract generally provides little or no guidance as to the pension rights (if any) of the employee. *Employment Rights Act 1996, s 1* ('*ERA 1996*') states that, within two months of the commencement of employment, the employer must provide a written statement of the essential terms of the employment and must include any terms and conditions (see *ERA 1996, s 1(4)(d)(iii)*) relating to 'pensions and pension schemes'. Generally, the information given will be limited, as *ERA 1996* in reality requires information to be given on access to a pension scheme, as opposed to the benefits which will be provided if an employee joins the pension scheme. Indeed, it would be risky for an employer to give express commitments in the employment contract as to the benefits to be provided under a final salary scheme as, until the winding-up of a pension scheme and the crystallisation of its liabilities occurs, an employer cannot be certain that there will be sufficient funds to meet the pension promise. There is less of a problem with money purchase arrangements.

Although the precise wording would have to be checked in any individual case, usually a contract will state that an employee may join the pension scheme if eligible to do so (for example, having completed a specified period of service) and membership will be subject to the provisions governing the scheme from time to time, which are summarised in the scheme booklet. The contract may also reserve to the employer the right to amend or terminate the pension scheme, or alternatively an employer may rely on the reference to the scheme booklet (which should, if properly drafted, contain such a caveat). In most instances, and as clarified by the High Court in *ITN v Ward [1997] PLR 131*, the trust deed will override the booklet in cases of inconsistency. This principle was more recently confirmed by the Court of Appeal (reversing the High Court judgment) in *Steria Ltd v Hutchison [2006] EWCA Civ 1551* and in *Bainbridge v Quarters Trustees Ltd [2008] EWHC 979 (Ch)*.

When it comes to employing a senior executive, the employer is likely to take more time over the drafting of that individual's service contract (which is less likely to follow a standard form), and one of the important clauses will usually deal specifically with the pension benefits to be provided (as opposed merely to access to the scheme).

In most cases the wording of the employment contract is unlikely to be of assistance in analysing pension rights, and it is designed to comply with statutory minimum requirements. The only employment 'right' is likely to be a right to join the scheme, if the employee satisfies the eligibility criteria.

In reality, an employee will obtain clearer information from the trustees of any occupational scheme, pursuant to the trustees' obligations under the disclosure requirements of *PA 1995* and *PA 2004* (for further details see CHAPTER 3 and APPENDIX II), than he will from his employer. Basic information about the scheme (*Occupational Pension Schemes (Disclosure of Information) Regulations 1996 (SI 1996/1655), reg 4* (the '*Disclosure Regulations*')) must be provided as a matter of course to each prospective member or, if this is not practicable, within two months of his becoming a member.

The Sweeney/Lewin independent 'Deregulatory Review of Private Pensions', published in July 2007, recommended a reform of the current prescriptive disclosure regime to a more principles-based regime, with members being given sufficient information to allow them to understand the benefits to which they will be entitled and to make decisions in their own best interests. The Government response in December 2007 indicated that this would gradually be tackled. The DWP's March 2009 consultation proposed deregulating certain areas (basic scheme information, annual reports, annual information and statutory money purchase illustrations). It aims to have legislation in place by April 2010.

The pension scheme documentation

7.3 The explanatory booklet or announcement will usually be designed to comply with the disclosure requirements of *PSA 1993*, *PA 1995*, *PA 2004* and the *Disclosure Regulations*. It will usually state that the scheme is established under a trust and is managed by trustees, that the booklet is explanatory only, and that the employees' rights are set out in the trust deed and rules, which are available for inspection or copies of which are available on application to the trustees. In practice it is uncommon for employees to exercise their rights to inspect the deed.

In addition, a statement will usually be incorporated saying that whilst the company has every intention of continuing the scheme it does reserve the right to modify or discontinue it at any time.

The application for membership will usually authorise the company to deduct any contributions payable by the employee from his remuneration and to remit these contributions to the trustees. This authority (which must be in writing and precede the first deduction) is required under *ERA 1996, s 13* (a consolidation of the *Wages Act 1986* provisions) and may be specifically incorporated within the contract of employment or in a separate agreement. This is an important fact which must be remembered when considering the merger of two or more schemes or the transfer of a group of employees into a new scheme. The authority to deduct contributions may be specific to the former scheme and may have to be renewed for the new scheme before any deductions are made.

The trust deed and rules will generally establish that the employee, if he joins the scheme and becomes a beneficiary of the trust, will become entitled to benefits in defined circumstances. The formal documentation will contain a power of amendment, exercisable by the employer with the consent of the trustees, or vice versa, or (less commonly) by one party solely. Rights already accrued may also be expressly protected (see also **7.10** below).

The employer will usually have power to discontinue contributions, following which the scheme will normally be wound up, although the trustees may have power to continue it as a closed scheme (see CHAPTER 5 for further details regarding winding-up of pension schemes and the priority order in which scheme assets are to be applied among the various classes of members). The benefits provided on winding-up will depend on the liabilities at that date, the value of the assets and the cost of purchasing annuities. If a defined benefit scheme is underfunded, an employee will be looking to the employer to make good his loss, and the *Occupational Pension Schemes (Employer Debt) Regulations 2005 (SI 2005/678)*, as amended, will come into play. If the scheme began to wind up before 6 April 2005 or, unless the scheme is a money purchase scheme, if a debt arose under *PA 1995, s 75* before that date, the *Occupational Pension Schemes (Deficiency on Winding Up etc) Regulations 1996 (SI 1996/3128)* (the '*Deficiency Regulations*') will instead apply. These two sets of Regulations value benefits on different bases, depending on the date of winding up and the status of the employee; therefore, in certain circumstances, employees will not receive their full entitlement. In addition, the employer's debt under these Regulations is an unsecured debt owed to the trustees from the employer; so, if the employer is insolvent, the employee will potentially receive nothing. However, the employee does have some security on an ongoing basis as a result of the scheme-specific funding regime (see CHAPTER 11) and the statutory priorities on wind up (see CHAPTER 5).

PA 2004 has improved member security to an extent, with the introduction of the Pension Protection Fund ('PPF'), which is designed to protect members of private sector defined benefit schemes in the event that their employer becomes insolvent with insufficient funds in the scheme (see CHAPTER 5). In summary, it is intended that members of the scheme who have reached normal retirement age will receive in full the pension to which they are entitled under the scheme and that members below retirement age will receive 90 per cent of the pension accrued to them prior to the assessment date, revalued to the date of payment but subject to an overall cap of £28,742.68 at age 65 for the year April 2009 to March 2010.

For a pension scheme established under trust, the employee's security therefore depends on a number of factors including the continued payment of contributions by the employer to ensure sufficient funding, and investment performance. It is difficult to ascertain what the employee's 'rights' against an employer are. His pension entitlement is enforceable against the trustees, who will look to the employer for additional funding, if required. If the scheme is in deficit, the employee's enforceable rights against the employer are statutory, and statute does not guarantee that a full pension (ie as promised under the trust documentation) will be paid.

What are the employer's obligations?

General

7.4 The employer must comply with the rights and obligations set out in the trust deed and rules governing the scheme. However, these do not cover every eventuality, and it is often necessary to look to case law for guidance.

Fiduciary duties – Mettoy *and* Icarus

7.5 *Mettoy Pension Trustees Ltd v Evans [1990] 1 WLR 1587* acknowledged (although the case did not hinge on this) that an employee's rights under a pension scheme trust are of a commercial and contractual origin; they derive from the contract of employment, with benefits being earned by virtue of service with the employer under those contracts and, where the scheme is contributory, by virtue of those contributions. Employees can therefore benefit from a pension scheme only by virtue of their employment, which in turn is governed by the employment contract. Similar issues were previously raised in *Kerr v British Leyland (1986) CA, reported [2001] WTLR 1071* and *Mihlenstedt v Barclays Bank International [1989] IRLR 522*, in which the judge stated that the scheme was 'established against the background of such employment and falls to be interpreted against that background'.

The judge in the *Mettoy* case concluded that the power apparently vested in the company to decide what to do with a surplus on winding up was a fiduciary power (ie a power conferred on the employer as 'trustee' of the power, effectively being one which had to be exercised in the best interests of the members and putting the employer in the same position as a trustee as regards the duties owed to members).

A similar decision was made in *Icarus (Hertford) v Driscoll [1990] PLR 1*, where the employer remained as trustee of the scheme following its insolvency (this was prior to the legislation requiring an independent trustee to be appointed in such a situation). It is therefore logical that the judge held the employer to be in a fiduciary position, as the employer was the actual, as opposed to a quasi, trustee. There was held to be a fiduciary power which the employer had to exercise in good faith, 'in the sense that he cannot act for reasons which are irrelevant or perverse'.

Employers should, therefore, bear in mind that the powers which they exercise may be those which a court would consider to be fiduciary in nature and should seek to ensure compliance with the associated duties accordingly.

Duty of good faith – the **Imperial** *case*

7.6 It is well established that under the contract of employment there exists a reciprocal duty of good faith on the part of both employers and employees. As a consequence of the *Imperial* case, this principle extends to the exercise of all the employer's powers and obligations under a pension scheme (*Imperial Group Pension Trust v Imperial Tobacco [1991] 2 All ER 597*). The decision in *Imperial* can be seen as the judiciary importing employment law concepts into the pensions arena: it was held that the company was under an implied contractual obligation of good faith in the exercise of its rights and powers under the pension scheme. The court also established the principle that the trust deed and rules were subject to the implied limitation that any rights or powers of the company should only be exercised in accordance with the obligation not seriously to undermine the relationship of trust and confidence existing between the employer and the employee. This duty of good faith, which arguably means little more than the employer having to act in a reasonable manner, is not the same as a fiduciary duty (see **7.5** above); the judge (Sir Nicolas Browne-Wilkinson V-C) explained that the company can have regard to its own interests (financial and otherwise) but only to the extent that in doing so it does not breach the obligation of good faith to its employees.

*Post-***Imperial**

7.7 The rights and obligations of an employer were considered by the High Court in May 1996 in the case of *Engineering Training Authority v Pensions*

Ombudsman [1996] PLR 409, this case being an appeal from a determination by the Pensions Ombudsman of maladministration on the part of the employer. The Ombudsman had jurisdiction at that time to consider the question of an employer's functions in relation to a pension scheme under the *Personal and Occupational Pension Schemes (Pensions Ombudsman) Regulations 1991 (SI 1991/588)* (which have subsequently been revoked and replaced by the *Personal and Occupational Pension Schemes (Pensions Ombudsman) Regulations 1996 (SI 1996/2475)*). The member was made redundant in May 1993. If he had been made redundant in September 1993, at age 50, he would have been entitled to an early retirement pension. In negotiations the employer agreed to keep the employee on its books until age 50 (agreeing that he could obtain an immediate pension without actuarial reduction) and the employee consented to this (by countersigning a letter to him from the employer). He then complained to the Ombudsman that the employer had not provided him with an enhancement (of six years' pensionable service) which was payable, at the employer's discretion, to employees retiring after age 47 and that he had been 'coerced' into signing away his pension enhancement rights. The court held that the Ombudsman does not have power 'to investigate complaints about the ordinary contractual relations between employer and employee', which are matters for an employment tribunal or a court. The Ombudsman's jurisdiction to investigate is confined to the employer's functions relating to the pension scheme.

Although this case deals essentially with the clarification of the jurisdiction of the Ombudsman, it is indicative of the uncertainty of the overlap between pension and contractual promises. Interestingly, in the appeal the Ombudsman tried to argue that even if the employer was not guilty of maladministration, the complaint should be upheld as the employer had breached the *Imperial* duty of good faith. The court was referred to the decision of the Court of Appeal in *Harris v Shuttleworth [1994] PLR 47*, which stated that for an employer to dismiss an employee and thus deprive her of an ill-health pension 'might very well amount to a breach of good faith on the part of the employer, giving the employee a separate remedy'. The judge thought that these submissions were inappropriate in the context of the appeal (having not been considered by the Ombudsman in his determination). However, it is possible in situations such as this that the employee concerned could (time limits permitting) launch a separate action.

The *Imperial* duty continues to be an extremely important legal principle, in both High Court cases and in the Ombudsman's jurisdiction. For example, the judge (Knox J) in *Hillsdown Holdings plc v Pensions Ombudsman [1997] 1 All ER 862* found that the employer had been in breach of the duty of good faith by threatening to suspend contributions and flood an overfunded scheme with new entrants if the trustees did not agree to merger proposals put forward by the employer. Similarly, the Ombudsman determined, in a complaint brought against the National Grid by two pensioners, that the power vested in an employer to distribute surplus had to be exercised in good faith and that, as the power was vested solely in the employer, the obligation approached a fiduciary duty, calling for the power to be exercised in the best interests of the scheme as a whole, without preferring the employer's interests. Inevitably, given the financial significance of the Ombudsman's determination, National Grid appealed the decision. The appeal (*[1997] PLR 157*) was heard by the High Court simultaneously with a summons taken out by National Power, upon whom the *National Grid* determination would have impacted. Part of the appeal hinged on the Ombudsman's view of the duty to distribute surplus approaching a fiduciary duty. Walker J concluded that there is an essential distinction between the duty of good faith and a fiduciary duty, being the right of the employer to look at its own interests. He stated that the Ombudsman had 'lost sight of that essential distinction', and felt that if the *Imperial* case had been heard before the *Mettoy* case, the judge in *Mettoy* could have come to a different conclusion. Although the duty of good faith may have aspects in common with a fiduciary duty, Walker J saw no reason to blend them together; he concluded that no evidence had been put before the Ombudsman to suggest that National Grid was in breach of its duty of good faith and that the Ombudsman had therefore erred in law. The Ombudsman's directions were consequently set aside by the High Court, but this decision was reversed by the Court of Appeal judgment (*[1999] PLR 37*), which in turn was reversed in the House of Lords in favour of the employers. However, the appeal was not concerned with the distinction between the duty of good faith and fiduciary duties, so the judgment of Walker J in that regard is still good law.

Later decisions emphasise the limits of the *Imperial* principle. In *University of Nottingham v Eyett [1999] 2 All ER 437* an employer was not obliged to warn an employee that he had not chosen the most advantageous course of action, where the employee was aware of his entitlement to a benefit and was taking a decision on ways to maximise it. In *Outram v Academy Plastics [2000] IRLR 499*, the Court of Appeal struck out a claim that an employer owed a duty of care to an employee who had resigned after 20 years' service and later rejoined the employer. Employers, it was held, do not owe a duty of care to advise scheme members faced with choices about pension matters, nor do they owe a wider duty in tort than in contract. If, however, an employer voluntarily undertakes to provide such advice, an implied duty not to give inaccurate, negligent or misleading advice may apply. *Outram* was cited in *Wirral Metropolitan Borough Council v Evans and another [2001] OPLR 73* and that judgment followed. It was held that there was no duty on the administrators to give advice to Mr Evans which would have prevented him from transferring his pension benefits to the scheme on unfavourable terms.

In *Crossley v Faithful & Gould Holdings Limited [2004] EWCA Civ 293, [2004] 4 All ER 447*, Dyson LJ, presiding, usefully analysed previous cases and concluded in paragraph 44 of the judgment that:

> 'The employer is not required to have regard to the employee's financial circumstances when he takes lawful business decisions which may affect the employee's economic welfare. There is no reason to suppose that he will even be aware of the details of those circumstances. Nor is it the function of the employer to act as his employee's financial adviser, that is simply not part of the bargain that is comprised in the contract of employment. There are no obvious policy reasons to impose on an employer the general duty to protect his employee's economic wellbeing. The employee can obtain his own advice, whether from his union or otherwise.'

Nevertheless, if an employer assumes the responsibility for giving financial advice to its employee, it is under a duty to take reasonable care in the giving of that advice. This principle was confirmed in *Lennon v Metropolitan Police Commissioner [2004] EWCA Civ 130, [2004] 2 All ER 266,* and cited in the *Crossley* case.

Can an employer contract out of the Imperial *duty?*

7.8 This issue was considered by the Ombudsman in a determination issued in May 1997 (*Poole v Trustees of the Cytec Industries (UK) Limited, Case reference F00088*). The Interim Trust Deed of the Cytec Scheme contained a provision which stated that 'in exercising any discretion, or power, or giving its agreement or consent under the Plan, an Employer may act in its absolute unfettered discretion and in its sole and exclusive interests'.

The Ombudsman determined that this provision could not operate to nullify the implied obligation of good faith, particularly as it appeared in an agreement made between two parties (the employer and the trustees), to the exclusion of the complainant. Additionally the Ombudsman held that the provision could not be allowed to operate so as to enable the employer to contract out of the Ombudsman's jurisdiction in respect of injustice caused by maladministration. He also commented that the exclusion was unusual and oppressive.

Would the Ombudsman's decision have been different if the offending provision had been printed in the booklet? Probably not, for the reasons set out in **7.19** below, but there is a lesson for employers here: if you wish to rely on a provision, make sure that it is drawn to the employees' attention, in a booklet or other scheme literature distributed to employees.

To whom is the Imperial *duty owed?*

7.9 In the *National Bus* determination (*1997 PLR 1*), the Pensions Ombudsman stated that the duty of good faith was owed by the employer to the trustees as well as to the employees. The duty is, therefore, also enforceable by the trustees against the employer. It seems likely that a court would hold that the duty is also owed to ex-employees and by implication, to those claiming through employees (ie spouses and dependants).

In the words of Walker J, 'the scope and limits of the *Imperial Tobacco* duty will no doubt be worked out, on a case by case basis, in coming years'. Employers must therefore take care when exercising their powers.

Termination and reduction of benefits

7.10 Although it is now beyond doubt, following *Barber* and *Coloroll*, that pensions are deferred pay, whether the employer has obligations (whether fiduciary or contractual, or arising from the duty of good faith) not to restrict, reduce or terminate the possibility of earning that future pay has yet to be tested in the courts. Given the wording of (or at least what could be considered to be the intention of) *PA 1995* and *PA 2004*, a successful challenge seems unlikely. However, in certain circumstances resulting from the particular drafting of scheme documents, such as highlighted in the *Lloyds Bank* case (see **7.11** below) and the *National Bus* determination (see **7.9** above), nothing can be taken for granted. Both of these cases indicate how carefully scheme documents have to be drafted and construed by trustees and employers, as a narrow interpretation is likely to be imposed by a court or the Pensions Ombudsman in the event of a dispute.

In ascertaining the crossover between pension and employment rights it is useful to focus on a scenario whereby the employer wishes to alter the level of benefits, either by terminating the pension scheme or by providing less beneficial benefits for future (or past) service. From a pure pensions viewpoint, the employer would have to consider the terms of the power of amendment (which may be jointly vested in the trustees and the employer and may have certain restrictions on how the power can be exercised), and the limitations imposed by *PA 1995, ss 67–67I*. In addition to these aspects, an employer would have to act in accordance with case law, in particular with the *Imperial* duty of good faith, and with the procedural requirements of *PA 2004* as to consultation with employees on the proposal (see **7.12** below). From an employment law perspective, both statutory and contractual issues may arise.

The issues arising where the employer wishes to terminate the scheme are much the same as those which arise where it wants to reduce future benefits under an ongoing scheme, since termination of a scheme may be regarded as the ultimate reduction in future accrual, ie to zero. Different considerations apply where the employer wants to reduce past service benefits.

Reduction of past service benefits

7.11 It has always been generally inadvisable to reduce an employee's past service benefits and in many instances this option will be precluded by the scheme's documentation. In addition, 'accrued rights and entitlements' became protected (from 6 April 1997) by *PA 1995, s 67*, as amended from 6 April 2006 by *PA 2004*, which replaced the original *s 67* with new *ss 67–67I*; these refer to 'subsisting rights' rather than 'accrued rights and entitlements' (see **12.18** below), though the two expressions cover much the same ground. The meaning of 'subsisting rights' is considered in **12.1** below. The new *s 67* is more flexible than the old in terms of what it permits, but the procedural requirements, eg information to members, are much greater. The Regulator's Code of Practice on modification of subsisting rights includes guidance on satisfying the information requirements.

The new *s 67* allows rule changes which modify members' subsisting rights, provided certain conditions are met. Protected modifications are those which would or might either convert defined benefit (DB) subsisting rights to defined contribution (DC) rights; or reduce a pension in payment; the written consent of all affected members (and survivors) must be obtained to these major changes. Detrimental modifications are those which are not protected modifications and which would or might adversely affect any subsisting right of an affected member (or survivor), ie which would or might alter the nature or extent of the entitlements or rights in a way that would or might result in less generous benefits for the affected member. To effect a detrimental modification, the trustees must obtain the written consent of affected members or obtain a certificate of actuarial equivalence or use a combination of both methods. As under the old *s 67* provisions, the trustees must formally approve the modification, no matter who has power to make amendments under the scheme rules. Before giving approval, they must ensure that all the requirements of *s 67* have been satisfied.

The issue of reduction of what were then referred to as accrued rights was considered by the High Court in *Lloyds Bank Pension Trust Corporation v Lloyds Bank plc [1996] PLR 263*. In that case the power of amendment was vested jointly in the trustee and the employer, but precluded (*inter alia*) alterations which would in the opinion of the actuary decrease 'the pecuniary benefits secured to or in respect of … members under the scheme'. The trustee and the company brought the court application to determine whether the trustee could agree to equalise benefits in accordance with a proposal put forward by the employer. The proposal effectively equalised male benefits up to the female level for the period 17 May 1990 to 30 April 2000 (at a cost of £100 million), but equalised female benefits down to the previous male level for the period 1 May 2000 onwards. The scheme also contained express provisions requiring member consent to any alterations. Although this case turns on its own facts and the peculiarity of the amendment power, the legal reasoning is of interest. The judge considered that, except with the requisite level of member consent, no amendment could be made either affecting accrued rights or future benefits and, accordingly, the court would not endorse the amendment.

Similar issues were considered by the Pensions Ombudsman in his determination in respect of the dissolution of the National Bus Company (see **7.9** above). The power of amendment was, subject to trustee consent, vested in the company, and contained a proviso that accrued rights could not be affected without obtaining written member consent. As part of a package offered by the company the trustee agreed to alter the basis of indexation on winding up. The Ombudsman considered that the indexation changes affected 'at least some members' benefits' and that accordingly consent had been required. As the trustee, even if acting innocently, had altered benefits in contravention of the power of amendment, the trustee was under an obligation to recover surplus monies paid to the Department of Transport, which inherited the rights and obligations of the company on its dissolution. On 1 June 1999 the Deputy Prime Minister announced that the Government had reached a settlement with the trustees and on 1 August 1999 paid over £355.77 million. What followed was the lengthy and difficult task of several court applications to assist the trustees to ensure the fair and equitable distribution of the returned monies.

The recent case of *Walker Morris Trustees Limited v Masterson [2009] EWHC 1955 (Ch)* is a useful reminder about the importance of properly applying the power of amendment. Most of the amendments which the trustees purported to make over a 30-year period were struck down (including *Barber* equalisation) because the trustees had failed to comply with the requirement of the amendment power to obtain a written opinion from the actuary that members' accrued rights would not be substantially prejudiced. The court held that the amendment rule clearly required the trustees always to seek the actuary's opinion, even where there could not possibly be any prejudice to members' benefits; and that *s 67* certificates issued by the actuary did not constitute the required written opinion, as *s 67* certificates are designed for a different purpose.

Termination of a scheme or reduction in benefits in an ongoing scheme

7.12 Arguably, termination of a pension scheme (other than cases of insolvencies, where a winding-up would often be automatically triggered) is the real test as to how far an employee has contractual rights against the employer, in addition to the established rights against the trustees under the trust deed and the employee's statutory rights. There is no clear case law on this issue.

As a point of employment law, the question is whether the employer would be in breach of contract by deliberately discontinuing the scheme, or whether it can rely on the express enabling power to terminate, contained in the trust deed and (generally) referred to in the booklet. In practice, an employer can terminate a pension scheme, provided it acts in accordance with the termination procedures contained in the governing documentation. Employers must, however, act very carefully to minimise the risk of any claims by employees and must have a valid reason for wishing to terminate the pension scheme. The most compelling reason will be that the employer simply cannot continue to operate the scheme because of its cost (a reason which has become more commonplace due to the additional costs arising under *PA 1995* and then under *PA 2004*).

If the employer sought to terminate all existing contracts of employment (by giving the appropriate notice) and issue new contracts reflecting the less favourable pension provision, this rather aggressive tactic would carry the risk of employees being able to argue that the unilateral change in their terms of employment constituted a fundamental breach of contract by the employer which would entitle them to resign and claim constructive dismissal. Additionally, the employer would have to have a good and substantial reason for wishing to act in this way, and the method of implementation would have to be fair.

Where the employer proposes to terminate the scheme it will generally be impracticable for it to seek the consent of all of the employees who are active scheme members, although this option may sometimes be chosen where the scheme has very few members. If the scheme is in deficit, the position of the deferred members and pensioners will also be affected. A period of consultation and/or negotiations with any trade unions may be appropriate, giving the employer an opportunity to make clear the reason for the changes, and also making it more likely that a court would consider that the employer had complied with the *Imperial* duty of good faith. Employment law obligations to provide information to, and consult with, trade unions or employee representatives may arise under *TUPE* in the case of a business transfer (see **7.24** below); under the collective dismissals legislation (*TULRCA*) in the case of large-scale redundancies; or under the *Information and Consultation of Employees Regulations 2004 (SI 2004/3426)* (the '*ICE Regulations*') in the case of other employment matters such as threats to employment, changes to terms and conditions of employment and the economic prospects of the business, but not where the *Pension Consultation Regulations*, referred to in the next paragraph, apply.

From April 2006 a separate set of regulations, the *Occupational and Personal Pension Schemes (Consultation by Employers and Miscellaneous Amendment) Regulations 2006 (SI 2006/349)* (the '*Pension Consultation Regulations*'), made under *PA 2004, ss 259–261*, introduced a new statutory requirement for employers to consult with employees in respect of 'listed changes' to occupational and personal pension schemes, including the cessation or reduction of future accrual. The announcement issued to members regarding an amendment to the scheme's trust deed and rules is no longer sufficient.

Although the obligation under the *Pension Consultation Regulations* is in addition to any of the other consultation requirements referred to above, the *ICE Regulations*, as amended, provide that employers are not obliged to consult about the same issues twice under the *ICE Regulations* and the *Pension Consultation Regulations*. However, if the proposed diminution of benefits is just one of a range of proposals by the employer, it may also be necessary to consult about those other proposals under the other requirements.

The *Pension Consultation Regulations* require employers to consult with active and prospective members of most occupational and personal pension schemes before certain changes may be made to a scheme in relation to future service benefits. In line with the *ICE Regulations*, the *Pension Consultation Regulations* now apply to employers of more than 50 employees (whether or not they are scheme members). The exemptions apply to each employer (irrespective of how many employers participate in a multi-employer scheme). Entirely excluded from the pensions consultation requirement are:

- in the case of occupational pension schemes, any employer in relation to:
  - a public service scheme;
  - a 'small scheme' (similar to the old 'SSAS');
  - a scheme with fewer than two members;
  - an employer-financed retirement benefits scheme;
  - an unregistered overseas scheme (having its main administration outside the EEA); and
- any employer in relation to a personal pension scheme where direct payment arrangements exist but no employer contributions fall to be paid towards the scheme.

The employer must give specified written information to all affected members and their representatives at least 60 days before the date on which it intends to take any decision (or series of decisions) to make a 'listed change'. The required information includes details of the listed change, its likely effects on the scheme and its members, and the timescale for implementation, and it must be accompanied by any relevant background information. The information must be clear and comprehensive enough to enable members' representatives to consider the effect of the proposed change. If there are no existing employee representatives, employers will have to arrange for their appointment or elections. If the employees do not appoint or elect representatives, employers will have to consult with all affected employees individually.

Listed changes are set out in *Pension Consultation Regulations, regs 8* and *9*, and include increasing the normal pension age; closing the scheme to new members; preventing or changing future accrual of benefits; changing some or all of the benefits provided under a defined benefit scheme to money purchase benefits; or changing (broadly, to the detriment of the members) the contributions required from members or provided by the employer.

Consultation 'in a spirit of co-operation, taking account the interests of both sides' then must take place with at least one of the specified employee representatives. The employer must then consider the responses received and, if the listed changes were proposed by a third party (eg the trustees or the principal employer), notify the third party in writing of the responses. The third party must then satisfy itself that consultation was carried out in compliance with the regulations. If no responses were received, the consultation would be deemed complete at the end of the consultation period.

The *Pension Consultation Regulations* were amended, from 6 April 2009, by the *Occupational, Personal and Stakeholder Pensions (Miscellaneous Amendment) Regulations 2009 (SI 2009/615)*, which have given the Pensions Regulator power to impose a civil penalty on an employer who has failed, without reasonable excuse, to comply with the consultation requirements (up to £5,000 on an individual and £50,000 on a company). Previously it was arguable that the regulations did not have much 'bite', as they laid down no specific sanction: the Regulator could have issued an improvement notice (under *PA 2004, s 13*), directing the person in default to take steps to remedy the contravention, but by that time it would generally have been too late, as the act which should have been consulted on would already have been implemented. There is now more incentive to comply with the consultation requirements, but there is still no direct power for the Regulator to impose a penalty on trustees for failure to comply.

How do the trustees fit in?

General

7.13 The trustees of a pension scheme have an overriding duty to act in the best interests of the beneficiaries, which usually means their best financial interests (see CHAPTER 3). If the power of amendment is vested solely in the employer, the trustees cannot control the outcome, save to ensure that the amendment complies with the requirements of *PA 1995, ss 67–67I* (except perhaps by way of court application in extreme circumstances, which could either be an injunction to prevent an amendment being made or an application for directions). When the power of amendment is vested in the trustees (or the trustees have to consent to the exercise of a power vested in the employer), the trustees must confine their considerations to the implications for the existing members (including deferred members and pensioners) only. Depending on the particular circumstances, the trustees may also wish to take into account the position of prospective beneficiaries (for example, if there was a waiting period before employees could join the scheme).

Whatever action the trustees take will depend very much on the circumstances; say, trustees are faced with a future reduction in benefits (for example, 60ths accrual to 80ths, or final salary to money purchase). They may be persuaded that the amendment is in the interests of all members if the only other alternative is that the scheme will be discontinued because the employer cannot (for sound commercial reasons) afford to continue the current level of promised benefits. In all but the rarest of cases it must be in the beneficiaries' best interests to have an ongoing scheme. This was highlighted in *Re Courage Group Pension Schemes [1987] 1 All ER 528*, where the judge stated that 'it is important to avoid fettering the power to amend the provisions of the scheme, thereby preventing the parties from making those changes which may be required by the exigencies of commercial life'.

The trustees may often find themselves in the position of arbitrators between an employer and employee if a dispute over a pension issue arises. Often trust deeds confer upon the trustees the power to reach decisions on any matter of doubt arising under the scheme documentation. Under *PA 1995, ss 50–50B* (as inserted by *PA 2004, s 273*, as amended by *PA 2007, s 16*), trustees of most occupational pension schemes have to put in place an internal dispute resolution (IDR) procedure, which since 6 April 2008 can be either single-stage, where the decision is made by the trustees, or two-stage, where a dispute may not be referred to the trustees until it has first been considered, and a decision made, by a 'specified person'. The final decision rests with the trustees. The Pensions Regulator has issued a Code of Practice on the subject. This requirement for a dispute resolution procedure does not, however, extend to disputes between a member and an employer. For further details of IDR, see CHAPTER 15.

In cases of dismissal or leaving service

7.14 When an employment contract is terminated, the leaving service rules of the scheme will apply and the employee will, if his rights have vested, become a deferred member. The trustees will be obliged, if the ex-employee so requests, to provide details of his options under the trust deed in accordance with the requirements of the *Disclosure Regulations* and the *Preservation Regulations*. If the employee takes no action to exercise an option available to him, he will simply continue to be treated as a deferred member.

Depending on whom the power to augment is vested in, the trustees may have to liaise with an employer on dismissal or redundancy packages (see **7.15** below).

Entitlements in cases of dismissal or redundancy

Redundancy

7.15 If an employee is entitled to a statutory redundancy payment, such a payment will be based upon his age, length of continuous employment and his gross average weekly pay (subject to a maximum of £380 a week with effect from 1 October 2009). For the purposes of *ERA 1996*, pay means either the remuneration payable under his contract or, alternatively, his pay based on his average hourly rate.

The *ERA 1996* definition of 'a week's pay' does not include any element relating to an employer's contributions to a pension scheme. Therefore, an employee's pension entitlement on redundancy will depend upon the wording of the scheme documentation. Generally, if the employee has been a member for less than two years he will be entitled to a refund of his contributions (less tax as calculated under *FA 2004, s 204, Schs 31, 36*) or a cash transfer sum, which the trustees may pay to another registered pension scheme; otherwise, he will become a deferred member. If he has at least three months', but less than two years', pensionable service, he will be entitled to either a refund of his contributions (less tax) or a cash transfer sum. It is also worth bearing in mind that some schemes, particularly ex-public sector ones, retain beneficial redundancy/early retirement provisions.

Unfair dismissal

7.16 Unfair dismissal is the dismissal of an employee entitled to protection under *ERA 1996* without a potentially fair reason or without following a fair procedure.

If an employee establishes that he has been unfairly dismissed (the burden of proof being on the employee to establish dismissal and on the employer to establish the reason for the dismissal and, effectively, that it was fair) he will usually be awarded compensation comprising a basic award, based on his weekly pay (subject to the statutory cap), age and length of service, and also to a compensatory award. Other alternative remedies include reinstatement or re-engagement, but are less common. The effect of a reinstatement or re-engagement order is that the previous terms and conditions remain in force so, for pension purposes, the employer and employee will simply have to pay arrears of contributions. This, of course, presupposes that the rules of the scheme allow the employee to rejoin.

The maximum basic award for claims where the effective date of termination is on or after 1 October 2009 is £11,400. This amount does not include benefits in kind. Under *ERA 1996, ss 123* and *124*, the compensatory award is such an amount as the employment tribunal considers just and equitable in all the circumstances, having regard to the loss sustained by the complainant, including loss of any pension benefit, subject to a current maximum of £66,200. The above figures are normally adjusted on 1 February every year. In 2009, however, owing to the economic climate, an adjustment to the cap on a week's pay was made in October 2009, with the next adjustment due to be made in February 2011. The tribunal has discretion to reduce any award if it believes that the complainant has caused or contributed to his dismissal or has failed to mitigate his loss by securing suitable alternative employment. An additional award is payable where reinstatement or re-engagement orders have not been complied with. This latter award does not include allowance for loss of pension benefits.

In practice, an employee may suffer loss of pension rights if he fails to find new employment or if his new employer does not operate a pension scheme or operates a less beneficial scheme. Compensation for loss of pension rights is often difficult to quantify. In the majority of employment tribunals cases a starting point for calculation is a 'rough and ready' style of calculation found in guidelines ('Compensation for Loss of Pension Rights' – Employment Tribunals), originally prepared in 1990 by the Government Actuary's Department in consultation with three employment tribunal chairmen and last updated in 2003. They require a loss to be viewed in three stages, namely:

(*a*) between the date of the dismissal and the date of the hearing (being the actual loss sustained, for example, the difference between an old and a new employer's benefit provision or, if the complainant is unemployed, between the scheme benefits and State scheme benefits);

(*b*) the loss of future pension rights to the date of retirement (which is essentially speculation on the part of the employment tribunal – it may even conclude that the employee's future earnings and benefits will never match his old package, thus the loss may continue over the remainder of his working life); and

(*c*) the enhancement of accrued pension rights.

The report also provides guidance on how tribunals should reach a just and equitable sum for compensation. It allows the parties to adduce actuarial evidence and breaks down the calculation into three areas:

(i) when attempting to calculate the loss of rights which would have accrued between the date of dismissal and the hearing, reference should be made to the contributions which the employer would have made during that period (although the report admits that this method is not technically correct);

(ii) for the calculation of loss of future pension rights between the date of the hearing and the date of retirement, the employment tribunal should estimate how long it will take for the applicant to enter equivalent employment;

(iii) when calculating the loss of enhancement of the pension rights accrued to the date of dismissal, no enhancement should be granted where the applicant is in any public sector scheme, where he is within five years of retirement or where the employment would have been terminated within one year. Otherwise a multiple (as set out in the report) will be utilised and the employment tribunal may also, at its discretion, apply a withdrawal factor, based on the likelihood of the complainant leaving service, being made redundant or fairly dismissed.

In a few cases the guidelines recommend the use of the 'substantial loss' approach: where it is generally considered that the employee will suffer a quantifiable continuing loss and where, for example, the employment was stable and unlikely to have been affected by economic cycles, where the employment lasted a considerable period of time and where the employee reached an age where he was less likely to seek new employment. The substantial loss approach involves using actuarial tables to assess the capitalised value of the pension rights which the employee would have accrued up to retirement. These tables use factors similar to those in the Ogden Tables for personal injury and fatal accident cases, although some of the assumptions used are different. Calculation under the substantial loss approach automatically includes compensation for loss of enhancement of accrued pension rights at the date of dismissal and for loss of pension rights from the date of dismissal to the date of the hearing, as well as for loss of future pension rights from the date of the hearing.

Which calculation method is used is a crucial issue, as the different methods can produce different results and make a substantial difference to the amount of compensation awarded in respect of pension losses. The guidance makes it clear that the ultimate decision as to the method of calculation to be used always rests with the employment tribunal.

Before the publication of the updated version of the guidance, the Employment Appeal Tribunal had ruled that there was no duty on employment tribunals to give precise effect to the guidelines (*Bingham v Hoboun Engineering Ltd [1992] IRLR 298*). Following the increase of the maximum compensatory award under all heads from £10,000 to £50,000 (£66,200 from 1 February

2009) (*ERA 1996, s 124(1)*), loss of earnings may now be less likely to be the major component of any compensatory award and arguably it is becoming more necessary for pension loss calculations to be precise.

Indeed, in *Clancy v Cannock Chase Technical College [2001] IRLR 331*, the Employment Appeal Tribunal noted that the guidelines were drawn up at a time when the compensatory award was set at £10,000. In the EAT's opinion, the significant raising of the cap meant that an accurate calculation of compensation for loss of pensions will be relevant (rather than reliance on the guidelines) in many more cases in the future. Evidently, this is not the view taken by the Government Actuary's Department.

In *Aegon v Roberts [2009] EWCA Civ 932*, the Court of Appeal made it clear that the calculation of compensation should not involve any 'double counting'. Here, the former employee had, unusually, found a new job with a higher salary and membership of a money purchase scheme after she had been made redundant (and the Employment Tribunal had found that this was also an unfair dismissal). However, the EAT awarded her compensation for continuing loss of final salary pension benefits, on the basis that she was unlikely ever to be able to join a final salary scheme in future as so few are open to new members. The Court of Appeal overturned the EAT decision, holding that pension benefits were just one part of the remuneration package; the EAT should not have separated the issues of earnings and pensions; and the higher salary should offset the less favourable pension.

Wrongful dismissal

7.17 If an employer dismisses an employee without good cause in breach of an obligation to give notice (either statutory or contractual) and the employee suffers loss as a result, it will be liable to pay to that employee damages for wrongful dismissal. The primary remedy is damages, normally equal to loss of earnings and other contractual benefits up to the earliest date upon which the contract could have been lawfully terminated by the employer. The aim of damages is to put the employee in the same position as he would have been had the contract been performed, although the employee is usually under a duty to mitigate his loss.

It is unlikely that an employer could successfully argue that it should not pay damages by reference to the pension scheme on the grounds that it could have terminated the scheme at any time in accordance with the trust deed. However, such a claim could be effective in respect of a single employer scheme.

In practice, most compensation payments will be negotiated between the employer and employee. For example, if a fixed-term contract was terminated two years before it could lawfully have been terminated, this period will be the starting point for the assessment of loss of pay and other benefits.

With a final salary arrangement, the employee would have been entitled to two years' additional pensionable service, perhaps taking into account an assumed pay rise if provision for this was made in the contract. If pay increases were not provided for in the contract, these will not be taken into account (ie the actual salary at the date of termination will be used), nor will any element of discretionary increases. The following three methods can be used to calculate the loss:

(*a*) The award of an additional two years' notional pensionable service to the employee under the rules of the scheme, dealing with the award under the augmentation provisions. The trustees would require payment of an additional contribution (generally a lump sum) by the employer to cover this (an actuary would be required to advise on the calculation of this contribution, and, depending on the employee's age, it may not be simply a case of utilising the general scheme contribution rate as the nearer an employee is to normal retirement date, the more costly this becomes).

(*b*) The most straightforward way of calculating the damages to be paid directly to the employee would be by reference to the employer contribution rate over the two-year period. This method would not produce an accurate result (effectively younger employees may be over-compensated) and is more appropriate for money purchase arrangements. However, if it is used, it should be subject to grossing up and discounting for early receipt if it is paid directly to the employee.

(*c*) Loss can also be calculated by reference to the difference in capital value of the benefits accrued to the effective date of dismissal and the capital value of the benefits which would have been accrued up to the end of the notice period. This is the most accurate method and actuarial advice will be required.

In a money purchase arrangement, the compensation will be calculated on the basis of the employer contributions which would have been made in the two-year period and an assumed investment return and (potentially) an allowance for salary increases. Similarly, discounting may apply.

Alternatively, it may be possible for the compensation to be paid as a contribution to the pension scheme. This may be advantageous to the employee, for example, if he is approaching retirement. It will be tax-deductible for the employer as an employer contribution to a registered pension if it is paid wholly and exclusively for the purposes of the trade (see HMRC Business Income Manual). It is likely that most contributions paid for this purpose will satisfy the test, but every case should be examined on its own facts.

It may be worth considering early retirement, to be funded by an additional amount of the damages being paid into the scheme, if the employee is over age 50 (or, for most employees, over age 55 from 6 April 2010: see CHAPTER 16). This can be tax-efficient from both an employer and employee viewpoint (although care has to be taken to ensure that the employee does not become liable to tax on the payment into the scheme as a benefit in kind). However, it may be less attractive if the amount does not compensate for the use of actuarial reduction factors. It would be necessary to involve the pension scheme trustees, as this would be an augmentation of the employee's pension benefits, and either trustee or company consent to the early retirement is likely to be required. (If the employee is entitled to pension benefits as of right under the trust deed, ie consent is not required, *Hopkins v Norcros [1994] PLR 27* confirmed that pension payments cannot be deducted from a wrongful dismissal award, thus leading to an element of double compensation.) Actuarial advice on the scope of the augmentation will also be required.

The employer's aim should ultimately be to negotiate a settlement which should be full and final, to preclude the bringing of further claims.

The express pension promise and GPPs

7.18 As already noted, it is highly unusual for an employer to give an express contractual commitment to provide specified pension benefits in a contract of employment, except perhaps in the case of senior executives. If such a commitment is made, the employee's pension rights, in the event of dismissal or redundancy, will depend entirely on the wording of the pension promise. If, for example, the contract states that the executive will be entitled to a pension of two-thirds of his salary at the date he leaves the employer, the executive will have a contractual right against the employer if those precise benefits are not paid.

It is, however, unlikely that a pension promise would be so widely drafted. Generally the promise will be contingent upon the executive remaining with the company until his normal retirement date, the benefits will be payable from his normal retirement date, termination conditions will usually be incorporated, and *FA 2004* restrictions will apply in the case of registered schemes. Employers should take great care in drafting the contract of employment, and not make any oral commitments.

Following 6 April 2006, with the introduction by *FA 2004* of more generous limits on contributions, it has become easier for employers to provide benefits for executives from a registered pension scheme without the need for a top-up arrangement, although this trend may be reversed once provisions of *FA 2009* come into force, as these will restrict higher rate tax relief on pension contributions (see CHAPTER 16).

A more common example of a contractual pension promise in today's climate is a Group Personal Pension, or GPP. This is a straightforward contractual arrangement between employer and employee. The employee joins the GPP, which will be administered by an insurance company. The employer's only commitment is to pay contributions on a fixed basis (for instance, a stated percentage of pensionable salary) for so long as the employee is employed by the employer.

Exclusion in deed and rules

7.19 Many trust deeds contain a clause to the effect that an employer has no liability to compensate employees for loss of pension rights on termination of employment. Case law makes it clear that the *Unfair Contract Terms Act 1977* ('*UCTA 1977*') applies to contracts of employment (for example, *Brigden v American Express Bank Ltd [2001] IRLR 94*). This means that it is unlikely that such a clause will be effective, as either it is not a term of the contract of employment (being contained in the rules of the pension scheme only and not referred to in the employment contract) or, if it is part of the contract, it will fail the test of reasonableness under *UCTA 1977, s 3*.

In addition, *ERA 1996, s 203* provides that, subject to a number of exceptions, any agreement precluding an individual from making an unfair dismissal claim is void. The most important exception to this is where an employee enters into a valid compromise agreement following receipt of independent legal advice. This will be a valid way to 'sign off' the employee's rights, provided that the conditions set out in *ERA 1996, s 203(3)* are met.

Lump sum death-in-service benefits

7.20 Is an employer liable for the payment of a lump sum benefit if an employee dies following a dismissal which is wrongful or unfair? Providing death-in-service benefits can be costly and most insurance policies will lapse when an employee leaves service (although for larger schemes which self-insure, the provisions of the trust deed will apply).

In wrongful dismissal cases the employer would be liable if the employee died during the notice period, although it is likely that the duty to mitigate loss would apply. In certain cases the trustees of a scheme may also be liable, as the Pensions Ombudsman ruled in the complaint by *Mrs E Richards* in connection with the Merchant Navy Ratings Pension Fund (May 1999). Consequently, an employee should make his own arrangements (and be compensated for the cost of so doing in his damages award) unless he is uninsurable as a single life (for example, he may be unable to pass a medical). Any action would subsist for the benefit of the estate of the deceased.

The situation is less clear-cut in cases of unfair dismissal. In such a situation the tribunal will make an award which it considers to be fair and reasonable, but bearing in mind the limits on compensation a wise employee would arrange his own life cover following the dismissal.

If an employee obtains a reinstatement or re-engagement order his employer should double-check the policy or rules to ensure that life cover continues and that the free cover limit is not breached.

Business reorganisations

Purchase of a company with its own scheme

7.21 If a company purchases the entire issued share capital of another company, the employees' pension rights will not be affected if the latter company operates its own pension scheme, as the scheme will simply remain in place after the sale.

Purchase of a business

7.22 The situation is different if an employer purchases a business or part of a business, in circumstances where the *Transfer of Undertakings (Protection of Employment) Regulations 2006 (SI 2006/246)* ('*TUPE*') apply. These *TUPE* regulations came into force on 6 April 2006, replacing the *Transfer of Undertakings (Protection of Employment) Regulations 1981 (SI 1981/1794)* ('*TUPE 1981*'). The provisions relating to occupational pensions in *TUPE* and *TUPE 1981* are substantially the same. In such a scenario, following the 'relevant transfer' the transferring employees become the employees of the purchasing employer. Their employment contracts are not terminated, and the rights and obligations under the contracts pass to the purchasing employer. Until 6 April 2005, most rights under occupational pension schemes did not transfer as a result of an exclusion contained in *TUPE 1981, reg 7* (now *TUPE, reg 10*). However, the position changed on 6 April 2005.

The law up to April 2005

7.23 *TUPE, reg 10* (previously *TUPE 1981, reg 7*) excludes 'occupational pension schemes' from the 'automatic transfer' effect of the regulations. *TUPE 1981* was intended to implement the *Acquired Rights Directive (Council Directive*

77/187/EEC), which states that protection will not be granted to supplementary company pension schemes but nevertheless expressly requires Member States to adopt 'the measures necessary' to protect the scheme members. This has been reinforced by an amending *Acquired Rights Directive (Council Directive 2001/23/EC)*, adopted on 12 March 2001, which effectively gives Member States the option of protecting pension rights under national legislation.

There have been a number of cases on the scope of *TUPE 1981*. In January 1992 in the case of *Warrener v Walden Engineering Co Ltd [1992] PLR 1*, the Hull Employment Tribunal was asked to consider employees' pension rights when, following a business sale, the new employer decided to discontinue all pension arrangements. The Tribunal stated that the benefits provided by the scheme had been 'part of the contract of employment' and that if a pension scheme is terminated an employee has a contractual right to an equivalent scheme, providing benefits no less beneficial, being set up in its place. This case was based on the argument that, as the pension scheme was contracted out of the State earnings-related pension scheme, it was not a supplementary pension scheme for the purposes of the *Acquired Rights Directive,* as implemented in the UK by *TUPE 1981, reg 7*.

In December 1992 came the case of *Perry v Intec Colleges Ltd [1993] PLR 56* in the Bristol Employment Tribunal. The decision in that case was reached on a different interpretation of *TUPE*; the complainant argued that *TUPE 1981* had failed to translate the aims of the *Acquired Rights Directive* into UK law (ie the subsidiary aim to protect employees). After the transfer no pension provision was to be made for the employees. It was held that the complainant was entitled to pension provision at least as beneficial as that which he had received prior to the transfer. It was suggested that, to compensate the employee adequately, the employer should make an equivalent percentage contribution to a personal pension scheme and should also make a lump sum payment to compensate for lost opportunity to enhance accrued pension benefits. In effect, the Tribunal was advocating double recovery.

In June 1993 the Employment Appeal Tribunal overturned the first instance decision in *Warrener* (*Walden Engineering Co Ltd v Warrener [1993] PLR 295*); meaning that an employer does not have to maintain the pension benefits enjoyed by employees prior to a business sale. The Employment Appeal Tribunal stated that a contracted-out scheme is a supplementary scheme (ie supplementary to the basic State scheme) for the purposes of the *Acquired Rights Directive*, as implemented in the UK by *TUPE 1981*, and accordingly, the employer was protected under the *reg 7* exclusion. In January 1996 this approach was sanctioned by both the High Court and the Court of Appeal in the case of *Adams & Ors v Lancashire County Council & Ors [1996] IRLR 154*. The judge stated that *TUPE 1981* required protection to be given to accrued rights only (which are protected as deferred benefits in the transferor employer's scheme by the preservation requirements now set out in *PSA 1993*).

On 15 May 1997 the High Court decision was upheld by the Court of Appeal (*[1997] IRLR 436*).

In *Hagen v ICI Chemicals and Polymers Ltd [2001] 64 PBLR*, the High Court held that a transferor had made a negligent misrepresentation when persuading its employees to accept a *TUPE* transfer, when it stated that their pension rights after the transfer would be 'broadly comparable' to their pre-transfer rights. The court held that 'broadly comparable' meant no more than 2 per cent difference whereas, in practice, some claimants would have been 5 per cent worse off. Liability for misrepresentations normally passes from transferor to transferee under *TUPE 1981* (*reg 5(2)(a)*). However, since the misrepresentation related to pension entitlement, and was caught by *reg 7*, liability remained with the transferor only.

One important exception to the exclusion of pension rights from *TUPE* comes under *reg 10(2)* (*TUPE 1981, reg 7(2)*) which attempts to implement *Article 3(3)* of the *Acquired Rights Directive* (now *Article 3(4)* of the *Acquired Rights Directive 2001*). *Article 3(4)* excludes from the automatic transfer provisions 'employees' rights to old-age, invalidity or survivors' benefits under supplementary company or inter-company pension schemes ...'. *TUPE, reg 10(1), (2)* stipulate that contractual provisions on occupational pension schemes do not transfer from the transferor to the transferee, except that 'any provisions of an occupational pension scheme which do not relate to benefits for old-age, invalidity or survivors shall be treated as not being part of the scheme'. For many years, it was unclear whether certain benefits provided under occupational pension schemes (for example, enhanced redundancy terms on early retirement, life assurance etc) fall within *reg 10(2)*. This question has been dealt with, to some degree, by the ECJ in *Beckmann v Dynamco Whicheloe Macfarlane Ltd, Case C-164/00, [2002] All ER (EC) 865*. The ECJ ruled that the exceptions contained in *Article 3(4)* of the *Directive* ought to be interpreted narrowly so as to apply only to old-age, invalidity or survivor benefits under occupational pension schemes falling due at the end of 'normal working life'. Other benefits, such as early retirement benefits and redundancy payments are excluded. (The decision in *Beckmann* was subsequently approved in *Martin and others v South Bank University C 4/01, [2003] PLR 329*: see **15.15** below.)

The Government has also made specific provisions regarding transfer of pension rights in the context of public sector transfers (see CHAPTER 14 for further details).

The law from April 2005

7.24 Following extensive consultation exercises since 1998, the Government introduced new pensions provisions which give limited protection to employees where the transferring employer has an occupational pension scheme. The protection extends to both scheme members and those eligible to join. Under *PA 2004, ss 257* and *258* and the *Transfer of Employment (Pension Protection) Regulations 2005 (SI 2005/649)*, which came into force on 6 April 2005, transferee employers must offer transferring employees:

(*a*) membership of the transferee employer's occupational defined contribution or defined benefit pension scheme or of a stakeholder scheme and make into the scheme matching contributions of up to 6 per cent of an employee's basic pay; or

(*b*) membership of an occupational defined benefit pension scheme which provides benefits the value of which is equal to no less than 6 per cent of an employee's pensionable pay (as set out in the scheme rules) for each year of employment together with the total amount of an employee's contributions, and employees are not required to make contributions in excess of 6 per cent of their pensionable pay; or

(*c*) membership of an occupational defined benefit pension scheme which satisfies *PSA 1993, s 12A* (ie the reference scheme test for contracting out).

It is interesting to note that the reference scheme test requirement may provide higher benefits than the transferring employer's scheme provided. It is also important to note that, because the *Transfer of Employment (Pension Protection) Regulations 2005 (SI 2005/649)* have not been amended and are not incorporated into *TUPE*, the transferee employer and employee can agree that the above protections will not apply and that different pension arrangements will operate. They can do this at any time after the employee becomes employed by the transferee.

Employers should always be cautious in situations where *TUPE* applies; if inferior pension provision is to be offered following a relevant transfer, providing the employees with alternative compensation may be the safest route and will go some way to forestalling industrial unrest. Transferor employers would be well advised to seek indemnity cover; although the judge in *Adams* confirmed that he did not believe that employees could claim against the transferor employer, this point has not yet been tested.

It is also important to remember that, under *TUPE*, transferors and transferees have onerous information and consultation obligations, and they are usually liable jointly for breach of these obligations. Proposed changes to the pension arrangements of the transferor's employees are likely to be 'measures' for the purposes of *TUPE, reg 13*, and the transferor will be obliged to consult with employee representatives about them. Although the transferor does not have to consult about measures envisaged by the transferee, the transferor is still required to inform employee representatives about the transferee's proposed measures. In practice, once information is provided, representatives will often start a discussion about the transferee's proposed measures (and a representative of the transferee may therefore attend meetings to answer questions). See **7.12** above for details of other information and consultation requirements.

Purchase of a subsidiary participating in its parent's scheme

7.25 Similar considerations to those outlined at **7.22** above would apply on the sale of a company which participates in a holding company pension arrangement, although *TUPE* itself would not apply. In practice if a new employer is unable to provide equivalent pension provision, alternative methods of compensation (for example, pay rises) should be considered.

Employer's lien

7.26 Many pension schemes permit a lien to be placed on benefits payable where the employee or ex-employee owes money to the employer or the trustees of a scheme resulting from criminal, negligent or fraudulent acts or omissions. Liens are now governed by *PA 1995, ss 91–94* and are an exception to the general rule that pension benefits cannot be assigned or forfeited. However, a lien rule can only operate with the agreement of the employee unless a court or arbitrator has made an order or award in the employer's favour (*PA 1995, ss 91(5)(d), 93(3)*). As an employee can insist on his statutory rights to payment of a guaranteed cash equivalent (see CHAPTER 6), trustees may be forced to pay benefits out before a court or arbitrator has considered the lien issue unless they obtain a time extension for the payment of the cash equivalent.

It should be borne in mind that a lien cannot attach to benefits deriving from transfer credits (unless the transfer is attributable to employment with the same or an associated employer and the transferring scheme contained an appropriate lien rule) (*Occupational Pension Schemes (Assignment, Forfeiture, Bankruptcy etc) Regulations 1997 (SI 1997/785), reg 3*), and no part of a guaranteed minimum pension or protected rights may be subject to deduction. The amount that can be recovered is limited to the lesser of the actuarial value of the employee's actual or prospective benefits and the amount of the monetary obligation owed to the employer or trustees of a scheme (*PA 1995, s 91(6)*).

Owing to the restrictions referred to above, and in particular the need for consent or a court order or decision of an arbitrator, lien rules are often difficult to operate in practice.

Maternity, paternity, adoption and parental absence

General

7.27 Rights relating to maternity, paternity, adoption and parental absence are among the employment rights which come under the heading of equality or equal treatment. Other equality issues (relating to sex, sexual orientation, part-time workers, fixed-term (temporary) workers, disability, race, religion or belief, age and gender reassignment) are dealt with in CHAPTER 9.

The requirements for the equal treatment of women on maternity leave, contained in the *Third Equal Treatment Directive 86/378/EEC,* led to the passing of the *Social Security Act 1989,* the relevant provisions of which came into effect on 23 June 1994. These provisions require benefits under occupational pension schemes to accrue for women on paid maternity leave in the same way as for women working normally, and by reference, therefore, to their full remuneration. Members pay contributions based upon their actual pay received, whether statutory or contractual, and pensionable service is treated as continuous notwithstanding the maternity absence.

Amendments to *Social Security Act 1989, Sch 5* have gradually extended these rights to employees on paid paternity leave (currently two weeks), parental leave (see below) and adoption leave to bring them in line with paid maternity leave. Further amendments were made by the *Work and Families Act 2006* ('*WFA 2006*'), with effect from April 2007. Under the Equality Bill, expected to obtain Royal Assent in Spring 2010, pregnancy and maternity are among the 'protected characteristics' which are subject to protection from discrimination, harassment and victimisation in specific areas, including pensions. The next paragraphs refer to maternity leave and pay, but similar provisions also apply to adoption leave and pay.

The legislation distinguishes between 'ordinary' maternity leave (OML) and 'additional' maternity leave (AML). The maximum period for both is 26 weeks. Generally, all pregnant employees who satisfy certain conditions (mainly in relation to notifications) are entitled to a period of OML. This applies regardless of the number of hours a woman works. *WFA 2006* removed the former length of service qualification for AML (bringing it into line with OML) for women whose expected week of childbirth (EWC) falls on or after 1 April 2007, so that an employee who qualifies for OML now qualifies also for AML. In practice, however, an employee must give notice, and thus be employed, by the 15th week before the EWC (see *ERA 1996, s 71*).

Most employees will be entitled to statutory maternity pay (SMP) from their employer (depending on their earnings and period of continuous employment) or to maternity allowance, paid by the State. *WFA 2006* extended the period in respect of which SMP is payable for women whose EWC falls on or after 1 April 2007, from 26 to 39 weeks, ie for part of the period of AML as well as the whole of the OML period. The Government has stated that it intends further to increase the SMP period to 52 weeks, but these plans have been shelved for the time being. *WFA 2006* also included scope to allow fathers and partners to 'take over' part of their spouse's or partner's maternity or adoption leave period. The Department for Business, Innovation and Skills began a consultation on draft regulations in September 2009, with the expectation that the new right will apply to parents of children due to be born or adopted on or after 3 April 2011.

Amendments to the *Sex Discrimination Act 1975* to remove the distinction between OML and AML were implemented by the *Maternity and Parental Leave etc and the Paternity and Adoption Leave (Amendment) Regulations 2008 (SI 2008/1966)* for women whose EWC falls on or after 5 October 2008. However, the principle remains that remuneration is an exception to the requirement not to deprive an employee on maternity leave of the benefit of her terms and conditions of employment; and the definition of 'remuneration' is unchanged. In the absence in the 2008 regulations of any clarification of the benefits which have to be provided to employees on AML, it is our view that the consequences of the legislation set out in **7.29** to **7.31** below remain unchanged.

In the case of *Boyle & others v Equal Opportunities Commission (C-411/96) [1998] All ER (EC) 879* it was stated that a condition limiting accrual of pensionable service to periods of paid OML was contrary to *Article 12* of the *Pregnant Workers Directive (EU Directive 92/85/EEC)*. The court said that the Directive required the period of OML to be pensionable regardless of whether the woman concerned was in receipt of pay. This means that the pensionable service of any woman who is a pension scheme member but who is not entitled to either contractual or statutory maternity pay (perhaps because she has recently become an employee) must continue during this minimum period (see *ERA 1996, s 71(4)*).

Under the *Employment Relations Act 1999*, qualifying employees with one year's continuous service have a right to take up to 13 weeks' unpaid parental leave in respect of a child for whom they have parental responsibility. This right must be exercised before the child's fifth birthday or fifth anniversary of adoption (18th birthday, if the child is disabled). An employee on parental leave is entitled to accrue pension benefits on the basis of actual pay received (under *Maternity and Parental Leave etc Regulations 1999 (SI 1999/3312), reg 18A*.

Contractual remuneration

7.28 As noted in **7.27** above, SMP is payable for 39 weeks for women whose EWC falls on or after 1 April 2007. The payment of contractual remuneration, ie payment under the employee's contract of employment, affects pension rights only in respect of maternity leave in excess of 39 weeks or if the contractual pay is higher than SMP.

Although the protection of pension rights during maternity absence can depend upon the payment of 'contractual remuneration', it is not clear what this includes. Employment legislation defines remuneration as comprising cash payments, whereas tax legislation includes benefits in kind within the definition. The safer approach is to treat remuneration as including all benefits in kind, for example, a company car. *Gillespie v Northern Health & Social Services Board [1996] All ER (EC) 284* confirmed that bonuses or pay increases granted during paid maternity absence, but which are backdated to the relevant pre-absence period, are to be reflected in the remuneration of those on paid maternity leave. SMP will also have to be recalculated if a backdated pay increase affects the average earnings which underlie the calculation of SMP. Essentially, *Gillespie* underlines the requirement in the *Social Security Act 1989* that pension rights accruing during a period of paid maternity absence reflect any increase to 'normal pay'.

Recently, the UK and European courts have had to revisit the so-called 'contractual remuneration during leave' question. These cases have taken the issues much further than in *Gillespie*. A number of these decisions have been reflected in amendments to the *Equal Pay Act 1970*.

In relation to pay rises, the ECJ in *Alabaster v (1) Woolwich plc; (2) Secretary of State for Social Security Case C-147/02 [2005] All ER (EC) 490* ruled that any pay rise, awarded from the time a woman falls pregnant and up to the end of her maternity leave, must be reflected in her higher SMP rate, contractual maternity pay, and the rate of pay on which she returns to work. This is the case even if the pay rise takes effect after the end of the period during which the higher rate SMP is payable.

Hoyland v Asda Stores Ltd [2005] IRLR 438 dealt with bonus entitlements during maternity leave. The EAT ruled that a woman must not be deprived of contractual bonus payments which are awarded to reflect work performance done at the time: (a) before the woman went on leave; (b) during which the woman was on a statutory compulsory maternity leave period; and (c) after the woman returned to work following maternity leave. The decision was upheld by the Court of Session, which confirmed that that it was lawful to reduce the bonus in respect of a period of absence on ordinary maternity leave because it fell within the exclusion in *Sex Discrimination Act 1975, s 6(6)*, which provides that the Act 'does not apply to benefits consisting of the payment of money when the provision of those benefits is regulated by the woman's contract of employment.' The bonus was a payment regulated by the employee's contract of employment notwithstanding that it was expressed to be discretionary because the bonus would not be paid but for the existence of the contract of employment. This decision should, however, be applied with caution owing to the varied nature and purpose of bonus provisions.

The ECJ decided in *North Western Health Board v McKenna [2006] All ER (EC) 455* that employers are not required to give full pay to women absent from work for a maternity-related illness, provided that they are treated in the same way as male employees on sick leave and that the level of pay they receive is not 'too low' so as to undermine the objective of protecting pregnant women. Here, the employee's sick pay was half her contractual pay; but whether a lower level, including the current level of statutory sick pay, would be 'too low' is not clear.

Final salary schemes

7.29 As already noted, the *Social Security Act 1989* provides for periods of paid maternity absence to count as pensionable service as if the woman was working normally, and for the accrual of benefits to continue on the basis of the pre-absence level of remuneration. As the employee's contributions are based upon actual pay and full final salary benefits accrue during the periods of paid absence, the employer will incur an additional cost to fund those benefits to compensate for any reduction in the amount of contribution paid by the employee.

Money purchase schemes

7.30 The position here is less clear, but money purchase schemes are not excluded from the scope of the legislation. Although the employee can only be required to contribute on the basis of actual pay received, the employer has to contribute at the full rate appropriate to the employee's pre-absence remuneration. It is also arguable that, as with the final salary schemes, the employer has to make good any shortfall in contributions (ie the difference between the contributions actually paid by the employee and those that would have been paid by her if she had been working normally) but this point is far from certain.

Death benefits

7.31 Benefits on death are treated in the same way as pension benefits, in that they must be continued during periods of paid maternity absence. On the death of an employee during such absence, death benefits will be calculated by reference to full pre-absence remuneration as if the employee had been working normally.

All of the requirements for equal treatment are clearly subject to the special provisions relating to paid maternity and family leave.

Additional changes

Time off for performance of duties and for training

7.32 Under *ERA 1996, s 58* (originally *PA 1995, s 42*), an employer must permit any employee who is a trustee of a scheme to take time off during working hours to allow him to perform all of his duties as a trustee or to undergo relevant training. The amount of time off, and any conditions imposed by the employer, must be reasonable having regard to the employer's business and the effect of the employee's absence. Any employee is entitled to be paid for any time taken off pursuant to this provision (*ERA 1996, s 59*). Under *PA 2004, ss 247–249*, in force from 6 April 2006, trustees are required to have 'knowledge and understanding' of the law relating to pensions and trusts and the principles relating to funding and investment. This issue is covered in detail in CHAPTER 3.

An employee can bring a complaint to an employment tribunal if he believes that his employer has failed to give him time off and failed to pay him (*ERA 1996, s 60*). He has three months from the date when the failure occurred in which to present his complaint, but the tribunal will have the power to extend this period if it is satisfied that it was not reasonably practicable for the complaint to be presented within the period.

If an employee's complaint is upheld, the tribunal can award such compensation at it considers just and equitable.

Right not to suffer detriment or to be unfairly dismissed

7.33 *ERA 1996, s 46* (previously *PA 1995, s 46*) states that an employer is not permitted to victimise an employee simply on the ground that he performed or proposed to perform his functions as a trustee of a scheme which relates to his employment.

Further, if an employee is dismissed and the reason (or the principal reason) for the dismissal is that the employee performed or proposed to perform any functions as a trustee, the dismissal is to be regarded as automatically unfair and the employee may be entitled to compensation (*ERA 1996, s 102*).

Any provision in a contract of employment (or in any other agreement) which purports to exclude or limit the right not to suffer detriment or to be unfairly dismissed is void (*ERA 1996, s 203(1)*).

Conclusion

7.34 It is difficult to classify pension provisions or an entitlement to pension benefits as an employment 'right', as in most instances employers do not have to provide pension arrangements. However, *PA 2004* has given employees a degree of protection following a business transfer and improved rights in relation to paternity and adoption leave.

On becoming a member of a pension scheme, an employee does obtain rights and entitlements, but primarily against the trustees of the scheme. The only contractual 'right' of the employee is to join the pension scheme if eligible to do so. Otherwise, it is easier to classify the rights of a member as being either statutory (for example, not to be discriminated against on various grounds) or common law rights, for example, the *Imperial* duty of good faith. Some of the cases referred to in this chapter clearly indicate the difficulties of differentiating between pension and employment issues. However, the basis of pension provision may, in time, move further towards a contractual as opposed to 'trusts' basis, although, as noted, the Government's default scheme for automatic enrolment is to be trust-based.

Chapter 8

Pensions and divorce

Introduction

8.1 Over the years there have been fundamental changes in the treatment of pension benefits in the context of divorce proceedings. These have arisen out of two different concepts for the treatment of pensions: earmarking and pension sharing, which were introduced by *PA 1995* and the *Welfare Reform and Pensions Act 1999* (*WRPA 1999*) respectively. This legislation has not only increased the awareness of divorcing couples of the comparatively high value that pension benefits may have in the context of the matrimonial assets as a whole, but has introduced sufficient flexibility to enable a fair settlement to be reached, whatever the divorcing parties' general and financial circumstances.

The family law courts generally had no jurisdiction over pension schemes in the context of divorce settlements until the introduction of *PA 1995* (*Brooks v Brooks [1995] All ER 257, HL* is the notable exception, although it is likely that this judgment is confined to its own facts and has now been superseded by legislation). That is not to say that the pension rights of parties to divorce proceedings were not taken into consideration prior to *PA 1995*, merely that the courts did not have the jurisdiction to make orders against pension schemes' trustees or scheme members, in respect of their pension benefits, when deciding how the parties' assets were to be split. This lack of options in law for the treatment of pension rights on divorce had long been a cause for dissatisfaction and was the subject of various reports which, in essence, recommended that the courts should have the power to split the pension rights on divorce, thereby creating a separate entitlement for the ex-spouse.

Despite an obvious desire for change, it took a number of years for legislation to appear on the statute books. The reason for this lies in the nature of pension schemes themselves. The majority of pension schemes were designed to be eligible for tax approval (see CHAPTER 16). The then requirements for obtaining exempt approved status prevented benefits being paid to any person who was not a member or a 'dependant' (as defined in the Glossary to the Revenue's Practice Notes, IR12 (2001)) of a member, and specifically prevented pensions from being assignable (subject to certain statutory exceptions) (IR12 (2001) PN 7.31). This had proved the main obstacle for the courts in the past because the governing trust deed of an exempt approved scheme would always contain a specific provision that benefits cannot be assigned. There was no mechanism to assign benefits to an ex-spouse so that they would become payable to the ex-spouse as of right, nor to provide for the ex-spouse on the death of the scheme member unless, first, the ex-spouse fell within the definition of 'dependant' and, secondly, the trustees exercised their discretion to pay the benefits to him or her in that capacity. This position has not changed to any material extent under *FA 2004*.

These issues have been addressed in legislation. However, it may still be appropriate for parties in some circumstances to leave the pension benefits intact and it is, therefore, useful to look at the issues which were relevant prior to the introduction of *PA 1995* and the earmarking regime.

Position prior to PA 1995

8.2 Prior to the introduction of *PA 1995*, the treatment of property on divorce in England, Wales and Northern Ireland was governed by *Matrimonial Causes Act 1973, ss 21–25* ('*MCA 1973*') (as amended by the *Matrimonial and Family Proceedings Act 1994*).

MCA 1973, s 25A(1) required the court to consider whether the financial obligations of each party towards the other could be terminated as soon after the grant of the decree as the court considered just and reasonable. This is known as a 'clean break'. It put the onus on the court to consider lump sum payments and property adjustment orders, rather than periodical payments orders (commonly known as maintenance payments), wherever possible and, if a maintenance payment order is made, to limit its duration if appropriate. A clean break will usually be appropriate where the couple is young, both are working and have no children or where the couple's assets are sizeable enough that they can be split in such a way that the ex-spouse will have sufficient resources on which to live.

Prior to amendment by *PA 1995*, *MCA 1973, s 25(2)* stated that the court should, when considering financial provision orders, have particular regard, amongst other matters, to the following:

'(*a*) the income, earning capacity, property and other financial resources which each of the parties to the marriage has or is likely to have in the foreseeable future, including in the case of earning capacity any increase in that capacity which it would in the opinion of the court be reasonable to expect a party of the marriage to take steps to acquire;

...

(*h*) in the case of proceedings for divorce or nullity of marriage, the value to each of the parties to the marriage of any benefits (for example, a pension) which by reason of the dissolution or annulment of the marriage, that party will lose the chance of acquiring.'

However, a problem of interpretation arose with the use of the words 'in the foreseeable future' in *MCA 1973, s 25(2)(a)* at that time. The approach adopted by the courts resulted in consideration being given only to those assets which a party could expect to acquire within the next ten years. Consequently, where a party to the divorce was more than ten years away from retirement, the value of his pension entitlements would not be taken into account. In any event, the court had no power over either the trustees or the assets of a pension scheme and so could not make an order re-allocating assets or obliging the trustees to make a payment to an ex-spouse. Therefore, even where pension rights fell within the definition of matrimonial property their value could only be taken into account in relation to the distribution of non-pension assets.

Under *MCA 1973, s 25(2)(h)*, the court was required to have regard to the value of any pension that a party to a divorce loses the chance of acquiring. It was not clear, however, to which benefits these provisions referred, ie to the member's pension, any cash lump sum payable on retirement, a spouse's pension payable on the death of the member and/or lump sum on a member's death in service.

The courts' inability to divide pension assets was problematical, particularly where there were insufficient non-pension assets to provide for the ex-spouse's needs. A common result was that in the divorce settlement the ex-spouse would be allocated the matrimonial home whilst the scheme member retained the pension rights. This often created both long and short-term problems; the party with the matrimonial home had realisable assets but no income on retirement, whereas the scheme member retained pension rights, to which he could not gain access to set up a new home, but was guaranteed a certain level of future income. An even worse scenario was where the pension rights were the only or the largest asset and, consequently, the court was unable to make any order which would adequately compensate the ex-spouse. Therefore, in many cases, this was not satisfactory for either party. It was against this background that *PA 1995, s 166* was introduced.

Earmarking – impact of PA 1995

General jurisdiction

8.3 The concept of earmarking was introduced by *PA 1995, s 166*. In general terms, earmarking introduced a means by which pension benefits could be used to pay either maintenance or a capital sum from the pension scheme direct to the ex-spouse on the member's behalf, but which would only become payable when entitlement arose under the pension scheme in respect of the member.

The powers of the courts regarding financial provision on divorce are still contained in *MCA 1973*, but s *25* was amended to introduce the concept of earmarking. *PA 1995, s 166* inserted new *ss 25B–25D* into *MCA 1973* with effect from 1 August 1996 which applied to petitions presented on or after 1 July 1996. *WRPA 1999* has subsequently made certain refinements to these sections which are reflected below. In essence, the earmarking provisions provide that the courts:

(*a*) must have regard to pension benefits which either party has or is likely to have or stands to lose the chance of acquiring because of the divorce and must ignore the words 'in the foreseeable future' contained in *MCA 1973, s 25(2)(a)* for this purpose (*MCA 1973, s 25B(1)*). With effect from 1 January 2006 this includes any PPF compensation either party has or is likely to have or stands to lose (*MCA 1973, s 25E*);

(*b*) have jurisdiction to make orders against the person responsible for the pension arrangement for payment of financial provision from a member's pension benefits to the other party when payment of those benefits falls due to the member (*MCA 1973, s 25B(4)*). The term 'person responsible' was introduced by *WRPA 1999, s 46(2)* and means, in the case of occupational pension schemes or personal pension schemes, the trustees and managers of the scheme. In the case of a retirement annuity contract, it means the provider of the annuity and, in the case of an insurance policy, the insurer;

(*c*) have power to direct a member as to the extent to which he may commute payments, thereby reducing the pension benefits payable to him, and have power to order payment of any lump sum following commutation to be made to the ex-spouse (*MCA 1973, s 25B(7)*);

(*d*) can direct trustees to exercise their discretionary powers in the event of the death of a member or pensioner in favour of the ex-spouse in whole or in part, and can also, where the member has power to nominate, require a member to nominate his ex-spouse for all or part of a lump sum payable on his death (*MCA 1973, s 25C*).

Essentially, the type of order that the court is empowered to make was not changed by *PA 1995*, merely the source of the payment. The order is in the form of either a deferred periodical payments (or maintenance) order or a lump sum order. The member's pension benefits remain in the scheme and are still attributable to the member but a proportion is payable directly to the ex-spouse. No separate entitlement is created in the scheme for the ex-spouse so payments only become due to the ex-spouse when they become due to the member and pension payments will stop automatically on the death of the member. As with all periodical payment orders, either party can apply to the court to have the amount varied (*MCA 1973, s 31*) and payments will cease on the re-marriage or death of the ex-spouse.

The amount due to the ex-spouse must be expressed as a percentage of the total amount of pension due to the member (*MCA 1973, s 25B(5)*). Such total amount can include the value of the member's GMP by virtue of the exclusion of the provisions relating to inalienability of GMPs (*PA 1995, s 91*) under *PA 1995, s 166(4), (5)*. Any lump sum payment made by the persons responsible for the pension arrangement shall discharge them of any liability to the member to the extent of the amount of the payment (*MCA 1973, ss 25B(6)(a), 25C(3)*) and, in the case of pension payments, any payments made by the person responsible for the pension arrangement shall be treated as a payment made by the member towards the discharge of his liability under the court order (*MCA 1973, s 25B(6)(b)*).

The duty of the court to consider a clean break was not affected by the changes introduced by *PA 1995*. In practice, therefore 'earmarking' orders against pension payments are likely only to be made where a clean break is not possible and a periodical payments order is appropriate. Such an order, however, gives the ex-spouse additional comfort and security because, instead of obtaining a deferred maintenance order payable by the member in retirement, the ex-spouse will now receive payments directly from the pension scheme. This removes direct dependency on the member for financial support and avoids the potential problems caused by non-compliance with an order by the member.

The amendments to *MCA 1973* by *PA 1995* (and *WRPA 1999*) specified the schemes against which the court can make orders. These are referred to as 'pension arrangements', a term introduced by *WRPA 1999, s 46(1)*, meaning an occupational pension scheme, personal pension scheme, retirement annuity contract, an annuity or insurance policy which is to give effect to the rights of an occupational pension scheme, or a personal pension scheme or an annuity purchased for the purpose of discharging liability for a pension credit (*MCA 1973, s 25D(3)*).

MCA 1973, s 25E, introduced by *PA 2004* with effect from 1 January 2006, and the *Divorce etc (Pension Protection Fund) Regulations 2006 (SI 2006/1932)* provide that, where the Pension Protection Fund assumes responsibility for an occupational pension scheme after an order has been made in relation to pension payments or commutation of pension benefits payable from that scheme, then the Board of the PPF is required to give effect to that order in relation to the member's PPF compensation.

Valuation of benefits for earmarking purposes

8.4 The question of the valuation of pension rights for earmarking is dealt with in the *Divorce etc (Pensions) Regulations 2000 (SI 2000/1123)* for divorce and nullity proceedings commencing on and after 1 December 2000. *Regulation 3* provides that, for the purposes of earmarking, benefits under a pension arrangement shall be calculated in the manner set out in *Pensions on Divorce etc (Provision of Information) Regulations 2000 (SI 2000/1048), reg 3*.

Pensions on Divorce etc (Provision of Information) Regulations 2000, reg 3 specifies that the basis of valuation depends on the category of member in question:

(*a*) For active and deferred members of occupational pension schemes, members of personal pension schemes and a person with rights contained in a retirement annuity contact, the statutory cash equivalent transfer value basis ('CETV') must be applied. Generally, the effective date for calculating the CETV is the date on which the request for the valuation was received by the person responsible for the pension arrangement. However, it should be noted that, under *Divorce etc (Pensions) Regulations 2000, reg 3*, the court can specify another date, if it considers it appropriate, such date not to be earlier than one year before the date of the petition and not later than the date on which the court is exercising its powers.

(*b*) In any other circumstances, *Pensions on Divorce etc (Provision of Information) Regulations 2000, reg 3* specifies that the value of benefits shall be calculated and verified in accordance with *Occupational Pension Schemes (Transfer Values) Regulations 1996 (SI 1996/1847), regs 7–7C, 7E(1)–(3)*, as amended.

Transfers of, and notices in relation to, earmarked benefits

8.5 Given that the courts' powers enable orders to be made for deferred maintenance payments, payable at some date in the future, it was necessary to make provisions permitting the transfer of the orders on the transfer of the member's accrued benefits to a new scheme (*MCA 1973, s 25D(1)(a)*). The *Divorce etc (Pensions) Regulations 2000 (SI 2000/1123)* provide for the person responsible for the transferring arrangement to give notice to the person responsible for the receiving arrangement in circumstances where an earmarking order is in force against a member who wishes to transfer his pension benefits. The effect of this notice is that the earmarking order will attach to the transfer credits granted in the receiving scheme and will be enforceable against the trustees of the receiving scheme.

Divorce etc (Pensions) Regulations 2000, reg 4 sets out the content of the notices which must be given to the receiving arrangement and the ex-spouse and the period within which they must be given. Notice must be given within the period provided by *PSA 1993, s 99* for the person responsible for the transferring arrangement to effect a transfer (usually six months) and before the expiry of 21 days after the person responsible for the transferring arrangement has made all required payments to the person responsible for the receiving arrangement (*Divorce etc (Pensions) Regulations 2000, reg 4(5)*).

Regulation 4(4) provides that the notice to the ex-spouse must contain the following particulars:

(*a*) the fact that the pension rights of the member have been transferred;

(*b*) the date on which the transfer takes effect;

(*c*) the name and address of the person responsible for the new arrangement; and

(*d*) the fact that the order made under *MCA 1973, s 23* is to have effect as if it had been made in respect of the person responsible for the new arrangement.

Regulation 4(3) provides that the notice to the person responsible for the new arrangement shall consist of:

(i) every order made under *MCA 1973* imposing a requirement on the person responsible for the transferring arrangement in relation to the rights transferred;

(ii) any subsequent orders varying the original order;

(iii) all information or particulars supplied by the ex-spouse under *Family Proceedings Rules 1991 (SI 1991/1247), r 2.70*, as amended (for example, address and bank details);

(iv) any notice given by the ex-spouse to the transferring trustees relating to a change of personal details or re-marriage; and

(v) where the rights of a member under the transferring scheme derive from a transfer from a previous scheme, any notices to the person responsible for the previous arrangement on the former transfer.

Under *Divorce etc (Pensions) Regulations 2000, reg 5*, notice is also required to be given by the person responsible for the arrangement to the ex-spouse, within 14 days of the occurrence of an event, when:

(*a*) it is likely that there will be a significant reduction in the benefits payable under the scheme in respect of the member (save where transfer of all benefits has been made or where market conditions have affected the value of the scheme's assets) (*Divorce etc (Pensions) Regulations 2000, reg 5(1)*); and/or

(*b*) a partial transfer of the member's accrued benefits has been made (*Divorce etc (Pensions) Regulations 2000, reg 5(3)*).

This notice shall state the nature of the event which has occurred and the extent of the reduction in benefits and, in the case of a partial transfer, the name and address of the person responsible for the receiving arrangement.

It should be noted that in the event of a partial transfer the order will remain with the original scheme and this may therefore give the member scope for the avoidance of the order. Nevertheless, because notice is given to the ex-spouse by the scheme, this gives the ex-spouse an opportunity to apply to the court for a variation of the original order.

An ex-spouse is required to give notice (*Divorce etc (Pensions) Regulations 2000, reg 6*) within 14 days to the person responsible for the arrangement subject to a court order where the particulars supplied by her cease to be accurate; where the ex-spouse has remarried or where, for any other reason, the order has ceased to have effect. The person responsible for the arrangement will be discharged of any liability to the ex-spouse to the extent of a payment where, by reason of the inaccuracy of the particulars supplied by the ex-spouse or the ex-spouse's failure to give notice of a change in details, it is not reasonably practicable for the person responsible for the arrangement to make a payment as required by the order and a payment is therefore made to the member instead (*Divorce etc (Pensions) Regulations 2000, reg 6(4)*).

Ambit of court orders

8.6 The courts were empowered to make deferred maintenance orders from 1 August 1996 where applied for in petitions presented after 1 July 1996, although any orders made could not take effect before 6 April 1997. In addition to making a deferred maintenance order from the pension arrangement, the court can also require a member to commute his pension when he retires, with part or all of the lump sum being paid to the ex-spouse (*MCA 1973, s 25B(7)*, see **8.3** above). Similarly in respect of benefits payable on the member's death, the court has the power to order the allocation of any lump sum and, even where payment of the lump sum is discretionary, the persons responsible for the pension arrangement can be ordered to pay all or part of it to the ex-spouse. In cases where the member himself has the power to nominate a beneficiary, the member can be required to nominate the ex-spouse.

As mentioned above the order must express the amount due to the ex-spouse as a percentage of the total amount due to the member. The order may also state the rate at which the payment is to increase annually and this may vary from the rates stated in the scheme rules. In relation to orders prior to 1 December 2000 which were stated to be for a fixed amount, it would also be necessary to consider whether or not allowance would need to be made for revaluation up to retirement and, further, to consider what the position would be were a member to retire and whether or not this earlier payment should be reflected in the ex-spouse's pension.

As mentioned in **8.3** above, the *Divorce etc (Pension Protection Fund) Regulations 2006 (SI 2006/1932)* came into force on 8 August 2006 and make necessary consequential amendments to give effect to *MCA 1973, s 25E* where the Board of the Pension Protection Fund assumes responsibility for a scheme.

Charging for earmarking orders

8.7 Charges by pension arrangements in relation to earmarking orders are permitted pursuant to *WRPA 1999, s 24* and *Pensions on Divorce etc (Charging) Regulations 2000 (SI 2000/1049), reg 10*. It is stated that the charges which a person responsible for a pension arrangement may recover in relation to an earmarking order are those charges which represent the reasonable administrative expenses which have been incurred or are likely to be incurred by reason of the order.

Pensions on Divorce etc (Charging) Regulations 2000, reg 3 deals with charges recoverable in respect of the provision of basic valuation information and provides that the person responsible for the pension arrangement may also recover the reasonable costs of providing such information to the extent that they would not have been required to provide such information in the ordinary course of disclosure in accordance with the *Occupational Pension Schemes (Disclosure of Information) Regulations 1996 (SI 1996/1655)* (the '*Disclosure Regulations*').

Disclosure

8.8 The provisions governing disclosure in relation to earmarking orders can be found in the *Pensions on Divorce etc (Provision of Information) Regulations 2000*. *Regulation 2* deals with the provision of the basic information which the person responsible for a pension arrangement can generally be required to disclose on request. These provisions apply equally to pension sharing and are set out in detail at **8.24** below.

Pensions on Divorce etc (Provision of Information) Regulations 2000, reg 10 deals with the provision of information after receipt of an earmarking order.

The person responsible for the pension arrangement must, within 21 days of receipt of the earmarking order, issue to both parties to the marriage a notice that includes the following, as appropriate:

(*a*) for an order in respect of pension rights that are not yet in payment, a list of the circumstances in respect of any changes of which the member or the ex-spouse must notify the person responsible for the pension arrangement;

(*b*) where the pension is in payment:

  (i) the value of the member's pension rights;

  (ii) the amount of those pension rights after the order has been implemented;

  (iii) the first date when a payment under the order is to be made; and

  (iv) the circumstances in respect of any changes of which the member or the ex-spouse must notify the person responsible for the pension arrangement;

(*c*) the amount of charges which remain unpaid by each party pursuant to *Pensions on Divorce etc (Charging) Regulations 2000, reg 3* (see **8.7** above) and in respect of complying with the order;

(*d*) information as to how and when these charges will be recovered.

Pension sharing

Introduction

8.9 The concept of pension sharing was first introduced, but not implemented, by the *Family Law Act 1996*. A lengthy consultation process then followed which culminated in the provisions contained in *WRPA 1999*.

In brief, the term pension sharing is used to signify a clean break approach towards dealing with pension rights. The aim is that the capital value of the pension will be divided between the parties with the effect that the rights of the member will be reduced by way of a 'pension debit' and the ex-spouse will be granted a 'pension credit' of the same amount. The primary advantage of pension sharing to an ex-spouse is that her rights are independent of those of the member and, in contrast with earmarking, will, therefore, continue beyond the death of the member and after the ex-spouse's remarriage.

The relevant sections of *WRPA 1999* came into force on 1 December 2000 and were in the form of insertions and amendments to *MCA 1973*, the provisions of *WRPA 1999, Parts III* and *IV*, and a number of statutory instruments.

Pension sharing is only available in proceedings commencing on or after 1 December 2000, the effective date for the new legislation (*Welfare Reform and Pensions Act 1999 (Commencement No 5) Order 2000 (SI 2000/1116)*). The provisions only apply to proceedings for divorce or nullity of marriage, and do not extend to judicial separation (*MCA 1973, s 24B(1)*). Subsequent case law has made it clear that the question of whether a decree nisi could be rescinded, to allow new divorce proceedings to be issued after 1 December 2000 thus enabling a pension sharing order to be made, is one for judicial discretion. In *S v S [2002] 13 PBLR* the court allowed rescission where both parties consented. However, in *Rye v Rye [2002] EWHC 956 (Fam)* the husband (who had the pension) successfully objected to rescission. The court held that *WRPA 1999* provides a clear cut-off date and in the absence of consent by both parties it would be an impermissible exercise by the court of its discretion to circumvent the statutory provision by rescinding the decree nisi.

The effect of the amendments to *MCA 1973* is that the courts now have the option to consider the possibility of granting a pension sharing order, if deemed appropriate, when considering ancillary relief (*MCA 1973, s 24B(1)*). Whilst it is open to the courts to make more than one sharing order in relation to a given set of divorce proceedings, the courts cannot make a pension sharing order in relation to a pension arrangement which is already the subject of a pension sharing order in relation to that marriage (*MCA 1973, s 24B(3)*). Moreover, the court cannot make a pension sharing order in respect of pension benefits which are already subject to an earmarking order (*MCA 1973, s 24B(5)*).

MCA 1973, s 21A states that a pension sharing order involves the court ordering that the 'shareable rights' of the member be shared for the benefit of the ex-spouse, with the order specifying the value of those rights to be transferred as a percentage of the total rights attributable to the member.

WRPA 1999, s 27(2) sets out the definition of 'shareable rights' as any rights under a 'pension arrangement' other than non-shareable rights of a description specified in regulations. As detailed at **8.3** above, the *WRPA 1999* definition of 'pension arrangement' (*s 46(1)*) is broadly termed. Indeed, the only exceptions to date appear to be excepted public sector schemes (*WRPA 1999, s 27(1), (3)*) by reference to the *Pension Sharing (Excepted Schemes) Order 2001 (SI 2001/358)* (being the schemes relating to the Prime Minister, Lord Chancellor and Speaker of the House of Commons) and the basic State pension.

PA 2008, Part 3 proposes to extend the principle of pension sharing to apply to PPF compensation by the creation of pension compensation sharing orders. The provisions relating to the pension compensation payable on the discharge of a pension compensation credit are set out in *PA 2008, Sch 5*, and the necessary amendments to *MCA 1973* are set out in *PA 2008, Sch 6*. Essentially, the courts will be able to make an order requiring an individual's PPF compensation rights to be shared on divorce/dissolution of civil partnership in the same way as ordinary pension rights. They cannot be made on rights which have already been shared using a normal pension sharing order or earmarking order in relation to the same marriage/partnership. The proposed mechanisms are very similar to normal pension sharing, but it is the PPF Board which is required to implement the order. It should also be noted that the ex-spouse will be paid compensation from the PPF. It is not envisaged that external transfer options will be permitted.

The Government is due to consult on draft regulations with a view to bringing the measures into effect on 6 April 2010. Subsequent editions will set out the provisions in full once they are in force.

Pension debits and credits

8.10 The person responsible for a pension arrangement is not required to implement the pension debit and pension credit until the pension sharing order has taken effect (*WRPA 1999, s 28(1)*). Pension sharing can also be provided under a 'qualifying agreement' between the parties to the marriage which takes effect on the dissolution of the marriage under the *Family Law Act 1996* (*WRPA 1999, s 28(1)(b)*). (A 'qualifying agreement' has only yet been defined for the purposes of Scottish law. The *Pensions on Divorce etc (Pension Sharing) (Scotland) Regulations 2000 (SI 2000/1051 (S5))* specify the requirements for an agreement to be a 'qualify agreement' for the purposes of *WRPA 1999, s 28(1)(f)(ii)*.

A pension sharing order cannot take effect unless the decree pursuant to which it has been made has been made absolute (*MCA 1973, s 24B(2)*). In addition, *s 24C* (by virtue of *Divorce etc (Pensions) Regulations 2000, reg 9*) provides that the order cannot come into effect earlier than seven days after the end of the period for filing notice of appeal against the order.

Once the pension sharing order has become effective, the member's shareable rights under the arrangement become subject to a 'debit' of the specified amount and the ex-spouse becomes entitled to a 'credit' of a corresponding amount, held as a right against the person responsible for the arrangement (*WRPA 1999, s 29(1)*).

Pension debits

8.11 The pension debit operates by reducing the member's current and future benefits under the pension arrangement by a specified percentage (*WRPA 1999, s 31*) on the transfer day (ie the date on which the order takes effect).

The benefits to be reduced must be 'qualifying benefits' (*s 31(3)*). A benefit is a qualifying benefit if the member's cash equivalent includes an amount in respect of it.

When a benefit is reduced by a pension debit each part of the benefit is reduced equally. Thus, for example, the GMP benefits of a member are reduced by the same percentage as the excess over GMP. *WRPA 1999, s 31(2)* clarifies how the percentage deduction rule applies for members who are in pensionable service on the transfer day. The debit is applied to the deferred pension to which the member would have been entitled had he left pensionable service on that day. The benefits of active members to be reduced by the pension debit therefore exclude any elements which would not be included in his deferred pension, such as a death-in-service lump sum.

Pension credits

8.12 The ex-spouse becomes entitled to the corresponding amount as a pension credit, made up of the same elements and in the same proportions as the benefits of the scheme member. An arrangement which is the subject of a pension sharing order may discharge its liability for the pension credit by conferring appropriate rights under that arrangement (an 'internal transfer') or by transferring the pension credit to another qualifying pension scheme or arrangement (an 'external transfer') (see **8.14** below).

Implementation period

8.13 The person responsible for the arrangement has a specified period within which to give effect to the provisions of the pension sharing order – this is known as the implementation period and is defined in *WRPA 1999, s 34(1)* as being a period of four months beginning with the later of the day on which the pension sharing order takes effect, and receipt by the person responsible for the arrangement of relevant documents (for example, the order itself and the order or decree of the divorce or annulment), and the information set out in *Pensions on Divorce etc (Provision of Information) Regulations 2000, reg 5* (this includes the names, addresses, dates of birth and National Insurance numbers of the divorcing couple). A further pre-condition of implementing the sharing order may be the payment of any charges due from the divorcing couple (see **8.25** below).

In the event that the order has not been implemented by the trustees of an occupational pension scheme within the implementation period they are required pursuant to *WRPA 1999, s 33(2)* to notify the Pensions Regulator ('the Regulator') within 21 days beginning with the day immediately following the end of the implementation period (*Pension Sharing (Implementation and Discharge of Liability) Regulations 2000, reg 2*) and *PA 1995, s 10* shall apply. The Regulator may, therefore, impose civil penalties if the trustees failed to take all such steps as were reasonable to discharge liability for the pension credit before the end of the implementation period. On application by the trustees, the Regulator may extend the implementation period under certain circumstances (*WRPA 1999, s 33(4)*). These circumstances are set out in *Pension Sharing (Implementation and Discharge of Liability) Regulations 2000, reg 3* and include the scheme being in wind up, ceasing to be contracted out, or where an extension is in the financial interests of the members of the scheme generally. The implementation period may also be suspended or postponed where one of the parties has made an application for leave to appeal out of time (*reg 4*).

Discharging liability for the pension credit

General position

8.14 The main body of the pension sharing legislation is aimed at the means by which the liability of the person responsible for the pension arrangement which is subject to a pension sharing order can be discharged in respect of the pension credit created. The relevant provisions can be found in *WRPA 1999, s 35* by reference to *Sch 5*, together with the *Pension Sharing (Implementation and Discharge of Liability) Regulations 2000*.

WRPA 1999, Sch 5 deals with funded (*para 1*), unfunded (*paras 2* and *3*) and 'other' (*para 4*) pension arrangements. This chapter will concentrate on the position for 'funded' schemes in *Sch 5, para 1*, ie pension credits derived from a funded occupational pension scheme or a personal pension scheme.

WRPA 1999, Sch 5, para 1(2) states that the trustees or managers of these types of arrangements may discharge their liability in respect of the pension credit by conferring rights under the relevant scheme on the ex-spouse with his or her consent, or otherwise in accordance with regulations. The conferring right under the relevant scheme is known as the 'internal transfer' option. Alternatively, under *Sch 5, para 1(3)* the liability may be discharged by paying the amount of the pension credit to the person responsible for a 'qualifying arrangement' (defined widely in *Sch 5, para 6*) with the ex-spouse's consent or otherwise in accordance with regulations. This is known as the 'external transfer' option.

The *Pension Sharing (Implementation and Discharge of Liability) Regulations 2000* set out the detail of these procedures under *reg 7*. In summary, for internal transfers (*reg 7(1)*) the consent of the ex-spouse must be obtained unless the ex-spouse has failed to provide this consent and has also failed to specify a suitable recipient scheme under the external transfer route.

An external transfer (*reg 7(2)*) must be made with the ex-spouse's consent unless the ex-spouse fails to provide this consent and he or she has also failed to consent to an internal transfer or the trustees did not offer the internal transfer route as an option in the first instance.

WRPA 1999, Sch 5, para 1(4) specifies that any consent to be given by the ex-spouse to an internal transfer option will be invalid unless it is given after receipt of a written notice of an offer to discharge liability by way of an external transfer and the consent is not withdrawn within seven days of receipt of such notice.

Death of ex-spouse prior to discharge of liability

8.15 *Pension Sharing (Implementation and Discharge of Liability) Regulations 2000, reg 6* specifies how a pension credit liability can be discharged when the ex-spouse dies after the liability has arisen but before it has been discharged. Essentially, any benefits the scheme provides must, subject to the rules of the scheme, be in the form of a lump sum payment; payment of a pension; payment of both a lump sum and a pension and/or the purchase of an annuity contract or insurance policy with a 'qualifying arrangement' (defined in *reg 11*).

Pros and cons of internal v external transfer options

8.16 When pension sharing was first introduced there was much debate about which option trustees should adopt as their policy for securing pension credits. Arguments against internal transfers are the added costs and the administrative burdens of an extra membership category; extended ongoing disclosure requirements and the need for extensive rule amendments to incorporate a new benefit structure and category of member. Moreover, the external option sits more easily with the 'clean break' motivation that gave rise to the pension sharing legislation in the first place.

The majority of funded occupational pension schemes have expressed a preference for the external transfer option, which avoids the problems outlined above. Concerns were, however, raised about the ability of trustees who were not authorised under *FSA 1986* (now *FSMA 2000*) to select a default external transfer destination without contravening *FSA 1986, s 191* (now *Financial Services and Markets Act 2000 (Regulated Activities) Order 2001*

(SI 2001/1544), art 37. However, the position has subsequently been clarified somewhat by the Financial Services Authority which, in a letter to the NAPF dated 2 February 2001, stated that, where trustees pay the pension credit to a designated default option provider, this will not amount to the purchasing of an investment which will be held for the purposes of the scheme and so falls outside the ambit of the definition of a specified activity for the purposes of the financial services legislation.

The question of the availability of a suitable 'qualifying arrangement' to receive external transfers (without the need for the ex-spouse's signature on a proposal form) has historically been a problem. In relation to the default option, generally the Department for Work and Pensions ('DWP') has clarified a few points that had arisen regarding the type of vehicle available for the default option:

(*a*) The default option should not be available until the former spouse has been given adequate opportunity to make his or her choice or to make a further choice where payment cannot be made in accordance with his or her wishes. Where the default option, nevertheless, comes into play the only options available are either an internal transfer or the purchase of an annuity or insurance policy.

(*b*) This gives rise to the question as to the type of annuity and insurance policy available for this purpose. A deferred annuity can be purchased but it is not clear what other 'insurance policy' can be used. It is not possible to transfer the credit to a personal pension scheme or stakeholder schemes without the consent of the former spouse.

(*c*) *Section 32* buy-out contracts would also seem not to be an option. This is because only pension *benefits* can be transferred to a *s 32* buy-out contract so it would only be in the event that an ex-spouse were to acquire a 'pension credit benefit' in the scheme that this could then be transferred out – and even in that case the consent of the ex-spouse would be required. In most cases there will be no pension credit benefit, only a pension credit liability to be discharged by the trustees. This appears to leave the purchase of an annuity as the only available external default option.

In practice this issue seems to have posed less of a problem than anticipated. An ex-spouse who agrees to a pension sharing order as part of the divorce settlement will have been notified of the trustees' policy and, where only an external transfer option is offered, is likely already to have made suitable arrangements before agreeing to such an order. There are however problematic cases where ex-spouses have failed or have refused to provide details of a provider, and where the amount of the pension credit is too small to be applied to purchase an annuity.

Pension credit benefits

General benefits and transfers

8.17 Where the trustees of a scheme choose to offer ex-spouses an internal transfer option, and the ex-spouse does not elect to transfer the pension credit to another arrangement, the ex-spouse will become an ex-spouse participant and will become entitled to pension credit benefits in the scheme.

WRPA 1999, s 37 inserts new *ss 101A–101Q* into *PSA 1993*, setting out the requirements relating to pension credit benefits under occupational pension schemes. The protection given to ex-spouses with pension credit benefits broadly reflects the existing provisions for early leavers from occupational pension schemes, including similar transfer rights to those of a deferred member. This legislation is supplemented by the *Pension Sharing (Pension Credit Benefit) Regulations 2000 (SI 2000/1054).*

Pension credit benefits are payable at 'normal benefit age', which means the earliest date at which a person who has a pension credit right is entitled to receive a pension by virtue of those rights (disregarding provisions as to early payment on grounds of ill-health). Normal benefit age must be between 60 and 65 and benefits cannot be taken in lump sum form before that age except in prescribed circumstances (*PSA 1993, s 101C*; *Pension Sharing (Pension Credit Benefit) Regulations 2000, Part II*). Essentially, this permits payment of a pension commencement lump sum, serious ill-health lump sum, trivial commutation lump sum or a winding-up lump sum.

Members with pension credit benefits are entitled under *PSA 1993, s 101F* to request that their cash equivalent be transferred to another occupational pension scheme or personal pension scheme which satisfies the necessary criteria, or be used to purchase an annuity, subject to certain requirements and restrictions set out in *Pension Sharing (Pension Credit Benefit) Regulations 2000, Part III*. *PSA 1993, s 101H* provides, in relation to salary related schemes, that a statement of entitlement must be provided by the trustees or managers, on the application of an eligible member, following which the eligible member has three months within which to request a transfer (*s 101G(1)*). The exceptions to this general rule are that an eligible member may not take a transfer if there is less than a year remaining before the member reaches normal benefit age or where any part of the benefit attributable to the member's pension credit rights has become payable (*s 101G(2)*). Where the trustees receive a transfer notice (ie a request for transfer) from an eligible member, *PSA 1993, s 101J* requires the trustees to comply with the notice within six months of the valuation date or the date on which the member reaches normal benefit age, if earlier. *Pension Sharing (Pension Credit Benefit) Regulations 2000, reg 26* states that extensions may be applied for from the Regulator in similar circumstances to those referred to at **8.13** above in relation to the extension of the implementation period. Otherwise, failure to comply with the transfer notice must be reported to the Regulator within 21 days beginning with the day immediately following the end of the period for compliance (*reg 25*). The Regulator may then impose civil penalties under *PA 1995, s 10* if the trustees failed to take all such steps as were reasonable to ensure that the notice was complied with.

Indexation

8.18 *Pension Sharing (Pension Credit Benefit) Regulations 2000, regs 32–35* provide that occupational pension schemes must apply indexation to the pension credit benefit derived from post-April 1997 rights excluding AVCs and money purchase benefits that come into payment after 6 April 2005. The indexation to be applied is 5 per cent per annum or the increase in the Retail Prices Index, whichever is lower in respect of pensions in payment prior to 6 April 2005 or where entitlement to the pension credit arose before that date, and 2.5 per cent per annum where entitlement to the pension credit arose on or after 6 April 2005.

MNT legislation

8.19 *PA 2004, ss 241–243* require the trustees of an occupational trust scheme to ensure that arrangements are in place to provide for at least one-third of the total number of trustees to be member-nominated trustees (MNTs). The nomination process must provide for active members and pensioner members (or organisations which adequately represent them) to be eligible to participate. Pension credit members do not fall within the definition of active members or pensioner members. Trustees may, however, choose to include them, having had regard to the principles of proportionality, fairness and transparency.

PA 1995, s 67

8.20 *PA 1995, s 67* (as amended by *PA 2004*) contains the 'Subsisting Rights Provisions' which apply to amendments to occupational pension schemes. Pension Credit members of an occupational pension scheme benefit from the protections of *s 67* by virtue of their inclusion in the definition of 'member' and the inclusion of 'pension credit rights' within the definition of 'subsisting right' (see *PA 1995, s 124*).

Any amendment of a scheme's rules, however, to give effect to the trustees' pension sharing policy and enable the application of a pension debit is excluded from the ambit of *s 67* by virtue of *s 67(3)*, which excludes from the 'subsisting rights provisions' modifications for a purpose connected with pension debits under *WRPA 1999, s 29(1)*.

Treatment on winding up

8.21 In the case of a scheme to which *PA 1995, s 73* applies (see CHAPTER 12), from 6 April 2005 the position of pension credits in the statutory order of priorities on winding up is referred to under *s 73(8)(b)*, where it is stated that benefits derived from pension credits are not to be treated as derived from voluntary contributions for the purposes of that section.

In the case of all other schemes, pension credits are to be accorded the same treatment on winding up as the rights of a pensioner member if they have come into payment and the rights of a deferred member if they have not come into payment (*WRPA 1999, s 38(2)*). This section overrides the provisions of the scheme to the extent that they conflict with it.

Valuation

8.22 In creating pension debits and credits under *WRPA 1999, s 29*, the pension sharing order is applied to the cash equivalent of the member's benefits (*WRPA 1999, s 30*). The specified percentage for reduction of a member's benefits is therefore the percentage of his or her cash equivalent of the relevant benefits on the valuation day (*WRPA 1999, s 29(2)*). 'Valuation day' is defined in *WRPA 1999, s 29(7)* as such day within the implementation period for the credit as the person responsible for the arrangement may specify by notice in writing to the member and ex-spouse.

For active members of occupational pension schemes, the cash equivalent is calculated in respect of the benefits to which the member would have been entitled to had his pensionable service been terminated on the day immediately prior to the transfer day, ie the day on which the pension sharing order takes effect (*WRPA 1999, s 29(4)*). *Section 30* provides for the calculation of the cash equivalent of these benefits to be carried out in accordance with the provisions set out in the *Pension Sharing (Valuation) Regulations 2000 (SI 2000/1052)*.

Pension Sharing (Valuation) Regulations 2000, reg 4 provides that cash equivalents are to be calculated in accordance with the *Occupational Pension Schemes (Transfer Values) Regulations 1996 (SI 1996/1847)* on the basis of such assumptions as the trustees determine, having taken the advice of the scheme actuary. In the case of an active member, his cash equivalent is required to be calculated on the assumption that the member had made a request for an estimate of cash equivalent as if his pensionable service were to terminate on the transfer day.

Occupational Pension Schemes (Transfer Values) Regulations 1996, reg 7D provides for the possibility of the cash equivalents being reduced where an insufficiency report has been obtained from the scheme actuary or where the trustees are treating the actuary's last relevant GN11 report as an insufficiency report.

It is important to note, however, that a reduction cannot be applied in circumstances where the pension credit liability is discharged by way of internal transfer or by way of external transfer without the ex-spouse's consent (*Pension Sharing (Valuation) Regulations 2000, reg 4(3)*).

Disclosure of information

8.23 *WRPA 1999, s 23(1)(a)* provides for regulations to impose requirements on the person responsible for a pension arrangement to supply information to certain parties in connection with the power to provide financial relief under *MCA 1973*. The *Pensions on Divorce etc (Provision of Information) Regulations 2000 (SI 2000/1048)* set out the details of these requirements.

At the beginning of the divorce process the person responsible for the arrangement must, on the request of a scheme member or spouse or pursuant to an order of the court, ensure that the following information is provided in connection with the divorce in accordance with *reg 2*:

(*a*) a valuation of the pension rights or benefits accrued under the pension arrangement, if requested by the member or the court;

(*b*) a statement that, if a member or the court requests, a valuation of the member's accrued benefits will be provided to the member or the court;

(*c*) a statement summarising the way in which any such valuation of the benefits disclosed is calculated;

(*d*) a statement of benefits included the valuation;

(*e*) a statement as to whether the person responsible for the arrangement intends to offer membership of the scheme to a person entitled to a pension credit (ie internal transfer) and, if so, the type of benefits available to the pension credit member under that arrangement;

(*f*) a statement as to whether the person responsible for the arrangement intends to discharge liability for a pension credit other than by offering membership to a person entitled to a pension credit (ie external option only);

(*g*) the schedule of charges to be levied by the person responsible for the arrangement; and

(*h*) any other additional information relevant to the sharing order requested by the court.

Therefore only a member or the court can require the valuation of a member's accrued benefits to be provided by the arrangement. Once requested it must be provided within three months beginning with the date of receipt of the request; or within six weeks of the date of receipt of the request if the member has notified the trustees that it is required in connection with financial relief in divorce proceedings; or within a shorter period if so ordered by the court (*reg 2(5)*).

All the other items of information set out above must be supplied within one month of receipt of the request, as long as the request makes it clear that this is a request in connection with divorce (*reg 2(6)*).

Regulation 4 sets out the information to be provided within 21 days of a notification that a pension sharing order or provision may be made, as follows:

(*a*) the full name and address of the pension scheme;

(*b*) whether the scheme is in winding up and, if so, the effective date of winding up and the contact details of the trustees or administrators;

(*c*) whether cash equivalents are subject to deductions;

(*d*) whether the trustees are aware of any other relevant court orders;

(*e*) any elements of the member's pension rights which are not shareable;

(*f*) details of how charges are to be paid;

(*g*) whether the member is a trustee of the scheme;

(*h*) whether the scheme may request details of the member's health from the member, if the order were to proceed; and

(*i*) whether the scheme requires any further information before implementation of the order.

Regulation 5 sets out the information required by the person responsible for the pension arrangement before the implementation period begins, as follows:

(i) In relation to the member – all names and former names; date of birth; address; National Insurance number; name of scheme to which the order relates and membership/policy number.

(ii) In relation to the ex-spouse – all names and former names; date of birth; address; National Insurance number; if the ex-spouse is also a member of the scheme from which the pension credit is derived, the membership/policy number.

(iii) Where the ex-spouse is transferring to another arrangement – the full name and address of that arrangement; the membership or policy number; details of the person able to discharge liability for the pension credit; in the case of rights transferring from an occupational pension scheme which is in winding up with a deficit, whether the ex-spouse has indicated she wishes to transfer the pension credit rights; and any further information the receiving arrangement may require.

Regulation 6 sets out the information to be provided after the death of the ex-spouse prior to liability having been discharged.

Regulation 7 sets out the information to be provided after receipt of the pension sharing order or provision, and *reg 8* the information to be provided after the implementation of a pension sharing order.

Charging

8.24 *WRPA 1999, s 41* and the *Pensions on Divorce etc (Charging) Regulations 2000 (SI 2000/1049)* provide for persons responsible for pension arrangements to recover charges in respect of pension sharing costs.

Costs are not recoverable unless the divorcing parties have been informed in writing by the person responsible for the pension arrangement of the intention to recover costs and a written schedule of the charges has been provided. *Pensions on Divorce etc (Charging) Regulations 2000, reg 2* provides that charges cannot, however, be recovered for the provision of basic information about pensions and divorce (pursuant to *Pensions on Divorce etc (Provision of Information) Regulations 2000, reg 2*), or for the provision of information in response to a notification that a pension sharing order may be made (*Pensions on Divorce etc (Provision of Information) Regulations 2000, reg 4*) unless that information has already been provided on the previous 12-month period, or the member has reached normal pension age or is within 12 months of normal pension age. Charges also cannot be recovered for the provision of a cash equivalent which is provided in accordance with *PA 1995, s 93A* or *94* or in accordance with the *Disclosure Regulations.*

Where charges are recoverable they can only be for the reasonable administrative expenses the arrangement will incur in connection with the implementation of the pension sharing order or the provision of information in connection with the divorce proceedings and must be directly related to the individual case (*Pensions on Divorce etc (Charging) Regulations 2000, reg 5*). The legislation does not define, however, what is meant by 'reasonable'. The National Association of Pension Funds has issued guidance on this point to its membership (see **8.26** below).

MCA 1973, s 24D has been introduced to give the courts power to include a provision in the order relating to the apportionment of charges between the parties. To the extent that the court is silent on the issue, *WRPA 1999, s 41(3)(b)* provides that the charges shall be attributable to the scheme member.

Pensions on Divorce etc (Charging) Regulations 2000, reg 7 permits the postponement of the start of the implementation period for a sharing order until specified charges are paid, provided that appropriate notice has been given to the parties in accordance with that regulation.

Regulation 9 provides for certain methods of recovery of the charges by the person responsible for the pension arrangement. Where the charges are not paid in cash, recovery can be by way of deduction from the pension credit; deduction from the member's accrued rights; deduction from pension where the pension is in payment; and deduction from payments of pension credit benefits (subject to certain conditions having been satisfied).

Reference should be made to the *Pensions on Divorce etc (Charging) Regulations 2000* for full details of the conditions and restrictions relating to the charging for information and pension sharing activities.

In relation to earmarking orders, charges for the provision of information are dealt with as described above. In relation to the costs associated with the implementation of an earmarking order, *Pensions on Divorce etc (Charging) Regulations 2000, reg 10* provides that the person responsible for the pension arrangement recovers reasonable administrative expenses which have been or are likely to be incurred by reason of the order.

NAPF recommended scale of charges

8.25

Pension sharing costs for active and deferred members

Step	Lower limit	Upper limit	Notes
Produce CETV quotation	£0	£0	1. This is a standard entitlement under regulations. 2. CETV refers to 'cash equivalent transfer value' – the value of pension rights from the scheme.
Additional CETV quotations	£150	£200	Any more than one quotation a year can be charged for.
Provision of other information	£0	Up to £250	Information which does not have to be provided free may be charged for. Cost will depend upon the nature and complexity of the enquiry.

Step	Lower limit	Upper limit	Notes
Processing a pensions sharing order ('PSO') – internal transfer, in DB or hybrid scheme	£1,950	£2,350	Includes allowance for future scheme admin costs of approximately £1,000.
Processing a PSO – internal transfer, DC scheme	£1,800	£2,200	It is recommended that if trustees will pay for annuity purchase advice on retirement an extra £500 can be charged.
Processing a PSO – external transfer, DB or hybrid scheme	£1,100	£1,550	
Processing a PSO – external transfer, DC scheme	£1,050	£1,450	

Pension sharing costs for pensions in payment

Step	Lower limit	Upper limit	Notes
Produce CETV quotation	£500	£800	There is no entitlement to this information under regulations.
Additional CETV quotations	£500	£800	There is no entitlement to this information under regulations.
Provision of other information	£0	Up to £250	Information which does not have to be provided free may be charged for. Cost will depend upon the nature and complexity of the inquiry.
Processing a PSO – internal transfer, in DB or hybrid scheme	£2,000	£2,550	Includes recalculation of CETV and recovery of pension arrears if the full amount is paid for a time after the pension sharing order.
Processing a PSO – external transfer	£1,300	£1,900	

Safeguarded rights

8.26 *WRPA 1999, s 36* inserted new *ss 68A–68D* into *PSA 1993* with the effect that 'safeguarded rights' were created where rights to future benefits under the scheme were attributable to a pension credit which is or includes contracted-out (or safeguarded) rights. The safeguarded rights formed the same percentage of the pension credit as the contracted-out (or safeguarded) rights formed of the member's cash equivalent. Despite the different terminology, safeguarded rights were treated in broadly the same way as contracted-out rights.

However, as part of the measures introduced to simplify pension provision, *PA 2008, s 100* and related repeals in *Sch 11* removed the provisions relating to safeguarded rights in *PSA 1993, Part IIIA*. Shared rights derived from contracted-out benefits are now treated in the same way as other shared rights.

Family Proceedings Rules

8.27 The procedures to be followed to obtain either an earmarking or a sharing order are set out in *Family Proceedings Rules 1991 (SI 1991/1247), r 2.70*, as amended.

The rule applies to applications for ancillary relief and sets out the obligations of the parties with regard to the provision of information relating to benefits which a party has or is likely to have under a pension scheme. For both earmarking and pension sharing the order must be specifically applied for on Form A or Form B. The court will then fix an appointment and, within seven days after receiving notification of the date of that appointment, the member must request that the person responsible for the pension arrangement(s) under which the member has or is likely to have benefits provides basic information set out in *Pensions on Divorce etc (Provision of Information) Regulations 2000, reg 2(2)*, ie the valuation of the member's pension rights (see **8.22** and **8.23** above).

Within seven days of receiving this information, the member shall send a copy of it to the other party together with the name and address of the person responsible for the pension arrangement(s). *Rule 2.70(4)* states that, where the member is already in possession of, or has requested, a relevant valuation of his benefits under the pension arrangement in question, then this request for disclosure need not be made (for these purposes a relevant valuation is one which has been furnished to the member within the 12 months preceding the date fixed for the first appointment).

If notice is given of intention to proceed with an application for a pension sharing order, the applicant must send a copy of Form A to the person responsible for the pension arrangement (*r 2.70(6)*). In the case of an application for an earmarking order the applicant must send the person responsible for the pension arrangement a copy of Form A; an address for the service of any notices on the applicant by the person responsible for the pension arrangement; an address to which payments can be remitted; and, if that address is a bank, sufficient details to enable payment to be made into the applicant's account (*r 2.70(7)*).

Within 21 days after service of a notice of application for an earmarking order under *r 2.70(7)*, the person responsible for the pension arrangement has the right under *r 2.70(8)* to require a copy of the statement in Form E supporting the application to be provided and the person responsible for the pension arrangement may within 21 days of receipt provide to the applicant, respondent and the court a statement in answer (*r 2.70(9)*). If the earmarking order is being applied for by way of consent order, the relevant information together with a copy of the draft order must be provided to the persons responsible for the pension arrangement and the order shall not be made until 21 days have elapsed without objections being made or the court has considered any objections (*r 2.70(11), (12)*).

Under *r 2.70(13)*, any order for ancillary relief, whether by consent or not, which includes either a provision for pension sharing or for earmarking must:

(*a*) in the body of the order state that there is to be provision by way of pension sharing or earmarking in accordance with the annex to the order; and

(*b*) be accompanied by an annex in Form P1 (for pension sharing) or Form P2 (for earmarking), setting out specified information. If there is more than one pension arrangement, an annex must be attached for each arrangement.

8.28 A new *r 2.70A* has been inserted into the *Family Proceedings Rules 1991* for pension arrangements which are either in an assessment period for the purposes of the Pension Protection Fund (PPF), or where the PPF has assumed responsibility for the pension arrangement.

Where the party with the pension rights receives notification that the pension arrangement is in an assessment period for the purposes of the PPF, the member must send a copy of the notification and the valuation summary to the other party at the time when the valuation information is being sent, or within seven days of receipt (*r 2.70A(2), (3)*). If the member subsequently receives notification that, following an assessment period, the PPF has assumed responsibility for the arrangement, the member must with seven days (i) send a copy of that notification to the other party, and (ii) request from the PPF a forecast of his compensation entitlement and then send that on to the other party within seven days of receipt (*r 2.70A(4), (5)*).

Overlap between earmarking and pension sharing

8.29 *MCA 1973, s 24B(5)* states that a pension sharing order may not be made in relation to the rights of a person under a pension arrangement if there is in force an earmarking order in relation to any of the member's benefits under the relevant schemes.

MCA 1973, ss 25B(7B) and *25C(4)* state, similarly, that the power to make an earmarking order may not be exercised in relation to a pension arrangement which is the subject of a pension sharing order in relation to the marriage in question or has been the subject of a pension sharing between the parties to the marriage.

Civil partnerships

8.30 The *Civil Partnership Act 2004* ('*CPA 2004*') came into force on 5 December 2005 and provides the opportunity for same-sex couples to obtain legal recognition of their relationship by registering as civil partners. The general principles behind *CPA 2004* are that registered civil partners will have access to rights and responsibilities similar to those of married couples, including employment and pension benefits, the duty to provide maintenance for a civil partner, the duty to provide maintenance for children of the partnership, and recognition under intestacy rules. See **9.32** onwards for more information.

A civil partnership is formed by signing a civil partnership document in the presence of witnesses and a civil partnership registrar, following which the civil partnership will end only on death, dissolution or annulment. *CPA 2004, Sch 5* makes provision for financial relief in connection with civil partnerships that corresponds to the financial relief available in connection with divorces after marriage under *MCA 1973*. *CPA 2004, Sch 5, Part 4* sets out full details in relation to pension sharing orders available on the dissolution or nullity of a civil partnership, and these provisions mirror in essence those set out in the preceding paragraphs of this chapter in relation to divorce. *CPA 2004, Sch 5, Part 6* sets out the provisions in relation to earmarking orders.

Consequential amendments have been made, therefore, to all relevant statutes and regulations referred to in the preceding paragraphs of this chapter to extend the provisions to apply on the dissolution of a civil partnership including, in particular, amendments to *MCA 1973* and *WRPA 1999*.

Chapter 9

Discrimination

Introduction

9.1 Much of the UK's anti-discrimination law is derived from the European Union. For example, the principle of equal pay for men and women is contained in *Article 157* of the *Treaty on the Functioning of the European Union* ('*TFEU*'), and the *Equal Treatment Framework Directive (2000/78/EC)* requires Member States to put in place legislation prohibiting discrimination in employment on the grounds of sexual orientation, age, disability and religious belief. In this chapter, it will be seen that this is a large and developing area of the law, and in some respects is relatively untested in a pensions context.

In addition, the UK Government is in the process of reforming UK equality laws and the *Equality Bill* was published on 27 April 2009. The Bill consolidates and amends existing discrimination legislation relating to age, sex, race, disability, sexual orientation and religion or belief. It is anticipated that the Bill will come into force in October 2010 (see **9.46** to **9.50** below for further information in relation to the *Equality Bill*).

A summary of relevant legislation and case law (UK and European) is set out at the end of the chapter.

Sex discrimination

9.2 In the UK, differential pension provision for men and women was, prior to the 1990s, the norm rather than the exception. The effect of EU law in prescribing requirements for equal treatment in pension schemes could no longer be ignored in the UK when the Court of Justice of the European Communities ('ECJ') confirmed in the *Barber* case (*Barber v GRE Assurance Group C-262/88 [1990] ECR I-1889*) that pensions were 'pay' for the purposes of the equal pay requirements of what was then *Article 119* of the *Treaty of Rome*, was then renumbered as *Article 141* by the *Treaty of Amsterdam* with effect from 1 May 1999, and is currently *Article 157* of the *TFEU* (following the *Treaty of Lisbon*).

Article 157 of the *TFEU* provides that:

> '1. Each Member State shall ensure that the principle of equal pay for male and female workers for equal work or work of equal value is applied.
>
> 2. For the purpose of this Article, "pay" means the ordinary basic or minimum wage or salary and any other consideration, whether in cash or in kind, which the worker receives directly or indirectly, in respect of his employment, from his employer.
>
> Equal pay without discrimination based on sex means:
>
> (*a*) that pay for the same work at piece rates shall be calculated on the basis of the same unit of measurement;
>
> (*b*) that pay for work at time rates shall be the same for the same job.'

The action in *Barber* was against the employer, not the pension scheme, as it was founded on the equal pay concept. In brief, Mr Barber was made redundant at the age of 52 and received various cash benefits, but was not entitled at that time to take his pension. A woman in the same position as Mr Barber would have been entitled to an immediate retirement pension in addition to redundancy pay. Mr Barber claimed successfully in the ECJ that pensions should be treated as pay under *Article 157* and that, in consequence, he should be entitled to the same benefits as a woman of the same age. However, the ECJ's decision was not retrospective and persons were not permitted (unless legal proceedings had already begun) to claim entitlement to benefits accrued in relation to service prior to the date of judgment, ie 17 May 1990.

The *Maastricht Protocol (No 2)* (the '*Maastricht Protocol*') annexed to the *EU Treaty* (7 February 1992) amended the then *Article 141* constraining its application (in relation to pensions) to benefits accrued after 17 May 1990.

Although decisions of the ECJ are not legislative in nature, they are binding upon those to whom they are addressed (see *Article 288* of the *TFEU*). Where EU law has direct effect, it will generally override UK law. The principle that *Article 157* has direct effect was established on 8 April 1976 by the *Defrenne (No 2)* case (*Defrenne v Sabena [1976] ECR 455*) which stated that 'direct effect' means that the protections given under *Article 157* apply directly to UK law without the need for any further national or European legislation. This was confirmed in the *Coloroll* case (*Coloroll Pension Trustees Ltd v Russell (C-200/91) [1995] All ER (EC) 23*), which also made it clear that *Article 157* can be relied upon by both employees and their dependants against trustees who are bound to observe the principles of equal treatment.

PA 1995 incorporates the general requirements for equal treatment in pension schemes (see *ss 62–66*). These cover not only the terms on which scheme members are treated but also the terms on which employees are admitted to membership. Thus, *PA 1995, s 62(3)* provides that in relation to such a 'term' that is '... less favourable to the woman than it is to the man, the term shall be treated as so modified as not to be less favourable'. These provisions came into force on 1 January 1996, but their operation is to some extent retrospective, as explained below. The requirements are overriding so schemes must comply with them, irrespective of the actual provisions in their governing documentation. *PA 1995, s 65* also empowers trustees of schemes with inadequate amendment powers in their governing documentation to make whatever rule amendments are necessary to ensure compliance with the equal treatment requirements without employer consent.

PA 2004 also contains equal treatment provisions. *Section 171*, which came into force on 6 April 2006, provides for the equal treatment of men and women in relation to the 'payment function' of the Board of the PPF. The Explanatory Notes to *PA 2004* state that *s 171* provides the mechanism to ensure that there is no discrimination between men and women arising from the use of the scheme rules when calculating entitlement to pension compensation. (see CHAPTER 5).

It can be seen that there has been no clear policy or decision of principle underlying the development of UK law in this area. Indeed, it had been thought that the implementation of sex equality in pension schemes was simply not practicable. The cost issue alone was a significant deterrent to equalisation. Pension matters were expressly excluded from the equal pay and sex discrimination legislation passed in the 1970s and 1980s. Thus, the law has grown in fits and starts, very much in reaction to developments in the EU. It is an area of law in which most of the major issues have now been resolved, although a few anomalies remain.

Access/eligibility

General

9.3 The principle of equal access to pension scheme membership was established in UK legislation by the *Social Security Pensions Act 1975*, with detailed provision contained in regulations (the *Occupational Pension Schemes (Equal Access to Membership) Regulations 1976 (SI 1976/142)*). These Regulations were subsequently superseded by the *Occupational Pension Schemes (Equal Treatment) Regulations 1995 (SI 1995/3183)* (the '*Equal Treatment Regulations*'). The relevant provisions of the *Social Security Pensions Act 1975* were re-enacted in *PSA 1993* (*s 118*, now repealed), and are now covered in *PA 1995, ss 62–66*.

The ECJ, in the 1994 judgments of *Vroege v NCIV Instituut C-57/93 [1994] ECR I-4541* and *Fisscher v Voorhuis Hengelo BV C-128/93 [1994] ECR I-4583*, unequivocally stated that, as well as entitlement to benefits, the right to join an occupational pension scheme also falls within the scope of *Article 157* of the *TFEU*, and is therefore covered by the prohibition on sex discrimination laid down by that Article. Therefore, this means that the direct effect of *Article 157* could be relied upon to claim (retrospectively) equal treatment from 8 April 1976 (the date of the *Defrenne* case when it was established that *Article 157* had direct effect). In these two judgments the ECJ confirmed the earlier decision in *Bilka-Kaufhaus GmbH v Weber von Hartz C-170/84 [1986] ECR 1607* that indirectly discriminatory entry conditions which could not be objectively justified were in breach of *Article 157* (see **9.4** below).

Part-time employees

Exclusion from membership – general

9.4 The exclusion of part-time workers from scheme membership may infringe *Article 157* if it can be shown that there has been indirect sex discrimination.

There are two types of sex discrimination: direct and indirect. Direct sex discrimination occurs where, for example, women are denied entry to pension schemes but men are not. Indirect sex discrimination occurs where, for example, the pension scheme eligibility requirements are such that they are to the detriment of a significantly greater proportion of women than men because considerably fewer women can comply with them. By applying such restrictions (without objective justification not dependent on sex), women are being indirectly discriminated against on grounds of sex because considerably more women than men are being detrimentally affected.

It has generally been the case that considerably more women than men work part-time and, thus, may suffer indirect discrimination. In the *Bilka-Kaufhaus* case, the ECJ stated that there would be a breach of *Article 157* if the exclusion of part-time workers affected a much greater number of women than men. Unfortunately, the ECJ did not expand on what it meant by 'a much greater number', nor did it specify a minimum number of hours that a part-timer must work in order to qualify for membership. Some light was shed on the latter point by the ECJ decision in *Nolte v Landesversicherungsanstalt Hannover C-317/93 [1996] All ER (EC) 212*, where it was decided that it was in that case permissible to avoid granting pension benefits to employees who work less than 15 hours per week, where the reason is to achieve a social policy unrelated to any discrimination on grounds of sex. Here, the ECJ agreed that the fostering of 'minor' employment, for which there was a social demand, was practicable only if it was excluded from the relevant compulsory insurance provisions.

In the case of *Regina v Secretary of State for Employment ex parte Seymour-Smith and Another Case C-167/97 [1999] ICR 447*, the ECJ considered among other questions the test for determining whether a measure adopted by a Member State had 'such a disparate effect as between men and women as to amount to indirect discrimination'. The ECJ stated that the best approach to this issue was to compare statistical evidence of the proportion of men and women able to satisfy the condition at issue and those unable to do so and to compare those proportions. If the statistics indicated that a 'considerably smaller percentage' of women than men were able to satisfy the condition, there was indirect sex discrimination unless the measure was justified by objective factors. In addition, a lesser but persistent and relatively constant disparity over a long period between men and women who satisfied the particular condition at issue could also amount to indirect sex discrimination.

Exclusion from membership with justification

9.5 Even if the workforce statistics suggest that there might be discrimination, a scheme will not have to admit part-timers if the employer can demonstrate that the exclusion can be explained by objectively justified factors unrelated to any discrimination on grounds of sex. In the *Bilka-Kaufhaus* case it was accepted that a rule that incidentally adversely affects more women than men may nevertheless be lawful. It is for national courts to decide whether a particular rule is or is not justifiable, but guidelines laid down by the ECJ suggest that the onus is on the employer to show that:

(*a*) the grounds put forward do not relate to the employee's sex;

(*b*) the grounds put forward relate to a real need of the employer; and

(*c*) the measures taken are appropriate and necessary to achieve the desired end.

An employer who can show, for example, that there is a genuine need to encourage full-time working patterns because they increase productivity or that part-timers will gain very little or nothing by joining a scheme that is contracted out instead of remaining with the State second pension, may be able to exclude part-timers without infringement of *Article 157*.

Part-timers' claims

9.6 The *Equal Treatment Regulations* came into force on 1 January 1996 to supplement the requirements for equal treatment relating to occupational pension schemes provided for in *PA 1995, ss 62–66*. The *Regulations* extended the scope of the *Equal Pay Act 1970* to cover pensions and consequently (in accordance with the then provisions of the *Equal Pay Act*) any claim had to be brought within six months of the end of the employment to which the claim related. In addition, claims were limited to two years' backdated membership.

The *Equal Treatment Regulations* also imposed the full cost of funding the excluded employee's benefits after 31 May 1995 on the employer.

The ECJ reviewed the validity of these time limits in *Preston v Wolverhampton Healthcare NHS Trust [2000] All ER (EC) 714*. This was followed by a referral to the House of Lords (*Preston (No 2) [2001] IRLR 237, HL*). The House of Lords confirmed that any national legislation was unlawful if it prevented service from being taken into account that was earlier than two years before the date of the claim. Therefore, pension benefits payable after the date of claim now have to be calculated by reference to all periods of service for which the employee should have been a scheme member (or, if later, from 8 April 1976 – the date of the *Defrenne* judgment). The House of Lords also held that the rules of procedure under the *Equal Pay Act 1970* which required that a claim for membership of an occupational pension scheme must be brought within six months of the end of the employment to which the claim relates, were not less favourable than those applying to a breach of contract claim. Therefore the six-month limitation did not breach the community law principle of 'equivalence'. The significance for employees of this decision is that claims must, at the latest, be filed within six months of leaving employment. Employers also have to be aware that claims may arise not only from current part-time workers, but also from those who have ceased employment within the last six months or those who left employment more than six months previously but filed their claims within the six-month period. The House of Lords made it clear that a series of short-term contracts can amount to a stable employment relationship and therefore employment does not terminate at the end of each individual contract. Further, time starts to run for bringing a claim only when that relationship is broken.

A Directions hearing was subsequently held in November 2001 in which further issues relating to the *Preston* decision were raised and test cases were selected for a full hearing. These hearings took place in June and July 2002 and certain aspects of the employment tribunal's decision were appealed to the Employment Appeal Tribunal ('EAT'). The EAT (*Preston v Wolverhampton Healthcare NHS Trust (No 3) [2004] IRLR 96*) made the following determinations:

(*a*) There is a breach of the *Equal Pay Act 1970* where membership of a scheme is compulsory for full-time workers but part-time workers are excluded.

(*b*) There is no breach of *Article 157* of the *TFEU* where membership of the scheme is compulsory for full-time workers but part-time workers are given the option of joining or not joining the scheme.

(*c*) There is no continuing breach of *Article 157* by an employer failing to inform a part-time employee of his entitlement to join the pension scheme, unless that failure was itself on discriminatory grounds. However, employees may have a breach of contract claim in such circumstances on the basis of the employer's implied obligation to inform employees of advantageous contractual terms.

(*d*) The six-month time limit for bringing a claim under the *Equal Pay Act 1970* begins to run when:

(i) either party indicates that further contracts will not be offered or accepted;

(ii) either party acts in a manner which is inconsistent with the relationship continuing;

(iii) the employer does not offer a new contract in circumstances where the periodicity of the preceding cycle of contracts indicates that it should have been offered;

(iv) either party stops treating the relationship as stable;

(v) the terms under which work is to be done alter radically;

(vi) since liability for occupational pension schemes does not transfer under *TUPE*, liability under the *Equal Pay Act 1970* and *Article 157* for the transferor's failure to provide equal access to a scheme remains with the transferor; and

(vii) following a *TUPE* transfer, time for bringing a claim against the transferor begins to run from the date the employee's employment with the transferee comes to an end. Although the EAT commented that an employee may be advised to take action shortly after a relevant transfer to lessen the risk of the transferor going out of business and 'disappearing'.

The last finding relating to *TUPE* was appealed. The House of Lords found that the time for bringing a claim begins to run from the date of the transfer (*Preston v Wolverhampton Healthcare NHS Trust (No 3) [2006] UKHL 13* also known as *Powerhouse Retail Ltd v Burroughs*).

The *Occupational Pension Schemes (Equal Treatment) (Amendment) Regulations 2005 (SI 2005/1923)* implement the rulings in the *Preston* case. The Regulations amend provisions of the *Equal Pay Act 1970*, *PA 1995* and the *Equal Treatment Regulations*. In accordance with the decision in the *Preston* case, the Regulations remove the two-year limit on backdating successful claims. In addition, the Regulations make the six-month time limit for bringing claims comply with EU law, in that claims must be brought within six months of leaving employment or the end of a stable employment relationship.

Finally, the Regulations remove an obligation on the employer to meet the cost of employee contributions where backdated access is granted.

In *Deutsche Telekom v Schroder C-50/96 [2000] ECR I-743* the ECJ confirmed that the *Defrenne* time limit does not prevent more favourable national legislation which may allow even further backdating of periods of service, ie prior to 8 April 1976, thereby going further than European legislation itself.

The right of access to a pension scheme for contract workers arose in the case of *Allonby v Accrington and Rossendale College [2001] IRLR 364 (CA)*. In 1996 the college terminated Mrs Allonby's part-time contract and employed her services through an employment agency instead. Mrs Allonby complained, inter alia, that she was no longer eligible for membership of the Teachers' Superannuation Scheme and that this amounted to discrimination. The Court of Appeal allowed Mrs Allonby's appeal from the decision of the EAT on the grounds that the employment tribunal had not adopted the correct approach to the question of whether the impact of the condition for continuous employment was proportionate and justifiable, and the case was remitted back to the employment tribunal for a further hearing on whether the employer had discriminated against the employee as a contract worker. The Court of Appeal also referred certain questions to the ECJ and, on 13 January 2004, the ECJ gave its judgment in *Allonby v Accrington and Rossendale College C-256/01 [2004] IRLR 224*. The ECJ considered and gave judgment on the questions referred to it by the Court of Appeal as outlined below:

(*a*) The first question concerned whether Mrs Allonby could bring an equal pay claim identifying a male full-time employee as her comparator (Mr J). The ECJ held that Mr J could not be a comparator for Mrs Allonby. Mr J was paid by the college and Mrs Allonby by an employment agency. There was no basis on which the differences in pay between Mrs Allonby and Mr J could be attributable to a single source. There was therefore no single body responsible for the inequality.

(*b*) The ECJ considered whether Mrs Allonby was entitled to the right to equal pay conferred by *Article 157*. The ECJ held that the right extends to all 'workers' but does not cover an independent provider of services who is not in a relationship of subordination with the person who receives those services.

(*c*) Where an equal pay claim relates to a private occupational pension scheme a 'worker' must identify, in the same undertaking, workers of the opposite sex who perform or have performed comparable work.

(*d*) Where the pension scheme is statutory, an equal pay claim could be pursued where the statistics support it, even in the absence of an actual comparator. This is on the basis that the legislation is the sole source of the unequal treatment, ie there is no requirement for the comparator.

(*e*) In order to succeed, Mrs Allonby would have to show that, among teachers who are 'workers' and fulfil all of the scheme's membership conditions except that of being employed under a contract of employment, there is a much higher percentage of women than men. It would be open for the college to objectively justify the difference in treatment.

In light of the ECJ's judgments, the Court of Appeal held, on 25 November 2004, that it would be appropriate to remit the case to the employment tribunal for determination of outstanding matters. It was held that the following issues required determination; (a) whether Mrs Allonby was a worker as ruled by the ECJ; (b) if so, whether the pension scheme had an adverse impact on her on the grounds that she was a woman; and (c) whether any such impact was justified.

The decision in *Allonby* was referred to in the case *British Airways Plc v Jessica Starmer [2005] IRLR 863*. It was held by the EAT that the employment tribunal was correct in finding that the decision of British Airways not to allow Mrs Starmer to work 50 per cent of her hours was a provision, criterion or practice which had a disparate impact and was not justified.

However, the *Allonby* decision was distinguished in *Shaikh v Department for Constitutional Affairs [2005] All ER (D) 154*. The claimant was a part-time tribunal chairman. He claimed equal access to the pension provision available to full time chairmen. However, the respondents denied the claim and stated that there was no comparable female chairperson engaged in like work or work of equal value. Relying on the decision in *Allonby*, the claimant asserted that there was no requirement for a comparator in this case as statute was the source of the unequal treatment. However, distinguishing *Allonby*, the EAT stated that there had to be a female comparator.

In the case of *Dacas v Brook Street Bureau (UK) Ltd [2004] EWCA Civ 217*, Mrs D worked for a local authority through an agency. She claimed unfair dismissal against both the agency (Brook Street) and the local authority. Brook Street appealed the EAT's decision that it was her employer. The Court of Appeal held that Brook Street was not Mrs Dacas' employer. It went on to say that there might be an implied contract of employment between Mrs Dacas and the local authority. If the local authority had been a party to the appeal then that question would have been remitted to the employment tribunal for decision. The importance of this decision for pensions is that the Court of Appeal is indicating that agency workers could be employees of the organisation they provide their services to. This is a move away from the previously generally held view that the individual's only contractual relationship was with the agency. If such workers can establish implied contracts of employment then they may well also, as employees, have rights to membership of pension schemes.

In *Astbury v Gist [2005] All ER (D) 165 (Apr)* the *Dacas* case was applied when the EAT found that the employment tribunal had been wrong in not carrying out a detailed factual assessment before reaching a conclusion as to whether or not there was an implied contract of employment between the worker and the end user. The case was remitted to the employment tribunal for a re-hearing. At this hearing it was determined that Mr Astbury was not an employee of the end user. Mr Astbury appealed and the case was heard by the EAT on 28 March 2007. The EAT dismissed Mr Astbury's appeal. It was stated, obiter, that the decision in *Dacas* did not sit 'comfortably with the structure of the employment protection legislation'.

See **9.33** below for further comment in relation to temporary/agency workers.

It may be possible for employees who are outside the statutory time limits for bringing a claim to the employment tribunal to complain to the Pensions Ombudsman. The Ombudsman took this view in his determination of *Mrs D Copnall (Case No F00828, 28 September 2000)*. He determined that failure to admit part-timers retrospectively to a pension scheme was maladministration. However, this finding was overturned on appeal to the High Court in *Glossop v Copnall [2001] PLR 263* on 5 July 2001 when Sir Andrew Morritt held that a trustee's failure to comply with the requirements of legislation is not of itself maladministration (in fact, Mrs Copnall had not complained of the matter which the Ombudsman held to be maladministration). The High Court held that trustees acted properly in waiting for the relevant decisions by the ECJ before granting backdated benefits.

The benefit of making a complaint to the Pensions Ombudsman is that the more generous limitation period of three years applies. The Ombudsman can also extend the three-year limitation period in exceptional cases where the complainant was unaware of the event giving rise to the complaint or if it was not reasonably practicable for the complaint to be made or referred within the three-year time limit. However, the Ombudsman is precluded from investigating complaints if proceedings have already been brought before the courts, and this includes employment tribunal claims (*PSA 1993, s 146(6)*).

With regard to the backdating of employee contributions where retrospective membership of a scheme has been granted, under the *FA 2004* employees can make unlimited contributions to a registered pension scheme during a tax year but may only get tax relief on contributions up to the higher of their total UK earnings or £3,600 (see CHAPTER 16).

On 21 June 2007, the ECJ gave its judgment in the case of *National Pensions Office v Jonkman (C-231/06)* concerning the right to require contributions from members in relation to backdated membership. The Court confirmed that members can be required to make good contributions for the period of backdated membership but that:

(*a*) any interest payable must compensate for inflation only; and

(*b*) there can be no requirement for the payment to be made as a single sum where that condition makes the payment impossible or excessively difficult in practice, in particular where the sum exceeds the annual pension payable.

Membership conditions

9.7 Some schemes/employers may impose membership conditions that indirectly discriminate against part-timers. An example of this type of practice was challenged in the complaint of Mrs E M Shillcock which was determined by the Pensions Ombudsman *(No F00317, 30 October 1997)*. In that complaint, the scheme rules required the lower earnings limit ('LEL') for national insurance contributions to be deducted when determining pensionable salary. Employees who earned less than the LEL were not eligible to join the scheme.

The Pensions Ombudsman ruled that this practice amounted to indirect discrimination against part-time employees earning less than the LEL. He said that only part of the LEL should have been deducted, representing the proportion that the employee's part-time hours bore to full-time hours. The decision was appealed to the High Court and the decision was overturned. It was held that the Pensions Ombudsman did not have jurisdiction to entertain a complaint regarding short service benefits. In addition, the LEL offset was not discriminatory and had it been so, the intention to provide integration with the State scheme would have been sufficient objective justification (*Uppingham School v Shillcock [2002] EWHC 641 (Ch)*).

The Part-time Workers Regulations

9.8 The *Part-time Workers (Prevention of Less Favourable Treatment) Regulations 2000 (SI 2000/1551)* (the '*Part-time Workers Regulations 2000*') came into effect on 1 July 2000 implementing *Directive 97/81/EC* as extended to the UK by *Directive 98/23/EC*. The Regulations require employers to treat part-time workers (not only employees) no less favourably than they treat comparable full-time workers. In addition, employers may not treat less favourably an employee who, having worked full-time, returns to work on a part-time basis after absence, compared with the way the employee was treated when he or she worked full-time. This is subject to the defence of objective justification. It will not be necessary for a part-timer to prove indirect sexual discrimination in order to claim entitlement to the same benefits as full-time workers. So, for example, part-time workers cannot be excluded from a pension scheme which full-time workers are entitled to join unless this exclusion can be objectively justified. Employers will have to ensure that there are no restrictive conditions relating to access to, and benefits under, the pension scheme for part-time workers.

However, as referred to above, treating part-timers less favourably than full-timers can be justified on objective grounds provided that it can be shown that the less favourable treatment is (*a*) to achieve a legitimate objective (for example, a genuine business objective); (*b*) necessary to achieve that objective; and (*c*) an appropriate way to achieve that objective.

To reflect the ruling in *Preston* (see **9.6** above), the *Part-time Workers (Prevention of Less Favourable Treatment) Regulations 2000 (Amendment) Regulations 2002 (SI 2002/2035)* (the '*Amendment Regulations 2002*') came into force on 1 October 2002. The *Part-time Workers Regulations 2000* (*reg 8(8)*) had limited the backdating of a claim to two years from the date upon which the complaint was presented, but this restriction has been removed (*Amendment Regulations 2002, reg 2*). In addition, the distinction between fixed-term and permanent contract employees has been removed, with the result that part-time workers on a fixed-term contract can now compare themselves with full-time workers on a permanent or fixed-term contract.

The first case under the *Part-time Workers Regulations 2000* to reach the Court of Appeal was *Matthews v Kent & Medway Towns Fire Authority [2004] EWCA Civ 844*. Mr Matthews worked as a part-time fire-fighter and complained that he was discriminated against compared with full-time fire-fighters, in particular by not being granted access to the pension scheme. The employment tribunal had dismissed the fire-fighters' claims on the basis that the part-time fire-fighters were employed on a different type of contract to full-time fire-fighters and the part-time fire-fighters were not engaged in the same or broadly similar work as full-time fire-fighters. The EAT dismissed the fire-fighters' appeal and their appeal against the EAT decision was dismissed by the Court of Appeal. The Court of Appeal found that the part-time fire-fighters were employed under the same type of contract as their full-time colleagues but that the Tribunal was correct in finding that the full-time fire-fighters carried out additional job functions not carried out by the part-time workers.

The part-time fire-fighters took their case to the House of Lords where judgment was reached on 1 March 2006 (*Matthews v Kent and Medway Towns Fire Authority [2006] All ER 171*). In summary, the fire-fighters' appeal was allowed and the case was sent back to the employment tribunal for reconsideration of the question whether part-time and full-time fire-fighters are engaged in the same or broadly similar work.

Following the House of Lords decision, the employment tribunal reconsidered and upheld the part-time fire-fighters' claim (*Matthews and others v Kent & Medway Town Fire Authority and others 6100000/2001 (ET)*).

It was held that:

- the part-time fire-fighters carried out the same or broadly the same work as full-time fire-fighters;
- the part-time fire-fighters were treated less favourably in terms of pension provision and sick pay; and
- the differences in treatment could not be justified.

The Fixed-term Employees Regulations

9.9 The *Fixed-term Employees (Prevention of Less Favourable Treatment) Regulations 2002 (SI 2002/2034)* came into force on 1 October 2002 implementing *EU Council Directive 1999/70/EC*. The Regulations require employers to treat fixed-term employees no less favourably than comparable permanent employees of the same employer, unless there is an objective justification for the difference in treatment. The Regulations also provide that, if a fixed-term employee is employed on a number of successive contracts for four years or more, the contract has the effect of a permanent contract unless the employer can objectively justify continuing employment on a fixed-term basis. The Regulations cover all employees under a fixed-term contract with the exclusion of apprentices, agency workers, the armed forces and those employed under a Government training scheme.

The Regulations cover, in addition to other contractual terms, pay and occupational pension schemes and thus access to pension arrangements and the level of benefits offered. However, the Regulations do not require term-per-term equality, providing the overall package offered is broadly comparable. Therefore, whilst in principle employers are required to offer fixed-term employees the same rights of entry to the pension scheme and the same benefits under it as they do for permanent employees; it may, be possible, in certain circumstances, to offer access on different terms, providing that the overall package of rights is comparable.

If an employer does not wish to offer entry to the main pension scheme for employees on fixed-term contracts, it might consider offering to make equivalent contributions to a personal arrangement. However, there may be a difficulty in showing that this benefit is 'at least as favourable' as that offered to permanent employees. An alternative would be for fixed-term employees, whom the employer does not want to admit to the pension scheme, to be paid a salary bonus equivalent to the value of the scheme membership, although this could give rise to industrial relations problems where permanent employees then ask for the bonus instead of scheme membership.

It should be noted that there is no direct claim under the Regulations by employees against trustees. However, this is an issue which trustees of schemes excluding fixed-term employees may wish to raise with the sponsoring employers. Under the automatic enrolment requirements due to commence in October 2012, employers will have to enrol fixed-term employees into a qualifying pension scheme (see CHAPTER 13).

Benefits

General

9.10 Although the matter of equal access to pension schemes has presented many difficulties, many more questions have been raised over the issue of equality in benefits and contributions. This arises, in the main, from the fact that benefit design and computation have been dictated by actuarial science which takes into account, among other matters, the differing mortality rates of the sexes. The *Barber* decision (17 May 1990) meant that immediate action had to be taken, and various measures were adopted to implement equalisation. Many, but not all, of the issues raised by the *Barber* decision were clarified in subsequent ECJ decisions (notably, the 1994 *Coloroll* decision (*Coloroll Pension Trustees Ltd v Russell C-200/91 [1994] ECR I-4389*)). It had been feared by employers that the equalisation of benefits would have to be fully retrospective. The ECJ in *Coloroll* confirmed that retrospection is only required in relation to benefits payable for periods of service from 17 May 1990. The reason for this limitation on equalisation of benefits for men and women is because it was held that Member States could argue that they had been led to believe that such discrimination was acceptable because of parallel EU legislation. In the case of *Quirk v Burton Hospital NHS Trust [2002] 24 PBLR* the Court of Appeal upheld the judgment of the EAT which held that the limitation is correct and equal treatment under *Article 157* in relation to scheme benefits does not apply to service prior to 17 May 1990.

The ECJ required employers and trustees to consider three time periods in respect of measures to equalise benefits under their schemes:

(*a*) the period up to 17 May 1990, when benefits need not be equalised;

(*b*) the period from 17 May 1990 to the date when scheme benefits are equalised, when benefits must be 'levelled up' (ie increased to the level enjoyed by the advantaged sex); and

(*c*) the period after the date when scheme benefits are equalised. Although

Article 157 itself permits benefits to be 'levelled up' or 'levelled down' in respect of this period, the UK decision in the *Lloyds Bank* case should be noted at this point (*Lloyds Bank Pension Trust Corporation Ltd v Lloyds Bank plc [1996] OPLR 181*). In this case, the High Court decided that future accrual rates could not be reduced to meet equalisation objectives. However, this may be a decision turning on the particular facts of the case (summarised in the table of cases at the end of this chapter), and certainly flows against the tide of the other main cases, notably *Smith v Avdel Systems Ltd C-408/92 [1994] ECR I-4435*.

Derived rights

9.11 The requirement for equality in pay and pensions applies also to spouses, survivors, dependants and others who are entitled to claim benefits through an employee's membership of a scheme. In *Ten Oever v Stichting Bedrijfspensioenfonds voor het Glazenwassers- en Schoonmaakbedrijf C-109/91 [1993] ECR I-4879* the ECJ confirmed that a survivor's pension falls within the scope of *Article 157*. Thus, any scheme benefit provided for the wife of a male member must also be provided for the husband of a female member. The ECJ in *Coloroll* confirmed that, as for members' benefits, the requirement for equal treatment only applies in relation to service from 17 May 1990, except for those claims brought before this date.

Transfers

9.12 Schemes which accept transfer payments in respect of benefits accrued since 17 May 1990 will bear the burden of equalisation as a consequence of any inadequacy in the transfer payments received. The ECJ considered (in *Coloroll*) that the rights accruing to an employee from *Article 157* cannot be affected by the fact that he changes his job and has to join a new scheme, with his accrued pension rights being transferred to the new scheme. However, in the event of an inadequate transfer payment being made, the ECJ envisaged the receiving scheme making a claim (under national law) against the transferring scheme for the additional sums required to equalise the benefits to be paid. In practice trustees of the receiving scheme will also obtain an indemnity from the transferring scheme to cover such additional sums as may be required.

It may be that transferring employees have a claim against both the trustees of the transferring scheme and of the receiving scheme. The *Acquired Rights Directive (77/187/EEC)* (replaced by *Directive 2001/23/EC*) was designed to safeguard employees' rights and ensure continuing employment following a transfer of a business undertaking. However, provisions contained in a contract of employment or collective agreement relating to an occupational pension scheme are specifically excluded. There have been a number of challenges to this pensions exclusion over the years (see, for example, **15.15** below for a discussion of the *Beckmann* and *Martin* cases).

The position of money purchase schemes which receive unequalised transfer payments is uncertain. Clearly, there would be serious practical difficulties in complying with the obligation to equalise, possibly entailing the re-allocation of funds in individual members' accounts. Arguably, the *Coloroll* decision does not encompass money purchase schemes (see **9.16** below) but pending clarification of the issue, the trustees of such schemes should act with great caution. For example, trustees should consider very carefully whether this would be an appropriate circumstance in which they should exercise any discretion (in the provisions of the scheme) to refuse transfers.

Bridging pensions

9.13 Bridging pensions aim to achieve a form of equality between men and women, by taking into account the earlier date from which women are eligible to receive the State pension. Thus, bridging pensions could be paid to both men and women who take early retirement at, say, age 55, and stop at age 60 for women, but continue to age 65 for men. In *Birds Eye Walls v Friedl M Roberts C-132/92 [1993] PLR 323*, the pension for a female ex-employee was reduced when she reached age 60, whereas a man would have received a full pension to age 65. The ECJ was asked whether bridging pensions where in breach of *Article 157*. The ECJ held that bridging pensions were not discriminatory because they were designed to remove an existing inequality arising as a consequence of the different ages that State pension commences for men and women. This decision can be criticised, however, in that it allows employers to reduce a pension on the assumption that a woman is in receipt of a full State pension, whether or not that is in fact the case. It is to be noted that *PA 1995, s 64(2)* and the *Equal Treatment Regulations* exclude bridging pensions paid in these circumstances from the ambit of the equal treatment rule contained in *PA 1995, s 62*. In addition, the *FA 2004* allows scheme pensions to be reduced when a member begins to receive a State retirement pension (*Sch 28, para 2*).

The decision in *Birds Eye* is difficult to reconcile with the decision in *Bestuur van het Algemeen Burgerlijk Pensioenfonds v Beune C-7/93 [1995] All ER (EC) 97*, where the ECJ held that it was unlawful for a scheme to make deductions in respect of the State pension where it had the effect of producing a lower pension for men but not women from the scheme. In the Netherlands, the Dutch State scheme gives married men a higher pension than married women.

Actuarial factors

9.14 The use of actuarial factors in funded final salary occupational pension schemes which vary according to sex was held by the ECJ in *Coloroll* not to fall within the scope of *Article 157*. This was so even though the amount of a transfer value for a man would be lower than for a woman in consequence of the actuarial factors used in the assessment of the capital sum transferred that are based on life expectancy which differs between men and women.

The issue of unequal transfer values had previously been considered in *Neath v Hugh Steeper Ltd C-152/91 [1993] ECR I-6935*. It considered that it is only the employer's commitment to the payment of a periodic pension at a particular level which constitutes pay within the meaning of *Article 157*. It decided that the funding arrangement by which the pension was to be secured falls outside the scope of *Article 157*. (Although this was confirmed in the *Coloroll* decision, the ECJ has made the position clear only in relation to final salary schemes.)

It was confirmed in *Neath* that as employees' contributions were deducted from salaries, employees' contribution rates must be the same for both men and women as they constitute an element of pay within *Article 157*. Thus, although contributions made by employees must be equal as between men and women, as these contributions are an element of their pay, employers' contributions are pitched to ensure the adequacy of the funds necessary to secure the future payment of periodic pensions and may be unequal due to the use of sex-based actuarial factors. Inequalities in the amounts of capital benefits or substitute benefits (for example, where a dependant's pension is payable in return for surrender of part of the member's annual pension or where a reduced pension is paid on early retirement) whose value can be determined only on the basis of the arrangements chosen for funding the scheme, were likewise considered to be outside the scope of *Article 157*.

PA 1995 (*s 64*) and the *Equal Treatment Regulations* (*reg 15*) expressly permit the use of actuarial factors which differ for men and women. It is stated that the equal treatment rule does not operate in relation to actuarial factors which differ for men and women in respect of the differences in the average life expectancy of men and women and which are determined with a view to providing equal periodical pension benefits for men and women. The difference in treatment is permitted only in relation to certain prescribed benefits as set out in *reg 15*.

Notwithstanding the above, the ECJ held on 11 September 2007 that the use by the Council of the European Union of different actuarial factors for men and women when calculating transfer values was unlawful sex discrimination (*Lindorfer v Council of the European Union C-277/04P [2009] All ER (EC) 569*). The *Lindorfer* case did not expressly overrule the decision in *Neath*, and UK schemes may still rely on the statutory exemptions relating to actuarial factors. However, the case suggests that the EU's opinion is moving against the use of sex-based actuarial factors. Therefore, although not required to do so, trustees may wish to consider the use of unisex actuarial factors.

The use of unisex actuarial factors is permitted. Unisex tables appear to be logical, and the aim of achieving equal contributions and equal benefits would seem to be desirable. However, as long as insurance companies remain outside the constraints of *Article 157* in their assessments of risk, this disparity with company pension schemes will distort the market.

Unisex annuity rates are already required in securing the protected rights element of contracted-out money purchase schemes and personal pension schemes (see CHAPTER 4).

Pre A-Day limits on maximum relievable contributions and maximum benefits available from exempt approved schemes have been replaced by the annual allowance and the lifetime allowance (see CHAPTER 16). Under *FA 2004, s 234,* when calculating the annual allowance a single factor of 10:1 is used to value the annual increase in benefits regardless of the sex or age of the member. In addition, *FA 2004, ss 214–219* provide that, when valuing DB benefits against the lifetime allowance, a single factor is used regardless of the age or sex of the member (normally 20:1).

Additional voluntary contributions

9.15 Equality principles apply to all pension benefits under a scheme and it is irrelevant whether they are attributable to employers' or employees' contributions. However, where the scheme does no more than provide the necessary arrangements for the management of contributions and payments of the resulting benefits (in relation to money purchase additional voluntary contributions) those resulting benefits are not covered by *Article 157*. Consequently additional benefits deriving from contributions paid by employees on a voluntary basis are not covered by *Article 157*, as these additional contributions are to secure benefits over and above those which they are entitled to expect by reason of their employment and cannot, therefore, be regarded as pay within the meaning of *Article 157*.

Money purchase benefits

9.16 In money purchase schemes, the pension commitment of the employer is an obligation to pay a defined level of contribution. The ECJ has not directly decided how the principle of equal treatment is to be applied to money purchase schemes. What has been established is that the commitment or 'promise' to the employee, which must be equal between men and women, is to be distinguished from the funding considerations, which are not covered by *Article 157*.

Whilst it is clear that employee contributions must be equal as between men and women, the position in relation to employer contributions is less certain. It is generally accepted that, as the employer in a money purchase scheme does not promise any particular level of benefit, the commitment is the contribution, and as such these must be equal. In schemes which use sex-based actuarial factors, it is not possible to have both equal contributions and equal benefits. If the *Neath* case applies to money purchase schemes, women are most likely to be the disadvantaged sex. This is because the capital sum built up will not secure the same amount of pension for a woman as for a man. Her periodic pension will be lower as it will take account of the expectation that she will live longer.

Therefore, until unisex actuarial factors are an accepted norm in the insurance domain, it would be safer for schemes to make the open market option available to members and let them make the arrangements for securing their benefits with the insurer of their choice. The member is not subject to the same constraints on trustees in securing a pension. On taking his capital sum from the scheme, the trustees are released from any further liability to the member, and it is for the member to buy the best pension he can in the annuity marketplace.

Retirement ages

State pension age and contractual retirement age

9.17 State pension age is being equalised over a ten-year period commencing in the year 2010. State pension age for women is due to increase to age 65 from April 2010. In addition, as a consequence of changes introduced by *PA 2007* (amending *PA 1995, s 126, Sch 4*), State pension age will be increased to age 68 by 2046.

Ascertaining the contractual retirement age is not as straightforward as it seems. If the contract of employment is silent on the retirement age, the established custom and practice will be looked at to determine when employees have retired in the past in relation to that particular position. However, the contractual retirement age must not be different for men and women doing the same job. (See **9.44** below for commentary on retirement ages in the context of age discrimination.)

In the ECJ case *Kutz-Bauer v Freie und Hansestadt Hamburg C-187/00 [2003] All ER (D) 327 (Mar)*, provisions allowing workers over 55 to work part-time applied only until the date on which the worker became entitled to a statutory old age pension. For most women this was 60 and for most men it was 65. It was held that this was capable of breaching the *Equal Treatment Directive* and it was for the national court to determine whether there was in fact indirect discrimination which could not be objectively justified.

It is possible (and permissible) for employers to have differing retirement ages for different positions, as long as the demarcation of positions is not sex discriminatory (whether direct or indirect). This principle was upheld in *Bullock v The Alice Ottley School [1992] IRLR 564* in which the Court of Appeal decided that a school's grounds and maintenance staff (who had a retirement age of 65) could have a different retirement age from its domestic staff (who had a retirement age of 60). However, where different groups of employees are treated in this way, the court will look very closely at the reasons given to justify the difference.

Retirement age under the pension scheme

9.18 Although the *Barber* case established beyond doubt that pensions were 'pay' and, in consequence, that pensions had to be equal for men and women, the questions as to how and from which date equalisation was to be implemented were not answered until later. These issues were addressed by the ECJ in the *Coloroll* and *Smith v Avdel* cases. In the *Smith v Avdel* case, the employer proposed to implement the *Barber* decision by raising the retirement age of women to that of men from June 1991. The change was implemented in relation to benefits paid in respect of service both before and after June 1991. The ECJ held that until equalisation measures had been taken, the only proper method of compliance with *Article 157* was to confer upon the disadvantaged sex those advantages enjoyed by the favoured sex, in respect of service after 17 May 1990. In the *Smith v Avdel* case this meant that, for the period between May 1990 and June 1991, the pension rights of men were to be calculated on the basis of the same retirement age as women.

Thus, from 17 May 1990 until the date of the equalisation of retirement ages, the pension rights of men had to be enhanced to correlate with the lower retirement age of women, ie 60. For the period prior to the date of the *Barber* decision, the ECJ determined that there was no requirement to equalise benefits.

With regard to the period following the date of equalisation, the ECJ stated that *Article 157* did not preclude equalisation measures which had the effect of reducing the benefits of the (previously) advantaged sex. *PA 1995, ss 62–66* (which aim to bring into statute the effect of *Barber* and the subsequent cases) do not preclude this either. However, neither *Article 157* nor *PA 1995* overrides trustees' duties to act in their members' best interests (or an employer's duty of good faith) and so these duties must still be borne in mind.

The equal treatment requirement was not, therefore, necessarily a victory for women. Where retirement ages have been equalised upwards, women will have to work for longer or face the risk of a reduction in their pensions if they still wish to retire at age 60. Further, sex-based actuarial factors may be applied which could further reduce the amount of pension received (although see **9.14** above and the case of *Lindorfer v Council of the European Union C-277/04P*). This would affect transfer values, which on transfer to a money purchase scheme would lead to unequal benefits. However, where a prospective pensionable service factor is used, for example, on ill-health early retirement, this can increase the resultant pension.

Conclusions and practical issues

General

9.19 Although some of the equality issues raised by the *Barber* case have now been settled, there is still much case law dealing with equalisation issues. There is also an increasing realisation that equalisation does not necessarily lead to equity. The main difficulty which has confronted many employers and trustees is how to implement the equal treatment requirement in their schemes.

Employers and trustees

9.20 It was unclear from the *Barber* decision whether *Article 157* imposed an obligation both on the trustees and the employer in respect of equal treatment. Whilst the primary obligation to implement equalisation falls upon the employer, the position of trustees was clarified by the ECJ in the *Coloroll* case. The ECJ confirmed that trustees in the exercise of their powers and in the performance of their obligations are also bound to observe the principles of equal treatment. Although the ECJ decisions are overriding, *PA 1995* clearly envisages schemes being amended so as to comply with the equal treatment provisions. *PA 1995, s 65* empowers trustees or managers of occupational pension schemes to make amendments by resolution where either they do not have the necessary amendment powers to implement the equal treatment requirements, or they do have powers available but the procedure for implementation is 'liable to be unduly complex or protracted' or 'involves the obtaining of consents which cannot be obtained, or can only be obtained with undue delay or difficulties'.

Review of scheme documentation

9.21 In as much as the equal treatment cases are overriding, clarity and consistency in the day to day application of the equal treatment principles can only be achieved if scheme documentation is brought into line with the current law. Although it would be hoped that most schemes have by now updated their documentation to reflect the equal treatment requirements, areas to look out for include:

(*a*) the definition of normal retirement age;

(*b*) conformity of the (equalised) normal retirement age under the scheme and the contract of employment;

(*c*) equality in early retirement terms, survivors' benefits, and transfer arrangements; and

(*d*) allowing trustees the discretion to grant enhanced benefits in individual cases.

Scheme amendments

9.22 As stated above (see **9.10** and **9.18**), employers and trustees must consider three time periods in respect of measures to equalise benefits under their schemes:

(*a*) the period up to 17 May 1990, when benefits need not be equalised;

(*b*) the period from 17 May 1990 to the date equalisation takes place, when benefits must be 'levelled up'; and

(*c*) the period after the date equalisation takes place, when benefits can be levelled up or down.

Careful scrutiny of the power of amendment will be necessary to ensure that any changes made are a valid exercise of that power. Amendment powers often contain an express restriction that accrued rights cannot be reduced without members' consent. Even in the absence of specific wording to that effect, such a restriction is consistent with a trustee's fiduciary duty to act in the best interests of the members and it is generally accepted to be consistent with the employer's duty of good faith towards its employees. Further, *PA 1995, s 67* imposes restrictions on scheme amendments which reduce 'subsisting rights'. In summary, subsisting rights are rights or entitlements which a member has accrued to or in respect of him to future benefits under the scheme rules. With effect from April 2006, *s 67* was amended by *PA 2004* and, under the new provisions, although schemes are not able to reduce the value of a member's subsisting rights, they are able to make changes to the nature of the rights, provided that the overall actuarial value of the affected person's subsisting rights is not reduced (see CHAPTER 12).

Where there is no amendment power, or inadequate provision, the power conferred by *PA 1995, s 65* must be used to implement the equal treatment requirements. The exercise of the statutory power may place the employer in a vulnerable position, as it is a power to be used by the trustees alone, and not, as is usually found in scheme provisions, either an employer's power or a joint power of the employer and the trustees.

The power of amendment is a fiduciary power and, as mentioned above, its exercise is, therefore, subject to a duty of good faith to the beneficiaries of the scheme. Thus, in seeking to amend the scheme to comply with the equal treatment requirements, the best interests of the whole membership must be considered. Following the decision in *Van den Akker v Stichting Shell PF C-28/93 [1994] ECR I-4527*, it is not possible to 'red circle' groups of members, ie to apply preferential benefits to a group of members who were exclusively women or men, unless the group delineation was objectively justified and, thus, not sex discriminatory.

There have been several cases concerning problems with the way schemes have sought to equalise benefits.

In *Betafence Limited v Veys and others [2006] EWHC 999 (Ch)*, the scheme provided men with a normal retirement age of 65 and women with a normal retirement age of 60. The scheme amendment power did not require amendments to be recorded in a formal document. Therefore, in 1991 the employer issued an announcement to members stating that from 1 October 1991, the normal retirement age for both men and women would be age 65. However, a member could retire from service from age 60 without incurring an early retirement reduction. Unfortunately for the company, this announcement had the unintended consequence of allowing male members to retire at age 60 without company consent, where previously consent had been required.

The case of *Trustee Solutions v Dubery [2006] 36 PBLR* considered whether a scheme amendment power had been validly exercised in 1992 to change the normal retirement date (NRD) relating to female members. The Colour Processing Laboratories Pension Scheme was a final salary scheme with a normal retirement date of 65 for male members and 60 for female members. In July 1992, the employer issued an announcement to female members informing them that, with effect from 1 October 1991, their normal retirement date would be age 65. In 2002, winding up of the scheme was triggered and the trustees sought directions from the court in relation to the following:

(*a*) whether the amendment power had been validly exercised in 1992;

(*b*) whether an estoppel arose so as to close the '*Barber* window'; and

(*c*) how the statutory priority order should be applied (see **9.25** below).

The scheme rules provided that amendments could be 'by any writing effected under hand by the Trustees and the Principal Company', provided that the amendments did not vary benefits already accrued.

Two documents were presented:

(*a*) a memorandum from the trustees to members dated 15 May 1992 setting out the options for equalising retirement ages for men and women and inviting members to a presentation; and (*b*) an announcement from the principal employer to female members dated July 1992 stating that the normal retirement date was being equalised at age 65.

The High Court held that there had been no valid amendment to the rules and no estoppel arose. It was held that 'under hand' meant a document that was signed. As neither of the documents met this requirement, the rules had not been validly amended and the Barber window remained open. In addition, it was stated that even if the documents had been signed, they were inadequate to amend the rules because the memorandum merely set out the options and the announcement did not come from the trustees. Although the third point (application of priority order) was the subject of an application to the Court of Appeal, no appeal was brought in relation to the first two issues (see **9.25** below).

In *Harland and Wolff Pension Trustees Limited v Aon Consulting Financial Services Limited [2006] EWHC 1778 (Ch)*, the trustees claimed that their advisers had failed to advise properly in relation to equalisation. As in the other cases, the scheme rules provided different retirement ages for men and women (63 and 60 respectively). The rules were amended retrospectively in September 1993 so that, from 17 May 1990, the normal retirement age for female members would be 63.

It was accepted that the rules of the scheme permitted retrospective amendments; however, the question before the court was whether the amendment satisfied the requirements of *Article 157.* The court held that although the amendment power was wide enough to permit the amendment in question, an amendment could not validly remove the free-standing rights granted by European law, ie following the *Smith v Avdel* case, until equalisation measures are taken, the only proper method of compliance with *Article 157* is to confer upon the disadvantaged sex those advantages enjoyed by the favoured sex in respect of service after 17 May 1990. Therefore, the court held that, for the period between 17 May 1990 and September 1993, the normal retirement age for male members was age 60.

In *Hodgson and others v Toray Textiles Europe Limited and others [2006] EWHC 2612 (Ch)* the trustees and the employer had sought to equalise members' normal retirement ages at 65 by issuing an announcement in May 1994. Doubts about the validity of this amendment led to a deed of amendment being executed in 2004.

Under the scheme amendment power, amendments had to be made by deed. However, the definition of normal retirement age itself provided that it could be subsequently altered, and there was no mention of a deed. The definition did not say who could amend members' normal retirement age, but all parties agreed that the consent of the employer, trustees and members was required. The court held that the 1994 amendment was ineffective and the announcements were not enough to alter the normal retirement age. Although the trustees and the employer might be said to have agreed the change, it would not be right to infer that members had consented to the change.

More recently, in the case of *Capital Cranfield Trustees Ltd v Beck [2008] EWHC 3181 (Ch)*, the High Court held that an announcement by the employer was not effective to equalise retirement ages. This case focused on whether the announcement amounted to a valid exercise of the power of amendment and/or a power in the definition of NRD, allowing the employer to determine a member's NRD. It was held that the announcement did not comply with the strict requirements of the amendment power. Also, it was concluded that the power contained in the definition of NRD could not be exercised in relation to a class of member.

Ill-health early retirement

9.23 Where the provisions of a scheme calculate ill-health pensions as inclusive of prospective service to normal pension age, a lowered normal pension age will operate to reduce the amount of pension payable. It is to be noted that, in respect of the 'levelling-up' period described at **9.10(*b*)** above, benefits calculated by reference to a member's prospective service to normal retirement age must be calculated by reference to the higher normal retirement date.

Contracted-out schemes/guaranteed minimum pensions (GMPs)

9.24 The issue of equalisation of GMPs (see CHAPTER 4) is fraught with difficulty, and the relevant provisions of *PA 1995, s 126* deal only with the future equalisation of the contracting-out arrangements. Neither the ECJ nor the Government has addressed all the difficulties that arise as a result of the fundamental design of GMPs correlating to the State scheme with its discriminatory pension ages. Specifically, the difficulties arise out of the methods of calculation and revaluation applied to the GMP element of a pension before and after State pension age is attained. The *Equal Treatment Regulations* permit pension increases to be paid at different rates on GMPs and pensions in excess of GMPs, in so far as the difference does not exceed the SERPS increase for the same period. The *Equal Treatment Regulations* do not, however, legalise the differences in benefits caused by the contracting-out legislation.

The determination by the Pensions Ombudsman in *Williamson* dated 7 January 2000 *(No: H00177)* restated the requirement to equalise GMPs. The Pensions

Ombudsman directed that the trustee and the company equalise GMPs in compliance with the equal treatment rule under *PA 1995, s 62*. However, he did not make any directions as to how this should be done and noted that:

> 'Parliament apparently concluded that salary-related schemes should have the flexibility and freedom to make their own arrangements as to how equalisation should be achieved.' (paragraph 37)

Furthermore, he expressed the view that the method of equalisation chosen should not be one that could lead to some members of the scheme being adversely affected.

The *Williamson* determination was subsequently overturned in the High Court in *Marsh Mercer Pension Scheme v Pensions Ombudsman [2001] 16 PBLR (28)* on the basis that the Ombudsman could not make a direction relating to the equalisation of GMPs and compliance with the equal treatment rules in *PA 1995, s 62* as the question was too wide-ranging and the nature and effect of the Ombudsman's direction was so uncertain that he was in error making it. The Ombudsman's jurisdiction did not extend to his making a decision on the question of equalisation of GMPs as this matter had an impact on other members of the scheme without allowing them the opportunity to put their case. Rimer J added that GMPs in isolation did not have to be equalised on the basis that they are not a distinct part of a pension scheme. However, the position as to whether total benefits should be equalised was undecided. Therefore, the issues as to the application of *Article 157* and the method of equalisation of GMPs remain undetermined and trustees currently attempting to wind up contracted-out final salary schemes are left with little guidance as to how to proceed.

The rulings of the European Court in *Bestuur van het Algemeen Burgerlijk Pensioenfonds v Beune C-7/93 [1995] All ER (EC) 97* and *Birds Eye Walls v Friedl M Roberts C-132/92 [1993] PLR 323* (see **9.13** above) appear contradictory in deciding whether a scheme may provide unequal benefits to men and women to remove an existing inequality as a result of the different ages that State pension commences for men and women. These two cases were considered by the High Court in *Uppingham School v Shillcock [2002] EWHC 641 (Ch)*, in its ruling that an LEL offset to integrate with the State scheme was not indirect sex discrimination and, had it been so, that it would have been objectively justified. This case would appear to support the argument that unequal GMPs are objectively justifiable if the intention is to integrate with the State scheme.

In the case of *Leadenhall Independent Trustees Limited v Welham [2004] All ER (D) 423 (Mar)*, the scheme was winding up with a surplus and the trustee sought directions from the court as to whether it had the power to allocate funds in such a way as to neutralise the gender discrimination of GMPs. The court said that the trustee could augment deferred benefits as there was express power in the governing documentation to do so. In the case of existing pensioners (for which there was no express power of augmentation) the court was not willing to say whether or not the trustee could augment benefits, nor was it prepared to state whether overriding EC equal treatment law could be applied. The court suggested that, if the trustee did decide to go ahead and augment benefits for pensioners, it should consider taking out trustee insurance.

PA 2007 amends *PSA 1993* so as to allow trustees of contracted-out defined benefit schemes to convert members' GMPs into normal scheme benefits, provided that actuarial equivalence is maintained. This should give schemes more flexibility in the benefits they can provide and should make it easier for members to transfer out their benefits if they wish. There must, however, be some question as to how the actuary will be able to confirm actuarial equivalence when the question of the equalisation of GMPs for men and women has not been resolved.

In April 2008, the PPF issued a consultation on equalising GMPs for PPF purposes, entitled 'Consultation on the requirement under section 179 of the Pensions Act 2004 to equalise compensation to allow for differences in the GMP formula'. This is specific to schemes in a PPF assessment period or which have transferred into the PPF. The issue of how to equalise GMPs for any other purpose remains unresolved.

The consultation was prepared on the basis of legal advice taken by the PPF in relation to its duties under *PA 2004, s 171*, which include ensuring that equal compensation is paid to comparable male and female members of schemes in the PPF.

On 29 October 2009, the PPF published its decision on how it is going to require schemes to equalise GMPs for PPF purposes. The 'decision' is still rather vague but does make it clear that all schemes entering an assessment period will be required to equalise GMPs for service on and from 17 May 1990.

Some of the main issues to come out of the 'decision' are:

- All schemes entering an assessment period will be required to equalise GMPs for service on and from 17 May 1990. PPF entry will be contingent on equalisation having been made.
- The method will be 'partial method 2', as set out in the consultation document. This is the comparison of the total male and female pension when the pension comes into payment, and annually (or possibly more frequently) once the pension is in payment. The pensioner should be paid the higher of the male or female estimate that applies in their particular case at each pension payment date.

- The PPF is considering issuing a standard amending deed to be used by trustees.
- The PPF considers trustees should be able to modify their schemes under *PA 1995, s 65* (the equalisation provision) if they do not otherwise have power to do so under the rules.
- *Section 179* valuations need not include equalised GMPs (this is to be kept under review, as it may disadvantage schemes which have equalised).

At the time of writing, there are some outstanding issues relating to comparators, and further work needs to be done in addressing detailed calculation requirements. Once this is completed, the PPF will be providing further information.

Winding up and mixed retirement ages

9.25 On 26 July 2007 the Court of Appeal handed down judgment in the case of *Cripps v Trustee Solutions Ltd and Dubery [2007] EWCA Civ 771*. The case concerned the division of assets among different groups of members on winding up. This decision will be of particular interest to trustees of defined benefit schemes which commenced winding up before 6 April 2005.

The question on appeal concerned which members fall into the priority pensioner category on winding-up, and for what portion of their benefits. The difficulty arose because male members of the scheme, who had been members since before May 1990, had accrued part of their benefits based on a retirement age of 65 and part on a retirement age of 60. The High Court had held that any member aged 60 or over as at the date winding-up commenced was in the pensioner priority category on winding-up for all his benefit (not just the tranche of benefit accrued with a retirement age of 60).

Mrs Cripps (a deferred member of the scheme who would have received a reduction in her benefit as a result of that decision) appealed. The Court of Appeal overturned the High Court judgment and ruled that those members aged between 60 and 64 on the date winding-up commenced will be in the pensioner priority category only for that portion of their benefits accrued with a retirement age of 60. Consequently, they are to be treated as being in the deferred category with a lower priority in relation to benefits accrued with a retirement age of 65.

In light of this decision, trustees of defined benefit pension schemes which are in the process of winding-up (where winding-up commenced before 6 April 2005) may need to review the manner in which benefits are secured.

The decision in *Cripps* was distinguished by the Court of Appeal in *Foster Wheeler Limited v Hanley & Others [2009] EWCA Civ 651*. The facts of *Foster Wheeler* are fairly typical. Prior to May 1990, female members of the scheme had an NRD of 60 and male members 65. From May 1990 to August 1993, all members accrued benefits based on an NRD of 60. The scheme rules were amended from 16 August 1993, giving all members an NRD of 65. The High Court had held that all members could receive their benefits as a single pension from age 60, with no early payment reduction applied to the tranche of benefit accrued with an NRD of 65. This gave a significant windfall to those members with substantial benefits accrued with an NRD of 65, as they would have expected a reduction for early payment before age 65. The employer appealed the High Court decision. The Court of Appeal was asked to consider three options:

- **Option 1** – a single pension calculated on the basis that all the benefits had fallen due for payment on the date of retirement (no reduction for early payment). This is the decision which had been reached by the High Court in *Foster Wheeler*.
- **Option 2** – a single pension with benefits accrued with an NRD of 65 reduced for early payment.
- **Option 3** – split pensions, ie a separate pension payable from each NRD. This had been the decision in the Court of Appeal in *Cripps v Trustee Solutions*.

The Court of Appeal concluded that, in this case, Option 2 was the correct approach. This would result in each member obtaining a single pension from age 60 comprising the benefits accrued with an NRD of 60 in full plus the benefits accrued with an NRD of 65 reduced for early payment.

The facts of this case turn on the detailed provisions of the scheme rules, and so Option 2 will not always be the correct answer. The Court of Appeal did, however, set down some guiding principles:

- where possible, effect should be given to *Barber* rights by adhering to the scheme provisions;
- if some departure is required, it should, so far as practicable, represent the minimum interference to both the substance and the form of scheme provisions;
- possible options should be compared, and consideration given in relation to each option as to whether effect can be given to *Barber* rights in some other way involving less interference with the rights of any party; and
- whether a particular valuation is appropriate will depend on the circumstances of the individual scheme.

Same-sex partners

Introduction

9.26 The legal position of same-sex partners was examined in the case of *Grant v South-West Trains Limited C-249/96 [1998] All ER (EC) 193*. This was an employment case involving the granting of travel concessions. South-West Trains refused to give travel concessions to Ms Grant's same-sex partner when she was promoted to a post at South-West Trains previously occupied by an employee whose opposite sex partner had obtained such concessions. The ECJ found that the refusal of the employer to grant the travel concessions in this case did not constitute discrimination prohibited by *Article 157* of the *TFEU* or *Council Directive 75/117/EEC* of 10 February 1975, as the condition imposed by South-West Trains applied in the same way to female and male workers. The ECJ said that Community law as it stood at that time did not cover discrimination based on sexual orientation. If the ECJ had decided in favour of Ms Grant, this would have had implications for pension benefits provided for unmarried couples which would have to be the same for all such couples irrespective of gender.

The European *Equal Treatment 'Framework' Directive (2000/78/EC)*, establishing a general framework for equal treatment in employment and occupation, requires Member States to enact legislation to prohibit discrimination on the grounds of religion or belief, disability, age and sexual orientation. The time limit for compliance was December 2003 for discrimination on the grounds of religion or belief or sexual orientation, and 2006 for discrimination on the grounds of age and disability. In the context of sexual orientation discrimination, the Directive requires that pension schemes which recognise unmarried heterosexual partners must also recognise same-sex partners. The Directive allows pension schemes which recognise married couples only to continue to do so.

The *Employment Equality (Sexual Orientation) Regulations 2003* (*SI 2003/1661*) (as amended) are designed to implement the Directive in respect of sexual orientation discrimination and outlaw discrimination in employment and vocational training on grounds of sexual orientation. The Regulations came into force on 1 December 2003 and protect heterosexuals, homosexuals and bisexuals.

The Regulations prohibit direct discrimination (ie treating people less favourably than others on grounds of sexual orientation) and indirect discrimination (ie applying a provision, criterion or practice which disadvantages people of a particular sexual orientation and which is not justified in objective terms) (*reg 3*).

As with other anti-discrimination legislation, the Regulations cover the terms of a person's employment. As is established law, this extends to the field of occupational pensions. The primary target of the Regulations as they apply to pension schemes would seem to be to prevent discrimination in respect of dependant's pensions (ie where the scheme rules provide that a pension may be paid to an unmarried opposite-sex partner but not to a partner of the same sex). If a scheme provides benefits to opposite-sex unmarried partners but not same-sex partners, then this would constitute direct discrimination.

The *Employment Equality (Sexual Orientation) (Amendment) Regulations 2003 (SI 2003/2827)* amended the Regulations to extend their provisions to the trustees and managers of occupational pension schemes. The amended Regulations make provision for every occupational pension scheme to be treated as including a 'non-discrimination' rule prohibiting discrimination contrary to the Regulations.

Originally, the Regulations provided that, if the scheme provides benefits to married partners but not unmarried opposite-sex partners, then there would be no discrimination, as *reg 25* states that it will not be unlawful discrimination if access to benefits is prevented or restricted by reference to marital status. This arises out of the Government's interpretation of the Directive's provision that it is without prejudice to national laws on marital status and benefits dependent thereon.

From 5 December 2005, *Employment Equality (Sexual Orientation) Regulations 2003, reg 25* was amended by the *Civil Partnership Act 2004 (Amendments to Subordinate Legislation) Order 2005 (SI 2005/2114)*. The amended *reg 25* extends the exemption for benefits conferred on married people and civil partners to the exclusion of all others.

In addition, following the introduction of the *CPA 2004*, a new paragraph was inserted into *Employment Equality (Sexual Orientation) Regulations 2003, reg 3* to ensure that the status of a civil partner is comparable to that of a spouse.

The *Equality Act 2006* received Royal Assent on 16 February 2006, giving the Secretary of State the power to make Regulations which outlaw discrimination in the provision of goods, facilities, services and education, the use and disposal of premises and the exercise of public functions on the grounds of sexual orientation. Pursuant to this power, the *Equality Act (Sexual Orientation) Regulations 2007 (SI 2007/1263)* came into force on 30 April 2007 and prohibit discrimination on grounds of sexual orientation in the areas mentioned above.

Civil partnerships

9.27 The *Civil Partnership Act 2004* ('*CPA 2004*') received Royal Assent on 18 November 2004. The Act provides for same-sex couples to obtain legal recognition of their relationship by registering as civil partners. Registered civil partners will have access to rights and responsibilities including, for example:

- employment and pensions benefits;
- the duty to provide maintenance for a civil partner;
- the duty to provide maintenance for children of the partnership; and
- recognition under intestacy rules.

There are certain eligibility requirements that must be satisfied before couples can register as civil partners. The couple must be of the same sex, both parties must be 16 years or over, neither party can be legally married or already a civil partner and the partner cannot be 'within prohibited degrees of relationship' (ie blood ties).

There are also various formalities involved in registering a civil partnership. The register has to be signed by the couple in the presence of the civil partnership registrar and two witnesses (see *CPA 2004, Part 2, Chapter 1*).

In a similar way to divorce, a civil partnership can only be dissolved or nullified by a court order (see *CPA 2004, Part 1*).

The Act impacts on pensions in a number of areas including:

- State pensions;
- survivor benefits;
- pension sharing; and
- *s 67* issues.

CPA 2004, s 255 contains an enabling power to allow a Minister of the Crown to amend, by statutory instrument, primary and secondary legislation relating to pensions in order to achieve the main purpose of the Act.

There are numerous statutory instruments that have been implemented in relation to the Act. In particular, the *Civil Partnership (Pensions and Benefit Payments) (Consequential, etc Provisions) Order 2005 (SI 2005/2053)* provides for a number of amendments to *PSA 1993*, *PA 1995* and *PA 2004*. In addition, the *Civil Partnership Act 2004 (Amendments to Subordinate legislation) Order 2005 (SI 2005/2114)* makes changes to the *Employment Equality (Sexual Orientation) Regulations 2003 (SI 2003/1661)* and the *Paternity and Adoption Leave Regulations 2002 (SI 2002/2788)*.

State pensions

9.28 *CPA 2004* makes a number of amendments to the *Social Security Contributions and Benefits Act 1992* so as to extend State pension rights to civil partners.

Survivor benefits

9.29 In contracted-out schemes a civil partner must be entitled to an equivalent widow's/widower's pension on the death of a member if the spouse will be entitled to a GMP (post-5 April 1988), protected rights or statutory reference scheme benefits on the death of a member. The changes to the contracting-out legislation are made by the *Civil Partnership (Contracted-out Occupational and Appropriate Personal Pension Schemes) (Surviving Civil Partners) Order 2005 (SI 2005/2050).* Non contracted-out benefits for civil partners must be provided in respect of pensionable service from 5 December 2005. Contracted-out schemes may need to amend their rules to comply with the new requirements. However, the provisions in relation to non contracted-out benefits are overriding. Employers and trustees may want to consider whether they wish to grant civil partners benefits in excess of the statutory minimum, ie benefits for all pensionable service back to April 1988 or benefits for all pensionable service.

The ECJ has ruled that the surviving registered life partner (the German equivalent of a UK civil partner) of a member of an occupational pension scheme was unlawfully discriminated against on grounds of sexual orientation where the national legislation had placed life partnership and marriage on an equal footing since 1 January 2005, but the scheme rules did not provide for survivor benefits for same-sex partners (*Tadao Maruko v Versorgungsanstalt der deutschen Bühnen C-267/06 [2008] All ER (EC) 977*). The ECJ refused to limit the period from which a registered partner had become entitled to survivors' benefits. This calls into question the UK's implementation of the *Equal Treatment Framework Directive*, as the *Employment Equality (Sexual Orientation) Regulations 2003 (SI 2003/1661)* allow schemes to restrict survivors' benefits for civil partners to periods of service from 5 December 2005 (when *CPA 2004* came into force) and contracted-out rights from 6 April 1988. If that implementation is held to be ineffective, it is likely that public service schemes will have to provide full retrospective entitlement for civil partners because of the direct effect of EU legislation on them. UK legislation would have to be amended to apply this to private schemes. Without either legislation or a test case in the courts, the point remains unresolved, but the issue may have to be considered, for example, in the case of outsourcing agreements.

Pension sharing

9.30 *CPA 2004, Sch 5, Part 4* provides the court with a power to make a pension sharing order on making a dissolution or nullity order in respect of the civil partnership and at any time afterwards.

It is provided under *Part 4* that a pension sharing order is an order which provides that one civil partner's 'shareable rights' under a 'specified pension arrangement' are to be subject to pension sharing for the benefit of the other civil partner. A 'specified pension arrangement' includes occupational and personal pension schemes. There is also power for the court to make earmarking orders (*CPA 2004, Sch 5, Part 6*).

PA 1995, s 67

9.31 As mentioned in **9.29** above, the requirement to treat civil partners in the same way as spouses from 5 December 2005 is overriding. However, the requirement to backdate contracted-out benefits is not overriding. Therefore, schemes will need to amend their rules (although some schemes may not need to where the rules contain a provision stating that they will comply with the contracting-out legislation as amended from time to time).

Before trustees and employers amend their schemes to give effect to the *CPA 2004*, regard must be had to the provisions of *PA 1995, s 67* (restriction on use of amendment powers). Consideration will have to be given to *s 67* in relation to documenting the contracting-out requirements mentioned above and also in cases where the employer and trustees wish to provide benefits beyond the statutory minimum and grant benefits for civil partners for all pensionable service or all pensionable service back to 1988.

Generally, trustees and employers should consult with their actuary and have regard to the provisions of their scheme. It had appeared that *s 67* was likely to be most problematic in circumstances where the scheme rules provide that where there is no spouse then children's pensions are payable or are increased. This is because incorporating benefits for civil partners may have the effect of reducing the benefit payable to the child or may mean that no children's pensions are payable at all. However, the *Occupational Pension Schemes (Modification of Schemes) Regulations 2006 (SI 2006/759)* exclude certain such amendments from the ambit of *s 67*.

Gender Recognition Act 2004

9.32 Case law and the *Gender Recognition Act 2004* have developed the law relating to transsexuals. In the case of *Goodwin v United Kingdom [2002] IRLR 664,* the European Court of Human Rights held that UK law was in breach of the *European Convention on Human Rights* in not allowing Ms Goodwin to marry or enjoy the benefits and burdens of her new gender. Ms Goodwin was a male-to-female transsexual who had been required to pay National Insurance contributions until the age of 65 as if she were a man. In particular, it was held that Ms Goodwin was entitled to the pension rights available to members of her new gender.

In its judgment of 10 April 2003 in *Bellinger v Bellinger [2003] 2 All ER 593,* the House of Lords considered the position of Mrs Bellinger, a transsexual woman who had undergone a marriage ceremony to a man in 1981. The Court of Appeal had declined to grant a declaration that the marriage was valid. The House of Lords held that the marriage was not a valid marriage but declared that the non-recognition of gender reassignment for the purposes of allowing transsexuals to marry was incompatible with the right to respect for private and family life and the right to marry guaranteed by *Articles 8* and *12* of the *European Convention on Human Rights.*

Also, in the case *KB v National Health Service Pensions Agency C-117/01 [2004] All ER (EC) 1089,* the ECJ confirmed that national legislation which prevents marriage (and therefore the enjoyment of certain pension benefits) to individuals who have undergone a sex change is in breach of EU law.

The *Gender Recognition Act 2004* received Royal Assent on 1 July 2004 and the Act's provisions came into force on 4 April 2005.

Under the Act, a person aged 18 or over may make an application to a Gender Recognition Panel for a gender recognition certificate on the basis of living in the other gender, or having changed gender under the law of a country or territory outside the UK. Where a gender recognition certificate is granted, the applicant's gender becomes for most purposes the acquired gender. The Act will allow transsexuals, on acquiring a gender recognition certificate, to marry in their acquired gender and be given birth certificates that recognise the acquired gender. *Gender Recognition Act 2004, Sch 5* deals with benefits and pensions.

There have been a number of post-*Gender Recognition Act* cases dealing with transsexuals' pension rights. In the case of *Grant v United Kingdom (2007) 44 EHRR 1,* a complainant (G) (a male-to-female transsexual) complained that the refusal by the Department of Social Security to pay her a State pension in 1997 at age 60 was in violation of her rights under the *European Convention of Human Rights.* The complaint was upheld, and it was stated that G was entitled to claim the lack of legal recognition from the date of the *Goodwin* judgment (see above). In addition, on 27 April 2006 the ECJ ruled in the case of *Richards v Secretary of State for Work and Pensions C-423/04 [2006] All ER (EC) 895.* In this case, R (who was born a male) underwent gender reassignment surgery in 2001. At age 60, R claimed State retirement pension but was denied on the basis that she had not reached the male retirement age of 65. The UK Government argued that national law was permitted to provide different State pension ages for men and women, and that EU law had not been breached because R's entitlement derived from national law. It was held that, although EU law allows Member States to discriminate in relation to State pension ages, the unequal treatment in question derived from R's gender reassignment, and not from the difference in State pension age. The case was referred back to the UK courts.

Temporary workers

9.33 On 22 October 2008, the European Parliament approved the European Commission *Directive 2008/104/EC* on Temporary Agency Work. All Member States have until December 2011 to ensure their own laws comply with the Directive. The Department for Business, Innovation and Skills has consulted, to 11 December 2009, on draft regulations to implement the Directive.

In summary, the purpose of the Directive is to ensure the protection of temporary agency workers and to improve the quality of temporary agency work by ensuring that the principle of equal treatment is applied to temporary agency workers (*Article 2*).

Article 5 provides:

> 'The basic working and employment conditions of temporary agency workers shall be, for the duration of their assignment at a user undertaking, at least those that would apply if they had been recruited directly by that undertaking to occupy the same job.'

The phrase 'basic working and employment conditions' is stated to include pay. However, draft Regulations exclude from the definition of pay 'any payment by way of a pension, gratuity or allowance ... in connection with retirement or loss of office'. The Department for Business, Innovation and Skills has indicated that pensions will be excluded from the scope of the Regulations. However, the wording referred to above does not appear wide enough to exclude pension contributions, as it only seems to cover payments out.

In brief, the Regulations:

- require temporary employment agencies (and, ultimately, employers), after a 12-week qualifying period, to give temporary workers the same pay, working hours, rest breaks and holiday that they would have received if hired directly by the employer;
- require employers, from day one, to allow temporary workers equal access to information about vacancies at the hirer, as well as to canteen, childcare and transport services; and
- leave agencies and employers vulnerable to legal action by temporary workers, the outcome of which may be an order to pay 'just and equitable' compensation.

Notwithstanding the proposed pension exclusion, agency workers are covered by the new personal accounts regime. Therefore, once the new regime is in force in 2012, agency workers will have to be enrolled into an automatic enrolment scheme. For the purposes of the personal accounts requirements, agency workers are defined in *PA 2008, s 89*. See CHAPTER 13 for more on automatic enrolment.

Disability discrimination

9.34 In brief, the *Disability Discrimination Act 1995* ('*DDA 1995*') makes it unlawful for employers to discriminate without justification against disabled persons:

(*a*) in the arrangements made for deciding who should be offered employment;

(*b*) in employment terms;

(*c*) by refusing to offer or deliberately not offering employment;

(*d*) in the opportunities which are afforded for promotion, transfer, training or other benefit; or

(*e*) by dismissing or subjecting them to any other detriment.

It is also unlawful for an employer to subject a disabled person to harassment (*DDA 1995, s 4*).

A person discriminates against a disabled person if, for a reason which relates to the disabled person's disability, he treats that person less favourably than he treats (or would treat) others to whom that reason does not (or would not) apply (unless he can show that the treatment is justified). This is known as disability-related discrimination and can be distinguished from direct disability discrimination discussed below. Disability-related discrimination can be justified if the reason for it is 'material to the circumstances of the particular case and substantial'. It is also provided that a person discriminates against a disabled person if he fails to comply with a duty to make reasonable adjustments imposed on him in relation to the disabled person. (*DDA 1995, s 3A*).

It is important to note that, as of 1 October 2004 (under the *Disability Discrimination Act 1995 (Amendment) Regulations 2003 (SI 2003/1673)*), the *DDA 1995* prohibits direct disability discrimination. The *DDA 1995* provides that a person directly discriminates against a disabled person if, on the grounds of the person's disability, he treats the disabled person less favourably than he treats or would treat a person not having that particular disability whose relevant circumstances, including his abilities, are the same as, or not materially different from, those of the disabled person. This form of unlawful treatment cannot be justified, unlike discrimination for a reason related to disability. (*DDA 1995, s 3A(5)*). In *Mayor and Burgess of the London Borough of Lewisham v Malcolm [2008] UKHL 43*, the House of Lords made it considerably harder to prove disability related discrimination. However, the Government intends to overturn the effects of this decision in the *Equality Bill*.

The *DDA 1995* implies an overriding 'non-discrimination rule' into occupational pension schemes (see *DDA 1995, s 4G*, as inserted by the *Disability Discrimination Act 1995 (Pensions) Regulations 2003 (SI 2003/2770)*). The trustees or managers of a scheme must refrain from discriminating against a disabled person in carrying out any of their functions in relation to the scheme (including in particular their functions relating to the admission of members to the scheme and the treatment of members of the scheme) and they must not subject a disabled person to harassment. It is not clear whether trustees may use the justification defence.

However, the non-discrimination rule does not apply to rights accrued and benefits payable in respect of periods of service preceding 1 October 2004 (the date the Regulations came into force amending the *DDA 1995*). Notwithstanding this, communications with members and prospective members about such rights and benefits are subject to the non-discrimination rule. (*DDA 1995, s 4G(4)*).

In addition, trustees and managers of occupational pension schemes have a duty to make reasonable adjustments in relation to provisions, criteria or practices (including scheme rules) which place a disabled member/prospective member at a substantial disadvantage compared with non-disabled members/ prospective members. There is also a requirement to make any necessary reasonable adjustments to physical features of premises occupied by the trustees/ scheme managers (*DDA 1995, s 4H*).

A person who believes that he has been discriminated against may bring a claim to an employment tribunal or, alternatively, against the trustees under the scheme's internal dispute resolution procedure (see CHAPTER 3).

The *DDA 1995* was amended further, with effect from 5 December 2005, by the *Disability Discrimination Act 2005* ('*DDA 2005*'). Amongst other things, the *DDA 2005* extends the definition of disability to include, from the point of diagnosis, persons who have cancer, HIV infection or multiple sclerosis. In addition, the requirement that a mental impairment ought to be a clinically well-recognised illness has been removed, thus further extending the scope of persons who are covered by the legislation.

Religion or belief discrimination

9.35 The *Employment Equality (Religion or Belief) Regulations 2003 (SI 2003/1660)* implement the provisions of the *Equal Treatment Framework Directive (Council Directive 2000/78/EC)* on discrimination on grounds of religion or belief. The Regulations, which came into force on 2 December 2003, outlaw less favourable treatment, victimisation and harassment, in the employment context, on grounds of religion or belief.

In the context of pensions, the Regulations provide that it is unlawful for the trustees or managers of an occupational pension scheme to discriminate, on the grounds of religion or belief, against a member or prospective member of the scheme in carrying out any of their functions in relation to the scheme (*reg 9A*). The prohibition does not apply to rights accrued or benefits payable in respect of periods of service prior to the coming into force of the Regulations. One area that trustees will need to consider in the context of religion or belief discrimination is the provision in DC schemes of investment options that comply with the requirements of different religions. Also, prospective members may be prevented from joining a DB scheme because of the way its assets are invested.

Age discrimination

9.36 *Council Directive 2000/78/EC* 'establishing a general framework for equal treatment in employment and occupation' was adopted on 27 November 2000. The purpose of the Directive (as stated in *Article 1*) is to 'lay down a general framework for combating discrimination on the grounds of religion or belief, disability, age or sexual orientation as regards employment and occupation'. Member States had until 2 December 2003 to implement its provisions into domestic law with the possibility of a three-year extension to 2 December 2006 for the age and disability aspects (*Article 18*).

The *Employment Equality (Age) Regulations 2006 (SI 2006/1031)* (the '*Age Regulations*') came into force on 1 October 2006 implementing the new EU age discrimination requirements in the UK. Implementation of the requirements relating to pensions was, however, delayed until 1 December 2006 to give the Government time to carry out a further consultation on the exemptions for pension schemes (the *Employment Equality (Age) (Amendment) Regulations 2006 (SI 2006/2408)*).

The pension exemptions were finalised on 10 November 2006 (the *Employment Equality (Age) (Amendment No 2) Regulations 2006 (SI 2006/2931)*).

The DWP has issued guidance in relation to the *Age Regulations* ('The Impact of the Age Regulations on Pension Schemes, Guidance on the Employment

Equality (Age) Regulations 2006 and their impact on occupational and personal pension schemes'). It provides some helpful (although non-binding) assistance in interpreting the *Age Regulations* and gives examples of how each exemption might work in practice.

What is discrimination on grounds of age?

9.37 Direct discrimination on grounds of age occurs when trustees treat a member or prospective member, or an employer treats a worker, less favourably than he treats others on grounds of age. Indirect discrimination occurs when an apparently age-neutral provision is applied which in fact disadvantages members or workers of a particular age or age group (*Age Regulations, reg 3*). Unlike other strands of discrimination, both direct age discrimination and indirect age discrimination can be justified.

The discrimination, direct or indirect, must be between people where the relevant circumstances are the same or not materially different. This means, for example, that employers could argue that the position of senior executives is not the same, or is materially different, to the rest of the workforce, thus enabling them to be provided with better benefits.

In relation to pensions, the *Age Regulations* apply only to rights accrued or benefits payable in respect of periods of pensionable service on or after 1 December 2006 (*Age Regulations, reg 11*). However, death-in-service benefits are not calculated based on a period of accrual, and the full amount of any benefit arising from a death on or after 1 December 2006 will be subject to the *Age Regulations*.

Exemptions from age discrimination requirements

9.38 There are a number of exemptions for pension schemes in *Age Regulations, Sch 2*. The exemptions will allow some, but not all, existing age-related rules and practices to continue. Key exemptions are set out in the following table.

Exemption	**Commentary**
Age-related contributions to money purchase schemes (*Sch 2, para 10*).	The aim of the different levels of contribution must be to equalise or make more nearly equal resulting benefits in respect of comparable periods of pensionable service to which members of different ages (who are otherwise in a comparable situation) will become entitled. In practice, this means that contributions for older members may be higher than for younger members, to reflect the fact that they will be subject to investment growth for a shorter period.

Exemption	Commentary
Maximum or minimum ages for admission including different ages for admission for different groups or categories of worker (*Sch 2, para 7(a)*).	The *Age Regulations* allow schemes to set a minimum or maximum age for admission and to set different ages for different categories of worker.
Minimum service requirement (*Sch 2, para 3A*).	In relation to admission to a scheme and the accrual of or eligibility for any benefit under the scheme, trustees and employers may impose a service requirement of up to five years. Any period of more than five years requires the employer to be satisfied that it is fulfilling a business need (for example by encouraging loyalty or motivation, or rewarding experience) and the trustees must obtain confirmation from the employer of this. The length of service can either be the actual length of service, or the length of service working at a particular level (ie the five-year period can run each time an employee is promoted). There is also an exemption at *reg 32* which allows employers to discriminate against members on the basis of length of service of up to five years.
Pension based on service (*Sch 2, para 19*).	Arguably, any benefit based on length of service is indirectly discriminatory (as younger workers are likely on average to have shorter service) but there is an express exemption allowing any difference in the amount of benefit attributable to differences in length of pensionable service as long as members in a comparable situation accrue a right to benefit based on the same fraction of pensionable pay.
Final pensionable salary (*Sch 2, para 24*).	There is an express exemption allowing a maximum cap to be placed on the salary to be taken into account when calculating a benefit (this could either be a cap equivalent to former HMRC limits, or a scheme-specific cap).
Maximum length of pensionable service (*Sch 2, para 21(2)*).	*Paragraph 21(2)* exempts any limitation on benefit where that limitation results from imposing a maximum number of years of pensionable service.
Targeted Benefits (*Sch 2, para 19A*)).	This exemption applies, for example, where an accrual rate is set so as to target a pension of two-thirds final pensionable salary at normal retirement date.

Exemption	**Commentary**
Closure to new entrants (*Sch 2, paras 25* and *25A*).	There is an express exemption allowing the closure of a scheme, from a particular date, to workers who have not yet joined it. There is also an exemption allow sections of schemes to be closed from a particular date to new entrants. A section of a scheme means: (*a*) any group of members who became eligible to join, or who joined, the scheme on, after or before a particular date on the basis that particular benefits will be provided to or in respect of those members or that a particular level of contributions will be paid in respect of those members; or (*b*) any group of members who became eligible to join, or who joined, the scheme as a result of a block transfer.
Normal retirement date (*Sch 2, para 14*).	Schemes may set a specific age as the earliest date at which a benefit becomes payable without consent and without actuarial reduction (other than in special cases such as ill health). This is referred to in the *Age Regulations* as the early retirement pivot age ('ERPA').
Early retirement (*Sch 2, paras 12* and *13*).	Schemes may include a provision setting a minimum age for the payment of or entitlement to benefits prior to ERPA (with or without consent). Any benefit paid between this minimum age and ERPA (other than on the grounds of ill health or redundancy) must be actuarially reduced and no added years awarded unless the practice can be objectively justified. The reduction must be on the basis that the aim is to reflect the fact that the benefit is paid before ERPA, which suggests that the aim should be cost neutrality. Where applicable, existing enhanced early retirement rules may continue to apply in relation to members, or prospective members, as at 1 December 2006. This exemption also applies to members as at 1 December 2006 who are subject to a subsequent bulk transfer. The enhancement may be on the basis of potential future service to 'normal pension age' (which is the earliest age at which a member is entitled to receive benefits), a fixed number of years of future service or by reducing or removing the actuarial reduction. Enhancement on any other basis may need to be justified.

Exemption	**Commentary**
Enhancement of benefits on ill health (*Sch 2, para 15*).	There is an express exemption allowing benefits payable on retirement before ERPA (see above) on the grounds of ill health to be enhanced on the basis of potential future service to 'normal pension age' (which is the earliest age at which a member is entitled to receive benefits), a fixed number of years' future service or by reducing or removing the actuarial reduction.
Calculation of death benefits (*Sch 2, para 15A*).	There is an exemption allowing death benefits to be enhanced by reference to prospective service to 'normal pension age' (which is the earliest age at which a member is entitled to receive benefits), a fixed number of years' future service or by reducing or removing the actuarial reduction. Enhancement on any other basis may need to be justified.
Bridging pensions (*Sch 2, para 16*).	The *Age Regulations* provide an exemption for bridging pensions whereby they can be reduced at any time between the ages of 60 and 65 by up to the level of State pension.
Requirements imposed by *FA 2004* (*Sch 2, para 30*).	*Paragraph 30* exempts any provisions relating to the entitlement to or payment of benefits under a registered pension scheme insofar as compliance is necessary to secure any tax relief or exemption available under *FA 2004, Part 4* or to prevent any charge to tax arising under that Part of that Act, whoever is liable in relation to such charge.

Which common practices are not exempt?

9.39 Many pension schemes require members to stop accruing benefits when they reach the scheme's normal retirement date (often age 60 or 65). There is no exemption allowing this to continue and it may be difficult to justify. Consideration should be given to allowing those employees still in service after normal retirement date to continue as active members of the scheme. This will include providing them with full life cover.

There is no general exemption for schemes continuing to apply former HMRC limits. There is a general exemption in relation to *FA 2004* requirements, but this is not wide enough to cover former HMRC limits. The exemption for 'sections' might allow trustees to treat class A, B and C members differently, but any age discriminatory provisions within each class would have to be justified. The fact that it was a previous HMRC requirement is unlikely on its own to be sufficient justification.

Do the exemptions comply with the Directive?

9.40 It has been suggested that some of the exemptions in the *Age Regulations* go beyond those authorised by *Article 6* of the *Equal Treatment Framework Directive*. If this is the case (and it would have to be decided by the courts), then the individual exemptions found to be outside the Directive will be struck down.

In the European case of *Birgit Bartsch v Bosch und Siemens Hausgerate (BSH) Altersfursorge GmbH C-427/06 [2009] All ER (EC) 113* the Advocate General gave his opinion in relation to a young spouse provision of a German pension scheme which prevented a widow from receiving a pension because she was more than 15 years younger than the deceased member. The Advocate General found that:

- Because the period for implementing the *Equal Treatment Framework Directive* had not expired, there was no discrimination contrary to EU law.
- However, such a provision would now be in breach of EU age discrimination laws.
- It might be possible to objectively justify such discrimination, ie the Member State might be able to show that it was an appropriate and necessary means of achieving a legitimate aim; but, because this young spouse clause prevented any payment to the widow, it went beyond what was 'appropriate and necessary'; a sliding scale might instead be acceptable, or payments starting only when survivors reached a certain age.

On 23 September 2009 the ECJ gave its judgment in the *Bartsch* case. The ECJ held that the claim could not succeed as the claim was brought before the time limit for transposition of the age discrimination requirements of the *Equal Treatment Framework Directive* had expired.

The provision in question prevented any pension at all being paid to the spouse. The *Age Regulations* allow for actuarial reduction in pension if a spouse is more than a specified number of years younger than the member. However, any scheme with a rule which could potentially allow for a reduction to zero might have to review its rules if future decisions of the ECJ follow the Advocate-General's opinion.

Justification

9.41 If an age-related practice/benefit rule does not fall within one of the exemptions, it may still be justified if it can be shown that it is a 'proportionate means of achieving a legitimate aim' (*Age Regulations, reg 3(1)*).

DWP guidance suggests that a legitimate aim might include business needs, efficiency, reducing staff turnover or providing promotion opportunities to retain good people. It is stated that, for the means of achieving that aim to be proportionate, there must be a balance between the discriminatory effect of a measure and the importance of the aim being pursued. Key to the proportionality test is whether there is a less discriminatory or non-discriminatory way of achieving the same aim.

Justification was considered by the EAT in March 2005 in the case of *Cross v British Airways [2005] 26 PBLR*. The claim against British Airways was for unfair dismissal and sex discrimination (the case was brought before the *Age Regulations* were in force) where employees had a normal retirement age of 55 but wished to continue working until the age of 60. The appeal by the employees was dismissed. The EAT referred to various previous cases, and in particular *Hampson,* which said:

> 'In my judgment "justifiable" requires an objective balance between the discriminatory effect of the condition and reasonable needs of a party who applies the condition.'

The key conclusion on justification in this case was that an employer/trustees seeking to justify a discriminatory practice cannot rely solely on considerations of cost. Cost can however be taken into account, together with other justifications if there are any.

There are a number of decisions of the employment tribunal and EAT which deal with the issue of justification and age discrimination.

On 10 October 2007, the employment tribunal handed down its decision in the case of a former partner in the law firm Freshfields who brought a claim based on age discrimination in relation to a 'pay as you go' pension arrangement (*Bloxham v Freshfields [2007] 53 PBLR*). In this case, the employment tribunal found that the less favourable treatment was based on age, but that it was justified. This is an employment rather than a pensions case, and as an employment tribunal decision it has no formal precedent value; however, it includes some useful arguments on less favourable treatment and on justification.

Key factors in the findings include:

- The arrangements as they stood discriminated against younger partners and it was legitimate to consider changing them – the question was whether the new arrangements were a proportionate response.
- There was a finite pool of money – if Mr Bloxham won, someone else of a different age would suffer.
- No one had put forward an alternative, less discriminatory, solution.

- Freshfields had tried to mitigate the effect of the change through transitional arrangements and there had been extensive consultation.

In *MacCulloch v ICI*, the EAT looked in some detail at the issue of justification in the context of a contractual redundancy scheme. Of particular interest in a pensions context is the EAT's finding that, in a scheme where there is a standard set of rules, the aims must justify the scheme as a whole, not just the treatment of the individual claimant; but the extent to which an individual is disadvantaged compared to his or her comparators is highly relevant to proportionality.

From a practical perspective, therefore, the trustees/employer in considering any objective justification that is needed for a potentially age discriminatory practice, need to consider whether in the first instance there is a legitimate need for having this practice/rule. They should then consider if there is a way of achieving the aim with a lesser degree of discrimination and, if so, change the practice/rule to use the lesser degree of discrimination. However, if this cannot be done, and retention of the practice/rule is desired, then they would need to rely on the legitimate aim that they consider justifies the practice/rule and keep all records as evidence of the objective justification.

Effect of a non-discrimination rule

9.42 Where there is a discriminatory provision in a pension scheme which is not exempt or justified, a non-discrimination rule will be implied into the scheme, overriding the provision and requiring trustees to refrain from doing any act which is unlawful under the *Age Regulations*. Trustees have power, subject in some circumstances to employer consent, to modify the scheme to secure conformity with the non discrimination rule (*Sch 2, para 2*).

It is generally thought that the effect of the non-discrimination rule will be that until the discriminatory provision is eliminated, the less favoured group will be levelled up to the benefits of the more favoured group. For example, if a scheme provided accrual at 1/80ths for those under 40 and 1/60ths for those over 40, all the members would have to be granted 1/60th benefit accrual from 1 December 2006 onwards. It may be open to the trustees and employer to later modify the scheme to provide for 1/80ths accrual for all, but that change could only take effect in relation to accrual on or after the date of the modification.

Flexible retirement

9.43 Since the *FA 2004*, schemes may offer flexible retirement, whereby an individual may draw all or part of his/her pension and remain in employment with the same employer. Prior to 6 April 2006, most members had to leave pensionable service in order to draw their benefits. Many schemes which are considering this option may wish to require a member taking flexible retirement to cease accrual in that scheme (and for the employer to offer another arrangement such as a stakeholder scheme). This raises the possibility of an indirect age discrimination claim from the flexible retiree, who could argue that the requirement to cease accrual impacted unfairly on members of his age.

The alternative approach is not to offer flexible retirement at all, and continue with existing practice, which could itself be discriminatory. The argument in this case could be that requiring a member to cease working before drawing a pension would indirectly discriminate against older workers, who are more likely to want to draw all or part of their pension, perhaps in conjunction with reducing their hours as they move towards full retirement.

In September 2007, the DWP issued a consultation document on flexible retirement and pension provision. The DWP's response to this consultation and draft regulations ('Flexible Retirement and Pension Provision Government Response to the Consultation and Draft Regulations') were published on 16 December 2008.

As referred to at **9.38** above, the *Age Regulations* contain a number of pensions related exemptions which mean that certain rules and practices connected with pensions are exempt from the prohibition on age discrimination. The draft Regulations published by the DWP in December 2008 set out alternative options for a further pensions exemption covering flexible retirement arrangements. The two versions of the exemption are:

- A wide flexible retirement exemption. This would permit any rule, practice, action or decision of an employer or occupational pension scheme trustee that stopped accrual of, or entitlement to, any further rights or benefits under the scheme during the flexible retirement arrangement. For the purpose of death benefits, the exemption provides that a member in a flexible retirement arrangement would be treated as a pensioner.
- A more limited option allowing occupational pension schemes not to provide the same death-in-service benefits in respect of members in flexible retirement arrangements as for active members, but to treat them for that purpose as pensioner members.

The draft Regulations define a 'flexible retirement arrangement' as an arrangement between a member and his employer under which the member reduces the hours worked or the grade in which he is employed after becoming eligible to receive all or part of the age related benefits payable under an occupational pension scheme. This definition will not include a member who takes all or part of their benefits but continues at the same grade with the same hours.

Consultation on the draft Regulations closed on 10 March 2009.

Age discrimination and retirement ages

9.44 The National Council on Ageing (NCA) persuaded the High Court that it should ask the ECJ whether the provision in the *Age Regulations* which permits enforced retirement at age 65 is lawful (*R (on the application of the Incorporated Trustees of the National Council for Ageing (Age Concern England)) v Secretary of State for Business, Enterprise and Regulatory Reform (24 July 2007)*). The NCA argued that the *Equal Treatment Framework Directive*, on which the *Age Regulations* are based, had not been properly implemented by the UK.

The *Age Regulations* permit employers to retire employees at the age of 65, provided they follow a specified statutory procedure, without needing to justify that decision. Employers *may* retire employees earlier, if they can justify the decision to retire on objective grounds.

NCA argued that the existence of a right for employers to impose a compulsory retirement age is in breach of the underlying Directive.

On 5 March 2009, the ECJ gave its judgment, stating that it was for the UK court to determine whether legislation which permits employers to retire employees at age 65 is justified by legitimate social policy objectives, such as those related to employment policy, the labour market or vocational training. The ECJ held that the *Equal Treatment Framework Directive* gives Member States the option to provide, within the context of national law, for differences in treatment on the grounds of age if they are objectively and reasonably justified by a legitimate aim, and the means of achieving that aim are appropriate and necessary.

The case was referred by the ECJ back to the High Court which ruled on 25 September 2009. The High Court found in favour of the Government and confirmed that its decision to adopt a default retirement age ('DRA') was 'legitimate and proportionate'.

On the issue of whether 65 was appropriate as the DRA, the court noted that the Government's review of the DRA (which it was announced on 13 July 2009 will take place in 2010) must give 'particular consideration to whether the retention of 65 can conceivably now be justified'. It was stated that, in 2006, 'there were powerful reasons why an age over 65 should have been adopted … the choice of 65 seems particularly odd in the light of subsequent thinking about pensionable age which is intended by the middle of the century to rise to 68'. It was added that, if the DRA had been adopted in 2009 instead of in 2006 or there had been no indication of an imminent review, the court would have concluded that the selection of age 65 as the DRA would not have been proportionate because of the discriminatory effect on those who are able and willing to work longer.

In October 2009 the Government commissioned a research project to assist in the 2010 review of DRA and called for evidence from interested parties in the following areas:

- the operation of the DRA in practice;
- the reasons that businesses use mandatory retirement ages;
- the impacts (positive and negative) on businesses, individuals, and the economy, of raising or removing the DRA;
- the experience of businesses operating without a DRA; and
- how any costs of raising or removing the DRA could be mitigated and benefits realised.

Race discrimination

9.45 The *Race Relations Act 1976* protects against discrimination connected with membership of a 'racial group', and makes it unlawful for a person to discriminate:

(*a*) in the arrangements made for determining who should be offered employment;

(*b*) in the terms on which employment is offered;

(*c*) by refusing or deliberately omitting to offer employment;

(*d*) in the way he/she affords access to opportunities for promotion, transfer or training, or to any other benefits, facilities or services, or by refusing or deliberately omitting to afford access to them; or

(*e*) by dismissing, or subjecting a person to any other detriment.

Harassment is also prohibited.

In a pensions context, the issue of race discrimination has been raised by the Gurkhas who continue to challenge the Ministry of Defence's pension arrangements. Under the arrangements, a large number of Gurkhas who retired before 1 July 1997 are not entitled to be transferred to the Armed Forces Pension Scheme. Issues of age discrimination have also been raised.

Equality Bill 2009

9.46 The *Equality Bill* was introduced into Parliament on 27 April 2009, and has two main stated purposes:

- to harmonise discrimination law; and
- to strengthen the law to support progress on equality.

The majority of the provisions of the Bill which may impact on pension schemes are covered by the first aim – essentially, it is a consolidation of discrimination law, with the current statutes and regulations being repealed and a new statutory structure introduced. It is understood that there is no intention to make substantive changes to discrimination law as it currently applies to pensions.

The legislation contains a list of 'protected characteristics' which are then subject to protection from discrimination, harassment and victimisation in specific areas – including pensions.

Protected characteristics

9.47 The protected characteristics are:

- age – by reference to a particular age or to a range of ages;
- disability – a physical or mental impairment having a substantial and long-term adverse affect on the ability to carry out normal day-to-day activities (guidance may be issued on what can be taken into account when determining if someone is under a disability);
- gender reassignment – where someone is proposing to undergo, is undergoing or has undergone gender reassignment;
- marriage and civil partnership;
- pregnancy and maternity;
- race;
- religion or belief;
- sex; and
- sexual orientation.

Occupational pension schemes

9.48 An occupational pension scheme must be taken to include a non-discrimination rule by virtue of which the 'responsible person' must not discriminate (directly or indirectly) in the carrying out of any of his functions in relation to the scheme. 'Responsible persons' include trustees and employers. According to the explanatory notes to the Bill, the new provision does not apply to 'pension rights built up or benefits payable for periods of service before the commencement date' but this is not made clear on the face of the Bill.

Some points of interest in the current draft of the Bill are:

- Exemptions to the non-discrimination rule relating to age may be specified by order. Consultation is required on any new exemptions which are not in use before any order comes into force. We would therefore expect that, at least initially, the current exemptions will be retained in an order.
- The sex equality provisions in the Bill are similar to the current requirements. If an occupational pension scheme does not include a sex equality rule, it is to be treated as including one. The Bill includes a power for the trustees, by resolution, to make sex equality alterations to the scheme. The sex equality rule will not apply where the trustees can show that the difference in treatment is because of a material factor which is not the difference of sex.
- Pension credit members are excluded from protection because their rights are derived from orders of the court rather than employment rights.
- Non-discrimination rules are already in place in relation to age, disability, religion or belief and sexual orientation. The Bill adds a requirement for a non-discrimination rule in respect of gender reassignment and marriage and civil partnerships.
- In relation to marriage and civil partnerships the Bill does not give non-married partners the right to the same benefits as married partners – *clause 13(4)* requires that the less favourable treatment must be because someone is married or a civil partner (not because someone is *not* married or a civil partner). Essentially, this would still allow schemes to offer those who are married or in civil partnerships benefits not available to those not married or in civil partnerships.

Insurance

9.49 A new requirement in the Bill is that a service provider must not discriminate in the terms on which it provides a service. This will include insurance companies. The new provisions will not apply to existing insurance policies entered into before the date of commencement. In addition, there is an exemption in relation to disability where the discrimination is relevant to the assessment of risk. This would appear to allow insurers both to require medical reports and to set premiums based on the results of those reports.

In relation to sex, gender reassignment, pregnancy and maternity, an exemption allows insurers to rely on specified actuarial data. Any differences in treatment must be proportionate according to the data.

There is currently no exemption in relation to age. However, in June 2009, the Government Equalities Office published a consultation on age discrimination in relation to the supply of services and public functions, and this includes a section on the financial services sector.

The Government has proposed three broad options for consultation:

- **Option 1** – allow different treatment on age only where it can be objectively justified. The concern here is that it might reduce the products providers are willing to offer and increase costs because of the costs/risks of individual justification.
- **Option 2** – create an exception which will allow different treatment where it is justifiable and in line with risk. Evidence of risk could be weighed against commercial factors – there would not have to be strict mathematical proportionality. Minimum and maximum age limits and age-banding would be allowed. There would have to be increased transparency (such as the publication of risk data) and better access/cross referrals.
- **Option 3** – a wide exemption for the financial services sector.

Option 2 is the Government's preferred option. If it is adopted, life cover for late retirees will remain an issue for trustees and employers. Consultation closed on 29 September 2009 and, at the time of writing, responses are currently being considered.

Trustees' power to amend

9.50 Previously, the Bill gave trustees an overriding power to modify their scheme rules by resolution to comply with the non-discrimination requirement only in relation to sex equality. A new amendment extends this to other types of discrimination. The result of this amendment is that trustees will be able to use the power in the same circumstances as currently apply under *PA 1995, s 65* (equal treatment):

- if they do not have power to amend; or
- if the amendment procedure is 'liable to be unduly complex or protracted' or 'involves obtaining consents which cannot be obtained or which can be obtained only with undue delay or difficulty'.

Tables of relevant legislation and case law

9.51 The following tables list relevant UK and European legislation and its main effect. The table of cases lists the main issues decided.

UK legislation	
Legislation	*Main effect*
Equal Pay Act 1970	Did not originally encompass pension schemes expressly. Amended by the *Occupational Pension Schemes (Equal Treatment) Regulations 1995 (SI 1995/3183)*, see below.
Social Security Pensions Act 1975	Required schemes to provide equal access to membership for both men and women (re-enacted in *PSA 1993* and now covered by *PA 1995*).
Race Relations Act 1976	The *Race Relations Act 1976* protects against discrimination connected with membership of a 'racial group'.
Pension Schemes Act 1993	Consolidated previous pensions legislation (*Social Security Act 1973, Social Security Pensions Act 1975, Social Security Act 1990*).
Pensions Act 1995	Imposes equal treatment requirements on scheme provisions in relation to pensionable service after 17 May 1990, and covers both access to schemes and benefits under schemes. It also empowers trustees to make changes unilaterally for the purpose of implementing equal treatment.
Disability Discrimination Act 1995	The *Disability Discrimination Act 1995* makes it unlawful for employers to discriminate against disabled persons.
Occupational Pension Schemes (Equal Treatment) Regulations 1995 (SI 1995/3183)	The Regulations supplement the requirements for equal treatment relating to occupational pension schemes provided for in *PA 1995, ss 62–66*.
Part-time Workers (Prevention of Less Favourable Treatment) Regulations 2000 (SI 2000/1551) (implementing *Directive 97/81/EC*)	The Regulations give part-time workers the right not to be treated less favourably than full-time workers working for the same employer under the same type of employment contract. Workers who change from full-time to part-time are also protected as they are to be treated no less favourably than they were before going part-time. The Regulations apply where the less favourable treatment is applied to a part-time worker which cannot be justified on objective grounds.

UK legislation	
Legislation	*Main effect*
Part-time Workers (Prevention of Less Favourable Treatment) Regulations 2000 (Amendment) Regulations 2002 (SI 2002/2035)	The Regulations remove the provision which had limited the backdating of a claim to two years from the date on which the complaint was presented. Additionally, provisions for comparators have been amended, removing the distinction between fixed-term and permanent contracts.
Fixed-term Employees (Prevention of Less Favourable Treatment) Regulations 2002 (SI 2002/2034) (implementing *Directive 1999/70/EC*)	The Regulations give fixed-term employees the right not to be treated less favourably than permanent employees of the same employer who are doing similar work unless there is an objective justification for the difference.
Employment Equality (Sexual Orientation) Regulations 2003 (SI 2003/1661) (implementing *Directive 2000/78/EC*)	The Regulations are designed to implement the Directive in respect of sexual orientation discrimination and outlaw discrimination in employment and vocational training on grounds of sexual orientation. The Regulations came into force on 1 December 2003 and protect heterosexuals, homosexuals and bisexuals.
Employment Equality (Sexual Orientation) (Amendment) Regulations 2003 (SI 2003/2827)	These Regulations extend the provisions of the *Sexual Orientation Regulations* to the trustees and managers of an occupational pension scheme. The Regulations make provision for every occupational pension scheme to be treated as including a 'non-discrimination' rule prohibiting discrimination contrary to the *Sexual Orientation Regulations.*
Disability Discrimination Act 1995 (Amendment) Regulations 2003 (SI 2003/1673)	Amend the *Disability Discrimination Act 1995* so as to prohibit direct disability discrimination.
Disability Discrimination Act 1995 (Pensions) Regulations 2003 (SI 2003/2770)	Amend the *Disability Discrimination Act 1995* in relation to occupational pension schemes.
Employment Equality (Religion or Belief) Regulations 2003 (SI 2003/1660)	Implement the provisions of the *Equal Treatment Framework Directive* in relation to discrimination on grounds of religion or belief.

UK legislation	
Legislation	*Main effect*
Gender Recognition Act 2004	Under the Act, a person aged 18 or over may make an application to a Gender Recognition Panel for a gender recognition certificate on the basis of living in the other gender, or having changed gender under the law of a country or territory outside of the UK. Where a gender recognition certificate is granted, then the applicant's gender becomes for most purposes the acquired gender.
Civil Partnership Act 2004	The Act provides for same-sex couples to obtain legal recognition of their relationship by registering as civil partners.
Disability Discrimination Act 2005	The *Disability Discrimination Act 1995* was amended, with effect from 5 December 2005, by the *Disability Discrimination Act 2005* so as to extend the definition of disability to include persons who have cancer, HIV infection or multiple sclerosis.
Occupational Pension Schemes (Equal Treatment) (Amendment) Regulations 2005 (SI 2005/1923)	Amend the provisions of the *Equal Pay Act 1970, PA 1995* and the *Equal Treatment Regulations* to reflect the *Preston* decision.
Transfer of Employment (Pension Protection) Regulations 2005 (SI 2005/649)	Provide a basic level of pensions protection for employees on a *TUPE* transfer who were, prior to the transfer, members of, or entitled to be members of, an occupational pension scheme.
Equality Act 2006	Received Royal Assent on 16 February 2006. One of the key elements of the Act is the creation of a new Commission for Equality and Human Rights.
Employment Equality (Age) Regulations 2006 (SI 2006/1031)	The Regulations came into force on 1 October 2006 implementing the new EU age discrimination requirements in the UK. Implementation of the requirements relating to pensions was, however, delayed until 1 December 2006, coming into force in amended form (*Employment Equality (Age) (Amendment No 2) Regulations 2006 (SI 2006/2931)*).

European legislation	
Legislation	*Main effect*
TFEU – Article 157 (formerly *119* and then *141* of the *EU Treaty*)	Each Member State shall ensure and subsequently maintain the application of the principle that men and women should receive equal pay for equal work.
Directive 75/117/EEC on equal pay	Requires Member States to introduce equal pay laws.
Directive 77/187/EEC on acquired rights	Original *'Acquired Rights Directive'* ensuring continuing employment following a transfer of the business undertaking (but excludes pension rights). Now replaced by *Directive 2001/23/EC.*
Directive 76/207/EEC on equal treatment	Requires Member States to prohibit sex discrimination in employment, but made no specific reference to pensions or social security (made under *Article 235*).
Directive 79/7/EEC on statutory benefits	Requires Member States to implement equal treatment in statutory social security schemes but excludes retirement ages, survivors' benefits, derived rights and maternity provisions.
Directive 86/378/EEC on equal treatment	Requires Member States to implement equal treatment in pension schemes and includes access, calculation of contributions and of benefits, retirement ages and maternity provisions. (NB following the various ECJ decisions on equal treatment, a revised directive has been issued – see below.)
Directive amending *Directive 86/378/EEC* (above)	Transposes the ECJ decisions on equal treatment onto the *1986 Directive*. Thus, those parts of the *1986 Directive* which provide for derogations from the principle of equal treatment are invalid as far as paid employees are concerned. However, the provisions of the *1986 Directive* relating to self-employed workers remain valid.
Directive 98/50/EC on acquired rights	Reinforces *Directive 77/187/EEC* and effectively gives Member States the option of protecting pension rights under national legislation.
Directive 2000/78/EC on equal treatment.	This Directive, establishing a general framework for equal treatment, requires Member States to enact legislation prohibiting discrimination on grounds of religion or belief, disability, age or sexual orientation.

European legislation	
Legislation	*Main effect*
Directive 2001/23/EC on acquired rights	Replaced previous *Acquired Rights Directive.*
Directive 2002/73/EC on equal treatment	Amends *Directive 76/207/EEC* in respect of sex discrimination and introduces two new definitions of harassment.
Directive 2008/104/EC on temporary agency work	A Directive to ensure the protection of agency workers.

Cases		
Decision	*Date*	*Main issues decided*
Defrenne v The Belgian State *Case No C-80/70 [1971] ECR 445*	1971	Distinguished between statutory pension provision and private occupational pension schemes, in that the former did not come within the scope of *Article 157*. Payments from the latter were not, in principle, to be excluded from the concept of 'pay' for the purposes of *Article 157*.
Defrenne v Sabena (No 2) *Case No C-43/75 [1976] ECR 455*	1976	Determination that *Article 157* had direct effect, and consequently could be enforced by individuals in Member States without the need for further legislation to implement it.
Bilka-Kaufhaus GmbH v Weber von Hartz *Case No C-170/84 [1986] ECR 1607*	1986	Exclusion of part-timers from scheme membership is unlawful where the reason for exclusion is discriminatory on grounds of sex. Here, the exclusion affected ten times as many women as men and could not be explained by any reason other than one based on sex discrimination, ie it was not 'objectively justified'.

Cases		
Decision	*Date*	*Main issues decided*
Barber v GRE Assurance Group *Case No C-262/88 [1990] ECR I-1889*	17 May 1990	Decided that a pension paid from a UK occupational pension scheme was 'pay' for the purposes of *Article 157* which requires equal pay for equal work. Also decided that the same retirement benefits 'package' available to a woman who is made compulsorily redundant, should also be available to a man in like circumstances, and that each element (as opposed to the totality) of a pay package must be equal.
Bullock v The Alice Ottley School *[1992] IRLR 564*	15 Oct 1992	Employers are permitted to have a variety of normal retirement ages for different types of workers, provided that the reason for the differences is not based upon direct or indirect sex discrimination.
Ten Oever v Stichting *Case No C-109/91 [1993] ECR I-4879*	6 Oct 1993	Temporal limitations of the *Barber* judgment clarified in that the direct application of *Article 157* can only substantiate a claim in respect of benefits (in this case, a widower's pension) relating to periods of employment on or after 17 May 1990, unless the claim is brought before that date.
Birds Eye Walls v Friedl M Roberts *Case No C-132/92 [1993] PLR 323*	9 Nov 1993	'Bridging' pensions do not infringe *Article 157*, as they are designed to remedy inequality (in this case, in taking into account the differing ages at which State pensions became payable).
Neath v Hugh Steeper Ltd *Case No C-152/91 [1993] ECR I-6935*	22 Dec 1993	Under a final salary scheme, it is the employer's commitment (ie the amount of pension promised) that must be equal, even though the use of sex-based actuarial factors may require unequal contributions from the employer to meet the funding requirements of the scheme.

Cases		
Decision	*Date*	*Main issues decided*
Coloroll Pension Trustees Ltd v Russell *Case No C-200/91 [1994] ECR I-4389*	28 Sep 1994	Determined that: • both employees and their dependants may rely on the direct effect of *Article 157* against a scheme's trustees (who are required to observe the principles of equal treatment); • equal treatment may be implemented by the 'levelling down' of benefits (ie reduction of the advantages enjoyed by one group of members to the level received by a less advantaged group) from the date of scheme equalisation; • retrospection is only in relation to benefits (including survivors' benefits) for periods of service after 17 May 1990; • the receiving scheme must make good any inadequacy in respect of an unequalised transfer payment made to it; and • AVC's and single sex schemes do not fall within the scope of *Article 157*.
Smith v Avdel Systems Ltd *Case No C-408/92 [1994] ECR I-4435*	28 Sep 1994	Retirement ages for women could not be raised to that of men for the period from 17 May 1990 to the date of equalisation, although this measure would not infringe *Article 157* in respect of service completed after the date of the change.
Van den Akker v Stichting Shell PF *Case No C-28/93 [1994] ECR I-4527*	28 Sep 1994	*Article 157* does not allow a uniform retirement age to be set whilst maintaining an advantage for women members. Equality can only be achieved by the 'levelling up' of benefits, ie for men to enjoy the same advantages of women members, for service after *Barber* to the date of equalisation.

Cases		
Decision	*Date*	*Main issues decided*
Algemeen Burgerlijk PF v Beaune *Case No C-7/93 [1994] ECR I-4471*	28 Sep 1994	Civil service pension schemes do come within the scope of *Article 157*.
Vroege v NCIV Instituut *Case No C-57/93 [1994] ECR I-4541*	28 Sep 1994	The right to join an occupational pension scheme is covered by *Article 157*, but falls outside the temporal limitations of the *Barber* judgment. This right continues to be governed by the *Bilka-Kaufhaus* judgment.
Fisscher v Voorhuis Hengelo BV *Case No C-128/93 [1994] ECR I-4583*	28 Sep 1994	As for *Vroege*, but also decided that administrators must comply with *Article 157*. Further, it confirmed that employees can claim retrospective membership although they cannot avoid paying backdated contributions.
Nolte v Landesversicherungsanstalt Hannover *Case No C-317/93 [1996] All ER (EC) 212*	14 Dec 1995	Exclusion of part-timers from membership is permissible, even where to do so affects more women than men, where the reason is to achieve a social policy unrelated to any discrimination.
Lloyds Bank (EC) Pension Trust Corporation Ltd v Lloyds Bank plc *[1996] OPLR 181*	24 Apr 1996	The rules of the scheme provided that 'pecuniary benefits secured' for members could not be reduced without their consent. The court refused to permit the trustees to amend the rules to reduce future benefits.
Grant v South-West Trains Limited *Case No C-249/96 [1998] All ER (EC) 193*	17 Feb 1998	This was an employment case involving the granting of travel concessions. South-West Trains refused to give travel concessions to Ms Grant's same-sex partner when she was promoted to a post at South-West Trains previously occupied by an employee whose opposite-sex partner had obtained such concessions. The ECJ said that Community law as it stood did not cover discrimination based on sexual orientation.

Cases		
Decision	*Date*	*Main issues decided*
Regina v Secretary of State for Employment ex parte Seymour-Smith and Another *Case No C-167/97 [1999] ICR 447*	9 Feb 1999	The ECJ considered, among other questions, the test for determining whether a measure adopted by a Member State had 'such a disparate effect as between men and women as to amount to indirect discrimination'.
Deutsche Telekom v Schroder *Case No C-50/96 [2000] ECR I-743*	10 Feb 2000	The *Defrenne* time limit of 8 April 1976 (backdated benefits can be claimed as far back as this date) does not prevent national legislation being more generous and backdating claims even further.
Preston v Wolverhampton *Healthcare NHS Trust* *Case No C-78/98 [2000] All ER (EC) 714 and [2001] IRLR 237 HL*	16 May 2000 and 8 Feb 2001	Claims by part-timers in respect of unlawful exclusion from scheme membership have to be made within six months of leaving service as required under national UK law. However, the maximum of two years' backdated benefits that can be awarded under the UK legislation is not valid, and backdated benefits can be claimed going as far back as April 1976. However, Member States are permitted to require that individuals making a claim pay any past contributions which they would have had to pay had they belonged to the scheme throughout the relevant period.
Marsh Mercer Pension Scheme v Pensions Ombudsman *[2001] 16 PBLR 28*	23 Feb 2001	The Pensions Ombudsman could not make a direction relating to the equalisation of GMP's and compliance with equal treatment rules in *PA 1995, s 62* as the matter was too wide-ranging for determination in such a manner. The Ombudsman was wrong to determine that the dispute was one affecting the scheme and all the members generally and also his direction requiring the rewriting of the scheme affected all the members. It was not within the jurisdiction of the Ombudsman to purport to decide equalisation of GMPs on behalf of all the other members of the scheme.

Cases		
Decision	*Date*	*Main issues decided*
Allonby v Accrington & Rossendale College *[2001] IRLR 364*	23 Mar 2001	Claim brought by a part-time lecturer who was no longer eligible for membership of the scheme by virtue of change in employment status – the lecturer's services were changed by the employer from being employed on a one year renewable contract with the employer to being employed through an employment agency while doing the same work. It was held by the Court of Appeal that the part-time lecturer was in a contract of employment for occupational pension purposes. As there could be a possible conflict with *Article 157*, *Allonby* was referred to the ECJ.
Glossop v Copnall *[2001] PLR 263*	5 Jul 2001	The Pensions Ombudsman's determination that the trustees' failure to comply with *Article 157* amounts to maladministration was incorrect. A mere error of law could not amount to maladministration.
Quirk v Burton Hospital *[2002] 24 PBLR*	12 Feb 2002	Mr Quirk, a male nurse, had been excluded by scheme rules from rights available to female nurses. Mr Quirk complained that the decision in *Barber* should be retrospective. It was held that the reason for the limitation on equalisation of benefits to 17 May 1990 was because Member States could reasonably have believed that such discrimination was lawful on the basis of parallel EU legislation. Therefore the limitation in *Barber* is correct and equal treatment under *Article 157* in relation to scheme benefits does not apply to service prior to May 1990.
Uppingham School v Shillcock *[2002] EWHC 641 (Ch)*	19 Apr 2002	The case overturned the decision of the Pensions Ombudsman and held that an LEL offset to integrate benefits with the State scheme was not indirect discrimination and, had it been so, it would have been objectively justified.

Cases		
Decision	*Date*	*Main issues decided*
Beckmann v Dynamco Whicheloe Macfarlane Ltd *Case No C-164/00, [2002] 64 PBLR, [2002] All ER (D) 05 (Jun)*	4 Jun 2002	This case held that benefits payable on redundancy under the *NHS Compensation for Early Retirement Regulations* transfer under *TUPE* and the *Acquired Rights Directive* ('*ARD*') despite the fact that they are calculated by reference to the same rules used to calculate normal pension benefits. Early retirement benefits and benefits intended to enhance the conditions of such retirement, paid before the end of a 'normal working life' in the event of dismissal for redundancy are not 'old age, invalidity or survivors' benefits' within the meaning of *Article 3(3)* of the *ARD* and thus are not subject to exclusion from transfer.
Goodwin v UK *[2002] IRLR 664*	11 Jul 2002	The European Court held that the UK was in breach of *Article 8* (right to respect for private and family life) and *Article 12* (right to marry and to found a family) of the *European Convention on Human Rights*. The UK had failed legally to recognise that Ms Goodwin who underwent 'gender re-assignment' surgery was female. Ms Goodwin was therefore required to pay NICs until age 65. Had her sex change been legally recognised, NICs would have ceased at age 60.
Bellinger v Bellinger *[2003] 2 All ER 593*	10 Apr 2003	The House of Lords held that the marriage was not a valid marriage but declared that the non-recognition of gender reassignment for the purposes of allowing transsexuals to marry was incompatible with the right to respect for private and family life and the right to marry guaranteed by *Articles 8* and *12* of the *European Convention on Human Rights*.

Cases		
Decision	*Date*	*Main issues decided*
Kutz-Bauer v Freie und Hansestadt Hamburg *Case No C-187/00 [2003] All ER (D) 327 (Mar)*	20 Mar 2003	Provisions allowing workers over 55 to work part-time applied only until the date on which the worker became entitled to a statutory old age pension. For most women this was 60 and for most men it was 65. It was held that this was capable of breaching the *Equal Treatment Directive* and it was for the national court to determine whether there was in fact indirect discrimination which could not be objectively justified.
Martin v South Bank University *Case No C-4/01 [2004] IRLR 74*	6 Nov 2003	It was decided by the ECJ that only benefits paid from the time when an employee reaches the end of his normal working life can be classified as 'old age' benefits within the meaning of *Article 3(3)* and are thus excluded from automatic transfer under *TUPE*.
Preston v Wolverhampton Healthcare NHS Trust (No. 3) [2004] IRLR 96	19 Dec 2003	Decision of the Employment Appeal Tribunal on a number of part-timer issues raised by the 2002 *Preston* case.
KB v National Health Service Pensions Agency *Case No C-117/01 [2004] All ER (EC) 1089*	7 Jan 2004	The ECJ confirmed that national legislation which prevents marriage (and therefore the enjoyment of certain pension benefits) for individuals who have undergone a sex change is in breach of EU law.
Allonby v Accrington and Rossendale College *Case No 256/01 [2004] IRLR 224*	13 Jan 2004	The ECJ's judgment on matters referred to it by the Court of Appeal following the 2001 *Allonby* case.
Leadenhall Independent Trustees Ltd v Welham *[2004] All ER (D) 423 (Mar)*	19 Mar 2004	The trustee of a scheme in surplus sought directions as to whether it had the power to augment benefits to neutralise the gender discrimination of GMPs.
Dacas v Brook Street Bureau (UK) Ltd *[2004] EWCA Civ 217*	19 Mar 2004	Court of Appeal decision indicating that agency workers could be employees of the organisation they provide services to.

Cases		
Decision	*Date*	*Main issues decided*
Matthews v Kent & Medway Towns Fire Authority *[2004] EWCA Civ 844*	2 Jul 2004	Case brought before the Court of Appeal under the *Part-time Workers (Prevention of Less Favourable Treatment) Regulations 2000 (SI 2000/1551)*. The EAT had held that a part-time fire fighter had not suffered less favourable treatment than full-time fire fighters despite being excluded access from the pension scheme. The fire fighters' appeal to the Court of Appeal was dismissed.
Cross v British Airways *[2005] 26 PBLR*	23 Mar 2005	This case looked at the expense involved in allowing employees to work later.
Astbury v Gist Ltd *[2005] All ER (D) 165 (Apr)*	14 Apr 2005	Application of the *Dacas* case in relation to agency workers.
British Airways Plc v Jessica Starmer *(2005) EAT [2005] IRLR 863*	6 July 2005	Application of the *Allonby* case.
Shaikh v Department for Constitutional Affairs *[2005] All ER (D) 154 (Sep)*	31 Aug 2005	Case distinguishing the *Allonby* decision in relation to the requirement for a 'comparator'.
Matthews v Kent and Medway Towns Fire Authority *[2006] All ER 171*	1 Mar 2006	Part-time fire-fighters case is remitted back to the employment tribunal.
Preston v Wolverhampton Healthcare NHS Trust (No 3) *[2006] UKHL 13*	8 Mar 2006	Decision of the House of Lords in relation to the point at which the time limit for a part-timer's claim begins to run following a *TUPE* transfer.
Richards v Secretary of State for Work and Pensions *Case No C-423/04 [2006] All ER (EC) 895*	27 Apr 2006	Case dealing with discrimination against transsexuals.

Cases		
Decision	*Date*	*Main issues decided*
Grant v United Kingdom *(2007) 44 EHRR 1*	23 May 2006	It was held that G (a transsexual) was entitled to claim a lack of legal recognition from the date of the judgment in *Goodwin v UK (2002).*
National Pensions Office v Jonkman *[2005] All ER (D) 47 Case No C-231/06*	21 Jun 2007	Decision of the ECJ in relation to back-dated employee contributions following a successful claim for backdated membership of the scheme.
R (on the application of the Incorporated Trustees of the National Council for Ageing (Age Concern England)) v Secretary of State for Business, Enterprise and Regulatory Reform *Case No C-388/07*	24 Jul 2007	The National Council on Ageing (NCA) persuaded the High Court that it should ask the European Court of Justice whether the *Age Regulations*, which permit retirement at age 65, are lawful.
Cripps v Trustee Solutions Ltd and Dubery *[2007] EWCA Civ 771*	26 Jul 2007	Court of Appeal decision relating to equalisation and the division of assets among different groups of members on winding up.
Bloxham v Freshfields *ET July 2007 [2007] PLR 375*	9–19 Jul 2007	Case before the employment tribunal looking at age discrimination and objective justification arguments.
Lindorfer v Council of the European Union *Case No C-277/04P [2009] All ER (EC) 569*	11 Sep 2007	Decision of the ECJ in relation to the use of sex based actuarial factors.

Cases		
Decision	*Date*	*Main issues decided*
Betafence Limited v Veys and Others *[2006] EWHC 999 (Ch)* *Trustee Solutions v Dubery* *[2006] 36 PBLR* *Harland and Wolff Pension Trustees Limited v Aon Consulting Financial Services Limited* *[2006] EWHC 1778 (Ch)* *Hodgson and Others v Toray Textiles Europe Limited and Others* *[2006] EWHC 2612 (Ch)* *Capital Cranfield Trustees Ltd v Beck [2008] EWHC 3181(Ch)*	2006–2008	Cases relating to equalisation and defective amendments.
Foster Wheeler Ltd v Hanley *[2009] EWCA Civ 651*	8 July 2008	The Court of Appeal allowed an employer's appeal against the High Court decision reached in November 2008. This case looked at the correct way to treat members with mixed retirement ages as a consequence of *Barber*.
Matthews and others v Kent & Medway Town Fire Authority and others 6100000/2001 (ET)	2008	The employment tribunal reconsiders the case of the part-time fire-fighters following a successful appeal to the House of Lords.
Tadao Maruko v Versorgungsanstalt der deutschen Bühnen *Case No C-267/06 [2008] All ER (EC) 977*	1 April 2008	ECJ decision relating to discrimination on the grounds of sexual orientations. This case has implications for the implementation of the *CPA 2004* in the UK.
Mayor and Burgesses of the London Borough of Lewisham v Malcolm *[2008] UKHL 43*	June 2008	Decision of the House of Lords which makes it considerably harder to prove disability-related discrimination.

Cases		
Decision	*Date*	*Main issues decided*
MacCulloch v ICI *Employment Tribunal*	22 July 2008	Decision of the EAT looking at the issue of age discrimination and justification.
Birgit Bartsch v Bosch und Siemens Hausgerate (BSH) Altersfursorge GmbH *Case No C-427/06 [2009] All ER (EC) 113*	23 Sept 2008	Consideration by the Advocate General of a young spouse provision of a German pension scheme which prevented a widow from receiving a pension because she was more than 15 years younger than the deceased member.

Chapter 10

Investment

Introduction

10.1 One of the fundamental duties of any trustee is to invest the monies under his control so as to produce income for his trust. In doing so, a trustee must act within the boundaries imposed on him by the trust instrument, by statutory restrictions and by case law. The duties and obligations are onerous and, consequently, many trustees prefer to delegate their powers to professional fund managers.

This chapter deals with the powers of trustees regarding the investment of the funds for which they are responsible and the duties imposed on them when exercising those powers. It considers how, and to whom, trustees may delegate their powers and briefly discusses the implications of the *Financial Services and Markets Act 2000* (*FSMA 2000*). Finally, it examines the protection afforded to trustees in respect of investment decisions. This chapter is particularly relevant to trustees of self-administered schemes, whether large or small, who will be more directly involved with investment activities than trustees of insured schemes.

Following the publication, on 6 March 2001 of the report by Paul Myners, 'Institutional Investment in the United Kingdom: A Review', the Government issued a voluntary Code of Best Practice on 2 October 2001, containing ten key principles which relate to the setting of investment objectives, and the method by which pension trustees should take investment decisions.

Although the Code of Practice is voluntary, the Myners' review recommended that there should be a subsequent review, to be commenced in March 2003, to establish how effective the voluntary Code had been in bringing about change. The Government said that, if change had not occurred in the methods by which trustees reached investment decisions by March 2003 on a voluntary basis, it would legislate. *PA 2004* introduces new knowledge and understanding requirements, which are dealt with at **10.51** below together with the Myners' Code of Practice. In December 2004, the Government released its review of progress in implementing the Myners' Principles.

The review found that progress in several key areas was behind schedule and recommendations were made to strengthen the principles. The National Association of Pension Funds (NAPF) agreed to undertake a further progress review in 2007 (see **10.51** below). In the light of the evidence and recommendations from the NAPF's progress review, the Government will consider the need for policy action, including whether to take forward any of the proposals suggested in 2004.

The meaning of investment

10.2 The classic statement of the legal meaning of the words 'invest' and 'investment' was given in the case *Re Wragg* in which Mr Justice Lawrence said that:

> 'Without attempting to give an exhaustive definition of the words "invest" and "investment" I think that the words "to invest" when used in an investment clause may safely be said to include as one of its meanings "to apply money in the purchase of some property from which interest or profit is expected and which property is purchased in order to be held for the sake of the income which it will yield".' (*Re Wragg [1919] 2 Ch 58* at 64)

On a strict interpretation, an asset purchased for some reason other than deriving an income would therefore not be an investment; for example, land that is purchased for the financial gain it will produce when it is sold will not be an investment unless it is let for a rent or produces some other income.

In recent years there have been indications of greater flexibility in the definition of investment. In *Marson v Morton*, Sir Nicolas Browne-Wilkinson V-C recognised that in the modern financial arena 'new approaches to investment have emerged putting the emphasis in investment on the making of capital profit at the expense of income yield' (*Marson v Morton [1986] 1 WLR 1343* at 1350). He gives the purchase of short-dated stocks (which give a capital yield but no income) and works of art as examples of common ways of investing and concludes that the mere fact that land is not income-producing should not be decisive on the question of whether it was bought as an investment.

The Pension Law Review Committee used the term investment to mean 'any application of assets, whether or not investments in the technical sense, and thus (including), for example, stock lending and borrowing' (Report of the Pension Law Review Committee, page 342). Unfortunately this approach was not adopted in *PA 1995*, which does not define 'investment'. Consequently there remains doubt as to the modern meaning of the term. The cautious approach must be to adopt the strict interpretation set out in *Re Wragg* in the absence of a more definitive modern definition.

Trading or investing?

10.3 Broadly speaking, registered pension schemes are not liable for income tax or capital gains tax on the investments they make (see **5.25** to **5.27** above for details of the taxation of pension schemes). However, in certain circumstances, HMRC may argue that trustees are not investing but are in fact trading. If a pension scheme is found to be trading, rather than investing, the transaction will fall outside the scope of the statutory tax exemptions and the trustees will be liable for the appropriate income tax. It is, therefore, important to determine whether the proceeds of the sale of an asset constitute the realisation of an investment, or are the profits of a trade.

Badges of trade

10.4 The 1954 Royal Commission (Cmd 9474, paragraph 116) identified 'six badges of trade' as being relevant in deciding whether a transaction is, or is not, to be treated as a trading transaction. These 'badges' are discussed below.

The subject matter of the realisation

10.5 Generally, property which does not yield an income is more likely to have been acquired for the purpose of trading rather than as an investment. A one-off transaction of the purchase of a type of property which yields no income followed by a profit on a sale has been held to be trading (*IRC v Fraser (1942) 24 TC 498*). However, dealing with an asset which does not produce an income, does not of itself necessarily imply trading; an asset can quite legitimately be purchased solely for the capital profit it will yield (*Marson v Morton [1986] 1 WLR 1343*). Some forms of property, such as manufactured articles, are usually purchased for trading and can only very exceptionally be an investment.

The length of the period of ownership

10.6 There is an inference of trading where property is realised within a short time of acquisition. However, if trustees can show a good reason for their actions the presumption that the trustees are trading may be rebutted. There is no doubt, however, that a quick sale helps to support the finding of trading, especially where other indications of trading are present (*Turner v Last (1965) 42 TC 517*; *Eames v Stepnell Properties Ltd (1966) 43 TC 678*).

The frequency or number of similar transactions by the same person

10.7 If there are repeated instances over a period of the same type of activity being carried out by trustees, the number of transactions may in itself give rise to a presumption of trading. In some cases, it may be conclusive proof (*Pickford v Quirke (1927) 13 TC 251*). However, much will depend on the reasons for the sale.

Supplementary work on or in connection with the property realised

10.8 If land is purchased and then developed for sale, there is often a suggestion that the trustees are to sell the property soon and thus enter into a transaction in the nature of trade. However, this is not necessarily the case; trustees may well refurbish a property simply in order to retain its marketability in the long term, which most prudent investors would, and probably should, do.

The circumstances that were responsible for the realisation

10.9 There are many situations that may arise which call for an asset to be sold very shortly after its purchase, for example, changes in market conditions or the payment of a large cash benefit. In such a situation it would be sensible for the trustees or their investment advisers to record in writing the reason for the sale so that any suggestion of 'trading' can be rebutted.

It should be remembered that one of the prime duties of a trustee is to exercise his duty of investment with diligence and prudence. Even if there may be a potential tax charge on grounds of trading, trustees should realise an asset, where appropriate, if not to do so would be a breach of trust. The duty of a trustee to invest prudently can be a very powerful weapon against allegations of trading.

Motive

10.10 The intention or motive of the trustees can be an important factor. There are cases in which the purpose of a transaction is clearly discernible, but where this is not so it may be sensible for the trustees or their investment advisers to note the reason for the purchase or the sale of an asset. In the absence of direct evidence of the trustees' intentions, motive can be inferred from the surrounding circumstances.

Application of the badges of trade

10.11 The 'badges of trade' are of general application to all types of transactions, where tax mitigation may be in question; they were not drawn up to apply solely to trustees or to pension schemes, and so may not always be relevant to dealings by pension scheme trustees. The onus of proving trading is, in reality, on HMRC, as far as occupational pension schemes are concerned (*Salt v Chamberlain (1979) 53 TC 143*) and there are presumptions to assist trustees who are accused of trading.

Presumption against trading

10.12 It is common practice for frequent changes to be made in a scheme's portfolio of Stock Exchange securities. Normally no inference of trading would be drawn from such changes. However, if there is evidence of a large turnover of a scheme's holdings, which appears to have been carried out pursuant to a deliberate and organised plan of buying and selling with a view to profit-making, it may be possible to infer that trading has taken place (*Cooper v C & J Clarke Ltd (1982) 54 TC 670*).

In the case of *Clark v British Telecom Pension Scheme [1999] 6 PBLR 21*, Lightman J overturned the earlier decision of the Commissioners of the Inland Revenue that profits received from the sub-underwriting of share issues by the trustees were not profits from trade rather than gains from investments and hence were not subject to tax. Lightman J found instead that the trustees had been involved in operations of a 'commercial character' for a period of years and the activity had all the hallmarks of trade being 'frequent (or habitual) and organised as well as extensive, business-like and for profit' (paragraph 31). However, the trustees of British Telecom Pension Scheme appealed and the Court of Appeal (*[2000] 21 PBLR 13*) held that the sub-underwriting activities of the trustees were an integral and indissoluble part of their investment activities. Income from the sub-underwriting was not therefore trading income and was exempt from tax by virtue of *ICTA 1988, s 592*. Lightman J's decision was therefore reversed. Appeal to the House of Lords was refused.

Powers given under the trust instrument

10.13 The majority of trust deeds governing pension schemes contain wide powers permitting investments in many areas. Trustees may also be given power to trade, but when such a power is missing there is a very strong argument against any allegation of trading; it is unlikely that a trustee will knowingly commit a breach of trust in order to trade.

Power of investment

10.14 A trustee's power of investment will derive from two sources; statute and the trust instrument.

Statutory power to invest

10.15 Prior to 6 April 1997, statutory powers of investment were conferred on trustees by the *Trustee Investments Act 1961* (*TIA 1961*) and, to a small extent, the *Trustee Act 1925*. Even before *PA 1995*, it was rare for a pension scheme to rely solely on the powers conferred by these Acts as they are very restrictive in the types of investments they permit. So far as pension scheme trustees are concerned, the provisions of *TIA 1961* have largely been replaced or superseded by the provisions of *PA 1995* and so are no longer generally relevant.

PA 1995, s 34(1) confers a wide power of investment on trustees by providing that they have the same power to 'make an investment of any kind as if they were absolutely entitled to the assets of the scheme; subject only to any restriction imposed by the scheme'. The power is also subject to the provisions of *PA 1995, s 36(1). Section 34(1)*, which takes effect as if it were contained in the scheme's governing documentation, was intended to aid trustees who were prevented from making some types of investment by an overly restrictive power of investment. However, the wording of the provision causes problems which were not intended. If the term 'investment' is narrowly construed, certain traditional assets including, arguably, group life policies, are not investments under *PA 1995,* and *s 34* alone would not permit trustees to purchase them. Consequently, trustees still need a carefully drafted investment power, allowing them specifically to undertake transactions, or to purchase assets, which fall outside the meaning of investment used in *Re Wragg [1919] 2 Ch 58.*

The trust instrument

10.16 It is common for trustees to be given power to invest, or otherwise apply the monies under their control in any manner which they could do if they were absolutely and beneficially entitled to the assets of the scheme and in any manner which they could do as trustees of a pension scheme. The second limb is necessary to allow trustees to invest in those investments, such as exempt unit trusts which are only available to trustees of funds which are not liable for income or capital gains tax. The ability to 'apply' the fund is designed to permit trustees to purchase assets which are not technically investments.

Trustees will generally be given specific power to purchase certain assets such as traded options, financial futures, life assurance contracts and assets which are to be held for capital growth rather than for the income they produce. Trustees may also be given power to underwrite new issues on the Stock Market and possibly the power to engage in stock lending. Trustees are sometimes given specific power to trade, but this is less common (see **10.13** above).

Trustees may also be given the power to commingle the assets of their scheme with the assets of one or more other schemes in a common investment fund, which will usually be set up under an independent trust. In order to continue to benefit from the tax advantages available to 'registered pension schemes', all schemes participating in such a fund must themselves be registered schemes.

It is also advisable to have express power in the trust deed to lease, charge and otherwise deal in and conduct the management of real property, and to have a general power to give indemnities and guarantees.

Notwithstanding the supposedly wide power of investment given in *PA 1995*, the investment provisions contained in most trust deeds will probably continue to spell out the powers of the trustees, since, if they do not, there is the possibility of the trustees exceeding their powers by inadvertently purchasing an asset which is not an investment and which cannot, therefore, be purchased under the power given by *PA 1995, s 34*.

Duties of trustees when exercising their investment power

10.17 When exercising their investment power, trustees must consider the duties imposed on them under the trust instrument, by statute and by case law. The main duties are set out in **10.18** to **10.22** below.

The duty to act in the best interests of the beneficiaries

10.18 One of the fundamental duties of a trustee is to exercise his powers in the best interests of the beneficiaries of the scheme and to act fairly between different classes of beneficiaries. In the context of an investment power, a beneficiary's best interests will generally mean his best financial interests. Consequently an investment power must generally be exercised so as to produce the best return possible, having regard to the level of risk involved (*Cowan v Scargill [1984] 2 All ER 750*).

The prudent man test

10.19 The basic duty of a trustee, when exercising his investment power, is to choose investments which are within the terms of his trust and, in selecting those investments, to 'take such care as an ordinary prudent man would take if he were minded to make (an investment) for the benefit of other people for whom he felt morally bound to provide' (*Re Whiteley (1886) 33 Ch D 347*).

The House of Lords decision in *Learoyd v Whiteley* sets out the principles which trustees must consider when exercising their investment power as follows:

> 'As a general rule the law requires of a trustee no higher degree of diligence in the execution of his office than a man of ordinary prudence would exercise in the management of his own private affairs. Yet he is not allowed the same discretion in investing the money of the trusts as

> if he were a person *sui juris* dealing with his own estate. Business men of ordinary prudence may, and frequently do, select investments which are more or less of a speculative character; but it is the duty of a trustee to confine himself to the class of investments which are permitted by the trust, and likewise to avoid all investments of that class which are attended with hazard.'
>
> (*Learoyd v Whiteley (1887) 12 AC 727*, Lord Watson at 733)

Sir Robert Megarry has reiterated and clarified the standard required of a trustee in exercising his powers of investment, making it clear that, in addition to the above, the duty 'includes the duty to seek advice on matters which the trustee does not understand, such as the making of investments, and on receiving that advice to act with the same degree of prudence' (*Cowan v Scargill [1984] 2 All ER 750* at 762).

PA 2004, ss 247 and *248* contain provisions concerning the 'requirement for knowledge and understanding' of trustees and impose more specific and onerous requirements for trustees of occupational pension schemes. This is dealt with further at **10.51** below.

However wide the provisions of an express investment power may be, the trustees are not absolved from their duty to consider whether a proposed investment is such that it is prudent and right for them, as trustees, to make it. The mere fact that a certain type of investment is authorised by the trust instrument or by statute does not mean that it is necessarily proper to invest in it. Even though, under *PA 1995*, trustees have power to invest at their absolute discretion and as if they were absolute owners, they should remember that they must act as trustees in exercising that power. Moreover, *PA 2004* amends *PA 1995, s 36* to ensure compliance with *Article 18(1)* of the *Pensions Directive (2003/41/EC)*. This directive requires investments to be carried out in accordance with the 'prudent person principle' as defined in the Directive. The detailed requirements are contained in the *Occupational Pension Schemes (Investment) Regulations 2005 (SI 2005/3378)* (the '*2005 Investment Regulations*'). The *2005 Investment Regulations* replaced the *1996 Investment Regulations* with effect from 30 December 2005, together with the changes to *PA 1995, ss 35* and *36* and the insertion of new *s 36A*.

When exercising their investment power, *PA 1995, s 36* requires trustees (and any fund manager to whom a discretion has been delegated) to exercise their powers of investment in accordance with the *2005 Investment Regulations*. These Regulations require that the trustees of a trust scheme (and any fund manager to whom any discretion has been delegated) must exercise their powers of investment, in accordance with the provisions of *reg 4*:

- The assets must be invested in the best interests of members and beneficiaries and, in the case of a potential conflict of interest, in the sole interest of members and beneficiaries.

- The powers of investment, or the discretion, must be exercised in a manner calculated to ensure the security, quality, liquidity and profitability of the portfolio as a whole.
- Assets held to cover the scheme's technical provisions must also be invested in a manner appropriate to the nature and duration of the expected future retirement benefits payable under the scheme.
- The assets of the scheme must consist predominately of investments admitted to trading on regulated markets; investments in assets which are not admitted to trading on a regulated market must in any event be kept to a prudent level.
- The assets of the scheme must be properly diversified in such a way as to avoid excessive reliance on any particular asset, issuer or group of undertakings and so as to avoid accumulations of risk in the portfolio as a whole. Investments in assets issued by the same issuer or by issuers belonging to the same group must not expose the scheme to excessive risk concentration.
- Investment in derivative instruments may be made only insofar as they:

  (*a*) contribute to a reduction of risks; or

  (*b*) facilitate efficient portfolio management (including the reduction of cost or the generation of additional capital or income with an acceptable level of risk),

  and any such investment must be made and managed so as to avoid excessive risk exposure to a single counter party and to other derivative operations.

Note that *reg 4* does not apply to a scheme that has fewer than 100 members but regard must still be had to the need for diversification of investments, in so far as appropriate to the circumstances of the scheme. *Regulation 9* of the *2005 Investment Regulations* also partially disapplies *reg 4* in respect of schemes being wound up.

PA 1995, s 36 also requires trustees to obtain and consider 'proper advice' before making any investment in order to ascertain whether the investment is suitable, having regard to the need for diversification (see **10.20** below) and whether it is in accordance with the statement of investment principles (see **10.23** below). *Section 36* (as amended by *PA 2004*) requires 'proper advice' to be taken on the question of whether the investment is satisfactory taking into account the requirements of the *2005 Investment Regulations*, some of which are referred to above, so far as relating to the suitability of the investments.

Broadly speaking, proper advice is advice from a person authorised under *FSMA 2000* in relation to investments covered by that Act. In any other case proper advice must be obtained from a person whom the trustees reasonably believe to be qualified by his ability in, and practical experience of, financial matters and to have the appropriate knowledge and experience of the management of the investments of pension schemes. Trustees must ensure that they obtain confirmation of the 'proper advice' given in writing in order to comply with the requirements of *PA 1995*.

Civil penalties can be levied if trustees fail to take all reasonable steps to ensure compliance with the requirements set out in *PA 1995, s 36* (see APPENDIX I).

The duty to diversify

10.20 Trustees are required to exercise their powers of investment in accordance with the requirements of the *2005 Investment Regulations* and *PA 1995, s 36(3), (4)*. The trustees and any fund manager to whom any investment discretion has been delegated must exercise their investment powers in particular in accordance with *2005 Investment Regulations, reg 4* which provides that 'The assets of the scheme must be properly diversified in such a way as to avoid excessive reliance on any particular asset, issuer or group of undertakings and so as to avoid accumulations of risk in the portfolio as a whole'.

In addition to the above requirements, *PA 2004* inserted a new *s 36A* into *PA 1995* concerning restrictions on borrowing by trustees, or the fund manager to whom any discretion has been delegated under *PA 1995, s 34*. The *2005 Investment Regulations* provide that they cannot borrow money or act as a guarantor in respect of the obligations of another person where the borrowing is liable to be repaid, or liability under a guarantee is liable to be satisfied, out of the assets of the scheme. This is stated not to preclude borrowing made only for the purposes of providing liquidity for the scheme and on a temporary basis.

The requirement imposed on the trustees to diversify is also important from the actuary's standpoint, particularly in mature schemes. Although the actuary does not advise between one investment and another he may, and frequently does, become involved in deciding investment policy and asset allocation of the scheme. The actuary will ascertain the liabilities of a scheme and will advise on the short, medium and long-term liabilities. He should then be able to advise on the various types of investment and, for example, how they should be split to allow the trustees sufficient cash funds to provide lump sum and pension benefits for the beneficiaries as they fall due.

The trustees, or more likely the fund managers, will look at the strategy for the short, medium and long-term cash needs which the actuary has mapped out and should select investments that meet those needs. Not only must they look at diversification from that standpoint but they must also look at diversification on a second level. Therefore, if a certain percentage of the fund has to be put in short-term investments, they should not put all of the fund designated for such purpose into one investment; they should spread the risk amongst a group of investments.

Moral and ethical considerations

10.21 There has been much discussion on the ability of trustees legitimately to consider moral and ethical considerations in preference to financial return on any particular investment.

Decided case law indicates that trustees cannot invest other than on the usual criteria (financial returns, security and diversification). However, if, for example, trustees wish to make an ethically acceptable investment which will produce a financial return that is at least as good as that produced by any other suitable (although perhaps not so ethically sound) investment, there is no reason why they cannot do so. Essentially, they must act with the standard of care and prudence required by the law. What the trustees cannot generally do is subordinate the interests of the beneficiaries to ethical or social demands (see *Cowan v Scargill [1984] 2 All ER 750*; *Bishop of Oxford v Church Commissioners [1991] PLR 185*; *Martin v The City of Edinburgh District Council [1989] PLR 9*). In some circumstances, trustees 'may even have to act dishonourably (though not illegally) if the interests of their beneficiaries require it' (*Cowan v Scargill [1984] 2 All 750* at 761).

However, although trustees cannot allow their own political, social and moral views to override financial considerations when making investments, they can in some circumstances be influenced by the views of the beneficiaries of the scheme. If all the beneficiaries are known to hold strong moral views on a matter '... it might not be for the "benefit" of such beneficiaries to know that they are obtaining rather larger financial returns under the trust by reason of investments in those activities than they would have received if the trustees had invested the trust funds in other investments' (*Cowan v Scargill [1984] 2 All ER 750* at 761). The circumstances where this principle could apply in relation to a pension scheme must be very limited, due to the inevitable divergence of opinions of a large number of beneficiaries.

The debate over whether trustees can, or even should, invest in so-called ethical or socially responsible investments has moved on. The *Occupational Pension*

Schemes (Investment, and Assignment, Forfeiture, Bankruptcy etc) Amendment Regulations 1999 (SI 1999/1849) amended the *Occupational Pension Schemes (Investment) Regulations 1996 (SI 1996/3127)* and came into force on 9 August 1999, except for the provisions relating to ethical/social/environmental investment policies and voting which came into force on 3 July 2000. These require the trustees to state in their statement of investment principles (a) the extent (if at all) social, environmental or ethical considerations are taken into account in the selection, retention and realisation of investments; and (b) their policy (if any) in relation to the exercise of the rights (including voting rights) attaching to investments. At *2005 Investment Regulations, reg 2* similar requirements for inclusion of reference to social, environmental or ethical considerations are provided.

Duty to review investments

10.22 A trustee's responsibility does not stop once he has made an investment; trustees have a duty to review the investments of the scheme from time to time. Although this is a continuing duty it will be particularly relevant in a scheme which is close to winding up as it may be advisable to match the investments of the fund with the liabilities of the scheme. Even where a scheme is wholly insured trustees should still review the position from time to time as it may be sensible for the trustees to consider changing the insurance company or to become self-administered.

Under *PA 1995, s 36*, trustees must consider at what intervals they should obtain 'proper advice' in respect of investments they retain and must then obtain and consider such advice accordingly (see **10.19** above regarding the meaning of 'proper advice'). In determining the appropriate intervals the trustees must consider the circumstances of the case and, in particular, the nature of the investment. It might, for example, be appropriate to review the scheme's gilt portfolio less frequently than its equity portfolio as equities are a more volatile investment than gilts.

Statutory obligations

Statement of investment principles

10.23 Under *PA 1995, s 35*, trustees must secure that a written statement of investment principles is prepared and maintained governing the decisions about investments for the purposes of the scheme and that that statement is reviewed and revised at intervals. Trustees (or the fund manager acting on their behalf) must exercise their investment power with a view to giving effect to the principles contained in the statement, so far as reasonably practicable (*PA 1995, s 36(5)*).

Section 35 should be read together with the provisions of *2005 Investment Regulations, reg 2*. Under these provisions, the trustees of the scheme must secure:

- that a statement of investment principles is prepared and maintained for the scheme (*PA 1995, s 35*); and
- that it is reviewed at least every three years and without delay after any significant change in investment policy (*2005 Investment Regulations, reg 2*).

The statement must cover, among other matters, the trustees' policy for securing compliance with *PA 1995, s 36* (see **10.19** and **10.20** above) and their policy about:

(*a*) the kinds of investments to be held;

(*b*) the balance between different kinds of investments;

(*c*) risks (including the ways risks are to be measured and managed);

(*d*) the expected return on investments;

(*e*) the realisation of investments;

(*f*) the extent (if at all) to which social, environmental or ethical considerations are taken into account in the selection, retention and realisation of investments; and

(*g*) their policy (if any) in relation to the exercise of the rights (including voting rights) attaching to the investments.

The agreed investment strategy set out in the statement of investment principles must accord with the general law discussed in **10.17** to **10.22** above, and be devised to reflect the liability position of the scheme in question.

PA 1995, s 35 and the requirements relating to statements of investment principles under the *2005 Investment Regulations* do not apply to a scheme which has fewer than 100 members or a scheme which is established by an enactment and is guaranteed by a public authority. For wholly insured schemes, although a statement of investment principles is required now, the requirements are modified and are less onerous (*2005 Investment Regulations, reg 8*).

Before a statement of investment principles is prepared or revised, trustees must:

(i) obtain and consider the written advice of a person whom they reasonably believe to be qualified by his ability in, and practical experience of, financial matters and to have the appropriate knowledge and experience of management of the investments of pension schemes; and

(ii) consult the scheme's sponsoring employer.

(*2005 Investment Regulations, reg 2*)

Where a scheme has more than one sponsoring employer, all the participating employers may nominate a person to represent them, in which case the trustees need only consult that person. Where the employers do not nominate a representative, each employer must be consulted individually unless all the employers notify the trustees to the contrary.

The Act does not define what is meant by 'consult'. Consultation does not mean consent; in fact, *PA 1995* specifically prohibits the exercise of any investment power being subject to the consent of the employer (*PA 1995, s 35(3)*). To comply with their duty to consult, trustees should allow the employer sufficient time to make representations and should ensure that they consider suggestions put forward by the employer with an open mind. If the trustees are obliged to consult all the employers, they may specify a reasonable period (which cannot be less than 28 days) within which the employers must make representations regarding the statement of investment principles; any representations made after the specified date can be ignored by the trustees.

The extent of the requirement to consult was considered in the case of *Pitmans Trustees v the Telecommunications Group plc [2004] PBLR 32, [2004] All ER (D) 143*. The Vice-Chancellor ('V-C') confirmed the above views, namely that, to comply with the consultation requirements then contained in *PA 1995, s 35(5)(b)*, trustees must go further than simply giving notice to the employer of the proposed changes to the statement of investment principles. Although no timeframe is prescribed in *s 35(5)(b)*, it was held that it is necessary to give adequate time for the employer to obtain and consider advice of its own on the proposals and to comment on the proposals. The V-C held that prior consultation is a pre-condition to the existence and exercise of the trustees' powers in *PA 1995, s 35* and, therefore, if prior consultation has not taken place, this pre-condition has not been satisfied, the power has not yet arisen and a purported exercise of it will be of no effect. The adoption of any revised statement of investment principles will be invalid as a result.

Trustees must confirm in their annual report whether they have produced a statement of investment principles in accordance with *PA 1995, s 35* and must also include a statement providing details of any investments which were not made in accordance with the statement of investment principles giving the reasons why and explaining what action has been or will be taken to resolve the position. A copy of the statement of investment principles must be provided to any member or beneficiary who requests it (*Occupational Pension Schemes (Disclosure of Information) Regulations 1996 (SI 1996/1655), reg 6*).

A failure to take all reasonable steps to prepare or maintain a statement of investment principles or to take advice from an appropriately qualified person could result in a trustee being fined (*PA 1995, s 35(6)*). See APPENDIX I.

Restrictions on employer-related investment

10.24 Trustees are under a statutory duty to ensure that not more than 5 per cent of the current market value of the resources of the scheme is invested in employer-related investments. Furthermore, none of the resources of a scheme may be invested in an employer-related loan or in any employer-related investment if it would involve the trustees entering into a transaction at an undervalue (see *PA 1995, s 40* and *2005 Investment Regulations, reg 12*).

In summary, employer-related investments are defined under *PA 1995, s 40* as:

(*a*) shares or other securities issued by the employer or by any person who is connected with, or an associate of, the employer (for definitions of connected and associated employers, see *PA 1995, s 123* and **14.81** below);

(*b*) land which is occupied by, or used by, or subject to a lease in favour of, the employer or by any person who is connected with, or an associate of, the employer;

(*c*) property (other than land) which is used for the purposes of any business carried on by the employer or by any person who is connected with, or an associate of, the employer;

(*d*) loans to the employer or any person who is connected with, or an associate of, the employer;

(*e*) other prescribed investments.

The *2005 Investment Regulations* contain the list of investments prescribed as employer-related investments at *reg 11*.

If any sums due and payable by a person (including, but not limited to, an employer) to the trustees of a scheme remain unpaid they are to be regarded, for the purposes of *PA 1995, s 40*, as a loan made to that person by the trustees and may consequently be treated as an employer-related investment.

The *2005 Investment Regulations* contain relaxations to the restrictions on employer-related investment at *reg 13*. For example, employer-related investments will not include certain types of insurance policies and additional voluntary contributions invested in employer-related investments with the written agreement of the member who paid the contributions.

Under *PA 1995, s 40*, if the resources of a scheme are invested in employer-related investments in excess of the maximum allowed, sanctions, in the form of a fine, could apply to any trustee who fails to take all reasonable steps to ensure compliance with the Act. Further, a trustee who agrees to make an employer-related investment is guilty of an offence and may be liable, in extreme cases, to imprisonment (see APPENDIX I).

The *2005 Investment Regulations* contain transitional provisions at *reg 14*.

The Financial Services and Markets Act 2000

10.25 The *Financial Services and Markets Act 2000* ('*FSMA 2000*'), which came into effect on 1 December 2001, provides for the regulation of the whole of the UK financial services and banking industry by a single regulator, the Financial Services Authority ('FSA').

Professional firms (solicitors, accountants and actuaries) who do not undertake FSA regulated activities such as providing investment advice are exempt from direct regulation by the FSA.

Such firms are also exempt if they only carry out certain restricted activities arising out of, or incidental to the provision of professional services.

It should be noted that, in the summer of 2009, both the Government and the Conservative Party issued White Papers on the future of financial regulation. Under the Government proposals, the FSA's powers would be increased and it would continue to be responsible for the regulation of financial institutions. The Conservative White Paper proposes a radical overhaul of the regulatory system through which the FSA and the existing tripartite system would be abolished and the prudential regulation of financial institutions would be the responsibility of a new Financial Regulation Division of the Bank of England. The Conservatives also propose to establish a new Consumer Protection Agency responsible for ensuring consumers are treated fairly.

Objectives of the FSA

10.26 The FSA has four principal objectives under *FSMA 2000*:

(*a*) maintaining market confidence;

(*b*) promoting public understanding of the financial system;

(*c*) the protection of consumers; and

(*d*) reducing financial crime, ie by the regulation of investment activities and persons authorised to carry on such activities.

Investment managers

10.27 Most investment managers providing financial services to pension scheme trustees classify their trustee clients as 'Professional Clients' under FSA rules which were amended in 2007 by the *Markets in Financial Instruments Directive*.

Prohibited activities

10.28 It is a criminal offence under *FSMA 2000, s 24* to carry out a 'regulated activity', without authorisation or exemption from authorisation.

What constitutes a regulated activity?

10.29 *FSMA 2000* and specifically the *Financial Services and Markets Act 2000 (Regulated Activities) Order 2001 (SI 2001/544)* (the '*Regulated Activities Order*') specify a wide range of regulated activities which include the following activities, namely:

(*a*) dealing in investments;

(*b*) arranging deals in investments;

(*c*) managing investments;

(d) advising on investments;

(*e*) establishing, operating or winding up a stakeholder pension scheme;

(*f*) establishing, operating or winding up a personal pension scheme;

(*g*) safeguarding and administering investments; and

(*h*) assisting in the administration and performance of a contract of insurance.

Specified investments, for the purposes of *FSMA 2000*, include shares and stocks, debentures, Government and public securities, certificates representing securities, units in collective investment schemes, rights under a stakeholder pension scheme or a personal pension scheme, options, futures, contracts for differences and rights under contracts of insurance (*Regulated Activities Order, Part III*). Land and cash are not investments for the purposes of *FSMA 2000*.

The position of the trustees

10.30 Ordinarily, where trustees deal, arrange deals or give advice in relation to investments, they are likely to benefit from the exclusions contained in the *Regulated Activities Order*. However, *Financial Services and Markets Act 2000 (Carrying on Regulated Activities by Way of Business) Order 2001 (SI 2001/1177), art 4* (the '*Business Order*') provides that trustees will be treated as carrying out the activity of managing investments by way of business, where assets are held for the purposes of an occupational pension scheme. An exception to this is where all 'day-to-day' decisions in the carrying on of that activity (except for certain exclusions in *Business Order, art 4(6)*) relating to securities or contractually based investments are taken by an authorised or exempted person or an overseas person who does not require authorisation. Most commonly trustees seek to benefit from this provision by delegating investment management activities to duly authorised fund managers.

The *Business Order* also provides that certain decisions relating to pooled vehicles will not be categorised as day-to-day decisions (see *Business Order, art 4(1)(b), (6)*).

The *Business Order* excludes decisions where trustees of occupational pension schemes are investing in pooled investment vehicles in general, if they have considered advice from a regulated person (as defined in the *Business Order*). Decisions to invest in such vehicles will not be caught by FSA regulation in those circumstances because the trustees in making these decisions will not be deemed to be managing investments by way of business.

Where a trustee undertakes investment management activities himself, he will need to be authorised under *FSMA 2000* and regulated by the FSA. The rules of the FSA are intended to ensure that those managing pension scheme assets are adequately trained and supervised and meet competence thresholds; that adequate records are kept; that proper investment contracts are entered into; and that adequate procedures exist to safekeep assets.

In supervising a fund manager (see **10.34** below), trustees must ensure that they do not inadvertently end up taking 'day-to-day' investment decisions which would require them to be authorised under *FSMA 2000*. There is no definition of 'day-to-day' in the *Business Order* but the FSA has issued guidance to trustees of pension schemes on the implications of *FSMA 2000* for them. The guidance is contained in the FSA's Perimeter Guidance Handbook, PERG 10.

The fact that decisions may be taken only infrequently does not, of itself, prevent a decision from being a 'day-to-day' decision. The nature of the decision, not its frequency, is the important factor. The fact that a trustee might only occasionally make decisions about buying new, or selling existing, investments would not prevent those decisions being day to day decisions. Similarly, frequent interventions outside scheduled review meetings with fund managers, or the making of recommendations to fund managers with a force amounting to a direction, might also amount to a 'day-to-day' decision. The guidance also makes it clear that 'day-to-day' decisions include decisions to 'buy, sell or hold particular investments'.

Trustees can make:

- strategic decisions (eg adopting a statement of investment principles; formulating general asset allocation policies; deciding the proportion of assets that should constitute particular investment categories; affecting the balance between income and growth; appointing new fund managers);
- decisions that need to be taken in exceptional circumstances (eg where the manager has a conflict of interest; where an investment decision raises sensitive policy considerations such as investments in certain territories; or following a change in fund managers which results in the scheme holding investments which a new fund manager does not want to take on); and
- day-to-day decisions about investments in pooled investment products, provided that they have first taken advice from an authorised, exempt or overseas person or an exempt or professional firm.

The guidance also makes it clear that persons other than trustees involved in pension schemes, be they employers, administrators, etc, will also require authorisation in circumstances analogous to those of trustees.

Care should also be taken when investing in common investment funds. These are usually established where an employer operates more than one pension scheme and it is decided to place all of the schemes' investments in one vehicle. Usually such arrangements are established to enable the participant schemes to benefit from the additional purchasing power, reduction in costs and wider market exposure that a larger investment arrangement may offer.

The selection and supervision of investment advisers

10.31 Quite apart from the *FSMA 2000* implications discussed in **10.25** to **10.30** above, many trustees will lack either the time or skill to manage directly their scheme's portfolio, and so will delegate their investment power to a professional fund manager. Although it is a fundamental rule of trust law that a trustee cannot delegate his powers and discretions, there are statutory exceptions to the rule and it can be overridden by the trust documents.

Position before PA 1995

10.32 *Trustee Act 1925, s 23* (now repealed) allowed trustees to employ and pay an agent to transact any business required in the execution of a trust. However, this provision did not allow a trustee to delegate the exercise of a discretion. The trustees still had to decide on the investments to be sold and purchased; the agent simply implemented the decisions made.

Trustee Act 1925, s 23 has now been replaced by *Trustee Act 2000, s 11*, which allows trustees to authorise any person to exercise any or all of their 'delegable functions' as their agent. Trustees may delegate any function other than:

(*a*) a function relating to the distribution of the assets of the trust;

(*b*) a power to decide whether payments from the trust funds should be made out of income or capital;

(*c*) a power to appoint trustees; or

(*d*) a power conferred by any other enactment or the trust instrument which permits the trustees to delegate their functions or to appoint a person to act as a nominee or custodian.

Trustee Act 1925, s 25 allows trustees to delegate the exercise of their discretions for a period of up to one year under a power of attorney, but does not explicitly allow for the remuneration of the person to whom the discretion has been delegated.

Due to the constraints of the statutory power to delegate, trustees are generally given power to delegate investment decisions and to appoint and remunerate advisers and agents, including investment advisers and fund managers, in their scheme's documentation.

Position after PA 1995

10.33 The statutory power allowing trustees to appoint agents and delegate the exercise of their investment power has been significantly extended from 6 April 1997 by *PA 1995*.

PA 1995, s 34 effectively permits delegation of investment decisions by the trustees where the delegation is:

(*a*) to a fund manager who is authorised under *FSMA 2000*;

(*b*) to a fund manager who is not authorised under *FSMA 2000, s 19* so long as any decisions made by that fund manager would not constitute activities of a specified kind under *FSMA 2000*;

(*c*) to a sub-committee of two or more trustees;

(*d*) in accordance with *Trustee Act 1925, s 25* (see **10.32** above).

Trustees cannot otherwise delegate any investment decision (*PA 1995, s 34(2)(b)*). As the provisions of *PA 1995* are overriding in this regard, even if the trust instrument permits delegation in other circumstances, it appears that the trustees cannot delegate outside the four situations referred to above. In the case of (*c*) and (*d*) above, the trustees' ability to delegate may be further restricted by the requirements of *FSMA 2000* (see **10.25** to **10.30** above).

PA 1995, s 34(2) permits trustees to delegate any discretion to make any decision about investments to a fund manager who is authorised under *FSMA 2000*. Provided that the trustees take all reasonable steps to satisfy themselves that the fund manager has the appropriate knowledge and experience for managing the investments of the scheme and is carrying out his work competently and complying with *PA 1995, s 36*, they will not be responsible for the acts or defaults of the fund manager. (See **10.19** above regarding the requirements of *s 36*, and see **10.34** below regarding supervision of a fund manager.)

PA 1995, s 34(5) provides that, subject to any restrictions imposed by the scheme, trustees may delegate investment decisions to a sub-committee of two or more of the trustees. However, in practice, the requirements of *FSMA 2000* may restrict the circumstances in which such a delegation would be appropriate. The trustees, or a person on their behalf, may also delegate decisions which do not constitute carrying on a regulated activity (within the meaning of *FSMA 2000*) to a fund manager who is not authorised under *FSMA 2000*. Trustees will remain liable for any acts or defaults of the sub-committee or the fund manager to whom the discretion has been delegated. However, if the trustees, or the person who delegated the discretion on their behalf, take all reasonable steps to ensure that such a fund manager has the appropriate knowledge and experience for managing the investments of the scheme and that he is carrying out this work competently and complying with *PA 1995, s 36*, the liability of the trustees for the acts and defaults of the fund manager can be excluded or restricted (see **10.50** below for discussion on restricting liability of trustees).

Although *PA 1995, s 34* gives trustees a power to delegate investment decisions, it does not give trustees explicit authority to remunerate any fund manager to whom such decisions have been delegated. The cautious approach is to ensure that the trust instrument contains power to remunerate fund managers although, arguably, there is an implicit power to do so. Although the statutory power to delegate investment discretions has certainly been widened by *PA 1995*, most trust deeds will probably continue to include some form of express powers of delegation. The relationship between the trustees and the fund manager they appoint is, and will continue to be, governed to a large extent by the terms of the agreement entered into between them.

PA 1995, s 47 requires an individual or a firm to be appointed by or on behalf of the trustees as fund manager if the assets of the scheme consist of or include investments (within the meaning of *FSMA 2000*) (see **10.29** above). The appointment of the fund manager must be made in writing and must specify the date on which the appointment is due to take effect, to whom the fund manager is to report and from whom the fund manager is to take instructions (*Occupational Pension Schemes (Scheme Administration) Regulations 1996 (SI 1996/1715), reg 5*).

Neither the Act nor the regulations made under *PA 1995, s 47* impose any requirements or restrictions regarding the qualifications or experience required of a person to be appointed as a fund manager. He does not, for example, have to be authorised under *FSMA 2000*. In reality trustees are likely to appoint the person to whom they have delegated their investment decisions but this is not a requirement of the Act. Indeed, on a literal reading of *PA 1995*, a fund manager appointed under *PA 1995, s 47* need play no role in the scheme whatsoever.

Supervision of a fund manager

10.34 Trustees have a general duty to supervise and monitor the performance of a fund manager. In particular, trustees should ensure that the fund manager is carrying out his work competently and complying with the requirements of *PA 1995* if they wish to benefit from the statutory exoneration provision contained in *s 34(4)*, which is applicable where an FSA authorised manager is appointed (see **10.33** above and **10.50** below). Supervising does not imply that the trustees should continually check up on their fund manager but it does impose an obligation to review his appointment from time to time. If the fund manager is regularly performing below the market performance or is outside the benchmark set by the trustees, the trustees should ask why this is and, if appropriate, consider whether they wish to continue their arrangement with that fund manager.

The liability of investment advisers

Duties arising from the agreement

10.35 As a matter of general contract law, a fund manager is obliged to act in accordance with the terms of his contract and must not exceed his authority or he will be liable for a breach of contract even if he acted in his client's best interests (*Fray v Voules (1859) 1 E&E 839*). A fund manager may be required to follow the trustees' instructions, but he cannot be obliged to commit an illegal act. It is not enough for the fund manager simply to follow the trustees' instructions and to observe to the letter the terms of his written agreement; he is in addition contractually bound to act with due care and skill. As a fund manager is remunerated for his services he must perform his duty exercising the care, skill and diligence which it is usual, necessary and proper for professional fund managers to employ.

FSMA 2000 has, to an extent, dictated the terms of the contractual relationship between fund manager and trustees. Under the FSA Rules a fund manager cannot generally manage the investments of trustees on a discretionary basis unless there is in place an investment management agreement regulating the rights and liabilities of the trustees and the investment manager. 'Standard' terms and conditions for discretionary fund management are now published by the Investment Management Association ('IMA'). We are informed by the IMA that the most recent edition of the standard terms was published in July 2007. Many fund managers do, however, prefer to use their own 'standard' terms and conditions. The fact that such contracts are described as 'standard', however, should not dissuade trustees from questioning their terms or seeking additional protections.

The agreement will also contain a schedule setting out specific investment guidelines agreed upon by the fund manager and the trustees. Some of the 'standard' terms deal specifically with the fiduciary duties imposed upon fund managers and, where appropriate, these are considered in **10.42** to **10.47** below. The following provisions in the standard terms are examples of provisions which could cause concern for trustees, particularly in light of *PA 1995*.

Investment discretion

10.36 The fund manager and the trustees must agree on any restrictions or objectives to be imposed on the fund manager. Trustees should consider supplying the fund manager with a copy of the investment power they are delegating to ensure that the fund manager does not inadvertently make an investment which is outside the scope of the power. Trustees may also wish to clarify the details of their statement of investment principles with the fund manager and to append it to the written agreement to seek to ensure that he exercises the investment power with a view to giving effect to the principles contained in the statement of investment principles (see **10.23** above and *PA 1995, s 36(5)*).

Liability

10.37 Typically, fund managers will attempt to limit their contractual liability. In particular, they will look to exclude liability for indirect or consequential loss (even where they have had prior notice of special circumstances concerning the possibility of such loss arising). It is not uncommon for managers to attempt also to avoid responsibility for the acts and omissions of delegates and agents. Trustees should be concerned to obtain protection in respect of these 'third parties', given that they will have little involvement in their selection and may have no direct contractual relationship with them.

Uninvested cash

10.38 The IMA's standard terms provide that where specified in the client-specific terms, the manager will be responsible for managing the cash balances of the Fund. If uninvested cash is to be held in a bank account, trustees should ensure that in doing so, the fund manager is obliged to comply with the requirements of *PA 1995* relating to the retention of money in a bank account (*PA 1995, s 49*; *Occupational Pension Schemes (Scheme Administration) Regulations 1996 (SI 1996/1715), reg 11*). Consideration should also be given to the application of the 'FSA's Conduct of Business Rules' concerning the treatment of client money.

Shareholder activism

10.39 The IMA's standard terms provide among other things that a copy of the fund managers's policy on shareholder activism is available on request. Trustees should consider whether they should impose any specific conditions on the fund manager in light of their possible duties to exercise voting rights (see **10.49** below).

Valuation and reports

10.40 Trustees will need to consider when they require reports to be made regarding the valuation of investments. In agreeing on a suitable time frame they should bear in mind their duty to supervise the fund manager and in particular whether the timing is appropriate to ensure that they are satisfied that the fund manager is carrying out his work competently and complying with *PA 1995, s 36* (see **10.19** above). It may also be appropriate to require the fund manager to disclose other documents and information in his possession on the reasonable request of the trustees and to allow auditors or other advisers to inspect these documents. Trustees should also seek to resist clauses which provide that, following a specified period after the trustees have received a valuation or report, they may no longer bring an action against the manager for any breach which occurred during the period to which the valuation or report relates.

Custodianship

10.41 If the fund manager is to make use of the services of a custodian (who may or may not be a party to the investment management agreement), the trustees should ensure that they have formally appointed that custodian in accordance with *PA 1995, s 47* and *Occupational Pension Schemes (Scheme Administration) Regulations 1996 (SI 1996/1715), regs 4, 5*; otherwise they will not be able to rely on his skill or judgment without the risk of incurring sanctions in the form of a fine and/or removal (see APPENDIX I).

The debate as to whether trustees must also appoint sub-custodians was closed as a result of the publication of the *Occupational Pension Schemes (Scheme Administration) Amendment Regulations 1998 (SI 1998/1494)*, which relieved trustees of this obligation and enables them to rely on the skill and judgement of sub-custodians appointed by the custodian, provided that written disclosure of the extent to which (if any) the custodian accepts liability for its sub-custodians' actions is made in the custody agreement. Any changes to the liability position must be immediately notified to the trustees by the custodian. The trustees should also check that the custodian they appoint has the appropriate *FSMA 2000* authorisation.

Where the custodian is not a party to the investment management agreement, it is likely that there will be a separate 'global custody agreement'. Whether custody is dealt with in the investment agreement or otherwise, it will be necessary to deal with a number of key areas in addition to core custody, including: settlement of transactions (contractual or actual); cash management; liability for sub-custodians; and foreign exchange transactions.

Investment management and custody agreements should always be carefully reviewed by trustees and their advisers before being entered into, as some of their terms (for instance, the extent to which the agreement seeks to exempt the fund manager or custodian from liability) can expose the scheme to significant liabilities.

Fiduciary duties

10.42 Because the fund manager is handling trust monies, it may be argued that his duties are not only contractual, but also fiduciary, ie they may have to be exercised in the best interests of the members. To the extent that the fund manager is a fiduciary, the following duties may be implied.

Duty not to delegate

10.43 The general duty not to delegate applies not only to trustees but also to their agents. An agency relationship is based on the confidence one person has in another, and so an agent is in principle prohibited from delegating his authority to another person or even appointing a sub-agent (see *Allam & Co*

Ltd v Europa Poster Services Ltd [1968] 1 All ER 826). Delegation is, however, permitted in certain circumstances. For example, where the employment of a sub-agent is usual in managing a client's investments and is not unreasonable or inconsistent with the express terms of any written agreement; or where the act delegated is purely administrative and one which does not require or involve confidence or discretion.

Usually the investment management agreement will expressly permit a fund manager to delegate or appoint sub-agents, often without the consent of the trustees. Fund managers will often include a provision to the effect that they are not liable for the actions of their sub-agents unless they are 'connected companies'. As trustees may have no direct contractual relationship with the sub-agent it is advisable for them to ensure that, if the fund manager is to be allowed to delegate or appoint agents, he remains liable to the trustees for their acts or defaults.

The fund manager must not put himself in a position where his duties to the trustees conflict with his own interests

10.44 This is no more than the application of the equitable maxim that a person in a position of trust must not put himself in a situation in which his interest and his duty would be in conflict. An extreme example is where a fund manager seeks to buy an asset from the trustees. He would be attempting to achieve the impossible: trying to achieve the highest price for the trustees and at the same time endeavouring to pay the lowest possible price himself.

The IMA's standard terms specifically address potential conflicts of interest. They allow the fund manager to effect transactions where conflicts arise but provide that the fund manager must ensure that such transactions are effected on terms which are not materially less favourable to the trustees than if the conflict or potential conflict had not existed. The agreement lists in the client-specific schedule conflicts where the fund manager is not able to manage them effectively and it also refers to the fund manager's Conflict of Interest policy which provides detail of actual or potential conflicts of interest and how these are managed. The agreement provides that, to the extent that any fiduciary or equitable duties arise as a result of the services to be provided under the agreement, these duties will not prevent or hinder the fund manager or associate in effecting customer transactions.

A fund manager appointed under *PA 1995, s 47(2)* must, on being appointed, confirm that he will declare any conflict of interest affecting his relationship with the trustees immediately he becomes aware of it or, if he is regulated under *FSMA 2000*, in accordance with the rules of the FSA. However, many managers will interpret the rules to allow them to give generic style disclosures in the investment management agreement, thus avoiding the impracticality of making prior disclosure on a case-by-case basis.

Duty not to accept bribes

10.45 This duty is self explanatory. If a fund manager accepts a payment which could constitute a bribe and conducts himself in the way proposed by the person offering the bribe, it will be presumed that he has been influenced by the bribe and has breached his duty to the trustees. This presumption is not rebuttable and the trustees' loss is considered to be at least the amount of the bribe.

The person offering the bribe, as well as the fund manager who receives it, will be criminally liable. The fund manager will have to repay or forego any commission, profit or remuneration to which he would otherwise have been entitled from the trustees (*Andrews v Ramsay & Co [1903] 2 KB 635*). The trustees will be able to dismiss the fund manager without notice (*Bulfield v Fournier (1895) 11 TLR 282*) and claim for the amount of the bribe plus interest from the date upon which the bribe was received.

The fund manager has a duty not to take advantage of his position or the trustees' property in order to acquire a benefit for himself

10.46 An investment manager is liable to account to the trustees for any profits he makes using confidential information acquired in the course of his appointment (*Peter Pan Manufacturing Corporation v Corsets Silhouette Ltd [1963] 3 All ER 402*). The provisions relating to insider dealing contained in the *Criminal Justice Act 1993* may also be relevant. Broadly speaking, dealings in securities of a company by an individual who holds unpublished price-sensitive information in respect of that company by virtue of his connection with the company are prohibited. There are similar provisions with regard to advising others to deal in the shares or debentures of the company, and in respect of the communication of unpublished price-sensitive information to others where that person might reasonably be expected to make use of it for the purpose of dealing.

Ultra vires

10.47 If trustees make an investment which under their investment power is barred or outside its scope they are acting *ultra vires*. *Hazell v Hammersmith and Fulham London Borough Council [1990] 2 WLR 17* raised the concept of *ultra vires* in connection with a local authority's funds as certain of the activities were beyond those permissible by the relevant Local Government

Act. An act which is *ultra vires* is generally void and may not be ratified. Fund managers should be made aware of the powers of the trustees on whose behalf they are acting as otherwise they may enter into *ultra vires* arrangements. Equally, trustees are advised to ensure that they restrict fund managers from inadvertently acting outside the trustees' powers by ensuring that the investment management agreement contains appropriate investment restrictions.

Liability for breach of trust by agents

10.48 It is possible for an agent of trustees to be held liable in respect of a breach of trust committed by the trustees for whom he is acting, and which he, as agent, has facilitated. To be liable, the fund manager would have knowingly to commit a wrongful act in relation to the scheme's assets; in effect, he would have to know that the trustees did not have authority to give the instructions he followed or take the action he took. A fund manager may also be liable where he turns a blind eye to what is an obvious breach of trust where an honest and reasonable man would have considered it such.

Unless fund managers are either aware that a breach of trust is being committed by the trustees concerned, or the situation is such that it is, or should be, obvious to any competent fund manager that this is the case, they are entitled to assume that the instructions given are bona fide and within the powers of the trustees. If a fund manager follows an investment policy which he knows to be outside the powers of the trustees he renders himself liable to an action for breach of trust.

The most crucial factor on which liability of a fund manager depends is the precise terms of the investment powers given to the trustees and whether the fund manager is aware of them. Consequently trustees should ensure that the fund manager is fully apprised of any restrictions on their powers of investment and appropriate restrictions should be built into the investment management agreement.

Voting rights as a consequence of share ownership – is it a trust asset?

10.49 In the UK a high proportion of all shares in publicly quoted companies are held by pension funds. Trustees have traditionally exercised their voting rights only in exceptional cases but the sheer size of their voting power begs the question: are trustees and any fund managers to whom they have delegated their discretions in some way responsible for the actions of the companies in which they invest?

The Cadbury Committee recommended that institutional investors should make positive use of their voting rights and should also disclose their policies on the use of voting rights. The National Association of Pension Funds has recommended that trustees should decide on their voting policy and that voting policy should be made public. Trustees should then exercise their votes prudently and in the interests of scheme beneficiaries.

There is no doubt that in the US this idea has progressed further than in the UK. Pension funds in the US have been obliged to exercise their voting rights since 1988 in respect of US companies. This duty was extended in 1994 to include overseas companies and the effect of this duty is being felt in the UK (see **10.51** below).

The legislators in the UK have, to date, resisted attempts to impose a similar obligation on trustees. The previous Government successfully resisted an attempt by the then opposition to include such a duty in *PA 1995*. Although it was felt that imposing a mandatory duty to exercise voting rights was contrary to the general aim of deregulation and would be too difficult to enforce, it was accepted that trustees, or fund managers on their behalf, should be encouraged to exercise their voting rights.

Even in the absence of a statutory duty to exercise voting rights, there is a strong case for arguing that some form of duty exists. Trustees have a clear duty to act in the best interests of their members and this includes protecting the value of, and the income derived from, an investment. There may be circumstances where this can only be achieved by voting for or against certain proposals and in such situations trustees may be open to attack if they simply make no voting decision whatsoever. It should be remembered that positively abstaining from voting can be a legitimate voting decision. The duty is perhaps not necessarily to vote but to consider whether, and if so how, to vote.

Arguably, fund managers to whom discretionary investment responsibilities have been delegated have fiduciary responsibilities similar to the responsibilities of trustees. Accordingly, if trustees have a duty to consider exercising voting rights, it follows that fund managers must also concern themselves with the running of those companies in which they invest trustees' monies.

In 2002, the Government gave its response (its 'consultation document') to the Myners' Review in which it stated at Principle 6 on Activism:

> 'The mandate and trust deed should incorporate the principle of the US Department of Labor Interpretative Bulletin on activism. Trustees should also ensure that managers have an explicit strategy, elucidating the circumstances in which they will intervene in a company; the approach they will use in doing so; and how they measure the effectiveness of this strategy.'

In October 2002, the Institutional Shareholders Committee (which consisted of the Investment Management Association, the Association of British Insurers, the National Association of Pension Funds and the Association of Investment Trust Companies) unveiled the publication of a new Statement of Principles entitled, 'The Responsibilities of Institutional Shareholders and Agents – Statement of Principles'. It was updated in 2005 and again in June 2007. It develops the principles set out in its 1991 statement 'The Responsibilities of Institutional Shareholders in the UK' and expands on the Combined Code of Corporate Governance of June 1998. It sets out best practice for institutional shareholders such as pension schemes and/or agents in relation to their responsibilities in respect of investee companies.

The 2007 Statement provides that institutional shareholders' primary duty is to those on whose behalf they invest such as the beneficiaries of a pension scheme and they must act in the best interests of their clients. The Statement provides that effective monitoring will enable institutional shareholders and/or agents to exercise their votes and, where necessary to intervene objectively and in an informed way. It is also provided that institutional shareholders and/or agents should vote in respect of all shares held directly or on behalf of clients whenever practicable to do so.

Trustee liability and protection

10.50 The ultimate responsibility for investment decisions lies firmly with the trustees. The duties placed on trustees regarding investment are onerous, and becoming more so, not only in terms of the legal principles governing the propriety of their actions, but also in terms of the types of investment vehicles now available. It would be a foolish trustee who did not take specialist advice regarding the exercise of his investment power and, in any event, this is a statutory requirement (*PA 1995, s 36*). However, taking advice will not, on its own, necessarily protect the trustee; he/she must still act honestly with reasonable care and prudence. The increased responsibilities of trustees in *PA 2004* should also be noted (see further at **10.51** below). The fiduciary duties and liability of fund managers are discussed at **10.42** and **10.48** above but the following particular points arise in relation to investment decisions.

Trustees will be liable for the acts or defaults of the fund manager if they fail to take reasonable care in choosing the fund manager or in fixing or enforcing the terms of his engagement (*Steel v Wellcome Custodian Trustees Ltd [1988] 1 WLR 167*).

Trustee Act 2000, s 23 gives trustees some protection by providing that a trustee is not liable for any act or default of an agent, nominee or custodian, or a permitted substitute, when entering into or reviewing the arrangements under which that person acts, unless the trustee has failed to comply with the applicable duty of care.

Case law considers 'wilful default' to include both positive acts and a 'want of ordinary prudence' (*Speight v Gaunt (1883) 22 Ch D 727*; *Re Chapman [1896] 2 Ch 763*). There have been cases to the effect that 'wilful default' should be interpreted in the company law context so that it includes a deliberate or reckless breach of duty but not a negligent breach of duty (*Re Vickery [1931] 1 Ch 572*). However, the safer and the generally more acceptable view of trustees' responsibilities is the former definition.

It is common sense that trustees should take care when selecting their advisers and agents, as would any man with common prudence, and further exercise reasonable and responsible supervision.

Many trust deeds attempt to mitigate trustees' responsibilities by widely drafted exoneration clauses. However, *PA 1995, s 33* limits the extent to which liability in respect of investment decisions may be excluded by providing that liability for breach of an obligation to take care or exercise skill in the performance of any investment functions exercisable by the trustees (or by a person to whom that function has been delegated under *PA 1995, s 34*) cannot be excluded or restricted by any instrument or agreement.

PA 1995 also offers some exoneration for trustees who delegate their investment discretion to a fund manager authorised under *FSMA 2000* in accordance with *PA 1995, s 34(2)*. The trustees will not be liable under *PA 1995* for the acts or defaults of such a fund manager provided they have taken all reasonable steps to satisfy themselves that he has the appropriate knowledge and experience and is acting competently and complying with the requirements of *PA 1995, s 36* (see **10.19** and **10.20** above) (*PA 1995, s 34(4)*).

In addition, *PA 1995, s 33* does not prevent trustees being exonerated under the provisions of the trust deed from liability for the actions of a fund manager to whom the trustees have delegated an investment discretion under *PA 1995, s 34(5)* (see **10.33** above).

Myners' Report: voluntary Code of Practice

10.51 The Myners' Report, published in March 2001, proposed a set of voluntary principles to be used by trustees of defined benefit schemes when taking investment decisions. There is a separate set of principles applicable to defined contribution schemes. The Government allowed schemes two years to comply with Myners (or explain why they could not), and it stated that it intended to conduct an 'audit' of Myners compliance in 2003.

In December 2004, the Government released its Review (Myners' Principles for Institutional Decision-making; Review of Progress, HM Treasury, 2004). The 2004 HM Treasury review of compliance found that, whilst progress was lacking in some areas, in others, trustees were complying with the Myners' Principles. The NAPF agreed to undertake a further review of compliance in 2007. The NAPF's Discussion Paper ('Institutional Investment in the UK Six Years On', January 2007) sought the views of a range of stakeholders on the Myners' Principles and was the start of the review process which was completed in October 2007. The NAPF review concluded that overall standards of governance of UK pension schemes had continued to improve, and that trustees' compliance with the principles had increased. The review made recommendations to bring the principles in line with current best practice, and replace the current ten principles with six high-level principles.

The Government accepted the NAPF's principal findings and recommendations. In particular, it agreed that the principles would be more effective if Government and industry developed them to be more flexible and high level, rather than prescribing how pension funds should manage specific aspects of their business.

In March 2008, the Government consulted on proposals to update the Myners' Principles and establish a new industry-led framework for their application. The consultation document generally endorsed the recommendations made by the NAPF in the October 2007 review. The Government reported that the majority of respondents supported its proposals. In particular, respondents supported the proposal to reduce the number of principles from ten to six higher-level, less prescriptive, principles suggesting only minor drafting changes. The Government's response to the consultation was published in late 2008. The Government made a small number of changes of emphasis, but the substance of the proposed principles remained unchanged. The updated principles and framework include:

(A) Principles

A smaller number of higher-level principles to provide more flexibility for different types of schemes in terms of their size, financial position and strategy to explain their investment decision-making process to stakeholders. The consolidated principles are:

(1) **Effective decision making** – decisions should be taken by persons with the skills, knowledge, advice and resources necessary to take them effectively and monitor their implementation. Trustees should also be able to evaluate and challenge the advice they receive and manage conflicts of interest.

(2) **Clear objectives** – investment objectives must be determined by

reference to each scheme's liabilities, strength of employer covenant and attitude to risk.

(3) **Risk and liabilities** – when reviewing their investment strategy, trustees should take account of the form and structure of liabilities, including the strength of employer covenant, the risk of employer default and longevity risk.

(4) **Performance assessment** – trustees should arrange for the formal measurement of the performance of the investments, investments managers and advisers, and also periodically make a formal policy assessment of their own effectiveness as a decision-making body and report on this to members.

(5) **Responsible ownership** – trustees should adopt, or ensure their investment managers adopt, the Institutional Shareholders' Committee Statement of Principles on the responsibilities of shareholders and agents. A statement of the scheme's policy on responsible ownership should be included in the statement of investment principles. Trustees should report periodically to members on the discharge of such responsibilities.

(6) **Transparency and reporting** – trustees should act in a transparent manner, communicating with stakeholders on issues relating to their management of investment, governance and risks, including performance against stated objectives. Trustees should provide regular communication to members in the form they consider most appropriate.

(B) Best practice guidance and trustee tools

The principles are linked to comprehensive best practice guidance and trustee tools, which should ensure a thorough consideration of the issues relevant to investment decision-making.

(C) Investment Governance Group (IGG)

The IGG is a joint Government and industry body, chaired by the Pensions Regulator. The IGG is responsible for decisions on the nature, scope and development of the principles, best practice guidance and trustee tools. The IGG will formally 'own' the updated principles, monitor their effectiveness and the quality of reporting against them, and make recommendations for improvements to investment decision-making and governance.

The Government has identified four main issues for the IGG to address as a priority. These include: updating the Myners' Principles for DC schemes; drafting specific principles and associated guidance for smaller schemes; drafting brief and practical guidance on the location and content of reporting by trustees (without inhibiting trustees' flexibility to inform members in the manner they think most effective); and updating the guidance for the Local Government Pension Scheme.

(D) Enforcement

A more robust approach to disclosure and industry debate, within the voluntary 'comply or explain' framework. The Government believes that high-quality disclosure and thoughtful debate reinforce the development and dissemination of best practice, encourage self-assessment against the principles, and improve accountability to members.

Given the increasingly complex investment decisions which trustees are required to make, it seems entirely sensible that trustees should seek to increase their knowledge and understanding of how investment markets work and, in particular, how charges operate in relation to investment decisions made by the trustees.

However, it seems equally valid that, where investment managers with a full discretionary mandate involve pension scheme trustees in complex financial transactions or instruments, they should clearly communicate the value of entering into such transactions in relation to the trustees' particular circumstances.

The Government threatened to legislate to incorporate the Myners' Principles into trustees' investment decision-making. This has resulted in the provisions contained at *PA 2004, ss 247–249*, which set out the level of knowledge that the Government now expects of trustees and which came into force in April 2006. Trustees and, where there is a trustee company, each individual who exercises any function which the company has as trustee of the scheme must be 'conversant with':

- the trust deed and rules of the scheme;
- any statement of investment principles;
- any statement of funding principles; and
- any other document recording policy for the time being adopted by the trustees relating to the administration of the scheme generally.

They must also have 'knowledge and understanding of':

- pensions and trust law; and
- principles relating to funding of occupational pension schemes and the investment of the assets of schemes.

The degree of knowledge and understanding required is that appropriate for the purposes of enabling the individual properly to exercise the function in question. A Code of Practice has been issued by the Regulator to provide practical guidance on the functions of trustees and the standards of conduct and practice expected. It has also produced the 'scope guidance' which lists items that trustees need to know and understand, together with a list of documents containing policy with which trustees may need to be familiar. At the time of writing, the Code of Practice on trustee knowledge and understanding is being revised. Much of the revised code reinforces existing practice, but there are some changes which may require additional study by some trustees.

Key changes in the new Code of Practice include:

- all references to 'trustee' will include a director of a corporate trustee;
- the chair of trustees must have full knowledge and understanding from the date of appointment and cannot take advantage of the 6-month period of grace allowed to other trustees;
- trustees of larger schemes who make investment decisions must all have the basic level of knowledge indicated in the scope guidance, even if they are not members of the investment committee;
- each trustee should read the scheme's trust documentation thoroughly;
- the trustee toolkit is required study for all trustees unless an appropriate alternative can be found; and
- the Regulator may make enquiries about a trustee's level of knowledge and understanding when discussing any regulatory issue.

Chapter 11

Funding, deficits and surpluses

Introduction

11.1 Most private sector occupational pension schemes in the UK are funded; assets are set aside, in advance, to provide a fund to meet the benefits ultimately payable (although death-in-service benefits are commonly insured). Public sector schemes are often unfunded or partially funded as they are, instead, backed by a Government guarantee. Before the changes to pension scheme taxation introduced from 6 April 2006 by *FA 2004* (see CHAPTER 16), it was quite common for higher-paid employees to be provided with benefits from an unapproved top-up scheme (possibly unfunded) but these are less common now that unfunded schemes have lost the tax advantages they previously enjoyed.

The first part of this chapter deals with the legal requirements imposed on trustees and employers regarding funding, in particular those contained in *PA 2004*. The second part of this chapter considers the implications of excessive funding and discusses the ways in which a surplus can be reduced.

Pre-PA 1995 requirements relating to funding

11.2 Until *PA 1995*, there was scant legislation relating to funding and no legislation which specifically required an employer to fund a pensions promise in advance. An employer could, quite legitimately, promise a pension to an employee and then make no financial provision for the benefit until it became payable. However, there were several controls which had implications in respect of funding:

(*a*) under the pre-6 April 2006 pensions tax regime, a Revenue requirement that an occupational exempt-approved scheme have an element of employer funding (there are now no specific HMRC requirements for employers to contribute to registered occupational pension schemes);

(*b*) under that former tax regime, limits on the tax reliefs available in respect of overfunded schemes (replaced from 6 April 2006 by a tax charge of 35 per cent on any payment to an employer (see **11.32** below);

(*c*) a requirement for contracted-out defined benefit schemes to obtain actuarial certificates at least triennially as to the scheme's ability to pay members' guaranteed minimum pensions in full if the scheme were to be wound up during the following three and a half years; and

(d) a requirement under the *Occupational Pension Schemes (Disclosure of Information) Regulations 1986 (SI 1986/1046)* for trustees of Revenue-approved schemes to produce an annual report which had to include an actuarial statement on long-term funding (now superseded by the requirements of *PA 1995*, *PA 2004* and the *Occupational Pension Schemes (Disclosure of Information) Regulations 1996 (SI 1996/1665)* (see **11.24** below).

Funding practice

11.3 Generally, employees prefer not to rely on their employer having the financial resources available to meet the pension commitment by the time benefits become payable. With an unfunded scheme, an individual could find that, when he comes to retire, the employer he worked for 20 years previously and who had promised him a pension has gone out of business. A properly funded scheme should ensure that members receive the pension due to them at retirement.

From the employer's perspective, making provision for future benefits as they accrue (as opposed to when they fall due) means that the employer can control its cash flow more easily and plan ahead; it is not faced with having to provide a costly benefit when its financial position may be poor. Also, in the case of registered schemes (and approved schemes before them), the tax advantages available in respect of contributions to the scheme and income and capital gains on assets held by the scheme (see CHAPTER 16) mean that the overall cost of providing benefits is reduced.

Most occupational pension schemes are funded in a way that aims to ensure that, by the time each member reaches retirement, there are sufficient funds to provide the benefits that have been promised. A scheme's governing documentation will normally contain rules specifying how the contributions payable by both the employer and the employees are to be determined. In most defined benefit schemes employees' contributions are fixed, with the employer meeting the balance required to pay the benefits promised (a 'balance of cost' scheme). The scheme-specific funding provisions contained in *PA 2004* require most funding decisions to be made by the trustees with the consent of the employer, overriding the provisions of scheme rules. These requirements are subject to modification depending on the exact provisions of the scheme rules and this is dealt with in more detail in **11.14** below.

The minimum funding requirement – Pensions Act 1995

11.4 *PA 1995, ss 56–61* introduced a requirement from 6 April 1997 that the value of a scheme's assets should be not less than the amount of its liabilities. This requirement, intended to increase the security of members' accrued pension rights, was referred to as the minimum funding requirement (MFR).

The MFR was a cyclical process consisting of three components: valuations, contribution schedules and annual certification. It applied to most exempt-approved defined benefit occupational pension schemes, the main exemptions being broadly the same as the exemptions under the *PA 2004* funding regime (see **11.5** below).

Where the most recent MFR valuation showed funding at less than 100 per cent, the scheme actuary had to provide an 'annual certificate' stating whether or not, in his opinion, the contributions payable were adequate for the purpose of securing that the MFR would continue to be met throughout the schedule period, or would be met by the end of the period. If the certificate expressed the opinion that the MFR would not be met in this way and the value of the scheme's assets was less than 90 per cent of its liabilities ('serious under-provision'), a new MFR valuation or a revised schedule of contributions was required, and, broadly, the employer had to increase the value of the assets within a set period to the 90 per cent level.

The MFR was intended to provide only a minimum level of funding. If, instead, the legislation had based the MFR on the cost of securing benefits by the purchase of annuities, the test would have been considerably stricter in terms of funding, but would have provided members with greater security. Pending the introduction of the new statutory funding objective under *PA 2004*, the Government gradually changed the basis for valuing scheme assets in various circumstances from the MFR basis to the buyout basis.

The MFR has now, in relation to valuations with an effective date on or after 22 September 2005, been replaced by the statutory funding objective (see **11.5** to **11.26** below). Schemes were permitted, under transitional provisions, to continue to operate under MFR valuations for effective dates up to 22 September 2008.

Pensions Act 2004 – statutory funding objective

The statutory funding objective

11.5 The statutory funding objective ('SFO') is the funding standard that replaced the MFR. In contrast to the 'one size fits all' approach adopted by the

MFR, the SFO is intended to enable individual schemes to adopt a funding strategy that is more appropriate to their specific circumstances. The provisions governing the SFO are set out in *PA 2004, ss 221–233* and the *Occupational Pension Schemes (Scheme Funding) Regulations 2005 (SI 2005/3377)* (the '*Scheme Funding Regulations*'). They apply to actuarial valuations with an effective date on or after 22 September 2005 but did not come into force until 30 December 2005 (because there was a delay in implementing (through *PA 2004*) certain provisions of *Directive 2003/41/EC* on the Activities and Supervision of Institutions for Occupational Retirement Provisions ('IORP'), including those relating to scheme funding, investment and cross-border schemes, which IORP required to be transposed into national law by 22 September 2005). The statutory provisions are supported by the Regulator's Code of Practice No. 3, *Funding defined benefits*. In May 2006 the Regulator issued a statement (updated in September 2008) on how it intended operating its powers in relation to scheme funding (see **11.16** below). It has since issued a number of statements reminding trustees that prudent scheme funding requires trustees to keep the scheme's funding position and the employer covenant under constant review, especially in the current economic climate.

The SFO applies to all defined benefit schemes unless exempted by regulations. The exemptions, listed in *Scheme Funding Regulations, reg 17*, are:

- statutory schemes guaranteed by a public authority;
- pay-as-you-go schemes;
- House of Commons pension scheme;
- certain schemes for overseas employees;
- an unregistered scheme with fewer than 100 members;
- a *s 615(6)* scheme which has fewer than 100 members;
- a scheme which has fewer than two members;
- a scheme which has fewer than 12 members, where all the members are trustees of the scheme and either:
  - the scheme rules require all decisions which fall to be made by the trustees to made by the unanimous agreement of the trustee/members; or
  - the scheme has a trustee who is an independent trustee in relation to the scheme for the purposes of *PA 1995, s 23* and is on the Regulator's register;
- a scheme which has fewer than 12 members, where a company is the sole trustee of the scheme and all the scheme members are directors of the company and either:

  - the scheme rules require all decisions made by the company in its capacity as trustee to be made by the unanimous agreement of the director/members; or
  - one of the directors is a trustee who is independent in relation to the scheme for the purposes of *PA 1995, s 23* and is on the Regulator's register;
- a scheme under which the only benefits provided for (other than defined contribution benefits) are death benefits, if the death benefits are secured by insurance policies or annuity contracts;
- a scheme which is the subject of a scheme failure notice under *PA 2004, s 122* or *130* (PPF);
- a scheme which is being wound up (see **11.18** below), or
- the Chatsworth Settlement Estate Pension Scheme.

The overriding statutory funding requirement is set out in *PA 2004, s 222*. It requires that a scheme must have 'sufficient and appropriate assets to cover its technical provisions'. The term 'technical provisions' means the 'amount required, on an actuarial calculation, to make provision for the scheme's liabilities'.

The *Scheme Funding Regulations* set down some requirements as to how to value assets and liabilities. The technical provisions are to be calculated in accordance with prescribed methods and assumptions. This must be an 'accrued benefits funding method' but it will be for the trustees to decide exactly which methods and assumptions are used for their scheme. In reaching this decision, the trustees will have to take into account certain matters. This will include taking advice from the actuary and in most cases obtaining the employer's agreement (see **11.14** below).

The statement of funding principles

11.6 Trustees are required to prepare, and from time to time review and if necessary revise, a statement of funding principles. This is a written statement setting out the trustees' policy for securing that the SFO is met.

Certain details to be included in the statement are set out in *PA 2004, s 223*. In particular, it must record any decisions by the trustees about the actuarial methods and assumptions to be used for calculating the scheme's technical provisions and the manner in which, and the period within which any failure to meet the SFO is to be made good. *Scheme Funding Regulations, reg 6* lists further matters to be covered in the statement and sets out the timescales within which the statement has to be prepared, reviewed and if necessary revised (see **11.12** below).

Actuarial valuations and reports

11.7 *PA 2004, s 224* requires trustees either to obtain an actuarial valuation annually, or, if they obtain an 'actuarial report' each year, they can obtain an actuarial valuation every three years. An actuarial report is a written report from the scheme actuary 'on developments affecting the scheme's technical provisions since the last actuarial valuation was prepared'.

The trustees must ensure that they obtain an SFO actuarial valuation or actuarial report within a prescribed period after the effective date. *Scheme Funding Regulations, reg 7* specifies 15 months in the case of the valuation (but see **11.12** below) and 12 months in the case of the report. The trustees must then ensure that a copy is made available to the employer within seven days of the trustees receiving it.

Certification of technical provisions

11.8 *PA 2004, s 225* requires that, when an actuarial valuation is carried out, the scheme actuary must certify that, in his opinion, the calculation of the technical provisions complies with the *Scheme Funding Regulations*. The certificate must include the actuary's estimate of the solvency of the scheme (*Scheme Funding Regulations, reg 7(4)*). This will usually be on a buyout basis but, where this is not possible, the actuary may substitute an alternative appropriate basis. The certificate should be included as part of the actuarial valuation document (see **11.7** above).

If the actuary cannot certify that the relevant legal requirements have been satisfied, he must report the matter in writing to the Regulator within a reasonable period following the date for receipt of the valuation by the trustees. The Code of Practice proposes ten working days as a reasonable period.

Recovery plan

11.9 Where an actuarial valuation shows that the SFO is not met on the effective date, ie that there is a shortfall, *PA 2004, s 226* requires the trustees to prepare a recovery plan or, if there is already a recovery plan in place, to review and revise the existing plan as necessary. The recovery plan must set out the steps to be taken to meet the SFO and the period within which this is to be achieved and it must be 'appropriate having regard to the nature and circumstances of the scheme' (*PA 2004, s 226(3)*). The recovery plan must be reviewed, and if necessary revised, where the trustees or managers consider that there are reasons that may justify a variation to it or where the Regulator has given directions under *PA 2004, s 231* as to the period within which, and manner in which, a failure to meet the SFO is to be remedied.

Scheme Funding Regulations, reg 8 requires the trustees to take account of the following:

- the asset and liability structure of the scheme;
- its risk profile;
- its liquidity requirements;
- the age profile of the members; and
- the recommendations of any person other than the trustees who (broadly) determines employer contribution rates without employer consent.

The Code of Practice provides that when devising a recovery plan, trustees should aim to eliminate the shortfall as quickly as the employer can reasonably afford. The trustees should ensure that the assumptions underlying the recovery plan are appropriate for the scheme. The Code of Practice lists matters the trustees should take into account, including:

- the employer's business plans and the likely effect any recovery plan would have on the employer's future viability;
- the scheme's membership profile (eg a shorter recovery period may be appropriate where most scheme members are already in receipt of a pension);
- any proposed changes to the membership profile (eg a bulk transfer);
- the ability of the trustees to pursue an employer should the scheme wind up;
- the employer's expenditure commitments;
- the value of any contingent security provided by the employer, bearing in mind both term and enforceability; and
- the likely outcome for members on the employer's insolvency.

The recovery plan must include the date by which the shortfall is expected to be eliminated (*PA 2004, s 226(2)*). The Code of Practice suggests that, except where the recovery period is less than one year, it should also include the date by which the amount of additional contributions to be made is half the amount of all the contributions due under the recovery plan (ie when half the shortfall will be eliminated). A copy of the recovery plan and the prescribed information must, except in prescribed circumstances, be sent to the Regulator within a reasonable period (the Regulator suggests ten working days) after it is prepared or revised. The prescribed information is a summary of the information contained in the relevant valuation and, where a plan has been revised on the initiative of the trustees (ie not by the intervention of the Regulator), an explanation of the reasons for the revision (*Scheme Funding Regulations, reg 8(7)*). The Code of Practice gives guidance on what the valuation summary should include.

Failure by trustees to take all reasonable steps to comply with the requirements for recovery plans can lead to civil penalties.

Schedule of contributions

11.10 Trustees must prepare, and from time to time review and if necessary revise, a schedule of contributions (*PA 2004, s 227*). This must be done within 15 months of the effective date of each actuarial valuation. The schedule of contributions must cover the period of five years from the date of its certification by the actuary, or the recovery plan period, if longer (*Scheme Funding Regulations, reg 10(2)*). The schedule of contributions has to show:

- the rates of contributions payable by the employer and active members of the scheme; and
- the due dates on or before which the contributions have to be paid.

The actuary is required to certify that the schedule of contributions is consistent with the statement of funding principles and either:

- the scheme meets the SFO and can be expected to do so for the period covered by the schedule; or
- the scheme can be expected to meet the SFO by the end of the period specified in the recovery plan.

If the actuary is unable to give this certificate, he must report this to the Regulator within a reasonable period after the end of the period within which the schedule is required to be prepared or revised. The Code of Practice suggests ten working days would be reasonable.

The schedule must be signed by the trustees and make provision for signature by the employer in order to signify his agreement to the matters included in it. See **11.16** below for the role of the Regulator where the trustees and the employer cannot reach agreement on the schedule of contributions.

Where the actuary considers that because of the possibility of significant changes in the value of scheme assets or technical provisions since the effective date of the latest valuation he is unable to certify the schedule as described above, he may sign a modified certificate (*Scheme Funding Regulations, Sch 2, para 12*).

Where the SFO was not met on the effective date of the most recent actuarial valuation, the trustees must send a copy of the schedule to the Regulator within a reasonable period of its completion. The Code of Practice suggests this should be within ten working days of the actuary certifying the schedule and that the recovery plan should be sent at the same time.

Again, failure by the trustees and the actuary to take all reasonable steps to comply with the requirements relating to schedules of contributions can lead to civil penalties.

Failure to make payments

11.11 The trustees must report late payment of contributions that are due under a schedule of contributions. *PA 2004, s 228* requires a report of late payment to be made to the Regulator and the members where the trustees have reasonable cause to believe that the failure to pay on time is 'likely to be of material significance in the exercise by the Regulator of any of its functions'. The Code of Practice sets out situations which are likely to be of material significance. These include where the employer appears to have been involved in fraudulent evasion, where there is an immediate risk to members' benefits and where contributions remain unpaid for 90 days. Situations unlikely to be of material significance include failures stemming from administrative lapses which have been remedied and cases where a claim has been made to the Redundancy Payments service. Reports to the Regulator should usually be made within ten working days, or earlier where an immediate report is required. Reports to members should be made within one month.

Similar reporting requirements and reasonable periods apply in the case of late payment of contributions to occupational money purchase schemes and to personal pensions (Codes of Practice Nos 5 and 6 respectively).

Any contributions that remain unpaid become a debt due from the employer to the trustees (*PA 2004, s 228(3)*).

Civil penalties may be imposed on an employer who fails without reasonable excuse to make a payment of contributions and to a trustee who has failed to take all reasonable steps to report the late payment. Failure to pay contributions in accordance with the schedule of contributions may also be a breach of law requiring a report to the Regulator under *PA 2004, s 70* (see CHAPTER 2).

Timing

11.12 Under the *Scheme Funding Regulations* the trustees have a period of 15 months from the effective date of the actuarial valuation in which to obtain the actuarial valuation, produce a statement of funding principles, set a schedule of contributions and (if necessary) produce a recovery plan. This means that by 22 December 2009 all schemes subject to the SFO should have put in place all the elements of the SFO following the effective date for their first valuation under the SFO. The MFR requirements relating to schedules of contributions, record keeping and late contributions continue to apply until the trustees have put in place a new schedule of contributions following their first SFO valuation.

The Code of Practice suggests that trustees draw up an action plan factoring in time for contingencies and to make allowance for taking actuarial advice, considering any recovery plan and reaching agreement with the employer, including bearing in mind that it may be necessary to consider modification of future accrual of benefits, which would require the employer to consult with affected members under *PA 2004, ss 259–261* (see CHAPTER 7).

Record keeping

11.13 Under *Scheme Funding Regulations, reg 11*, trustees are required to keep records of:

(*a*) all contributions made to the scheme, showing separately:

  (i) the aggregate amounts of contributions paid by or on behalf of active members and the dates on which they were paid;

  (ii) the voluntary contributions paid by each member; and

  (iii) the aggregate of the contributions paid by or on behalf of each employer and the dates on which they were paid;

(*b*) all contributions and payments made to secure any increase required to meet a serious shortfall; and

(*c*) any action taken by the trustees to recover:

  (i) any contributions which are not paid on the date on which they are due; and

  (ii) any debt which has arisen under *PA 1995, s 75(2)* or *(4)* (deficiencies in the assets).

Role of the employer

11.14 The intention behind the *PA 2004* scheme funding requirements is for there to be a partnership approach, with the trustees working with the employer to develop an appropriate funding strategy for their scheme. A number of the requirements set out in the legislation are primarily the responsibility of the trustees. However, under *PA 2004, s 229*, trustees are required to obtain the consent of the employer in relation to the following key issues:

- any decision about the methods and assumptions underlying the technical provisions;
- the content of the statement of funding principles;

- any recovery plan; and
- the schedule of contributions.

This requirement for employer consent is modified where the existing scheme rules give the trustees power to set contributions without reference to the employer (*Scheme Funding Regulations, Sch 2, para 9*):

- where the trustees have power under the scheme rules to determine contribution rates (and no one else is permitted to reduce the rate or suspend contributions), the consent requirements set out above are replaced by a requirement for the trustees to *consult* with the employer only;
- where the trustees have power, subject to conditions, to set the contribution rate (and no one else is permitted to reduce the rate or suspend contributions) then, provided the conditions are satisfied, the consent requirements set out above are replaced by a requirement for the trustees to *consult* with the employer only.

However, the Code of Practice recommends that, in either situation, the trustees should nevertheless seek to obtain the employer's agreement.

The Regulations also impose the following additional conditions:

- Where the scheme rules provide for the contribution rate to be determined by or 'in accordance with the advice of' someone other than the trustees, and without the agreement of the employer, then the trustees must take account of the recommendations of that other person on the methods and assumptions for calculating the technical provisions and on the preparation of any recovery plan (but not the schedule of contributions itself or the statement of funding principles) (*Scheme Funding Regulations, regs 5(3)* and *8(2)(e)*). It is not clear whether 'in accordance with the advice of' bites only where the trustees are bound by the scheme rules to follow the advice or also where the trustees are obliged only to take that advice into account but retain a discretion to make the determination themselves. In the latter case, the trustees may then be obliged only to consult with the employer (under *PA 2004, s 229*, as modified by *Scheme Funding Regulations, Sch 2, para 9*) and follow the recommendations of the other person.
- Where the scheme actuary has the power under the scheme rules to determine the contribution rate without the agreement of the employer, the trustees must determine the rate with the consent of the employer (in accordance with *PA 2004, s 229*) with an additional requirement that the actuary may only certify the schedule of contributions if the contributions are no less than they would have been had the actuary

determined the rate (*Scheme Funding Regulations, Sch 2, para 9(5)*). From 6 April 2009 this applies where, and to the extent that, the actuary has the sole power under the scheme rules to determine any (not just all) of the employer contribution rates without the employer's agreement and applies only to the extent of that power; ie where the actuary has that power under the scheme rules only in certain circumstances, the balance of power is not shifted to the actuary in all other circumstances as well (*Occupational, Personal and Stakeholder Pensions (Miscellaneous Amendment) Regulations 2009 (SI 2009/615), reg 18*).

In many schemes, the application of the above provisions may not be straightforward and detailed advice may be required at the outset in order to establish which procedures the trustees are required to adopt. See further **11.33** below.

Where it is necessary to obtain the consent of the employer, what happens where the employer does not agree? There are two consequences of failure to agree, which are set out in *PA 2004, s 229*:

- the trustees may modify future service accrual by resolution, with the employer's consent; and
- the trustees must report the failure to agree to the Regulator who has wide powers to intervene.

Where modification for future accrual is being considered and the trustees have power under the scheme rules to fix contributions, they need only consult the employer with regard to the proposed changes (*Scheme Funding Regulations, Sch 2, para 9*). Any modification must not adversely affect subsisting rights. Modifications must be in writing and must be notified to the active members within one month of the modification taking effect. Where trustees have unilateral power of amendment under the scheme's trust deed and rules, this may not be diluted by *s 229* and, in those circumstances, the trustees could exercise the power of amendment without the consent of the employer. As noted in **11.12** above, modification of future accrual of benefits would require the employer to consult with affected members under *PA 2004, ss 259–261* (see CHAPTER 7).

Role of the actuary

11.15 *PA 2004, s 230* sets out certain circumstances where trustees must obtain the advice of the scheme actuary. The trustees must obtain advice before:

- making any decision about the methods and assumptions to be used in calculating the scheme's technical provisions;
- preparing or revising the statement of funding principles;

- preparing or revising a recovery plan;
- preparing or revising the schedule of contributions; and
- modifying the scheme as regards future accrual of benefits in the event of failure to agree with the employer.

The Regulations require the actuary to have regard to professional guidance. GN49, issued by the Faculty and Institute of Actuaries and subsequently adopted by the Board for Actuarial Standards, is currently the relevant guidance note.

Powers of the Regulator

11.16 The Regulator has a range of powers designed to ensure that the scheme funding requirements are complied with by trustees and employers. These powers are set out in *PA 2004, s 231* and include the ability to modify future service benefits and to impose a schedule of contributions, a statement of funding principles or a recovery plan where the trustees have failed fully to comply with the statutory requirements, the actuary has been unable to give a certificate or the trustees and the employer have been unable to reach agreement where required.

The Regulator's Code of Practice provides guidance on the steps that it expects the trustees to take in order to reach agreement with the employer before reporting to the Regulator.

In May 2006 the Regulator issued a statement on how it intended to exercise its powers in relation to scheme funding. This statement, updated in September 2008, sets out the principles underpinning its regulatory approach and deals with how it might identify schemes which pose the greatest risk.

The suggested principles under which it will operate are:

- **protecting members** – schemes should aim to be funded so that they can pay all benefits promised to members as they fall due;
- **scheme-specific** – each scheme needs to take account of its specific circumstances, including the strength of the employer;
- **risk-based** – regulatory function should be focused on those schemes that pose the greatest risk to members' benefits and to the PPF (see below);
- **proportionate** – trustees are required to correct any shortfall as quickly as the employer can reasonably afford;
- **preventative** – where possible, to act before risks materialise;

- **practicable** – to operate within the constraints of the information and resources available
- **referee not player** – it is the responsibility of trustees and employers, with the help of their advisers, to ensure that schemes are fully funded.

In order to identify schemes at risk, the proposal is that the Regulator will look for three triggers:

- imprudent technical provisions;
- inappropriate recovery plans; and
- non-agreement between trustees and employers.

The 'technical provisions' trigger involves the Regulator comparing the *s 179* (PPF risk-based levy valuation) and FRS17/IAS19 liabilities, and then looking at the strength of the employer covenant to assess whether the trigger has come into operation. If it has, the Regulator will look more closely at the mortality improvement assumptions; if these give cause for concern, it will usually ask trustees to justify their assumptions in the light of the advice they have obtained.

The technical provisions and recovery plan triggers are not to be regarded in isolation; the Regulator will look at the interaction between them. The triggers it will look for in relation to recovery plans are:

- the recovery period is longer than ten years (or it is less than ten years but the Regulator believes that the employer can reasonably afford to pay off the shortfall more quickly);
- the recovery plan is significantly back-end loaded (higher contributions towards the end of the period); and
- the underlying assumptions, especially investment assumptions, appear inappropriate, unrealistic or over-optimistic.

Trustees and employers must show that they have taken both appropriate advice and all available steps to minimise the risk of the funding position deteriorating further.

If the employer is unable to pay contributions at the required level, the Regulator may require trustees and employers to consider modifying future accrual of benefits if they have not properly considered this option.

As already noted, the *PA 2004* funding regime requires trustees and employers in most cases to try to reach agreement on a number of issues. If they are unable to reach agreement on funding, the Regulator expects trustees to provide details of negotiations with the employer and of the reasons for non-agreement and to demonstrate that they have 'explored all reasonable avenues', eg alternative dispute resolution (ADR) and mediation. If its initial intervention does not resolve the disagreement, the Regulator has a range of powers available to it, including modifying future accrual of benefits, imposing a schedule of contributions and issuing a freezing order (stopping future accrual). *PA 2008, s 132* gives the Regulator additional powers to intervene, from 26 January 2009, where the methods and assumptions underlying the technical provisions fail to comply with prescribed requirements.

The Regulator has published on its website examples of scheme funding documents which include typical content and suggest how it could be presented:

- statement of funding principles;
- recovery plan;
- schedule of contributions;
- summary funding statements.

Multi-employer schemes

11.17 The *Scheme Funding Regulations* modify *PA 2004* so that, where there is a sectionalised scheme, the SFO provisions apply to each section as if it were a separate scheme. A sectionalised scheme is one where contributions and assets are allocated to a particular section and cannot be used for the purposes of any other section.

For non-sectionalised multi-employer schemes, provision is made for a single employer (nominated by the other employers or under the scheme rules) to agree matters with the trustees. If no nomination has been made:

- the agreement of all employers must be sought to the matters referred to in *PA 2004, s 229(1)* (the methods and assumptions to be used in calculating the scheme's technical provisions; the statement of funding principles; any recovery plan; and the schedule of contributions) unless an employer has expressly waived its rights under that section; and
- in the case of a modification of the scheme as to future accrual, the agreement of all the employers must be obtained (*Scheme Funding Regulations, Sch 2, paras 1, 2*).

In *Hearn v Dobson [2008] EWHC 1620 (Ch)*, the High Court considered the interaction of the *PA 2004* funding regime and the definition of 'employer' in *PA 1995, s 124* in relation to a multi-employer scheme where all but one employer had ceased to participate. It held that 'employer' for this purpose did not include an employer which employed no active members, so this scheme had only one employer. Therefore, it was not a multi-employer scheme for the purposes of the SFO and it was not open to the trustees to segregate the assets relating to each participating employer and treat each separate fund as a separate scheme.

Schemes in winding-up

11.18 Schemes which commenced winding-up before 30 December 2005 are not subject to the new scheme funding regime. Schemes which commence winding-up on or after 30 December 2005 are subject to a limited requirement to obtain from the scheme actuary an annual estimate of the solvency position (*Scheme Funding Regulations, reg 18*). However, a relaxation was introduced from 6 April 2009: a segregated section of a multi-employer pension scheme which is winding up is exempt from *PA 2004* funding requirements where certain criteria are met (*Occupational, Personal and Stakeholder Pensions (Miscellaneous Amendments) Regulations 2009 (SI 2009/615), reg 18*).

Where an occupational pension scheme in respect of which a recovery plan has been prepared under *PA 2004, s 226* begins to wind up during the recovery period specified in the recovery plan, *PA 2004, s 231A* requires the trustees to prepare a winding-up procedure as soon as reasonably practicable. This must set out the action and the estimated time to be taken to establish the scheme's liabilities, to recover assets and to discharge liabilities; and, to the extent that the trustees or managers have sufficient information to do so, indicate which accrued rights or benefits (if any) are likely to be actuarially reduced.

The winding-up procedure must be appropriate having regard to the nature and circumstances of the scheme and may be reviewed, and if necessary revised, where the trustees consider this appropriate. They must send a copy of any winding-up procedure to the Regulator as soon as reasonably practicable after it has been prepared or revised.

Civil penalties apply to trustees who have failed to take all reasonable steps to comply with these requirements.

Schemes with fewer than 100 members

11.19 Domestic (as opposed to cross-border) schemes with fewer than 100 members on the effective date of the most recent actuarial valuation made under the SFO need not obtain annual actuarial reports nor issue annual funding statements (see **11.24** below) between their triennial valuations. If the membership reaches 100 at any time during a year then an annual report will be required. Members for this purpose include active, deferred, pensioner and pension credit members (*Scheme Funding Regulations, Sch 2, para 11*).

Cross-border schemes – European Economic Area

11.20 Stricter funding requirements apply to these schemes. IORP requires that a scheme operating cross border must be 'fully funded at all times'. The *Scheme Funding Regulations* require that such schemes must meet the SFO requirements at all times and have annual actuarial valuations; each valuation must be signed by the actuary and received by the trustees within one year of its effective date. 'Cross border' originally referred to EU Member States, but this was extended from 26 November 2007 to all EEA States once the three EEA Member States which are not also EU Member States had adopted IORP.

Application for authorisation and approval to operate a cross-border scheme must be made to the Regulator. The *Occupational Pension Schemes (Cross-border Activities) Regulations 2005 (SI 2005/3381)*, which came into force on the same date as the *Scheme Funding Regulations*, set out how the Regulator is to perform its functions in relation to cross-border schemes; and the Regulator has published guidance as well as application forms.

A new scheme must meet the SFO within two years of the date of application for authorisation; an existing scheme which is becoming cross-border for the first time must meet the SFO at the date of application. In both cases, this means without the use of a recovery plan, as a cross-border scheme is not permitted to rectify its underfunding through the use of a recovery plan. Note that the 'fully funded' requirement applies to the entire scheme and not only to the cross-border element of it (although the Regulator has power to order ring-fencing of assets in certain circumstances, eg misappropriation).

Regulatory own funds requirement

11.21 The *Occupational Pension Schemes (Regulatory Own Funds) Regulations 2005 (SI 2005/3380)*, which also came into force on 30 December 2005, require that, where an occupational pension scheme itself, rather than an employer, covers any liability for risks linked to death, disability or longevity, guarantees any investment performance, or guarantees to provide defined benefits, the scheme must have additional assets (free of foreseeable liabilities) above its technical provisions (the regulatory own funds requirement, ROFR) of at least 4 per cent of the scheme's technical provisions, plus 0.3 per cent of the amount by which the total amount which the scheme would be obliged to pay on the immediate death of all members of the scheme exceeds the technical provisions (calculated on the basis of the scheme's annual report and accounts). Actuarial valuations are required annually, and the scheme's statement of funding principles must include the policy for securing that the ROFR is met.

If the ROFR was not met as at the effective date of the actuarial valuation, the trustees must ensure it is met within two years and must send the Regulator a report of the steps to be taken. The Regulator may modify the scheme as regards future accrual of benefits, give directions as to the calculation of the ROFR and may also impose a schedule of contributions. Penalties under *PA 1995, s 10* apply to trustees who fail to take all reasonable steps to ensure compliance with the requirements of the regulations.

Regulation 15 exempts from the ROFR certain kinds of schemes which are not cross-border schemes. These are broadly the same as the exemptions from the *Scheme Funding Regulations*. A scheme which begins winding up on or after 30 December 2005 will not be exempt from the ROFR unless the trustees ensure that they receive, before the end of each scheme year following the scheme year in which winding-up begins, the actuary's estimate of the solvency of the scheme as at the end of the preceding scheme year (*reg 16*).

Contracting out

11.22 Where a scheme is contracted out on the 'reference scheme' basis, either the resources of the scheme must be sufficient to enable the scheme to meet the SFO or the actuary must have certified that, in his opinion, the rates shown in the schedule of contributions are such that the SFO can be expected to be met by the end of the period specified in the recovery plan (*Occupational Pension Schemes (Contracting-Out) Regulations 1996 (SI 1996/1172), reg 18*).

Reporting to the Regulator

11.23 The following must be reported to the Regulator:

- The actuary must report if he is unable to certify that the calculation of technical provisions is made in accordance with the Regulations. The Code of Practice suggests that this should be done within ten working days of the deadline for certifying the technical provisions.
- The actuary must report if he is unable to certify the schedule of contributions. The Code of Practice suggests that this should be done within ten working days of the deadline for certifying the schedule.
- A copy of any recovery plan must be sent (see **11.9** above).
- Failure to pay in accordance with the schedule of contributions (see **11.11** above).
- Failure to agree any matter with the employer (see **11.14** above). The Code of Practice suggests that this should be done within ten working days from the relevant deadline.

Failure to report could give rise to civil penalties.

Disclosure to members

11.24 The funding regime includes a requirement to disclose certain documents to any member, potential member, the spouse or civil partner of any member or potential member, any beneficiary or any recognised trade union who requests it, either by making them available to inspect or by providing copies (*Occupational Pension Schemes (Disclosure of Information) Regulations 1996 (SI 1996/1655), reg 7* (the '*Disclosure Regulations*'), as amended by the *Scheme Funding Regulations*). The trustees must disclose on request:

- the latest actuarial valuation and any actuarial report;
- the certified schedule of contributions;
- the statement of investment principles;
- the statement of funding principles;
- actuarial reports subsequent to the latest valuation;
- any recovery plan; and
- any outline of the winding-up procedure prepared or revised under *PA 2004, s 231A*.

The trustees must also, as a matter of course, send an annual funding statement to all members and beneficiaries of schemes subject to the SFO. *Disclosure Regulations, reg 5(12ZA)* and *Sch 2, paras 17–22* set out what the annual funding statement must contain:

- a summary, based on the most recent valuation, of the extent to which the assets were sufficient to cover the technical provisions;
- an explanation of any change in the funding position since the date of the last funding statement (or in the case of the first funding statement, since the last actuarial valuation);
- the actuary's estimate of solvency contained in the latest actuarial valuation;
- a summary of any recovery plan;
- information as to whether the scheme has been modified at the direction of the Regulator, or subject to directions of and or bound by a schedule of contributions imposed by the Regulator together with an explanation of the circumstances in which this occurred; and
- whether any payment of surplus has been made to the employer and, if so, the amount of the payment.

The Code of Practice recommends that trustees consider including additional information such as a summary of the scheme's investment policy, a reference to the Pension Protection Fund and a list of the funding and related documents available on request. The Code states that the annual funding statement should normally be provided within three months from the date by which valuations or reports must be obtained.

Interplay between SFO and scheme rules

11.25 As noted in **11.14** above, the application of the SFO to the rules of many schemes may not be straightforward. This has already been demonstrated in two cases.

In *British Vita [2007] EWHC 953 (Ch)* the rules of the scheme, which had not yet had its first valuation under *PA 2004*, allowed the trustees to demand additional contributions from the employer. The trustees exercised this power. The employer argued that the scheme was subject to the statutory funding regime, and therefore the trustees and employer were required to agree a schedule of contributions. The High Court held that until the first contribution schedule was produced under the SFO regime the trustees' power to demand additional contributions under the scheme's own rule remained valid. It was left open as to whether the rule would survive once a *PA 2004* schedule of contributions was in place. Because the case subsequently settled, there was no appeal, so this question currently remains unanswered.

In *Allied Domecq (Holdings) Ltd v Allied Domecq First Pension Trust Ltd and another [2008] EWCA Civ 1084* the Court of Appeal upheld the judgment of the High Court that the scheme rules gave the scheme actuary unilateral power to set the contribution rate without the agreement of the employer; this power was unaffected by powers of the trustees to apportion contributions among employers and to set the time period for past service deficit contributions, which were held to be separate limbs of the relevant rules. This case, of course, turns on the exact wording of the rules, but it gives a useful insight into the interaction between the legislation and individual scheme rules.

Other actuarial valuations

11.26 *PA 2004* introduced two new statutory actuarial valuations: the '*s 143* valuation' applies only to those schemes being considered for entry to the Pension Protection Fund ('PPF'), and its purpose is to ascertain whether the scheme has sufficient assets to cover its liabilities for benefits at the PPF level as well as the expenses of winding up; and the '*s 179* valuation' is required for all schemes eligible for the PPF for the purpose of calculating each scheme's risk-based levy (see CHAPTER 2).

Schemes in deficit

11.27 The position of deficits in schemes in winding-up, or where an employer ceases to participate, is dealt with in CHAPTER 14.

There are also a number of consequences for an ongoing scheme which is in deficit. The exact impact will depend upon the basis upon which the deficit has been assessed. For example:

- (domestic) schemes in deficit on an SFO basis will be subject to a recovery plan (see **11.9** above) and may come under the scrutiny of the Regulator (see **11.16** above);
- schemes funded at less than 140 per cent on a PPF (*s 179*) basis (see **11.26** above) will be subject to the PPF risk-based levy, and the greater the deficit, the higher the levy will be subject to a cap (see CHAPTER 2);
- schemes showing a deficit on a *s 179* basis will be required to report more notifiable events than those which do not (see CHAPTER 2);
- schemes showing a deficit on a number of bases may be subject to clearance applications for employer-related events under the moral hazard provisions (see CHAPTER 14).

What is a surplus?

11.28 Although widely used, the expression 'surplus' is not a legally defined term. It is generally said to exist when the actuarially estimated value of a scheme's assets at a certain date exceeds the actuarially estimated value of its liabilities at that date.

When a scheme is winding up, a surplus is easy to identify, as the cost of securing the liabilities of the scheme in a given manner will ultimately be known, as will the value of the assets of the scheme. On a winding-up, a surplus will exist if there are any funds remaining after all the benefits have been secured.

An ongoing scheme, however, could be either in deficit or in surplus at any given time depending on the actuarial method and assumptions used for the valuation. A 'surplus' in an ongoing scheme is simply the actuary's prediction, based on a given method and on a certain set of assumptions, that the scheme will have more than sufficient assets to cover its liabilities over a certain period.

An employer may tend to see a surplus in an ongoing scheme as representing past overfunding. Trustees may see it as representing a reserve fund, providing security in the event of the cost of the benefits being more than the actuary anticipated or the investments of the scheme failing to perform to the level hoped for. Members will sometimes regard a surplus in an ongoing scheme as 'spare' money that could be used for immediate benefit increases. However, arguably there can be no certainty of a surplus unless and until the scheme is wound up and all benefits secured. Any surplus in an ongoing scheme is notional, as any number of events could happen which would eradicate it.

Why surpluses are an issue

11.29 During the 1980s a huge growth in the value of investments, coupled with a reduction in the workforce, led to many schemes having substantial surpluses. Sometimes, these were so large that even the suspension of contributions by employers and employees was insufficient to eliminate them over a foreseeable period. Many employers began to look for ways to extract what appeared to be superfluous assets in their pension schemes.

At the same time, the Government became concerned that the tax advantages conferred on occupational pension schemes meant that it was losing valuable tax revenue from the assets in these overfunded schemes. *FA 1986* removed some of the tax advantages for exempt approved schemes, prompting some employers to remove a surplus from a scheme or to take contribution holidays or improve scheme benefits to eradicate surplus. Some members and trustees of pension schemes became increasingly concerned that employers were unjustly appropriating part of their schemes' funds, resulting in the reduction of scheme security and the loss of any possibility of increased benefits. The treatment of a surplus in an ongoing scheme gave rise to controversy.

In recent years, surplus has become much less of an issue, as many defined benefit schemes have moved into deficit. This has resulted in the closure of many defined benefit schemes (either to future accrual or to new members) and their replacement with defined contribution schemes. However, surpluses can still arise and it is necessary to know how to deal with them if they do.

Who owns a surplus?

Ongoing schemes

11.30 A surplus in an ongoing scheme may be considered notional, but the debate over the ways in which it can be used is very real. In most defined benefit schemes the employer's contribution will be the balance of the cost of providing the benefits promised. One of the easiest ways of dealing with a surplus is, therefore, simply to adjust the employer's contribution rate. However, trustees and beneficiaries may argue that a surplus will not necessarily have arisen because the employer has paid excessive contributions; it could be due to high investment growth on the assets purchased by both the employer's and members' contributions, or to members leaving a scheme at a faster rate than that assumed by the actuary for the purposes of his valuation. In such a situation the issue of who owns the surplus is inevitably raised.

The courts have been asked in a number of cases to consider the use of a surplus and, in particular, the members' right to share in the surplus. These cases have generally recognised that, in a defined benefit scheme where an employer would be required to meet any deficit, it would be inequitable for the employer not to benefit at all from any surplus. There has, however, been a gradual shift away from the proposition that any surplus belongs solely to the employer while the scheme is ongoing.

In *Re Courage Group's Pension Schemes [1987] 1 All ER 528*, Millett J considered that, although members did not have an absolute legal right to participate in the surplus in their scheme, they were entitled to have it dealt with by consultation and negotiation between them and the employer. He rejected the argument that members were entitled, as of right, to a contribution holiday, as any surplus arising from past overfunding in a balance of cost scheme arose primarily from the employer. However, he drew a distinction between the employer using a surplus to fund a contribution holiday and requiring a payment out of the scheme. In the latter situation the trustees could, and should, press for generous treatment of members and the employer could be expected to be influenced by the desire to maintain good industrial relations with its workforce.

When considering how to deal with a surplus, it should be remembered that an employer can have regard to its own interests (financial and otherwise) but only to the extent that in doing so it does not breach the obligation of good faith to its employees and former employees (*Imperial Group Pension Trust Ltd v Imperial Tobacco Ltd [1991] 2 All ER 597*: see CHAPTER 7).

The issue of who owns a surplus continues to be subject to debate. The starting point should of course be the terms of the trust deed and rules of the particular scheme. The position would currently seem to be that members do not have an absolute right to any surplus but may have a legitimate expectation of benefit improvements, particularly where the trustees have a discretion as to the use of a surplus. When considering the use of a surplus the employer is, however, obliged to keep an open mind and consider arguments put forward on behalf of the members. (See *Stannard v Fisons Pension Trust Ltd [1992] 1 PLR 27* and *LRT Pension Fund Trustee Co Ltd v Hatt [1993] PLR 227.*) Much will depend on the respective powers of the trustees and the employer under the scheme's governing documentation and the relative bargaining position of the parties.

The courts have recognised that, if employers were to be prevented from taking contribution holidays, they might simply freeze or wind up the scheme, replacing it with one which is funded so as to avoid a surplus arising. This point was accepted by the judge in *The National Grid Company plc v Laws [1997] PLR 157*, which in 2001 progressed to the House of Lords. It was emphasised in the Court of Appeal that the treatment of surplus depends on the construction of the terms of the scheme, a view supported by the Court of Appeal in *Stevens v Bell (British Airways) [2002] PLR 247*.

Schemes which are winding up

11.31 A scheme's trust deed and rules will generally include a rule setting out how the fund is to be distributed on a winding-up. This rule should include a provision relating to how any assets remaining after all the liabilities have been secured are to be used. Usually there will be a power to increase benefits and/or make a payment to the employer. In some instances the provision will simply provide that all assets remaining should be paid to the employer.

If the rules do not contain provisions regarding the use of a surplus the general principles of trust law will have to be considered. Essentially, where funds are transferred to a trust and it subsequently transpires that those funds are not needed for the purposes of the trust, the trustees hold those funds for the benefit of the person who provided them on a 'resulting trust'. A resulting trust does not arise where the person who provided the money never intended to receive any of it back, so if the rules of the scheme specifically provide that no payment can be made to an employer (on a winding-up or otherwise) a resulting trust cannot arise.

How a surplus should be dealt with in the absence of a valid rule was considered by Scott J in *Davis v Richards Wallington Industries Ltd [1991] 2 All ER 563*. A resulting trust in favour of the members of the scheme was excluded largely on the grounds that, as the scheme provided salary-related benefits, two members who paid in the same monetary amount in contributions could be entitled to benefits of a different value; so a resulting trust was unworkable as between the different groups of beneficiaries. Consequently, any resulting trust had to be in favour of the employer. Again, the point was made that, in a balance of cost scheme, any surplus was to be treated as being provided first and foremost by the employer's contributions.

HMRC requirements relating to the reduction of surpluses

11.32 Legislation restricts the tax advantages available to registered occupational pension schemes if they are in surplus (so that the Government does not lose potential tax revenue). The current restriction (since 6 April 2006) is in the form of by a tax charge of 35 per cent on payments to employers (*FA 2004, ss 177, 207*) combined with the requirements of *PA 1995, s 37* (see CHAPTER 5 and **11.33** below).

Pensions Act 2004 – position from 6 April 2006

Ongoing schemes

11.33 *PA 1995, s 37* introduced, with effect from 6 April 1997, certain requirements which had to be satisfied before a repayment of surplus could be made to an employer. These included an increase in all pensions by 5 per cent LPI and requirements to give advance notice to members.

PA 2004, s 250 substituted a new *PA 1995, s 37* with effect from 6 April 2006. The new *s 37* provides that, where power is conferred on the employer, or any other person, to make payments to the employer, that power may be exercised only by the trustees. The power to repay surplus may only be exercised if:

- except in the case of a scheme subject to the regulatory own funds requirement (see **11.21**), the trustees have obtained a written valuation prepared and signed by an actuary (usually the scheme actuary);
- there is a certificate in force which meets prescribed requirements (see below) and specifies the maximum amount which may be paid to the employer;
- the payment does not exceed the maximum amount specified in the certificate;
- the trustees are satisfied that it is in the interests of the members that the power is exercised in the manner proposed;
- there is no freezing order in force under *PA 2004, s 23*; and
- notices have been given to members in accordance with prescribed requirements.

The *Occupational Pension Scheme (Payments to Employer) Regulations 2006 (SI 2006/802)* (the '*Payments to Employer Regulations*'), which also came into force on 6 April 2006, provide that valuation methods similar to those under the *Scheme Funding Regulations* should be adopted. Alternatively, trustees may rely on an SFO valuation (see **11.7** above) for 15 months from the effective date of the valuation. The maximum amount of any refund payment to the employer will be the amount by which the value of the assets exceeds the buy-out liabilities, as shown in the actuary's certificate for this purpose (*Payments to Employer Regulations, regs 5, 7*).

Where the trustees intend making a payment to the employer, the prescribed requirements for the notice (*Payments to Employer Regulations, reg 10*) are:

- a statement that the trustees have decided to make a payment;
- the payment amount;
- the date the payment is to be made (at least three months from the date of the notice and not later than the last day on which the valuation certificate is valid for the purposes of *s 37(4)(e)*; and
- a statement that the member may, within one month of the date of the notice, request a copy of the relevant valuation certificate (which the trustees must then provide within one month of their receiving the request).

Where a payment is made, notice must be given to the Regulator within one week (*Payments to Employer Regulations, reg 11*).

Where the scheme is an insured money purchase scheme, a payment may be made to the employer where all the liabilities in respect of the relevant member, beneficiary or estate have been satisfied and there are assets remaining in relation to that member (*Payments to Employer Regulations, reg 8*).

Transitional powers in *PA 2004, s 251* provide trustees with a power to resolve to allow payments in accordance with the new *PA 1995, s 37*. Any such resolution may be made only once, must be made within five years of the provisions coming into force (ie by 6 April 2011), and is subject to notice being given to the employer and members. No payment may be made to an employer unless a resolution has first been made by the trustees under *PA 2004, s 251*.

Schemes in winding-up

11.34 If a registered scheme commences winding up on or after 6 April 2006, any power conferred on the employer or the trustees to distribute assets to the employer on a winding-up cannot be exercised unless the requirements set out in *PA 1995, s 76* and *Payments to Employer Regulations, regs 15–17* are satisfied. These can be summarised as follows:

- the liabilities of the scheme must have been fully discharged;
- where there is any power under the scheme to distribute surplus assets to any person other than the employer, that power must have been exercised or a decision must have been made not to exercise it; and
- notice must have been given to scheme members, in accordance with the prescribed requirements, of the proposal to exercise the power.

Where the trustees or employer propose to exercise the power to make a payment, they must take all reasonable steps to ensure that each member is sent a written notice divided into two parts. The first part must:

- inform the member as to the trustees' estimate of the value of assets remaining and the persons or classes of person to whom, and in what proportions, it is proposed that they should be distributed and whether the requirements of *PA 1995, s 76(3)* are satisfied;
- invite the member to make written representations before a specified date (not earlier than two months from the date the first part of the notice is given); and
- advise the member that the second part of the notice will be issued if they intend to proceed with the proposal and that no assets will be distributed until at least three months after the date on which the second part of the notice is furnished to him.

The second part of the notice must be given after the date specified (see second point above) and at least three months before the power is exercised and must:

- contain the information referred to in the first point above, including any modifications to the proposal; and
- advise the member that he may make written representations to the Regulator before a specified date (not earlier than three months from the date on which the second part of the notice is furnished to him) if he considers *PA 1995, s 76(3)* is not satisfied.

Where the Regulator receives written representations from a member before expiry of the second part of the notice, or obtains from any other source information sufficient to raise a doubt as to whether the requirements of *PA 1995, s 76(3)* have been met, the Regulator may notify the trustees or employer (as appropriate) that the power should not be exercised until the Regulator has confirmed in writing that it is satisfied. Where the three-month time limit has expired and the trustees or employer have heard nothing from the Regulator, they should ask the Regulator for written confirmation that it has not received any representations or information (*Payments to Employer Regulations, regs 16, 17*).

Schemes with more than one employer

11.35 Where a scheme has more than one employer and is divided into two or more sections, the requirements of the Act relating to payments to the employer for both ongoing schemes and schemes which are winding up apply as if each section of the scheme were a separate scheme (*Payments to Employer Regulations, reg 18*) if the provisions of the scheme are such that:

(*a*) different sections of the scheme apply to different employers or groups of employers;

(*b*) contributions payable to the scheme by an employer or by its employees are allocated to that section; and

(*c*) a specified part or a proportion of the assets of the scheme is attributable to each section and cannot be used for the purposes of any other section (or cannot be used for those purposes except on a winding-up).

Trust law requirements relating to the reduction of surpluses

Powers under the trust instrument

11.36 The ways in which a reduction may be achieved may be restricted by the terms of a scheme's trust deed and rules. Usually, these will be wide enough to let the employer and the trustees decide on benefit improvements or a contribution holiday. However, the trust deeds of many schemes established before 1970 include a restriction on the power of amendment to the effect that no amendment can be made which would permit scheme funds to be paid to the employer. It is debatable whether such a restriction can be validly removed; much will depend on the circumstances and the exact wording of the power of amendment. Before agreeing to a payment to the employer, trustees should carefully check all previous trust deeds to ensure that the power of amendment has not been inappropriately amended in the past.

Even if the amendment is possible, trustees must consider whether, in agreeing to it, they are acting in the best interests of the beneficiaries. They may be offered benefit improvements for the beneficiaries in return for making the amendment and subsequently making a payment to the employer. Trustees must balance the security of members' interests in the fund against the benefit improvements on offer when deciding whether to agree to the amendment. The decision is not easy and trustees must consider carefully the propriety of making the amendment when the benefit improvements on offer are relatively small.

Exercise of trustees' powers

11.37 Before agreeing to a payment of surplus to the employer (or, where the trust deed requires their agreement, to an employer's contribution holiday), trustees should obtain independent legal advice and should also consider whether they are subject to any conflicts of interest. For example, a trustee who is also a director of the employer may have difficulty maintaining his impartiality and fulfilling his duties as a trustee. In some circumstances, it may be necessary to appoint independent trustees (see CHAPTER 3).

In exercising their powers, trustees must act in the best interests of the beneficiaries and must act impartially as between the different groups of beneficiaries. If, for example, an agreement was reached between the employer and the employees' representatives, it would indicate that active members find the proposal satisfactory, but the trustees would still have to consider the interests of deferred members and pensioners. Trustees have a duty to negotiate the best bargain they can in the circumstances, taking into consideration the relative balance of power between themselves and the principal employer (see *Re Courage Group's Pension Scheme [1987] 1 All ER 528*). The employer also has obligations to the membership; it must ensure that it is not acting in breach of its implied obligation of good faith (see *Imperial Group Pension Trust Ltd v Imperial Tobacco Ltd [1991] 2 All ER 597*). In practice, it is difficult to see how the trustees can justify making any payment to the employer unless they have also secured some clear advantage (usually benefit improvements) for the beneficiaries.

Chapter 12

Reconstruction and winding up

Introduction

General

12.1 In this chapter the word 'reconstruction' is used to denote some significant change in the nature or structure of an employer's pension arrangements. Such a reconstruction will typically involve:

(*a*) a scheme amendment;

(*b*) a bulk transfer of assets and liabilities between different schemes operated by the same employer (or by employers within the same group); and/or

(*c*) the winding-up of a scheme.

Amendments

12.2 Examples of scheme amendments which are significant enough to be regarded for the purposes of this chapter as reconstructions include:

(*a*) converting a defined benefits scheme into a defined contributions scheme;

(*b*) closing a scheme to future entrants;

(*c*) amending a scheme so that no further benefits accrue under it; or

(*d*) amending a scheme as part of a wider exercise, so as to enable the parties to make bulk transfer payments to other schemes (see **12.3** below) and/or wind up the scheme (see **12.4** below).

Scheme amendments are dealt with further in **12.8** to **12.29** below.

Bulk transfers

12.3 Bulk transfers of assets and liabilities between schemes operating within the same group of employers have become increasingly common in recent years. Typical cases include:

(*a*) bulk transfers from a defined benefit scheme to a defined contribution arrangement; or

(*b*) bulk transfers between defined benefit schemes operating within the same group of employers, so as to replace two or more defined benefit schemes with a single, larger defined benefits scheme. Some of the advantages of having a single, larger scheme are that:

 (i) it avoids the inefficiency for employers of operating some overfunded schemes and some underfunded schemes;

 (ii) administrative costs for a single scheme should be lower owing to economies of scale;

 (iii) a single, larger fund may justify the trustees in pursuing some investment opportunities which might be considered too risky in relation to a smaller fund; and

 (iv) less time and resources overall need be spent on compliance with statutory requirements as there will be only one scheme (rather than several) in relation to which these requirements need to be met.

Bulk transfers are considered further in **12.30** to **12.53** below.

Winding up

12.4 A winding-up occurs when a scheme is terminated and its assets are used to secure the scheme's benefits through other means (typically, by purchasing annuities or making transfer payments to other schemes).

The circumstances in which schemes go into winding-up are varied, but some examples are:

(*a*) where the purpose of the winding-up is to make a bulk transfer to another scheme, often for one of the purposes referred to in **12.3** above;

(*b*) where the employers can no longer afford to run the scheme. The employment law implications of this are considered in CHAPTER 7; or

(*c*) where a scheme (perhaps with few, if any, remaining active members) has become too small to justify the cost of continuing to operate it as a separate scheme.

Winding-up is dealt with in more detail at **12.54** to **12.78** below.

Before dealing further with these areas, it is worth looking at some of the key considerations which will determine how far it is possible to achieve a scheme reconstruction.

Key considerations

Powers

12.5 The trustees and the employers need to be certain that they have the necessary powers to carry out any proposed reconstruction. If, for example, the trustees were to accept a bulk transfer from another scheme in circumstances where they had no power under their trust deed to do so, they could subsequently be challenged by the members and held liable for resulting losses even though the trustees had at the time taken all available steps to ensure that the arrangement was in the members' best interests.

The question of whether the parties have the necessary powers will be determined primarily by the scheme's trust deed and rules. If therefore it is intended, for instance, to amend a scheme, it should be checked that the governing documentation does not impose restrictions on the power of amendment which the proposed alteration would infringe.

The *Pensions Act 2004* (*PA 2004*) has a further bearing on whether the parties have the necessary powers. The effect of the Act in some areas is to restrict the exercise of certain powers which a scheme's rules (when read in isolation) appear to confer, and in other areas the effect is to give wider powers to the trustees. For instance:

(*a*) *Pensions Act 1995* (*PA 1995*), *s 67* introduces certain restrictions on the exercise of the power of amendment, which is modified by *PA 2004, s 262* with effect from 6 April 2006 (dealt with further in **12.18** below); and

(*b*) where a registered defined benefit scheme begins to be wound up after 5 April 1997, any power in the trust deed to apply the assets in respect of pensions or other benefits becomes exercisable by the trustees (even if the trust deed confers that power on another party, such as the employer) (*PA 1995, s 73A(9)*).

It is not sufficient, however, for the employers and the trustees simply to have the necessary powers to carry out the reconstruction; they must ensure that in exercising those powers they act in a manner consistent with their duties as employers (see **12.6** below) and trustees (see **12.7** below) respectively.

Employers' duties

12.6 Many scheme reconstructions are initiated by employers, often prompted by funding concerns. An employer should ensure that its proposals do not contravene its contractual commitments towards its employees in relation to pensions. These commitments will be set out primarily in employees' written terms and conditions of employment (although references to pensions in such documents are usually brief). There will, in addition, be written announcements or booklets issued to the employees explaining the scheme. The position as regards the interaction of all the various Scheme documentation, particularly as to which prevails, had been the subject of many cases over the years and despite the Court of Appeal's ruling in *Steria*, the matter may be far from settled for good. This is considered in more detail in **7.3** above.

Employers are also under an implied contractual duty of good faith (*Imperial Group Pension Trust Ltd v Imperial Tobacco Ltd [1991] 1 WLR 589*). The nature of this duty is that both employers and employees are obliged to act in a manner which is consistent with a relationship of mutual trust and confidence between them. Failure to do so can amount to a breach of contract.

This implied duty of good faith (unlike the more onerous duties placed on trustees) does not require the employer to act solely in the best interests of those to whom the duty is owed; an employer is entitled also to take its own commercial interests into account. It is not possible to give a definitive statement as to what would and would not amount to a breach of that duty. However, the following instances, which can be expected to amount to a breach of the duty of good faith, may be useful as guidelines:

(*a*) a refusal by the employer even to consider (as opposed to considering and then rejecting) alternative proposals put forward by the trustees;

(*b*) putting forward proposals which discriminate between employees (or groups of employees) without justification;

(*c*) threatening to suspend contributions unless the trustees agree to the proposals (*Hillsdown Holdings plc v Pensions Ombudsman [1996] PLR 427*); or

(*d*) threatening never to grant further pension increases unless the parties agree to the proposals (*Imperial Group Pension Trust Ltd v Imperial Tobacco Ltd [1991] 2 All ER 589*).

CHAPTER 7 considers the duty of good faith in further detail (from **7.6** above).

Trustees' duties

12.7 Trustees' powers are of a fiduciary nature, which means that they must exercise them in the best interests of the persons for whose benefit those powers were conferred. In most cases, this will be the scheme's present and past members (and any of their family or dependants who may have an interest in the scheme as a consequence of their membership).

Trustees may also owe a duty towards the employer when exercising certain of their powers. For instance, if the scheme rules give the trustees a discretion to pay surplus assets to the employer on winding-up, they must at least take the employer's interest into account. However, their duties towards scheme members are undoubtedly more onerous than an employer's duty of good faith towards its employees (described in **12.6** above).

This mismatch between the trustees' duties and those of the employer can give rise to a potential conflict of interests between the two sides and trustees should, therefore, seek separate advice wherever such a conflict exists. In the absence of separate advice, trustees may find themselves vulnerable to criticism if their decisions are subsequently called into question by scheme members; even if the trustees have acted entirely in their beneficiaries' best interests, it may be harder to convince the Pensions Ombudsman (or a court) of this if independent advice has not been obtained. In recent years, the Pensions Regulator has put particular focus on the appropriate treatment of conflicts of interest, and both trustees and employers should ensure they are aware of the Regulator's guidance on the subject and deal with situations that may potentially arise having regard to such guidance.

The terms of the trust deed (as qualified by *PA 1995* and *PA 2004* – see **12.5** above) will be relevant, in that any conflict is likely to be less of an issue if the trustees simply have no power to do anything other than implement the employer's proposals; however, such instances are rare (and will become even more so in the future as *PA 2004* shifts the balance of power further from the employer to trustees).

Conflicts can arise not only as between employers and trustees, but also as between the trustees of separate schemes. This may happen where a bulk transfer of assets and liabilities from one scheme to another is under consideration, as the trustees of the two schemes will owe their duties to different groups of beneficiaries. Where there is a conflict, separate advice should again be sought.

Amendments

General

12.8 Scheme reconstructions very often involve amending a scheme, either because the reconstruction itself takes the form of a fundamental change to the scheme's rules, or because an amendment is required to enable the employers or the trustees to make (or receive) a bulk transfer and/or wind up the scheme.

The main ways in which an occupational pension scheme may be amended are:

(*a*) in accordance with a power of amendment contained in the scheme's trust documents;

(*b*) by a court order;

(*c*) by means of a modification order granted by the Pensions Regulator ('the Regulator'); or

(*d*) by a trustees' resolution passed under a specific provision in *PA 1995* or *PA 2004*.

The first of these methods is by far the most common, but it is worth summarising the others before considering the scheme's own power of amendment in more detail.

Court order

12.9 A court order to vary the terms of a trust may be available in the following limited circumstances:

(*a*) On application by the trustees (or, less likely, a beneficiary) under *Trustee Act 1925, s 57*. The basis for any such application must be that the trustees do not have the necessary investment or administrative powers which they need to deal in some particular way with the trust property. The court will need to be convinced that the proposed transaction is expedient.

(*b*) On application to the court under the *Variation of Trusts Act 1958*. This Act (which is not normally used in relation to pension schemes) enables the court to approve amendments on behalf of beneficiaries.

(*c*) Under the court's inherent jurisdiction to vary trusts. The court will generally only exercise this jurisdiction in circumstances where some matter concerning the scheme has in any event come before the court.

Modification orders

12.10 The Regulator has powers under *PA 1995, ss 69–71* to grant orders for the modification of occupational schemes (other than public service schemes) in certain circumstances.

There are two purposes for which the Regulator may grant an order in this context (*PA 1995, s 69*), as illustrated in the following table:

	Who may apply for order	**Orders which may be granted**
Where the purpose, in the case of a registered scheme which is being wound up, is to enable assets remaining after the liabilities have been fully discharged to be distributed to the employer (and all other relevant requirements for that distribution have been met).	The trustees.	• Order authorising the trustees to modify the scheme; or • order modifying the scheme.
Where the purpose is to enable the scheme, for the period from 6 April 1997 to 5 April 1999, to be so treated that an employment to which it applies may be contracted out (see **chapter 4**).	The trustees, the employer or any person other than the trustees who has power to alter the rules of the scheme.	• Order authorising such persons (not restricted to parties to the application) as the Regulator thinks appropriate to modify the scheme; or • order modifying the scheme.

The Regulator may only make such an order if it is satisfied that the desired result cannot be achieved without one, or that it can only be achieved in accordance with a procedure which is liable to be unduly complex or protracted (or involves the obtaining of consents which cannot be obtained without undue delay or difficulty) (*PA 1995, s 70*).

There is provision for such a modification to be retrospective. The modification order may be made or complied with even if the scheme rules or other legal requirements would otherwise prevent it (*PA 1995, s 71*).

Where an application is made to the Regulator under the *Winding-up Notices and Reports Regulations 2002 (SI 2002/459)*, such application will be subject to the following conditions:

(*a*) it must set out the modification required and specify what effect (if any) it may have on benefits;

(*b*) it must specify the reasons for the modification;

(*c*) it must identify any previous application for a modification order made to a court or to the Regulator;

(*d*) it must confirm that the employer is subject to an insolvency procedure;

(*e*) it must specify whether the modification order will reduce the value of the assets; and (*f*) it must contain a statement that notices have been given to members of the scheme and any other relevant persons together with the relevant date(s) where such notice is given.

A member of the scheme in respect of which a notice has been given has the right to make representation to the Regulator within one month of any notice to request a modification order. Before the Regulator considers any application for a modification order it will require:

(i) a copy of the documents which govern the scheme;

(ii) a copy of any actuarial advice on the effect or otherwise of the modification order on the scheme's assets;

(iii) a copy of any legal advice in relation to the application for a modification order;

(iv) a copy of any court determination in relation to the application for a modification order or any similar order; and

(v) a copy of any determination by trustees or managers to wind up the scheme.

Trustees' statutory power to amend

12.11 Subject to limited exceptions (primarily public service schemes), trustees have power under *PA 1995, s 68* to amend a scheme by resolution with a view to achieving any of the following purposes:

(*a*) (subject to the consent of the employer) to extend the class of persons who may receive benefits in respect of the death of a member;

(*b*) to enable the scheme to conform with arrangements required by *PA 1995* prior to 6 April 2006, and by *PA 2004* with effect from 6 April 2006, in respect of the appointment of member-nominated trustees or member-nominated directors (see CHAPTER 3);

(*c*) to enable the scheme to comply with requirements imposed by the Pension Protection Fund in relation to any payment to be made by that body; or

(*d*) to enable the scheme to conform with certain other specified provisions of *PA 1995* and *PA 2004*.

The *Occupational Pension Schemes (Modification of Schemes) Regulations 2006 (SI 2006/759)* prescribe additional circumstances in which trustees have the power to modify schemes under *PA 1995, s 68*. These are to take into account the provision of *FA 2004* and to adopt provisions relating to survivors' benefits for civil partners. There are further sections of *PA 1995* and *PA 2004* and their accompanying regulations which enable the trustees to modify the scheme by resolution for specific purposes. For example, *PA 1995, s 65* enables trustees to alter the scheme in line with the requirements for equal treatment as between men and women (see CHAPTER 9).

Scheme's own power of amendment – general

Need for power

12.12 An occupational pension scheme may well continue in operation for several decades. During that time, it will almost certainly need to be adapted to cater for circumstances which could not reasonably have been predicted at the outset. For this reason, it is essential that the documents governing the scheme contain a power of amendment.

If no amendment power is included in the interim deed, it may still be possible to adopt a suitable power in the scheme's definitive deed, to take effect retrospectively to the date of the interim deed (*Re Imperial Foods Ltd Pension Scheme [1986] 2 All ER 802*).

The consequences of omitting the power from the definitive deed will be more serious and render it unlikely that a power of amendment can validly be inserted into the documents at a future date. It may still be possible subsequently to adopt a power of amendment, if it can clearly be shown that it had always been intended to include the power but that it was omitted by mistake; however, this would involve a court application.

Exercise of power

12.13 The exercise of any power of amendment must be carried out by the persons, and in accordance with any requirements (for instance, that there be a deed), specified in the provision conferring that power. The vast majority of amendment powers require some involvement by both the principal employer and the trustees before the scheme may be amended.

To the extent that an employer is involved in the exercise of the power, it must act in accordance with its implied duty of good faith towards its employees (see **12.6** above). In the rare cases where an employer has power to amend without requiring the agreement of the trustees, the courts can be expected to scrutinise the exercise of that power particularly strictly.

The trustees' duties are more onerous, as mentioned earlier in **12.7** above. Some examples of the sorts of amendments which trustees may and may not properly agree to are considered in **12.23** to **12.29** below. At this point, however, it is enough to say that trustees must not, as a matter of trust law, agree to amendments which reduce benefits earned before the amendment power is exercised (whether or not immediately payable).

Whoever exercises the power of amendment must do so for the purpose for which it was conferred, namely (unless the trust deed indicates otherwise) to promote the purposes of the scheme. Any statement in the trust deed as to the scheme's main purpose may therefore be relevant to the validity of a subsequent amendment. However, this purpose need not remain fixed indefinitely, and it was recognised in the *Courage* case that a scheme's underlying purpose may change gradually as a scheme evolves over a period of time (*Re Courage Group's Pension Schemes [1987] 1 WLR 495*).

The *Courage* case itself provides an example of scheme amendments which were successfully challenged in court as not promoting the schemes' purposes. There were three schemes involved, whose principal employer had recently been acquired by a new owner. The aim of the amendments was to enable the new owner (who had no genuine relationship with the members and was already negotiating to sell the existing principal employer) to be substituted as the schemes' new principal employer, and so gain some benefit from the schemes' surplus funds. This conflicted with the purpose for which the schemes had been established, which was the provision of retirement benefits. The judge specifically commented upon the fact that the new owner was not recognisably the successor to the business or workforce of the company for which it was intended to be substituted.

The case of *Harwood-Smart v Caws [2000] PLR 101* arose following the compulsory liquidation of the employer. The trustees asked the court to determine whether they had to use any surplus to increase benefits to Revenue maxima prior to making any repayment to the employers. It was found in favour of the beneficiaries rather than the employers. The original trust provisions on winding-up had required any surplus to be used to enhance benefits to Revenue maxima prior to making any payment to the employers. The power of amendment contained a specific prohibition on paying any part of the fund back to the employers. However, the power of amendment had itself been subsequently amended and been used to amend the winding-up provisions to permit refunds to be paid to the employers without increasing members' benefits in excess of their entitlement. The court found that this power of amendment was invalid.

In the other recent case of *Bestrustees v Stuart [2001] PLR 283*, the BAI pension scheme amended its normal retirement age to 65 for all members following the case of *Barber v GRE [1990] ECR I-1889* in the European Court of Justice in 1990. This case arose around the ambiguity of how and when the decision was made to amend the rules to effect equalisation. As the employer was also trustee, the issue of consent by the other party did not arise. The amendment to the rules was found to be of limited effect. The scheme was in deficit and in the process of being wound up while its assets were used to apply for a decision in circumstances where it was suggested that the professional trustees should have exercised their discretion.

In *Sovereign Trustees Ltd v Glover [2007] EWHC 1750 (Ch)*, the High Court emphasised the need to comply with the scheme's power of amendment in order for amendments to be valid.

The trust deed and rules of a group defined benefit scheme included specific provisions regarding amendment. Following a review of the scheme by benefit consultants on the principal employer's instructions, the then trustees wrote to all active members to inform them that the company was introducing changes to the scheme: from 1 April 1998, future service benefits would be provided on a money purchase basis. From that date, contributions and benefits were paid on the basis that the scheme had been amended. Two of the three trustees had passed a resolution that 'the Company's proposals be accepted in full'. The question for the court was whether the money purchase section of the scheme had been validly created.

The court ruled that the resolution was not effective to amend the scheme; it merely recorded the adoption of a policy now for implementation later by amendments made in accordance with the rules. Accordingly, the money purchase section of the scheme had not been validly created.

The outcome of this case is not surprising, but it reinforces the need to ensure that amendments are made in accordance with the scheme's power of amendment and that when resolutions are passed it is clear to all concerned precisely what the scope of that resolution is. Further, where employer consent is required to an amendment, that requirement is not satisfied merely by fact that the amendment was originally proposed by that employer.

More recently in *Walker Morris Trustees Ltd v Masterson and another [2009] EWHC (Ch)* the trustees' failure to take actuarial advice, as required by the amendment rule, led to the amendments made since 1974 being declared invalid.

The power of amendment allowed the trustees, with the consent of the principal employer, to amend the definitive deed by deed and to amend the rules by deed or resolution. It also required a written opinion from the actuary that members' rights 'secured in terms of the Scheme prior to the [effective date of the amendment]' would not be substantially prejudiced. The main issue was that there was no evidence that the actuary's written opinion had been sought or obtained for any of the amendments.

The first question was whether the amendment rule required the trustees to seek the opinion of the actuary even in cases where there could not possibly be any prejudice to members' benefits. The judge (Mr Justice Peter Smith) looked at a number of cases on the interpretation of pension schemes. He found that the clause was clear and it did require the trustees to seek the opinion of the actuary in all cases. He accepted that this gave an unfortunate result but that it did not arise out of an overly literal or technical interpretation of the deed, but from the trustees having ignored the clear provision. The consequence of this is that none of the amending deeds were valid.

The court went on to consider whether those amendments which were supported by a *s 67* certificate could stand (on the basis that the actuary had been involved). It was held that *s 67* certificates are designed for a different purpose and could not be used to save the proposed amendments.

Effect of winding-up

12.14 It is unlikely that a power of amendment can be exercised once winding-up has started, unless the terms of that power and the other provisions of the scheme rules indicate a contrary intention (*Thrells v Lomas [1992] PLR 233.*) However, a power of amendment can probably be exercised (unless the scheme rules indicate otherwise), after an employer has given notice to wind up a scheme, but before that notice has expired (*Municipal Mutual v Harrop [1998] PLR 149*).

Many trust deeds include wording to the effect that the trusts of the scheme will cease once winding-up begins, and this can be taken to include any amendment power. Others include a provision to the effect that amendments may be made during the winding-up stage, in which case the power will continue to be exercisable.

If a scheme's winding-up rule has not been triggered, but the scheme has become closed to new entrants or benefits have ceased to accrue, the power of amendment remains exercisable unless the scheme rules suggest that it does not.

Retrospective amendments

12.15 A power of amendment may be worded so as to permit scheme amendments to take effect from a date earlier than the date on which they are made. Retrospective amendments may validly be made under such a power, although the requirements of *PA 1995, s 67* (as amended by *PA 2004, s 262*) will usually apply (see **12.18** below).

If the power of amendment does not expressly allow retrospective alterations, the position is less certain. In reality, a court's decision on the validity of a purportedly retrospective amendment in these circumstances may depend on the nature of the change. A retrospective amendment made simply to ensure compliance with some statutory requirement would probably be upheld; a more controversial alteration might not.

Not surprisingly, therefore, the judge in *Municipal Mutual v Harrop [1998] PLR 149* disallowed a retrospective amendment which would have taken away vested rights. He also decided that the amendment could not be upheld on the grounds that its purpose was to correct an error in the scheme rules.

Restrictions

12.16 An amendment will not be valid if it infringes restrictions written into the amendment power under which it is made. Some of the more common restrictions found in amendment powers are as follows:

(*a*) That no amendment may be made which would alter the main purpose of the scheme. This reflects the general law on scheme amendments (see **12.13** above).

(*b*) That no amendment may be made which would result in surplus assets being returned to the employers. Such restrictions were built into some older trust deeds in order to comply with requirements of tax approval which no longer apply. *PA 1995* has introduced provisions to overcome restrictions of this nature in certain circumstances (see **12.10** above).

(*c*) That no amendment may reduce pensions in payment or accrued benefits. This adds nothing to existing trust law principles; the position is now reinforced by *PA 1995* (see **12.18** below).

(*d*) That amendments (or amendments of a certain nature) may be made only with the members' consent. Sometimes the members concerned are simply not contactable; *PA 1995* helps to relieve this problem.

Of course, an amendment will not be valid if it infringes overriding legislation.

Amending a power of amendment

12.17 The presence of unwanted restrictions in an amendment power raises the question of whether those restrictions can be removed by amending the power of amendment.

If the trust deed states that the amendment power can itself be amended, then this should be possible. However, if the restriction being removed is one which can only serve to protect members' interests, the change may be hard for the trustees to justify.

If there is no express power to amend the power of amendment, it will generally not be possible (without a court order or modification order) to remove restrictions which have been there since the scheme was established; widening the amendment power in this way would be like introducing an amendment power where none had previously existed.

However, removing a restriction which did not exist at the scheme's inception but was introduced at a later date may present less of a problem. The nature of the restriction being removed, how it arose, and how long it has been in place, are likely to be relevant.

It is not usual for the parties to wish to introduce restrictions where none previously existed. Were the trustees to do so, they would be in breach of the general trust law duty not to fetter their own discretion (although it is possible for that duty to be excluded by an express provision in the trust deed).

Statutory protection of entitlements and accrued rights

General

12.18 Since 6 April 1997, under *PA 1995, s 67*, any power conferred by an occupational pension scheme (other than a public service pension scheme) to modify the scheme could not be exercised 'in a manner which would or might affect any entitlement, or accrued right, of any member of the scheme acquired before the power is exercised' unless the statutory requirements were satisfied. These provisions were replaced from 6 April 2006 by *PA 2004, s 262*, which replaces *PA 1995, s 67*.

Under the original provisions of *s 67*, consideration had to be given to whether an amendment would or might affect accrued rights or entitlements. Under the new *s 67*, the question is whether the power to modify is being used to make what is called a regulated modification. A regulated modification is either:

(*a*) a protected modification; or

(*b*) a detrimental modification,

or is both.

A protected modification is a modification which would or might result in the reduction of any pension in payment; and/or a modification which involves converting defined benefit rights into defined contribution rights.

A detrimental modification is a modification that would or might adversely affect the subsisting rights of any member of the scheme or any survivor of a member of the scheme. A detrimental modification is the type of modification under the original *s 67* provisions that can only be made if member consent is obtained.

Any exercise of a power to make a regulated modification is voidable unless certain conditions are satisfied. These conditions are as follows:

(*a*) In the case of each affected member for protected modifications (converting defined benefit rights into defined contribution rights or reducing pensions in payment) the consent requirement must be satisfied and for detrimental modifications (those which would or might adversely affect subsisting rights) either the consent requirement or the actuarial equivalence requirement must be satisfied.

(*b*) In respect of all regulated modifications the trustee approval requirements and the reporting requirement must be satisfied.

(i) The trustee approval requirement

Before the trustees can approve any proposed modifications, they must be satisfied that the actuarial requirements set out below have been complied with. Only then can the trustees decide to exercise the power of amendment and give effect to the proposed modifications.

(ii) The trustee reporting requirement

Trustees must take reasonable steps to notify members of the decision taken regarding the modification, within a reasonable period of it being made, and before the modification takes effect. The Code of Practice suggests that a 'reasonable period' to notify members would be within one month of the decision.

(*c*) In summary there are three pre-conditions to make a regulated modification which are consent or actuarial equivalence requirements, trustee approval requirement and reporting requirement.

Under the new provisions the consent requirement is made up of two components which are the informed consent requirement and the timing requirement.

The consent requirement

12.19 The consent requirement is satisfied if the trustees give information to members explaining the proposed modification, the trustees notify members that they may make representations to the trustees about the modification, members are notified that the consent requirements apply and the member then gives his consent to the proposed modification in writing.

Once the member has given his consent, the timing requirement is satisfied if the modification takes effect within a reasonable period after the giving of consent.

The actuarial equivalence requirement

12.20 The actuarial equivalence requirement applies in relation to a detrimental modification that is not a protected modification (ie a modification which would involve or might adversely affect subsisting rights but not a modification which involves converting defined benefit rights into defined contribution rights or reducing pensions in payment) and where the trustees determine that this test is to apply.

The actuarial equivalence test has three aspects which are the information requirement, the actuarial value requirement and the actuarial equivalence statement requirement.

(*a*) *The information requirement*

Under this requirement, trustees must, before the modification is made, take all reasonable steps to provide affected members with information in writing that adequately explains:

- the nature of the modification
- the effect on the members
- that the members may make representations to the trustees and how to do so.
- what constitutes actuarial equivalence and how it will be achieved.
- that the members should consider whether they need to take independent financial advice.

What constitutes taking 'all reasonable steps' to provide the above information, will vary depending on the particular circumstances. The Pensions Regulator's Code of Practice No 10 'Modification of subsisting rights' contains the following suggestions:

- Where the affected members are still employed by the employer, use of internal post or email may be appropriate.
- In the case of other members, the use of post will usually be appropriate, although where contact has been lost, the trustees

should consider using the local newspapers to alert the deferred members to the proposals and invite them to get in contact.

The members must be given reasonable opportunity to make representation to the trustees about the proposed modifications. The Code of Practice contains guidelines on how trustees should manage this. The Regulator expects members to be given at least four weeks to make representations. However, this will vary according to the number of members and complexity of the modifications.

Members should be able to contact the trustees during this period and ask any questions they may have, and answers should be given as soon as is reasonably practicable.

- Once representations have been received, the trustees must take time to consider them, obtain any further advice and hold discussions with the employer to identify whether any changes to the proposals are necessary in light of the representations.
- If changes to the proposals are needed, the trustees must consider whether this renders the modifications materially different, and legal and actuarial advice might be sought on this. If the changes are deemed material, the information requirement will need to be recommenced so that members have an opportunity to comment on the amended proposals.

If the changes are not deemed material, the trustees will have fulfilled the information requirement.

(*b*) *The actuarial value requirement*

This requirement is satisfied if the trustees have taken steps to secure that 'actuarial value' will be maintained. Actuarial value is maintained if the actuarial value, immediately after the time at which the modification takes effect, of the member's subsisting rights is equal to or greater than the actuarial value of his subsisting rights immediately before that time.

(*c*) *The actuarial equivalence statement*

The final condition of the actuarial equivalence requirement is that trustees obtain an actuarial statement, usually from the scheme actuary, within a reasonable period after the effective date of the modification.

The statement must certify that at the time the proposed modification took effect, the actuarial value of each affected member's subsisting rights immediately after the change is no less than it was immediately before the change. The Code of Practice specifies 'a reasonable period' to be one month in this instance.

Civil penalties

12.21 The new *PA 1995, s 67* provides that, where a modification is held to be voidable, then civil penalties under *PA 1995, s 10* may be applied to any trustee who has failed to take all reasonable steps to secure that the modification was not voidable.

Affected schemes

12.22 The new *PA 1995, s 67* applies to any power conferred on any person by an occupational pension scheme to modify the scheme. The new provisions do not apply to a public service pension scheme or a 'prescribed scheme' or a scheme of a 'prescribed description'.

Examples

12.23 The following examples consider some of the scheme amendments which an employer might wish to make, and whether the trustees could properly agree to them.

It is assumed for this purpose that the scheme's amendment power is wide enough to allow the amendments proposed but that agreement between the employer and the trustees is required.

The employer's decision to make these amendments and whether such decision accords with its contractual obligations will be governed by the principles outlined in **7.6** to **7.10** above.

Reduction of past service benefits

12.24 Trustees should think carefully before agreeing to an amendment which reduces any benefit earned before the amendment power is exercised (whether payable immediately or from some time in the future). If the trustees were to agree to such amendment, it would arguably be a breach of trust (quite apart from the requirements of *PA 1995, s 67*).

Sometimes an employer will propose a method of recalculating all past service benefits which appears to represent a general benefit improvement but, on closer examination, disadvantages a small number of members. The trustees should not agree to the proposals unless they are revised to remove that detriment; it is no defence to a breach of trust action brought by a disadvantaged minority that the arrangements benefit the majority.

Reduction of future service benefits

12.25 Trustees should not agree to a reduction in future benefit accrual without compelling reasons. For example, if the likely outcome of the trustees refusing to agree to the reduction is that the employer will arrange for the scheme to be wound up the trustees may take the view that they are acting in the best interests of their members by agreeing to the change. Trustees do also owe a duty to the employer (see CHAPTER 3), and are not required to push the company into paying more than it can genuinely afford. This is also a matter which may need to be considered when negotiating scheme funding (see **chapter 11**). There is always a difficult balance for trustees to strike between the protection of future service benefits and ensuring the security of benefits accrued to date. Consideration of the strength of the employer covenant can be particularly important in this context.

Amending the scheme so that no further benefits will accrue in the future

12.26 This is simply a more drastic version of **12.25** above, and so the same principles apply.

Closing the scheme to future entrants

12.27 The proposal here will be that an amendment is made to the scheme's eligibility rule so that no further members may join the scheme in the future. This will not necessarily cause the trustees significant problems as the main effect of the amendment will be to exclude individuals who have never belonged to the scheme and to whom the trustees will, therefore, not normally owe a duty. It may raise age discrimination issues for the employer.

However, some schemes impose a 'waiting period' for membership, so that an employee has to complete, say, six months' service before he is allowed to join the scheme. Individuals currently serving this 'waiting period' can be regarded as being contingently entitled to benefits from the scheme, and the trustees would usually, therefore, be well advised (unless the scheme is seriously underfunded) to insist that the closure to new entrants does not affect these particular individuals.

Introduction of different benefits for future joiners

12.28 The concern here is very often that the new benefits package is (or is capable of being) less generous than the one for current members. The issues which this raises for trustees are similar to those in **12.27** above, in that the individuals to be affected by the amendment will not yet be scheme members.

The same considerations as regards anyone serving a 'waiting period' will apply.

Conversion to defined contribution

12.29 An employer may continue to operate its defined benefits scheme on the existing basis for current members, but decide that future joiners should be admitted to membership on a defined contribution basis only. This is an example of the sort of amendment described in **12.28** above.

The trustees will face harder decisions if they are asked to agree to an amendment which will convert the current defined benefit scheme members to a defined contribution basis for future accrual (and possibly also for past service benefits).

The trustees, acting on actuarial advice, should not hesitate where appropriate to seek from the employer improvements in the defined contribution benefits being offered. This might take the form of:

(*a*) a more generous method of conversion (if it is proposed to convert past service benefits);

(*b*) an increase in the employer's future contributions; or

(*c*) possibly even some form of 'defined benefit underpin' for the members involved, so that their eventual benefits will not dip below a given level.

The employer may be prepared to compromise on at least some of these points in order to see the conversion go ahead. The improvements will also make the exercise easier for the employer to justify to its employees.

The trustees should seek actuarial advice as to how the employer's proposals will compare with the existing defined benefit basis. Applying the principles set out in **12.24** and **12.25** above, the position will normally be as follows:

(i) The trustees should have no difficulties in agreeing to the proposals in relation to any member whom those proposals will clearly benefit.

(ii) The trustees should not agree to the proposals in relation to any member for whom the risks or other disadvantages of those proposals outweigh any advantage.

(iii) If neither of the above applies in relation to a member, the trustees should generally be reluctant to permit the conversion to take place without his consent. In seeking his consent, the position should be explained fully to him in terms which he can understand and which clearly draw his attention to any risks involved. He should also be advised to seek independent financial advice. If he decides to consent, he should be asked to sign a consent form which states that the decision reached is his own and that the trustees will not be held responsible for it.

In some circumstances, the trustees may justifiably go further than this towards accommodating the employer's proposals (for instance, if the future service benefits offered are genuinely the best which the employer can afford). However, in no circumstances should the trustees allow a reduction in the value of a member's accrued benefits. The conversion of past service defined benefits to a defined contribution basis will be a protected modification and require consent under *PA 1995, s 67* (see **12.18** above).

Bulk transfers – general

Background

12.30 Some of the reasons for making bulk transfers of assets and liabilities between schemes operating within the same group of employers were outlined in **12.3** above. The matters that arise in relation to bulk transfers vary to some extent according to whether or not the transferring scheme has begun to be wound up before the time of the transfer (see **12.45** to **12.53** below). Here, however, some general issues are considered.

Members' consents to transfer

12.31 An advantage of obtaining members' consents to the transfer is that, if matters have been properly and clearly explained to the members, they are less likely to feel aggrieved about the transfer arrangements later on.

However, the fact that members' consents are being sought in no way relieves the trustees of the responsibility to ensure that the arrangements are in the members' best interests. The consent form which members are asked to sign may contain a statement discharging the transferring trustees from any further liability, but it may not be possible for trustees to rely on this discharge if it is later shown that they did not take proper steps to protect their members.

In seeking consents, care should be taken not to give unauthorised investment advice contrary to the *Financial Services and Markets Act 2000* (explained further in **10.25** above) and members should be encouraged to seek independent financial advice before taking a decision.

In reality, however, obtaining the consent of the entire membership will often be impractical, particularly in relation to deferred pensioners, some of whom are likely to have moved house and not advised their former employer or the trustees of their new address. Transfers to other occupational pension schemes (but not to personal pension schemes) are therefore permissible without the need for members' consents, but only if:

(*a*) either:

(i) the scheme rules expressly permit transfers to be made without consent; or

(ii) the transferring scheme is a registered defined benefit scheme, the transfer follows the commencement, after 5 April 1997, of the winding-up of that scheme and the requirements dealt with in **12.56** to **12.57** below are met; and

(*b*) either:

(i) both schemes apply to employment with the same employer (which is generally taken to mean that the two schemes must have at least one participating employer in common); or

(ii) it is a bulk (as opposed to an individual) transfer, either resulting from a financial transaction between the employers or where the employers are 'connected' for the purposes of the legislation (*Occupational Pension Schemes (Preservation of Benefit) Regulations 1991 (SI 1991/167), reg 12(2)* (the '*Preservation Regulations*'));

(*c*) an actuarial certificate (often called a 'GN16', this being the number of the Guidance Note issued by the Institute and Faculty of Actuaries regulating the preparation of such certificates) is given to the effect that:

(i) the transfer credits in the receiving scheme for each member are broadly no less favourable than the rights being transferred; and

(ii) there is good cause to believe that the award of discretionary benefits (or discretionary benefit increases) in the receiving scheme will be broadly no less favourable than any established custom of awarding discretionary benefits (or discretionary benefit increases) in the transferring scheme (*Preservation Regulations, reg 12(3)*). For this purpose, the actuary may make an allowance for any amount by which the transfer credits under the receiving scheme are more favourable than the rights to be transferred; and

(*d*) in relation to contracted-out arrangements (see **chapter 4**) the transfer is not of such a kind that members' consents are required as set out in **4.33** above. These requirements used to be particularly onerous in relation to protected rights but the *Protected Rights (Transfer Payment) (Amendment) Regulations 2005 (SI 2005/2906)* permit, from 28 November 2005, the bulk transfer of protected rights to a contracted-out defined contributions scheme or the defined contribution section of a mixed benefit scheme, without members' consent; provided that the amount is at least equal to the value of the cash equivalent and transferring members must either be given at least three months' notice and have the opportunity to object, or be given at least one month's notice; subject to an actuary's statement that a member's rights will be broadly no less favourable (see CHAPTER 4). At the time of writing, it is arguable (but by no means certain) that these requirements do not apply so long as the transferring scheme is a registered defined benefits scheme, the transfer follows the commencement, after 5 April 1997, of the winding-up of that scheme and the requirements dealt with in **12.56** to **12.57** below are met.

Where a transfer is to be made without consent, information about the proposed transfer and details of the value of the rights to be transferred (including rights in respect of death in service benefits and survivors' benefits) must be given to each member affected not less than one month before the proposed transfer is due to take place (*Preservation Regulations, reg 12(4B)*).

The ability to transfer without consent in these circumstances applies only to past service benefits. Future service benefits cannot accrue without consent in the receiving scheme; this would amount to compulsory scheme membership contrary to *Pension Schemes Act 1993* (*PSA 1993*), *s 160*.

Even where all the above conditions are met, the trustees may not exercise a discretion to make a transfer unless they are satisfied that it is in their members' best interests.

Issues for trustees to consider

12.32 The matters to be borne in mind by the trustees in deciding whether they are doing the best for their members will vary according to the circumstances, but the following issues are amongst those which will most commonly arise. It is assumed here that the trustees have some discretion as to whether the transfer takes place.

Benefits

12.33 The employers may offer benefit improvements in order to encourage the trustees to agree to the transfer. If improvements are not offered, the trustees should seek them (particularly if, without any, there is no advantage for their members in the transfer going ahead). This is potentially an issue for both the transferring and receiving trustees.

The transferring trustees should examine closely the benefits which are offered in respect of the transfer and guard against the possibility of agreeing to proposals which result in any person's benefits being reduced. Trustees' duties in relation to changes in benefits were considered in **12.23** to **12.29** above in the context of scheme amendments. The same principles apply in relation to transfers, so that trustees will be in breach of trust if they agree to a transfer which reduces any person's past service benefits, and only exceptionally may they agree to a transfer which reduces future benefits (for instance, in the circumstances outlined in **12.25** above).

The transferring trustees should also consider the Revenue issues relating to loss of protection of tax-free cash amounts and loss of enhanced protection that may occur if certain requirements are not satisfied. See **15.42** for more detail. Additionally, as scheme mergers often involve not just the bulk transfer of accrued benefits but also the future provision of benefits in the 'new scheme', employers and trustees should carefully consider the potential impact of the 'anti-forestalling' tax legislation introduced from 22 April 2009, as this could potentially be a significant issue for certain members.

Funding disparity

12.34 Another issue is the comparative funding levels of the transferring and receiving schemes. If, for example, the trustees of an ongoing scheme are considering whether to make a bulk transfer, they should seek advice as to the solvency of both the transferring and receiving schemes respectively. If the transferring scheme is significantly better funded than the receiving scheme, the transferring trustees should question whether they can justify making a transfer which would, in effect, put their members into a worse funded scheme than the one to which they presently belong.

How much of an issue this is will depend not only on the extent of the funding disparity but also on other factors. For instance, both schemes might be well funded, but the receiving scheme only slightly less so than the transferring scheme. In these circumstances the transferring trustees could properly take the view that the modest funding disparity was outweighed by any more significant advantages of the transfer, such as:

(*a*) better benefits to be provided by the receiving scheme;

(*b*) provisions in the receiving scheme's rules creating greater scope than under the transferring scheme for surplus assets to be used for benefit improvements; or

(*c*) a likelihood of the receiving scheme's future investment performance significantly outstripping that of the transferring scheme (perhaps because the receiving scheme is much larger – see **12.36** below).

If the funding disparity remains an issue, the transferring trustees should impose conditions upon the employers (and, where appropriate, the receiving trustees) before agreeing to make the transfer. These conditions might typically include one or both of the following:

(i) That a benefit improvement be granted in respect of the members to be transferred.

(ii) That any surplus to be transferred from the transferring scheme be subject to some measure of 'ringfencing' in the receiving scheme. The aim of ringfencing is to ensure that assets transferred from the transferring scheme are subject to safeguards for the benefit of the transferring members in the receiving scheme. This is done by amending the rules of the receiving scheme, so as (in this context) to give the transferring members prior rights over other members as regards the transferred assets in relation to such matters as:

- any use of surplus assets to grant benefit improvements;
- the calculation of future transfer values paid from the receiving scheme; and/or
- the distribution of assets on a winding-up of the receiving scheme. However, such an amendment may be partly or wholly ineffective if the receiving scheme subsequently goes into winding-up with insufficient assets to meet all its liabilities. This is because of the winding-up requirements in *PA 1995* and *PA 2004* which, at least to some extent (as explained further in **12.68** to **12.73** below), override the scheme's rules.

The employer may well insist that any 'ringfencing' provisions only remain effective for a specified period of time. In agreeing to a suitable period, the trustees should consider actuarial advice as to how long the surplus might otherwise have lasted in the transferring scheme.

The transferring trustees are likely to have less negotiating power, however, if their scheme has gone into winding-up.

If, conversely, the receiving scheme is better funded than the transferring scheme, then similar considerations in reverse will have to be borne in mind by the receiving scheme's trustees before they exercise any discretion under the terms of their trust deed to accept the transfer.

Comparison of balance of powers

12.35 The trustees of an ongoing scheme ought also, before agreeing to make a transfer, to consider the 'balance of powers' (as between the employers, on the one hand, and the trustees, on the other) under the provisions of their own scheme and compare it with the corresponding balance in the receiving scheme. If the receiving scheme's balance of powers is overall less favourable towards the trustees (and therefore the beneficiaries) than under the transferring scheme, then the transferring trustees should again question whether they can properly make the transfer.

An unfavourable shift in the balance of powers may be compensated for by other factors; for instance, if the receiving scheme is significantly better funded than the transferring scheme, provides better benefits, or (as mentioned in **12.36** below) has better prospects for future growth. If this is not the case, however, then the trustees should consider obtaining from the employer some benefit or safeguard for their members before agreeing to the transfer. This might take the form of:

(*a*) an immediate benefit improvement in respect of the transferring members; or

(*b*) amendments to the receiving scheme to make its balance of powers more favourable to the trustees, at least in so far as that scheme will ultimately relate to the transferring members. Where surplus assets are being transferred, any such amendment will be another form of 'ringfencing' as referred to in **12.34(ii)** above. The difference here, however, is that the purpose of the ringfencing will be to protect the transferring members' interests against those of the employers (rather than against those of the other members).

The issue will not be as acute for the transferring trustees if their scheme is already in winding-up.

Long-term future of schemes and employer covenant

12.36 It is increasingly difficult to predict the long-term stability and growth of any pension scheme, but it is nevertheless an issue which trustees should bear in mind. The overall financial circumstances of a scheme's sponsoring employers may give a clue as to the scheme's future. Another factor is the scheme's size.

Many transfers of the sort discussed in this chapter are from smaller schemes to larger schemes. Larger funds tend to bear proportionately lower administrative costs (owing to economies of scale) and may be able to pursue a successful investment strategy which might not realistically be available to a smaller scheme. Additionally, it is sometimes the case that the receiving scheme has a principal employer at its helm that is higher up the corporate chain and may enjoy a better employer covenant than the transferring scheme's principal employer. This should theoretically provide better security of benefits for members. However, trustees should be wary of relying too heavily on the size of a scheme or an improved employer covenant to justify a transfer which would not otherwise be in their members' best interests.

It is comparatively rare for trustees to be asked to agree to a transfer to a smaller scheme within the same group of employers. The trustees should make certain that there is a clear advantage for their members (most probably in the form of benefit improvements) should this happen.

Of course, if the transferring scheme is already being wound up, that scheme will not have any long-term future for the trustees to consider.

Other ways of securing benefits on a winding-up

12.37 If the transferring scheme is in the course of being wound up, some of the issues mentioned above may be less relevant, as members will not have the alternative simply of remaining in the transferring scheme. Instead, the transferring trustees should satisfy themselves that any bulk transfer will be on terms which serve their members at least as well as the other courses of action available (such as transfers to personal pension schemes or purchasing annuities).

Contracted-out schemes

12.38 Further requirements apply in relation to contracted-out schemes. These requirements are dealt with in **4.42** above.

Transfer agreement

12.39 It is advisable for the parties involved to enter into a formal transfer agreement where the terms of the arrangement which has been entered into can be clearly set out. The parties will usually be the trustees of the two schemes and each scheme's principal employer. The terms of any such agreement will vary enormously depending on the circumstances, but **12.40** to **12.44** below describe the provisions which will most often be included.

Some of these are, in reality, scheme amendments. The parties could, as an alternative, deal with these areas in separate deeds of amendment relating to the two schemes, but it is often more convenient to deal with all matters relating to the transfer in a single document. However, it is not uncommon for a benefit harmonising exercise to be carried out prior to the transfer exercise in an attempt to make the transfer process run more smoothly. Care should be taken to ensure that, if the transfer agreement is to amend either of the schemes, it complies with all the relevant requirements of that scheme's power of amendment (for instance, by being in the form of a deed).

The agreement will typically cover the following areas.

Amendments to the transferring scheme

12.40 Amendments to the transferring scheme may be necessary to:

(*a*) permit the parties to make the bulk transfer; and/or

(*b*) grant any benefit improvements which the transferring trustees require as a condition of their making the transfer. Alternatively, there may be some form of augmentation of benefits carried out between the trustees and the employer immediately prior to transfer.

Transfer amount

12.41 This may be stated as a specific sum (subject to a market value adjustment and/or increase for late payment) or the agreement may simply set out the method by which the amount is to be calculated (perhaps by reference to an actuary's letter appended to the agreement). If the agreement provides for the transferring scheme's entire assets to be transferred, then the precise calculation of the amount becomes less of an issue.

Past service benefits

12.42 The benefits to be provided in the receiving scheme in relation to the transfer payment should be clearly stated.

Amendments to the receiving scheme

12.43 Amendments may be required in relation to the receiving scheme, for instance, to:

(*a*) permit the parties to accept the transfer;

(*b*) incorporate any special future service benefits in relation to the transferring members which have been agreed;

(*c*) grant any benefit improvements for the receiving scheme's existing members which the receiving trustees require as a condition of their accepting the transfer; and/or (*d*) incorporate any 'ringfencing' provisions (as referred to in **12.34(ii)** and **12.35(*b*)** above) which have been agreed between the parties as a condition of the transfer being made.

Indemnity

12.44 The transferring trustees may seek an indemnity from the receiving trustees in relation to any claims which might be brought against them in relation to the transferring members. The receiving trustees should of course consider how this might affect their own members' interests. Any such indemnity will normally exclude matters where there has been an element of bad faith or dishonesty by the transferring trustees and be limited, for instance, to that part of the receiving scheme's assets which is attributable to the transfer payment.

To the extent that these assets may be insufficient fully to indemnify the transferring trustees, one or more of the employers may agree to indemnify the transferring trustees for the difference; however, care should be taken not to infringe the provisions of the *Companies Act 2006* regarding companies indemnifying their own officers (referred to in further detail at **3.61** above).

Bulk transfers – specific issues where winding-up has not commenced

Background

12.45 The questions of whether there is power to make a bulk transfer, and how any transfer payment is to be calculated, will attract different answers depending on whether or not the transferring scheme has gone into winding-up at the time of the transfer. The date on which a scheme commences to be wound up for this purpose is governed by *PA 1995, s 124(3A)–(3E)* (or, for schemes commencing winding-up before 6 April 2005, by *Occupational Pension Schemes (Winding-up) Regulations 1996 (SI 1996/3126), reg 2* (the '*Winding-up Regulations*')).

Where winding-up has not commenced (or is not even expected to happen), the position is as set out in **12.46** and **12.47** below. (The corresponding position where winding-up has commenced is dealt with in **12.48** to **12.52** below.)

Power to make bulk transfers

12.46 Whether there is power to make a bulk transfer out of a scheme which is not in winding-up depends upon the terms of that scheme's trust deed and rules. If there is power to make the transfer, much will depend on whether the trust deed and rules place that power primarily with the employers or with the trustees. For instance:

(*a*) the principal employer might have power to direct the trustees to make a transfer, with the trustees having no right of refusal;

(*b*) the principal employer might have power to request the trustees to make a transfer, with the trustees having a discretion as to whether or not they act on that request;

(*c*) the trustees might have power to initiate a transfer, subject only to the employer's consent. This gives the trustees a greater degree of control than in (*b*) above since, in putting their proposals to the employer, the trustees are effectively requiring the employer to consider those proposals in a manner consistent with its implied duty of good faith (see **12.6** above);

(*d*) the trustees might have power to make a transfer, subject only to consultation with the employer. So long as a genuine consultation procedure is carried out, this does not require the trustees actually to obtain the employer's consent; or

(*e*) the trustees might have power to make a bulk transfer without any form of reference to the employer being required.

Amount to be transferred

12.47 Similarly, the calculation of the transfer amount is governed by the trust deed and rules, subject to members' statutory entitlements to a minimum of the cash equivalents of their accrued benefits (see **6.44** above) (although underfunding in the transferring scheme may justify a reduction of cash equivalents – see **6.51** above for further details on the reduction of cash equivalents).

Trust deeds vary considerably as to how the transfer amount is to be calculated. Some examples are as follows:

(*a*) The matter might be left entirely to the discretion either of the principal employer or of the trustees, often subject to the requirement that they first consider the advice of the actuary (which advice the trust deed may or may not require them to accept, but in practice may be hard to reject without good reason).

(*b*) More commonly, the deed will leave the decision as to the amount to one of the two parties – either the principal employer or the trustees – subject to the consent of the other.

(*c*) The trust deed might (particularly if it is an older one) have the effect of requiring that the transfer payment represent a share of the overall fund in respect of the members being transferred. In an underfunded scheme, this would mean the transferring members bearing a proportion of the brunt of any overall deficit in the transferring scheme. In an overfunded scheme, by contrast, the transfer payment would have to include a share of any surplus.

(*d*) The trust deed might (especially if it is a relatively modern one), seek to give the employers maximum control in relation to active members by specifying that the transfer payment be the lesser of:

(i) their statutory cash equivalents; and

(ii) the amount which would be available to be applied in respect of them were the scheme to be wound up,

(which is, effectively, the minimum which the law will allow) subject to the principal employer's sole discretion to direct a greater amount.

Bulk transfers – specific issues where winding-up has commenced

Preliminary

12.48 This section now addresses the questions of whether there is power to make a bulk transfer, and how any transfer payment is to be calculated, from a scheme that has begun to be wound up. (The corresponding position where the transferring scheme has not gone into winding-up is dealt with in **12.45** to **12.47** above.)

Power to make bulk transfers on winding-up

Winding-up started before 6 April 1997

12.49 In these circumstances, the existence of a power to make bulk transfers on winding-up, and the question of who may exercise that power, is governed by the scheme's trust deed and rules.

Care should be taken to check whether any bulk transfer-out power under those documents may be exercised during the winding-up stage. A transfer-out power which is intended for use whilst the scheme is ongoing may well cease to be exercisable after winding-up has commenced, depending on the exact wording of the scheme documents.

Winding-up started after 5 April 1997

12.50 *PA 1995, s 74* gives the trustees of registered defined benefit schemes which commence winding-up after 5 April 1997 the power to make bulk transfers even if there is no power to do so in the scheme rules (so long as the requirements in **12.68** to **12.69** below are met). Whether trustees have power to make a transfer from a scheme to which *PA 1995. s 74* does not apply will continue to depend upon the trust deed and rules.

Many schemes' rules give the principal employer a power to direct the trustees to make a bulk transfer. Any such power in a registered defined benefit scheme where winding-up has started after 5 April 1997 needs to be considered in the context of *PA 1995. s 73A(9)*. If it amounts to a power 'to apply the assets of the scheme in respect of pensions or other benefits', as the power will no longer be exercisable by the principal employer it will be exercisable by the trustees instead.

Amount to be transferred on a winding-up

Winding-up started before 6 April 1997

12.51 The amount to be transferred in these circumstances will depend upon the trust deed and rules. However, a minimum of the statutory cash equivalents of members' accrued benefits (see **6.40** above) must be transferred (although cash equivalents may be reduced to take account of underfunding – see **6.47** above for further details on the reduction of cash equivalents).

In the unlikely event of the transferring scheme being regarded by HMRC as overfunded, there may be difficulties in transferring the surplus to another scheme.

Winding-up started after 5 April 1997

12.52 The position as set out in **12.51** above is subject to two further points in relation to registered defined benefits schemes where winding-up instead commences after 5 April 1997:

(*a*) if the scheme is underfunded, the amount of the transfer payment in respect of any given person must be consistent with the sums required to be allocated towards the scheme's various liabilities under the new statutory order of priorities (*PA 1995, s 73*, summarised in **12.68** to **12.69** below); and

(*b*) under *PA 1995*, any power given by the scheme's rules to a person other than the trustees (the principal employer, for instance) 'to apply' scheme assets during winding-up 'in respect of pensions or other benefits' will become exercisable by the trustees and not by that person. *PA 1995* prevents an employer from directing the trustees to transfer less than the amounts required under the new statutory order of priorities (see **12.68** to **12.69** below) but does not affect an employer's power under the scheme rules to decide whether the transfer amount should include any surplus.

Bulk transfers – overview

12.53 The following table provides an overview of the requirements governing bulk transfers as described in this chapter.

	1. Where the transferring scheme has not gone into winding-up	*2. Where the transferring scheme has gone into a winding-up which commenced before 6 April 1997*	*3. Where the transferring scheme has gone into a winding-up which commenced after 5 April 1997*
A. Issues for trustees	Before exercising any discretion enabling the transfer to go ahead, issues which the trustees should consider may include: • the effect of the transfer on members' benefits (issue for transferring trustees and receiving trustees – see **12.33**); • any disparity between the funding position of the transferring scheme and that of the receiving scheme (issue for transferring trustees and receiving trustees – see **12.34**); • the 'balance of powers' in the receiving scheme as compared with that in the transferring scheme (issue for transferring trustees – see **12.35**); • the long-term futures of the transferring and receiving schemes and employer covenant (issue for transferring trustees – see **12.36**); and • if the transferring scheme is already being wound up, the comparative merits of other ways of securing benefits (issue for the transferring trustees – see **12.37**).		

<table>
<tr><th></th><th>1. Where the transferring scheme has not gone into winding-up</th><th>2. Where the transferring scheme has gone into a winding-up which commenced before 6 April 1997</th><th>3. Where the transferring scheme has gone into a winding-up which commenced after 5 April 1997</th></tr>
<tr><td>B. Members' consents</td><td colspan="2">Members' consents are required unless:
• scheme rules permit non-consent transfers;
• either:
(a) both schemes relate to employment with the same employer; or
(b) it is a bulk transfer either resulting from a financial transaction between the employers or where the employers are 'connected';
• actuarial certificate GN16 is given;
• members are notified at least one month before transferring; and
• contracting-out requirements do not require members' consents.</td><td>Members' consents are required unless:
• either:
(a) both schemes relate to employment with the same employer; or
(b) it is a bulk transfer either resulting from a financial transaction between the employers or where the employers are 'connected';
• actuarial certificate GN16 is given;
• members are notified at least one month before transferring; and
• either:
(a) scheme rules permit non-consent transfers; or
(b) the transferring scheme is a registered defined benefits scheme and the requirements mentioned in 12.68 to 12.69 are met; and
• any contracting-out requirements for members' consents are met.</td></tr>
</table>

	1. Where the transferring scheme has not gone into winding-up	*2. Where the transferring scheme has gone into a winding-up which commenced before 6 April 1997*	*3. Where the transferring scheme has gone into a winding-up which commenced after 5 April 1997*
C. HMRC approval	Prior to 6 April 2006, HMRC permission had to be sought in advance of transfer. If the transferring scheme is overfunded on HMRC basis, HMRC may refuse to agree to the transfer of that surplus to another scheme.		
D. Contracting out	Further requirements may apply if either the transferring scheme or the receiving scheme is contracted out, depending on the circumstances (see **4.33**).		As for columns 1 and 2, except that, if the transferring scheme is a registered defined benefits scheme, it may be sufficient to meet the requirements by notifying the Regulator.
E. Do trustees have power to make a bulk transfer?	Depends on scheme rules.	Depends on scheme rules.	If transferring scheme is a registered defined benefits scheme, yes. Otherwise, depends on scheme rules.
F. Can the employer(s) require the trustees to make a bulk transfer?	Depends on scheme rules.	Depends on scheme rules.	Depends on scheme rules except that, if any such power of the employer (in a registered defined benefits scheme) amounts to a power 'to apply the assets of the scheme in respect of pensions or other benefits', that power becomes exercisable by the trustees and not by the employer(s).

	1. Where the transferring scheme has not gone into winding-up	*2. Where the transferring scheme has gone into a winding-up which commenced before 6 April 1997*	*3. Where the transferring scheme has gone into a winding-up which commenced after 5 April 1997*
G. How is the transfer payment calculated?	As set out in the scheme rules, but subject to: • H below where the transferring scheme is in deficit; and • C above where the transferring scheme has a surplus.	As set out in the scheme rules, but subject to: • H below where the transferring scheme is in deficit; and • C above where the transferring scheme has an HMRC surplus.	As set out in scheme rules, but subject to: • H below where the transferring scheme is in deficit; • C above where the transferring scheme has a surplus; and • the fact that, if a registered defined benefits scheme's rules give to any person other than the trustees (eg the employers) power 'to apply the assets of the scheme in respect of pensions or other benefits', that power ceases to be exercisable by that person and becomes exercisable instead by the trustees.
H. Deficit: may the scheme rules provide for the transfer payment to be reduced to take account of underfunding in the transferring scheme?	Yes, so long as members are not denied their statutory cash equivalents. Some reduction of cash equivalents is, however, permissible in cases of underfunding (see **6.51**).	Yes, so long as members are not denied their statutory cash equivalents. Some reduction of cash equivalents is, however, permissible in cases of underfunding (see **6.51**).	Yes, subject: • (in relation to a registered defined benefits scheme) to complying with the statutory order of priorities (as explained in **12.68** to **12.69**); and • (in relation to other schemes) as set out in column 2.

	1. Where the transferring scheme has not gone into winding-up	*2. Where the transferring scheme has gone into a winding-up which commenced before 6 April 1997*	*3. Where the transferring scheme has gone into a winding-up which commenced after 5 April 1997*
I. Surplus: may the scheme rules provide for the transfer payment to include a share of any surplus in the transferring scheme?	Yes, but see C above where there is a surplus.	Yes, but see C above where there is a surplus.	Yes, but subject to: • C above where there is a surplus; and • the fact that, if a registered defined benefits scheme's rules give to any person other than the trustees (eg the employers) power 'to apply the assets of the scheme in respect of pensions or other benefits', that power ceases to be exercisable by that person and becomes exercisable instead by the trustees (see **12.52**).

Winding-up – general

Triggering events

12.54 The events which will trigger a winding-up of a scheme will depend upon the scheme's governing trust deed and rules. These might typically provide for a winding-up of the scheme to be triggered upon the earliest of:

(*a*) the expiry of a notice to the trustees by the principal employer, requiring that the scheme be wound up;

(*b*) the trustees resolving to wind the scheme up and notifying the principal employer accordingly;

(*c*) the principal employer being in arrears in its contributions to the scheme and failing to rectify the position within a specified period of the trustees formally requesting it to do so;

(*d*) the principal employer going into liquidation; and

(*e*) the expiry of a specified period from the date on which the scheme was established.

Many trust deeds and rules will, in some of these circumstances, give the trustees a discretion to continue operating the scheme (with a new principal employer, where appropriate) rather than wind it up immediately; this is dealt with further in **12.57** below.

Application to the Regulator

12.55 In the unlikely event of the employer or the trustees wishing to wind up a scheme and there being no power in the trust deed enabling them to do so, the Regulator may, under *PA 1995, s 11*, authorise or direct a winding-up if:

(*a*) the scheme (or any part of it) ought to be replaced by a different scheme;

(*b*) the scheme is no longer required; or

(*c*) it is necessary in order to protect the interests of the generality of the scheme members.

It should only rarely be necessary to resort to an application to the Regulator, and the Regulator is unlikely to make such an order without a compelling case being made to it. Alternatively, it may in exceptional circumstances be necessary to apply to the court for directions to wind up a scheme.

Disclosure requirements

12.56 The intention of the Regulator's disclosure requirements is to shorten the time between the instigation of termination of a pension scheme and its completion. An outline of the Regulator's requirements is as follows:

(*a*) the trustees must notify the Regulator where a scheme has been in the process of winding-up for more than three years;

(*b*) the trustees must notify the Regulator in writing every 12 months about current progress;

(*c*) the trustees must provide a member of the scheme with a copy of any report sent to the Regulator within two months of a request being made;

(*d*) the Regulator has the power to speed up the winding-up process of a scheme, where it deems it appropriate;

(*e*) the scheme's sponsor or administrator must notify the Regulator in the absence of an independent trustee where an independent trustee is required;

(*f*) an independent trustee must be appointed by the official receiver or insolvency practitioner where relevant within three months of the date such appointment was required;

(*g*) the trustees must notify the Regulator within one month in the absence of an independent trustee where an independent trustee is required;

(*h*) the administrator must notify the Regulator within one month where the scheme has no trustees;

(*i*) the trustees and the employer (if appropriate) must keep a written record of any decisions to wind up a scheme;

(*j*) the trustees can seek a modification order from the Regulator to wind up a scheme.

Where the trustees have not complied with the requirements to wind up a scheme, they will have to provide justified reasons to the Regulator for not doing so. This may include copies of statements from the scheme's actuary or auditor. Delays in winding up which are allegedly caused by awaiting information from HMRC on contracting-out issues are expected to be reduced. Trustees may be fined by the Regulator in the event of unjustified delays in winding up a scheme.

Deferral of winding-up by trustees

Power under scheme rules

12.57 Some scheme rules give the trustees power, even after the winding-up rule has been triggered, to defer winding the scheme up. Examples of circumstances where the trustees might wish to defer winding-up are:

(*a*) where annuity rates are low at the time when the winding-up rule is triggered and the trustees wish to wait for them to rise, so placing the fund in a better position to secure the benefits with an insurance company;

(*b*) where the trustees are awaiting a clarification of the law without which winding-up may prove risky (the initial uncertainty over the European Court's *Barber* decision – see CHAPTER 9 – being an example); or

(*c*) where the scheme's winding-up rule has been triggered by the principal employer going into receivership and the trustees expect the business to be sold to a new owner who is committed to the continued funding and operation of the scheme.

A scheme rule enabling the trustees to defer winding-up in these circumstances may or may not permit the trustees to take steps during the deferral period (for example, requiring further employers' contributions) which would create further liabilities for the employers.

Statutory power

12.58 Where winding-up has not commenced before 6 April 1997, there is in some circumstances a statutory power to defer winding-up for those trustees who do not have such a power under their scheme rules.

This statutory power is conferred by *PA 1995, s 38(1)* and is available only where (in particular):

(*a*) there is no power to defer winding-up in the scheme's trust deed and rules (*s 38(1)*);

(*b*) it is not a defined contribution scheme (*s 38(3)(a)*);

(*c*) the scheme:

- has at least two members;
- is registered (or formerly approved) or a relevant statutory scheme; and
- is not a tax approved (or formerly tax approved) small self-administered scheme (see CHAPTER 13) (*Winding-up Regulations, reg 10(1)*); and

(*d*) a 'relevant insolvency event' has occurred in relation to any of the scheme's employers and that event is, under the scheme rules, an event triggering a winding-up of the scheme. A 'relevant insolvency event' is defined in *PA 1995, s 75*, but in broad terms it means the commencement of an employer's bankruptcy or an employer going into liquidation. If the scheme has no active members, anyone who was an employer in relation to the scheme when the scheme last had active members will count as an employer for this purpose (*Winding-up Regulations, reg 10(1)(a), (2)*).

Where trustees exercise this new power, they may not allow new members to join the scheme during the deferral period. However, *PA 1995, s 38(2)* does allow them to decide:

(i) that contributions will not continue to be payable; or

(ii) that benefits will not continue to accrue,

during deferment, but not to stop increases to accrued rights.

Winding-up priorities

12.59 Whilst winding-up is being deferred, some active members are likely to become deferred pensioners, others to become pensioners, and so on. These changes of status are important because, should the scheme be wound up with insufficient assets to secure all the benefits, some membership categories (such as pensioners) may have preferential rights over others. This is less important since new statutory winding-up priorities were introduced from 6 April 2005 (see **12.73** below).

Trustees who defer winding-up now have a limited degree of scope under *Winding-up Regulations, reg 5* for deciding the date at which membership status (for instance, whether a person is an active member or a pensioner) is to be determined for this purpose.

Disclosure requirements

12.60 Any decision to defer winding-up (whether reached under the scheme rules or under *PA 1995, s 38*) or to fix a date for determining winding-up priorities (whether reached under the power referred to in **12.59** above or under any other power) must be recorded and members must be informed of the decision within one month (*Winding-up Regulations, reg 11*).

If the trustees do not defer winding-up, or when any period of deferral comes to an end, the winding-up process will start.

The process

Overview – methods of securing the liabilities

12.61 The securing of the scheme liabilities where a scheme is being wound up varies accordingly to when the winding-up began. There are three time periods to consider as set out below.

Winding-up begins before 6 April 1997

12.62 Where winding-up started before 6 April 1997, the winding-up process for securing the benefits was governed primarily by the scheme rules. The winding-up of pension schemes can take many years so there may still be a handful of schemes where a pre-1997 winding-up has not yet completed. There will be a difference between one scheme and another but the following matters will usually be covered in scheme rules.

(a) Expenses

Most scheme rules will provide for an amount to be set aside out of the assets to cover scheme expenses. The costs will depend upon a number of factors including the complexity of the scheme, the size of the scheme and any problems encountered in the winding-up.

(b) Purchase of annuities

From the remaining assets, the rules will normally provide for the trustees to secure the benefits by purchasing annuities from an insurance company. Where there are insufficient assets, an order of priorities in accordance with which the trustees must apply the assets will normally be established and this is set out in the rules.

(c) Transfers

As an alternative to purchasing annuities, most schemes will allow the trustees to transfer benefits to other retirement benefits schemes or personal pension schemes or other approved arrangements.

Winding-up begins after 5 April 1997

12.63

(a) Statutory power to secure benefits

Where the winding-up of a scheme commences after 5 April 1997, *PA 1995, s 74* gives trustees of an approved defined benefits scheme, the power to secure members' benefits.

(b) Options available

PA 1995, s 74 and the *Winding-up Regulations* provide that trustees of defined benefits schemes which commenced winding-up after 5 April 1997 are treated as having discharged any liability in respect of scheme benefits so long as they have arranged for the discharge of that liability in one or more of the following ways:

- by making transfer payments to other occupational pension schemes (*PA 1995, s 74(3)(a)*);
- by making transfer payments to personal pension schemes (*PA 1995, s 74(3)(b)*);
- by purchasing annuities from insurance companies (*PA 1995, s 74(3)(c)*);
- by transferring the benefits of an annuity contract or insurance policy to the member concerned (or his dependant) (*Winding-up Regulations, reg 8(4)*);

- in certain limited circumstances, relating to insolvent contracted-out schemes, paying sums to the Department for Work and Pensions (*Winding-up Regulations, reg 8(5)*),

provided that any transfer value quotation issued to a member must be accompanied by a statement informing him that the value of his guaranteed cash equivalent may be affected by the winding-up of the scheme, that a decision to take a guaranteed cash equivalent should be given careful consideration and that the member should consider taking independent financial advice prior to any transfer payment from the scheme being made.

(c) Notice to members

When securing a member's benefits in accordance with *PA 1995, s 74* trustees must also give to the member to whom the liabilities relate (or if the member is deceased to his beneficiaries), a notice in writing of the proposed discharge (a 'discharge notice') (*Winding-up Regulations, reg 6(2)(a)*.

(d) Statutory discharge

In order to be discharged when securing members' benefits, the *Winding-up Regulations* provide that the trustees must comply with the requirements relating to: (i) the contents of the discharge notice (*reg 7*, as mentioned above; and (ii) other prescribed requirements, such as whether the individual's consent is required (*regs 6, 8*).

Winding-up Regulations, reg 9 confirms that these requirements are in addition to (and do not replace) certain requirements of *PSA 1993, s 32A* in relation to the discharge of protected rights on winding-up and any scheme rules reflecting those requirements.

The Financial Assistance Scheme, introduced by *PA 2004*, may provide assistance to underfunded schemes winding up in this period. This is covered in more detail at **2.42** above.

(e) Other trustee protections

There are other protections available for trustees on scheme wind-up also. One is a '*s 27* notice'. This is a mechanism under *Trustee Act 1925, s 27* to protect trustees from further claims after completion of the winding up. Trustees seeking to rely on *s 27* must advertise in both the *London Gazette* and a newspaper local to the scheme, giving notice that they intend to distribute trust property and requiring people having an interest to make a claim within a specified period (of at least two months). After this, the trustees are not liable to anyone to whom they did not have notice of. However, as seen in the case of *MCP Pension Trustees Ltd v AON Pension Trustees Ltd [2009] EWHC 1351 (Ch)*, liability will not be escaped if the trustees already had notice of beneficiaries, even if that was historical and the details had then been lost.

Trust deeds and rules often contain protection for trustees so that they are indemnified as far as legally possibly from the scheme and/or the employer. Once the scheme has finally wound up, however, the underlying protection of through scheme assets is lost and, as such, trustees often seek to negotiate an ongoing employer indemnity or preferably 'run off' and 'missing beneficiary' insurance. Whilst it may be possible, subject to the provisions of the particular scheme's trust deed and rules, to obtain 'missing beneficiary' insurance from scheme assets, it is very unlikely (unless specifically authorised by the rules) that trustees could use scheme assets to purchase 'run off' cover for their own protection, as this would have no benefit for the scheme's beneficiaries. It would, therefore, be down to the trustees to negotiate purchase of this cover by the employer on their behalf.

Winding-up begins on or after 6 April 2005

12.64 If the scheme began to wind up on or after 6 April 2005, it is necessary to consider the extent to which the changes introduced by *PA 2004* impact on the methods of securing members' benefits to those matters set out in **12.63** above, in particular the extent to which the Pension Protection Fund is relevant.

Impact of the Pension Protection Fund ('PPF')

12.65

(a) The PPF – General

The PPF was established on 6 April 2005. The legal framework is set out in *PA 2004, ss 107–220, Schs 5–9* and associated regulations.

In summary, schemes eligible for protection by the PPF have to pay the PPF levies. In return, members of those schemes may be entitled to compensation from the PPF if the employer becomes insolvent. Where the employer cannot become insolvent in a normal sense (for example, public bodies or unincorporated charities), the trustees or the Regulator must inform the PPF when they become aware that the employer is unlikely to continue as a going concern. The PPF represents an additional method of securing members' benefits if the sponsoring employer is insolvent. For this to be possible certain qualifying conditions have to be satisfied.

(b) Conditions for entry

There are a number of conditions for entry in *PA 2004, Part 2* and related regulations, in particular the *Pension Protection Fund (Entry Rules) Regulations 2005 (SI 2005/590)*.

(i) *Eligible schemes*

PA 2004 provides that certain pension schemes will not be considered an eligible scheme for the purposes of gaining entry to the PPF. In order to be considered to be eligible, the pension scheme:

- must not be a defined contributions scheme (*PA 2004, s 126(1)(a)*);
- must not be a prescribed scheme (*PA 2004, s 126(1)(b)*; and *Pension Protection Fund (Entry Rules) Regulations 2005, reg 2*;
- must not have started winding-up before 6 April 2005 (*PA 2004, s 126(2)*). The date on which a scheme starts to wind up is usually determined by reference to the scheme rules; and
- except in certain circumstances, must not have entered into a legally enforceable compromise agreement, in connection with a debt payable by the employer under *PA 1995, s 75* (deficiencies in the assets).

The circumstances when a *s 75* debt can be compromised without preventing a pension scheme from being an eligible scheme are set out in *Pension Protection Fund (Entry Rules) Regulations 2005, reg 2(2)–(7)*. In summary, this is where one of the following applies:

- the PPF has validated an actuarial statement that the compromise is above the PPF level of benefits; or
- the compromise was part of an arrangement under *Companies Act 1985, s 425* (power of company to compromise with creditors or members); or
- the PPF Board acting as creditor of the pension scheme has entered into a legally enforceable agreement with the employer on behalf of the trustees; or
- a scheme apportionment arrangement, a regulated apportionment arrangement, a withdrawal arrangement or an approved withdrawal arrangement under the *Occupational Pensions Schemes (Employer Debt) Regulations 2005* is in place.

(ii) *Qualifying insolvency events*

For a scheme to be considered for entry to the PPF, a qualifying insolvency event must occur in relation to the sponsoring employer. The insolvency event must have occurred on or after 6 April 2005 (this is discussed in more detail in CHAPTER 5).

(c) PA 1995, s 75 and the PPF

A key case was heard in late 2006 regarding a proposed reallocation of a future *s 75* debt as part of a corporate restructuring. The employer and trustees in *L v M [2007] 1 PBLR, [2006] EWHC 3395 (Ch)* wanted comfort that the proposed reallocation would not subsequently preclude entry of the scheme into the PPF.

M was the sole employer of the scheme and L was a trustee. In order to continue in business and retain its employees, M proposed to restructure its finances, including its obligations to the pension scheme.

The *Pension Protection Fund (Entry Rules) Regulations 2005* exclude from eligibility a scheme where 'at any time, the trustees or managers of the scheme enter into a legally enforceable agreement the effect of which is to reduce the amount of any debt due to the scheme under *section 75* of the *1995 Act* which may be recovered by, or on behalf of, those trustees or managers'. The main purpose of the legal proceedings was to get comfort that this provision would not be triggered if M's proposals were agreed.

The proposals to reallocate the future debt were held not to fall foul of the *Pension Protection Fund (Entry Rules) Regulations 2005*. At the time the arrangements were to be put in place, there would be no *s 75* debt due (as the reallocation was to be made before the winding-up was triggered). It was not enough that the agreement had the effect of reducing a debt which would or might become due as a result of a triggering event in the future.

However, the court made no findings as to when a *s 75* debt, once triggered, actually comes due. It is clear that any attempt to reallocate or compromise a *s 75* debt once it has been certified by the actuary would preclude PPF entry unless the detailed requirements of the *Pension Protection Fund (Entry Rules) Regulations 2005* in relation to the compromise of debts are followed, but what remains unclear is the effect of any attempts to modify the allocation or compromise of *s 75* debts between the date of trigger and the date of actuarial certification and, in particular, the significance of the date as at which the assets and liabilities are calculated for the purposes of the debt.

Multi-employer schemes

The position prior to 6 April 2008

12.66 Where a solvent employer ceased to participate in a multi-employer scheme on or after 2 September 2005 but prior to 6 April 2008, it became liable for a debt on a buy-out basis, or it had to enter into a withdrawal arrangement with one or more guarantors. The details were set out in the *Occupational Pension Schemes (Employer Debt) Regulations 2005 (SI 2005/678)*, (the '*Employer Debt Regulations*').

Where such a withdrawal agreement was put in place, the departing employer remained liable for a debt on the minimum funding requirement basis (less the value of any liabilities relating to its former employees which had been transferred out) plus the expenses associated with its withdrawal. The guarantors were responsible either for the balance of the buy-out debt as at the date the employer withdrew or for the amount that would be payable had the employer withdrawn at a future 'guarantee time' – the guarantee time being the date the scheme commences winding-up, the date no solvent employers remain, or a date when the Regulator directs the guarantors to pay. A withdrawal agreement remained in force until the scheme had completed winding-up, the Regulator issued a notice stating that it was no longer required, or it was replaced by another withdrawal agreement.

The terms of the withdrawal agreement had to be approved by the Regulator. They could only be approved where the Regulator was of the opinion that the agreement satisfied the conditions laid down in legislation and that the guarantors had sufficient resources such that the debt was likely to be met. When an approved withdrawal agreement was in force, the guarantors had to notify the Regulator of certain events, including any decision which would result in the debt not being paid in full or any change in control of the guarantor.

The position from 6 April 2008

12.67

(a) General

The Regulator's lack of flexibility under the pre-6 April 2008 regime to defer payment of the debt using the pre-existing 'withdrawal agreement route' was much criticised. Broadly, the Regulator could only approve a withdrawal agreement when the employer did not have the assets to pay the debt in full. In many cases, trustees and employers were agreeing in advance to amend the scheme rules (as was permitted by the legislation) to apportion the debt so that a smaller debt fell on the departing employer. From 6 April 2008, changes to the way in which employer debts are calculated and apportioned in defined benefit pensions schemes were introduced by the *Occupational Pension Schemes (Employer Debt and Miscellaneous Amendments) Regulations 2008* (and, from 15 April 2008, by the *Occupational Pension Schemes (Employer Debt – Apportionment Arrangements) (Amendment) Regulations 2008*, as amendments to the *Employer Debt Regulations*. The stated intention of the changes was to frustrate any attempts to use apportionment as a method to abandon a scheme, whilst retaining flexibility for employers in corporate transactions and restructurings. Some of the changes may well assist in easing difficulties encountered under the pre-6 April 2008 regime – but may have thrown up new problems.

The changes generally affected only multi-employer schemes, with the exception of the changes to the calculation of assets and liabilities, which impact on all *s 75* debts. Money purchase assets and liabilities are expressly excluded, and employers of members with only money purchase benefits are excluded from the definition of employer. A key change from the pre-6 April 2008 position is a new definition of employment-cessation event.

Under the *Employer Debt Regulations*, there are now five ways of dealing with the debt:

- liability share (the default position);
- scheme apportionment share;
- regulated apportionment share;
- withdrawal arrangement; and
- approved withdrawal arrangement.

(b) Employment-cessation event

The new definition is similar to but slightly different from the old one, which used to refer to employment of persons in the description of employment to which the scheme relates. Now, an employment-cessation event in relation to a multi-employer scheme is an event which is not an insolvency event and which, subject to the provisions discussed below, occurs on the date on which:

- an employer has ceased to employ at least one active member of the scheme (which arguably could mean an active member for life cover only); and
- at least one other employer who is not a defined contribution employer continues to employ at least one active member (removed in the draft Regulations but now restored).

Note that closure to future accrual of the scheme as a whole was not, and is still not, an employment cessation event.

(c) Period of grace

A 'period of grace' has been introduced to alleviate the problem of a debt being triggered inadvertently. An employer, on ceasing to employ active members, may within one month give the trustees a period of grace notice, a notice in writing that it intends, during the period of 12 months from the employment-cessation event, to employ at least one person who will be an active member. This defers the triggering of the debt, and the employer continues to be an employer in relation to the scheme. A debt will arise as at the date of the original cessation event if the employer:

- does not employ an active member within that period;
- becomes insolvent; or
- changes its intention during the 12-month period, in which case it must notify the trustees.

There is, therefore, no option for using a period of grace notice as a tool to manipulate when the debt will actually trigger.

Once the employer employs an active member (either before or after the notice is given), the period of grace comes to an end.

The period of grace notice cannot be given if the employer is aware of any intention that the scheme should, during the 12-month period, become a frozen scheme (defined as a scheme which has ceased to have active members).

In theory, this provision may assist where an employer's last active member leaves employment, which in the past may have inadvertently triggered a debt. However, it will not assist where a multi-employer scheme is closed to new entrants (unless the employer can employ somebody who is already an active member – perhaps from another group company), nor will it assist if the notice is not served within one month of the triggering event. This latter requirement may result in the provision being less useful than it appears, as the fact that a debt has been triggered is often not discovered for more than one month.

(d) Liability share – default position

The 'liability share' rule applies in the absence of:

- a scheme apportionment share;
- a regulated apportionment share;
- a withdrawal arrangement; or
- an approved withdrawal arrangement.

The liability share is essentially the proportion of the total difference between assets and liabilities based on the liabilities attributable to employment with the departing employer divided by the liabilities attributable to employment with all employers. The liability is calculated on an annuity buy-out basis, ie the estimated cost of buying annuities to secure the benefits.

This is similar to the previous position, but there is a change in how the liabilities referable to each employer are assessed. These now only include liabilities arising during or as a result of pensionable service with that employer (including transfers in) but, where the trustees are unable (at least, without disproportionate cost) to determine the exact liabilities attributable to an employer, all the liabilities will be attributable to the most recent employer, or they will be attributable in a reasonable manner to one or more employers. If this is not possible, the 'orphan' liabilities will not be attributed to any employer.

Because the *Employer Debt Regulations* now include the details of how scheme actuaries should calculate deficiencies in scheme assets, the Board for Actuarial Standards has withdrawn actuarial guidance note GN19 in relation to all deficiency calculations made by reference to dates on or after 6 April 2008.

If a bulk transfer payment is made out of the scheme in relation to the outgoing employer, its liability share can be reduced by the amount of a relevant transfer deduction, provided that the liabilities and corresponding assets are transferred out within 12 months. Similar provisions apply in the case of withdrawal arrangements and approved withdrawal arrangements, but not apportionment arrangements.

(e) Scheme apportionment arrangement

This is an arrangement under the scheme rules (it must be written into the rules) which satisfies the conditions below and to which the trustees and either the exiting or remaining employer(s) consent. Which employer(s) will be required to consent depends on whether the exiting employer is paying more or less than the 'liability share'. If it is paying more than the liability share, then its consent will be needed. If it is paying less than the liability share (which is more likely), it will be the remaining employer(s) to whom all or part of the exiting employer's liability has been apportioned. The other conditions to be met, apart from the consent requirements, are that the arrangement:

- provides for the employer to pay a 'scheme apportionment arrangement share' instead of its liability share;
- where that amount is less than the liability share, apportions all or part of the difference to one or more of the remaining employers;
- is entered into before, on or after the applicable time;
- sets out the amount of an employer's scheme apportionment arrangement share;

- meets the funding test (unless one of the exceptions applies – see (*i*) below); and
- may set out when the 'amount apportioned' is to be paid.

In practice, the trustees will want to specify when the amount apportioned is to be paid.

Where scheme rules do not currently permit the trustees to enter into a scheme apportionment arrangement or a regulated apportionment arrangement, a rule permitting apportionment can be introduced, either by amendment of the deed and rules of the scheme or by resolution of the trustees. Since 6 April 2008, the *Employer Debt Regulations* give trustees power under *PA 1995, s 68*, after consulting such employers under the scheme as they think fit, to modify the scheme by resolution to achieve this, even if the scheme rules would enable them to modify the scheme in a different manner. This change represented a shift from the previous position, where the trustees could modify the scheme by resolution only if there was no other way of achieving the modification.

(f) Regulated apportionment arrangement

This is designed to be used in restructuring situations where the trustees consider that there is a reasonable likelihood that the scheme will enter a PPF assessment period in the next 12 months or where an assessment period has already commenced but not ended. It is an arrangement under the scheme rules which broadly:

- provides for the employer to pay a 'regulated apportionment arrangement share' instead of the employer's liability share;
- where that amount is less than the employer's liability share, apportions all or part of the difference to one or more of the remaining employers;
- is entered into before, on or after the applicable time;
- sets out the amount of an employer's regulated apportionment arrangement share;
- may set out when the remainder is to be paid; and
- where a PPF assessment period has not already commenced, satisfies the following conditions:
  - the trustees and the employer/any employer to whom all or part of the employer's liability has been apportioned consent to the arrangement;
  - the arrangement and any amendments to it are approved by the Regulator by a notice of approval (issued only if the Regulator considers it reasonable); and
  - the PPF does not object.

All the conditions are equivalent to those for a scheme apportionment arrangement, except that the funding test is replaced by Regulator approval and the requirement for the PPF not to object.

This arrangement allows apportionment of a smaller amount of debt in order to avoid employer insolvency, enabling the employer to continue to trade free of the pension liabilities. It will be used only where the potential recovery to the PPF is greater than putting the employer through an insolvency process. Trustees should in practice not agree to the arrangement unless it is structured so that PPF entry is still achievable on the insolvency of the remaining employer(s).

(g) Withdrawal arrangement

This is intended to offer a simpler alternative to the previous 'approved withdrawal agreement'. It operates in a similar way, but does not require Regulator approval and can be entered into before, on or after the employment-cessation event.

The cessation employer must pay an amount of at least the 'withdrawal arrangement share'. This is equal to or, with employer agreement, greater than 'amount A'. Amount A is broadly the employer's share of the shortfall on a scheme funding (not buyout) basis. The guarantors are liable for 'amount B', a floating or a fixed amount payable on certain events occurring, including the agreed payment date, the scheme commencing winding-up, and a relevant event occurring in relation to the last employer.

The conditions are quite stringent: the trustees may enter into a withdrawal arrangement with the cessation employer and guarantor(s) only where they are satisfied that:

- the funding test is met (the same as the first limb of the funding test for a scheme apportionment arrangement) (see (*i*) below); and
- the guarantors have sufficient financial resources at the date the arrangement is entered into to be likely to be able to pay amount B – the guarantors will therefore need quite significant assets to meet this test.

On the face of it, withdrawal arrangements have costs and speed advantages; however, if clearance is required, some of those advantages will be lost.

(h) Approved withdrawal arrangements

The provisions are similar to the previous 'approved withdrawal arrangements' entered into by the cessation employer, the trustees and a guarantor, with the approval of the Regulator, and which may be given before or after the employment-cessation event. This is the only withdrawal arrangement option if the exiting employer wishes to pay less than the scheme funding basis shortfall.

The old requirement has been removed whereby the Regulator could approve an agreement only where the resources of the guarantors were such that the *s 75* debt was more likely to be met if the agreement was approved. It has been replaced by new conditions which give the Regulator significantly more flexibility than under the old regime:

- the amount the cessation employer proposes to pay as its approved withdrawal arrangement share must be less than amount A;
- the trustees must have notified the Regulator that the funding test is met (the same test as for withdrawal arrangements under (*g*) above) (see (*i*) below); and
- the Regulator must be satisfied that it is reasonable to approve the arrangement having regard to such matters as it considers relevant, including:
  - the potential effect of the employment-cessation event on the method or assumptions used to calculate the scheme's technical provisions;
  - the financial circumstances of the proposed guarantors;
  - the amount of the cessation employer's 'liability share';
  - the amount of the proposed approved withdrawal arrangement share and, where there is likely to be a relevant transfer deduction, an estimate of the amount the cessation employer will pay if the transfer is completed; and
  - the effect of the proposed arrangement on the security of members' benefits.

(i) Valuation of assets and liabilities

From 6 April 2008, changes to the valuation of assets and liabilities were made which impose new responsibilities on trustees. These apply to single employer schemes as well as to multi-employer schemes. The provisions require assets to be determined, calculated and verified by the trustees. There is express provision for an updated valuation since the last accounts to be used where the trustees, after consulting the actuary and the employer, so decide.

Where the scheme is not winding up and there is a previous withdrawal arrangement or approved withdrawal arrangement, amount B is included as an asset if the trustees are reasonably satisfied that, at the applicable time, the guarantors will have sufficient financial resources to be likely to pay amount B.

Liabilities (including all winding-up expenses except the cost of annuities) must be determined by the trustees and calculated and verified by the actuary based on the actuary's estimate of the cost of purchasing annuities. He must estimate the cost of purchasing the annuities to secure the benefits on terms he considers to be both consistent with those in the available market and sufficient to satisfy the scheme's liabilities in respect of pensions and other benefits or, where he considers that it is not practicable to make an estimate on this basis, in such manner as he considers appropriate in the circumstances.

(j) Funding test

The funding test is designed to prevent scheme apportionment being used to abandon the scheme. The test is met if the trustees are reasonably satisfied that:

- when the arrangement takes effect, the remaining employers will be reasonably likely to be able to fund the scheme so that, after the applicable time, it will have sufficient and appropriate assets to cover its technical provisions; and
- the arrangement will not adversely affect the security of members' benefits as a result of any:
  - material change in circumstances that would justify a change to the method or assumptions last used in calculating the scheme's technical provisions; or
  - material revision to any existing recovery plan.

The first limb of the funding test applies to scheme apportionment arrangements, withdrawal arrangements and approved withdrawal arrangements. The second limb applies only to scheme apportionment arrangements. Neither limb applies to regulated apportionment arrangements.

The *Employer Debt Regulations* expressly provide that the first limb of the test may be met if the trustees consider that the remaining employers are able to meet the relevant payments as they fall due under the statutory schedule of contributions (revised as necessary).

The funding test does not have to be met in the case of a scheme apportionment arrangement if:

- the proposed employer scheme apportionment share is greater than the liability share, ie above buyout level (though few employers will wish to pay more than buyout); or
- the scheme has commenced winding up and the trustees are satisfied that it is likely that the employer would be unable to pay the liability share, if it applied, but will be able to pay the scheme apportionment share.

(k) Proposed relaxations for future corporate restructurings

It is proposed that the Regulations be further amended (from 6 April 2010, if implemented) so as to provide additional flexibility in certain types of corporate restructurings (see CHAPTER 15 for more detail).

Timing and order in which benefits are secured

12.68 The order in which the trustees must secure members' benefits when a scheme is being wound up varies according to when the winding-up began. There are four time periods to consider:

- before 6 April 1997;
- 6 April 1997 to 9 May 2004;
- 10 May 2004 to 5 April 2005; and
- on or after 6 April 2005.

A statutory priority order was introduced for the first time by *PA 1995*. The policy intention behind having a statutory priority order is that when a scheme is wound up in deficit, the assets are divided amongst scheme members as fairly as possible.

The provisions of *PA 1995, s 73* (preferential liabilities on winding-up) and the *Winding up Regulations* imposed a statutory overriding priority order from 6 April 1997 where a scheme was winding-up and it was subject to the statutory minimum funding requirement.

A new transitional priority order was introduced for schemes that commenced winding-up after 9 May 2004 (*Occupational Pension Schemes (Winding Up) (Amendment) Regulations (SI 2004/1140)*).

PA 2004 introduced changes to *PA 1995, s 73*. A different winding-up priority order therefore applies for schemes where winding-up starts after 6 April 2005.

Time at which winding-up starts

12.69 The relevant legislation determines the time at which the wind-up starts. The relevant legislation is *Winding-up Regulations, reg 2* and *PA 1995, s 124(3A)–(3E)*.

Scheme rules

If the scheme is winding up under the scheme rules, then it is necessary to consider whether the rules specify a time for the winding-up to start. If they do not, the *Winding-up Regulations* provide that the time at which winding-up starts is the later of:

(*a*) the time when the trustees (or whoever has the power) decide that the scheme wind up starts; and

(*b*) the earliest date when there are no members in pensionable service.

If the rules do specify a time and the trustees have decided not to defer the winding-up of the scheme, the winding-up starts on the later of:

(*a*) the date as specified in the scheme rules; and

(*b*) the earliest date when there are no members in pensionable service.

Order of the Regulator

If the winding-up has been triggered by the Regulator, the time at which winding-up starts depends on whether or not a time is specified in the relevant order. If a time is specified, this is the time for winding-up to start. If the order is silent, the winding-up will start on the effective date of the order.

PPF assessment period

If an assessment period has been triggered in relation to the scheme, the PPF rules set out in *PA 2004* will apply in relation to the time at which winding-up starts. This is discussed at **12.65** above.

Before 6 April 1997

12.70

No statutory framework

Prior to *PA 1995*, there was no statutory framework to govern how the assets of a pension scheme were to be allocated where there was a deficit. Contracted-out defined benefit schemes were required to adopt an order of priorities which afforded higher priorities to guaranteed minimum pensions over the non-guaranteed minimum pensions element of deferred pensioners' benefits. Most pension schemes had a winding-up rule that included a list of priorities in accordance with which the assets of the scheme were to be distributed on a winding-up.

Typical priority order

Typically, the order of priorities in a contracted-out scheme might be as follows:

(*a*) pensions and other benefits in payment together with benefits payable to those over normal pension age and still in service;

(*b*) guaranteed minimum pensions not yet in payment, equivalent pension benefits under the *National Insurance Act 1965* and State scheme premiums;

(*c*) deferred pensions and other benefits for early leavers;

(*d*) deferred pensions and other benefits for scheme members when the winding-up began as if they had left service;

(*e*) augmentation of benefits within Inland Revenue limits;

(*f*) payment of any remaining surplus to the employers.

Additional voluntary contributions normally have absolute priority on winding-up provided certain conditions are met. The purpose of these conditions is to ensure that the additional voluntary contributions fund can be regarded as a totally separate fund, the distribution of which will not affect the ability of the scheme to meet its liability for the basic benefits which the scheme provides.

Winding-up started from 6 April 1997 to 9 May 2004

12.71 The priority order for a scheme that started winding-up at any time from 6 April 1997 to 9 May 2004 is set out in *PA 1995, s 73*, as modified by the *Winding-up Regulations*.

When considering the provisions of *PA 1995, s 73* and the associated provisions of the *Winding-up Regulations*, it is necessary to ignore the changes made to that section by *PA 2004, s 270*. This is because the *Pensions Act 2004 (Commencement No 2, Transitional Provisions and Consequential Amendments) Order 2005 (SI 2005/275)* confirms that *PA 2004, s 270* does not come into force for all purposes. The new wording is not effective to the extent that it affects *PA 1995, ss 73* and *74* as they apply immediately before 6 April 2005 to a scheme in winding-up at that time. The question of whether or not a scheme was in winding-up at that time is determined under *Winding-up Regulations, reg 2* or *PA 1995, s 124* (as appropriate).

PA 1995, s 73(2), as it applies to schemes in wind-up before 6 April 2005, requires that the assets of the scheme must be applied first towards satisfying the amounts of the liabilities mentioned in *PA 1995, s 73(3)*. If the assets are insufficient to satisfy the amounts in full, the earlier paragraphs of *PA 1995, s 73(3)* take priority over the later paragraphs.

Any assets remaining after allocating these amounts in this way must then be used to satisfy any remaining liabilities, in the order of priorities set out in the scheme's own rules (*PA 1995, s 73(4)*).

The priority order in *PA 1995, s 73(3)* is as follows:

First priority – additional voluntary contributions benefits

Either in defined contributions form or added years. If added years, the benefits must be identified by the trustees as being accrued by reference to additional voluntary contributions.

Second priority – pre-1997 insurance policies

These are the liabilities secured where:

- the trustees are entitled to benefits under an insurance contract entered into:
  - *before* 6 April 1997; and
  - in order to secure all or part of the scheme's liability for any benefit payable in respect of one particular person whose entitlement to payment of a benefit has arisen (and for any benefit which will be payable in respect of him on his death); and
- either:
  - the contract may not be surrendered; or
  - the surrender value does not exceed the liability secured (excluding liability for pension increases).

This exemption for insurance policies only applies to policies taken out *before* 6 April 1997 and where they have been taken out after this date, they may need to be surrendered in order to comply with *PA 1995, s 73*.

Third priority – liability for benefits to which entitlement to payment has arisen and benefits which will be payable in respect of the person so entitled upon his death (excluding pension increases)

This will cover pensions in payment from the scheme and should also cover postponed pensioners (where a member has postponed taking benefits after normal retirement age) and any lump sum death benefits that arose prior to the commencement of the winding-up.

Fourth priority – contracted-out benefits and refunds of contributions

Fifth priority – liabilities for increases to pensions referred to in the second and third priorities above

Where the increases to the pension arose prior to the date on which the winding-up started, then they form part of the benefit liability as at that date and enjoy higher priority than post-wind up increases.

Sixth priority – liabilities for increases to pensions referred to in the fourth priority above

Seventh priority – other liabilities for accrued benefits (including pension increases)

This category is mainly for the deferred pensioners (including those with pension credits). Where the scheme is contracted out, it will cover non-guaranteed minimum pension benefits (as the contracted-out benefits currently have higher priority). For schemes that are not contracted out, a much larger proportion of the benefits will fall into this priority.

It also covers future pensions or other future benefits attributable (directly or indirectly) to pension credits (including increases to pensions).

Winding-up started from 10 May 2004 to 5 April 2005

12.72 A new transitional priority order was introduced for schemes that commenced winding-up after 9 May 2004.

The main changes from the priority order that applied before 10 May 2004 is that: (i) increases on pensions in payment now fall below deferred benefits; and (ii) no priority is given to contracted-out benefits.

The transitional priority order is as follows:

First priority – additional voluntary contributions benefits

Either in defined contributions form or added years. If added years, the benefits must be identified by the trustees as being accrued by reference to additional voluntary contributions.

Second priority – pre-1997 insurance policies

These are the liabilities secured where:

- the trustees are entitled to benefits under an insurance contract entered into:
  - before 6 April 1997; and
  - in order to secure all or part of the scheme's liability for any benefit payable in respect of one particular person whose entitlement to

payment of a benefit has arisen (and for any benefit which will be payable in respect of him on his death); and

- either:
  - the contract may not be surrendered; or
  - the surrender value does not exceed the liability secured (excluding liability for pension increases).

This exemption for insurance policies only applies to policies taken out *before* 6 April 1997 and where they have been taken out after this date, they may need to be surrendered in order to comply with *PA 1995, s 73.*

Third priority – liability for benefits to which entitlement to payment has arisen and benefits which will be payable in respect of the person so entitled upon his death (excluding pension increases)

This will cover pensions in payment from the scheme and should also cover postponed pensioners (where a member has postponed taking benefits after normal retirement age) and any lump sum death benefits that arose prior to the commencement of the winding-up.

Fourth priority – liabilities for pensions or other benefits which have accrued to or in respect of any members of the scheme (excluding increases to pensions) and refunds of contributions

- Future pensions, or other future benefits, attributable (directly or indirectly) to pension credits (but excluding increases to pensions); and
- refunds of contributions for members with less than two years' service.

Fifth priority – liabilities for increases to pensions referred to in the second and third priorities above

Where the increases to the pension arose prior to the date on which winding-up started, then they form part of the benefit liability as at that date and enjoy higher priority than post-wind up increases.

Sixth priority – liabilities for increases to pensions referred to in the fourth priority above

Winding-up started on or after 6 April 2005

12.73 *PA 2004, s 270* replaces *PA 1995, s 73.* These provisions only apply for schemes that start to wind up on or after 6 April 2005. The *Occupational Pension Schemes (Winding up etc) Regulations 2005 (SI 2005/706)* (the

'*Winding-up Regulations 2005*') have been issued pursuant to revised *PA 1995, s 73*, also with effect from 6 April 2005.

The intention behind the requirements is to ensure that the winding-up provisions work in harmony with the provisions of *PA 2004* and associated regulations that establish the PPF and its procedures. They are intended to ensure that individual scheme members will be no worse off where their scheme winds up than they would be if the PPF were instead to assume responsibility for the scheme and pay compensation to members.

PA 1995, ss 73, 73A and *73B* do not apply in relation to any liability for an amount by way of pensions or other benefits which a person became entitled to payment of, under the scheme rules, before the start of the winding-up (*PA 1995, s 73B(6)*). Nor do they apply to liabilities for money purchase benefits (*PA 1995, s 73(10)*).

The statutory priority order now set out in *PA 1995, s 73(4)* is as follows:

First priority – pre-1997 insurance contracts

This is a contract of insurance entered into before 6 April 1997 to secure certain scheme liabilities which may not be surrendered, or the amount payable on surrender does not exceed the liability secured by the contract (*PA 1995, s 73(5)*).

Second priority – liability for benefits to the amount of the corresponding PPF liability

This is the cost of securing the benefits that would be payable to a member under the pension compensation provisions if the PPF assumed responsibility for the scheme in accordance with *PA 2004* (*PA 1995, s 73(5)*). This means the pension compensation provisions set out in *PA 2004* are modified in certain respects (*PA 1995, s 73(4)(b)*).

Third priority – additional voluntary contributions benefits

Under the post-2005 priority order additional voluntary contributions benefits (other than money purchase benefits) have been demoted from their top priority position to a lower priority. This is linked to the compensation mechanism within the PPF. The PPF compensation formula swallows up payments from additional voluntary contributions. As a result of this additional voluntary contributions (except those that have been turned into added years) fall behind the benefits for which PPF compensation is paid.

Fourth priority – any other liability in respect of pensions or other benefits

Once the PPF liabilities have been given priority, all other remaining benefits of members of the scheme are secured. In practice, this means that contracted-out benefits have no priority which fits with the position under the PPF. The fourth priority order will simply apply to all remaining benefits which are to be secured by the scheme.

Moving down the priority order

12.74 Once it has been established which priority order applies when securing members' benefits, the trustees have to work down the priority order securing benefits until they run out of funds. It is important to establish which category of membership applies to each individual member of the scheme – this is done by reference to the 'crystallisation date'. It is then necessary to decide how much to apply to each category. *PA 2004* has given the trustees powers to make adjustments to the benefits of certain members that have to be secured which in turn has an impact on the amount to be applied for those members.

Crystallisation date

12.75 It is important to note that the status of the beneficiary (ie pensioner, deferred member) as at the date the scheme starts to wind up dictates the level of priority. This date is referred to as the 'crystallisation date'. *Winding-up Regulations, reg 4* confirms the meaning of the crystallisation date. This is the date when the scheme starts to wind up; or if the trustees have determined to postpone winding-up, such earlier date, prior to the actual winding-up which is fixed by the rules of the scheme.

Until recently, there had been an amount of uncertainty as to how the pension rights of members who had been affected by the *Barber* decision who have benefits accrued based on two or more normal retirement dates (typically 60 and 65) (for more see CHAPTER 9) should be treated under *PA 1995, s 73* for schemes commencing wind-up between 6 April 1997 and 5 April 2005.

In *Cripps v Trustee Solutions Limited and Dubery [2007] EWCA Civ 771* the Court of Appeal held that members who had a lower normal retirement age (because of the *Barber* judgment) for part of their pension should receive priority under the 'third' priority (set out in **12.72** above) under *PA 1995, s 73* for this part of their pension if they were over that age at the crystallisation date and the remainder would be in the relevant lower priority. This 'splitting' was a change from established practice, which was predominantly based on the requirement of HMRC to pay a pension from a single date.

In *Foster Wheeler Ltd v Hanley & Ors [2008] EWHC 2926 (Ch)* the Court of Appeal overturned the High Court's decision that all benefits could be paid from age 60 unreduced, and held there was a legal principle that any amendments to the scheme rules that were required to give effect to *Barber* rights should represent the 'minimum interference' with the scheme's provisions. In this case, all that was required to give effect to *Barber* was to disapply the requirement to obtain the company's consent to the early retirement pension, as the payment of a single pension would more closely track the scheme rules than split pensions would. The result in that case was that all benefits could be paid from age 60, but the portion of pension accrued based on a normal retirement date of 65 must be reduced for early payment.

How much to apply to each category

12.76 *Winding-up Regulations, reg 4* sets out how the liabilities are calculated under *PA 1995, s 73*. A number of amendments have been made to *Winding-up Regulations, reg 4* as the amount to be applied to each category has increased over time.

(a) The sum needed to secure pensions in payment plus minimum funding requirement value of other benefits

This amount applies where the members' rights crystallised before 19 March 2002. It also applies where all of the participating employers in the scheme immediately before the start of the winding-up were insolvent.

The liabilities for benefits other than pensions in payment should be calculated in the manner specified in *Occupational Pension Schemes (Minimum Funding Requirement and Actuarial Valuations) Regulations 1996 (SI 1996/1536), regs 7(2), (3), (7)–(10)* and *8(2)*. The liabilities do not include the expenses involved in meeting them and therefore the actuary should include no allowance for the buy-out costs.

(b) Buy-out costs for pensions in payment and future increases plus minimum funding requirement value of other benefits

This is the amount to apply to each category where:

- the rights crystallised on or after 19 March 2002, but before 11 June 2003; and
- the participating employers were not insolvent immediately before the start of winding-up.

The amount to apply for pensioners is calculated as the cost of buying annuities in the market. The calculation of the minimum final requirement liabilities is as set out above but expenses are included. This reflects the position set out in the *Winding-up Regulations*.

(c) Buy-out costs for all benefits

This is the amount to apply to each category under *Winding-up Regulations, reg 4* where:

- the winding-up started on or after 11 June 2003;
- the date chosen for calculating the statutory winding-up debt falls on or after 15 March 2004; and
- the participating employers were not insolvent immediately before the start of the winding-up.

This change was introduced in March 2004 but was made retrospective to June 2003 because this is the time at which the change to buy-out costs was first announced by the Government.

Further changes were made in February 2005, so that if the winding-up commenced on or after 15 February 2005, the amount to apply is the buy-out costs for all benefits whether or not the employer participating in the scheme is solvent or insolvent. The buy-out costs for this purpose include full winding-up expenses.

(d) Actuarial Guidance Note GN19

The scheme actuary calculates the value of the liabilities for the purposes of *PA 1995, s 73*. Actuarial Guidance Note GN19 gives the actuary guidance with regard to calculation of the scheme liabilities. The actuary must certify that the calculation made of the liabilities is made in accordance with GN19. GN19 has been withdrawn for all winding-ups commencing on or after 1 December 2008.

New powers for trustees to make adjustments

12.77 *PA 1995, ss 73A* and *73B* confirm that, during the winding-up period, no benefits may accrue to members under the scheme rules and no new members can be admitted to the scheme. The benefits to be secured are those that apply on the crystallisation date. However, the *Winding-up Regulations* permit the trustees to make adjustments to certain scheme liabilities in limited circumstances. These powers are intended to prevent the amount of the scheme's liabilities being increased after the date on which the winding-up starts. This is consistent with the PPF rules in *PA 2004*.

(a) Early leavers

Members of the scheme who have completed more than three months' pensionable service but less than two years' pensionable service at the time that the scheme starts to wind up, are deemed to have chosen the contribution refund option on the day that winding-up commenced (*PA 1995, s 73(9)*; *Winding-up Regulations 2005, reg 5*). The trustees must therefore provide benefits for them on this basis.

(b) Discretionary awards

If someone has exercised a power under the scheme rules to pay a discretionary award to a member in the winding-up period, the trustees can reduce the member's benefits if the effect of the discretionary award is to increase the scheme's liabilities. The adjustment will ensure that the total benefits for that member do not exceed the amount of their benefits immediately before the day that winding-up commenced (*PA 1995, s 73A(7), (8)*; *Winding-up Regulations 2005, reg 6*). If the date of winding-up is backdated because an assessment period has been triggered and a withdrawal notice given, the adjustment takes effect from the date that the award takes effect, rather than the date on which winding-up is treated as having started.

Where a discretionary award takes effect during the winding-up period, the trustees must provide the affected member with a notice in writing within one month explaining that the trustees may make an adjustment to the award at a future date.

(c) Survivors' benefits

If a member dies during the winding-up period and a survivor's pension comes into payment, the trustees can reduce the survivor's benefits if the effect of the payment is to increase the scheme's liabilities. The adjustment will ensure that the total benefits payable in respect of the member do not exceed the amount of the member's benefits immediately before the day that winding-up commenced (*PA 1995, s 73A(7), (8)*; *Winding-up Regulations 2005, reg 7*). If the date of winding-up is backdated because an assessment period has been triggered and a withdrawal notice given, the adjustment takes effect from the date that the entitlement to benefits arises, rather than the date on which winding-up is treated as having started.

Where the entitlement to a survivor's benefit arises during the winding-up period, the trustees must provide the affected member a notice in writing within one month explaining that the trustees may make an adjustment to the benefits at a future date.

(d) Death benefits

Where a member dies before winding-up commenced but the trustees do not confirm a beneficiary's entitlement to death benefits until after the start of the winding-up, those benefits will be treated as having arisen before the commencement of winding-up (*PA 1995, s 73B(8)*; *Winding-up Regulations 2005, reg 8*). This means that they will be excluded from the scheme liabilities for the purposes of the winding-up provisions in *PA 1995, s 73*.

(e) Benefits discharged during an assessment period

The PPF rules in *PA 2004, Part 2* allow certain liabilities to be validly secured during an assessment period. Where this happens those liabilities will be excluded from the scheme liabilities for the purposes of the winding-up provisions in *PA 1995, s 73* (*PA 1995, s 73B(6)*; *Winding-up Regulations 2005, reg 10*).

Defined contributions schemes

12.78 *PA 1995, ss 73, 73A, 73B* and *74* do not apply and defined contributions (or money purchase) schemes are not eligible for PPF protection. In normal circumstances, at retirement the trustees will have purchased for existing pensioners an annuity with their money purchase 'pot' and this will be transferred into the name of the member on winding-up. Deferred members' 'pots' will then be applied to purchase an annuity or will be transferred to another approved arrangement. The issue of 'priorities' is therefore not strictly relevant. Assets and liabilities in respect of money purchase benefits are excluded from scheme assets and liabilities of mixed benefit schemes for the purposes of *PA 1995, s 73*. Typically, this will mean that additional voluntary contributions will fall outside the statutory priorities (*PA 1995, s 73(10)*).

A facility enabling the trustees to deduct winding-up costs from members' defined contributions accounts prior to applying them for transfer/buy-out needs to be included. Schemes where there is a defined benefits and defined contributions section should make it clear that defined contributions assets cannot be used to subsidise a deficiency in the defined benefits section. By the same token, defined contributions members may not necessarily expect to share in a defined benefits surplus.

Sanctions against trustees under PA 1995

12.79 Trustees who disregard the provisions of *PA 1995* as summarised in this chapter may be subject to prohibition orders and civil penalties. Further details appear in the table set out in APPENDIX I.

Chapter 13

Personal pension schemes and personal accounts

Introduction

13.1 This chapter describes personal pension schemes, self-invested personal pension schemes and stakeholder schemes. Unless stated otherwise, the descriptions given in this chapter with regard to personal pension schemes (with the exception of self-invested personal pension schemes) also apply to stakeholder schemes. This chapter also sets out the new personal accounts regime.

13.2 Personal pension schemes are now another form of 'registered pension scheme' and subject to the tax rules contained in *FA 2004*. Much of the statutory framework relating to personal pension schemes is the same as that for other registered pension schemes and is found in CHAPTER 16 of this book. Whereas, in past editions of this book, this chapter was, at times, a lengthy description of the benefits that a personal pension scheme could provide, that task is now undertaken, in common with coverage of all registered pension schemes, by CHAPTER 16.

Historically, HMRC 'approved personal pension' schemes were governed largely by tax legislation, most notably *ICTA 1988*. The changes introduced by *FA 2004*, which came into force on 6 April 2006 ('A-Day'), represented a significant change to that legislative framework. Before A-Day, it was necessary to conduct a detailed examination of *ICTA 1988, Part XIV, Chapter IV* in order to understand the benefits provided by a personal pension scheme. These provisions were different to those applicable to occupational pension schemes, which were found in *ICTA 1988, Part XIV, Chapter I.*

13.3 *PA 2008* sets out the structure of the personal accounts regime, to be phased in from 2012. Every employer will have to make arrangements for the automatic enrolment of all 'jobholders' aged between 22 and State pension age who have 'qualifying earnings', ie gross earnings (including bonuses, etc) between £5,035 and £33,540, into a 'qualifying scheme' or the default personal accounts scheme, a trust-based occupational DC scheme to be regulated by HMRC and the Pensions Regulator. A 'qualifying scheme' can be an occupational pension scheme or a 'workplace personal pension scheme', ie a group personal pension, a stakeholder pension or a group self-invested personal pension. For further details, see **13.39** onwards below.

An historical perspective

13.4 The forerunner of the personal pension scheme was the 'retirement annuity contract' ('RAC'). RACs were first introduced in the 1950s. They subsequently became governed by *Income and Corporation Taxes Act 1970, s 226* and consequently are often referred to as '*s 226* policies'. The most significant distinctions between RACs and personal pension schemes were:

(*a*) RACs were only available to the self-employed and those in non-pensionable employment (ie broadly speaking, employment where the employer did not provide a pension scheme); an individual could not leave an occupational pension scheme and take out an RAC if he remained employed by the sponsoring employer of that occupational scheme;

(*b*) an individual's employer was not permitted to contribute to an RAC but could contribute to a personal pension scheme (*ICTA 1988, s 620,* now repealed); and

(*c*) insured personal pension schemes allow individuals to contract out of the second-tier State scheme ('S2P') (formerly the State Earnings Related Pension Scheme ('SERPS')) via an 'Appropriate Personal Pension Scheme' ('APPS') – there was no such facility under an RAC (*PSA 1993, s 43(1)*).

Although RACs are still in existence and contributions can still be made to them, it has not been possible to establish a new RAC since 1 July 1988.

The concept of personal pensions was introduced by the *Social Security Act 1986* and they first became available on 1 July 1988. The main reason for the introduction of personal pensions was to allow individuals who did not have access to a company sponsored group scheme (or who wanted to leave such a scheme whilst still employed by the sponsoring employer, ie to 'opt out') the opportunity of building up their own pension entitlement. The ability of an employee to opt out of their occupational scheme was one of the major factors in the pensions mis-selling scandal and has resulted in many providers of personal pension schemes having to pay substantial compensation in order to reinstate those individuals who were mis-sold personal pensions back into their previous occupational schemes. Personal pension schemes were also designed to give individuals the opportunity (of their own volition) to contract out of SERPS on an individual basis.

The introduction of the concept of the Self-Invested Personal Pension Scheme ('SIPP') in the 1989 Budget led to even more choice in retirement provision by giving the member the opportunity to become involved in decisions about the investment of contributions. SIPPs have tended to attract higher earners because of the higher costs of administration and the general complexity of such arrangements.

Originally, the requirements for a SIPP (in addition to those personal pension requirements already set out in HMRC's Practice Notes) were outlined in Memorandum No 101 published in October 1989. This Memorandum was superseded by the Personal Pension Schemes Practice Notes IR76 (2000) and, in particular, by the *Personal Pension Schemes (Restriction on Discretion to Approve) (Permitted Investments) Regulations 2001 (SI 2001/117)* which came into force on 6 April 2001. Both of these have subsequently been superseded by *FA 2004* and the new regime that came into force on A-Day. However, even after A-Day, SIPPs and other 'Investment-Regulated Pension Schemes' (see *FA 2004, s 174A, Sch 29A*) are still effectively limited in the investments that they can make; this is discussed in more detail at **13.24** below.

Personal pension schemes, like occupational pension schemes, had to be approved by HMRC if they were to benefit from the full range of tax advantages. The *Finance (No 2) Act 1987* introduced legislation governing the approval and tax treatment of personal pension schemes. This legislation was then consolidated in *ICTA 1988, ss 630–655* which, as mentioned above, was then repealed and replaced by *FA 2004*.

The Regulator

13.5 One change introduced by *PA 2004* of particular relevance to personal pensions is that the Regulator includes personal pensions as well as occupational pensions within its remit. This means that the Regulator is able to use the raft of powers that are available to it under *PA 2004* in relation to personal pension schemes. These powers are discussed in CHAPTER 2.

Establishing a personal pension scheme

Personal pension scheme providers and the FSA

13.6 A personal pension scheme would only be approved by HMRC if it had been established by a permitted provider (*ICTA 1988, s 632*, now repealed). After 6 April 2006 (but before 6 April 2007), both trust-based and non-trust-based personal pension schemes had to be established by one of the entities then listed in *FA 2004, s 154(1)*. These entities were largely the same as those found in the repealed *ICTA 1988, s 632*.

As from 6 April 2007, an application to register a pension scheme may be made only if the pension scheme is an occupational pension scheme or has been established by a person with permission under *FSMA 2000* 'to establish in the United Kingdom a personal pension scheme or a stakeholder pension scheme' (*FA 2004, s 154(1)*). This reflects the FSA's new role regulating the establishing, operating and winding-up of personal pension schemes.

The FSA, in its Perimeter Guidance Manual ('PERG'), describes what it considers to be involved in 'establishing', 'operating' and 'winding-up' a personal pension scheme. In particular, PERG highlights that in a trust-based scheme the establisher will 'usually be the person who executes the trust as Provider'. Furthermore, it goes on to highlight that 'there will usually only be one person who establishes the scheme', and that 'the activity of establishing a personal pension scheme ceases once the scheme is established'. The effect of this is that an 'establisher' who had established a scheme prior to 6 April 2007 would not require authorisation for establishing a personal pension scheme 'unless they intended to establish a new scheme after that date' (PERG 12.2). They would, however, require authorisation if they wished to continue to 'operate' it beyond that date.

PERG also describes what is involved in operating a personal pension scheme. It states that the operator 'is the person responsible to the members for managing and administering the assets and income of, and the benefits payable under, the scheme in accordance with the relevant pensions and tax legislation, the scheme's constitution and the regulatory system'. It is likely that, in most instances, this will be the same person as the scheme administrator under *FA 2004*. However, this may not always be the case, especially in SIPPs where a separate scheme administrator is appointed alongside a trustee. In such a situation, PERG highlights that 'it may be the case that (the trustees) are operating a scheme jointly with the Scheme Administrator by virtue of the responsibilities they assume under the trust deed for management and administration of the scheme's assets'. Generally, this will not be the case if the trustee is nothing more than a bare trustee (though this is not always a suitable option in all circumstances). However, an examination of the trustees' duties and powers under the Rules is necessary to decide whether authorisation as an 'operator' is required (PERG 12.2).

PERG also clarifies that, despite the fact that a member of a SIPP may have the right to direct where the assets of that scheme will be invested, it will not result in him being considered to be an 'operator'.

It should be noted that the FSA regulates the single activity of 'establishing, operating and winding up' schemes, even though the establisher and the operator may be different entities. As the FSA only authorises firms that conduct business on an on-going basis, there may be difficulties for providers who establish schemes infrequently, as they may need to apply for FSA authorisation on each occasion, or persuade the FSA to allow them to retain their authorised status during periods of inactivity.

The administrator

13.7 The scheme administrator of a registered pension scheme is the person who is, or persons who are, appointed in accordance with the rules of the pension scheme to be responsible for the discharge of the functions conferred or imposed on the scheme administrator under *FA 2004, Part 4* (in particular, *s 270*). The person who was the administrator of an approved scheme before A-Day will, on A-Day, have automatically become the administrator of that scheme for the purposes of *FA 2004*.

The two main areas of responsibility for the administrator are reporting matters to HMRC and paying certain tax charges. These provisions are discussed in more detail in CHAPTER 16.

Registering a personal pension scheme

Personal pension schemes

13.8 Prior to 6 April 2006, approval for a personal pension scheme was granted under *ICTA 1988, Part XIV, Chapter IV*.

In order to obtain HMRC approval under that regime, it was necessary (under *ICTA 1988, s 633,* now repealed) to satisfy HMRC that the sole purpose of the scheme was the provision of benefits on retirement or death and to comply with HMRC's requirements relating to how these benefits are provided. The HMRC had published Model Rules (coded IMR 2003) for personal pension schemes and, if these were incorporated in full without amendment, the scheme would usually be granted approval very quickly. SIPPs would also need to have included the relevant additional provisions for conditions applicable to SIPPs in addition to the Model Rules.

Personal pension schemes were restricted from amending the Model Rules without obtaining HMRC's prior consent. However, this requirement was relaxed after A-Day. HMRC's Pension Update 156 (issued October 2005), confirmed that 'changes to personal pension scheme rules effective on or after 6 April 2006 should not be sent to APSS [and] where a personal pension scheme is using the HMRC Integrated Model rules the prior consent of HMRC will not be needed where the rule change takes effect on or after 6 April 2006'.

As a result of A-Day, many personal pension schemes are seeking to amend their governing documentation and move away from the restrictions contained in the Model Rules. In the interim many schemes have overlaid their rules with an amending deed that allows them to take advantage of the flexible benefits to found in *FA 2004*, pending a more comprehensive re-write.

Pension schemes, be they personal or occupational, now 'register' with HMRC rather than seek approval and this is discussed in CHAPTER 16.

Benefits payable from a personal pension scheme

General

13.9 A personal pension scheme is a defined contribution scheme (also known as a 'money purchase scheme'). The benefits it can provide are determined by the level of contributions paid into it and the amount of investment growth achieved on those contributions. The main legislative control on funding is the tax treatment of contributions and benefits by reference to the Annual and Lifetime Allowance (see CHAPTER 16). However, the specific rules of a scheme that has not yet been amended to take into account the changes brought about by A-Day may contain restrictions on benefits and contributions.

The only benefits that a personal pension scheme could provide were, until May 1995, annuities payable to the member on his retirement, annuities payable to his spouse and/or dependants on his death and a lump sum payable on the retirement of the member or on his death. HMRC previously imposed conditions on the type of annuity which could be provided and on the amount of cash lump sum which could be taken. In May 1995, HMRC made it possible for a member to defer purchasing an annuity and instead make income withdrawals (known as 'income drawdown') from the scheme.

Prior to A-Day, the benefits that a personal pension scheme could provide stemmed from the provisions of *ICTA 1988*. The relevant parts of *ICTA 1988* were repealed from 6 April 2006. The benefits that can be provided by a registered pension scheme after 6 April 2006 are now covered in CHAPTER 16.

Pension date

13.10 The rules of a personal pension scheme will usually allow the member to choose the date on which he retires but, generally, the date must not be before age 50 (55 from April 2010) nor after age 75. The date on which a member chooses to receive his benefits is referred to as his 'pension date'.

HMRC used to allow a pension date earlier than age 50 if it were satisfied that the member's occupation was one in which people usually retired before the age of 50. For example, if HMRC was satisfied that a member was a professional athlete, the rules of the scheme could allow that member to choose a pension date of age 35. The following is a list of occupations where HMRC permitted a pension date to be set that is lower than age 50 (the list is now found in the *Registered Pension Schemes (Prescribed Schemes and Occupations) Regulations 2005 (SI 2005/3451)*).

Profession or occupation	**Retirement age**
Athletes	35
Badminton players	35
Boxers	35
Cricketers	40
Cyclists	35
Dancers	35
Divers (saturation, deep sea and free swimming)	40
Footballers	35
Golfers	40
Ice hockey players	35
Jockeys – flat racing	45
Jockeys – national hunt	35
Members of the reserve forces	45
Models	35
Motor cycle riders (motocross or road racing)	40
Motor racing drivers	40
Rugby league or rugby union players	35
Skiers (downhill)	30
Snooker or billiards players	40
Speedway riders	40
Squash players	35
Table tennis or tennis (including real tennis players)	35
Trapeze artists	40
Wrestlers	35

Since 6 April 2006, it has no longer been permissible to have a normal minimum pension age of less than 50 (age 55 from 2010), except in cases of ill-health (*FA 2004, s 165*). However, where an individual had an existing actual or prospective right to take their benefits earlier than age 55, they may still be able to do so subject to fulfilling certain conditions. The detailed conditions are set out in *FA 2004, Sch 36, paras 19–23* and RPSM03106010, and can be summarised as follows:

- the scheme must have been approved by HMRC immediately prior to A-Day; and
  - as at 10 December 2003, the member must have been entitled under the rules of the scheme to a pension from an age earlier than 55; or
  - as at 5 April 2006, the member had an actual or prospective right under the pension scheme to a pension from an age of less than 50 and the member was in a prescribed occupation (see list above).

The age at which the member has the right to take a pension on 10 December 2003 or 5 April 2006, as relevant, will be their protected pension age (subject to all the statutory requirements being met). This is dealt with in more detail in CHAPTER 16.

General benefits payable in respect of a member

13.11 As personal pension schemes are essentially nothing more than defined contribution or money purchase arrangements, the benefits available will be the same as those listed for other money purchase arrangements in CHAPTER 16.

Contributions

Contributions from 6 April 2006

13.12 Post 6 April 2006, a member is entitled to make unlimited contributions to any registered pension scheme. However, tax relief will only be given on a relievable pension contribution made by a relevant UK individual and will be subject to the annual allowance. These are discussed in more detail in CHAPTER 16.

Tax treatment

Tax relief for member's contributions

13.13 Since 6 April 2006, the rules relating to the tax treatment of personal pension schemes have been absorbed into the *FA 2004*. This is discussed in more detail in CHAPTER 16. A personal pension scheme will generally obtain tax relief at source.

Contracting out of the State earnings related pension scheme

Appropriate personal pension schemes (APPS)

13.14 Contracting out is dealt with in detail in CHAPTER 4.

An individual can currently contract out of S2P either through an occupational pension scheme (where this is available to him) or through an APPS. A properly constituted APPS must have a current 'appropriate scheme certificate' in force. Such a certificate can only be issued once a scheme complies with the statutory requirements. (*PSA 1993, s 9(5)*).

An APPS can only be an appropriate scheme if it is a scheme which is, or is treated as, registered under *FA 2004, s 153* (*Personal Pension Schemes (Appropriate Schemes) Regulations 1997 (SI 1997/470), reg 2*). On 1 October 2008, regulations allowing protected rights to be held in SIPPs came into force, and SIPPs are now able to apply for contracting-out certificates as 'appropriate schemes' (*Personal and Occupational Pension Schemes (Amendment) Regulations 2008 (SI 2008/1979)*).

There are detailed requirements relating to the continuing supervision of APPSs by NISPI. These include the need to notify NISPI in writing of any changes in scheme details, and the requirement to give members certain information.

Stakeholder schemes must be contracted out (*WRPA 1999, s 1(10)*). This is either as an Appropriate Personal Pension Stakeholder Pension Scheme ('APPSHP') or as a Contracted-out Money Purchase Stakeholder Pension Scheme ('COMPSHP').

It should be noted that, as a result of *PA 2007* and *PA 2008*, it is intended that contracting out for defined contribution schemes (including all personal pension schemes) will be abolished. This will take place no earlier than 2012.

Minimum contributions

13.15 Minimum contributions equate to the age-related rebate paid by the DWP based on earnings between the lower earnings limit and upper accrual point (*PSA 1993, s 45*, as amended). The rules of an APPS may provide for the payment of contributions in addition to minimum contributions.

Protected rights benefits

13.16 Unless the rules of an APPS provide otherwise, the whole of the fund will be treated as 'protected rights'. This means that all the stringent provisions relating to protected rights would then have to apply to all the rights in the scheme. Consequently, the rules of the scheme will usually contain a specific definition of what constitutes protected rights. For a general discussion on protected rights, see CHAPTER 4.

When a scheme's rules define protected rights, they must include all or any of the following:

(*a*) minimum contributions;

(*b*) protected rights transferred from another personal pension scheme or occupational pension scheme;

(*c*) guaranteed minimum pensions transferred from an occupational pension scheme;

(*d*) any 'incentive payments' made by the DWP;

(*e*) payments representing basic rate relief from income tax on the member's share of minimum contributions (*PSA 1993, s 10*; *Protected Rights Regulations, reg 3*).

Protected rights benefits become payable as a pension through the purchase of an annuity at State pension age. The requirement for indexation of pensions arising from a member's protected rights fund under a personal pension scheme was removed where the pension was secured on or after 6 April 2005 (*PA 1995, s 162*, as amended by *PA 2004, s 279(2)*).

Protected rights cannot be assigned, suspended or forfeited.

Death of member and protected rights pension

13.17 In the event of the death of the member, either before or after taking protected rights pension benefits, a spouse's or civil partner's pension will be payable where relevant.

If the member dies after the pension has commenced, the survivor's pension will be 50 per cent of the pension the member was receiving at his or her death. If the member dies before the pension has commenced, the survivor's pension will be 50 per cent of the pension that would have been payable to the member (*PSA 1993, ss 28, 29*).

The spouse's/civil partner's pension must generally be payable until he or she dies, re-marries or enters a civil partnership while under State pension age (see CHAPTER 4).

Transfer of protected rights

13.18 Protected rights may be transferred to another pension arrangement that is permitted to accept such a transfer, including:

(*a*) another APPS or APPSHP;

(*b*) a contracted-out or previously contracted-out occupational pension scheme including a COMPS (or COMPS part of a COMBS), COMPSHP or COSRS (or COSRS part of a COMBS); or

(*c*) certain overseas occupational pension schemes.

Consent is generally required. These requirements and the transfer of contracted out rights in defined contributions schemes more generally, are discussed in greater depth in CHAPTER 4.

Personal pension protected rights premium

13.19 Prior to 6 April 1997, if an APPS ceased to be contracted-out or if the member wished to cease being in contracted-out employment, the member could regain the entitlement from SERPS by the payment of a Personal Pension Protected Rights Premium ('PPRP') to the DWP. This option is not available post-6 April 1997, so the scheme must either retain the protected rights in deferred form, or buy them out by purchasing a suitable annuity.

Transfer values

The right to a cash equivalent

13.20 Prior to A-Day, personal pension schemes were subject to specific restrictions and obligations, in respect of both transfers in and transfers out. The *FA 2004* rules regarding transfers now apply (although note the specific requirements in relation to APPS at **13.18** above). The *FA 2004*'s requirements are discussed in more detail in CHAPTER 16.

Disclosure of information

13.21 The trustees (or the provider) are responsible for disclosing certain information to the member. In particular they must provide certain basic information about the scheme to every new member within 13 weeks of joining (*Personal Pension Schemes (Disclosure of Information) Regulations 1987 (SI 1987/1110)*, as amended).

Information relating, in particular, to the amount of contributions credited to the member, the value of the member's protected rights, and the value of the member's accrued rights other than those protected rights must be given to the member annually. In addition, further information must be given to each member before his retirement.

In relation to each scheme year commencing on or after 1 October 1987, the trustees must make available to every member a copy of an annual statement containing specified information.

Investment

13.22 Once again, most of the restrictions that were specific to personal pension schemes under *ICTA 1988* and IR76 (2000) have been removed and, generally, personal pension schemes are subject to the same restrictions as other registered pension schemes (although see the provisions relating to investment regulated pension schemes at **13.23** below). General investment provisions are dealt with in CHAPTERS 10 and 16.

With stakeholder schemes the investment choice is likely to be more restricted than that available under general insured personal pension schemes and, much more restricted than the choice available to SIPPs. This is because of the much stricter control placed on costs; the annual management charge levied on a stakeholder scheme cannot exceed 1 per cent of the member fund per year (1.5 per cent for the first ten years for members who joined after 6 April 2005). This will inevitably lead to a limited range on offer. It should also be noted that members cannot be required to select an investment choice, so a stakeholder scheme will need a default investment fund.

SIPP investment restrictions

13.23 The main principle behind a SIPP is that the member retains control over the investment of contributions. The member can choose the type of investments (subject, of course, to HMRC requirements discussed below and any restrictions contained in the rules of the scheme).

In recognition of the role that the member plays in investment decisions, SIPPs were, historically, subject to stricter regulation of investment than other types of pensions schemes. Originally, the requirements relating to the types of investments that members could make were set out in Memorandum No 101. These were subsequently extended and clarified by the *Personal Pension Schemes (Restriction on Discretion to Approve) (Permitted Investments) Regulations 2001 (SI 2001/117)*), which set out a comprehensive list of permitted investments. Those regulations have now lapsed.

Investment after 'A-Day'

13.24 The intention was that the new tax regime would impose few restrictions on investment. *FA 2004, s 186(1)* states simply that 'no liability to income tax arises in respect of: (a) income derived from investments or deposits held for the purposes of a registered pension scheme ...'. Investments are discussed in more detail in CHAPTERS 10 and 16.

For SIPPs, this would have represented a significant change from the restrictions imposed by the *Personal Pension Schemes (Restriction on Discretion to Approve) (Permitted Investments) Regulations 2001 (SI 2001/117)* and mentioned at **13.23** above. As a result, many professional trustees offering SIPPs were exploring and actively marketing investment in residential properties and exotic investments such as wine and antiques. However, the Government, in the Pre-Budget Report on 5 December 2005, indicated that investments in residential property and exotic investments would not attract tax relief. HMRC produced a technical bulletin indicating that this 'U-turn' was to '... prevent people benefiting from tax relief in relation to contributions made into self directed pension schemes for the purpose of funding purchases of holiday or second homes and other prohibited assets for their or their family's personal use'.

As a result, *FA 2006, Sch 1* introduced amendments to *FA 2004* in relation to investments in 'taxable property' by 'investment regulated pension schemes' ('IRPS'). Most of these provisions are to be found in *FA 2004, Sch 29A*.

Both occupational and personal pension schemes can be IRPSs (see CHAPTER 16). However, for the purposes of personal pension schemes, and therefore this chapter, an IRPS is a scheme where one or more members, or a person related to a member, is or has been able (directly or indirectly) to direct, influence or advise on the manner of investment of any sums held for the purposes of the scheme (*FA 2004, Sch 29A, para 1(2)*).

The restrictions in FA 2004, Sch 29A

13.25 *FA 2004, s 174A* provides that, where a pension scheme acquires an interest in 'taxable property', and it is held for the purposes of an arrangement under the pension scheme relating to the member, then that pension scheme will be treated as having made an unauthorised payment to the member (see CHAPTER 16 for details of the unauthorised payment regime). Subsequent improvements to that property will also constitute an unauthorised payment, as will the conversion of non-residential property to residential use.

The provisions in *FA 2004, Sch 29A* provide the definitions and details required to operate *s 174A*, and relate to schemes that hold a direct or indirect interest in 'taxable property'. Taxable property includes 'residential property' (*FA 2004, Sch 29A, paras 7–10*) and 'tangible moveable property' (*FA 2004, Sch 29A, para 11*).

Types of taxable property

Tangible moveable property

13.26 Tangible moveable property is not defined in *FA 2004, Sch 29A, para 11* and it does not appear to be defined anywhere else in tax legislation. HMRC Taxable Property Guidance describes it as 'things you can touch and move. Examples are art, antiques, jewellery, fine wine, boats, classic and vintage cars, stamp collections and rare books'.

However, the *Investment-regulated Pension Schemes (Exception of Tangible Moveable Property) Order 2006* (*SI 2006/1959*) does specify particular items that are not to be regarded as taxable property for the purposes of *FA 2004, Sch 29A*. These include:

(*a*) gold bullion (defined as gold of a purity not less than 995 thousandths, which is in the form of a bar, or of a wafer, of a weight accepted by the bullion markets); and

(*b*) any item of tangible moveable property (whose market value does not exceed £6,000) that:

   (i) is held by a vehicle (within the meaning of *FA 2004, Sch 29A, para 20(2)*) solely for the purposes of the administration or management of the vehicle;

   (ii) in which the relevant IRPS does not hold an interest directly; and

   (iii) where a member of the pension scheme or a person connected with such a member does not occupy or use, or have any right to occupy or use, the property.

Residential property

13.27 Residential property is defined in *FA 2004, Sch 29A, para 7* as:

(*a*) a building that is used or suitable for use as a dwelling;

(*b*) any land consisting of or forming part of the garden or grounds of such a building (including a building on any such land) which is used or intended for use for a purpose connected with the enjoyment of the building;

(*c*) a hotel or similar accommodation, unless it is a whole hotel (*FA 2004, Sch 29A, para 13(2)*); or

(*d*) a beach hut.

Building includes a structure and part of a building or structure (*FA 2004, Sch 29A, para 7*). HMRC's guidance provides that:

(*a*) if a building includes a large number of separate flats, these are each treated as separate buildings;

(*b*) if a building includes a shop with a wholly separate flat, these are separate buildings. A flat is wholly separate if it has a separate entrance and has no inter-connection with other parts (other than a communal hallway); and

(*c*) if a building comprises part which is used for commercial purposes, such as a shop with an interconnected residential area such as a flat, then the whole will be treated as suitable for residential purposes.

However, the following are not considered to be residential property (*FA 2004, Sch 29A, para 8*):

(*a*) a children's home;

(*b*) a student hall of residence;

(*c*) residential care homes for people by reason of old age, disability, past or present dependence on alcohol or drugs, or past or present mental disorder;

(*d*) a hospital or hospice; or

(*e*) a prison or similar establishment.

Furthermore, *FA 2004, Sch 29A, para 10* provides that residential property is not taxable property where 'Condition A' or 'Condition B' is met:

- **Condition A**: The property is, or is to be, occupied by an employee, who is not a member or connected with a member of the pension scheme, nor connected to the employer and is required as a condition of employment to occupy the property.
- **Condition B**: The property is, or is to be, occupied by a person, who is not a member or connected with a member of the pension scheme and is used in connection with business premises held as in investment of the pension scheme.

HMRC's guidance gives an example for Condition B as a flat above a shop where the shop is leased from the scheme and the flat is occupied by the trader in connection with his business.

Land and buildings in the process of development becomes residential property from the point when it is first suitable for use as a dwelling – this will usually be when works are substantially completed and a certificate of habitation issued.

Holding taxable property

13.28 The provisions contained in *FA 2004, Sch 29A* apply where taxable property is held either directly or indirectly. *FA 2004* defines both.

Direct holdings

13.29 This applies to interests which are held jointly, in common or alone where the person:

(*a*) holds the property or any estate, interest, right or power in or over the property;

(*b*) has the right to use the property, or participate in arrangements relating to its use;

(*c*) has the benefit of any obligation, restriction or condition affecting the value of any estate, interest, right or power in or over the property; or

(*d*) is entitled to receive payments determined by reference to the value of or income from the property.

FA 2004, Sch 29A, para 15 goes on to specify a number of exemptions to the general principles of direct holding, related to holding assets through insurance products.

Indirect holdings

13.30 This applies to interests that are held jointly, in common or alone where the person holds an interest in a person who holds a direct or indirect interest in the property. It also includes circumstances where one person makes another a loan to acquire property.

Holding an interest includes participating in a collective investment scheme under *FSMA 2000, s 235* (*FA 2004, Sch 29A, para 18*) and holding an interest in a trust (*para 19*).

However, there are three exceptions where schemes will not be taken to have an indirect holding:

(*a*) Real Estate Investment Trusts ('REITs') set up under *FA 2006, Part 4* (*FA 2004, Sch 29A, para 22*).

(*b*) Vehicles meeting certain conditions, where the pension scheme and associates own 10 per cent or less and there is no right to have private use of any taxable property. The conditions are that the vehicle must hold at least £1 million of assets, or at least three assets which consist of an interest in residential property, and no asset exceeds 40 per cent of the total value of the assets held directly by the vehicle. The vehicle must be a non-close company and it must not have the purpose of holding animals for sport (eg race horse syndicates are not allowed). The pension scheme's interest in the vehicle must also meet certain conditions: it must not be for the purpose of enabling a member or a person connected with such a member to occupy or use the property, and the scheme should not have more than a 10 per cent interest in the vehicle (direct or indirect) (*FA 2004, Sch 29A, para 23*). Where the interest increases without any new holding being taken (for example by another participant leaving), there will be no charge to tax unless the increase was as part of a deliberate device to avoid tax (*FA 2004, Sch 29A, para 29* and RPSM07109430).

(*c*) Holding through a 'trading vehicle' which must satisfy four conditions:

  (i) the main activity is carrying on a trade, vocation or profession;

  (ii) the pension scheme, alone or with associated persons, does not have control;

  (iii) neither a scheme member nor person connected is a controlling director of the vehicle nor of any other vehicle which holds a direct or indirect interest in the vehicle; and

  (iv) the pension scheme does not hold an interest for the purpose of enabling a member or connected person to occupy or use the property (*FA 2004, Sch 29A, para 21*).

The guidance states that this is to allow schemes to invest at arm's length in commercial trading concerns without worrying about any 'tangible moveable property' which is being used by the company for its trade. The guidance may therefore imply that this does not include trading concerns holding residential property.

Stamp duty

13.31 *FA 2003* replaced stamp duty on land transactions with stamp duty land tax with effect from 1 December 2003 (for Stamp Duty Land Tax ('SDLT') see **13.33** to **13.34** below). However, stamp duty remains chargeable on some transactions in relation to securities.

In specie transfers

13.32 If securities are owned by the trustees of a registered pension scheme and are transferred in specie for no consideration other than the liability of the receiving trustees of another registered pension scheme to pay the retirement benefits represented by the value of the securities concerned, HMRC accept that the value of the securities being transferred does not attract *ad valorem* stamp duty (which would otherwise be charged at 0.5 per cent) (HMRC's Stamp Taxes Manual, para 9.75).

No *ad valorem* stamp duty will arise in respect of the agreement for the transfer of assets from the transferring scheme to the receiving scheme, because the assumption of the liability by the trustee of the receiving scheme to provide pension benefits to members of the transferring scheme is not chargeable consideration for stamp duty purposes. However, all transfer documents executed on or before 12 March 2008, that give effect to the transfer of stock or marketable securities from the transferring scheme to the receiving scheme, are liable to a fixed duty of £5. Fixed duties were abolished for documents executed on or after 13 March 2008 (*FA 2008, s 99, Sch 32*).

Stamp duty land tax (SDLT)

13.33 SDLT came into effect on 1 December 2003 and replaced stamp duty with regard to land transactions (*FA 2003, s 42*). Unlike stamp duty, which is a document-based tax and charged voluntarily, SDLT is a transaction-based, self-assessed tax. HMRC have published the SDLT Manual, setting out how the rules are applied in practice.

Purchases of property by the trustees of occupational and personal pension schemes and retirement annuity contracts are liable to SDLT at the appropriate percentage rate. If the property is subject to a mortgage, SDLT is payable on the equity value and the amount of the debt assumed by the purchaser (*FA 2003, Sch 4, para 8*).

Stamp duty on the taking of a lease was also abolished with effect from 1 December 2003 and replaced by SDLT (*FA 2003, s 56, Sch 5*). The basis of valuation of the lease to arrive at the SDLT payable is different from stamp duty and the amount of SDLT payable is likely to be greater than the former stamp duty. The taking of a lease by the trustees of any registered pension scheme from 1 December 2003 is liable to SDLT.

The trustees of a SIPP are liable to pay SDLT in the circumstances outlined in the second and third paragraphs above.

In specie transfers

13.34 Where a property in the UK owned by the trustees of a registered pension scheme forming part or the whole of an in specie transfer of a member's retirement benefits is transferred between registered occupational and personal pension schemes and RACs from 1 December 2003, the value of the property is not liable to SDLT. This is because, in HMRC's view, the assumption by the trustees of the receiving pension scheme to provide retirement benefits does not constitute chargeable consideration for the property transaction.

If the property being transferred in specie is subject to a mortgage or legal charge, the mortgage/legal charge is not liable to SDLT. This is because HMRC will not treat the assumption of the outstanding debt as chargeable consideration.

A pension fund may borrow money and may grant a mortgage or other charge over land as security. For SDLT purposes, it is necessary to consider the borrowing and the mortgage separately in the context of a transfer. If the transferee fund, or trustees of a transferee fund, assume an existing liability of the transferor fund or trustees of the transferor fund to repay borrowing or otherwise bring about the release of the transferor fund or trustees of the transferor fund from the debt, and they do so as part and parcel of such transfer, then HMRC will not treat *FA 2003, Sch 4, para 8* as meaning that there is chargeable consideration given for the land transaction.

A land transaction for no consideration is exempt from notification under *FA 2003, s 77*. Where there are linked transactions and one element is liable for SDLT, even though it is not notifiable, but other transactions are notifiable, then HMRC would expect the non-notifiable element of tax due to be added to the tax paid in the land transaction return for the notifiable element (SDLT Manual 31745).

Certain transactions made in connection with the ending of a marriage, or a civil partnership, are exempt from SDLT. There transactions are those made between the parties to the marriage or civil partnership as a result of certain types of court order, an agreement between the spouses in contemplation of or in connection with the dissolution or annulment of their marriage or civil partnership, or their judicial separation or a separation order. The exemption is not available if the transaction involves someone other than the spouses or civil partners (SDLT Manual 00550).

Stakeholder schemes

13.35 Stakeholder schemes were introduced by the Government in an attempt to increase pension coverage for the UK working population. One of the main driving forces was that stakeholder schemes were to be low cost. They were originally introduced by the *Welfare Reform and Pensions Act 1999* ('*WRPA 1999*') and the first stakeholder schemes were available from April 2001.

13.36 It is a requirement that a stakeholder scheme, in order to be recognised as such, has to be registered with the Regulator and with HMRC.

In order for the stakeholder scheme to be registered with the Regulator, the scheme provider or the trustees must demonstrate that the scheme complies with certain criteria. The trustees or stakeholder manager must complete a registration form and declaration that the scheme will comply with the registration conditions, and return this together with the registration fee to the Regulator. Where the scheme is set up under trust, the trustees or directors of a corporate trustee must also complete a questionnaire about their eligibility to act as a trustee. The stakeholder manager or trustees will receive notification of registration from the Regulator. Once registration has been confirmed, the stakeholder pension scheme can be marketed.

The criteria that the scheme must comply with are set out in *WRPA 1999, s 1* and the *Stakeholder Pension Scheme Regulations 2000 (SI 2000/1403)* (the '*Stakeholder Regulations*'), as amended, as follows:

- The scheme must provide money purchase benefits (within the meaning of *PSA 1993, s 181*).
- The scheme must not restrict membership on the basis of a member's financial status, the amount of contributions to be made, or the manner in which contributions will be made to the scheme.
- The scheme must provide an investment option that is subject to lifestyling – this is where, during the years leading up to retirement, a member's pension is gradually moved into less volatile investments, therefore providing greater security as they approach retirement.
- The trustees or manager of the scheme must appoint a reporting accountant in accordance with the requirements of *Stakeholder Regulations, reg 11*.
- The scheme must use all contributions, income or capital gains arising from the investment of contributions, and the value of rights under the scheme, in a way that results in the provision of benefits for members, the only exceptions to this being the deductions permitted under *regs 13, 14, 14A, 14B* and *14C*.
- The scheme's winding up rules, must state that:
  - (*a*) if the scheme ceases to be registered under *WRPA 1999, s 2*, the scheme begins winding up on the date on which the Regulator notifies the scheme in writing that it is no longer registered;

(*b*) if the trustees or manager fix a time for winding up the scheme for any reason other than (*a*) above, the winding up of the scheme shall commence at the earliest time fixed by the trustee or manager as the time from which steps for the purposes of winding up are to be taken;

(*c*) the trustee or manager must notify the employer in writing, within 2 weeks from the date winding up commenced, of the fact of and reason for the winding up;

(*d*) for contributions made to a scheme after the date that winding up commences, the contributions made by the member should be repaid to him/her and the remainder to the employer;

(*e*) winding up rights under the scheme shall be discharged by the trustees or manager within 12 months of the commencement of winding up by the making of transfer payments to other stakeholder pension schemes or in accordance with requests by one or more members or beneficiaries; and

(*f*) if the scheme fails to complete winding up within 12 months, the trustees or manager must notify the Regulator of that fact within one month of failing to complete the winding up.

- The scheme's trustees or manager must comply with the requirements of *PSA 1993, s 113* and associated regulations in providing members and potential members with relevant information about the scheme.
- The scheme must accept transfer payments from other pension schemes, contracts and schemes that became registered pension schemes by virtue of *FA 2004, Sch 36, para 1(1)(f)*, retirement annuity contracts, and other relevant annuity and insurance policies.
- The scheme must be a registered pension scheme under *FA 2004, s 153*.
- The trustees or manager of the scheme, or the scheme's fund manager, must ensure that the funds are invested with due regard to the need for diversification and suitability, having first obtained and considered proper advice from an authorised person.
- The scheme must accept any contribution of £20 or more. The minimum contribution may not be above £20.
- The trustees or manager of the scheme must provide members with an annual benefit statement in accordance with the requirements of *reg 18*.
- In the event that the scheme changes the rules or manner in which charges and deductions are made, the trustees or manager of the scheme must provide members with an explanatory statement within one month of making the change.

- The trustees or manager must ensure that the assets of the scheme are invested in accordance with *reg 8*. Where the assets are invested in a with-profits fund, the trustees or manager must ensure that the requirements of *reg 15* are complied with.
- If the scheme is an occupational pension scheme, it is specified in a contracting-out certificate in relation to all categories of employment to which the scheme relates; and if the scheme is a personal pension scheme, it is an appropriate scheme within the meaning of *PSA 1993, s 7(4)*.
- The trustees or manager must make a declaration at least once a year that the scheme has complied with the relevant regulations relating to expenses and charges, the scheme's systems and controls, and accounts and records. The trustees or manager must obtain a statement from the scheme auditor or reporting accountant that, in their opinion, the declaration was reasonable.

13.37 Unless exempt, an employer of 'relevant employees' has to select a stakeholder pension scheme that the employees could join if they wish.

A 'relevant employee' includes all employees of [the employer] employed in Great Britain and also, in the case of an employer resident or incorporated in any part of Great Britain, all employees of his employed outside the United Kingdom, but with the exception, in the case of any employer, of any employees of his:

(*a*) who have worked for the employer continuously for three months or more;

(*b*) who are not eligible to join an occupational pension scheme run by the employer;

(*c*) who have earnings above the Lower Earnings Limit (see *PSA 1993, s 181*); and

(*d*) who are not prevented from contributing to a UK pension scheme (*WRPA 1999, s 5(9)*; *Stakeholder Regulations*).

Membership of the scheme is not compulsory, and an employer does not have to contribute on behalf of the employee. The exemptions, whereby, if one of them is satisfied, there is no obligation upon the employer to arrange access to a stakeholder scheme, are to be found in *Stakeholder Regulations, regs 22, 23*. These exemptions include:

(*a*) The employer already offers an occupational pension scheme that all relevant employees over the age of 18, and who have more than five years' possible future service before normal pension age, are eligible to join within one year of commencing work with the employer.

(*b*) The employer employs fewer than five people.

(*c*) If the employer already offers to make contributions to a personal pension scheme in respect of that employee, providing that the scheme:

   (i) is receiving a contribution from the employer of at least 3 per cent of the employee's basic pay (note that an employer does not have to count overtime, commission or bonuses when calculating this figure);

   (ii) does not penalise members for ceasing contributions or transferring their entitlements; and

   (iii) is offered to every employee who would in law have access to a stakeholder scheme (ignoring anyone under the age of 18).

(*d*) Employees who declined to join the employer's occupation pension scheme when eligible and are now excluded.

(*e*) Employees who do not satisfy the residency test for the UK.

13.38 A stakeholder scheme can either be established on a contract basis or a trust basis. If established on a contract basis, it must be a personal pension scheme. If it is established on a trust basis, it could either be occupational or personal (depending on the person establishing it). In the majority of cases, stakeholder schemes will be established under contract. Careful consideration would need to be given when establishing a stakeholder scheme under trust because much of the regulatory framework that some employers will be trying to avoid by not establishing a pure occupational pension scheme will, in fact, apply equally to a trust-based stakeholder scheme. For example, a trust-based stakeholder scheme needs to appoint a scheme auditor and the requirement to ensure that there is suitable diversification of investments as described in *PA 1995*.

The employer is obliged to discuss with eligible employees and any representative organisations the employer's plans for the stakeholder pension scheme and which stakeholder scheme it would like to designate. There is flexibility here in how this is achieved, for example, by way of a meeting or by giving details in writing and then asking for feedback. Once the consultation process is completed, it is the employer who makes the final decision. The employees may, despite the employer setting up a stakeholder scheme, decide to join a different stakeholder scheme (or not join a scheme at all). If an employee already contributes to another pension scheme, that can continue, or they may choose to transfer to the employer's new stakeholder scheme, or contribute to both.

All stakeholder schemes are obliged to have a statement of investment principles. Therefore, proper advice must be taken by the trustees or manager to ensure diversification and the appropriateness of the investments selected.

Further requirements related to with-profits funds (that can be offered under stakeholder schemes) which include the ring fencing of those with-profits funds so those funds are only available to stakeholder schemes.

Automatic enrolment

Introduction

13.39 From 1 October 2012, employers will be under a duty to comply with the requirements of a new pensions regime. The 'automatic enrolment' regime, the broad structure of which is set out under *PA 2008* and which is to be delivered by the Personal Accounts Delivery Authority ('PADA') (see CHAPTER 2), will oblige employers to make arrangements for automatic enrolment, of all 'jobholders' aged between 22 and State pension age who have 'qualifying earnings', into a scheme which meets certain requirements (a 'qualifying scheme') which may include an employer's scheme or the Government's default arrangement. A 'qualifying scheme' can be an occupational pension scheme or a 'workplace personal pension' (ie a group personal pension, a stakeholder pension or a group self-invested personal pension). Jobholders may opt out of the regime but employers must not offer any inducement to do so. There will be an automatic triennial re-enrolment, and those jobholders who are younger or older than the target age band may choose to opt in.

13.40 There are some significant distinctions between the automatic enrolment system and the requirements of the stakeholder regime which it will effectively replace. Under the stakeholder regime, employers with five or more qualifying employees must nominate a stakeholder scheme and inform employees that it is available to them. There is, however, no obligation for employers to contribute to that scheme. In contrast, under the automatic enrolment regime, all employers employing 'jobholders' are under a duty both to provide a pension scheme and to contribute to that scheme, including on behalf of those who choose to opt in (see **13.55** below).

13.41 Three DWP consultation papers have been issued in 2009 in relation to the new regime. The first and third (published in March and September 2009) relate broadly to the duties of employers. The second, produced jointly by the DWP and PADA, relates to the Government's default scheme. Each of these consultations included sets of draft regulations.

Responses to the March consultation have now been published. However, the final details of the new regime are far from settled.

There has been a variety of responses from employers and pensions advisers to the Government's proposals, ranging from discussions about the timescales involved in establishing the automatic enrolment regime and the default scheme, expressing concern about the suitability of default investment options which may be made available to scheme members, to identifying potential problems in specific areas such as how automatic enrolment may impact on individuals who have registered for enhanced protection under *FA 2004* (see CHAPTER 16) or who might otherwise qualify for mean-tested benefits in retirement.

Responses to the DWP's September consultation are due to be circulated in autumn 2009, when the results of a PADA consultation on investment options are also to be published. Regulations are not due to be laid before Parliament until 2010.

This section, therefore, summarises some of the key elements of a new regime which is not yet fully in force and whose legal framework remains under construction.

The need for a new regime

13.42 It has been widely predicted that increased life expectancy and low birth rates will lead to a major increase in the percentage of the adult population over 65 years of age in the next 50 years. The Government Actuary's Department projects that, by 2050, the ratio of 65-year-olds and over to 20- to 64-year-olds will increase from 27 per cent to 48 per cent. Against this background of greater longevity and faced with the prospect of an ageing population, governments have been increasingly concerned with the relative decrease in pension saving in the UK under both State and occupational schemes. HMRC has estimated that around 7 million people in the UK are not saving enough to deliver the pension income they are likely to want, or expect, in retirement.

In recent years, the Government has sought various means to address this problem, the automatic enrolment regime being one of the latest and most high profile. The steps taken to implement this new regime are also in part a response by the Government to the perceived failure of the stakeholder regime introduced by *WRPA 1999* which was also designed to encourage saving across the UK's working population in order to deliver appropriate future retirement income.

The Pensions Commission and the White Papers of 2006

13.43 In 2002, a Pensions Commission was established to review the regime for UK private pensions and long-term savings. The Commission produced three reports. One of the key conclusions of those reports was that substantial reform to the State pension system was necessary in order to make it both fairer and more comprehensible. Having analysed pension provision in other countries, the Commission suggested that this reform might be achieved in the UK by a system of nationally administered individual accounts, and the application of enrolment to pension saving schemes at national and at individual employer level, as well as a modest minimum level of matching employer contributions to ensure that savings are clearly beneficial to all savers.

The Pensions Commission also recommended the introduction of a system of automatic enrolment. This was chosen in preference to both the current voluntary system, which was perceived as insufficient, and to compulsion, which the Commission suggested would not account for the diversity of individual preference and was likely to prove unpopular.

Following the recommendations of the Pensions Commission, the Government published two White Papers for consultation in 2006, introducing its proposal for automatic enrolment with a minimum employer contribution into either a workplace pension, or a new Government default scheme. In light of the responses to the White Papers, the DWP decided on the following measures:

- creating a Government default scheme as a trust-based defined contribution occupational pension scheme;
- phasing in requirements for minimum employer contributions over three years;
- setting an annual cap on contributions to the scheme at £3,600; and
- giving PADA executive powers to enable it to set up a system of automatic enrolment

DWP Consultations and draft Regulations

13.44 The DWP has subsequently issued further and more detailed consultation papers on its proposals. The first, issued in March 2009, contained details of employer duties for the automatic enrolment regime, information requirements, deduction of contributions, postponement, and opting out of the new regime. The consultation was accompanied by two sets of draft regulations – the *Pensions Regulator (Delegation of Powers) Regulations* and the *Pensions (Automatic Enrolment) Regulations*.

A second consultation was issued by PADA and the DWP jointly in April 2009, giving some detail of the Government's default scheme, and invited comments on three further draft regulations: the *[ ] Pension Scheme Order*, the *Transfer Values (Disapplication) Regulations*, and the *Rules of the [ ] Pension Scheme*. The incomplete titles of two of these draft regulations reflect the fact that the Government had originally referred to the scheme as 'personal accounts', but this term is no longer used by the Government and has not yet been replaced. It is referred to below simply as 'the Scheme'.

The *Scheme Order* and *Rules* will together form the constitutional documents of the Scheme. It is proposed that the trustee of the Scheme will be a new trustee corporation comprised of between 9 and 15 members.

A third consultation, *Workplace Pension Reform – Completing the Picture*, was issued on 24 September 2009, seeking views on:

(*a*) arrangements for implementing the reforms, including measures to manage the burden on business;

(*b*) remaining elements of the employer duty requirements including pay reference periods, voluntary joining for individuals not eligible for automatic enrolment, and changes to the 19-day rule;

(*c*) the quality requirements for pension schemes; and

(*d*) elements of the compliance regime, including information to be provided to the Regulator, sanctions and penalties, giving further information on employer duties, including re-enrolment and opt-ins, quality requirements and self-certification for qualifying schemes, as well as setting out some details of compliance issues.

The September consultation builds on the responses to the earlier 2009 consultation papers and invites comments on five further draft regulations, including the draft *Occupational and Personal Pension Schemes (Automatic Enrolment) Regulations 2010*. This final consultation closed on 5 November 2009.

The automatic enrolment regime

The automatic enrolment requirement

13.45 With effect from its relevant 'staging date', each employer must make arrangements to enrol all 'jobholders' (see **13.46** below) aged between 22 and 65 on the first day of their employment into a pension scheme which meets specified requirements (a 'qualifying scheme' – see **13.60** below), which may include the employer's own scheme or the Scheme. Automatic enrolment will therefore be triggered by:

(*a*) implementation of the new regime, if the jobholder meets the above criteria;

(*b*) the jobholder starting work and meeting the qualifying criteria; or

(*c*) meeting the criteria whilst in work by reaching the age of 22 and having qualifying earnings.

The date on which one of these events first occurs in relation to a jobholder is known as the 'automatic enrolment date'.

Jobholders and qualifying earnings

13.46 For the purposes of the automatic enrolment requirement, a 'jobholder' is defined as a worker who is working or ordinarily works in Great Britain under the worker's contract, is aged at least 16 and is under 75, and is a person to whom 'qualifying earnings' are payable by the employer in the relevant pay reference period. Where a jobholder has more than one employer or a succession of employers, the requirement applies separately in relation to each employment.

13.47 '**Qualifying earnings**' is defined as being that part of a person's gross earnings in a pay reference period of 12 months that is more than £5,035 and not more than £33,540. These figures may be altered in proportion to any change to the length of the pay reference period either above or below 12 months. 'Earnings' means sums of any of the following descriptions payable to the person in connection with the employment:

(*a*) salary, wages, commission, bonuses or overtime;

(*b*) statutory sick pay under *Social Security Contributions and Benefits Act 1992, Part 11*;

(*c*) statutory maternity pay under *Part 12* of that Act;

(*d*) ordinary statutory paternity pay or additional statutory paternity pay under *Part 12ZA* of that Act; and

(*e*) sums otherwise prescribed as earnings for these purposes.

Qualifying earnings are assessed over the 'pay reference period'. This will usually be the period over which a jobholder is regularly paid, with a period of 12 months for those who earn less than the threshold over a 12-month period but has isolated periods when he earns more than the weekly equivalent.

The staging process

13.48 The reforms are due to be phased in over a three-year staging period. The current implementation date for the new regime is 1 October 2012, the first of three 'staging dates'. The largest employers will be brought into the regime in the first year, and the smallest employers in the final year. Employers who begin to trade after October 2012 will be part of the last group to be phased in (regardless of size).

Employers will have the option to bring forward their implementation date, subject to informing the DWP of their intention and proving they are sufficiently advanced in their preparations.

Relationship with stakeholder requirements

13.49 In light of the new automatic enrolment requirements, the current duty on employers under the stakeholder regime will be removed by *PA 2008*. There will be transitional provisions requiring employers to continue to operate a payroll deduction facility for existing stakeholder plan member contributions. This obligation will end when the member chooses to end contributions or leaves the particular employment.

Action from automatic enrolment date

13.50 In relation to occupational pension schemes, employers must within one month from the automatic enrolment date take the necessary steps to complete the automatic enrolment process, as well as provide written enrolment information to the jobholder and provide certain information about jobholders to the scheme. Membership must be effected from the automatic enrolment date.

The automatic enrolment date will be:

- for a worker who, on his employer's staging date, satisfies the criteria for a jobholder (age and qualifying earnings), on that date; or
- for any other worker, the date on which he meets the criteria, whether he does so on first starting work for the employer or later (eg because he reaches age 22 after starting work for the employer and/or his salary reaches the qualifying earnings level).

13.51 In relation to workplace personal pension schemes, employers must within one month of the automatic enrolment date (see **13.50** above) make arrangements with the provider to ensure that the jobholder receives key information on the terms and conditions of the scheme, as well as provide written enrolment information to the jobholder and certain information to the scheme about the jobholders. The jobholder is deemed to have entered into an agreement to become an active member of the personal pension scheme with effect from the automatic enrolment date on the later of the date on which the provider gives the jobholder the key information about the terms and conditions of the scheme and the date on which the employer gives the jobholder the enrolment information.

Details of the information which must be made available are set out at **13.70** below.

Opting out

13.52 The draft *Occupational and Personal Pension Schemes (Automatic Enrolment) Regulations 2010* provide some detail on the process of opting out of the new regime.

A jobholder who has been automatically enrolled may opt out by giving the employer a signed opt-out notice in the form scheduled to the draft regulations. This may be in paper or electronic form.

The opt-out notice must be available from the scheme (and may not be provided by the employer). In the case of an occupational pension scheme, the notice must be received by the employer within one month after the day on which the jobholder becomes an active member of the scheme or the day on which he receives the enrolment information (whichever is the later). In the case of a workplace personal pension scheme, the notice must be given within one month after the day on which the agreement is 'deemed' (see **13.51** above).

Where the employer is given a valid opt-out notice, the employer must inform the relevant scheme that the notice has been received. Where an opt-out notice is found to be invalid, the employer must inform the jobholder and explain the reason for the invalidity. In such circumstances, the opt-out period will be extended to six weeks, so the jobholder has an opportunity to resubmit the notice without losing the chance to opt out.

PA 2008 prohibits employers from offering inducements which encourage workers to give up future membership of a pension scheme or to opt out of automatic enrolment (*PA 2008, s 54*).

'Inducement' is not defined, but the Regulator has stated in the 'Pensions Reform' section of its website that it considers inducement to be 'any action taken by the employer for the sole or main purpose of encouraging an individual to opt out of, or cease being an active member of, a qualifying pension scheme'. There are certain clear examples of inducements, such as offering higher salaries or one-off bonus payments, that would fall foul of this rule. However, employers should also consider whether flexible benefit packages would be considered inducements. The Regulator has used the example of holidays or company cars being offered rather than a pension. This could be at risk of breaching the ban on inducements. The Regulator has also stated on its website that an employer 'is of course free to offer alternative benefits in addition to the 3 per cent pension contribution but may breach their duty if such rewards were offered in a way that were mutually exclusive to the minimum 3 per cent contributions'.

Where opt-outs do occur, employers and schemes will have to refund contributions within one month or by the second payday from and including the day the jobholder gives notice to refund contributions, whichever is the later.

Automatic Enrolment Timeline

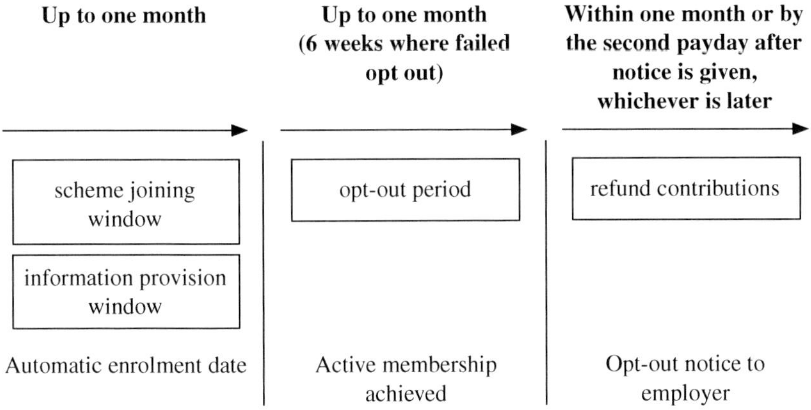

13.53 Currently, pension contributions deducted from a worker's earnings must be paid over to the trustees or manager of the scheme within a 19-day period, commencing with the end of the month in which the amount is deducted (*Scheme Administration Regulations, reg 16*). Under the automatic enrolment regime, contributions must be deducted on the first occasion the jobholder is paid after his automatic enrolment date. As jobholders have a 30-day window from the end of the joining window to opt out from the scheme, due to the 19-day rule there will be times when contributions are deducted by the employer and paid to the trustees during the opt-out window. If a jobholder then chooses to opt out, employers would have to pay over contributions to the trustees and then subsequently refund the jobholder, creating a significant administrative burden.

The DWP has proposed an extension to the 19-day requirement in relation to those payments deducted during the joining window and the opt-out period. During this period, the deadline for payment of the contributions to the trustees will be the 19th day of the second month following the month in which the jobholder's automatic enrolment date applies. This means that contributions will not have to be paid to the scheme until the opt-out period has ended. In all other months, the employer must comply with the 19-day requirement.

Re-enrolment

13.54 *PA 2008* requires employers to make arrangements for 'jobholders' who have previously opted out to be automatically re-enrolled with effect from the automatic re-enrolment date. It is currently proposed that jobholders should be automatically re-enrolled every 3 years if they continue to work for the same employer. Any person changing jobs during those 3 years and moving to a new employer would be automatically enrolled into a pension scheme by his new employer.

In order to minimise the administrative burden on employers, the date which has been agreed on for re-enrolment is 3 years from the employer's staging date, so that there is no requirement for each individual jobholder to have his own separate re-enrolment date.

Where jobholders have left pension saving within the previous 12 months, they will be exempt from automatic re-enrolment. If a jobholder opts out of the scheme at any other stage, however, he will be automatically re-enrolled on the automatic re-enrolment date and will have to opt out again if necessary.

For those individuals who lose jobholder status (because their earnings fall below £5,035 or because they are no longer considered as working in Great Britain) but then regain it, the re-enrolment date will be the day that the status of jobholder is reinstated.

Opting in

13.55 Jobholders who are not automatically enrolled can give their employer notice requiring the employer to arrange for them to be opted into an automatic enrolment scheme. There are two categories of individuals who will not qualify for automatic enrolment but who may request to join the pension scheme:

- **Jobholders aged over 16 and under 22 or over State pension age but under age 75**: employers will be required to inform these individuals in writing that they have a right to join an automatic enrolment scheme, the process for opting in, what it means for them and how to get more information on pension saving. Where the jobholders inform their employers in writing that they want to join the scheme, employers will have a duty to treat them as jobholders eligible for automatic enrolment and will have to follow the normal automatic enrolment process. Jobholders may request to opt in once in a 12-month period.
- **Individuals earning less than £5,035 per annum**: these individuals have the right to join a tax registered pension scheme, but do not have the right to an employer contribution. Employers will have a duty to inform these individuals in writing that they have the right to join a pension

scheme. Where a worker instructs the employer in writing that they wish to start saving in a pension, the employer must make arrangements for them to become an active member of a tax registered scheme. This need not be the same automatic enrolment scheme used for jobholders.

Postponement of automatic enrolment

13.56 The draft *Occupational and Personal Pension Schemes (Automatic Enrolment) Regulations 2010* enable an employer to postpone the automatic enrolment of a jobholder for a maximum period of three months if they automatically enrol the jobholder into a qualifying scheme that is:

(*a*) a qualifying defined benefit scheme;

(*b*) a defined contribution scheme (occupational or personal) under which (broadly) the employer contributes 6 per cent, and the total contributions are at least 11 per cent, of qualifying earnings, on an ongoing basis (compared to the minimum contribution levels for defined contribution schemes of 3 and 8 per cent respectively); or

(*c*) a hybrid scheme meeting conditions to be specified in the September consultation (see **13.61** below).

Within one month of the automatic enrolment being postponed, the employer must give the jobholder written information about:

- the reasons for postponement;
- the date on which automatic enrolment will commence; and
- how to obtain further information about pensions and saving for retirement.

Once the postponement period is complete, the jobholder must be automatically enrolled into the scheme and the employer must not take any steps to prevent the jobholder from remaining in that scheme for a minimum period of three months after the end of the postponement period, with contributions remaining at the above levels.

Options for employers

13.57 Options that employers might consider include:

Option one: the Government's default scheme as the company's only/main pension provision

13.58 The Government's default scheme is a trust-based occupational DC scheme to be set up and operated by PADA and regulated by HMRC and the Pensions Regulator.

This option outsources the administrative burden of the pension scheme, removing the employer's responsibility of being the pension provider. This could be an attractive option for employers, as their only responsibility would be to enrol employees and provide contributions. This is also likely to involve a 'levelling down' of contributions; employers would be moving to the minimum 3 per cent contribution level (see Option Four below). Levelling down could create contractual and employee relations problems and would almost certainly trigger consultation requirements under the *Occupational and Personal Pension Schemes (Consultation by Employers and Miscellaneous Amendment) Regulations 2006 (SI 2006/349)* (see **13.69** below and CHAPTER 7). This option may not be appropriate for employers with a significant number of higher earners, as annual contributions to the scheme are to be limited to £3,600 and there are severe restrictions on transfers out. Many employers may need to consider a top-up pension scheme in addition to the default scheme (see **13.68** below).

Option Two: using existing pensions arrangements

13.59 Where an employer decides to use its own existing scheme, it must, subject to regulations and the DWP's guidance notes, satisfy itself and certify that the scheme is a 'qualifying scheme' (see **13.60** to **13.66** below). In certain circumstances, certification may be provided by the scheme actuary. This option would also allow postponed automatic enrolment, subject to the prescribed conditions being met (see **13.56** above).

An increase in cost is likely with this approach, especially for employers who currently have a low take-up for their pension scheme, as the percentage of employees joining the scheme will swell under an automatic enrolment system.

Scheme amendments are likely to be needed, so employers should be considering in advance how they will comply with the requirements set down by *PA 2008, s 16*. There may be scope for levelling down contributions or accrual in an existing scheme whilst retaining 'qualifying scheme' status (see **13.67** below).

Qualifying schemes and the quality requirement

13.60 A pension scheme is a 'qualifying scheme' in relation to a jobholder (J) if:

(*a*) the scheme is an occupational pension scheme or a personal pension scheme,

(*b*) the scheme is registered under *FA 2004, Part 4, Chapter 2*, and

(*c*) while J is an active member, the scheme satisfies the 'quality requirement' in relation to J.

The quality requirements for different types of scheme are set out in *PA 2008, ss 20–27*, are discussed in the DWP's September consultation paper, and are summarised in the table below:

Type of scheme	**Quality requirement**
Defined contribution (occupational or personal pension scheme)	Employer contribution of 3 per cent of qualifying earnings and a total contribution of 8 per cent of qualifying earnings (phased in over three years).
Contracted-out defined benefit scheme	Qualifies by being contracted out.
Contracted-in defined benefit scheme	Must provide benefits from age 65 of 1/120ths of the average of the last three years' qualifying earnings, multiplied by number of years in pensionable service.
Hybrid scheme	The relevant requirements for each section, as set out above.
Non-UK schemes	Must meet the relevant criteria for UK schemes, plus the scheme must provide an income for retirement, and scheme must be regulated by a regulatory body.

UK money purchase schemes

13.61 *PA 2008* provides that a money purchase scheme that has its main administration in the United Kingdom satisfies the quality requirement in relation to a jobholder if, under the scheme:

(*a*) the jobholder's employer must pay contributions in respect of the jobholder;

(*b*) the employer's contribution, however calculated, must be equal to or more than 3 per cent of the amount of the jobholder's qualifying earnings in the relevant pay reference period; and

(*c*) the total amount of contributions, however calculated, must be equal to or more than 8 per cent of the amount of the jobholder's qualifying earnings in the relevant pay reference period.

Contributions to the qualifying scheme will, however, be phased in over a transitional period as follows:

Phased Contributions: Defined Contribution Schemes		
Year (from 2012)	Employer	Total
Years 1 to 3	1 per cent	2 per cent
Year 4	2 per cent	5 per cent
Year 5 onwards	3 per cent	8 per cent

UK defined benefits schemes

13.62 A defined benefits scheme that has its main administration in the United Kingdom satisfies the quality requirement in relation to a jobholder if the jobholder is in contracted-out employment.

13.63 A defined benefits scheme that has its main administration in the United Kingdom satisfies the quality requirement in relation to a jobholder who is not in contracted-out employment if it satisfies the 'test scheme' standard in relation to that jobholder.

A scheme satisfies the test scheme standard in relation to a jobholder where the pensions to be provided for the relevant members of the scheme are broadly equivalent to or better than the pensions which would have been provided to them under the test scheme.

The test scheme is a theoretical benchmark occupational pension scheme, allowing for a pension to be provided from age 65 and allowing for an accrual rate of at least 1/120ths of average qualifying earnings in the last three tax years preceding the end of pensionable service, multiplied by the number of years of pensionable service, up to a maximum of 40 years.

In applying the test scheme standard, the pensions to be provided for relevant members must be considered as a whole. The draft *Occupational and Personal Pension Schemes (Automatic Enrolment) Regulations 2010* provide that a scheme actuary or employer may not certify that a scheme meets the test scheme standard if the pensions to be provided for more than 10 per cent of relevant members are not broadly equivalent to the pensions which would be provided to them under a test scheme. The DWP has issued draft guidance which sets out in more detail the process for certifying that the test scheme standard is met, including the circumstances in which an employer may self-certify, the circumstances when the actuary must certify, and how sampling can be used.

UK hybrid schemes

13.64 A hybrid scheme that has its main administration in the United Kingdom satisfies the quality requirement in relation to a jobholder, broadly, where it satisfies the quality requirements for defined benefit schemes and money purchase schemes in proportion to the benefits that the scheme provides which are defined benefits or money purchase benefits. Qualifying conditions applying to hybrid schemes will be governed by specific regulations. A draft set of regulations, the *Hybrid Scheme Quality Requirement Rules 2010*, was included in the DWP's September consultation and includes further detail as to how the requirements may be met in relation to different types of hybrid scheme.

UK personal pension schemes

13.65 Personal pension schemes satisfy the quality requirement in relation to a jobholder if the following conditions are met:

(1) All of the benefits that may be provided to the jobholder under the scheme are money purchase benefits.

(2) In relation to the jobholder, there is an agreement between the provider of the scheme and the employer under which:

  (*a*) the employer must pay contributions in respect of the jobholder; and

  (*b*) the employer's contribution, however calculated, must be equal to or more than 3 per cent of the amount of the jobholder's qualifying earnings in the relevant pay reference period.

(3) If there is a shortfall, there is an agreement between the provider of the scheme and the jobholder under which the jobholder must pay contributions which, however calculated, are equal to or more than the shortfall. 'Shortfall' for these purposes is the difference (if any) between the employer's contribution in respect of the jobholder, and 8 per cent of the amount of the jobholder's qualifying earnings in the relevant pay reference period.

(4) There are direct payment arrangements (within the meaning of *PSA 1993, s 111A*) between the jobholder and the employer.

Contributions will be phased in as set out in **13.61** above.

Other types of pension scheme

13.66 *PA 2008* allows for further provision to be made by regulations on the quality requirement in relation to non-UK occupational pension schemes (see

PA 2008, s 25), and in relation to personal pension schemes to which *FSMA 2000* does not apply (see *PA 2008, s 27*).

Option Three: use existing pensions arrangements but level down

13.67 Employers have the option of keeping employees in an existing scheme (altering it where necessary to become a 'qualifying scheme') but reducing the employer contributions to the minimum contributions level of 3 per cent, or levelling down benefits to the 'test scheme' standard.

The attraction of this option is clear; it could save employers significant amounts of money if they currently provide a more generous pension scheme to their employees.

The 'levelling down' of pension scheme benefits is a major concern that has been raised by critics of the automatic enrolment regime. How many employers will choose this option remains to be seen.

Levelling down could create contractual and employee relations problems and would almost certainly trigger consultation requirements under the *Occupational and Personal Pension Schemes (Consultation by Employers and Miscellaneous Amendment) Regulations 2006 (SI 2006/349)* (see **13.69** below and CHAPTER 7). Careful consideration must also be given to any restrictions to the scheme's power of amendment.

Option Four: use the Government's default scheme and provide a top-up

13.68 Employers who wish to outsource the administration of their pension scheme but aim to give employees higher contributions than 3 per cent could consider this final option. An employer can enrol its employees in the Government's default scheme, but also include more than the minimum 3 per cent contribution (although this would be restricted to total contributions of £3,600 per jobholder).

In order to recruit and retain higher earners, it is likely that the employer would have to provide additional benefits outside the default scheme, perhaps through offering to contribute to personal pension schemes for certain employees.

Consultation requirements

13.69 If any of the four options set out above involves a 'listed change' to the employer's current pension scheme, as defined in the *Occupational and Personal Pension Schemes (Consultation by Employers and Miscellaneous*

Amendment) Regulations 2006 (SI 2006/349), the employer must embark on a consultation process with a trade union, elected representative or directly with the employees. 'Listed changes' include closing a scheme to new members, stopping accrual of all benefits, reducing employer contributions, and introducing or increasing member contributions (see CHAPTER 7).

Employer disclosure requirements

13.70 Employers have significant disclosure duties under the draft *Occupational and Personal Pension Schemes (Automatic Enrolment) Regulations 2010*. They will need to provide information to both the trustees/scheme manager and the members themselves, as set out below.

Information to be provided by the employer to the scheme

13.71 The employer must provide the following information relating to the jobholder to the trustees or manager of an occupational pension scheme or the personal pension scheme provider within one month of the automatic enrolment date:

(*a*) name;

(*b*) date of birth;

(*c*) postal residential address;

(*d*) gender;

(*e*) automatic enrolment date;

(*f*) postal or individual electronic work address (the latter where available);

(*g*) national insurance number (where the employer already have this information or within one month of receiving it);

(*h*) details of remuneration (if available);

(*i*) the jobholder's personal email address (if the employer holds this information); and

(*j*) the value, if any, of contributions payable by:

  (i) the employer; and

  (ii) the jobholder (where requested and the employer can provide it).

Enrolment information

13.72 The following information must be given to all relevant jobholders in writing within one month of their automatic enrolment date:

(*a*) a statement which includes the words 'the object of automatic enrolment is to encourage jobholders to make pension savings';

(*b*) the jobholder's automatic enrolment date;

(*c*) the name, physical and electronic contact details of the scheme into which the jobholder is to be enrolled;

(*d*) the value of contributions that will be made into the scheme by the employer;

(*e*) the value of contributions that will be deducted from the jobholder's remuneration and made to the scheme;

(*f*) confirmation as to whether tax relief will be through net pay arrangements or relief at source arrangements;

(*g*) a statement that the jobholder may remain an active member of the scheme without employer interference unless the jobholder is or becomes an active member of another qualifying scheme;

(*h*) that the jobholder has a right to opt out of the scheme;

(*i*) the opt-out period applicable to the jobholder;

(*j*) that opting out can only occur through the completion of the opt-out notice and its submission to the employer;

(*k*) that the opt-out notice must be obtained from the scheme;

(*l*) an explanation of how the notice may be obtained from the scheme;

(*m*) that opting out can means that the jobholder will be considered not to have become an active member of the scheme on that occasion;

(*n*) that, after a completed opt-out notice is received by the employer, any contributions paid by the jobholder will be refunded to the jobholder by the employer;

(*o*) that a jobholder who opts out may later opt in;

(*p*) that a jobholder who opts out or who ceases active membership of an automatic enrolment scheme will be automatically re-enrolled into such a scheme by the employer; and

(*q*) details of where to obtain further information about pension and saving for retirement.

Compliance and the role of the Pensions Regulator

13.73 The Regulator will be charged with policing the automatic enrolment regime. In the DWP's September consultation, it is stated that the compliance approach to the new regime will aim to be:

- Effective – the DWP will aim to maximise compliance across all employers.
- Efficient – using HMRC and other available data in a cost-effective way.
- Graduated – warning notices first, followed by a penalty.
- Proportionate – there will be a right of appeal against financial notices.
- Risk based – the Regulator will weigh up costs and benefits of any compliance action.
- Simple – enforcement will be feasible and understood by employers.

The *Pensions Regulator (Delegation of Powers) Regulations 2009 (SI 2009/1888)* enable the Regulator to delegate a number of its powers, including its enforcement powers under *PA 2008*, to third parties.

Duty to register with the Pensions Regulator

13.74 Employers will be required to provide information about how they have met their automatic enrolment duties via a process of registration.

It has been proposed that the following information will be required from employers at registration:

- Information that enables the Regulator to identify and contact them.
- Information about the action they have taken to enrol their jobholders into pension saving and where those jobholders have opted out.
- Where they do not have to enrol individuals in pension saving, an explanation of why this is the case.
- Information about their pension arrangements to enable the Regulator to match an employer to their pension arrangement.
- Employers will be required to register within 9 weeks after their staging date. This will enable employers who have undertaken automatic enrolment to provide information about jobholders who have left the pension scheme during the one-month opt-out period.
- Employers will have to re-register every 3 years. It is expected that re-registration will follow automatic re-enrolment.

Duty to keep records

13.75 Employers, trustees and managers of pension schemes and pension providers will be required to keep certain records to enable the Regulator to check compliance. Employers will be required to keep records relating to:

- pension arrangements they have made;
- the enrolment of jobholders;
- the opt-in and opt-out processes; and
- the pension contributions they have made.

Employers will be required to keep most of these records for a period of 6 years, which is the maximum time allowable under *PA 2008, s 60.*

Contravention of employer duties

13.76 *PA 2008* expressly provides that contravention by an employer of its automatic enrolment duties (including minimum contributions) does not give rise to an action for breach of statutory duty.

However, an employer who 'wilfully' fails to comply with certain requirements (that is, the right to opt in, automatic enrolment and re-enrolment) will be guilty of an offence, liable on conviction to imprisonment or a fine or both (see *PA 2008, s 45*).

13.77 The Regulator will have the power to:

- issue a formal 'compliance notice' to an employer who is in default, directing them to take steps to remedy the contravention;
- issue notices including notices requiring employers to provide information and pay any unpaid contributions; and
- order penalties including fixed or escalating penalties that will increase the longer they remain unpaid.

There will be a flat rate 'wake-up call' fixed penalty of £500. Escalating penalty notices will depend on the size of the employer (from £50 per day for one to four workers, to £10,000 per day for 500 or more workers). Those receiving a penalty notice will have 28 days to request a review. As mentioned in **13.73** above, the *Pensions Regulator (Delegation of Powers) Regulations 2009 (SI 2009/1888)* enable the Regulator to delegate a number of its powers, including its enforcement powers under *PA 2008*, to third parties.

Chapter 14

Commercial transactions

Introduction

General

14.1 This chapter considers the pensions implications of buying or selling a company or business. The value of the pension liabilities concerned can be very substantial and in some cases may exceed the value of the company or business itself, particularly where there is a defined benefit scheme involved. It is therefore essential that the main pensions issues arising from such a transaction are considered and addressed at an early stage in the negotiations. This was never more so than since the enactment of the *Pensions Act 2004* ('*PA 2004*') where the concept of 'moral hazard' in relation to pension schemes was introduced. There are now provisions in *PA 2004* and subordinate legislation that specifically deal with this issue, including the clearance procedure with the Regulator, whereby parties to a transaction can seek the Regulator's confirmation that it will not issue a contribution notice or financial support direction as a result of the transaction in contemplation. Since its introduction, the clearance procedure has been subject to revisions by the Regulator in the light of its experience and how the legislation is being interpreted. Amendments made to the 'Employer Debt' regulations have also ushered in an era when employers are required to stand behind their pension schemes' obligations to a greater extent. The *PA 2004* provisions as well as the amended 'Employer Debt' regulations are explored in more detail throughout the chapter.

Type of scheme

14.2 Inevitably, much will depend upon the type of scheme involved. However, pensions will tend to feature most prominently in the negotiations where the employees affected by the sale belong to a defined benefit scheme. The majority of these schemes would have been exempt approved under *ICTA 1988, Part XIV, Chapter I* prior to 6 April 2006, and are now registered pension schemes pursuant to *Finance Act 2004* ('*FA 2004*'), *Part 4* and will also frequently be contracted out (see CHAPTER 4).

This chapter therefore focuses on those transactions where the employees concerned belong to a registered, contracted-out defined benefit occupational pension scheme. The implications for other types of scheme are considered at the end of the chapter.

Type of sale

14.3 The course of the pensions negotiations will depend largely upon:

(*a*) whether the sale is of shares or of assets (see **14.14** below); and

(*b*) whether or not the sale will require a transfer of assets and liabilities between schemes. The circumstances which will typically give rise to such a transfer are described further in **14.20** below.

Funding

14.4 A preliminary point to establish, which will set the tone of subsequent negotiations, is the funding position of the scheme providing benefits for the employees of the company or business which is being sold.

Where employees' benefits are to be transferred from the seller's scheme to a scheme of the purchaser following completion (see **14.20** below), the funding level is likely to affect the sum which is transferred from the seller's scheme and consequently the level of past service benefits to be granted in the purchaser's scheme following the transfer (unless the purchaser can negotiate a shortfall clause – see **14.46** below).

Where instead the purchaser is to take over the entire scheme (see **14.21** below), the funding level may impact on the profitability of the company or business being purchased. For example, a well-funded scheme may reduce future liability for the company to contribute (so boosting profits) but, conversely, an underfunded scheme may require an immediate injection of cash to raise its funding level.

These situations are likely to affect the negotiation of the contract wording and, of course, the purchase price itself. In some instances, the funding level of the pension scheme may be of such concern to the purchaser that it is not prepared to acquire the target company unless the pension deficit has been addressed. Although the compromise of pension scheme deficits has to date been relatively under-utilised as a means of dealing with funding shortfalls when selling the entire issued share capital of a company, this may become more commonplace in the future as means of ensuring that the transaction proceeds, especially where the target or its holding company are in financial difficulty. These issues are dealt with in more detail below and further information on the Statutory Funding Objective, which was brought into effect from 30 December 2005 under *PA 2004*, can be found at CHAPTER 11.

Warranties and indemnities

14.5 It is common in a sale and purchase agreement for both warranties and indemnities to be agreed to deal with specific issues of concern to the parties, often points which have arisen during the course of negotiations and the due diligence exercise.

A *warranty* is a statement of fact made by one party to the contract (usually the seller). An example of this may be that the benefits provided by the scheme have been fully equalised as between men and women as required by law (see CHAPTER 9). This statement may then be disclosed against in the disclosure letter (see **14.12** below) to negate the effect of the statement to some extent, for example, by the disclosure that guaranteed minimum pensions have not yet been equalised. In such a circumstance the purchaser may seek to obtain an *indemnity* to the effect that the seller will indemnify the purchaser for the costs of equalising benefits, should this cost be incurred by the purchaser after completion.

The main difference between a warranty and an indemnity is the level of protection given to the party for whose benefit it is given and the method by which each is enforced. To enforce a warranty, the party seeking to benefit must take steps to enforce the contract. Unless a breach of warranty is agreed by both the parties, this is likely to involve proceedings, incurring costs and delays.

By contrast, an indemnity requires the party who granted the indemnity to reimburse the other party for specified losses which have been incurred. There is no requirement for the indemnified party to mitigate his loss or to take steps to prove any wrongdoing by the indemnifying party. Consequently an indemnity offers not only more protection than a warranty to the purchaser but also considerably less inconvenience in obtaining a remedy.

Due diligence

14.6 Due diligence is the name given to the fact-finding exercise which takes place before and during negotiation of the contract. The purchaser will be concerned to find out as much information as possible about the company or business it is seeking to acquire, to ascertain not only what potential liabilities there are but also to ensure that these are quantifiable and that protection, in the form of warranties and indemnities, is sought from the seller where appropriate.

In the context of pensions, the purchaser will wish to see, for example, a copy of the trust deed and rules, the scheme's booklet and full details of employees (including salary levels). Where a company with its own scheme is being purchased, as opposed to a transfer payment being received, more extensive information will be sought, as the purchaser will effectively be inheriting the whole scheme. The results of the due diligence exercise may result in re-negotiation of the purchase price or the seeking of further warranties and indemnities. Due diligence is considered in further detail below.

The sale documents

The sale agreement

Parties

14.7 The distinction between share sales and assets sales is considered in **14.14** below, but in either case the main parties to the agreement will be the seller and the purchaser respectively. There may also be other parties including, for example, guarantors.

The important point to bear in mind is that the trustees of the respective pension schemes are unlikely to be parties to the agreement and, consequently, there will be no contractual relationship between them. In any event, trustees may not under normal circumstances fetter a future exercise of their discretion and so making them a party to the agreement would be of little comfort to either the seller or the purchaser when the calculation of the transfer payment and the granting of past service benefits take place a few months after completion of the agreement (*Stannard v Fisons Pension Trust Ltd [1992] 1 PLR 27*).

This is relevant when the pensions schedule is negotiated. It may be impossible for a party to agree to procure that a certain event occurs, because the scheme rules place that event in the hands of the trustees. An example of this would be where the rules of the purchaser's scheme provide that past service benefits are granted entirely at the trustees' discretion. Where this is the case, the principal company or an adhering employer cannot guarantee that a certain level of past service benefits will be granted. The most the purchaser is likely to agree to in such circumstances is that it will use its best endeavours to procure that the specified event will take place.

The extent to which the parties can hold out for a greater commitment will therefore generally depend on who has the relevant power under the trust deed and rules and (if it is the trustees) the extent to which the principal employer or an adhering employer (subject to any overriding legislation) has control over the trustees' actions. An exception to this, however, is the transfer payment. In the context of transfer payments, the purchaser should seek to place the seller in such a position that, should the trustees pay less than the contractually defined transfer payment, the seller will be bound to make up any shortfall – see **14.46** below.

Warranties

14.8 The pensions warranties will usually appear in the part of the agreement which sets out all the warranties (not just those relating to pensions) being given by the seller. Sometimes, however, where there is a schedule to the agreement dealing with other pensions issues (typically a transfer payment – see **14.9** below) the pensions warranties may appear in that schedule instead. Where this happens, the seller should take care to ensure that any clauses in the agreement that limit the scope of the warranties also extend to the warranties in that schedule. The purchaser, on the other hand, may wish to seek to disapply any general limitations from the pension warranties schedule. Sellers can also seek to limit the warranties by 'awareness', and purchasers should be wary of this practice and understand exactly what this means. Usually an explanation is provided within the definitions section, which will confirm that phrases such as 'as far as the seller is aware', or 'to the best of the seller's knowledge' shall be deemed to refer to actual knowledge of the seller or the seller's knowledge after making due and careful enquiries for instance. If the seller is not prepared to remove the limitation the purchaser can seek to extend the definition to include the scheme administrator and/or the trustees of the scheme, for additional comfort.

It is common for parties to enter into a 'disclosure letter' of the same date as the main agreement (see **14.12** below). To the extent that a warranty is disclosed against, this will negate the effect of the warranty. An example of this has already been given in **14.5** above.

The warranties that a purchaser requires will vary considerably according to the nature of and the circumstances surrounding the transaction and are dealt with later on in this chapter in the contexts in which they arise.

Pensions schedule

14.9 Where the transaction involves a transfer of assets and liabilities from a scheme operating within the seller's group to one to be set up (or already established) by the purchaser, its holding company or one of its subsidiaries, there will normally be detailed provisions specifying how this is to happen. In the vast majority of cases, these will be set out in a schedule to the agreement, dealing specifically with pensions.

Other provisions

14.10 Other provisions may be included either in the pensions schedule (where there is one) or in the main body of the agreement.

These might include indemnities (see **14.5** above), for instance, in relation to equalisation issues (see CHAPTER 9) or as a consequence of obligations that may be inherited as a result of case law such as the *Beckmann* and *Martin* cases (see **14.15** below). Another example might be a provision which seeks to adjust the purchase price for any past overfunding or underfunding that may emerge where the purchaser is to inherit the scheme in its entirety (see **14.27** to **14.29** below).

Consistency with scheme rules

14.11 Any action to be taken in connection with the transfer of benefits from one scheme to another will need to be carried out in accordance with the respective scheme's rules. It is therefore important that both parties are aware of the provisions in the schemes' rules governing each particular issue. One example of this is where the transaction involves a transfer payment and the scheme rules require a different method of calculation from that specified in the sale agreement. Other examples are given in the course of this chapter.

The disclosure letter

14.12 As mentioned briefly above, the disclosure letter documents the agreement between the parties on the information which has been provided during the due diligence exercise and acts to limit or negate the effect of the warranties given in the sale and purchase agreement. The disclosure letter is a letter from the seller to the purchaser which is likely to set out first certain general statements of agreed information (such as records at Companies House) and will then go on to provide specific disclosures against specific warranties.

Purchasers should seek to ensure that the wording of disclosures is specific and to the point. From the perspective of the seller, by contrast, it will often be desirable to make general disclosures, or make reference to a bundle of documents (thereby making an effective disclosure without drawing attention to specific areas about which the purchaser should be concerned or, at least, aware). From the purchaser's point of view, it is important to receive as much specific information as possible to ensure that it is informed of all potential and actual liabilities and can take these into account when negotiating the sale and purchase agreement.

Actuary's letter

14.13 It will be seen later in this chapter that, particularly where the transaction involves a transfer payment from the seller's scheme, it may be necessary to agree a calculation method and assumptions for valuing the scheme's liabilities. Although there is no reason in principle why these assumptions cannot be set out in the agreement itself, they will usually be covered separately in a letter from the seller's actuary to the purchaser's actuary and countersigned by the purchaser's actuary by way of agreement. The letter should be clearly identified in the pensions schedule, attached as an appendix and referred to where relevant.

Shares or assets

The distinction

14.14 For the purposes of this chapter, a share sale takes place when the seller is selling all of the issued share capital of a company. In such a situation the identity of the company remains the same; it is the underlying ownership of the company which has changed. The purchaser inherits through its ownership of the company all the company's pre-existing contracts including (of particular relevance to pensions) contracts of employment and deeds which the company has entered into in relation to a pension scheme.

An asset sale takes place when all or part of a business is being sold to the purchaser. In such a transaction the purchaser will take on only specific contracts, premises and employees of the company selling the business and will only assume those liabilities specified in the agreement.

Practical implications

Employment aspects

14.15 Following a sale of shares there is no change in the employment relationship between the company and its employees. The employment contracts will stay intact and the employees therefore will enjoy the ongoing benefit of any contractual provisions, including any that relate to pensions.

This contrasts with the position of employees on an asset (or business) sale where their employment contracts are transferred to a new employer. Whilst the *Transfer of Undertakings (Protection of Employment) Regulations 2006 (SI 2006/246)* ('*TUPE*') contain provisions to transfer contractual employment rights to the purchaser, *reg 10* makes an exception in relation to 'so much of a contract of employment … as relates to an occupational pension scheme …'. However, any provisions of an occupational pension scheme which do not relate to benefits for old age, invalidity or survivors are excluded from the *reg 10* exception described above, and will therefore pass to a purchaser.

The first case in which the status of such benefits was raised in the courts was the case of *Frankling v BPS Public Sector Ltd [1999] IRLR 212, [1999] ICR 347, EAT*. The Employment Appeal Tribunal refused the employee's claim that the previous entitlements to early retirement pensions and compensation on redundancy were not part of the scheme and therefore transferred under *TUPE*. The Employment Appeal Tribunal considered that the rights still related to old age, they were just triggered by redundancy. The employee's leave to appeal was granted but the action was settled before it reached appeal.

This was followed by the case of *Beckmann v Dynamco Whicheloe Macfarlane Ltd, Case C-164/00 [2002] 64 PBLR; [2002] All ER (D) 05 (Jun)*. Katia Beckmann was a former NHS employee whose employment transferred to Dynamco Whicheloe Macfarlane under *TUPE*. She was subsequently dismissed on redundancy grounds and claimed entitlement to an early retirement pension and other lump sum benefits, on the basis that these had transferred under *Article 3* of the 1977 *Acquired Rights Directive (77/187/EEC)* (now repealed). *Article 3(3)* excludes the provision of 'employees' rights to old-age, invalidity or survivors' benefits under supplementary company or inter-company pension schemes outside the statutory social security schemes in member states'. A reference was made to the European Court of Justice ('ECJ'), and the ECJ decided that 'it is only benefits paid from the time when an employee reaches the end of his normal working life as laid down by the general structure of the pension scheme … that can be classified as old age benefits, even if they are calculated by reference to the rules for calculating normal pension benefits'. As a result, the right to an early retirement pension on redundancy was held to transfer. The judgment was short and still gives rise to concern amongst pensions professionals.

Beckmann is considered further at **14.52** below.

Following on from *Beckmann*, another case was subsequently referred to the ECJ in which additional questions were posed. In *Martin v South Bank University [2004] 1 CMLR 472, [2003] All ER (D) 85*, Martin and others transferred into a private pension arrangement following the transfer of their employment from the NHS to South Bank University. The claimants subsequently opted to take early retirement and claim an early retirement redundancy pension.

Nine questions were referred to the ECJ on the assumption that rights contingent upon both dismissal and premature retirement pass under *TUPE*. These included:

(*a*) Is an employee's right to the payment of early retirement benefits and lump sum compensation:

- on redundancy;
- in the interests of the efficiency of the service;
- on organisational change; or
- a right to 'old age, invalidity or survivors' benefit'?

(*b*) May an employee agree to waive benefits if the purchaser's scheme does not entitle the employee to the same benefits if the employee:

- joins the purchaser's scheme; or
- joins the purchaser's scheme and transfers his past service pension rights to the purchaser's scheme?

(*c*) Where a purchaser and employee agree that the employee will take premature retirement on less generous terms than under the seller's scheme, what criteria should a national court use to establish if the transfer is the reason for that agreement (a reconsideration of *Tellerup Foreningen af Arbejdsledere (Tellerup) v Daddy's Dance Hall [1988] ECR 739* – employment terms can be varied, provided that the transfer is not the reason for the variation)?

When the Advocate General's opinion was handed down it was dubbed 'Beckmann revisited'. Early retirement benefits and benefits intended to enhance the conditions of such retirement, paid in the event of dismissal to employees who have reached a certain age, did not relate to 'old-age, invalidity or survivors' benefits'. The right did therefore transfer.

On the *Daddy's Dance Hall* issue, rights cannot be waived, but could be varied within the parameters of that case – whether the transfer is the reason for the variation can only be answered on all the facts of the case. However, changes in the law or in the purchaser's economic position may suggest that the reason is something other than the transfer.

The Advocate General did not give a view on the impact of a transfer of past service rights.

The ECJ gave its decision on 6 November 2003. It upheld the Advocate General's opinion, but gives no guidance on the issue of in what circumstances the transfer may not be considered to be the reason for the change.

However, as regards waiving rights, the ECJ considered that as the protection was imposed as a matter of public policy, an employee could not waive his rights.

So what will transfer under *TUPE*? It is likely that redundancy benefits payable under an occupational pension scheme will transfer, and it is certainly arguable that other benefits payable before normal retirement date may transfer. The matter will undoubtedly give rise to further litigation, as the issues are clarified in the courts. In the meantime, there are a number of interesting issues raised by the case law:

(*a*) Must benefits be replicated in a purchaser's scheme in all respects? *Mitie Management Services Limited v French [2002] IRLR 513, [2002] All ER (D) 150 (Sep)* provides some authority for not having to replicate unjust, absurd or impossible features. Replacement benefits, for example salary increases, may need to be offered instead.

(*b*) When is the transfer going to be considered to be the reason for the change? Can it be argued that an employee agreeing to join the purchaser's scheme post transfer constitutes a variation of terms by mutual consent as opposed to a waiver?

(*c*) Does it make a difference whether past rights are transferred? What happens if an employee is told that if his past service benefits are not transferred, any benefits will be limited to future service?

(*d*) Can *Beckmann/Martin* be distinguished? The *Beckmann* pension was only payable to normal retirement age – the rights under a private sector scheme may be payable for life.

PA 2004 pension protection on the transfer of employment

14.16 Criticisms of the exclusion of occupational pensions from the ambit of *TUPE* (except in relation to *Beckmann* and *Martin*-type benefits) have led to the introduction of limited protection for employees pursuant to *PA 2004*, introduced with effect from 6 April 2005. Where an employer acquires employees on or after that date, as a result of a business purchase governed by *TUPE*, the new employer will be required to provide a minimum level of pension protection where the employee was an active member of, or eligible to become a member of, the seller's occupational pension scheme prior to the transfer.

From 6 April 2005, *PA 2004, ss 257, 258* and the *Transfer of Employment (Pensions Protection) Regulations 2005* (*SI 2005/649*) have therefore brought in limited protections for the pension position of employees who are involved in a business transfer governed by *TUPE*. To qualify for the protection, certain conditions must be met:

- there must be a relevant transfer within the meaning of *TUPE*;
- by virtue of that transfer, the employees cease to be employed by the transferor and become employed by the transferee;

- at the time immediately before the employee becomes employed by the transferee, there is an occupational pension scheme in relation to which the transferor is the employer;
- the employees being transferred were either active members of the scheme, were eligible to become members of the scheme, or were in a waiting period before becoming eligible; and
- if the transferor's scheme provided money purchase benefits, (i) for active members the transferor was required to make contributions to the scheme or elected to contribute, even though there was no requirement for it to do so, and (ii) for those who were not active members but were eligible to join or would have been eligible after completing a waiting period, the transferor would have been required to contribute if they had been active members.

If the above conditions are met, the new employer will now be required, as a condition of the employee's contract of employment, to offer the transferred employees membership of:

(*a*) the transferee employer's occupational defined benefit or hybrid scheme, and the scheme must provide benefits worth at least the equivalent in present value of 6 per cent of a member's pensionable pay (excluding the member's own contributions) for each member. The employee will not be required to contribute more than 6 per cent of pensionable pay; or

(*b*) an occupational money purchase scheme or a stakeholder arrangement where it is up to the employee to decide on the amount of contributions which the employer will then be required to match, up to a 6 per cent prescribed maximum.

Unlike the position generally under *TUPE*, these protections can be disapplied in relation to a contract or contracts of employment if the employee(s) and the new employer agree alternative terms (see *PA 2004, s* 258(6)).

It is worth noting that the definition of occupational pension scheme in *PSA 1993* has been amended by *PA 2004* to the effect that schemes providing only death-in-service benefits are excluded from the definition. Consequently, such schemes will not be covered by the occupational pension scheme exemption and will transfer under *TUPE*.

Employer's debt

14.17 We shall see later in this chapter (see **14.64** onwards below) that, where the seller's scheme is underfunded, the sale may give rise to a statutory debt payable to the trustees by the purchaser or by the company that it is buying. It will be seen, however, that the extent of this problem will normally be less on an asset purchase than on a purchase of shares (see **14.87** below), unless of course the purchaser as part of a share purchase insists on acquiring the company free of all pension liabilities, in which case further considerations apply, including notifiable events requirements and the possibility of clearance being sought from the Regulator.

Deed of substitution

14.18 Circumstances may arise where an asset sale results in the employment contracts of all of the scheme's active members being transferred to the purchaser. In such a situation, it may be appropriate for the entire scheme to become the purchaser's responsibility. This will typically require the execution of a deed substituting the purchaser as the scheme's new principal employer. In most cases, the execution of such a deed will be entirely consistent with *Re Courage Group's Pension Schemes [1987] 1 WLR 495* (outlined in **12.13** above).

A share sale is generally less likely to give rise to a deed of substitution. However, one example of where this might be appropriate would be where the seller is the scheme's principal employer but the subsidiary being sold employs all or the majority of the scheme's active members.

Whether the sale will give rise to a transfer payment

General

14.19 The scope, nature and extent of the contractual provisions required in the sale and purchase agreement will generally depend on whether or not a transfer payment is anticipated. In most cases, the question of whether there is to be a transfer will be dictated largely by the structure of the pension arrangements and of the sale (see **14.20** and **14.21** below) but the parties may nevertheless be able to agree some alternative approach (see **14.22** below).

Circumstances involving a transfer

14.20 The following circumstances will normally give rise to a transfer payment:

(*a*) where the company being sold is one of a number of companies which participate in the seller's scheme; or

(*b*) on an asset sale, where some but not all of the scheme's active members are to have their employment transferred to the purchaser.

Transactions such as these are discussed further in **14.31** to **14.63** below.

Circumstances not involving a transfer

14.21 The following circumstances will not usually give rise to a transfer payment:

(*a*) the sale of a company with its own scheme; or

(*b*) an asset sale, where all of the scheme's active members are to have their employment transferred to the purchaser and the purchaser is to be substituted as the scheme's new principal employer (see **14.18** above).

In these cases, the purchaser will effectively be taking over the whole of the scheme, as it will be buying (or, alternatively, becoming) its principal employer. This is considered further in **14.23** below.

Other approaches

14.22 The general principles outlined in **14.20** and **14.21** above may sometimes be overridden if the parties agree to structure matters differently.

One example of this would be where the vast majority of the active members were to be affected by the transaction, but not all of them. In these circumstances, rather than provide for a transfer payment to be made in respect of most the scheme's active members, the parties might decide instead to arrange for the purchaser to be substituted as the scheme's principal employer (and then for a transfer payment to be made back to another scheme within the seller's group in respect of the minority of active members whose employment was to remain with the seller).

The parties will need to satisfy themselves that the course of action proposed will be one which can be achieved under the terms of the scheme rules (particularly as the co-operation of the trustees, who will not be parties to the agreement, may be required). Even if the scheme rules themselves do not appear to present a problem, the agreement may still fail if it is inconsistent with the purposes of the scheme; *Re Courage Group's Pension Schemes [1987] 1 WLR 495* (see **12.13** above) is perhaps the best known example of this happening.

In some cases, the purchaser may refuse to accept any responsibility for past service benefits at all, so that the employees concerned simply become deferred pensioners in the seller's scheme. The industrial relations consequences of such a step do of course need to be borne in mind and the employment law position carefully considered in all the circumstances (see CHAPTER 7); in this respect, there may be a difference depending on whether it is a share or asset sale, in view of the employment law distinction mentioned in **14.15** above.

Transactions where the purchaser takes over the whole scheme

Protection of purchaser

General

14.23 Where the purchaser is, in effect, to take over the whole of the seller's scheme (see **14.21** above), its main concern will be to obtain as much protection as possible from any liabilities associated with the seller's scheme which arose prior to completion. This is especially the case because the scheme will relate not only to those current employees being acquired by the purchaser, but also to past employees with benefits (whether deferred or in payment) under the scheme. It is not surprising, however, that purchasers are becoming increasingly reluctant to acquire companies with defined benefit liabilities. This is a result of many factors, including unpredictability of costs, continually improving mortality rates and low inflation.

Where, however, a scheme is to come within the purchaser's group after completion, protection will take the form of thorough due diligence, warranties and, in relation to areas of particular concern, indemnities. There may also be negotiation on payments into the scheme by the seller to address funding concerns.

Due diligence

14.24 The purchaser should seek to ensure that its advisers have the opportunity to examine as much as possible of the scheme's documentation at an early stage.

At the very least, this should cover the scheme's governing trust documents, the latest actuarial valuation report (and any subsequent actuarial advice), booklets and announcements issued to members (as well as references to pensions in contracts of employment and service agreements), recent annual reports and accounts and sufficient membership data to enable the purchaser's advisers to take a view on the costs of the scheme's ongoing liabilities.

The purchaser should also seek to obtain copies of the HMRC approval letter or proof of registration under the *FA 2004* requirements and any contracting-out certificates. Other relevant matters are trustees' minutes, copies of investment management agreements (and other advisers' appointment letters), insurance policies, transfer agreements with the trustees of other schemes, the statement of investment principles and any proposals to review or revise it, the schedule of contributions, the current statement of funding principles and any proposals to review or revise it, documentation relating to member-nominated trustee arrangements and details of the scheme's internal dispute resolution procedure.

Additionally and pursuant to *PA 2004*, the purchaser should also be raising inquiries regarding whether any breaches of the law have been reported to the Regulator by the trustees of the scheme or the seller (not to mention the scheme's advisers or other persons involved in the administration) under *PA 2004, s 70* or if any reportable matters have arisen in relation to the scheme in accordance with *PA 2004, s 69* and the corresponding Codes of Practice for both. Purchasers will also want to know if the seller has been the subject of a contribution notice or if a financial support direction is in place (*PA 2004, ss 38, 43*) in relation to the scheme, as such funding obligations could be inherited going forwards. Both contribution notices and financial support directions are discussed in further detail at **14.77** and **14.82** below. Furthermore, a purchaser should also be making enquiries as to whether there are any withdrawal arrangements or apportionment arrangements in place in relation to the scheme, or whether there are any circumstances that might give rise to such arrangements.

The aim should be to build up a full picture of the scheme including funding levels, liabilities, the balance of powers between the employers and the trustees and compliance with *PA 1995* and *PA 2004*. This knowledge will all be important as part of the negotiation process.

Warranties

14.25 The more comprehensive the warranties that the purchaser is able to obtain from the seller, the safer he will generally be. For maximum protection, the agreement may stipulate that the warranties apply not only as at the date of the agreement but also (if later) the date of completion. Even if the seller gives warranties but then discloses against them, the purchaser will at least be in a better position to know where any problems lie.

Some examples of the warranties that a purchaser should seek are:

(*a*) that there are no schemes or similar commitments (whether legally binding or not) relating to the employees, except those that have been disclosed;

(*b*) that the documents provided to the purchaser are true and complete;

(*c*) that the scheme is a registered scheme in accordance with *FA 2004, Part 4* and there is no reason why the scheme should be de-registered;

(*d*) that the scheme is contracted out (where appropriate) (see CHAPTER 4) and the necessary contracting-out certificates have been issued;

(*e*) that the scheme complies with all legal requirements for the equalisation of benefits as between men and women;

(*f*) that the scheme, its trustees and the employers have complied with all applicable statutory requirements;

(*g*) that the information contained in the latest actuarial valuation report is complete and accurate in all respects and that nothing has happened since its effective date which would have an adverse affect on its conclusions;

(*h*) that no debt has arisen under *PA 1995, s 75* (as amended);

(*i*) the rate of employers' contributions;

(*j*) that all contributions due have been paid in accordance with the trust deed and rules and as required by the scheme's schedule of contributions;

(*k*) that no changes have been made (or proposed or announced) to the scheme's eligibility requirements, contribution rates or benefits;

(*l*) that all risk benefits are validly insured with an insurance company of good repute on normal terms for persons in good health;

(*m*) that there are no court proceedings and no complaints (whether under the scheme's internal dispute resolution procedure, or to The Pensions Advisory Service ('TPAS') or to the Pensions Ombudsman) in progress, pending, threatened or anticipated;

(*n*) that no contribution notices or financial support directions have been issued by the Regulator in relation to the scheme;

(*o*) that no employee has ever become employed by the seller as a result of a transfer pursuant to *TUPE*;

(*p*) that no professional adviser has had cause to report breaches of the law in accordance with *PA 2004, s 70*;

(*q*) that no unauthorised payments under *FA 2004, Part 4* have been made from the scheme since 6 April 2006;

(*r*) that the seller has complied with its obligations in respect of stakeholder pension arrangements in accordance with the *Welfare Reform and Pensions Act 1999*; and

(*s*) that the scheme is eligible for the Pensions Protection Fund and all applicable levies have been paid by the trustees or the sponsoring employer.

The purchaser may seek more extensive warranties than these, and the seller, conversely, will often aim to limit their scope. For instance, the seller may wish to restrict the warranties to matters of which it is aware, which in turn may lead to negotiations as to what extent of knowledge the contract should deem the seller to have. The seller will be particularly cautious with regard to any funding warranty, as a breach of this can prove extremely expensive.

Indemnities

14.26 Either party may seek indemnity protection from the other in respect of matters where there is some particular risk involved.

Purchasers, therefore, frequently require indemnities against the costs of benefits not having been equalised as between men and women in respect of past service (see CHAPTER 9). Another area which may give rise to an indemnity is the possibility of an employer's debt becoming payable under *PA 1995, s 75* (as amended) (see **14.64** to **14.74** below) and claims relating to *Beckmann/Martin* type benefits where the transaction is subject to the provisions of *TUPE*.

Funding

General

14.27 The importance to a purchaser of having a funding warranty has already been mentioned in **14.25** above.

A separate (but related) issue arises where the scheme is understood to be overfunded or underfunded on an ongoing basis and it is agreed that there should be some payment between the parties following the sale (usually as an adjustment to the purchase price) to compensate. Where this happens, the respective parties' actuaries will normally negotiate a method and assumptions for determining the amount of overfunding or underfunding; the calculation itself is then carried out after completion.

(It is common for these issues instead to be dealt with at an earlier stage, as part of the purchase price negotiations. The most likely reason for dealing with the matter by means of a post-completion adjustment would be that there was insufficient information as to the scheme's funding position at the time of sale.)

It should be noted that, where a scheme is overfunded but ongoing, *PA 2004, s 250* has amended *PA 1995, s 37* further to restrict the ability for payments to be made to the employer from a defined benefit scheme. Trustees will in the future only be able to make payments where the scheme is funded in excess of the buy-out level and the other requirements of *PA 1995, s 37* have been complied with, such as the member notification requirements.

Underfunded scheme

14.28 Where the scheme is underfunded on an ongoing basis, the purpose of the compensating payment will, in effect, be to relieve the purchaser of the costs of bringing the funding up to that level.

The sum which the scheme will require, therefore, will be the amount by which the scheme's assets fall short of the value calculated in accordance with the agreed actuarial method and assumptions. The seller, however, will be reluctant to pay more than is necessary to achieve this, and so (instead of paying the sum directly into the scheme) may propose to pay it to the purchaser net of the standard rate of corporation tax, on the basis that corporation tax relief will become available to the purchaser's group when it is remitted to the trustees. (The seller may be particularly concerned that the payment should be used to restore the scheme's funding position rather than to benefit the purchaser, and so expressly require that the purchaser pay the sum into the scheme as soon as it is received.)

The purchaser will not necessarily be satisfied with this approach. For instance, the purchaser's group may prove not to be making profits when the time comes, in which case it will derive no benefit from the theoretical availability of corporation tax relief. Alternatively, even if the purchaser is making profits, the sum involved may be treated by HMRC as a special contribution (see CHAPTER 5), in which case the tax relief would have to be spread over a period of years.

A compromise position would be for the payment to be made to the purchaser gross of corporation tax, on condition that the purchaser take steps to avail itself of corporation tax relief on paying the sum into the scheme and account to the seller for the value of that relief.

Overfunded scheme

14.29 Where the scheme has a surplus on an ongoing basis, the purpose of a compensating payment (which would instead be from the purchaser) is very different, as are the considerations affecting its calculation.

The payment would be a form of recognition that, before the sale, there was an overfunded scheme within the seller's group from which the seller might have gained some benefit in the future. Following the sale, the seller no longer has that opportunity, which has passed to the purchaser instead.

It would probably be inappropriate for the purchaser to pay to the seller the whole of this surplus. This would presume that it was open to the scheme's employers to acquire the full present value of the scheme's surplus, which is not the case for a number of reasons:

(*a*) Only in exceptional cases may an employer receive a refund of surplus assets from its scheme, and even then the scheme rules may require that substantial benefit increases be granted first. Previous legislation also required this. From 6 April 2006, pursuant to *PA 1995, s 37*, as amended by *PA 2004, ss 250* and *251*, certain conditions will need to be satisfied before any refund of surplus can be made. For example, the scheme will need to show that it is funded at buy-out level on an actuarial basis; the trustees will need to confirm that they are satisfied such a payment would be in the interests of the members; and the Regulator must not have issued a freezing order against the scheme which is in force. Any such refund would, in any event, be subject to a 35 per cent tax charge (see *FA 2004, s 207*). These issues are considered in more detail in CHAPTER 11.

(*b*) It is more likely that the employer could benefit from the surplus by means of a reduction in its contributions or even a contributions holiday. However, it is by no means certain that the whole of the surplus could be used in this way. For example, if the scheme rules give the trustees a say in the matter, then it is likely that at least some of this surplus would instead have to be used for benefit improvements.

(*c*) Even if the employer is able to take a contributions holiday in respect of the entire surplus, the benefit of that holiday will only gradually be realised over a period of time. An immediate payment to the seller in lieu of that contributions holiday, therefore, ought not to be equal to the entire surplus, but should be discounted to take into account the fact that (unlike a contributions holiday) the benefit to the seller is immediate.

It can be seen from this that agreeing a suitable method for ascertaining the amount of the compensatory payment is likely to prove complex. Often the matter will instead be dealt with between the parties before the sale as part of the purchase price negotiations.

Change of trustees

14.30 Usually, the scheme's trustees will be directors, employees or a subsidiary company of the seller. If the trustees are to remain with the seller's group following completion, it will generally be appropriate for them to be replaced as trustees by individuals or by a company within the purchaser's group. The contract may expressly provide for this to be done, and may even require that a deed of removal and appointment of trustees be one of the completion documents.

Considerations may also arise in relation to the issue of member-nominated trustees. This is addressed further in **14.88** below.

Transactions involving a transfer payment

General

14.31 Where the transaction involves a transfer payment (see **14.20** above), the sale agreement may provide for the company being sold (or, in the case of an asset sale, the purchaser) to participate in the seller's scheme on a transitional basis for a temporary period after completion. This is not always the case, however, and the following paragraphs, from **14.32** to **14.52** below, assume that there is to be no such transitional period.

The further issues which will become relevant if there is to be a transitional period are considered later in this chapter (see **14.53** to **14.63**).

Methods of calculating transfer payments

Past service reserve

14.32 There are several ways of calculating a bulk transfer payment. Of these, a 'past service reserve' calculation is the one which seeks to produce a sum which is sufficient to provide past service benefits which are equal overall to the benefits that the transferring members could otherwise have expected to receive in respect of their completed membership of the seller's scheme had there been no sale.

A past service reserve transfer payment is calculated by reference to the length of past pensionable service of the members concerned, but with present pensionable salaries being increased by an actuarially assumed rate of future salary growth. The calculation will also require other assumptions to be made, for instance, in relation to the future mortality rates, inflation, rates of withdrawal by members from pensionable service and investment growth.

The figure produced by this calculation will ultimately depend upon the assumptions used. These assumptions should normally therefore be agreed between the respective parties' actuaries before the contract is signed. Two very slightly differing sets of assumptions can produce vastly different results and consequently these negotiations are often hard fought. In reality, the relationships between the assumptions (for instance, the extent by which investment returns are assumed to exceed future salary growth) may have a greater impact on the final calculation than the assumptions themselves.

The purchaser's actuary will normally wish to see a copy of the scheme's most recent actuarial valuation report, so that he can form a view as to whether the assumptions on offer are consistent with the way in which the scheme as a whole is funded. The seller may refuse to make the valuation report available, but the purchaser may still be able to obtain it through links with members or with trades unions to whom the trustees can be required by law to provide a copy in accordance with the *Occupational Pension Schemes (Disclosure of Information) Regulations 1996 (SI 1996/1655)* (see summary at APPENDIX II).

The valuation report may reveal that the assumptions on offer will produce a smaller transfer payment than would the long-term funding assumptions recommended by the actuary for the purpose of calculating employer's contributions. The purchaser may then argue that the scheme's long-term funding assumptions should be used instead. The seller's likely response would be that a policy decision had been taken to fund the scheme using more cautious assumptions than were strictly necessary or that different assumptions were appropriate to the group of employees being transferred.

Sensitivity about the scheme's funding assumptions is not the only reason why a seller may prefer not to make a copy of the valuation report available. Other reasons might be that:

(*a*) the valuation shows that the scheme is in surplus, and this may encourage the purchaser to press for a greater transfer payment; or

(*b*) the valuation shows that the scheme is weakly funded, which in turn may lead the purchaser to ask for an indemnity in respect of any employer's debt that may arise. This aspect is explained further in **14.64** onwards below.

Past service reserve plus share of surplus

14.33 The purchaser may seek a transfer payment that is calculated on a past service reserve basis but which also includes a proportionate share of any surplus funding in the seller's scheme over and above that.

Although the scheme rules will be relevant, it has been widely accepted since Walton J's decision in *Re Imperial Foods Ltd Pension Scheme [1986] 2 All ER 802* that there is no reason in principle why a purchaser (or the receiving trustees) should expect the transfer payment to include a share of any surplus. The rationale for this view is that, in an ongoing scheme whose rules will require the employers to increase their contributions to make good any underfunding that arises in the future, a surplus in the scheme as at a given time simply reflects the fact that the employers are temporarily ahead with their contributions. The so-called surplus does not represent 'spare' money that should necessarily be available to a receiving scheme.

Transfer payments including a share of a surplus are therefore now comparatively rare. However, they can still occur where, for instance, a very substantial proportion of the seller's scheme's liabilities is to be transferred in circumstances where the seller's scheme's rules will make it difficult for the trustees to justify not transferring a share of the surplus, or require a 'share of fund' transfer value to be paid.

Where this does happen, the seller can be expected to require an increase in the purchase price. The manner in which this should be calculated is complex, but it will be governed by the same considerations as have been mentioned in the context of **14.29** above.

Cash equivalents

14.34 We saw in CHAPTER 6 that a member's 'cash equivalent' is the statutory amount which he may be entitled by law to require the trustees to transfer to another scheme. In most cases, cash equivalents will produce a lower figure than would a past service reserve. This is primarily because the cash equivalent calculation does not provide for future salary growth.

Where a seller proposes that the transfer payment be restricted to cash equivalents, this may be because the seller's scheme is too precariously funded to be able to pay more. If this is so, the purchaser may request a shortfall payment from the seller representing the difference between the cash equivalents and the higher amount which a past service reserve calculation would have produced (see **14.46** below) or alternatively seek a reduction in the purchase price. If the seller is not prepared to accede to either of these requests, then there is likely to be an adverse impact on the past service benefits which the purchaser's scheme will be able to offer, unless the purchaser is prepared to make up the shortfall itself. The employment law and industrial relations of this will have to be considered (see CHAPTER 7), as well as the possibility instead that past service benefits simply be left in the seller's scheme (rather than transferred).

Sometimes a seller will offer only cash equivalent transfer payments, even though its scheme can afford to pay more. The scheme rules are likely to be especially relevant in such cases; it may well be that they require the trustees to pay more than the seller is offering.

Reduced cash equivalents

14.35 It may be the case, where the trustees of the seller's scheme have requested an insufficiency report from the scheme actuary, that the trustees decide to reduce the cash equivalent pursuant to *Occupational Pension Schemes (Transfer Values) Regulations 1996, reg 7D* (as amended by the *Occupational*

Pension Schemes (Transfer Values) (Amendment) Regulations 2008 which came into force on 1 October 2008).

Matters the trustees are likely to take into account when deciding whether it is appropriate to reduce cash equivalents include the degree of underfunding, the strength of the employer covenant and any recovery plan. The problems which this can raise for the purchaser are essentially the same as those mentioned in **14.34** above, only even more acute. The purchaser should also be particularly concerned about the risk of an employer's debt arising, as explained further in **14.64** below.

Other possibilities

14.36 There are, of course, other ways of calculating a transfer payment. For instance, it could be calculated as an agreed percentage of (for example) the amount needed to meet the statutory funding objective ('SFO') as more fully explained in CHAPTER 11 in respect of the transferring members' past service benefits. So, a scheme which, being funded at 104 per cent of the scheme's SFO, could afford to pay more than the statutory cash equivalents but was unable to pay a reasonable past service reserve, might pay transfer payments equal to 104 per cent of the SFO in respect of the members concerned.

Timescales, mechanics and calculation adjustments

Timescales and mechanics

14.37 In the absence of a transitional period (see **14.53** onwards below), the mechanics of the transfer provisions will tend to revolve around two key dates.

The first of these is the date of completion of the sale which, for pension purposes, will be the date on which the relevant employees' pensionable service in the seller's scheme will terminate.

The second of these is the date on which the transfer payment becomes payable.

The length of time that is to pass between the completion date and the payment date will be determined by the sale agreement. In most cases the agreement will provide for certain steps to be taken between the two dates. In a typical agreement, these might include:

(*a*) Following the completion date, members are to be invited to join the purchaser's scheme for future service and advised that if they do elect to join they will have a right to transfer their past service benefits to the purchaser's scheme.

(*b*) The members are to be given a period in which to decide whether to elect for such a transfer. This will normally involve their signing and returning a consent form, and the sale and purchase agreement will often provide for that form to include a discharge from the member to the seller's scheme's trustees (and possibly the seller) in respect of any further liability for past service benefits. The information given to members should recommend that they obtain independent financial advice (see CHAPTER 10).

(*c*) Once that period has expired, the parties know which members have elected to transfer. The parties then instruct their actuaries to liaise with a view to calculating the transfer payment in accordance with the method of calculation previously agreed between them. There will usually be a set timescale for this.

(*d*) Once the calculation of the transfer payment has been agreed, there is a short further period allowed for, at the end of which the payment becomes due. If it has been agreed that the transfer be paid in cash, the transferring trustees may need to realise assets during this period. Alternatively, the parties and their actuaries may agree certain in specie transfers of assets.

Timing adjustment

14.38 A past service reserve transfer payment will in these circumstances be calculated as at the date of completion, as that will be the date on which pensionable service terminated and the benefits therefore crystallised.

However, as explained in **14.37** above, the transfer payment will not actually become payable until some time after that. Some provision therefore needs to be included in the agreement specifying how the transfer payment is to be adjusted in respect of the period from completion until the date on which it becomes payable.

An interest calculation can be used, but this may not take proper account of the effects of investment conditions during the period in question. If, for instance, share values were to soar ahead of the agreed interest rate during this period, then the seller's fund would benefit disproportionately from this, whereas the purchaser's fund would not benefit from it at all. Conversely, were investments instead to fall in value, the effect of an agreed interest rate would be to exacerbate the impact of this upon the seller's fund, whilst the purchaser's fund would remain insulated from the adverse conditions.

The actuaries may therefore agree a market related 'timing adjustment' in respect of this period. In effect, this means that the past service reserve figure is to be adjusted by a formula representing movements over the period in a notional portfolio consisting of (for instance) 85 per cent equities and 15 per cent gilts. The actuaries will discuss and agree the formula to be used before the sale agreement is signed. The respective schemes' investment strategies can be expected to have some bearing on these discussions.

Interest

14.39 If the transfer payment is not paid until after it has fallen due, a further adjustment will be necessary in respect of the period of late payment.

This may be dealt with simply by continuing to apply the timing adjustment for that further period, but the purchaser may consider that the sale agreement should require a more punitive adjustment as payment by that stage will be overdue. One approach would be to continue to apply the timing adjustment, but to make the sum resulting from it subject to an agreed rate of interest in respect of the period of delay.

Voluntary contributions

14.40 The agreement should also provide for the transfer of assets arising from the payment of money purchase voluntary contributions by those members who elect to transfer their past service benefits. Because of the money purchase nature of these, this will be a simpler provision than those parts of the agreement dealing with the transfer of defined benefit liabilities.

Disputes clause

14.41 There may be circumstances in which, following the sale, the actuaries are unable to agree the calculation of the transfer payment as required by the sale agreement. Alternatively, the sale agreement may require that the past service benefits to be granted by the purchaser's scheme should be equal in overall value to the amount of the transfer payment; this is another area where the actuaries may fail to agree.

Most pensions schedules therefore include a clause providing for disagreements of this nature to be referred to an independent actuary. The clause will normally provide for the independent actuary to act as expert (rather than as arbitrator) as this is generally suitable for disputes of this nature and is less formal than arbitration. The agreement should also make provisions as to who is to bear the expert's costs; for example, whether these are to be borne between the parties equally or, alternatively, as the expert may direct.

Revenue issues

14.42 Previous editions of this book have set out the Revenue requirements relating to consent to bulk transfers and preservation of a member's continued rights following a transfer. Both of these requirements ceased to exist from 6 April 2006. There are, however, new considerations to take into account following *FA 2004*.

Loss of protection of cash

14.43 Where a member of a scheme had a right as at 5 April 2006 to a tax-free cash lump sum which exceeded the new 25 per cent pension commencement lump sum limit and this is preserved by the transitional protection contained in *FA 2004, Sch 36, para 31* (see CHAPTER 5), then a transfer to a new arrangement can cause such protection to be lost unless the following conditions are satisfied:

(*a*) the member must not have applied for enhanced protection or primary protection;

(*b*) the value of the prospective lump sum as at 5 April 2006 was less than £375,000; and

(*c*) the transfer is a 'block transfer'.

A transfer is a 'block transfer' if it is a single transfer of all the assets of at least two members and either:

(i) the member was not a member of the receiving scheme before the transfer; or

(ii) he has been a member of the receiving scheme but for no longer than 12 months.

Loss of enhanced protection

14.44 In relation to ensuring no loss of enhanced protection for any member, it is necessary to consider the provisions of *FA 2004, Sch 36, para 12* (as amended by *FA 2007, Sch 20*). In summary, this states that, for enhanced protection to be retained on transfer, the transfer must be a 'permitted transfer'.

In terms of *para 12(7)*, a transfer is a permitted transfer if *sub-para (8)* applies and the aggregate of the amount of the sums and the market value of the assets is, applying normal actuarial practice, equivalent before and after the transfer.

Sub-paragraph (8) requires the transfer to comply with one of the following:

(*a*) it is a transfer to a money purchase scheme;

(*b*) it is a transfer 'in connection with the winding-up of the pension scheme under which the arrangement is made' and the rights transfer to employment with the same employer;

(*c*) it is a transfer in connection with a TUPE transfer; or

(*d*) it is a transfer to comply with life assurance only benefits contrary to *Pensions Act 2004, s 255*.

Contracting out

14.45 Separate requirements apply to the transfer of contracted-out benefits. The relevant law is summarised in CHAPTER 4, starting at **4.75**.

Shortfall and excess clauses

Shortfall clause

14.46 As has been mentioned already, the trustees will not be a party to the sale agreement and so will not be bound by its terms. Consequently, except in those cases where the seller's scheme's rules enable the seller to direct the amount of the transfer payment, there can be no guarantee that the trustees of that scheme will in fact transfer the amount provided for in the sale agreement. The purchaser will have particular cause for concern if the funding position of the seller's scheme suggests that its assets may prove insufficient to justify the transfer payment which the parties have negotiated.

The purpose of a shortfall clause, therefore, is to protect the purchaser (and the purchaser's scheme) from the possibility of the trustees transferring less than the amount which the seller and the purchaser have agreed. The clause will require a payment by the seller itself (or by a company in its group) to achieve this. The principles surrounding the shortfall payment (including the tax considerations) will be those that have already been considered in the context of **14.28** above.

Excess clause

14.47 An excess clause is essentially the converse of a shortfall clause. Whereas a shortfall clause requires a payment from the seller, should the trustees of the seller's scheme pay less than the agreed transfer payment, an excess clause requires a payment from the purchaser should they pay more.

A seller might insist that, in order to be even-handed, any shortfall clause in the agreement should be accompanied by a mirror-image excess clause. The purchaser, however, may take the view that the seller's trustees will only exceed the negotiated transfer payment if they are satisfied that their scheme can afford it. Consequently, many excess clauses are expressed so as only to apply to the extent that the trustees have transferred the excess by mistake.

The purchaser's scheme

Type of scheme

14.48 The course of action which ought to create the least disruption to the continuing accrual of members' pension benefits will be a properly funded transfer payment to a defined benefit scheme of the purchaser, containing similar provisions to those of the seller's scheme.

Often, however, the purchaser will not have an existing defined benefit scheme and the number of employees to be transferred may simply not be enough to make the establishment of a defined benefit scheme specifically for them financially viable. In these circumstances, the purchaser might instead offer membership of a money purchase scheme or agree to pay contributions to personal pension schemes in relation to the employees concerned.

The seller will normally require a commitment in the sale agreement that the receiving scheme should be registered under the *FA 2004*, so that the seller's scheme may properly make the transfer to it. The contracted-out status of the purchaser's scheme should also be addressed, in view of the requirements referred to in **14.46** above.

One related point concerns announcements which the seller may have made about the purchaser's scheme. When contemplating making announcements to members about an impending sale, sellers will need to bear in mind the case of *Hagen v ICI Chemicals and Polymers Ltd [2001] 64 PBLR, [2001] All ER (D) 273 (Oct)*. This has already been referred to at **7.23** above. In the light of this case, the seller may want to leave as much detail as possible to be explained by the purchaser, whilst still complying with its duty to provide certain disclosures under *TUPE*. The sellers should ensure that communications are, as far as possible, recorded in writing and that they take legal advice.

Past service benefits

14.49 If the sale agreement provides for a past service reserve transfer payment to a defined benefit scheme, the seller is likely to require some commitment as to what past service benefits the purchaser's scheme will provide. The seller may prefer that these be determined in the same manner as applies for the calculation of benefits under the seller's scheme, but this could prove impractical for the purchaser if its own scheme has a different benefit structure.

Instead, the purchaser may (if it is satisfied that the transfer payment will be sufficient) be prepared to agree that the past service benefits will be broadly equivalent (or, if the purchaser agrees to go further than that, at least equal in value) overall to those earned in the seller's scheme; the seller, in turn, may consider that this should be tightened so as to apply separately in respect of each member. The agreement may have to make it clear how benefits are to be valued for this purpose.

A more stringent line that a seller could take would, in effect, be to insist that the whole of the transfer payment is used to provide past service benefits in respect of the employees concerned. This would prevent the purchaser from using any part of the sum to fund a reduction in employers' contributions or to provide benefits for other scheme members. Much will depend upon the trust deeds and funding positions of the respective schemes, but a purchaser may well be reluctant to accept such a suggestion on the ground that it places a more onerous obligation upon it than would previously have applied under the seller's scheme.

Indeed, the purchaser may be reluctant to give any commitments as to the level of past service benefits at all if it has doubts about the adequacy of the transfer payment being offered.

Where the transfer is to be made to a money purchase scheme, the question of past service benefits is less controversial. These will normally be whatever the value of each member's portion of the overall transfer payment provides.

Future service benefits

14.50 Purchasers are generally reluctant to commit themselves in the sale agreement to a specific level of benefits in respect of future service. This is partly because to do so would in most cases be a more onerous obligation than the seller itself had ever assumed, but more particularly because it would fetter the future running of their business.

A purchaser which has decided initially to provide defined benefits might, therefore, be prepared to commit itself to a particular benefits structure as at the date when the employees join the scheme, but reserve the right to amend or discontinue the scheme at any time after that. In the comparatively rare cases where the purchaser agrees to maintain a particular benefit structure (perhaps because it is receiving a generous transfer payment), this will only normally apply for a limited period.

Transfer agreement

14.51 The nature of the purchaser's scheme and the benefits under it will generally tend to be of greater concern to the transferring trustees than they are to the seller itself. These trustees may even have adopted a practice of requiring receiving trustees to enter into a transfer agreement with them, dealing specifically with these issues, before they will agree to make a particular transfer payment. The ability of trustees to take such a stance will depend on the balance of powers in the transferring scheme.

However, where this is the case, the seller may require that a form of transfer agreement is attached to the sale agreement and that the seller's obligations in relation to any transfer are dependent upon the purchaser's scheme's trustees entering into such an agreement with the seller's scheme's trustees.

Transfer agreements, and examples of the matters that they will frequently cover, are considered in CHAPTER 12, at **12.35** onwards.

Due diligence, warranties and indemnities

14.52 Where the purchaser will not be inheriting the whole of the seller's scheme, it may not require the same level of warranty protection as described in **14.25** above. This is particularly so in the absence of a transitional period (see **14.31** above) (or, in the case of a share purchase, the company it is buying), as the purchaser will not be participating in the seller's scheme following completion.

The purchaser should still, however, request a complete copy of the scheme's trust deed and rules and obtain a warranty as to its accuracy. There are two main reasons for needing to see this. The first is to enable the purchaser to satisfy itself that its provisions will not be such as to prevent the agreed pensions schedule from being implemented. If, therefore, the rules show that the power to make bulk transfer payments rests solely with the trustees, then (particularly if the scheme appears to be poorly funded) the purchaser will be forewarned of the importance of obtaining a shortfall clause (see **14.46** above).

The other reason is to enable the purchaser to ascertain the contributions and benefits structure in the seller's scheme; with this in mind, the purchaser should also seek to obtain copies of members' booklets and should also require a warranty that no changes to the information shown have been proposed or announced. This (together with appropriate membership data) should enable the purchaser's actuary to assess the likely costs to the purchaser of providing the same benefits for future service and suggest what alternative approaches might be available. This information should also reveal any particular expectations the members may have that could prove expensive for the purchaser, such as generous early retirement provisions on redundancy.

The purchaser ought also to request a copy of the latest actuarial valuation report and obtain warranties to the effect that nothing has happened since its effective date which might adversely affect its findings. An understanding of the scheme's funding position will help the purchaser to take a view as to how large a transfer payment it can realistically negotiate. Where there is some indication of underfunding, this will again alert the purchaser to the possible need for a shortfall clause (see **14.46** above) and an indemnity in respect of any employer's debt that may arise (see **14.64** onwards below).

Warranties should also be sought as to the registered status of the seller's scheme (as, broadly, a transfer can be made without adverse tax consequences if it counts as a 'recognised transfer' – a type of authorised payment (see CHAPTER 5)) and also its contracted-out status (because of the requirements referred to briefly in **14.45** above and set out in CHAPTER 4).

Another area of concern is the equalisation of benefits as between men and women as required by law (see CHAPTER 9). The purchaser should seek a warranty that these requirements have been met, as a member who is entitled to bring a claim based on a scheme's failure to equalise can also sue the trustees of another scheme to whom the benefits in question have been transferred. If successful, such a claim can prove expensive. It is therefore common for purchasers also to seek an indemnity against this eventuality.

The current state of concern arising from the case of *Beckmann v Dynamco Whicheloe Macfarlane Ltd, Case C-164/00 [2002] 64 PBLR; [2002] All ER (D) 05 (Jun)* (see **14.15** above) may lead to purchasers and sellers negotiating who will bear the commercial risk that a particular scheme benefit will pass following this case. Purchasers may seek indemnities or an adjustment to the purchase price in this connection. They should consider relevant provisions of the seller's scheme very carefully and ask their actuary to cost these pension rights.

Transitional periods

General

14.53 Transactions involving a transfer payment fall into two main categories, depending upon whether the employees concerned:

(*a*) cease to be active members of the seller's scheme from the completion date; or

(*b*) continue to be active members of the seller's scheme for a transitional period following the completion date.

The purchaser may wish to have the benefit of a transitional period if it has no suitable scheme in place to receive the transfer payment (or provide future service benefits) and requires a period of time in which to establish one.

In the context of a share sale, this will simply be a case of the company continuing to participate in the scheme for a temporary period after it has been sold out of the seller's group. In an asset sale, by contrast, it will mean the purchaser (or employer of the transferring employees) being admitted to the seller's scheme as a participating employer, but only for the agreed transitional period commencing on the completion date.

Previously in this chapter we have considered only those cases where there is no transitional period. Where there is to be a transitional period, further considerations will apply.

HMRC

14.54 The position prior to 6 April 2006 was that any period of participation by an employer which was not (or had ceased to be) associated with the scheme's principal employer required the agreement of HMRC. In the past HMRC usually agreed to a period of participation not exceeding 12 months.

This requirement fell away with effect from 6 April 2006 and the position is now that non-associated employers are able to participate in a scheme and/or allow previously associated employers receiving a transfer of employees following a business transfer to participate for longer than the previously permitted period of 12 months on completion of the transaction. This may give rise to 'balance of power' issues (for example, is admission subject to trustee consent under the trust deed and rules governing the scheme?) and consideration will be required as to whether the participation of a non-associated employer would be consistent with the main purpose of the scheme (ie where the scheme in question has been established for the benefit of the employees and directors of the principal and associated employers).

Role of trustees

14.55 Before agreeing to a period of temporary participation, the seller should check its scheme rules to see if the trustees have a discretion as to whether or not to permit this. If so, then the seller will not be in a position to *procure* a transitional period in the sale agreement, and should ensure that the level of commitment required of it under the sale agreement is consistent with those rules.

In most instances, the trustees should be amenable to the agreement of a transitional period of participation, but circumstances may arise where they are not (for instance, if the trustees anticipate that the temporary employer intends to grant artificially high pension increases, to the detriment of the scheme's funding position).

The sale agreement will normally seek to regulate the terms upon which the company or purchaser is to be permitted to participate, as we shall see below. This is another area, therefore, where the rules of the sellers' scheme and the scheme's actuarial assumptions will need to be checked. This can be particularly relevant in the context of contributions, which is considered next.

Employers' contributions

14.56 The parties may either leave the question of contributions during the transitional period to be determined in accordance with the scheme rules, or they can agree a specific rate.

If, for example, the seller's scheme is overfunded and the participating employers are enjoying a contributions holiday, the seller is likely to prefer to specify a fixed contribution rate, probably equal to the long-term contribution rate which the actuary would be recommending if the scheme was evenly funded on an ongoing basis. This, of course, is because the purchaser will have made no contribution towards the surplus that has arisen and so the seller will not wish to see the purchaser derive any benefit from it.

Conversely, the employers may all be paying very high contributions following an unfavourable actuarial valuation report. In these circumstances, the purchaser can be expected to request a lower, specified rate.

Even where a specified rate of contribution is agreed, it may in fact be the seller's scheme's trustees (rather than the seller) who have the power to decide contribution rates under the scheme rules. If, therefore, the parties have agreed a fixed rate which tends to favour the purchaser, then the purchaser may also seek an indemnity from the seller against the possibility of the trustees requiring a higher rate.

Expenses

14.57 Expenses arising during the transitional period may take the form of:

(*a*) administrative expenses; or

(*b*) the cost of insuring risk benefits.

They may form part of the contribution rate required to be paid by the purchaser during the transitional period, or be specified in the agreement as a further sum to be paid in addition to those contributions.

Limit on salary increases

14.58 One of the actuarial assumptions by reference to which the seller's scheme is funded will relate to future salary increases. A transitional period presents some risk to the seller of the temporarily participating company granting salary increases during that period which significantly exceed this assumption.

Such an increase will inflate the seller's liabilities for deferred pensions in respect of those members affected by the transaction who elect not to transfer to the purchaser's scheme. It may also increase the amount of the transfer payment, depending on the circumstances (see **14.62** below). This, of course, will be detrimental to the funding of the seller's scheme.

The seller may therefore insert a provision requiring the purchaser to procure that pay increases do not rise by more than a certain percentage during the transitional period (often a percentage consistent with the scheme's assumptions). Whether this presents a problem for the purchaser will depend on whether it anticipates granting such increases. If not, then the purchaser may choose to accept the restriction, but with the qualification that the increases may be granted with the consent of the seller (usually not to be unreasonably withheld or delayed).

Other obligations of the purchaser during the transitional period

14.59 The sale agreement may also require the purchaser to procure that, during the transitional period, it (or, where appropriate, the participating employer owned by it):

(*a*) will comply with all the provisions of the seller's scheme which apply to it as a participating employer;

(*b*) will not exercise any discretion which it may have in relation to the seller's scheme without the seller's consent (usually not to be unreasonably withheld or delayed);

(*c*) will not by any act or omission prejudice the scheme's exempt approved or contracted-out status;

(*d*) will not take any steps which might increase the transfer payment; and (*e*) will nominate the seller to act on its behalf in relation to the member-nominated trustee arrangements and its right to be consulted about the scheme's statement of investment principles.

Obligations of the seller during the transitional period

14.60 Obligations of the seller under the sale agreement in respect of the transitional period might be as follows:

(*a*) to keep the scheme in full force and effect;

(*b*) not to increase benefits in relation to the members concerned; and

(*c*) not to take any steps which might reduce the transfer payment.

Date as at which past service liabilities are calculated

14.61 The date as at which the transfer payment should be calculated may be either:

(*a*) the completion date; or

(*b*) the end of the transitional period.

One of these alternatives may be more consistent with the scheme's trust deed and rules than the other. A number of issues will arise depending upon which of the two dates is to apply:

(i) If the completion date is used, an addition should be made to the calculation of the transfer payment representing the contributions paid by the participating employer in respect of the transferring members, and by the transferring members themselves, during the transitional period (less any part of the employer contributions which relates to the expenses mentioned in **14.57** above).

(ii) If the end of the transitional period is used, then the issue of salary increases during the transitional period (see **14.58** above) becomes particularly relevant, as increases in excess of the assumptions will inflate the calculation of the transfer payment.

(iii) If the end of the transitional period is used, then the timing adjustment (which, in the absence of a transitional period, would operate from the completion date – see **14.38** above) should instead operate from the end of the transitional period.

Admission of new members during the transitional period

14.62 If during the transitional period the purchaser does not have any other scheme in place, it may wish to have new members employed by it (who were not members before completion) admitted to the seller's scheme during that period. The seller's views on this are likely to depend on the administrative implications.

It may be that the seller will draw a distinction between:

(*a*) applicants who were employed by the company (or within the business) before completion but were at that time serving a 'waiting period' before they could become eligible to join; and

(*b*) applicants who are recruited as employees by the new owners after completion,

and agree only to admit the first of these two groups.

Due diligence, warranties and indemnities

14.63 The purchaser should obtain the same information, and seek the same protections, as mentioned in **14.52** above.

In addition, however, the fact that there will be a temporary period of participation in the seller's scheme will necessitate a careful review of the participating employers' obligations under the scheme's trust deed. The issues in relation to employers' contributions have already been mentioned (see **14.56** above) including the possible need for an indemnity from the seller. A review of the scheme's latest actuarial valuation report may (depending on how recent it is) give some indication as to whether this is likely to be an issue.

The purchaser should also check to see whether the trust deed (or any other document) contains an indemnity by the participating employers in favour of the trustees. If so, more extensive warranties may be necessary to satisfy the purchaser that there is no matter in respect of which it might become liable under that indemnity.

Employer's debt

The new position

14.64 We saw in CHAPTER 12 (see **12.68** onwards) that there are certain circumstances where *PA 1995, s 75* may render an employer liable for a debt to the trustees of an underfunded scheme.

Some of those circumstances are especially relevant in the context of this chapter. The *Occupational Pension Schemes (Employer Debt) Regulations 2005 (SI 2005/678)* (the '*Employer Debt Regulations*'), were amended by the *Occupational Pension Schemes (Employer Debt and Miscellaneous Amendments) Regulations 2008*, which came into force on 6 April 2008 and were then subsequently amended by the *Occupational Pension Schemes (Employer Debt – Apportionment Arrangements) (Amendment) Regulations 2008* from 15 April 2008. The changes are intended to make the operation of the *Employer Debt Regulations* more flexible, whilst at the same time encouraging employers to stand behind their pension liabilities.

If a statutory debt is triggered under *PA 1995, s 75* as a result of a company ceasing to participate in a scheme, for example following the sale of the company out of the group, the company being sold will have to make an immediate payment to fund its statutory debt, calculated on a full buy-out basis (with effect from 2 September 2005, pursuant to the *Occupational Pension Schemes (Employer Debt etc) (Amendment) Regulations 2005 (SI 2005/2224)*), together with any 'cessation expenses'.

As set out in **14.53** above, purchasers may, in some circumstances, want to participate in a seller's pension scheme if they do not have appropriate arrangements for the transferring employees to join on completion. Similarly, when a company is being sold which is a participating employer in a multi-employer defined benefit pension scheme, that company will, at the time of completion, withdraw from those arrangements. Parties to such transactions need to be aware that the withdrawal of a company from a defined benefit arrangement may give rise to a *s 75* debt if:

(*a*) the scheme is one to which *s 75* relates (which, in practice, covers most defined benefit pension schemes – see **12.69** above);

(*b*) an insolvency event has not occurred;

(*c*) the employer has ceased to employ at least one active member of the scheme (which could mean an active member for life cover only); and

(*d*) at least one other employer who is not a defined contribution employer continues to employ at least one active member (an 'employment-cessation event').

(See *PA 1995, s 75(4)*, as modified by *Employer Debt Regulations, reg 6*.) Note that closure to future accrual is not an employment-cessation event, and money purchase assets and liabilities are expressly excluded. There is also a new definition of 'defined contribution employer' in *Employer Debt Regulations, reg 2*.

Under the original 2005 employer debt regulations, when a debt was triggered it had to be paid in full, unless either (i) the scheme rules allowed for the debt to be apportioned amongst the employers in a different manner from the statutory formula, or (ii) an approved withdrawal agreement was entered into with the trustees and approved by the Regulator, where the withdrawing employer paid a smaller amount ('amount A') and another person guaranteed the difference ('amount B') between amount A and the full amount of the buyout debt on the happening of certain events, eg the commencement of winding-up of the scheme.

The 'old' approved withdrawal agreement route as a means of deferring payment of the debt was widely criticised as being inflexible. Broadly, the Regulator could approve a withdrawal agreement only if it was more likely that the debt would be paid if the agreement were entered into than if it were not. Therefore, if the employer had enough assets to pay the debt in full, a withdrawal agreement could not be approved. In many cases, trustees and employers were agreeing in advance to amend their scheme rules (as was permitted by the legislation) to apportion the debt, so that a smaller debt fell on the outgoing employer. Case law suggested that apportionment agreements had to be entered into before the debt was triggered; otherwise, the scheme might be barred from ever entering the PPF.

Many employers considered it inequitable that the (original) employer debt legislation required the employer in certain circumstances to accelerate the funding of the scheme and fund it to a higher level than that for an ongoing scheme under the *Pensions Act 2004* ('*PA 2004*'), namely, at a prudent level but not as high as the buyout level. A further problem was that significant actuarial costs could be incurred in calculating the amount of the employer debt, and the necessary data was not always available for this purpose.

Under the amended *Employer Debt Regulations*, there are now five ways to deal with the debt, and these are summarised at **14.66** to **14.71** below.

Dealing with the debt

Period of grace (Employer Debt Regulations, reg 6A)

14.65 An employer, on ceasing to employ active members, may, within one month give the trustees a period of grace notice, which is a notice in writing that it intends, during the period of 12 months from the employment-cessation event, to employ at least one person who will be an active member. This defers the triggering of the debt, and the employer continues to be an employer in relation to the scheme. A debt will arise at the date of the original cessation event if the employer:

(*a*) does not employ an active member within the 12-month period;

(*b*) becomes insolvent; or

(*c*) changes its intention during the 12-month period, in which case it must notify the trustees.

Once the employer employs an active member (either before or after the notice is given), the period of grace comes to an end. Whilst this provision may assist where an employer's last employee leaves employment, it is difficult to see how it could be used in the context of corporate transactions.

Liability share – default position (Employer Debt Regulations, regs 5, 6(4)–(7))

14.66 The *Employer Debt Regulations* introduced five ways of dealing with the employer debt, and the first is the 'liability share', which will apply in the absence of any of the four alternatives. The liability share is an amount equal to the liability proportion of the full buyout debt. The liability proportion is a fraction K/L where:

K = the amount of a scheme's liabilities attributable to an employer, and

L = the total amount of the scheme's liabilities attributable to employment with all the employers.

Only liabilities arising during or as a result of pensionable service with that employer (including transfers in) and not as a result of pensionable service with any other employer under the scheme will be included. However, where the trustees are unable (or without disproportionate cost) to determine the exact liabilities attributable to an employer, all the liabilities will either be attributable to the most recent employer or they will be attributable in a reasonable manner to one or more employers.

Scheme apportionment arrangement (Employer Debt Regulations, reg 6B)

14.67 This is an arrangement under the scheme rules (it must be written into the rules) which satisfies the conditions below and to which the trustees, the exiting employer and/or any remaining employer(s) to whom all or part of the exiting employer's liability has been apportioned consent. Which employer will be required to consent depends on whether the exiting employer is paying more or less than the 'liability share'. If it is paying more, its consent will be needed. If it is paying less than the liability share (which is more likely), then it will be the remaining employer(s) to whom all or part of the exiting employer's liability has been apportioned who will need to consent. The other conditions to be met, apart from the consent requirements, are that the arrangement:

(*a*) provides for the employer to pay a 'scheme apportionment arrangement share' instead of its liability share;

(*b*) where that amount is less than the liability share, apportions all or part of the difference to one or more of the remaining employers;

(*c*) is entered into before, on or after the applicable time;

(*d*) sets out the amount of an employer's scheme apportionment arrangement share;

(*e*) meets the funding test (unless one of the exceptions applies) - see **14.71** below; and

(*f*) may set out when the 'amount apportioned' is to be paid.

In practice, trustees will want to specify when the amount apportioned is to be paid.

Where scheme rules do not currently permit the trustees to enter into a scheme apportionment arrangement or a regulated apportionment arrangement (see **14.68** below), a rule permitting apportionment can be introduced, either by amendment of the deed and rules of the scheme or by resolution of the trustees. The *Employer Debt Regulations* give trustees power under *PA 1995, s 68*, after consulting such employers under the scheme as they think fit, to modify the scheme by resolution to achieve this, even if the scheme rules would enable them to modify the scheme in a different manner.

As concerns were voiced that trustees might use this power to impose on one employer significant liabilities without consent, the *Employer Debt Regulations* were amended by the *Occupational Pension Scheme (Employer Debt – Apportionment Arrangements) (Amendment) Regulations 2008 (SI 2008/1068)* from 15 April 2008 to introduce an employer consent requirement.

Regulated apportionment arrangement (Employer Debt Regulations, reg 7A)

14.68 This is designed to be used in restructuring situations where the trustees consider that there is a reasonable likelihood of the scheme entering a Pensions Protection Fund ('PPF') assessment period in the next 12 months or where an assessment period has already commenced but not ended. It is an arrangement under the scheme rules which broadly:

- provides for the employer to pay a 'regulated apportionment arrangement share' instead of the employer's liability share;
- where that amount is less than the employer's liability share, apportions all or part of the difference to one or more of the remaining employers;
- is entered into before, on or after the applicable time;
- sets out the amount of an employer's regulated apportionment arrangement share;
- may set out when the remainder is to be paid; and

- where a PPF assessment period has not already commenced, satisfies the following conditions:
  - the trustees and the employer/any employer to whom all or part of the employer's liability has been apportioned consent to the arrangement;
  - the arrangement and any amendments to it are approved by the Regulator by a notice of approval (issued only if the Regulator considers it reasonable); and
  - the PPF does not object.

All the conditions are equivalent to those for a scheme apportionment arrangement, except that the funding test is replaced by Regulator approval and the requirement that the PPF does not object.

This arrangement allows apportionment of a smaller amount of debt in order to avoid employer insolvency, enabling the employer to continue to trade free of the pension liabilities. It will be used only where the potential recovery to the PPF is greater than putting the employer through an insolvency process.

Withdrawal arrangement (Employer Debt Regulations, reg 6C, Sch 1A)

14.69 This is intended to offer a simpler alternative to the 'old' approved withdrawal agreement. It operates in a similar way but does not require Regulator approval and can be entered into before, on or after the employment-cessation event.

The cessation employer must pay an amount of at least the 'withdrawal arrangement share'. This is equal to or, with employer agreement, greater than 'amount A'. Amount A is broadly the employer's share of the shortfall on a scheme funding (not buyout) basis. (If there has been no *PA 2004* valuation yet, the amount is calculated broadly in accordance with the *PPF Valuation Regulations* with certain adjustments.) The guarantors are liable for amount B, a floating or a fixed amount payable on certain events occurring, including the agreed payment date, the scheme commencing winding-up, and a relevant event occurring in relation to the last employer.

The conditions are quite stringent: the trustees may enter into a withdrawal arrangement with the cessation employer and guarantor(s) only where they are satisfied that:

- the funding test is met (the same as the first limb of the funding test for a scheme apportionment arrangement) – see **14.71** below; and

- the guarantors have sufficient financial resources at the date the arrangement is entered into to be likely to pay amount B – the guarantors will therefore need quite significant assets to meet this test.

On the face of it, withdrawal arrangements have costs and speed advantages; however, if clearance is required (see **14.83** below), some of those advantages will be lost.

Approved withdrawal arrangement (Employer Debt Regulations, reg 7, Sch 1A)

14.70 The new provisions are similar to the 'old' approved withdrawal arrangements entered into by the cessation employer, the trustees and a guarantor, with the approval of the Regulator, which may be given before or after the employment-cessation event. This is the only withdrawal arrangement option if the exiting employer wishes to pay less than the scheme funding basis shortfall.

The previous requirement, that the Regulator could approve an agreement only where the resources of the guarantors were such that the *s 75* debt was more likely to be met if the agreement was approved, has been removed. It has been replaced not by the 'sufficient financial resources' test used for the new withdrawal arrangements (see **14.70** above), but by new conditions which give the Regulator significantly more flexibility than under the old regime:

- the amount the cessation employer proposes to pay as its approved withdrawal arrangement share must be less than amount A;
- the trustees must have notified the Regulator that the funding test is met (the same test as for withdrawal arrangements under *Employer Debt Regulations, reg 6C*); and
- the Regulator must be satisfied that it is reasonable to approve the arrangement, having regard to such matters as it considers relevant, including:
  - the potential effect of the employment-cessation event on the method or assumptions used to calculate the scheme's technical provisions;
  - the financial circumstances of the proposed guarantors;
  - the amount of the cessation employer's 'liability share';
  - the amount of the proposed approved withdrawal arrangement share and, where there is likely to be a relevant transfer deduction, an estimate of the amount the cessation employer will pay if the transfer is completed; and

– the effect of the proposed arrangement on the security of members' benefits.

There is a practical problem if it cannot be established, before a withdrawal arrangement or approved withdrawal arrangement is entered into, whether the amount to be paid is above or below amount A, as it is then not possible to work out which option to choose.

The funding test (Employer Debt Regulations, reg 2(4A))

14.71 The funding test is designed to prevent scheme apportionment being used to abandon the scheme. Once the scheme has had its first valuation under the scheme funding provisions of the *PA 2004*, the test is met if the trustees are reasonably satisfied that:

- when the arrangement takes effect, the remaining employers will be reasonably likely to be able to fund the scheme so that, after the applicable time, it will have sufficient and appropriate assets to cover its technical provisions; and
- the arrangement will not adversely affect the security of members' benefits as a result of any:
  - material change in legal, demographic or economic circumstances that would justify a change to the method or assumptions last used in calculating the scheme's technical provisions; or
  - material revision to any existing recovery plan.

The first limb of the funding test applies to scheme apportionment arrangements, withdrawal arrangements and approved withdrawal arrangements. The second limb applies only to scheme apportionment arrangements. Neither limb applies to regulated apportionment arrangements.

The *Employer Debt Regulations* expressly provide at *reg 2(4C)* that the first limb of the test may be satisfied if the trustees consider that the remaining employers are able to meet the relevant payments as they fall due under the statutory schedule of contributions (revised as necessary).

The funding test does not have to be met in the case of a scheme apportionment arrangement if:

- the proposed employer scheme apportionment share is greater than the liability share, ie above buyout level (although few employers are likely to wish to pay more than buyout); or
- the scheme has commenced winding up and the trustees are satisfied that it is likely that the employer would be unable to pay the liability share if it applied but will be able to pay the scheme apportionment share.

14.72 On a business and asset sale, no debt on the new employer is likely to arise as long as the purchaser is not admitted to participate in the seller's scheme for a transitional period. However, if the purchaser does participate in the seller's scheme, then as some of the liabilities will be attributable to employment with that employer it could be liable for some of any statutory debt that may arise when it ceases to participate.

Clearly the possibility of a *s 75* debt arising will have a significant impact on the viability of a proposed transaction and the value of a withdrawing company. The *Employer Debt Regulations* are in themselves a complex piece of legislation and should be considered in detail in the event that the purchaser is acquiring a company which participates in a multi-employer scheme.

See also CHAPTER 12 regarding when multi-employer schemes are treated as being divided into separate schemes for debt purposes.

The new arrangements – summary

14.73

Arrangement	Amount of debt to be paid	Applicable conditions	Is the Regulator's approval required?	Is clearance required?	Is it a notifiable event?
Liability share (default position)	Buyout	N/A	No	No	No
Scheme apportionment arrangement ('SAA')	Any	Trustee and employer consent Must meet the funding test unless the SAA arrangement is greater than the liability share or in certain circumstances when the scheme is winding up): (i) remaining employers reasonably likely to be able to fund to the technical provision level; and (ii) security of members' benefits not adversely affected	No	Yes, if entered into retrospectively Yes, if entered into in advance unless: (i) increases debt immediately payable by an employer who can afford it; or (ii) alternatives too costly or complex and actuary's best estimate of unmodified debt is immediately payable; or (iii) no net reduction of employer covenant	Yes, if entered into retrospectively (notifiable by trustees)
Regulated apportionment	Any	Trustee and employer consent PPF does not object	Yes	Yes, if type A event	No

Arrangement	Amount of debt to be paid	Applicable conditions	Is the Regulator's approval required?	Is clearance required?	Is it a notifiable event?
Withdrawal arrangement	At least amount A (employer's share of liabilities on scheme funding basis)	Satisifies conditions in *Employer Debt Regulations, Sch 1A* Funding test met: remaining employers reasonably likely to be able to fund to technical provisions level Guarantors have, at date arrangement entered into, sufficient financial resources to be likely to pay amount B	No	Yes, if detrimental to scheme's ability to meet its liabilities (eg if guarantee insufficient)	No, but certain events notifiable by guarantors
Approved withdrawal arrangement	Less than amount A	Funding test met: remaining employers reasonably likely to be able to fund to technical provisions level	Yes	Yes, if it has a related type A event (eg if guarantee insufficient)	No, but certain events notifiable by guarantors

Employer Debt Regulations: proposed further changes

14.74 Many employers have expressed concern that the *Employment Debt Regulations* place unnecessary barriers to corporate restructuring. This is because the current regime requires an employer which has ceased to participate in a defined benefit pension scheme to immediately pay its share of any shortfall between the scheme's assets and liabilities on a full buy out basis, unless the debt is apportioned to other participating employers or part of the liability is transferred by way of a withdrawal arrangement, in accordance with the *Employer Debt Regulations*.

Under the new proposals, where there is a corporate restructuring and one employer's assets and pension liabilities are transferred to another, then as long as prescribed steps are followed, no debt will arise.

The DWP issued a consultation on the *Occupational Pension Schemes (Employer Debt and Miscellaneous Amendments) Regulations 2010* (the '*Draft Regulations*') in September 2009. The consultation closed on 19 November 2009. If implemented, the *Draft Regulations* are due to come into force on 6 April 2010.

The *Draft Regulations* would, if implemented, introduce relaxations for certain types of corporate restructurings. They amend the *Employer Debt Regulations* (with consequential amendments to some other regulations, such as the *Pensions Protection Fund (Entry Rules) Regulations 2005*) and are intended to relax the effect of the *Employer Debt Regulations* in the case of corporate restructuring between two employers: the 'exiting employer' and the 'receiving employer', where the latter takes over the former's responsibilities in relation to the pension scheme.

Under the new arrangements (which are additional to the existing methods of reducing the *s 75* debt), where a corporate restructuring meets the prescribed conditions, an event which would otherwise be an employment-cessation event will not be treated as such, and no *s 75* debt will arise.

The new arrangements can be used for a number of one-to-one transactions in a multi-employer scheme; transactions where there are a number of exiting employers and a single receiving employer can also take place, provided each transaction is carried out on a one-to-one basis.

Draft Regulations, reg 7 inserts new *regs 6ZA, 6ZB* and *6ZC* into the *Employer Debt Regulations*. These contain the new definition of 'employment-cessation event' and provide for a 'general easement' and a 'de minimis easement': an employment-cessation event will not occur if there is a restructuring within new *reg 6ZB* or *6ZC*, provided that the event which would otherwise be an 'employment-cessation event' takes place 'on the same date' as the transfer of assets, employees and pensions obligations to the receiving employer. The de minimis easement is intended to apply where small-scale corporate restructurings are being undertaken (also described as 'minor housekeeping restructurings').

The receiving employer must have its head office in the UK; the two employers must be part of the same multi-employer scheme and must be 'associated', as defined in *Insolvency Act 1986, s 435*. The exception to the 'associated' requirement is where an employer is changing its legal status, eg becomes a company registered under the *Companies Act*: this will no longer be an 'employment-cessation event' provided it falls within one of the easements.

If introduced, the new easements require specific steps to be carried out in a specific order. Some steps apply to both the general and the de minimis easements (including assessments of the likelihood of the insolvency of either employer), but the key difference between the two is as follows:

- The general easement focuses on the employer covenant: under the 'restructuring test' the trustees must be satisfied that the receiving employer will, after completion of the restructuring, be at least as likely as the exiting employer to meet (a) all of the exiting employer's liabilities in relation to the scheme, and (b) its own liabilities in relation to the scheme calculated immediately before completion.
- The de minimis easement instead requires the trustees to decide, using the figures contained in the most recent *s 179* valuation and scheme return, whether they are satisfied specified conditions are met:
  - the scheme's assets are at least equal to its protected liabilities as shown on the most recent *s 179* (PPF) valuation;
  - the number of scheme members in respect of whom defined benefits arose as a result of pensionable service with the exiting employer is less than 2 per cent of the total number of scheme members in respect of whom defined benefits have arisen;
  - the liabilities relating to the relevant members must not exceed a prescribed sum; and
  - broadly, in a rolling period of three years, no more than 5 per cent of scheme members can be included in transactions under new *reg 6ZC*.

There are also a number of disclosure and reporting requirements which must be followed by the trustees and employers.

The *Draft Regulations* also include some other technical amendments, such as clarifying scheme apportionment arrangements and regulated apportionment arrangements.

There can be no doubt that the proposals do provide some assistance for corporate group restructurings and, as long as the draft procedures are followed, there will be no crystallisation of the employer debt in purely internal reorganisations. However, one major limitation is that it will only apply to one-to-one transfers. Where one company's assets and liabilities are to be split between a number of companies, a debt will still be triggered. The DWP are consulting further on whether a multiple transaction within a single group of companies should also be subject to the easement and what additional safeguards would be required. The new proposals will also assist where an employer changes its legal status, as the new easements will apply.

Whether the above proposals remain in their current form following the consultation remains to be seen, but what is apparent is a shift towards acknowledging that greater flexibility is required to ensure that transactions involving multi-employer pension schemes and group restructurings are not frustrated by the current legislation, whilst at the same time ensuring that employers continue to stand behind their pension liabilities.

Moral hazard

History

14.75 Since April 2005, the Regulator has had new powers to prevent employers 'dumping' their defined benefit liabilities upon the Pensions Protection Fund and to increase member security. These so-called 'moral hazard' provisions and resultant Regulator's powers are of particular relevance to corporate transactions. Two of the Regulator's new powers include the ability to issue contribution notices, requiring specified persons to make contributions to pension arrangements, and to issue financial support directions, requiring certain persons to put in place financial support arrangements for a pension scheme. These new powers together with the new 'clearance procedure' for corporate transactions are set out in further detail below.

The revised position

14.76 In April 2008, the DWP issued a consultation document on its proposed changes to the Pension Regulator's moral hazard powers under *PA 2004, ss 38–54* (contribution notices and financial support directions). In the Regulator's statement dated 25 April 2008, it was noted that the proposed changes were to help 'ensure adequate protection is in place so that members' benefits and the Pension Protection Fund are not put at risk'.

The major changes affect contribution notices: there is a new 'material detriment' test, the 'lack of good faith' requirement has been removed, there is a revised test of reasonableness, and a new Code of Practice has been issued by the Regulator. There are also changes in relation to bulk transfers and the test for imposing financial support directions.

We explore in more detail (see **14.77** to **14.82** below) the changes that came into force with retrospective effect from 14 April 2008.

Contribution notices

14.77 The Regulator may, in accordance with *PA 2004, s 38* (as amended by *PA 2008* on 26 November 2008, with retrospective effect to 14 April 2008) issue a contribution notice to an employer or person *connected* with or an *associate* of the employer (see **14.81** below) where there is an act or failure to act and:

(*a*) the 'material detriment test' is met (see **14.79** below); or

(*b*) the main purpose, or one of the main purposes of the act or failure, was to:

- prevent the recovery of all or part of the statutory debt; or
- prevent the statutory debt becoming due, to compromise or otherwise settle or reduce that debt.

Previously, the final limb of this test required there to be a lack of good faith. This has now been removed, making it easier for the Regulator to impose a contribution notice.

These provisions do not apply to money purchase schemes or other prescribed schemes (as set out in the *Pensions Regulator (Contributions Notices and Restoration Orders) Regulations 2005 (SI 2005/931)*.

The contribution notice will require the person to pay a specified sum into the scheme, or to the PPF where the PPF has assumed responsibility for the scheme. This specified sum could be of an amount up to the total shortfall of any *s 75* debt (or even where there is no debt yet due, the total assessed shortfall as if a *s 75* debt were due from a solvent employer, ie in practice this would mean the full buy-out cost).

A contribution notice may be issued in relation to a series of acts rather than requiring the test to be met in relation to a single act (*PA 2004, s 38(12), (13)*) and, where a transfer has been made from a scheme, the Regulator may issue a contribution notice in relation to the transferor scheme, the transferee scheme, or both (*PA 2004, s 39A*).

Reasonableness test

14.78 The Regulator can only impose a contribution notice if it considers that it is reasonable to impose liability on a person. When deciding what is reasonable, it must have regard to the extent to which, in all circumstances of the case, it was reasonable for the person to act, or fail to act, in the way that the person did and have regard to such other matters as the Regulator considers relevant (*PA 2004, s 38(3)(d)*), including:

- the degree of involvement of the person in the act or failure to act;
- the relationship which the person has or has had with the employer (including where the employer is a company, whether the person has had control of the employer within the meaning of *Insolvency Act 1986, s 435(10)*);
- any connection or involvement which the person has or has had with the scheme;
- if the act or failure to act was a notifiable event for the purposes of *PA 2004, s 69*, any failure to notify;
- all the purposes of the act or failure to act (including whether a purpose of the act or failure was to prevent or limit loss of employment);
- the value of any benefits which directly or indirectly the person receives, or is entitled to receive, from the employer under the scheme;
- the likelihood of relevant creditors being paid and the extent to which they are likely to be paid;
- the financial circumstances of the person; and
- such other matters as may be prescribed (which has not yet been brought into force under *PA 2004, s 38(7)(g)*).

The legislation is retrospective and the Regulator can issue a contribution notice in relation to an act or failure to act which occurred on or after 27 April 2004 and before any assumption of responsibility for the scheme by the Pension Protection Fund (limited overall to a six-year 'look back' period).

Purchasers should therefore be seeking confirmation from the seller that no contribution notices have been issued by the Regulator and remain unpaid in relation to a pension scheme if acquiring the entire issued share capital of the target company. See **14.25** above for further details on suggested warranties.

The material detriment test

14.79 For the purposes of *PA 2004, s 38*, the material detriment test is met in relation to an act or failure to act if the Regulator is of the opinion that 'the act or failure has detrimentally affected in a material way the likelihood of accrued scheme benefits being received' (*PA 2004, s 38A(1)*).

In deciding whether an act meets the material detriment test, the Regulator must have regard to matters it considers relevant, including (*PA 2004, s 38A(4)*):

- the value of the assets or liabilities of the scheme or any relevant transferee scheme and the effect of the act or failure on the value of those assets or liabilities;
- the scheme obligations of any person and the effect of the act or failure on any of those obligations;
- the extent to which any person is likely to be able to discharge any scheme obligation in any circumstances and the extent to which any act or failure to act might affect that; and
- other matters which may be prescribed.

Under *PA 2004, s 38B* there is a statutory defence to the material detriment test where the person against whom the Regulator intends issuing a contribution notice can show **each** of the following:

- he gave due prior consideration (such that a reasonably diligent person would have done – *s 38B(6)*) to the extent to which the act or failure to act might have a materially detrimental effect on accrued scheme benefits;
- as a result and where relevant, he took all reasonable steps to eliminate or minimise any potential detriment identified; and
- in all the circumstances prevailing at the time of the act or failure to act, it was reasonable for him to conclude that accrued benefits would not suffer a material detriment.

When issuing a warning notice that it intends to issue a contribution notice under the material detriment test, the Regulator must inform the recipient that this defence is available.

The Regulator is also required to issue a code of practice setting out the circumstances in which it expects to issue contribution notices as a result of the material detriment test being met. As a result, Code of Practice No 12 entitled 'Circumstances in Relation to the Material Detriment Test' was issued on 29 June 2009 (the 'Code').

The Code confirms that, in order to issue a contribution notice by reference to the material detriment test, the Regulator must be of the opinion that:

- the act or failure to act has been materially detrimental to the likelihood of the accrued scheme benefits being received (whether the benefits are to be received as benefits under the scheme or otherwise) (there are factors which must be considered, when they are relevant, in determining whether there has been material detriment to the act or failure to act);
- the statutory defence is not met in relation to the act or failure to act; and
- it is reasonable to impose liability on the person to pay the sum specified in the contribution notice, having regard to:
  - the extent to which, in all the circumstances of the case, it was reasonable for the person to act, or fail to act, in the way the person did; and
  - such other matters as the Regulator considers relevant.

The circumstances in which the Regulator expects to issue a contribution notice as a result of being of the opinion that the material detriment test is met are:

- the transfer of the scheme out of the jurisdiction;
- the transfer of the sponsoring employer out of the jurisdiction or the replacement of the sponsoring employer with an entity that does not fall within the jurisdiction;
- the transfer of liabilities of the scheme to another pension scheme or arrangement which leads to a significant reduction of the:
  - sponsor support in respect of the liabilities; or
  - funding to cover the liabilities;
- a business model or the operation of the scheme which creates from the scheme, or which is designed to do so, a financial benefit for:
  - the employer; or
  - some other person;

  where proper account has not been taken of the interests of the members of the scheme, including where risks to members are increased.

The Regulator has helpfully provided examples of circumstances which would not normally give rise to a contribution notice under the material detriment test, which include:

- the payment of a routine annual dividend in the normal course of business
- buying out pensioner liabilities with a properly selected regulated insurer

- the weakening of an employer covenant due to poor trading because of market conditions
- granting security where proper mitigation is provided to the trustees.

Further details can be found at www.thepensionsregulator.gov.uk/guidance/examplesMaterialDetriment.aspx.

The Regulator has also published guidance for employers involved in corporate transactions, which reminds employers of the importance of understanding the effect any transaction may have on the pension scheme and on the sponsor's ability to meet the liabilities. This guidance can be found at www.thepensionsregulator.gov.uk/employers/CorporateTransactions.aspx.

Future changes

14.80 On 19 October 2009, the DWP issued a consultation on how the Regulator must calculate the amounts to be paid under a contribution notice following the transfer of accrued rights of two or more members of a pension scheme to another work-based pension scheme to which *s 75* does not apply. The consultation period ran until 11 December 2009.

The new *PA 2004, s 39A* (as inserted by the *Pensions Act 2008*) allows contribution notices to be issued where transfers are made from the original defined benefit scheme. The consultation relates to the regulations to be made under *s 39A*.

The draft *Pensions Regulator (Contribution Notices) (Sum Specified following Transfer) Regulations 2010* provide for two scenarios in respect of the calculation:

- the first is where the transfer itself is the act (or part of a series of acts) in relation to which the conditions for issuing a contribution notice have been met. In this scenario, the amount under the contribution notice is the full liability relating to the transferring members less any transfer payment actually made; and
- the second is where the transfer is not part of the offending act. In this scenario, the contribution notice may specify all or part of the full shortfall relating to the transferring members.

The draft regulations are due to come into force in 2010.

'Connected' and 'associated'

14.81 The Regulator can only issue a contribution notice to a person if that person was at any time in the relevant period:

(*a*) an employer in relation to the scheme; or

(*b*) a person connected with, or an associate of, the employer.

These are complex definitions. In summary, a person is '*connected*' with a company if:

(i) he is a director or shadow director of the company or an associate of such a director or shadow director; or

(ii) he is an associate of the company (see *Insolvency Act 1986, s 249*).

'*Associate*' (as defined under *Insolvency Act 1986, s 435*) is widely drawn and includes corporate bodies and private individuals such as husbands, wives, civil partners and relatives. The definition is complex and includes as associates partners, trustees, employers and employees and companies if the person has control or if he and his associates have control of the company. For example, a person can be associated with a company if he and one or more of his associates jointly hold one third of the company's voting rights in that company or in another company which has control of it. A company can also be an associate of another company where a person controls one company and his associate (or he and his associate jointly) controls the other. Consequently, the definition could potentially catch a number of individuals or companies within a group structure – even unrelated companies could be treated as associated with each other and potentially brought into the scope of the Regulator's powers.

Financial support directions

14.82 *PA 2004, ss 43–50* provide the Regulator with the power to issue a financial support direction to the employer and persons connected and associated with the employer. The purpose of a financial support direction is to ensure that groups of companies stand behind their pension liabilities and do not leave them with the weakest member of the group and, in turn, with the Pension Protection Fund.

The Regulator may issue a financial support direction if it is of the opinion that an employer to the scheme is a 'service company' or is 'insufficiently resourced'.

A company will be a *service company* if, at the relevant time, it is a company as defined in *Companies Act 2006, s 1(1)*, it is an employer in the group, and its turnover is 'solely or principally derived from amounts charged for the provision of the services of the employees of (this company) to other members of the group' (*PA 2004, s 44(2)*).

A company is *insufficiently resourced* if, at the relevant time (*PA 2004, s 44(3)*, as amended by *PA 2008*):

- the employer has insufficient net assets to enable it to meet the amount which is a prescribed percentage (50 per cent) of the estimated *s 75* debt in relation to the scheme; and

EITHER

- there is at that time a person who qualifies under the legislation and whose resources are not less than the relevant deficit, which is the amount which is the difference between:
  - the value of the resources of the employer; and
  - the amount which is the prescribed percentage (50 per cent) of the estimated *s 75* debt;

OR

- there are, at that time, two or more persons who qualify under the legislation and:
  - they are connected with or associates of each other; and
  - the aggregate value, at that time, of the resources of those persons is not less than the relevant deficit.

Under the definition of *insufficiently resourced*, the Regulator is now able to look at the aggregate resources of the group and its associates when considering whether a company is insufficiently resourced, rather than having to identify a single company. In addition to the widening of the 'insufficiently resourced' definition, the *Pensions Act 2008* also made changes to the provisions relating to transfers. Where a transfer has been made out of a scheme, the Regulator may issue a financial support direction in relation to the transferor scheme, the transferee scheme, or both (*PA 2004, ss 43A, 43B*).

The *Pensions Regulator (Financial Support Directions etc) Regulations 2005 (SI 2005/2188)* (the '*FSD Regulations*') came into force on 1 September 2005 and were amended by the *Pensions Regulator (Miscellaneous Amendment) Regulations 2009 (SI 2009/617)* with effect from 6 April 2009.

A financial support direction ('FSD') in relation to the scheme is a direction which requires the person or persons to whom it is issued to secure:

(*a*) that financial support for the scheme is in place within the period specified in that direction;

(*b*) that thereafter financial support or other financial support remains in place while the scheme is in existence; and (*c*) that the Regulator is notified in writing of prescribed events (as set out in *FSD Regulations, reg 4*) in respect of the financial support as soon as reasonably practicable after the event occurs.

PA 2004 provides that financial support arrangements can mean making all the members of a group jointly and severally liable for the whole or part of an employer's pension liabilities or making a holding company liable for the whole or part of a subsidiary employer's pension liabilities.

To make an FSD, the Regulator has to be satisfied it is reasonable to do so. Among the factors the Regulator has to take into account to decide whether it is reasonable to make an FSD is 'the value of any benefits received directly or indirectly by that person from the employer'.

Where there is a disposal of an employer the Regulator may need to be informed of this as the disposal is a notifiable event. If the Regulator thinks an FSD is appropriate both seller and purchaser would be included as 'associates' and the relevant event would usually be fixed as the disposal date. In accordance with *FSD Regulations, reg 5* (as amended), a company remains 'associated' for 24 months (with effect from 6 April 2010) after the disposal. Prior to this date, the 'look back' of 24 months is reduced by a period equal to the number of complete months then remaining until 6 April 2010. Accordingly, companies planning a disposal may wish to apply to the Regulator for clearance.

Purchasers, therefore, need to be aware that the company they are acquiring could potentially be the subject of an FSD for up to 24 months after the transaction has completed. Careful and early due diligence will be required of the corporate structure and any pension schemes relating to the company in question to put this matter beyond doubt and, where necessary, relevant warranties and indemnities should be sought from the seller.

Clearance

History

14.83 As a consequence of the powers of the Regulator brought into effect by *PA 2004*, a statutory clearance procedure was introduced to give greater certainty to parties considering transactions involving companies with defined benefit schemes. Assurance could be gained by the persons involved by requesting and obtaining a clearance statement from the Regulator to the effect that the actions in contemplation would not later cause the Regulator to exercise its powers to issue a contribution notice or a financial support direction. According to the original guidance issued by the Regulator:

> 'Clearance was introduced with the underlying aims being:
>
> - the protection of jobs, particularly where clearance is needed to prevent the employer becoming insolvent; and
> - the continuation of appropriate deal activity involving employers with defined benefit schemes.'

Historically, there were three classifications of events, as follows:

- **Type A**: specified events which were financially detrimental to the ability of the defined benefit scheme to meet its pension liabilities and where clearance may have been appropriate;
- **Type B**: events that did not affect a pension creditor and clearance was not necessary; and
- **Type C**: events that suggested a deterioration of the employer's covenant which may have been outside the control of the employer. Type C events included all type A events, although not all Type C events were notifiable or specified events.

This has now been amended, and only type A events may be eligible for clearance.

The revised position

14.84 Updated guidance was issued by the Regulator in June 2009 to reflect legislative changes and the introduction of the material detriment test (see **14.79** above) (the '2009 Guidance').

Given the complex nature of some corporate transactions, the 2009 Guidance is aimed at professional advisers working alongside trustees and employers in considering events that may have a detrimental impact upon the pension scheme.

Clearance applications are voluntary but they do provide certainty to those who may be liable to the imposition of a contribution notice or financial support direction. In terms of timescales for the Regulator to issue a clearance statement, regard will be had to any reasonable timescales or deadlines the applicant may have, but the timescales for dealing with an application will be reduced if applicants carry out the steps proposed in the 2009 Guidance, which include:

- involving trustees and sharing relevant information;
- ensuring that any trustee conflicts have been dealt with;
- ensuring advice has been taken and any opportunity to mitigate has been discussed; and

- informing the risk and funding team of the likely application, providing an outline of the event and making them aware of any timescales and external deadlines.

Once issued, the clearance statement will bind the Regulator unless there is a material change in circumstances.

The 2009 Guidance advises that, in line with its commitment to operate in a risk-based and proportionate manner, the Regulator expects a clearance statement to be sought only in relation to type A events. Type A events are all events that are *materially detrimental* to the ability of the pension scheme to meet its liabilities.

Type A events

Under the new 2009 Guidance, type A events fall into two categories: employer-related events, and scheme-related events:

Employer-related events

For employer-related events, there will need to be:

- a comparison of the employer covenant before and after the type A event;
- an assessment of whether any weakening in the employer covenant is to such a degree that the event could be considered to be materially detrimental to the ability of the scheme to meet its liabilities; and
- the identification of whether the scheme has a relevant deficit.

The 2009 Guidance suggests that it is important to carry out these three steps in this order, because the outcome of the first two steps may determine what basis should be used for the relevant deficit.

A detrimental event (including a type A event) will have one or more of the following effects, either immediately or in the near future:

- it prevents the recovery of the whole or any part of the employer's *s 75* debt;
- it prevents the employer's *s 75* debt becoming due or compromises the *s 75* debt;
- it reduces the amount of the employer's *s 75* debt which would otherwise become due; or
- it weakens the employer covenant, because it has an impact on the ability of the employer to meet its ongoing funding commitments to the scheme

or it reduces the dividend that would be available to the scheme in the event of employer insolvency.

As the assessment of the possible impact of a type A event may be a complex process, the 2009 Guidance suggests that, where trustees feel they may not have the necessary financial or legal skills to allow them to assess an event, they should consider obtaining independent professional advice or document the reasons why no such advice has been sought.

A type A event will not be an employer-related event unless the scheme has a relevant deficit, and the general rule is that it will usually be the highest of the scheme's deficits according to the following bases:

- FRS17/IAS19 (current accounting standards);
- *s 179* (PPF levy basis);
- technical provisions (scheme funding basis, where available); and
- ongoing (following scheme valuation, where technical provisions are not yet available).

An exception to the general rule regarding the relevant deficit is where an employer-related event is significantly materially detrimental to the scheme's ability to meet its liabilities. Also, where there are 'going concern' issues, the scheme is in wind-up or there is scheme abandonment, the relevant deficit will be measured on the *s 75* basis.

Examples of employer-related events provided in the 2009 Guidance include:

- a change in priority, eg the granting or extending of a fixed or floating charge over assets of the employer or the wider group;
- a return of capital, eg dividend payments; share buy backs; repayment of subordinated debt; and distributions in specie, including de-mergers;
- a change in group structure, including a change in control;
- a change to the employer in relation to a scheme;
- granting or repayment of inter-company loans; and
- business and assets sales.

Scheme-related events

Examples of scheme-related events that could also be type A events are set out in the 2009 Guidance and include:

- compromise agreements;
- apportionment of a scheme's deficit;

- non-payment of all or any part of a *s 75* debt for an unreasonable period (eg more than 12 months); or
- an arrangement that has the result of preventing a *s 75* debt from triggering.

In relation to both *employer-related* events and *scheme-related* events, where a type A event has been identified, the parties should consider and agree the most appropriate mitigation. Various different types of mitigation are listed in the 2009 Guidance, ranging from additional contributions through to more complicated parent and intra-group guarantees.

The 2009 Guidance also advocates that trustees should generally adopt the approach of a bank that has advanced a large unsecured loan. This concept has been retained from the original guidance published in 2005.

Parties wishing to apply for clearance should complete the Pension Regulator's standard application form (available on the Pension Regulator's website at www.thepensionsregulator.gov.uk) and provide the information requested, which includes:

- any relevant documents relating to the effect of the event on the scheme or actions taken to improve the position of the scheme;
- any independent reports that the trustees have commissioned in respect of the events described in the application;
- where the trustees have not taken independent advice, the document recording this decision together with the trustees' view of the events described in the application;
- a copy of the current and complete winding-up power from the scheme's trust deed and rules;
- a copy of the most recent actuarial valuation of the scheme, recovery plan and schedule of contributions;
- a copy of the assumptions used in assessing the scheme deficit on an FRS17/IAS19 basis; and
- copies of any withdrawal arrangements, any proposed rule amendments and existing apportionment rules.

The standard form issued by the Regulator for use for a clearance application invites the applicant to request that the Regulator issues one or more of the following statements:

> 'In the Regulator's opinion ...:
>
> - it would not be reasonable to impose any liability on the applicant under a contribution notice issued under *s 38*.

- it would it would not be reasonable to impose the requirements of a financial support direction, in relation to the scheme, on the applicant.'

In addition, the Regulator has a power to grant a clearance statement in relation to contribution notices which states that in its opinion and in the circumstances described in the application, the applicant would not be a party to a an act or a deliberate failure to act. However, this would require significantly more evidence and, therefore, extensive due diligence, which would take much more time.

14.85 As mentioned above, the Regulator can issue a contribution notice to a person requiring an amount up to and including the *s 75* debt which is due from an employer, or the *s 75* debt which might become due on the winding up of a scheme, to be paid to the scheme or the PPF if the Regulator is of the opinion that a person was a party to an act or deliberate failure to act and:

- the material detriment test is met in relation to that act or failure to act; or
- the main purpose or one of the main purposes of the act or failure to act was:
  - to prevent the recovery of the whole or part of a *s 75* debt which was or might become due from an employer in relation to the scheme; or
  - to prevent such a debt becoming due, to compromise or otherwise settle such a debt, or to reduce the amount of such a debt which would otherwise become due (see **14.79** above).

Under the 2009 Guidance, it is clear that the material detriment test can still apply, whether or not the benefits accrued at the time of the relevant act or omission are still to be received from the scheme (ie where there has been a subsequent transfer or buy out), and the Regulator will disregard payments which might be received from the PPF. So, employers and trustees cannot use the PPF as an argument that members have not suffered a detriment. This is not, however, set out in the Code of Practice No 12 entitled 'Circumstances in Relation to the Material Detriment Test' which was issued on 29 June 2009 and seems not to fit in with the material detriment test as set out in *PA 2004, s 38A*, which provides that:

> 'the act or failure has detrimentally affected in a material way the likelihood of accrued scheme benefits being received (whether the benefits are to be received as benefits under the scheme or otherwise).'

There is a reminder in the 2009 Guidance that the material detriment test is not the same as a type A event. Therefore, even where the material detriment test is met, there may not always be a type A event (and so clearance may not always be available). For example, the material detriment test will apply whether or not there is a relevant deficit in the scheme.

Clearance will not be available just in relation to the material detriment test. The clearance process is based on the reasonableness approach, rather than looking at the various individual limbs of the legislation.

Abandonment

14.86 The Regulator issued its latest guidance on 'abandonment' in December 2008. The December 2008 Guidance is updated to reflect changes to the 2009 Guidance on clearance. Otherwise, the substance of the 2008 abandonment guidance remains largely the same as the 2007 Guidance.

The abandonment of a pension scheme occurs where the sponsoring employer severs its links with the scheme without providing the scheme with sufficient funds or assets to compensate for losing the ongoing support of its employer. Where trustees of a defined benefit scheme are asked by the employer supporting the scheme to consider:

- the transfer of liabilities in whole, or in part, to another employer; and/or
- a change in control, or significant restructuring of the employer (or group of companies associated with the employer) that results in the substantial reduction in the financial strength of the employer who will in sponsor the scheme.

It is possible that such arrangements may be materially financially detrimental to the pension scheme, and the trustees are expected to negotiate robustly and seek mitigation prior to agreement.

Commercial activities may give rise to issues of abandonment, for example, where the proposal results in the current employer severing its links with the pension scheme without meeting its obligations to the scheme or the scheme is transferred to another employer that is unable to meet the full buyout costs of the scheme's liabilities. Trustees will need to be able to recognise that such arrangements may result in the abandonment of the scheme, exposing members to an increased risk that their benefits may not be provided in full and increasing the chances of the scheme entering the Pension Protection Fund.

The Regulator expects the trustees' starting point to be that any arrangement that breaks the link with the existing employer may not be in the best interests of the members unless the full *s 75* debt is paid, or unless the scheme remains supported by an employer of substance and the scheme is suitably compensated for any negative change in the strength of the employer's covenant (eg a guarantee).

The guidance is also stated to be applicable to all cases where an arrangement could result in the employer breaking the link with the scheme (or a significant proportion of the members of the scheme), without the payment of an appropriate proportion of the scheme's potential *s 75* debt or, where a debt has actually fallen due, without obtaining approval for a withdrawal arrangement. It is also applicable where there will be a restructuring of the employer, or group of companies associated with the employer, such that the scheme is no longer supported by an employer of substance.

The guidance recognises that any proposed arrangement will no doubt be very complex and that it is essential for trustees to obtain independent advice to obtain an analysis and explanation of the implications for the scheme. Trustees and employers are expected to report to and consult with the Regulator on any arrangement that may result in the abandonment of the pension scheme, at an early stage in the process. The Regulator has a number of powers at its disposal if it is felt that the proposed arrangement would result in the scheme being abandoned, including contribution notices and financial support directions (see **14.77** and **14.82** above) as well as powers to prohibit, suspend and appoint trustees of pension schemes, and to wind a pension scheme up.

The full guidance can be found on the Regulator's website at www.thepensionsregulator.gov.uk/guidance/abandonment/index.aspx.

Parties' positions

14.87 The purchaser should be concerned about the risk that he may be entering into a transaction which may gives rise to a debt payable by him or by the company he is buying. Even if the purchaser can persuade the seller to indemnify him against any such debt, there remains the possibility that a considerable period of time might pass before the actuarial calculations are complete and the debt is notified to the purchaser. There is a risk that, by this stage, the seller may no longer be in a financial position to meet the indemnity. As well as an indemnity, therefore, the purchaser may ask the seller to procure that the scheme will be valued, and the amount of any debt notified, within a set timescale.

None of this is likely to appeal to the seller, especially if the scheme's funding is indeed weak. The prospect of an indemnity will be particularly unattractive if the seller is promising a past service reserve transfer payment backed up by a shortfall clause (see **14.46** above).

The possibility of an employer debt arising may, therefore, present major issues for the parties, and this highlights the need for early due diligence in relation to the scheme's funding position. It may, however, be possible to lessen the impact of the legislation by structuring the deal, for example, as an asset sale rather than a company sale, or to enter into one of the new arrangements permitted by the *Employer Debt Regulations*, as amended by the *Occupational Pension Schemes (Employer Debt and Miscellaneous Amendments) Regulations 2008* (see **14.64** above), so that the purchaser has certainty over the amount of any debt that may arise as a consequence of the transaction. The following table sets out some of the options available to a purchaser, depending upon the structure of the transaction:

	Potential size of debt	**Reason**	**Options**
Company sale, no transitional period	Could be huge.	The purchaser acquires all the company's liabilities. The company may have participated in the seller's scheme for years and be responsible for a huge proportion of the overall debt (calculated on a full buy-out basis). This will relate not only to the company's present employees, but also to pensioners and deferred pensioners formerly employed by it.	• restructure the deal so it becomes an asset sale; • amend the trust deed and rules governing the scheme to introduce a scheme apportionment arrangement; • enter into an approved withdrawal arrangement or a withdrawal arrangement; • request the seller to make good the deficit prior to completion; or • adjust the purchase price to take into account the pension scheme liabilities that will be acquired on completion.
Company sale with transitional period	Larger still.	As above, except that the extra period of participation will increase any debt still further.	Same considerations as above, but the purchaser would want to ensure that it is only responsible, if at all, for any *s 75* liabilities arising solely in relation to its period of participation.

	Potential size of debt	Reason	Options
Asset sale, no transitional period	Nil (assuming the seller of the assets continues to have some employees in the scheme following completion).	No employer will be ceasing to participate in the seller's scheme.	
Asset sale with transitional period	Smaller debt than for corresponding company sale (again, assuming the seller of the assets continues to have some employees in the scheme following completion).	The purchaser will have participated in the seller's scheme only for a short time following completion, and so be responsible for a (probably small) proportion of any overall deficit.	Indemnification required from the seller that the purchaser will only be liable for those debts arising whilst a participating employer. A review of the trust deed and rules also necessary to ensure that other debts cannot be apportioned to the purchaser. In practice, very few purchasers are likely to want to take up this option.

Member-nominated trustees

14.88 A commercial transaction of the sort considered in this chapter may cause the trustees to review the appropriateness of the member-nominated trustee arrangements (see CHAPTER 3).

Public sector transfers

14.89 Bulk transfers from schemes such as the Principal Civil Service Pension Scheme and other public service pension schemes, of which the Government Actuary's Department is scheme actuary, have separate requirements which must be satisfied if a bulk transfer payment is to be made into a receiving scheme. These situations arise primarily when an outsourcing contract is entered into with a Government body or agency.

In order for the Government Actuary's Department to agree to the transfer of public service scheme benefits, the receiving scheme must satisfy prescribed criteria. These criteria relate generally to the level of benefits to be provided and the balance of powers in the receiving scheme. The Government Actuary's

Department will usually provide a standard pensions schedule setting out its requirements but its provisions can be negotiated to a limited extent, subject to the circumstances of a particular case. Some schemes may be required to make amendments to the scheme rules to satisfy the Government Actuary's Department's criteria. If the necessary criteria are satisfied, the Government Actuary's Department will issue either a 'certificate of broad comparability' or a 'passport'.

The distinction between the passport and the certificate of broad comparability is that the passport attaches to the receiving scheme and is valid for more than one transfer in, only ceasing to be of general application if the Government Actuary's Department's requirements change. A passport is more usually applied for when a new scheme is being established specifically to receive public service transfers. By contrast, a certificate of broad comparability will be required for all schemes without a passport on each occasion on which it is proposed that a transfer be made.

Of course, not all outsourcing contracts lead to a transfer of benefits. The *Local Government Pension Scheme (Amendment etc) Regulations 1999 (SI 1999/3438)* provided a new method of addressing pensions on the transfer of employment in the context of local government outsourcing. This method is to admit the new employer to participate in the Local Government Pension Scheme (the 'LGPS'). The new employer must enter into an admission agreement with the administering authority, and may also have to acquire an indemnity or bond (*Local Government Pension Scheme (Administration) Regulations 2008 (SI 2008/239), reg 6(5)* (the '*Administration Regulations*'). The *Local Government Pension Scheme (Administration) (Amendment) Regulations 2008 (SI 2008/3245)* make amendments to the *Administration Regulations*, in particular *reg 3*, which disapplies *Administration Regulations, reg 16(6)* so that, where a Local Government Pension Scheme member transfers employment by way either of a TUPE transfer or of a transfer which is treated as if TUPE applies, his membership of the Local Government Pension Scheme is treated as if it were continuous. *Regulation 3* applies with effect from 28 June 2008 in relation to England and Wales.

The need for an indemnity or bond was previously an absolute requirement, but this changed under the *Local Government Pension Scheme (Amendment) (No 2) Regulations 2003 (SI 2003/3004)*. The requirement now is that, where a new employer will provide services or assets in connection with the function of an existing 'Scheme Employer' (the outsourcing authority), as a result of the transfer of the service or assets by means of a contract or other arrangement, that 'Scheme Employer' must:

> '... carry out an assessment, taking account of actuarial advice, of the level of risk arising on premature termination of the provision of the

service or assets by reason of the insolvency, winding-up or liquidation of the transferee admission body.'

It is only 'where the level of risk identified by the assessment is such as to require it' that the prospective new employer is required to enter into an indemnity or bond. This means that where there are only a handful of employees transferring, for example, there may no longer be a need to go to the expense of providing an indemnity or bond. Where such a document is required, banks usually present their own 'standard', which is then considered by the outsourcing authority's lawyers.

Historically, the financial risk for a contractor participating in the LGPS was one that contractors seemed to accept, despite having no control over any part of the management or investment of the scheme. However, contractors are now becoming increasingly alive to the various risks associated with becoming an admitted body, which include:

- the relevant section of the LGPS being in deficit at the transfer date, and therefore the risk of the contractor, at some stage, subsidising that deficit;
- the risk of employer contribution rates to the LGPS increasing;
- having little or no control over the investment and management of LGPS funds, which in turn has an effect on the level of contribution required from local authorities and contractors; and
- the risks associated with ceasing participation in the LGPS. Here, the contractor may have to pay a lump sum under *Administration Regulations, reg 38* and it is difficult for a contractor to price for this risk at the outset of a contract.

The disadvantages noted above have to be considered in light of the advantages for a contractor participating in the LGPS. These include:

- the contractor avoiding the high costs of sponsoring its own defined benefit scheme; and
- complying with the requirements of the Fair Deal, and reducing the risk of a complaint from a transferred employee under the Best Value Authorities Staff Transfers (Pensions) Direction 2007 (see **14.90** and **14.91** respectively below).

Often, contractors now seek to manage these known risks by refusing to accept liability for any underfunding of the LGPS prior to the transfer of the employees, capping its ongoing contributions to the fund and/or passing the deficit on exit back to the letting authority.

As a consequence, the negotiation of the admission agreement and indemnity or bond is usually a lengthy process and should be started as soon as the overall contract negotiations begin.

The Fair Deal

14.90 The requirement for the new contractor to provide either broadly comparable pension arrangements or admission to the LGPS is contained in Government guidance published in June 1999 and updated in June 2004. The HM Treasury 'Guidance to Departments and Agencies: Staff Transfers from Central Government: A Fair Deal for Staff Pensions' dated June 1999 as annexed to the Cabinet Office 'Statement of Practice – Staff Transfers and the Public Sector' dated January 2000 ('Fair Deal') provides guidance on protecting all public service employees, including those transferring to a contractor under a Private Finance Initiative ('PFI') and Public-Private Partnership ('PPP') contracts.

The Fair Deal guidance essentially provides the public service employees with protection that is two pronged, covering past and future service rights. In respect of future service, the contractor must offer future service benefits which are 'broadly comparable' to the public service sector scheme they have left, which will be assessed by the Government Actuary's Department. The guidance explains that this means that there shall be 'no identifiable employees who will suffer material detriment overall'. If an individual will suffer, that individual must be awarded compensation (for example, a salary increase).

To protect past service, the contractor's scheme must be prepared to accept a bulk transfer, and 'day for day' transfer credits must be provided (or an equivalent basis as recommended by the Government Actuary's Department shall apply). The further guidance issued by HM Treasury and entitled 'The Fair Deal for Staff Pensions: Further Guidance – Fair Deal for Staff Pensions: Procurement of Bulk Transfer Agreements and Related Issues Guidance Note' dated June 2004 ('Fair Deal 2004') builds on the principles set out in the Fair Deal and clarifies the practical aspects of its application. One important point to note is that the Fair Deal and the subsequent Fair Deal 2004 guidance only apply to contracts let after the date of the Fair Deal. Therefore previous outsourcing contracts awarded prior to June 1999 will not be caught by the principles set out in the guidance on any subsequent re-let of those original contracts (although authorities may still wish to adopt such an approach voluntarily).

As a consequence of this guidance, the outsourcing process has been tightened up, but there could be some unwelcome side effects for contractors. Detailed pension information will have to be given by the contracting authority at the outset of the tendering procedure (this will be required before any shortlist of contractors is drawn up) and the transfer terms (ie the credits to be awarded in the contractor's scheme) will have to be settled at an early stage. This will have costs implications for the contracting authority. It is possible that delays will also occur further down the line. The Government Actuary's Department will be required to provide a full analysis of the terms of the transferring and receiving schemes, which must be made available to unions and employees. A reasonable period is to be allowed for discussion, and no contractual terms can be settled in that period.

The Best Value Authorities Staff Transfers (Pensions) Direction 2007

14.91 *Local Government Act 2003, s 101* allows for the Secretary for the Department for Communities and Local Government (DCLG) (previously the Office of the Deputy Prime Minster) to issue directions to best value authorities in England and Wales to provide how employment and pensions matters will be treated in the contracting of services.

The Direction under *Local Government Act 2003, s 101* came into force on 1 October 2007 and applies to 'best value authorities', ie those listed in *Local Government Act 1999, s 1.*

The new Direction sets out the standard of pensions protection with effect from 1 October 2007 by protecting the future service of former authority employees whose employment is transferred to a contractor. Authorities will be required under the new Direction to ensure via the contract governing the outsourced services that the contractor will secure pension protection for the employees with pension rights that are 'the same as' or 'broadly comparable to or better than' the pension provision the employees enjoyed prior to transfer. In addition, the transferred employees must be given a direct right to enforce the pensions protection against the contractor.

The cost allocation involved with protecting the pensions of the transferring employees is often the key consideration for authorities negotiating with possible contractors. Experience has shown that whilst contractors have been willing to undertake to provide the agreed level of pensions protection going forward, in practice, they have not been willing to pay for this protection.

The Direction provides statutory protection for authority employees who are compulsorily transferred to a new employer as part of an outsourcing or procurement project. However, *Local Government Act 2003, s 102* only protects the future service of the transferred employees. There is no statutory protection for the treatment of their past service benefits accumulated whilst an employee of the authority. In contrast, past service benefits are covered by the Fair Deal provisions (see **14.90** above), where the authority is required to seek agreement that the contractor will provide, where a bulk transfer will take place, day for day past service credits in the contractor's scheme.

As a consequence of this lack of statutory protection for past service benefits, it would seem that the interaction between the Direction and the Fair Deal remains uncertain. It may result in a shift in focus away from the requirements of the Fair Deal and consequently, from the protection for the employees' past service if the contractor can demonstrate compliance with the new statutory requirements of the Direction. The concern is that there may be a weakening of the Fair Deal, arising as result of its lack of statutory status being brought sharply into focus by the Direction. Whether or not this will become an issue may depend on the future appetite of contractors to set up or maintain a broadly comparable scheme.

The popularity of the admitted body route has increased, and if this trend continues then employees will maintain continuity of service in LGPS and the issue of past service protection and levels of service credits fall away. (In this context, it is interesting to note that the information circulated by the Department for Communities and Local Government indicates that admitted body status would 'appear to satisfy' the requirements contained in the Direction.)

The two-tier requirements

14.92 Local authorities have been subject to the 'Code of Practice on Workforce Matters' since 2003. The Code prevents the emergence of a two-tier workforce in cases where local authority employees are contracted out to a service provider by ensuring that new recruits are employed on terms and conditions that are, overall, no less favourable than those transferred local authority public sector employees.

In pension terms, the Code requires the contractor to offer new employees 'working alongside' former local authority employees 'reasonable pension arrangements' which can include:

- membership of the LGPS; or
- membership of the employer's contracted-out final salary pension scheme; or
- membership of an employer's defined contribution occupational pension scheme (or stakeholder scheme) to which the contractor must match contributions up to a maximum of 6 per cent.

Compliance with the Code's obligations (including pension provision) is likely to be a contractual provision within the main contract.

Further details regarding public sector transfers are to be found at **7.22** above.

Other types of scheme

Money purchase schemes

14.93 Where the seller's scheme provides money purchase benefits, the issues are considerably simpler.

In the context of a money purchase occupational scheme, the warranties will focus far less on the sufficiency of the scheme's assets and more on the extent of the liability to contribute (and whether all the contributions due have been paid). There may still, however, be some defined risk benefits, and the purchaser should seek the necessary disclosures and warranty as to the insurance of these.

If the circumstances give rise to a transfer payment (see **14.20** above), the amount to be transferred will effectively be the sums in the transferring members' money purchase accounts, rather than involving complex valuation methods and assumptions.

If the purchaser is taking over the entire scheme (see **14.21** above), it will also require warranties to satisfy itself that the scheme complies with all relevant legal requirements. However, as illustrated by the table at **1.16** above, money purchase arrangements are less heavily regulated than defined benefit ones. Money purchase assets and liabilities are expressly excluded from the scope of *PA 1995, s 75* in the *Employer Debt Regulations*, as amended by the *Occupational Pension Schemes (Employer Debt and Miscellaneous Amendments) Regulations 2008* (see **14.64** above).

If the scheme is a personal pension arrangement, the purchaser will want to see the documentation setting out the contribution promise and information indicating the costs of those contributions. It will also need a warranty that all contributions due have been paid (and that there has been no proposal or announcement to pay higher contributions).

Small self-administered schemes

14.94 Most small self-administered schemes ('SSASs') are money purchase arrangements and so the same principles as mentioned in **14.93** above apply. These are less regulated than other types of scheme in many respects, although the purchaser should seek warranties that provide comfort in relation to the scheme's compliance with the general legislative requirements that apply to such schemes.

Often the company which the purchaser is buying will be the principal (or only) employer of the SSAS and the sellers will be the scheme members. The sellers (who in these circumstances will probably also be trustees of the SSAS) will wish to retain control over their scheme and so may, as a term of the sale agreement, require that the purchaser executes a deed of amendment transferring (so far as possible) the company's powers under the scheme rules in relation to the SSAS to the trustees. The purchaser may be happy to do this, as long as it is protected from any further liabilities in relation to the SSAS.

Unregistered schemes

14.95 The purchaser should seek to obtain as much information as it can about any unapproved/unregistered schemes that there may be.

Much of the legislation that applies to other schemes does not apply to unapproved/unregistered arrangements. This will to some extent lessen the level of warranty protection that the purchaser will require, although in assessing the costs of these arrangements it should be borne in mind that the early leaver legislation (see CHAPTER 6) may apply (even to unfunded arrangements).

The key difference, however, between an unapproved/unregistered arrangement and any other type of scheme will, of course, be its tax treatment. This is considered in further detail in CHAPTER 5.

Conclusion

14.96 This chapter is only an overview, but it should be sufficient to illustrate the complexity and the possible costs implications of pension arrangements in negotiations for the sale or purchase of a company or business. The potential impact of pensions issues for both the seller and the purchaser should therefore never be underestimated, and the sooner these are addressed the better the chances of the deal progressing to a successful conclusion for both sides. This has never been more so than since the introduction of the Regulator's powers to issue contribution notices and financial support directions by *PA 2004*, and the more onerous level of debt calculation on the withdrawal of a participating employer in a multi-employer defined benefit arrangement.

The Regulator's clearance procedure can provide the parties to a transaction with greater certainty where the transaction involves a company with a defined benefit scheme. Clearance provides the parties with assurance via the clearance statement that their proposed activities will not later be found to fall foul of the legislation. Similarly, the new arrangements permitted under the *Employer*

Debt Regulations, as amended by the *Occupational Pension Schemes (Employer Debt and Miscellaneous Amendments) Regulations 2008*, provide the parties to a transaction with a number of ways to deal with a *s 75* debt in the event that an employment-cessation event arises (see **14.64** above). Further changes are also in the pipeline to assist with internal reorganisations, which will be welcomed and will assist with the continuance of merger, acquisition and restructuring activity for employers with defined benefit arrangements.

Chapter 15

Pensions dispute resolution and litigation

Introduction

15.1 Whilst there has always been scope for disputes to arise over pension schemes, there has been a dramatic growth in this area since the early 1990s. The reasons for this include the increased regulation of pension schemes, the introduction of public bodies to police such schemes, the authority of the Office of the Pensions Ombudsman to adjudicate upon disputes, the introduction of internal dispute resolution procedures and increased public awareness.

The 1990s began with the high-profile *Maxwell* scandal, followed by disputes over large surpluses in various privatised industries. The new millennium witnessed a slump in the stock market causing large pension deficits, the high-profile *Equitable Life* case, the increasing cost of annuities, the closure of final salary pension schemes and the widely publicised 'pensions crisis'. The more recent 'credit crunch' has impacted both occupational and personal pensions in ways which may not be clear for some time. These events have together served to increase public awareness about pension rights.

Pensions disputes have also been affected by further legislation. Pensions 'simplification' under the *Finance Act 2004* has increased the scope for disputes, including complaints against advisers, where scheme members' rights have changed, often in highly complex ways. The *Pensions Act 2004* saw the replacement of OPRA with the new Pensions Regulator ('the Regulator'), with wider powers to regulate schemes. For example, with the introduction of the so-called 'moral hazard' provisions, the Regulator has powers to seek contributions to underfunded pension schemes from entities other than the employer, and the actual or threatened exercise of such powers may give rise to a new area of disputes in the future. The Pensions Ombudsman's remit has been widened, and a number of complaints have now been brought before him as Ombudsman for the Board of the Pension Protection Fund (the vast majority relating to the PPF levy). Appeals against decisions made by the scheme manager under the Financial Assistance Scheme's internal review procedure have further widened the range of disputes referred to the Ombudsman.

As a consequence, the management and resolution of disputes has become an increasingly important factor for trustees in the administration of pension schemes. Trustees are now all too aware that their decisions may be subject to a complaint by an affected member. Similarly, employers, faced with increasing deficits in their pension schemes which they have to fund and which have implications for their balance sheets, are confronted with difficult decisions that impact on their employees.

In addition to the above more hostile types of disputes, less hostile litigation often arises in the context of the day-to-day administration of pension schemes. Trustees, in particular, can apply to court to resolve ambiguities or mistakes in pension scheme documents, and to seek approval of a proposed course of action which has certain consequences for the scheme.

The particular relationships of the parties involved in a pension scheme distinguish pensions disputes from normal commercial disputes. This chapter is not intended to be an exhaustive narrative of every type of dispute and procedure. Instead, it is intended to provide an overview of the principal forums for dispute resolution, and, in relation to litigation through the courts, to highlight some of the issues that may arise in pensions cases, including the use of alternative dispute resolution ('ADR') to settle disputes.

Non-court forums for dispute resolution

Internal dispute resolution procedure ('IDRP')

15.2 *PA 1995, s 50* introduced a requirement for trustees of occupational pension schemes to implement a two-stage IDRP to deal with disputes by members and other beneficiaries about matters concerning the scheme. *Section 50*, together with the *Occupational Pension Schemes (Internal Dispute Resolution Procedures) Regulations 1996 (SI 1996/1270)*, originally set out the detail of who can make a complaint, the information it should contain and how it should be dealt with.

PA 2004, s 273 was due to make a number of key changes from April 2006. However, the original section was not brought into effect. Instead, replacement provisions were enacted in the *Pensions Act 2007* ('*PA 2007*') and came into force on 6 April 2008. The new legislation inserted new *ss 50, 50A* and *50B* into *PA 1995*, where the main IDRP requirements are set out. The 1996 Regulations were replaced by the *Occupational Pension Schemes (Internal Dispute Resolution Procedures Consequential and Miscellaneous Amendments) Regulations 2008* (the '*IDRP Regulations*'), which also came into force on 6 April 2008. There are three main changes in the new provisions, providing for the option of a single-stage process, less prescriptive time limits, and changes to the information requirements. IDRP is discussed in more detail in CHAPTER 3.

IDRP should be capable of resolving the majority of the common complaints made by members and beneficiaries against the trustees and managers. It should be noted, however, that a complaint is exempted from the IDRP if proceedings have already been commenced in a court or other tribunal, or where the Pensions Ombudsman has already commenced an investigation. IDRP is also not the appropriate avenue for pursuing a complaint against an employer, as such complaints fall outside the scope of the procedure.

If the trustees do not implement any 'decision' made under the IDRP which requires implementation, the Pensions Ombudsman would be likely to determine that such failure constitutes 'maladministration' by the trustees, in the event that the member were to complain to him. Also, if the complainant is not satisfied with the 'decision' under the IDRP, the member may refer his complaint to TPAS (see below) and/or the Pensions Ombudsman (the Pensions Ombudsman will ordinarily require a complainant to have made full use of the IDRP before accepting a complaint for investigation).

Complaints to The Pensions Advisory Service ('TPAS')

15.3 TPAS (formerly known as OPAS) provides free advice and assistance to members of the public who have a complaint about their occupational or personal pension scheme and will seek to resolve a dispute by negotiation and correspondence between the parties. The success of this forum depends to a great extent on the willingness of the parties, as any suggested resolution proposed by TPAS is not directly enforceable. If TPAS cannot resolve the member's complaint, the complaint may then be submitted to the appropriate Ombudsman for resolution. The Pensions Ombudsman encourages individuals complaining to him to have consulted TPAS first. The contact details of TPAS can be found at **2.43** above.

Other forums

Financial Services Authority ('FSA') and Financial Ombudsman Service ('FOS')

15.4 Where a person has a complaint about the sale and marketing of a pension arrangement, the complaint may be investigated by the FSA (which regulates the industry) or the FOS (which settles disputes between consumers and financial institutions). If the complaint involves a financial product or service, the FOS requires the complaint to be submitted first to the firm involved to be considered under its internal complaints procedure. If the complainant is unhappy with the firm's final response to the complaint, or eight weeks have elapsed from the date the complaint was submitted without a final response from the firm, the complainant has six months in which to submit the complaint to the FOS. The FOS will first seek to resolve the complaint through an informal process of mediation. If that is unsuccessful, the FOS will conduct a full investigation into the complaint and issue a written determination which is binding on the firm (to a limit of £100,000 plus interest and costs).

Further information, the relevant forms and contact details can be found on the FOS website: www.financial-ombudsman.org.uk.

The Pensions Regulator

15.5 On 6 April 2005, the Regulator became the new regulatory body for work-based pension schemes in the UK, replacing the Occupational Pensions Regulatory Authority (known as 'Opra'). The Regulator regulates the compliance by trustees of occupational pension schemes with *PA 1995* and *PA 2004* and has a wide range of enforcement powers. A summary of those powers can be found at **2.12** above, and the Regulator's contact details are given at **2.32** above. Details of the penalties the Regulator can impose are summarised in APPENDIX I. In particular, where the Regulator considers that there has been a breach of the law it can require corrective action to be taken. Further, where it is believed that an employer is deliberately seeking to avoid its obligations to its pension scheme, the Regulator has powers to issue contribution notices, financial support directions and restoration orders for the purpose of restoring value to the pension scheme, thus reducing the exposure of the Pension Protection Fund to an underfunded scheme. The exercise of these powers by the Regulator can potentially be challenged, giving rise to possible areas for disputes in the future. The Regulator's Determination Panel issued its first determination notices imposing financial support directions on 15 June 2007 in schemes sponsored by Sea Containers Services Limited. However, despite an interim decision on disclosure, the substantive issue was not ultimately brought before the Pensions Regulator Tribunal on appeal, and only a handful of appeal decisions, chiefly on procedural or ancillary matters, have been published to date.

Employment tribunals

15.6 Disputes concerning an employee's rights under an occupational pension scheme may also be dealt with during the course of employment tribunals. This is discussed in more detail in CHAPTER 7.

Divorce proceedings

15.7 Disputes over pension benefits also arise in the context of divorce proceedings. This is dealt with in more detail in CHAPTER 8.

Complaints to Pensions Ombudsman ('PO')

15.8 The role of the PO, his jurisdiction and a summary of the applicable procedure is set out in CHAPTER 5 and at **2.44** to **2.46** above. The PO is not permitted to investigate or determine a complaint if proceedings have already been commenced in any court or employment tribunal in connection with matters to which the complaint relates, unless the proceedings have been discontinued without a settlement binding on the complainant. The court has the power to stay court proceedings concerning matters which are the subject of a complaint or dispute before the PO (*PSA 1993, ss 146, 148*). Although the PO reported in 2008/09 that the average time for completed investigations from the date of initial application was 18.5 months, steps have been taken both to streamline the provision of determinations and to clear the 'backlog' of cases over 12 months old. The PO has issued a guide for trustees and employers on 'How to avoid the Pensions Ombudsman' which can be downloaded from the PO's website. It provides a useful insight as to how the PO expects trustees and employers to fulfil their roles in relation to pension schemes.

Determination

15.9 A determination given by the PO is final and binding on the complainant and any person responsible for the management of the scheme to which the complaint relates (subject to being overturned, on appeal, by the court). The PO has the power to direct any person responsible for the management of the scheme to take, or refrain from taking, such steps as he may specify. Any determination of the PO is enforceable in a county court as if it were a judgment or order of that court (*PSA 1993, s 151*).

The PO's determination or direction must be in writing and state the grounds upon which it is made. A dissatisfied party may ask for the court's permission to appeal the determination on a point of law. The appeal is heard in the High Court (*PSA 1993, s 151(4)*) (see **15.12** below).

Human Rights Act 1998

15.10 The *Human Rights Act 1998* (*HRA 1998*) has been in force since October 2000. *Article 6(1)* of the *European Convention on Human Rights*, which *HRA 1998* incorporates into English law, provides that, in the determination of a person's civil rights and obligations, everyone is entitled to a fair and public hearing within a reasonable time by an independent and impartial tribunal established by law. Following doubts which were raised in connection with the office of the PO in this context, the PO obtained and published an opinion from counsel as to whether *Article 6(1)* applies to investigations by the PO and, if so, whether the PO's practice and procedure satisfy the principles set out in *Article 6(1)*. That opinion is available on the PO's website (www.pensions-ombudsman.org.uk). It concludes that *Article 6(1)* does apply and that the PO's practice and procedure in relation to the holding of oral hearings and otherwise are broadly compatible with *Article 6*. A party to a complaint to the PO can request an oral hearing, although this is not a common occurrence. However, particular criticism from legal commentators has been levied in the past at the role and influence of the PO's staff in investigating complaints and producing determinations, and it remains to be seen whether the PO's practice and procedure will be subject to a successful challenge in the High Court under *Article 6(1)*.

Court proceedings

Introduction

15.11 Litigation through the courts has, traditionally, been regarded as costly, time consuming and unpredictable. It is not surprising, therefore, that the PO and TPAS are attractive alternative forums in which beneficiaries of pension schemes may pursue their claims. However, court proceedings may be unavoidable in some circumstances, such as where a determination of the PO is appealed; where the trustees seek the court's directions on a pensions issue; or where the claimant has no other available forum in which to pursue the claim. Set out below is a summary of the most common types of applications that are made to the court in pensions disputes and a basic explanation of the various procedures under the *Civil Procedure Rules 1998 (SI 1998/3132)*, as amended (the '*CPR*'), which govern the procedure in the civil courts.

Types of application to court

Appeals from the PO

15.12 *PSA 1993, s 151* provides a right of appeal to the High Court on a point of law arising out of a determination given by the PO. This can extend to the way in which the Ombudsman has found on questions of fact: in *AF Blakemore & Son Ltd v Machin [2007] EWHC 963 (Ch)* the High Court found that the Ombudsman had made a determination of fact in the face of the evidence and remitted the decision to an oral hearing before the Ombudsman.

Any such appeal will be heard in the Chancery Division of the High Court. The procedure is set out in *CPR Part 52* and the *Practice Direction on Appeals*. The party lodging the appeal – the 'appellant' – must file a notice of appeal (known as the 'appellant's notice') at the High Court within 28 days after the date of the PO's determination. A copy must also be served on the PO and the respondent (see *Practice Direction on Appeals, para 17*). The appellant's notice should be in a form prescribed by the *CPR* (Form N161) and set out the grounds for the appeal, the arguments in support of those grounds, the decision sought from the appeal court and any evidence in support of the appeal. It should be accompanied by a skeleton argument (a summary of a party's submissions) and a bundle of relevant documents.

The other parties to the appeal are referred to as 'respondents', and may include the PO as a respondent. A respondent can ask the appeal court to uphold the PO's determination for reasons different from or additional to those given by the PO, in which case that respondent must file a 'respondent's notice' within 14 days of being served with the appellant's notice. Like the appellant's notice, the respondent's notice should be in a prescribed form (Form N162), accompanied by a skeleton argument and bundle of relevant documents.

It is important to note that the time limits referred to above are strict and cannot be varied without the court's permission. This means that once the PO has issued a determination, the parties should take immediate steps to consider whether they wish to appeal and, if so, prepare the relevant documents. Both the appeal notice and the skeleton arguments should be prepared with care because a party will not be able to rely in the appeal on a matter not contained in the appeal notice without the permission of the court. An appeal does not operate as an automatic stay of the determination of the PO unless the court or the PO permits otherwise.

The appeal will be limited to a review of the PO's determination unless the court considers that, in the circumstances, it would be in the interests of justice to hold a rehearing. Oral evidence and evidence which was not before the PO are not allowed to be introduced in the appeal unless the court orders otherwise. The court has power to affirm, set aside or vary any determination made by the PO; refer any claim or issue back to the PO for determination; order a new hearing before the PO; and make orders for the payment of interest on any monies awarded and the parties' costs.

In practice, whilst an employer may have the resources to fund the costs of an appeal, an individual complainant may be reluctant to pursue an appeal given the costs of mounting the appeal and the risk of being ordered to pay the respondent's costs if the appeal is lost. In such circumstances, the potential appellant may consider applying for a prospective costs order (which is discussed in more detail at **15.36** below) before pursuing an appeal.

In certain appeals the PO may decide that he wishes to participate but, if he does, he will expose himself to a risk that, if he loses, the court may order him to pay the costs of the appeal (*Moore's (Wallisdown) Ltd v Pension Ombudsman [2002] 1 All ER 737*). For this reason, the PO has indicated a reluctance to participate in appeals, except where the issue is of wider public relevance. This approach was reflected in the 2003 case of *Legal & General Assurance Society Ltd v CCA Stationery Ltd [2003] EWHC 2989 (Ch), [2003] All ER (D) 233*, in which the court requested the PO's participation in the appeal but the PO declined because of the costs risk. The result was that the appeal hearing went ahead without the participation of the respondents.

The decision of the High Court may be appealed to the Court of Appeal. The court's permission is required and will only be granted if it is considered that the appeal would raise an important point of principle or practice, or there is some other compelling reason to hear it. The Court of Appeal's judgment may, with the court's permission, be appealed to the UK Supreme Court.

It is relevant to note that, in general, recent attempts to seek judicial review of the PO's determinations, as an alternative to pursuing an appeal under the procedure explained above, have failed. In those cases, the court referred to the appeal procedure as being the more appropriate means of determining the issues. The case of *R (on the application of Parish) v Pensions Ombudsman* (the two hearings are reported at *[2009] EWHC 32 (Admin)* and *[2009] EWHC 969 (Admin)* respectively) is a recent exception. There, the Ombudsman declined jurisdiction on the basis that the complaint was already the subject matter of a judicial review against the public sector employer. The claimant then issued a further application for judicial review against the Ombudsman, which was upheld.

Seeking directions from the court

15.13 The court has a wide jurisdiction to provide directions to trustees on matters relating to the administration of a pension scheme (see *CPR Part 64* and the *Practice Directions* to it). Applications to court for such directions usually concern issues arising out of the trustees' exercise of a discretion or a power under the pension scheme's trust deed or rules, or where the meaning of the scheme's trust deed or rules is unclear or ambiguous. For example, the trustees may seek the court's direction because:

(*a*) they are uncertain whether or not a proposed course of action is within their powers;

(*b*) they wish to seek the court's blessing to a proposed course of action which may have a significant impact on the scheme (for example, application for a *Beddoe* order – see **15.34** below); or (*c*) they wish to surrender the exercise of a discretion to the court because they are unable to arrive at a decision for some reason (for example, conflict of interest, deadlock).

Such applications are commonly referred to as 'construction' or 'directions' applications.

Where a question has arisen as to how the terms of a trust deed should be interpreted and the trustees have obtained a written opinion from a counsel of at least ten years' standing, in the absence of a dispute over the issue, the trustees may apply to the High Court (under *Administration of Justice Act 1985, s 48*), without the need for a hearing, for an order authorising the trustees to take the proposed steps in reliance on the opinion. This abbreviated procedure has the potential of providing a relatively speedy and cost-efficient resolution of the issue. However, it is not appropriate where there may be a dispute over the proposed construction (for example, where the construction is not clear and is potentially favourable to one category of member over another). Where there is, or is likely to be, a dispute, a full application to court will be required.

These types of application are not usually of a particularly hostile nature (unless the employer and/or the beneficiaries take exception to what is proposed) and may be distinguished from proceedings in which the trustees' actions are being challenged by a third party, which are usually more hostile.

Directions applications are usually brought under the simplified *CPR Part 8* procedure (which is discussed in more detail in **15.21** below).

Claims by/against a third party

15.14 These are claims which involve the trustees and third parties, ie parties external to the trust. For example, they may include claims by trustees against their professional advisers for professional negligence or a claim by trustees against a former trustee for breach of trust. They are usually hostile in nature and are usually brought under the *CPR Part 7* procedure (which is discussed in more detail in **15.22** below).

Rectification

15.15 Where an error is discovered in the drafting of a pension scheme document, such that the document does not reflect accurately the true common intentions of the trustees and the employer, and that error cannot be resolved completely by other means (for example, by the proper construction of the document, or by the use of any applicable amendment power which does not offend *PA 1995, s 67*), the trustees may apply to the court to rectify the error.

Basically, in order to succeed the trustees would have to provide credible evidence that the error did not reflect accurately the clear and common intentions of the trustees and employer when the wording in the document was drafted. They would have to prove that there is no other effective remedy available, that the mistake is of significant importance such that it justifies the court making an order for rectification and that in all the circumstances it is appropriate to grant rectification (for example, there are no legal bars to rectification).

Given the importance of documentary and oral evidence to a rectification application, it is usually made using the *Part 7* procedure (see **15.22** below), unless there is no dispute on the facts, in which case the *Part 8* procedure may be more appropriate (see **15.21** below). The trustees and the employer will both be parties to the application and a representative beneficiary (see **15.26** below), or more than one where appropriate, is usually appointed to represent the beneficiaries of the scheme. As a result of the evidential burden on trustees, rectification applications are usually not straightforward, particularly where another party objects to the proposed rectification. They are often made in conjunction with, and as an alternative to, an application for a declaration that the offending document can be properly construed to give effect to the parties' instructions, which, if successful, would mean that the trustees would no longer need to pursue the alternative rectification application. The judgment in the recent case of *Colorcon Ltd v Huckell [2009] EWHC 979 (Ch)* involved rectification of a definitive deed which allowed revaluation of pensions in deferment at 5 per cent per annum, rather than, as intended, at 5 per cent LPI. The court confirmed that there are no special restrictions applying to rectification of pension documents. It also held that no outward expression of accord is necessary as a matter of law (as had been suggested in previous cases), and that the behaviour of the parties following the execution of the deed could stand as evidence of the intention itself: this included administration of benefits on the basis of 5 per cent LPI, and scheme reports and member booklets published and circulated in subsequent years stating that 5 per cent LPI was the correct figure.

Outline of procedure

Issues for consideration before commencing court proceedings

15.16 Before embarking on court proceedings, a claimant should consider, in particular, the following important factors:

(*a*) Is the claim being brought within any relevant limitation period prescribed by law? If not, the claim may be time barred.

(*b*) How will the costs of the proceedings be funded and paid? (Some relevant issues on costs are discussed in **15.30** below.)

(*c*) Who will be the parties to the proceedings?

(*d*) What remedy is sought and will it be an effective remedy?

(*e*) What are the merits of the application?

The answers to these questions will assist a claimant in determining not only whether to commence proceedings in the civil courts, but also the strategy to be adopted in progressing the claim, including whether to pursue alternative dispute resolution methods ('ADR', for which see **15.38** below). The decision to commence court proceedings should not be taken lightly, because once commenced, the claimant cannot unilaterally withdraw them without having to pay the other party's costs (unless the other party or the court agrees otherwise).

Trustees' obligations to disclose information to a beneficiary

15.17 Beneficiaries and trustees should be aware that the beneficiary may request disclosure by the trustees of certain 'trust documents', which the trustees may be legally obliged to disclose, without the need for litigation. This may assist a beneficiary's investigation into a matter. It is a common law principle that trustees are obliged to disclose 'trust documents' to beneficiaries who have a fixed (as opposed to discretionary) interest in a trust (including a pension scheme) (*O'Rourke v Darbishire [1920] AC 581, [1920] All ER Rep 1*). This obligation has been based on the principle that beneficiaries have the 'proprietary' right to the documents held by the trustees. Trust documents include the trust deed, rules, accounts and all documents relating to the trust, including minutes or trustee meetings. It may also extend to legal advice obtained by the trustees on behalf of the scheme, although not usually legal advice obtained in respect of the beneficiary's claim against the trustees or legal advice paid for by the trustees themselves rather than out of trust monies.

This disclosure obligation has not, however, extended to disclosing the trustees' deliberations on and reasons for exercising their discretionary powers under the scheme in a particular way. Therefore, trustees have not had to disclose any document evidencing their reasons and deliberations on that issue, unless there is evidence of improper conduct (*Re Londonderry's Settlement, Peat v Walsh [1964] 3 All ER 855*; *Wilson v Law Debenture Trust Corporation plc [1995] 2 All ER 337*). If the trustees fail to disclose the disclosable trust documents, they may be ordered by a court to pay the costs of any application that the beneficiary may make to the court to compel such disclosure.

However, this obligation has been affected by two subsequent decisions.

(*a*) In *Schmidt v Rosewood Trust Ltd [2003] UKPC 26, [2003] 3 All ER 76* the court appeared to move away from the 'proprietary right' as the underlying rationale of the obligation and, instead, asserted the court's inherent power to supervise the administration of trusts, and right to order disclosure of any trust documents if it is considered appropriate in all the circumstances. This potentially widens the scope of the disclosure obligation not only in terms of the range of documents that could be disclosable but also the type of beneficiary who may be entitled to disclosure. As a Privy Council decision, it is not binding on the English court or the PO, but nonetheless is of highly persuasive authority. It remains to be seen how this is further applied in practice by the court. However, the PO has already confirmed that he regards it as highly persuasive authority (see his determination in April 2005 in *Mr B Cameron (M00949)*).

(*b*) The PO indicated in a determination in 2002 (*Allen v TKM Group Pension Trust Ltd [2002] PLR 333*) that he considered it to be 'good administrative practice' for pension trustees to give reasons for their decisions and to make minutes of trustee meetings available to beneficiaries with a legitimate interest in the matter, even when exercising discretionary powers. Where he could see no good reason for trustees withholding disclosure of their reasons, he was prepared to determine that the trustees were guilty of maladministration. Given the above, trustees who receive a request for documents should consider it carefully, with appropriate advice, before deciding whether to reject it or the extent to which it should be complied with.

(See also a trustee's disclosure obligations pursuant to relevant pensions statutes and regulations at **3.21** above and APPENDIX II.)

Pre-action protocols

15.18 The *CPR* set out steps that the court will expect the parties to undertake before proceedings are commenced. In particular, the court will expect all parties to have complied in substance with the terms of any applicable 'pre-action protocol' in the *CPR*. Whilst there is presently no specific protocol applicable to all types of pension disputes, there is a protocol which applies specifically to professional negligence claims (for example, a trustee's claim against his professional advisors for negligence).

Where there is no specific protocol that applies to the dispute in issue, the *Practice Direction on Pre-Action Conduct* (set out in the *CPR*) sets out a pre-action procedure that parties should seek to adhere to with the intention of avoiding litigation in so far as possible. The procedure specified includes the following, although this may be revised by the parties to suit their particular circumstances, provided that the revisions are reasonable:

(*a*) Each party should act reasonably in exchanging information and documents relevant to the claim and generally in trying to avoid the necessity for the start of proceedings.

(*b*) The claimant should write to the defendant setting out its claim. The letter should:

- give sufficient and concise details to enable the recipient to understand and investigate the claim without extensive further information;
- enclose copies of the essential documents which the claimant relies on;
- ask for a prompt acknowledgment of the letter, followed by a full written response within a reasonable stated period (for many claims, a normal reasonable period for a full response may be one month);
- state whether court proceedings will be issued if the full response is not received within the stated period;
- identify and ask for copies of any essential documents not in his possession which the claimant wishes to see;
- state (if it is so) that the claimant wishes to enter into mediation or another alternative method of dispute resolution; and
- if the recipient is not legally represented, refer to the Practice Direction and draw attention to the court's powers to impose sanctions for failure to comply with this practice direction.

(*c*) The defendant should acknowledge the claimant's letter in writing within 14 days of receiving it and should state when the defendant will give a full written response. If this is longer than the period stated by the claimant, the defendant should give reasons why a longer period is needed.

(*d*) The defendant's letter should, as appropriate, accept the claim in whole or in part and make proposals for settlement, or state that the claim is not accepted. If the claim is accepted in part only, the response should make clear which part is accepted and which part is not accepted.

(*e*) If the defendant does not accept the claim, or part of it, the response should:

- give detailed reasons why the claim is not accepted, identifying which of the claimant's contentions are accepted and which are in dispute;
- Set out details of any counterclaim or contention that the claimant is partly or wholly to blame for the problem complained of;

- enclose copies of the essential documents which the defendant relies upon;
- enclose copies of documents asked for by the claimant, or explain why they are not enclosed;
- identify and ask for copies of any further essential documents not in his possession which the defendant wishes to see; and
- state whether the defendant is prepared to enter into mediation or another alternative method of dispute resolution (and, if not, why not).

(*f*) The claimant should provide requested documents within a reasonably short time or explain in writing why he is not doing so, and reply as defendant to any counterclaim.

(*g*) If the claim remains in dispute, the parties should promptly engage in appropriate negotiations with a view to settling the dispute and avoiding litigation.

It should be noted that any documents disclosed by either party in accordance with the above procedure, may not be used for any purpose other than resolving the dispute, unless the other party agrees. Further, if the dispute requires the assistance of an expert, the Practice Direction suggests that the parties should, wherever possible and to save expense, engage a single agreed expert (for example, if an actuary is required to provide a valuation). It should be noted that the court retains a power to refuse an expert's report sought by a party at this stage or refuse that party to claim the costs of an expert report in any subsequent proceedings.

It is important that a party follows this procedure, or any agreed revised procedure, as the court has an express power to apply costs and other sanctions in the event of a party's non-observance.

Whilst the above procedure provides for limited voluntary disclosure of documents, the *CPR* also provides a mechanism, in certain circumstances, for a potential claimant to apply to the court for an order obliging a potential defendant to anticipated proceedings to disclose documents before those proceedings are commenced (see *CPR, r 31.16*), although the party making the application will usually have to pay the other party's costs of the application and of complying with any order made.

Procedure in the civil court

15.19 Court procedure in civil cases is governed by the *CPR*. With the exception of appeals, court proceedings are initiated by the issue and service of a claim form (which replaces the 'writ' and 'originating summons'). There are two principal procedures under the *CPR* for issuing a claim (as opposed to an appeal) – the *Part 7* and *Part 8* procedures. They are discussed in more detail below. The *Part 7* procedure is the most commonly used procedure in claims involving third parties because such cases involve disputes of fact. The *Part 8* procedure is the standard procedure for directions applications by trustees.

Once proceedings have been commenced, the court will allocate the case to one of its three tracks:

(*a*) *Small claims track*: This is for claims worth less than £5,000. It is designed to be an inexpensive and less formal, expedited procedure, in which the strict rules of evidence do not apply. Expert evidence is not allowed without the court's permission and the court allows a party, its lawyer or a lay representative to present its case at the hearing. The court may, if all parties agree, deal with the claim 'on paper' (ie without a hearing).

(*b*) *Fast track*: This is for claims worth between £5,000 and £25,000. It involves an abbreviated but more formal procedure designed to allow for a trial within a reasonably short timescale, assuming a settlement cannot be reached.

(*c*) *Multi-track*: This is for claims worth over £25,000. It is the most formal procedure of the three tracks, as a result of which cases usually take longer to be determined and are more costly.

Claims issued under the *Part 8* procedure are automatically allocated to the multi-track, whereas *Part 7* claims will be allocated to the appropriate track, according to the value of the claim.

Case management powers

15.20 In all proceedings, the court has wide case management powers. When exercising any power under, or interpreting any rule in, the *CPR*, the court must give effect to what is known as the 'overriding objective'. The overriding objective stipulates that the court must deal with cases justly (see *CPR Part 1* for a full definition). This includes dealing with the case expeditiously and fairly, and in ways which are proportionate to the amount of money involved; the importance and complexity of the case; and to the financial position of each party. The parties themselves are also required to help the court to further the overriding objective.

The court also has wide powers to penalise parties for their conduct in the proceedings by, for example, disallowing all or any part of their costs, or ordering them to pay another party's costs or, in more serious instances, by striking out their case. As a result, parties should aim to meet time deadlines imposed by the court and conduct themselves appropriately.

Part 8 procedure

15.21 The *Part 8* procedure is simpler and is designed to be more efficient than the *Part 7* procedure. The *Part 8* procedure should be employed where the court's decision is required on a question which is unlikely to involve a substantial dispute of fact or where a Practice Direction permits or requires its use for that type of proceedings. In pensions cases, a trustee's application for directions (see **15.13** above) is required to be brought under the *Part 8* procedure. Whilst third party claims (see **15.14** above) and claims for rectification (see **15.15** above) may also be brought under the *Part 8* procedure, such claims will often involve a substantial dispute of fact so the *Part 7* procedure is usually more appropriate. The court may, at any time, disapply the *Part 8* procedure to any proceedings brought under it. *Part 8* claims are automatically allocated to the multi-track.

An outline of the *Part 8* procedure is as follows:

(*a*) *Issue and service of claim form*

The *Part 8* claim form is in a prescribed form and should set out, among other things, the question(s) for determination by the court, the remedy sought and the legal basis for that remedy. Any evidence upon which the claimant wishes to rely at the hearing of the claim should accompany the claim form (set out either in the claim form or in a witness statement, but in both cases verified by a signed statement of truth).

(*b*) *Acknowledgment of service*

The defendant must acknowledge service of the claim form within 14 days by filing at court, and serving on all parties, the prescribed form. In acknowledging service, the defendant should state whether the claim is contested, whether a different remedy is sought, or whether use of the *Part 8* procedure is itself disputed. Unlike under the *Part 7* procedure, the defendant does not have to serve a defence. Failure to acknowledge service will result in the defendant not being able to take part in the hearing of the claim without the court's permission.

(*c*) *Evidence*

If the defendant wishes to rely on evidence at the hearing, that evidence, in the form of a witness statement with any relevant documents exhibited to it, should be filed and served at the same time as the acknowledgment of service. The claimant then has 14 days in which to serve any evidence in reply, unless an extension of time can be agreed with the defendant(s) or is ordered by the court.

(*d*) *Case management directions*

The court may give case management directions when the claim form is issued. It is more usual, however, for the court to give directions after the defendant has acknowledged service or the time limit for acknowledging service has expired. The parties are encouraged to agree, so far as is possible, appropriate case management directions for the court's approval. The court may give such directions without a hearing or by calling a case management conference. Such directions may include the disclosure of documents (see **15.23** below), the exchange of further witness statements (see **15.24** below), the preparation and exchange of expert reports (see **15.25** below), and any other steps that may be necessary for the efficient management of the claim.

(*e*) *Hearing of claim*

The hearing of the claim will take place in open court before a judge, unless the court permits it to be held in private. Written evidence may not be relied on by a party at the hearing unless it has been served in accordance with the rules or the court gives permission. At the hearing, each party's legal representatives make their oral submissions to the judge. The judge may require or allow a party to give oral evidence at the hearing and may require a witness's attendance for cross-examination.

(*f*) *Judgment*

After hearing the parties' submissions, the judge will either hand down the judgment at the end of the hearing or may reserve judgment to a future date (in order to allow time for the judge to consider and draft the judgment).

In applications by trustees for directions in the administration of a pension scheme, the court's *Practice Direction B* to *CPR Part 64* provides additional guidelines, which include the following:

(i) *Confidentiality*

If the confidentiality of the directions sought is important (such as in a *Beddoe* application – see **15.33** below), the claim form should only give a general description of the remedy sought, with a more detailed explanation set out in the trustee's witness statement.

(ii) *Representative parties*

The trustees should consider carefully which beneficiaries should be 'representative parties' (see **15.26** below). It may not be necessary for a representative of each class of beneficiary in the pension scheme to be joined as a party to the proceedings because the trustees may be able to present the arguments for or against the application on behalf of some classes of beneficiary (although trustees will need to consider carefully whether it is prudent for them to pursue this course in the circumstances of the application). If the trustees are unable to decide which categories of beneficiaries to join as defendants (for example, where there are many members and categories of interest), the trustees may apply to issue the claim form without naming any defendants (under *CPR, r 8.2A*). At the same time, they may apply to the court for directions as to which persons to join as parties.

(iii) *No defendants required*

If the trustees consider that the court may be able to give the directions sought without hearing from any other party, they may apply for permission for the claim form to be issued without naming any defendants (*CPR, r 8.2A*). However, in *Re Owens Corning Fibreglass (UK) Pensions Plan Ltd [2002] PLR 323* where a trustee applied for the court's approval of a compromise without informing the beneficiaries, the court indicated that, in most such cases, it would be desirable that potential beneficiaries, or their representatives (for example, their union representatives or the pensions committee) be informed about the proposed arrangement and of any related application to the court to allow them to make their views known. The court indicated that, but for overriding considerations specific to that case, as the beneficiaries had not been informed, it would have adjourned the hearing to allow the beneficiaries to be told of the proposed compromise.

(iv) *Requirement for a hearing*

The court will always consider whether it can deal with the application on paper without the need for a hearing. If the trustees and/or the defendant(s) consider that a hearing is needed, they should state so, with reasons, in their evidence. If the court deals with the application on paper and refuses the application, the parties will be given an opportunity to request a hearing.

(v) *Trustees' evidence*

The trustees' evidence, which is given by witness statement, should disclose fully any matters which are relevant to the application, failing which they may not be protected by the court's order. It should indicate the significance of the proposed course of action for the scheme; include a valuation of the trust assets (ie include the latest actuarial valuation, updated as may be appropriate); describe the membership profile; if a deficit on winding up is likely, it should describe the priority provisions and their likely effect; explain the significance of the proposed litigation or other course of action for the trust; and why the court's directions are required.

(vi) *Consultation with beneficiaries*

The trustees' evidence should also describe what, if any, consultation there has been with beneficiaries, and the results of that consultation. As general guidance, unless the members are few in number, the court will not expect any particular steps by way of consultation with beneficiaries (including, where relevant, employers) or their representatives to have been carried out in preparation for the application. If no consultation has taken place, the court may direct that meetings of one or more classes of beneficiaries are held to consider the subject matter of the application, possibly as a preliminary to deciding whether a representative of a particular class ought to be joined as a defendant.

Part 7 procedure

15.22 The *Part 7* procedure is used if the *Part 8* procedure is inappropriate (for example, there is a substantial dispute of fact). The majority of third party claims (see **15.14** above) will therefore be brought under this procedure. The *Part 7* procedure usually requires more procedural steps prior to the trial than the *Part 8* procedure. An outline of the *Part 7* procedure is as follows:

(*a*) *Claim form and particulars of claim*

The claimant issues and serves a claim form which sets out a basic summary of the claimant's claim. Unlike the *Part 8* procedure, the claimant's case is set out in a separate particulars of claim, which contains a detailed description of the claim and the facts on which the claimant relies.

(*b*) *Acknowledgment of service*

Having been served with the claim form and particulars of claim, the defendant has 14 days to file an acknowledgment of service in the prescribed form, indicating whether it admits the claim, admits part of the claim but contests another part, or contests the entire claim. If the defendant fails to acknowledge service within the prescribed time limit and no extension of time has been agreed, judgment in default may be entered in the claimant's favour.

(*c*) *Defence (and counterclaim if relevant)*

If the defendant contests all or part of the claim, unlike under the *Part 8* procedure, the defendant must prepare, file and serve a defence within 14 days after being served with the particulars of claim (if no acknowledgment of service has been filed) or 28 days after service of the particulars of claim (if an acknowledgment of service has been filed). If a defence is not filed within the prescribed time limit and no extension of time has been agreed, judgment in default may be entered in the claimant's favour. If the defendant wishes to make a counterclaim against the claimant, this should be served with the defence.

(*d*) *Reply (and defence to counterclaim if relevant)*

If the claimant wants to allege facts to answer those alleged in the defence, the claimant may serve a reply. If the defendant has served a counterclaim, the claimant must, at the same time as serving the reply, serve a defence to the counterclaim, failing which judgment in default may be entered in the defendant's favour on the counterclaim.

(*e*) *Case management directions*

The court will allocate the case to one of the three court tracks (see **15.19** above) and give case management directions. These typically involve the following (in chronological order):

(i) disclosure and inspection of documents (see **15.23** below);

(ii) exchange of witness statements (see **15.24** below); and

(iii) exchange of expert reports (if necessary), followed by meetings of the experts in order to narrow the issues in dispute (see **15.25** below).

(*f*) *Trial*

The trial of the claim takes place before a judge in open court, at which each party's advocate makes oral submissions, and the witnesses and experts give oral evidence and are cross-examined. At the conclusion of the trial the judge will hand down a written judgment (or reserve judgment as in a *Part 8* claim) and will make any appropriate costs orders.

Disclosure of documents

15.23 Disclosure in the context of court proceedings is the process by which each party discloses to the other parties to the claim relevant documents within that party's control and in respect of which privilege is not being claimed. The disclosure process aims to ensure that each party has sight of the material that is available to the other parties so that each party can prepare adequately before trial of the proceedings. Disclosure of documents is not always ordered under the *Part 8* procedure (see **15.21** above), whereas 'standard disclosure' is usually ordered under the *Part 7* procedure (see **15.22** above).

Standard disclosure requires a party to disclose those 'documents' on which it relies, as well as those which adversely affect its own case or another party's case or which support another party's case. The word 'documents' has a wide meaning and includes anything in which information of any description is recorded (for example, paper documents, computer files, film, video, photographs). It includes electronic documents, such as emails, databases, saved documents and other electronic communications, stored on a computer's hard drive or a server or a back-up system, or on other electronic devices and media. A party must conduct a reasonable search for, and disclose, documents within its control (ie where the party has or had a right to possess it, inspect it or take copies of it.) Disclosure usually takes the form of the parties exchanging a list of documents in a form prescribed in *CPR Part 31*. There are specific guidelines in relation to electronic documents (see *section 2A.1* of the *Practice Direction* to *CPR Part 31*).

A party is entitled to inspect and take copies of the documents disclosed by another party. However, a party giving disclosure may object to the inspection of certain documents on the grounds that they are legally privileged from inspection (an analysis of the various types of privilege that may be relied upon is outside the scope of the chapter). It should be noted that, as the duty to give disclosure continues to the end of the case, a party should take care when creating new documents in case they also need to be disclosed. A party who gives inadequate disclosure may be compelled by the court to give further disclosure. If a party fails to disclose a document, it may not rely on that document at the trial of the proceedings without the court's permission and, ultimately, if in breach of its obligations, a party may be held to be in contempt of court. (The rules of disclosure are set out in *CPR Part 31* and should be distinguished from trustees' obligations to disclose information to members under common law and under various pensions statutes and regulations, for which see **3.22** and **15.16** above and APPENDIX II.)

Witness statements and affidavits

15.24 A fact which needs to be proved by the evidence of a witness must, as a general rule, be proved at the trial of the case by the oral evidence of that witness under oath. At any other hearing (ie before the trial) the fact may be proved by the written evidence of the witness (ie in a witness statement or affidavit). A witness statement is a written statement of a witness's evidence. It is signed by the witness and contains a statement that he believes the facts in it are true (a 'statement of truth'). If a witness makes a false statement without an honest belief in its truth, proceedings for contempt of court may be brought. Witness statements have largely replaced affidavits (a written sworn statement), although there may be occasions where an affidavit is still required. There are strict rules governing the form and content of witness statements and affidavits (see *CPR Part 32* and the *Practice Direction* to it).

Expert evidence

15.25 Expert evidence is frequently required in pension disputes to assist the court. For example, an expert actuary may be required to give an opinion on the valuation of the assets and liabilities of the pension fund or certain benefits under a pension scheme. The court has wide powers to control the use of expert witnesses in litigation because they are usually expensive and lengthen the proceedings. Expert evidence is restricted to that which is reasonably required to resolve the proceedings and a party may only call an expert with the permission of the court. In certain circumstances, the court may direct that expert evidence on an issue is to be given by a single expert, jointly instructed by both parties. The expert's overriding duty is to the court and not to the instructing or paying party. An expert will usually give his evidence in the form of a written report, which the parties exchange. Often the court will direct the parties' experts, following the exchange of reports, to meet in order to identify the technical issues in the proceedings and, where possible, reach agreement on those issues. An expert may be called to give oral evidence and be cross-examined at the trial of the action. (See *CPR Part 35* and the *Practice Direction – Experts and Assessors* for the rules and guidelines on the use of experts. In applications for directions, it is often the case that, where a party needs some statistical analysis carried out in relation to the scheme, to save costs, the parties agree to instruct the scheme actuary to carry out this work as, in effect, an expert (although this may not be appropriate in all cases, in which case the parties will need their own independent actuary expert).)

Representation orders

15.26 It is a basic rule under the *CPR* that, where the party making a claim is seeking a remedy to which another person is jointly entitled, every other person who is so jointly entitled to that remedy must be joined as a party to the proceedings, unless the court orders otherwise (*CPR, r 19.3*). There is no limit to the number of parties who may be joined to a claim (*CPR, r 19.1*). This rule is designed to prevent a multiplicity of proceedings for similar claims and is of particular relevance to litigation involving pension schemes (for example, trustees' applications for directions). Whereas the number of trustees of a pension scheme will be small, the number of beneficiaries under the scheme, who may be entitled jointly to a remedy, can be large – often amounting to hundreds, thousands and even tens of thousands. However, for each member or beneficiary of a scheme to be a named party to the litigation in accordance with the basic principle described above would give rise to a procedural and logistical burden which would seriously impair the efficient resolution of the litigation. That said, trustees require certainty that any order made by the court will be binding on all beneficiaries. The practical solution, therefore, is to appoint a party to represent the interests of other similarly interested parties. That party is known as a 'representative party' and may be appointed under two alternative provisions of the *CPR*:

(*a*) If more than one party has the same interest in a claim, the claim may be commenced, or the court may order the claim to be continued, by or against one or more of those parties as representatives of the other parties. Any judgment or order made by the court in the proceedings will bind all the persons represented in the claim (but may only be enforceable by or against a person who is not a party to the proceedings with the consent of the court) (see *CPR, r 19.6*).

(*b*) In claims concerning the assets of a pension scheme or the meaning of a document, the court may appoint, prior to or after the claim has commenced, a party to represent persons who are (i) unborn, or (ii) cannot be found, or (iii) cannot be easily ascertained. It may also appoint a party to represent a class of persons who have the same interest in a claim and either one or more members of that class fall within (i), (ii) or (iii) above, or if the court considers that the appointment would further the overriding objective of dealing with the claim justly (see **15.20** above) (see *CPR, r 19.7*).

If a representative party has been appointed, the court must give its approval to any compromise of the proceedings, and will only do so where it considers that the compromise is for the benefit of all the represented persons. Any judgment or order made by the court will bind all represented persons unless the court orders otherwise, but can only be enforced by or against a person who is not a party to the claim with the court's consent.

Practical considerations

15.27 Given the frequently large membership of a pension scheme, representation orders provide a practical way for proceedings to be pursued in an efficient and timely manner, and provide certainty for the trustees that the judgment handed down will bind all affected beneficiaries. Where there is more than one distinct category of beneficiaries with a similar interest, it may be necessary to join more than one representative party. As each representative party will require legal representation, the court will usually seek to keep to a minimum the number of representative parties to minimise the costs as much as possible, particularly where the costs are being borne by the pension fund.

Trustees should therefore give proper consideration, at an early stage, as to who should be an appropriate representative party. A proposed representative party should not have a conflict of interest and should have sufficient mental capacity and availability to provide proper instructions to his legal representatives throughout the expected length of the proceedings. If the trustees in *Part 8* proceedings are undecided as to who or how many representative parties should be appointed or cannot find a willing volunteer, they may issue the claim form without naming the defendant(s) and seek the court's directions – (see also (iii) in **15.21** above).

An additional factor is the question whether a person whose interests are represented in proceedings by a representative party may challenge the representation order or challenge a settlement approved by the court on the grounds that it is a breach of that person's right to a fair trial under *Article 6* of the *European Convention on Human Rights*. Published commentary has suggested that there are no grounds in *Article 6* for a challenge to the provisions of the *CPR* on representation orders (Lester & Pannick, *Human Rights Law and Practice*, 2nd ed (2004)), and the courts have now given guidance.

Article 6 is likely to be of more relevance where a settlement is approved by the court and is binding on a person represented in the proceedings by a representative party, without that person having had a chance to state his own case. When applying for the court's approval of a settlement, it is common practice for each representative party to obtain a written legal opinion on the merits of the compromise, the purpose of which opinion is to assist the judge in his consideration of whether the settlement is for the benefit of all the persons represented.

To further reduce the risk of a successful challenge, trustees should consider giving proper notice of the proceedings to all the persons represented (in so far as they can be ascertained) before the compromise is put to the court for approval. Such notice should set out the terms of the proposed compromise, a beneficiary's right to object to the compromise and his right to be joined in as a separate party to the proceedings.

This approach was deemed 'desirable' by the court in *Re Owens Corning Fibreglass (UK) Pensions Plan Ltd [2002] All ER (D) 191*. In that case, the court indicated that it would, but for other factors, have adjourned the application to allow the beneficiaries to be informed. In *Smithson v Hamilton [2008] EWCA Civ 996*, the court was inclined to agree with commentary that there were no grounds for challenge under *Article 6*. However, this was not the basis of the court's decision. Instead, taking a pragmatic view as to what was likely to prevent further dispute on the part of represented pension scheme members, the court took a step similar to that contemplated in *Owens Corning* and delayed the effective date of the order while members were informed of the proposed compromise.

If a person objects to being represented in an action, a practical solution may be for that person to be joined as a party in his own right (although that person will run the risk that he will have to bear his own legal costs in the event that the court does not permit his costs to be paid from the pension fund). In the recent case of *Re PD Teesport Limited [2009] EWHC 1693 (Ch)* (an interim application in the Pilots National Pension Fund litigation), the trustee had put in place a proposed scheme of representative parties and, for case management reasons, argued that additional parties who were already represented should not be joined in their own right. The applicant sought joinder on several grounds, including *Article 6* rights. The court, while granting joinder on other grounds, held that 'there is no breach of *Article 6* merely because a person has no direct access to the Court but only access through a representative, even where that representative is not of his own choosing'.

Trustees representing beneficiaries' interests

15.28 Where proceedings are brought by or against trustees without joining any of the beneficiaries of the pension scheme, any judgment or order made in those proceedings will bind the beneficiaries, unless the court orders otherwise. The court may order otherwise if it considers that the trustees could not or did not in fact represent the interests of those persons in the proceedings (see *CPR, r 19.7A*). Trustees should therefore consider carefully whether they can and are properly representing the beneficiaries' interests in such proceedings, because if they cannot or are not, it may be necessary to appoint an additional representative party.

Group litigation

15.29 Where there are a number of individual claims by separate persons which all give rise to common or related issues of fact or law (for example, claims by individual members of a pension scheme against the trustees for a breach of trust that has caused each of them loss and which has arisen out of the same facts), the court may order each of the cases to be managed together under a group litigation order. This should be distinguished from a representation order, where each person represented has the same interest in the outcome of a claim. A group litigation order is a useful and efficient mechanism in circumstances where each of the claims is individually small, but collectively large. In principle, it allows for an efficient and cost-effective method of determining the claims. (The detailed provisions relating to group litigation orders can be found in *CPR, r 19.11* and the related *Practice Direction*.)

Costs in litigation

15.30 The issue of costs is central to the assessment of whether or not to pursue or defend a claim, what strategy to adopt, in which forum the matter should be pursued, settlement considerations, and whether alternative dispute resolution methods should be explored. It is also an important factor that the court considers when it exercises its case management powers.

General principles

15.31 The court has a broad discretion to award costs (*Senior Courts Act 1981, s 51*). In deciding what costs order (if any) to make, the court will take into account all the circumstances, including the conduct of the parties before and during the litigation, whether a party was only partly successful and any offers of settlement (*CPR, r 44.3*). The court may penalise a party by denying it costs where it does not approve of that party's conduct or where the party has recovered a lesser amount than a previous offer of settlement which it rejected. Where the court orders a party to pay another party's costs, the amount of those costs will be assessed by the court, unless it can be agreed between the parties. The court may assess those costs summarily at the hearing itself, or conduct a separate detailed assessment of those costs after the hearing. In small claims track cases the court will only award limited costs and will assess those costs at the hearing. In fast-track cases the trial costs of the advocate that are awarded are also limited. In multi-track cases, there is no prescribed limit on the costs that can be recovered and the amount of those costs will be assessed by the court.

When ordering a party's costs to be assessed, the court will state the basis on which those costs will be assessed. There are two bases:

(*a*) *Standard basis*: This is the usual basis ordered. On this basis the court will only allow costs which are proportionate to the matters in issue and will resolve any doubt which it may have over a specific cost incurred in favour of the paying party.

(*b*) *Indemnity basis*: The court will resolve any doubt it may have over a specific cost incurred in the favour of the receiving party.

The receiving party can expect to recover more of its costs under the indemnity, rather than standard, basis. However, it is important for parties to appreciate that on neither basis is the receiving party ever likely to recover 100 per cent of its costs. Indeed, under the standard basis, the receiving party may recover as little as 60 per cent of its costs (or even less). This should be borne in mind at the outset of litigation and when considering offers of settlement.

The general rule followed by the court is that the winner's assessed costs are paid by the loser. In pensions cases involving third parties (see **15.14** above), this rule will usually apply. However, there are special rules that apply to trustees' costs and the costs of applications for directions brought in relation to the administration of a pension scheme. These are discussed below, in **15.32** onwards.

Solicitors are obliged to discuss with clients involved in litigation the possibility of purchasing an 'after-the-event' insurance policy to cover the potential liability to pay costs (his own and/or the other party's) in the event of an unsuccessful outcome. Such policies are yet to make a significant impact in the arena of pensions litigation, but are likely to be of most relevance in the future to claims against or by third parties.

Trustees' costs

15.32 Where a trustee is a party to proceedings in his capacity as trustee, as a general rule he is likely to be entitled to an indemnity out of the trust fund for his legal costs (which may include costs that the trustee is ordered to pay to another party) to the extent that they are not recovered from or paid by another person (*CPR, r 48.4*) and provided they are properly incurred. In such cases, those costs will be assessed on the indemnity basis. The court may order otherwise if it considers that the trustee has, in all the circumstances, acted improperly (see *section 50A* of the *Practice Direction* to *CPR, r 48.4*). By way of example, in *Mark Niebhur Todd v Judith Cobb Lady Barton & Others [2002] 2 WTLR 469*, the court disallowed a proportion of a trustee's costs which related to an application made by him which the court considered to be unnecessary.

Indemnity and power in trust deed

15.33 A pension scheme's trust deed may contain an indemnity clause which indemnifies the trustees against any costs and liabilities incurred in taking certain action for the benefit of the pension scheme. It may also give the trustees a power to agree to pay from the pension fund the costs of certain other parties to litigation. In the event that the trustees have, and exercise, such a power by agreeing to pay the costs of another party to the litigation (for example, in an application to court for directions), it is prudent for the trustees to enter into a formal agreement with that party stipulating what costs may be payable under that agreement and a mechanism for the trustees to control the level of costs incurred. The trustees' prior approval to large items of proposed expenditure (for example, expert witness fees, counsel's fees) should also prudently be sought by that party.

In applications to court concerning the administration of a pension scheme, if the trustees have and exercise properly a power to agree to pay the costs of another party to that application, the court will presume, when assessing the amounts of costs payable under that agreement, that (unless the agreement states otherwise) the costs have been reasonably incurred and are reasonable in amount (see *CPR, r 48.3*). In such a case, a prospective costs order (see **15.36** below) is not required and the trustees are entitled to recover out of the pension fund any costs of another party which they pay pursuant to such agreement (*para 6.2* of *Practice Direction A to CPR Part 64*).

Beddoe orders

15.34 The proviso to the general rule entitling a trustee to an indemnity out of the trust fund for its costs (see **15.32** above) is that the costs must have been 'properly incurred'. If they are improperly incurred, a trustee may incur personal liability for those costs. To determine what costs are properly incurred, the court will examine all the circumstances of the case including whether the trustee obtained the court's directions before bringing or defending proceedings, acted in the interests of the scheme or some other interest or conducted himself unreasonably. If trustees propose to commence or defend proceedings against or by a third party, they are able to protect themselves from this risk of personal liability by applying at an early stage for the court's directions on their proposed course of action (this is known as a '*Beddoe*' application, following the Court of Appeal judgment in *Re Beddoe, Downes v Cottam [1893] 1 Ch 547*). If the court sanctions the proposed action, the trustees can proceed in the comfort that the court regards their action as being proper and reasonable.

A *Beddoe* application is treated as a directions application under *CPR Part 64* (see **15.13** above). The application must be made in separate proceedings under the *Part 8* procedure (see **15.21** above). The trustees should be the claimant and the beneficiaries of the pension scheme the defendants. In the event that a beneficiary is a party to both the main proceedings and the *Beddoe* application and has an interest which conflicts with that of the trustees, the trustees should exercise care not to disclose to that beneficiary privileged information (for example, the legal advice of the trustees' lawyer), and that beneficiary may be excluded from all or part of any hearing of that *Beddoe* application.

In a *Beddoe* application, the court is asked to express its view on whether the action proposed by the trustees is proper. To enable the court to express a considered view, the trustees' application should be supported by evidence (in the form of witness statements) giving full disclosure of, among other things, the proposed course of action and the strengths and weaknesses of the trustees' case. This means that the trustees must include in their evidence the advice of an appropriately qualified lawyer on the prospects of success, and other relevant matters to be taken into account, including a costs estimate for the proceedings, any known facts concerning the means of the opposing party to the proceedings, and a draft of any proposed statement of case (see *Practice Direction B to CPR Part 64* for a fuller description of what matters should be included in the evidence and for guidelines on trustee consultation with beneficiaries). If the trustees fail to reveal in full to the court the strengths and weaknesses of their case, they may expose themselves to personal liability, even if the court grants the *Beddoe* order sought.

Depending on the nature of the case, the *Beddoe* application will either be dealt with on paper, without the need for a hearing, or will be referred to a judge in which case a hearing will usually be necessary. If the court allows the trustees to pursue the litigation proposed, it may do so only up to a particular stage in the litigation, thereby requiring the trustees to make a further *Beddoe* application in order to proceed beyond that stage.

However, whilst the above process may afford trustees protection from personal liability for the costs they will incur, the court has become increasingly critical about the tendency of trustees to seek, at considerable cost to the pension scheme, *Beddoe* consent for steps which are clearly in the interests of the pension scheme. This concern is reflected in the court's *Practice Direction* which states as follows:

> 'There are cases in which it is likely to be so clear that the trustees ought to proceed as they wish that the costs of making the application, even on a simplified procedure without a hearing and perhaps without defendants, are not justified in comparison with the size of the fund or the matters at issue.'
>
> (*paragraph 7.2* of *Practice Direction B* to *CPR Part 64*)

Trustees should therefore consider carefully, with their legal advisers, the appropriateness of incurring the expense of making a *Beddoe* application. Equally, trustees should have regard to the uncertainties of litigation, even in the most apparently clear cut of cases, and the risk that if *Beddoe* consent is not sought prior to taking a step, the trustees may be held personally liable for their costs (unless they can prove to the satisfaction of the court that they were properly incurred). An assessment of the risk of proceeding without *Beddoe* protection must, therefore, be made by trustees with their legal advisers at the outset. One alternative to incurring the costs of a *Beddoe* application may be for the trustees to seek an indemnity from the employer, particularly if the employer is ultimately liable under the pension scheme's trust deed to make up any shortfall in the assets of the fund.

Beneficiaries' costs

15.35 The indemnity enjoyed by trustees (which is discussed in **15.32** above) is not shared by beneficiaries who are parties to proceedings. However, the court has traditionally sought to divide trust litigation into three categories when considering which party should pay the costs of those proceedings (following the decision in *Re Buckton, Buckton v Buckton [1907] 2 Ch 406*):

(*a*) Proceedings brought by trustees for the court's guidance on the construction of the trust deed or a question arising in the course of the trust's administration. In such cases, the costs of all parties are usually treated as 'necessarily incurred for the benefit of the fund' and ordered to be paid out of the fund on an indemnity basis (such an application is usually brought under *CPR Part 64*).

(*b*) Applications which are brought by someone other than the trustees, but which raise the types of issues as in (*a*) above and would have justified an application by the trustees. In this case, the costs are also usually treated as being 'necessarily incurred for the benefit of the fund' and ordered to be paid out of the fund on an indemnity basis (whilst such an application may be made under *CPR Part 64*, the *Practice Direction B to CPR Part 64* only relates to applications made by trustees, and not other parties).

(*c*) Proceedings in which a beneficiary is making a hostile claim against trustees or another beneficiary. The costs of such proceedings are usually treated in the same way as ordinary litigation and the winner's costs are usually paid by the loser, unless the winner has, in some way, conducted himself inappropriately in connection with the litigation or is only a partial winner or has failed to win more than a previous offer of settlement from the loser.

These are known as *Buckton* categories 1, 2 and 3 and the court still deems these general guidelines applicable, albeit that it now takes a more robust attitude towards costs (*D'Abo v Paget (No 2) [2000] WTLR 863*). There is a costs risk to both the trustees and the beneficiaries in the third category of claims, which is a principal reason why trustees generally seek *Beddoe* consent before pursuing or defending such proceedings, and why beneficiaries prefer to avoid such costs risk and pursue their complaints through the PO. It is often difficult, in practice, to assess whether a particular claim is a category 2 or 3 type claim, but given the costs consequences, it is important to reach a conclusion before embarking upon the litigation.

Prospective costs orders

15.36 Whilst the principles in *Buckton* provide a useful guide to what the likely costs order will be at the conclusion of the proceedings, a party may require greater comfort at the outset of the proceedings that its costs will be paid out of the fund no matter what the outcome of the proceedings. For example, a representative beneficiary may not wish to become a party in the proceedings if there is a risk that he will incur a personal liability for his, and other parties', costs of the proceedings. In applications to the court concerning the administration of a trust (ie under *CPR Part 64* – see **15.13** above), if the trustees do not have, or decide not to exercise, a power to agree to pay the costs of another party to the application, the trustees or the party concerned may apply to the court for an order that the costs of any party (including the trustees) shall be paid out of the assets of the pension scheme. These are known as 'prospective costs orders' (formerly as 'pre-emptive costs orders') and provide the applicant with the comfort that his costs of the proceedings will be paid, no matter what the outcome of the proceedings.

In *Buckton* category 1 and 2 cases (see **15.35** above) at the conclusion of the case the court will usually follow the general rule that the parties' costs (including those of any beneficiary) are paid out of the assets of the pension scheme.

This makes the grant of a prospective costs order at an earlier stage in the case less problematic. A difficulty arises, however, in *Buckton* category 3 cases (hostile claims against the trustees). This is because in *Buckton* category 3 cases, the general rule is that the loser pays the winner's costs. This makes it difficult to make an assessment at any time prior to the full trial as to the likely outcome and therefore the likely costs order the court would make. In the leading case of *MacDonald v Horn [1995] 1 All ER 961* the court overcame this difficulty by deciding that an action by a member of a pension scheme to compel the trustees or others to account to the fund was analogous to what is known as a 'derivative action' by a minority shareholder on behalf of a company. In those circumstances a minority shareholder was entitled to a prospective costs order under the principle in *Wallersteiner v Moir (No 2) [1975] 1 All ER 849*. On this basis, the court held that a member of a pension scheme could also be entitled, by analogy, to a prospective costs order in those circumstances. When deciding whether to exercise its discretion to make such an order, the court has in each case a duty, under the *CPR*, to give effect to the overriding objective of dealing with cases justly. This includes ensuring, so far as possible, that the parties are on an equal footing and dealing with the case in a way which is proportionate to the financial position of each party. Such factors are particularly relevant in the pensions context, as the beneficiary who is a party to the case can often be a pensioner with limited financial resources.

Further guidance was given by the court in *Laws v National Grid [1998] PLR 295* where it considered that a prospective costs order should be made where the amount of money in issue is large, the matter in issue affects a large number of persons, the case involves difficult issues of law or fact, and the person applying for the order has substantial support from others in a similar position. In the subsequent case of *Chessels & ors v BT plc & ors [2002] PLR 141*, the court refused to grant a prospective costs order to a beneficiary to whom it had granted permission to appeal the court's judgment. The court followed the principle that prospective costs orders indemnifying a third party should only be made where the court is satisfied that no other orders can properly be made by the court which is to hear the substantive proceedings. The appeal in this case would, if successful, only benefit a relatively small number of beneficiaries of the scheme, was not for the benefit of the scheme as a whole, and was hostile litigation of the *Buckton* category 3 type in which the court usually awards the winner his costs. The court also reiterated the principle that the fact that the pension scheme had substantial assets, and was in surplus, was not relevant to whether or not it should grant the prospective costs order.

Applications for prospective costs orders can be made at any time during the proceedings but are usually made at the outset, or before a hearing. In the witness statement supporting the application the trustees and the applicant (if different) must give full disclosure of the relevant matters which show that the case is one which falls within the category of cases where a prospective costs order can properly be made. Ordinarily, the court will seek to deal with such an application on paper, without the need for an oral hearing, but if the trustees or any other party think a hearing should be held, they should set out their reasons in the evidence that they file at court. A model form of prospective costs order for straightforward cases is set out in the court's *Practice Direction A* to *CPR Part 64*. It allows for a party's solicitor to request from the trustees monthly sums on account and for that party's costs to be subject to a detailed assessment by the court on the indemnity basis, unless agreed. It also indemnifies the party against any costs that it is ordered to pay to another party to the proceedings. When granting a prospective costs order the court may set a limit on the costs to be paid (as in *Re AXA Equity & Law Life Assurance Society plc (No 1) [2001] 2 BCLC 447*).

Alternative dispute resolution

Introduction

15.37 Alternative dispute resolution ('ADR') is the generic phrase used to describe alternative means of resolving a dispute other than by a trial in court. The use of ADR has developed rapidly in recent years and its importance is actively promoted by the courts. Under the *CPR*, the court is obliged when using its active case management powers to encourage parties to use an ADR procedure if it considers it appropriate and to facilitate the use of such procedure (*CPR, r 1.4(2)(e)*). Further, when trustees apply for *Beddoe* approval concerning actual or possible litigation, they are required to state, in the witness statement they prepare in support of their application, whether they have proposed or undertaken, or intend to propose, mediation by ADR, and if not why not (*para 7.5* of *Practice Direction B to CPR Part 64*).

In the case of *Halsey v Milton Keynes General NHS Trust [2004] EWCA Civ 576, [2004] All ER (D) 125*, the Court of Appeal provided some guidelines on the court's approach to ADR (mediation in particular) and to penalising parties who fail to agree to pursue ADR. In summary:

(*a*) Although the court may encourage parties to seek to resolve a dispute through ADR in the strongest terms, it would not order parties to undertake ADR against their will.

(*b*) As an exception to the general rule that the loser would be ordered to pay the winner's costs, the court may penalise a party, by making an alternative costs order, if that party has acted unreasonably in refusing to agree to ADR.

(*c*) The burden is on the loser to show why the winner acted unreasonably.

(*d*) In deciding whether a party had acted unreasonably in refusing to agree to ADR, the court will consider the following, non-exhaustive factors:

- Is the nature of the dispute suitable for ADR? Not every dispute is suitable for ADR, for example, a directions application concerning the construction of the pensions deed may be unsuitable for settlement.
- What are the merits of the case? A party, who reasonably believes that he has a strong case, may reasonably not wish to compromise his position through ADR.
- Have any other settlement methods been attempted before? A history of unsuccessful attempts at resolving the dispute may justify a decision not to agree to ADR.
- What are the likely costs of ADR? If the costs of ADR are likely to be disproportionately high, this may justify a party not agreeing to it.
- Will ADR cause unreasonable delay? Pursuing ADR will require the commencement or continuation of proceedings to be stayed which may cause unreasonable delay to the resolution of the dispute.
- Will ADR have a reasonable prospect of success? The more remote the prospect of ADR resulting in a settlement, the more reasonable a court is likely to regard a refusal by one party to agree to ADR.

(*e*) All members of the legal profession should routinely consider with their clients whether their client's disputes are suitable for ADR.

These principles have been applied by the court in subsequent cases. For example, in *P4 Ltd v Unite Integrated Solutions plc [2006] EWHC 2924 (TCC)*, the court made a costs order in favour of a party which made only a nominal recovery, in part because of its opponent's unreasonable failure to mediate. By contrast, in *Daniels v Commissioner of Police for the Metropolis [2005] EWCA Civ 1312*, the Court of Appeal applied the *Halsey* decision and decided that where a defendant, particularly a public body, regularly faced unmeritorious claims which it chose to contest rather than settle, the court would be slow to view such conduct as being unreasonable. In *Re Midland Linen Services Ltd sub nom Chaudry v Yap & Ors [2004] EWHC 3380 (Ch)*, even though a party had offered mediation which was refused by the other party, the court viewed the refusal to mediate as not being unreasonable because it was questionable whether the party offering the mediation was sufficiently serious in pursuing it and, given the relationship between the parties, whether a mediation would have resulted in a resolution. These cases demonstrate that the court will consider the facts of each case in deciding whether there has been unreasonable conduct. The factors to be taken into account were recently considered further in *Corby Group Litigation v Corby DC [2009] EWHC 2109 (TCC)*.

Types of ADR

15.38 There are different forms of ADR, but the principal ones are as follows:

(*a*) *Mediation.* This is the most common form of ADR. It is a private, without prejudice process of negotiation between the parties, facilitated by an independent qualified mediator. It is non-binding so that a settlement can only be achieved if the parties agree. It is discussed in more detail below.

(*b*) *Conciliation.* This is a more formal form of mediation, and often involves the use of a formal conciliation service (such as ACAS). The 'conciliator' will often take an active role (ie proffering his views) in the negotiations.

(*c*) *Expert determination.* This is where the parties agree to refer a (usually) technical issue in dispute for a binding determination by an independent expert. For instance, a pension scheme's trust deed or rules may provide for an actuarial issue to be determined by an independent actuary, or the pensions schedule in a sale and purchase agreement may provide for expert determination in the case of disputes.

(*d*) *Adjudication.* Like an expert determination, this usually involves the parties agreeing to submit the dispute for determination by a neutral third party (for example, a retired judge or experienced lawyer).

(*e*) *Arbitration.* The process of arbitration takes place in a statutory framework which sets out various rules of conduct. It is common for commercial contracts to contain 'arbitration clauses' which require all disputes to be referred to arbitration. The arbitrator is usually a suitably qualified independent third party who determines the dispute, acting as a judge. The procedure can closely mirror that of court litigation. It is designed to be flexible and less procedural than court litigation. However, it is often regarded as being as time consuming and expensive as court proceedings.

Mediation

15.39 Mediation is the most common form of ADR adopted to settle disputes. Once the parties to a dispute have agreed to mediation, the next step is to appoint a mediator. The Centre for Early Dispute Resolution ('CEDR') and ADR Group are two of the most well known bodies that can assist parties in finding and appointing an appropriate mediator and setting up the mediation. They have lists of accredited and suitably experienced mediators. CEDR offers a dedicated Pensions Mediation Service in conjunction with the National Association of Pension Funds ('NAPF'). The Association of Pensions Lawyers also maintains a list of mediators with pensions experience (see its website: www.apl.org.uk).

The costs of the mediator(s) (there can be more than one if the parties wish) are usually borne equally by the parties. The costs of a mediation can be substantial as they may include the costs of the mediator, room hire and the costs of the parties' lawyers in preparing for and attending at the mediation. Before the mediation takes place, it is common for each party to exchange brief summaries of their case, if necessary accompanied by supporting documents. The mediation is usually attended by a senior person from each party who has the authority to negotiate and enter into a settlement agreement. The mediation often commences by each party giving an oral summary of its case to the other party in front of the mediator. The mediator may ask questions to clarify a point. Each party then retires to its own private room, and the mediator will visit each party in turn to discuss the structure of a possible settlement and the issues which each party should consider as part of the negotiations. Through this process of 'shuttle diplomacy' the mediator can gauge what possible terms of settlement may be agreeable to the parties and make appropriate suggestions to the parties to facilitate a settlement. As the process is without prejudice and non-binding, a settlement will only be achieved if both parties agree to it.

Practical considerations

15.40 Pension disputes between trustees and third parties are usually hostile, and in such cases, ADR may provide an efficient means of resolving the dispute, thereby avoiding the costs and risk of litigation. As stated above, trustees who seek a *Beddoe* order are required to tell the court whether a mediation has been or will be proposed. This means that trustees must factor into their consideration from the outset the potential for a mediation (or other appropriate form of ADR) as the court is likely to be interested. Further, trustees who have the benefit of a *Beddoe* order (see **15.34** above), may wish or need to seek the court's approval of any settlement (although trustees have a power under *Trustee Act 1925, s 15* to enter into a settlement), in which case this should be made clear to the other parties and may affect the choice of ADR method.

Claims against trustees by individual members may also be amenable to ADR, even if those disputes have been referred to the PO rather than the court.

Directions applications (see **15.13** above) are not always suitable for resolution by ADR. Some applications, by their nature, are not suitable to ADR (for example, where the trustees are requesting the court's approval of a proposed transaction or are surrendering their discretion to the court). Where ADR is possible, there are a number of practical issues which will require consideration, including the following:

(*a*) Trustees will usually want to avoid negotiating with all the beneficiaries under the pension scheme, not only for logistical reasons but also the difficulty of reaching agreement with all of them. To facilitate negotiations trustees may, therefore, seek the appointment of a representative party with whom they may negotiate. This necessitates the commencement of proceedings prior to ADR being commenced.

(*b*) Where a settlement is agreed, the trustees may seek the court's approval to that settlement (for example, if a *Beddoe* order has been granted or is sought, or where a representative party has been appointed). In any such application to the court, it is common practice for the trustees and/or the representative party to obtain and present to the court a legal opinion on whether the proposed settlement is in the interests of the members of the pension scheme (see **15.27** above). This means that the court will not examine the proposed settlement on a purely commercial basis, but will also consider to what extent the proposed terms reflect the legal merits of the members' case(s). Further, to produce a reasoned opinion, documents may have to be disclosed and exchanged, if disclosure has not already taken place.

Whilst such factors may provide practical hurdles to be overcome in order for ADR to lead to a successful resolution of the dispute, the advantages of ADR (notably, the potential for a relatively quick, private and less costly settlement of the dispute at an early stage) may justify its use as a means of resolving the dispute. Indeed, parties' solicitors are now expected by the court to consider, in every dispute, the appropriateness of ADR. In all cases, careful consideration should be given as to which form of ADR is most appropriate. If a party is considering rejecting an offer of ADR, it should first consider the guidelines given by the court in *Halsey*. This may assist in an assessment of whether the rejection is likely to be considered unreasonable, as a refusal to agree to ADR could potentially expose that party to costs sanctions by the court.

Chapter 16

Taxation of registered schemes

Section A

Introduction

16.1 The previous eight pension taxation regimes were replaced by a single integrated pension tax regime from 6 April 2006 ('A-Day'). The regime applies to all 'registered pension schemes' (the equivalent of pre A-Day tax approved pension schemes). The new provisions are contained in *FA 2004* (as amended by subsequent Finance Acts) and follow the proposals outlined in the joint Treasury and Inland Revenue consultation paper, 'Simplifying the taxation of pensions; increasing choice and flexibility for all', published December 2002. The concept is simple. Tax relievable contributions can be made to build up benefits in a tax approved environment up to a lifetime allowance. There is nothing to stop tax relievable contributions being made to enable an individual to build up benefits with a value in excess of the lifetime allowance but, if the lifetime allowance is exceeded, there is an additional tax charge (the lifetime allowance charge) on any excess when the benefits come into payment. The restrictions that existed until A-Day on the form in which benefits can be taken in different types of pension schemes have been simplified. All types of registered pension schemes are able to pay members any type of payment which is treated as an authorised member payment under *FA 2004*. If an unauthorised member payment is made by a registered pension scheme, there can be penal tax charges. Details of how HMRC operates the regime in practice can be found in the Registered Pension Schemes Manual ('RPSM'), available at www.hmrc.gov.uk.

This chapter is intended to give an outline of the tax treatment of registered pension schemes, including both occupational and personal pension schemes. It will then consider the continued relevance of pre A-Day Revenue limits after A-Day to pension schemes as a result of the *Registered Pension Schemes (Modification of the Rules of Existing Schemes) Regulations 2006 (SI 2006/364)* (the '*Modification Regulations*'). Unless steps are taken to disapply the *Modification Regulations*, pension schemes will not be able to pay out benefits in excess of pre A-Day Revenue limits for a period of five years (or possibly longer) after A-Day. For the reasons discussed in this chapter, many occupational pension schemes may choose not to disapply all or some of the existing pre A-Day Revenue limits, or will write similar requirements into their rules as scheme limits. Pre A-Day Revenue limits may, therefore, still be applicable after A-Day. Under the *Modification Regulations* the scheme administrator also has discretion not to make any payment which could have been paid by a tax approved scheme before A-Day but which counts as an unauthorised payment on and after A-Day.

The tax treatment of unapproved pension schemes established before A-Day and non-registered pension schemes established on and after A-Day is considered from **16.120** below.

Treatment of existing tax approved schemes

16.2 Pension schemes which were already tax approved before A-Day automatically became registered schemes from A-Day unless they took action to opt out (*FA 2004, Sch 36, paras 1, 2*). This included:

(*a*) Private sector defined benefits and defined contributions retirement benefit schemes that were previously approved on a discretionary basis under *Income* and *Corporation Taxes Act 1988, Part XIV, Chapter I* (‘*ICTA 1988*’) – including free-standing AVC schemes.

(*b*) Relevant statutory schemes (more commonly known as public sector schemes) defined in *ICTA 1988, s 611A*, such as the Local Government Pension Scheme.

(*c*) Certain deferred annuity contracts used to secure pension benefits under (*a*) and (*b*) that do not provide for the immediate payment of benefits. These deferred annuity contracts were not previously approved before A-Day (note this category does not cover most annuities used to secure benefits under an occupational pension scheme which come into payment immediately, for example, on a scheme wind up).

(*d*) A retirement annuity contract or retirement annuity trust scheme previously approved under *ICTA 1988, s 620* or *621* or a substituted contract within the meaning of *ICTA 1988, s 622(3)*. These were the only type of policy that could be taken out by the self-employed and individuals without access to an occupational pension scheme before personal pension schemes were introduced with effect from 1 July 1988.

(*e*) Personal pension schemes previously approved under *ICTA 1988, Part XIV, Chapter IV*, which includes most stakeholder pension schemes and ‘group personal pension schemes’.

(*f*) Former approved schemes (often referred to as 'old code schemes'). These schemes were schemes approved before 1970 but have not been re-approved as new code occupational pension schemes.

There are transitional provisions in *FA 2004, Sch 36, para 4*, which will determine who will be the scheme administrator where a pre-existing approved scheme was treated as becoming a registered pension scheme on A-Day. In the case of:

(i) retirement benefit schemes referred to in (*a*) above, relevant statutory schemes referred to in (*b*) above and a former approved superannuation fund referred to in (*f*) above, the person who was administrator of the scheme immediately before A-Day became the administrator on A-Day. In the case of a retirement benefits scheme under (*a*) this will generally be the trustees;

(ii) deferred annuity contracts under (*c*) or retirement annuity contracts under (*d*) above, the trustees of the pension scheme or the insurance company that is party to the contract in which the pension scheme is comprised became the scheme administrator at A Day;

(iii) personal pension schemes referred to in (*e*) above, the person who is referred to in *ICTA 1988, s 638(1)* immediately before A-Day (being a person resident in the United Kingdom who was responsible for the management of the scheme) will become the scheme administrator.

The responsibilities of the scheme administrator are discussed later in this chapter.

Application to become a registered pension scheme on or after A-Day

16.3 Any new pension scheme established on or after A-Day is required to make an application to HMRC to be registered (*FA 2004, s 153*). The application is made by the person who will become the scheme administrator.

An application to register must contain any information reasonably required by HMRC and must be accompanied by the required declaration by the scheme administrator (see below) and any other declarations reasonably required by HMRC (*FA 2004, ss 153(2), 270*).

At the date of writing, the declarations required are that:

(*a*) the scheme meets all the conditions to be a registered pension scheme;

(*b*) information supplied in the application is correct and complete to the best of the scheme administrator's knowledge and belief;

(*c*) the scheme administrator understands that false statements may lead to a penalty and/or prosecution and may lead to the scheme being de-registered; and

(*d*) the instruments or agreements by which the scheme is constituted do not entitle any person to unauthorised payments (see **16.24** below) (RPSM02101010).

Registration is made online by the completion of a form by the person agreeing to be the scheme administrator.

An application to register a pension scheme may be made only if the pension scheme is an occupational pension scheme or has been established by a person with permission under *FSMA 2000* to establish a personal pension scheme or stakeholder scheme.

There is no longer a requirement in the tax legislation that the only type of occupational pension scheme that can be registered as a registered pension scheme must be set up under irrevocable trusts. However, this has been replaced by an equivalent requirement in *PA 2004* that if an occupational pension scheme has its main administration in the UK, the trustees or managers of the scheme cannot accept any payment to fund benefits for or in respect of its members unless the scheme is established under irrevocable trusts (*PA 2004, s 252*). The trustees or managers can be liable to penalties if they accept a funding payment to an occupational pension scheme in breach of this requirement.

An occupational pension scheme that does not restrict membership to its own employees can be a registered pension scheme and can include employees of other non-associated employers. Before A-Day the general rule was that a non-sectionalised occupational pension scheme (ie not a multi-employer scheme for non associated employers) had to restrict membership to employees of associated employers to obtain and retain exempt approved status. If the rules of an occupational pension scheme for associated employers were to be changed after A-Day to allow employees of non-associated employers to join, consideration would need to be given as to whether this is consistent with the main purpose of the scheme which will often be to provide pension benefits for employees working in the undertaking of the sponsoring employer establishing the scheme and associated employers. However, cases do suggest that the main purpose of a trust can change over time.

The scheme administrator of a pension scheme that is registered on or after A-Day is the person who is, or persons who are, appointed in accordance with the rules of the pension scheme to be responsible for the discharge of the functions conferred or imposed on the scheme administrator of the pension scheme under *FA 2004, Part 4* (*FA 2004, s 270*). A person or persons can only become the scheme administrator if the person or one of the persons is resident in the UK or another State which is an EEA Member State, or a non-EEA Member State and has made the required declaration to HMRC. The required declaration is a declaration that the person:

(*a*) understands that the person will be responsible for discharging the functions conferred or imposed on the scheme administrator of the pension scheme under *FA 2004, Part 4*; and

(*b*) intends to discharge those functions at all times, whether resident in the UK or another State that is an EEA Member State or a non-EEA Member State.

Responsibilities of the administrator

16.4 The administrator is responsible for the discharge of certain functions under *FA 2004* (see **16.81** to **16.92** below on scheme administration) and is liable to pay certain tax charges (*FA 2004, ss 270–274*). In certain circumstances, the trustees of the registered pension scheme or, failing that, certain other persons who fall next down a statutory priority order set out in *FA 2004, s 272* (including the sponsoring employer of an occupational pension scheme) can be liable as scheme administrator if:

(*a*) there is no scheme administrator; or

(*b*) the person who is the scheme administrator cannot be traced; or

(*c*) the person who is the scheme administrator is in serious default.

There are further default provisions under *FA 2004, s 273* which can make members of the pension scheme liable as scheme administrator in certain circumstances to pay the tax that was due under *s 239* (scheme sanction charge) or *s 242* (de-registration charge) where the tax has not been paid.

Finding your way round FA 2004

16.5 Finding the relevant provision in *FA 2004* can sometimes be difficult. *FA 2004* was amended before it came into force by *FA 2005* and has been amended again by successive Finance Acts up to and including *FA 2009*).

The main provisions relating to pensions in *FA 2004, Part 4* are as follows:

(*a*) *Chapter 1* (Introduction) – defines some key concepts used in *FA 2004*, some of which are discussed below (*ss 149–152*);

(*b*) *Chapter 2* (Registration of Pension Schemes) – is about the registration and deregistration of pension schemes (*ss 153–159*);

(*c*) *Chapter 3* (Payments by Registered Schemes) – is about the payments that may be made by registered pension schemes and related matters (*ss 160–185*);

(*d*) *Chapter 4* (Registered Payments: Tax Reliefs and Exemptions) – deals with tax reliefs and exemptions in connection with registered pension schemes (*ss 186–203*);

(*e*) *Chapter 5* (Registered Pension Schemes: Tax Charges) – imposes tax charges in connection with registered pension schemes (*ss 204–242*);

(*f*) *Chapter 6* (Schemes that are not Registered Schemes) – is about some schemes that are not registered schemes (*ss 243–249*);

(*g*) *Chapter 7* (Compliance) – makes provisions about compliance (*ss 250–274A*);

(*h*) *Chapter 8* (Supplementary) – contains interpretation and other supplementary provisions (*ss 275–284*).

The schedules relating to the tax treatment of registered pension schemes are as follows:

(i) *Schedule 28* – Registered pension schemes: authorised pensions – supplementary:

Part 1 – Pension Rules;

Part 2 – Pension Death Benefit Rules;

(ii) *Schedule 29* – Registered pension schemes: authorised pensions – supplementary:

Part 1 – Lump Sum Rule;

Part 2 – Lump Sum Death Benefit Rule;

(iii) *Schedule 30* –Registered pension schemes: employer loans;

(iv) *Schedule 31* – Taxation of benefits under registered pension schemes;

(v) *Schedule 32* – Registered pension schemes: benefit crystallisation events – supplementary;

(vi) *Schedule 33* – Overseas pension schemes: migrant member relief;

(vii) *Schedule 34* – Non-UK schemes: application of certain charges;

(viii) *Schedule 35* – Pension schemes etc: minor and consequential changes;

(ix) *Schedule 36* – Pension schemes etc: transitional provisions and savings:

Part 1 – Pre-commencement pension schemes;

Part 2 – Pre-commencement rights: lifetime allowance charge;

Part 3 – Pre-commencement benefit rights;

Part 4 – Other provisions.

Key definitions

16.6 *FA 2004* makes use of certain key definitions set out in *ss 150–152* that are, in the main, borrowed or adapted from pre A-Day requirements. Other important *FA 2004* definitions can be found in *ss 275–280*, and are discussed later in the chapter.

'**Arrangement**' in relation to a member of a pension scheme, means an arrangement relating to the member under the pension scheme (*FA 2004, s 152*). Arrangement is a concept borrowed from the regime that applied to personal pension schemes before A-Day and is now applied generally to all types of registered pension schemes. Typically personal pension schemes were set up before A-Day so that the funds invested on behalf of the member were divided into multiple arrangements so that the member could just vest part of his benefits at any one time. Under the new regime it is possible to have multiple arrangements under an occupational pension scheme that vest at different times. There are different types of arrangement under the new regime, the main ones being 'money purchase agreements' (which are sub-divided into 'cash balance arrangements' and 'other money purchase arrangements') and 'defined benefits arrangements'.

'**Occupational pension scheme**' means a pension scheme established by an employer or employers and having or capable of having effect so as to provide benefits to or in respect of any or all of the employees of:

(*a*) that employer or those employers;

(*b*) any other employer,

whether or not it also has or is capable of having effect so as to provide benefits to or in respect of other persons (*FA 2004, s 150(5)*).

'**Pension Scheme**' means a scheme or other 'arrangements', comprised in one or more instruments or agreements, having or capable of having effect so as to provide benefits to or in respect of persons:

(*a*) on retirement;

(*b*) on death;

(*c*) having reached a particular age;

(*d*) on the onset of serious ill-health or incapacity; or

(*e*) in similar circumstances (*FA 2004, s 150(1)*).

A pension scheme is a 'registered pension scheme' at any time if it is registered under *FA 2004, Part 4, Chapter 2* (*FA 2004, s 150(2)*).

'**Personal pension scheme**' is not defined in *FA 2004*. The term is not used as the provisions relating to registered pension schemes apply at an arrangement level. The definition of 'personal pension scheme' under *PSA 1993* provides that:

(*a*) it is not an occupational pension scheme; and

(*b*) it is established by a person with permission under *FSMA 2000* to establish a personal pension scheme (*FA 2004, s 154(1)*).

The lifetime allowance and benefit crystallisation events

16.7 The tax regime sets a personal lifetime allowance for all pension savings in registered pension schemes. The standard lifetime allowance for each tax year is as specified in an order made by the Treasury (*FA 2004, s 218(3)*). For the tax year 2009/10, the standard lifetime allowance is set at £1.75 million, and for the tax year 2010/11 it is set at £1.8 million (*Registered Pension Schemes (Standard Lifetime and Annual Allowances) Order 2007 (SI 2007/494)*). The Government has announced that the standard lifetime allowance will be frozen at the 2010/11 level for the following five tax years.

The lifetime allowance available to an individual can be increased in certain circumstances by multiplying the standard lifetime allowance by a lifetime allowance enhancement factor (see below).

The amount of the individual's lifetime allowance available is tested on 'benefit crystallisation' events occurring in relation to an individual such as a pension coming into payment, a lump sum death benefit being paid, or on the commencement of income withdrawal (see below). For money purchase arrangements the amount applied under a pension policy or under the member's account to provide pension or other benefits on a benefit crystallisation event will be tested against the individual's lifetime allowance (Benefit Crystallisation Event 4 – *FA 2004, s 216*). For defined benefits arrangements, a pension coming into payment is valued using a standard valuation factor of 20:1 (Benefit Crystallisation Event 2 – *FA 2004, ss 216, 276*). For example, when a defined benefits pension of £35,000 comes into payment, it will be valued at £700,000 for the purpose of assessing how much of the lifetime allowance is available. This factor is based on certain assumptions with regard to the benefits the scheme will offer. Schemes offering more generous benefits can negotiate a higher factor with HMRC (*FA 2004, s 276(2)*). On a benefit crystallisation event occurring, the member's lifetime allowance is then reduced by the percentage of the lifetime allowance used up. So, in the previous example, if the pension of £35,000 per annum came into payment in the tax year 2009/10 when a standard lifetime allowance of £1.75 million was available, this will have used up two-fifths of a member's standard lifetime allowance. Three-fifths of the lifetime allowance will still be available on future benefit crystallisation events.

When pension benefits come into payment, the member will need to be informed of the percentage of the lifetime allowance that is being used up by the pension. The member will then need to confirm whether he has sufficient lifetime allowance remaining after taking into account other pension benefits that have already come into payment. To perform the calculations, the scheme administrator may need details of the percentages of the lifetime allowance used up by previous benefit crystallisation events. If the pension provided by the scheme takes the member over the lifetime allowance (or if the lifetime allowance has already been used up), then the benefits will be subject to a lifetime allowance charge (*FA 2004, s 214*). The lifetime allowance charge for sums in excess of the lifetime allowance will be 25 per cent, or 55 per cent if the excess funds are taken as a lump sum (*FA 2004, s 215*).

The scheme administrator and the member will generally be jointly and severally liable to pay the lifetime allowance charge (*FA 2004, s 217(1)*). However, when a benefit paid on the death of a member gives rise to a lifetime allowance charge, the person to whom the benefit is paid is liable (*FA 2004, s 217(2)*).

In practice (other than in death benefit cases), the scheme administrator of registered pension schemes (assuming their governing documentation permits them to do so) should deduct the lifetime allowance charge and make net payments to the member or other recipient. The scheme administrator should account to HMRC for the tax due in the next quarterly return (see **16.84** below) and pay the tax within 45 days of the end of the quarter in which the charge arose (see RPSM11105390). The scheme administrator then gives details of the lifetime allowance due, how the amount was calculated, and whether the amount due has been accounted by them within three months of the benefit crystallisation event (see RPSM11105390).

The scheme administrator can, in certain circumstances, apply to HMRC to be absolved from any liability to meet the lifetime allowance charge where:

(*a*) the scheme administrator reasonably believed that there was no liability to the lifetime allowance charge in respect of the benefit crystallisation event; and

(*b*) in all the circumstances of the case, it would not be just and reasonable for the scheme administrator to be liable to the lifetime allowance charge (*FA 2004, s 267(2)*; RPSM11105330).

It is therefore important to keep documentary evidence of the information requests made to the member and the responses received.

Lifetime allowance – transitional provisions

16.8 Three main options enable rights accrued prior to A-Day to be protected from the recovery charge (see RPSM, Chapter 3).

(a) Primary protection

Primary protection is available to individuals with pension benefits in excess of £1.5 million at 5 April 2006 (being the standard lifetime allowance for the 2006/07 tax year) (*FA 2004, Sch 36, paras 7–11*). Individuals claiming primary protection can continue to make tax relieved contributions to accrue further benefits under registered pension schemes after A-Day. The value of their rights will be the individual's individual lifetime allowance, expressed as a percentage of the standard lifetime allowance. This will then be indexed in line with the lifetime allowance. For example, a member with accrued benefits valued at £3 million on A-Day could register a figure of 200 per cent. If, when that member came to draw his benefits, the standard lifetime allowance had increased to £2 million, his personal lifetime allowance would be £4 million (see RPSM03100050).

To claim primary protection, the individual must have notified HMRC of his intention to rely on this protection no later than 5 April 2009.

(b) Enhanced protection

As an alternative to primary protection, an individual (whether their pension benefits were above or below the lifetime allowance at A-Day) could opt for enhanced protection (*FA 2004, Sch 36, paras 12–17A*). Enhanced protection fully protects the value of the individual's pension rights on A-Day. Such rights will not be subject to the lifetime allowance charge when they are brought into payment. Effectively this means that, if the value of the rights increases faster than the increase in the standard lifetime allowance, the individual will still be protected from the lifetime allowance charge (see RPSM03100040).

To take advantage of this option, there can be no further accrual of defined benefit or cash balance rights above a specified level of indexation, and no contributions can be paid to increase pension rights in defined contributions arrangements on or after A-Day. No benefits can be taken as a lifetime allowance excess lump sum while a claim to enhanced protection is in place.

Where an individual has made a valid notification of his intention to rely on enhanced protection, it will remain in force until he loses it because he fails to comply with the conditions for enhanced protection. If enhanced protection is lost the individual will revert to primary protection if he has claimed this as well (see below) or the standard lifetime allowance if he has not claimed primary protection.

To claim enhanced protection, an individual must have notified HMRC of his intention to rely on this protection no later than 5 April 2009.

(c) Enhanced protection with primary protection

Individuals with pension rights valued at more than £1.5 million at A-Day may have notified HMRC that they wished to claim both enhanced protection and primary protection. If they did so, the claim for enhanced protection will take precedence. The protection will operate on an enhanced protection basis until it is lost (see RPSM03100060).

When enhanced protection ceases, the protection will default to primary protection for benefit crystallisation events after enhanced protection is lost. In some circumstances primary protection will apply to the benefit crystallisation event which causes enhanced protection to be lost.

Enhanced lifetime allowance when an individual acquires pension credit rights that relate to pensions that came into payment on or after 6 April 2006

16.9 If, following a divorce, an ex-spouse of a scheme member acquires pension credit rights under a pension sharing order (see CHAPTER 10) that are derived from a pension that came into payment on or after 6 April 2006, that pension will have already been tested against the lifetime allowance. To avoid the same pension being tested again for lifetime allowance purposes the ex-spouse who has acquired the pension credit rights is entitled to a lifetime allowance enhancement factor (*FA 2004, s 220*). Notice has to be given to HMRC of intention to claim the lifetime allowance enhancement factor.

Enhanced lifetime allowance where the member acquired pension credit rights before 6 April 2006

16.10 An individual who, prior to 6 April 2009, gave appropriate notification to HMRC may have increased the standard lifetime allowance by a 'pre-commencement pension credit factor'. This was an available option where the individual (other than an individual who had claimed primary protection) had acquired pension credit rights under the pension scheme as a result of a pension sharing order being made before 6 April 2006 (*FA 2004, Sch 36, para 18*).

Enhanced lifetime allowance where member is a relevant overseas individual

16.11 An individual may also be able to increase the standard lifetime allowance by a 'lifetime allowance enhancement factor' on a benefit crystallisation event if, during any 'active membership period' of a registered scheme, he is a 'relevant overseas individual' (see *FA 2004, s 221* and **16.80** below). Broadly this means that, if the individual did not receive tax relief on any contributions made to a UK registered scheme while he was accruing benefits in the scheme (other than tax relief on contributions of up to £3,600 where he has been resident in the previous five years), his lifetime allowance can be enhanced.

Reduction in lifetime allowance to reflect the value of pensions in payment before 6 April 2006

16.12 Pre A-Day pensions are only considered for lifetime allowance purposes if there is a benefit crystallisation event on or after 6 April 2006. Broadly, on the first benefit crystallisation event occurring on or after 6 April 2006, it is assumed that a benefit crystallisation event occurred immediately before that date in relation to all the individual's pre-commencement pensions. The amount crystallised is the value of the individual's pre-commencement pension rights. Generally, this will be 25 times the annual rate or rates at which the relevant pension is, or pensions are, payable to the individual at that time. In the case of unsecured pension or alternatively secured pension, the value is the maximum amount that may be paid in the unsecured pension year or alternatively secured pension year calculated in accordance with the Pension Rules (*FA 2004, Sch 36, para 20*).

Reduction to lifetime allowance where member has a protected normal minimum pension age

16.13 If a member has a protected normal minimum pension age of below age 50 (or age 55 from 2010) (see **16.29** below) the amount of the member's lifetime allowance is generally reduced by 2.5 per cent for each complete year falling between the date of the benefit crystallisation event and the date he will reach his normal minimum pension age (*FA 2004, Sch 36, para 19*).

Benefit crystallisation events in more detail

16.14 The different types of 'benefit crystallisation events' are set out in a table contained in *FA 2004, s 216*. The table refers to various types of 'authorised payments' under the new regime which are described in more detail later in this chapter (see **16.22** to **16.62** below). The expressions used in the table are defined in *FA 2004, Sch 32*, which sets out details of how the amounts crystallised should be calculated. Reference should be made to RPSM, Chapter 11 for a comprehensive treatment of the subject.

	Benefit crystallisation event	**Amount crystallised**
1.	The designation of sums or assets held for the purposes of a money purchase arrangement as available for the payment of *unsecured pension* to the individual. Where a member with money purchase arrangements still has any uncrystallised funds at age 75 the individual is treated as having designated the funds under the arrangement for the payment of unsecured pension immediately before the member reached age 75 (*Sch 28, para 8*). Uncrystallised funds held under 'hybrid arrangements' immediately before age 75 are dealt with in the same way so there is a deemed crystallisation event immediately before age 75 (*FA 2004, Sch 28, para 8(2)* and *Sch 32, para 5*).	The aggregate of the amount of the sum and market value of the assets designated.
2.	The individual becoming entitled to a *scheme pension*.	RVF × P 'RVF' or the 'Relevant Valuation Factor' will generally be 20 but in certain circumstances a higher RVF can be agreed with HMRC by the scheme administrator. 'P' is broadly the amount of pension which will be payable to an individual in the 12 months from the date the individual becomes entitled to it.

	Benefit crystallisation event	Amount crystallised
3.	Pension increases which: (*a*) exceed the threshold annual rate; and (*b*) exceed by more than the permitted margin the rate at which it was payable on the day on which the individual became *entitled* to it. The 'threshold annual rate' is, in effect, an increase to the scheme pension, compared to the *scheme pension* a year ago, not exceeding the greatest of 5 per cent, RPI or £250. Where the Relevant Valuation Factor for converting the *scheme pension* is greater than 20:1, a higher figure than 5 per cent may be agreed with HMRC. The 'permitted margin' is a notional ongoing cost of living increase since the *scheme pension* came into payment and is measured as an annual rate of increase of the greater of 5 per cent (or higher figure agreed with HMRC) or RPI. A registered pension scheme that has 50 or more pensioner members may increase some or all of those *scheme pensions* beyond the threshold rate and the permitted margin without triggering this benefit crystallisation event where: (*a*) the same rate of increase is applied at the same time to all the *scheme pensions* that are in payment in respect of a particular class of pensioner members under the scheme; and (*b*) there are at least 20 pensioner members in that particular class. This is to allow schemes to award benefit augmentations to groups of members without triggering a benefit crystallisation event.	RVF × XP 'RVF' or the 'Relevant Valuation Factor' will generally be 20, but in certain circumstances a higher factor can be agreed with HMRC by the scheme administrator (see opposite). 'XP' will be broadly the amount by which the increase in the pension exceeds the 'permitted margin'.

	Benefit crystallisation event	**Amount crystallised**
4.	The individual becoming entitled to a *lifetime annuity* purchased under a *money purchase arrangement.*	The aggregate of the amount of such of the sums, and the *market value* of such of the assets, representing the individual's rights under the *arrangement* as are applied to purchase the *lifetime annuity* and any *relevant dependant's annuity.*
5.	The individual reaching the age of 75 when prospectively entitled to a *scheme pension* or a lump sum (or both) under a *defined benefits arrangement.*	(RVF × DP) + DSLS 'RVF' or the 'Relevant Valuation Factor' will generally be 20, but in certain circumstances a higher factor can be agreed with HMRC by the scheme administrator. 'DP' is broadly the annual rate of the scheme pension to which the individual would have been entitled if, at the date the individual reached age 75, the individual acquired an actual right to receive it. 'DSLS' is the amount of free-standing lump sum (ie not a commutation lump sum) the individual would have been entitled to at age 75 if the individual had taken the lump sum.
5A.	The individual reaching the age of 75 having designated sums or assets held for the purposes of a money purchase arrangement available for the payment of unsecured pension.	The aggregate of the amount of the sums and the market value of the assets representing the individual's unsecured pension fund under the arrangement less the aggregate of amounts crystallised by benefit crystallisation event 1 in relation to the arrangement and the individual.
6.	The individual becoming entitled to a *relevant lump sum.*	The amount of the lump sum paid to the individual.

	Benefit crystallisation event	Amount crystallised
7.	A person being paid a *relevant lump sum death benefit.* A *relevant lump sum death benefit* is a defined benefits lump sum death benefit or an uncrystallised funds lump sum death benefit.	The amount of the *relevant lump sum death benefit.*
8.	The transfer of sums or assets held for the purposes of, or representing accrued rights under, any of the relevant pension schemes so as to become held for the purposes of or to represent rights under a *qualifying recognised overseas pension scheme* (see **16.65** below).	The aggregate of the amount of any sum transferred and the market value of any assets transferred.
9.	Any event prescribed in regulations made under *FA 2004, s 164(1)(f)* so provide. Certain payments which have been paid in error are prescribed as benefit crystallisation events by the *Registered Pension Schemes (Authorised Payments) Regulations 2009 (SI 2009/1171).*	An amount determined in accordance with the regulations. Under the regulations made, the amount crystallised is the amount of the payment which is deemed to be authorised for the purpose of *FA 2004, 164(1)(f).*

If an unauthorised member payment is made, this will not count as a benefit crystallisation event but there will be various adverse tax consequences (see **16.25** to **16.28** below).

Contributions and the annual allowance

Tax relief on employee contributions

16.15 Tax relief on employer and employee contributions is dealt with in RPSM, Chapter 5. Broadly, any member may make unlimited contributions to a registered pension scheme during a tax year. However, to qualify for tax relief on a contribution it must be a 'relievable pension contribution' made by a 'relevant UK individual' (see *FA 2004, s 188(1)* and RPSM05100030). See also **16.19** below for specific provisions applicable to high earners.

A 'relievable pension contribution' is broadly any contribution paid by or on behalf of a member of the pension scheme other than any contributions made after age 75; contributions made by employers and age related or minimum payments under the contracting-out requirements (see *FA 2004, s 188(2)*). Transfers in and pension credits granted under a registered pension scheme do not count as relievable pension contributions (*FA 2004, s 188(4), (5)*).

An individual is a 'relevant UK individual' (*FA 2004, s 189*) if they:

(*a*) have relevant UK earnings chargeable to income tax for that tax year;

(*b*) are resident in the UK at some time during that tax year;

(*c*) were resident in the UK both at some time during the five tax years immediately before the tax year in question and when they became a member of the pension scheme;

(*d*) have for that tax year general earnings from overseas Crown employment subject to UK tax (as defined by *Income Tax (Earnings and Pensions) Act 2003, s 28* ('*ITEPA 2003*'); or

(*e*) are the spouse or civil partner of an individual who has for the tax year general earnings from overseas Crown employment subject to UK tax (as defined by *ITEPA 2003, s 28*).

'Relevant UK earnings' are:

(i) employment income such as salary, wages, bonus, overtime, commission providing it is chargeable to tax under *ITEPA 2003, s 7(2)*;

(ii) income chargeable under *Income Tax (Trading and Other Income) Act 2005, Part 2* ('*ITTOIA 2005*'), that is income derived from the carrying on or exercise of a trade, profession or vocation (whether individually or as a partner acting personally in a partnership);

(iii) income chargeable under *ITTOIA 2005, Part 3* derived from UK furnished holiday lettings business;

(iv) income arising from patent rights (*FA 2004, s 189(7)*);

(v) general earnings from an overseas Crown employment which are subject to tax in accordance with *ITEPA 2003, s 28* (*FA 2004, s 189(2)*).

Members will generally be given tax relief on the greater of £3,600 per annum or 100 per cent of their relevant UK earnings that are chargeable to income tax for the tax year on the individual's own contributions (*FA 2004, ss 188, 190*).

If relevant UK earnings are not taxable in the UK due to *ICTA 1988, s 788* (double taxation agreements), those earnings are not regarded as chargeable to income tax and will not count towards the annual limit for relief (*FA 2004, s 189(3)*).

A relevant UK individual under (*c*) who has no *relevant UK earnings* in a tax year may still qualify for tax relief on contributions to a registered pension scheme up to the basic amount in any tax year (currently £3,600) (see *FA 2004, s 190(2)*). However, the individual will only be able to claim this if the arrangement operates the 'relief at source' system – tax relief cannot be given where the scheme operates the 'net pay system' (*FA 2004, s 191(7)*).

A transfer by an individual of shares that have been acquired under an SAYE option scheme or appropriated to the individual under a share incentive plan to a registered pension scheme can count as a tax deductible contribution in certain circumstances (*FA 2004, s 195*).

Tax relief on employer contributions

16.16 Employers will generally be able to claim a deduction in profits chargeable to UK tax in the year the contributions are made. Relief is not automatic; it will be considered in accordance with the normal rules in relation to deductibility of business expenses (see *ICTA 1988, s 74(1)(a)*; and *ITTOIA 2005, Part 2*). The pensions legislation amends the normal rules applying to allowable deductions (*FA 2004, s 196*). In particular:

(*a*) a pension payment is not treated as a capital payment if it otherwise would have been; and

(*b*) a deduction can only be given for the accounting period in which the contribution is paid.

Spreading of tax relief may occur on contributions in excess of £500,000 if the contribution to a registered scheme exceeds 210 per cent of the contribution paid in the previous chargeable period. The spread is generally as follows:

(i) £500,000 or over and less than £1 million – two years;

(ii) £1 million or over and less than £2 million – three years;

(iii) £2 million or over – four years (*FA 2004, s 197*).

If a contribution is made to discharge any liability of the employer under the debt on employer requirements of *PA 2004, s 75* (see CHAPTER 14), this will be treated for tax purposes as if it were the payment of a contribution by an employer under a registered pension scheme (*FA 2004, s 199*).

As was the case before A-Day, employees will not be taxed as a benefit in kind on any employer contributions (*FA 2004, ss 188(3)(b), 201*; *ITEPA 2003, ss 307, 308*).

FA 2008 introduced provisions intended to prevent the rules applying to the spreading of tax relief on employer contributions to be avoided by routing payments through another company. The provisions relating to indirect contributions are contained in *FA 2004, s 199A* and apply to payments made on or after 10 October 2007, except any made under a contract entered into before 9 October 2007. Essentially, where a large contribution is routed through another company then it will still be caught by the spreading rules.

As a general rule contributions made by persons other than employers or members will be treated as member contributions and will not be tax deductible but there are exceptions (see RPSM05100040).

Employees may in certain circumstances be able to obtain tax relief on contributions to certain foreign pension schemes under the 'migrant member relief' provisions of *FA 2004* (see **16.80** below).

Annual allowance tax charge if contributions exceed the annual allowance

16.17 As explained above, there are no limits on the maximum amount of employee or employer contributions that can be made under a registered pension scheme but tax relief will not be granted above the annual limit for relief. There will also be a 40 per cent tax charge (annual allowance charge) on the member if the combined member and employer contributions or the value of benefits that accrue, in any year exceeds the annual allowance for that tax year (*FA 2004, s 227*). Additional tax charges will apply to certain high earners (see **16.19** below).

The annual allowance for each tax year is as specified in an order made by the Treasury (*FA 2004, s 228(2)*). For the tax year 2009/10, the annual allowance is set at £245,000, and for the tax year 2010/11 it is set at £255,000 (*Registered Pension Schemes (Standard Lifetime and Annual Allowances) Order 2007 (SI 2007/494)*). The Government has announced that the annual allowance will be frozen at the 2010/11 level for the following five tax years.

If the aggregate of the *pension input amounts* to all registered pension schemes of the individual exceeds the annual allowance in a *pension input period*, the individual will be taxed on the excess at 40 per cent (*FA 2004, ss 227, 229*). There will be no test, however, against the annual limit in the pension input period in which the individual dies or becomes entitled to benefits under the arrangement (*FA 2004, s 229(3)*). If the individual has multiple arrangements and has not crystallised the benefits under the other arrangements, the test will still apply to any pension input amounts in respect of the other arrangements.

The initial 'pension input period' will begin on the date of commencement of accrual in a defined benefits or cash balance arrangement or the date of commencement of contributions in a money purchase arrangement other than a cash balance arrangement. Unless it is changed, the initial pension input period will end on the anniversary of the start date and subsequent pension input periods will end on the day before the next anniversary. There is flexibility to change the pension input period (see *FA 2004, s 238*).

In a defined benefits arrangement the 'pension input amount' is the increase in the adjusted capital value of the individual's rights under the arrangement during the pension input period that ends in the tax year (*FA 2004, ss 234, 235, 236* and *238*). The value of the pension that accrues is generally calculated by multiplying the gross annual value of the pension at the beginning and the end of the pension input period by 10 (*FA 2004, s 234(4), (5)*). Any free-standing lump sum is then added on.

In a money purchase arrangement other than a cash balance arrangement, the 'pension input amount' is the amount of any employer and employee contributions paid in the pension input period that ends in the tax year (*FA 2004, s 233*). Any protected rights contributions are ignored (*FA 2004, ss 233(2), 238*).

In a cash balance arrangement the 'pension input amount' is the adjusted amount of increase in the value of the individual's rights under the pension input period of the arrangement that ends in the tax year (*FA 2004, ss 230, 231, 232* and *238*).

It is the responsibility of the individual, not the administrator, to declare on his tax return if his 'pension input amount' exceeds the annual allowance (*FA 2004, s 227(2)*, and see RPSM06100120). The individual (not the scheme administrator) is responsible for paying this tax. However, administrators of defined benefits occupational pension schemes may want to put systems in place to provide high earners with information to ensure that the pension input figure does not exceed the annual allowance.

Different methods of obtaining tax relief

16.18 There are three methods of obtaining tax relief. The method that applies will depend on the type of pension scheme (*FA 2004, ss 192–194*, and see RPSM05101310).

Personal pension schemes must operate the 'relief at source' arrangement under which the individual makes his relievable pension contribution, after deducting a sum equivalent to basic rate tax, and the scheme administrator then claims back a sum equal to the basic rate of tax from HMRC. A higher rate taxpayer can also obtain tax relief at the higher rate by making a claim when he fills in his tax return or by way of adjustment to his PAYE code. Relief at source enables individuals who have earnings below £3,600 or no relevant UK earnings to claim tax back on contributions of up to £3,600 (*FA 2004, s 192*).

Occupational pension schemes can continue to use a 'net pay arrangement' instead of 'relief at source' as long as the member is an employee of a sponsoring employer of the pension scheme and all the other contributing scheme members who are employees of the same employer are also receiving tax relief under the net pay arrangement (*FA 2004, s 191(3)*). A net pay arrangement allows the employer to give relief at source so employees are only taxed on their net pay after the pension contributions are deducted (*FA 2004, s 193*).

The third type of arrangement for obtaining tax relief on contributions is 'relief on making of a claim' (*FA 2004, s 194*). Broadly the member makes the contribution to the pension scheme and then claims tax relief from HMRC on their relievable pension contributions.

High earners

16.19 The Budget on 22 April 2009 announced a number of changes which will affect pension provision for high earners from 6 April 2011. The key change to pensions is the restriction of tax relief to the basic rate on pension contributions for individuals with income of £150,000 or more.

With effect from April 2010, a year before the introduction of the above measures:

- there will be an additional higher rate of income tax of 50 per cent for taxable income above £150,000; and
- the basic personal allowance for income tax for individuals with incomes above £100,000 will be reduced by £1 for every £2 until the allowance is reduced to nil.

From April 2011, when the restrictions on tax relief on pension contributions for individuals with income of £150,000 or more are introduced, tax relief will be given on employee contributions at the marginal rate of 50 per cent for individuals earning £150,000, but this will be tapered down until it becomes 20 per cent, ie basic rate, for those earning over £180,000; and a benefit-in-kind tax charge on employer contributions will apply.

The Pre-budget report in December 2009 widened the effect of the new provisions, taking into account employer contributions for those earning £130,000 or more.

It will not be possible to circumvent the restriction by paying in large contributions or changing the defined benefit accrual rate before April 2011. 'Anti-forestalling' measures, starting on 22 April 2009, prevent large additional pension contributions from being made before 6 April 2011. This applies to both employer and member contributions and to further accrual in defined benefits arrangements. The original anti-forestalling proposals for high earners allowed higher rate tax relief only on pension contributions of £20,000 per annum (although existing regular contributions in excess of this would be protected). In response to criticisms of these measures and, in particular, the adverse impact on those who did not have a pattern of making at least quarterly pension contributions, *FA 2009* contains a relaxation of provisions originally announced in April 2009.

A 'special annual allowance charge' will be payable if:

- the individual's income is £150,000 or higher;
- his normal ongoing regular pension savings or defined benefit accrual (to be known as 'protected pension inputs') are increased compared to previous years and that increase was not agreed before 22 April 2009; and
- his total pension savings (not just the excess over previous years), ie employer and member contributions/further accrual under a defined benefits arrangement, exceed the 'special annual allowance'.

The 'special annual allowance' has three bands of protection:

- anyone can contribute up to £20,000 in the years 2009/10 and 2010/11, even if they have no pattern of previous contributions;
- those with previous contributions to a money purchase arrangement may contribute up to £30,000 per annum, or the average of the last three years' contributions if less; and
- those with a regular (at least quarterly) pattern of previous contributions may continue at their protected level. The protected level will depend on factors such as: whether there was a pre-22 April 2009 contractual agreement to make regular contributions; whether contributions were in fact paid; and whether the amounts paid were the same or varied. HMRC have published guidance on protected contributions.

Full tax relief at the higher rates will be given up to the special annual allowance limit. Above that, tax relief will be at basic rate only. The special annual allowance tax charge – the difference between the highest rate of income tax and basic rate – will be levied on the individual, collected via the self-assessment tax return.

These provisions are transitional, and will cease in 2011 when higher rate tax relief on pension contributions for high earners is restricted.

The special annual allowance will be additional to the existing annual allowance (but there will be no double recovery of tax relief), and the value of an individual's pension savings for the special annual allowance will be calculated in a similar way to that for the existing annual allowance.

It will not be possible to avoid the anti-forestalling measures in the period up to 6 April 2011 by means of salary sacrifice arrangements agreed on or after 22 April 2009, as the amount of the sacrifice will be 'added back'; nor can they be avoided by means of any other type of arrangement which has as its main purpose (or one of its main purposes) to secure that an individual's income is less than £150,000. In these circumstances, the individual's income will be deemed to be £150,000.

Where the special annual allowance is exceeded, scheme administrators will, scheme rules permitting, be able to make a contributions refund lump sum (but not before the end of the tax year, or it will be an unauthorised payment) and account to HMRC for the tax charge on it.

The combined effect of all these measures is a significant reduction in the advantages for high earners of saving for retirement in a registered pension scheme, and the anti-forestalling/anti-avoidance measures have not left scope for additional pension saving before the new restrictions take effect in 2011.

Authorised and unauthorised payments

Move from a discretionary to a mandatory tax regime

16.20 The majority of UK occupational pension schemes were approved before A-Day on a discretionary basis under *ICTA 1988, Part XIV, Chapter I*. The types of benefits that could be provided without jeopardising HMRC approval were set out in the Occupational Pension Scheme Practice Notes on Approval of Occupational Pension Schemes (IR12 (2001)), as amended. The types of benefits that could be provided under personal pension schemes before A-Day were set out (on a non-discretionary basis) in *ICTA 1988, Part XIV, Chapter IV*.

Under the new regime, the types of 'authorised payments' that can be made by all registered schemes are set out in *FA 2004, Part 4*. If a registered pension scheme makes 'unauthorised member payments' or 'unauthorised employer payments' there can be adverse tax consequences for both the recipient and the scheme administrator (see below). In an extreme case if:

(*a*) in any 12-month period the *scheme chargeable payment percentage* (broadly most unauthorised payments) exceeds 25 per cent of the market value of the scheme's assets;

(*b*) the scheme administrator fails to pay a substantial amount of tax (or interest on tax) due from the scheme administrator by virtue of *FA 2004, Part 4*;

(*c*) the scheme administrator fails to provide information required to be provided to HMRC by virtue of *FA 2004, Part 4* and the failure is significant;

(*d*) any information contained in the application to register the pension scheme or otherwise provided to HMRC is incorrect in a material particular;

(*e*) any declaration accompanying that application or the provision of other information to HMRC is false in a material particular; or

(*f*) there is no scheme administrator,

HMRC has power to withdraw registration of the pension scheme (*FA 2004, ss 157, 158*). These are the only grounds on which deregistration can occur. There is an appeals procedure against deregistration (*FA 2004, s 159*).

HMRC only has power to withdraw registration from an entire pension scheme and not from an arrangement or arrangements in a pension scheme (see RPSM04105020 and onwards for further commentary). It does, however, have power to treat registered schemes as separate schemes in certain circumstances (*FA 2004, s 274A*). In practice, de-registration is unlikely to happen in a large occupational pension scheme, and HMRC is likely to enforce compliance through the tax charges that will fall on the administrator and the member if unauthorised payments are made. The trustees of occupational pension schemes and administrators of other registered pension schemes may, however, want to ensure that their existing rules or other scheme documentation do not provide for the payment of unauthorised payments. There are certain benefits or payments that were permitted under HMRC requirements for approval prior to A-Day that may be unauthorised under the *FA 2004* tax regime.

Activities of registered pension schemes to be restricted to retirement-benefit activities

16.21 Under the pre A-Day tax regime, for an occupational pension scheme to retain its status as an exempt approved scheme under *ICTA 1988, Part XIV, Chapter I*, it had to meet the 'sole purpose' test, ie in exercising its discretion to approve schemes. HMRC required them to be bona fide established for the sole purpose of providing 'relevant benefits', and continued approval was dependent on the sole purpose being maintained. There is no longer a requirement under *FA 2004* to meet the sole purpose test. However, under *PA 2004*, the trustees or managers of occupational pension schemes with their main administration in the UK have an obligation to secure that the activities of the scheme are restricted to 'retirement benefit activities' (*PA 2004, s 255*). Broadly, 'retirement benefit activities' are operations relating to retirement benefits and activities arising from operations relating to retirement benefits. 'Retirement benefits' are defined as:

(*a*) benefits payable by reference to reaching, or expecting to reach, retirement; and

(*b*) benefits that are supplementary to benefits within (*a*) and that are provided on an ancillary basis in the form of payments on death, disability or termination of employment or in the form of support payments or services in the case of sickness, poverty or need, or death.

Trustees of registered schemes can be fined by the Regulator if the scheme has activities that are not retirement-benefit activities and the trustee or manager has failed to take all reasonable steps to secure that the activities of the scheme are limited to retirement-benefit activities (*PA 2004, s 255(3)*).

Authorised member payments

16.22 The only authorised payments a registered pension scheme can make to or in respect of a person who is or has been a member are:

(*a*) pensions permitted under the 'pension rules';

(*b*) pensions permitted under the 'pension death benefit rules';

(*c*) lump sums permitted by the 'lump sum rule';

(*d*) lump sums permitted by the 'lump sum death benefit rules';

(*e*) recognised transfers;

(*f*) scheme administration member payments (ie payments made for the purposes of the management or administration of the scheme such as the payment of wages or salary or fees to persons engaged in administering the scheme);

(*g*) payments made under a pension sharing order or provision; and

(*h*) other payments permitted under HMRC regulations (*FA 2004, ss 164–174, Schs 28, 29*).

Included within (*h*) above are regulations which provide that certain payments to or in respect of members that would otherwise be unauthorised payments are regarded under the legislation as authorised payments (*FA 2004, s 164(1)(f)*; *Registered Pension Schemes (Authorised Payments) Regulations 2009 (SI 2009/1171)*). These payments include (subject to the satisfaction of conditions) pensions and lump sums that have been paid in error by scheme administrators or insurance companies, and 'stranded pots' which do not otherwise satisfy all of the conditions relating to the payment of trivial commutation lump sums. In the case of payments in error, the 'deemed authorisation' has retrospective effect from 6 April 2006. In other cases, the payments are only to be regarded as authorised if made on or after 1 December 2009 (see **16.47** below).

Authorised employer payments

16.23 The only payments which a registered scheme that is a private sector occupational pension scheme is authorised to make to or in respect of a sponsoring employer are:

(*a*) authorised surplus payments;

(*b*) compensation payments (ie payments made to an employer in respect of a member's liability to the employer in respect of a criminal, fraudulent or negligent act or omission);

(*c*) authorised employer loans;

(*d*) scheme administration employer payments; and

(*e*) other payments permitted under HMRC regulations (*FA 2004, ss 175–184*).

Unauthorised member payments

16.24 Any payment made to or in respect of a member that is not an authorised member payment will be an unauthorised payment with the various tax consequences discussed below (*FA 2004, s 160(2)*). There are also provisions which may deem a payment to be an unauthorised member payment including where:

(*a*) value shifting of assets occurs (*FA 2004, s 174*);

(*b*) a member of a registered pension scheme assigns or agrees to assign (or surrenders or agrees to surrender) any benefit to which they (or any dependant) have an actual or prospective right to under the scheme other than in certain permitted circumstances, such as the making of a pension sharing order (*FA 2004, ss 172, 172A*);

(*c*) there is an increase in rights on death of a connected person (*FA 2004, s 172B*);

(*d*) an asset held for the purposes of a registered pension scheme is used to provide a benefit other than a payment to a member, or a member of the member's family or household;

(*e*) if unallocated contributions are allocated to a member who is connected with the employer or any other person connected with the employer above a certain permitted level (*FA 2004, s 172C*);

(*f*) if the contributions made in respect of a member, or the capital value of the benefits that accrue in a pension input period in respect of a defined benefits arrangement, a cash balance arrangement or a hybrid arrangement relating to a member, exceed a certain amount where the member is connected with the employer or a person connected with a sponsoring employer (*FA 2004, s 172D*);

(*g*) direct or indirect investment in prohibited assets (for example, residential property or fine wines or vintage cars) by a self-directed pension scheme (see **16.69** below and CHAPTER 13).

Tax consequences of making unauthorised payments – unauthorised payments charge

16.25 Unauthorised payments can give rise to punitive tax charges and, in an extreme case, deregistration of the scheme.

If an unauthorised member payment is made, generally the member will be liable to an 'unauthorised payments charge' of 40 per cent of the value of the payment (*FA 2004, s 208(2)(a)*).

If the unauthorised member payment is made, after the member's death the recipient is subject to an 'unauthorised payment charge' of 40 per cent of the value of the payment (*FA 2004, s 208(2)(b)*).

If an unauthorised employer payment is made the sponsoring employer in respect of whom the payment is made is subject to an unauthorised payment charge of 40 per cent of the value of the payment (*FA 2004, s 208(2)(c)*).

Tax consequences of making unauthorised payments – unauthorised payment surcharge

16.26 An unauthorised member payment surcharge of 15 per cent may also be payable by a member where unauthorised payments in any 12-month period exceed 25 per cent of the value of that member's rights under the scheme (*FA 2004, s 210*).

An unauthorised employer payment surcharge may also be payable of an extra 15 per cent, broadly, where unauthorised employer payments in any 12-month period exceed 25 per cent of the value of scheme assets (*FA 2004, s 213*).

Tax consequences of making unauthorised payments – scheme sanction charge

16.27 In addition to the liability for the 'unauthorised payment charge', the scheme administrator will be subject to a 'scheme sanction charge' in respect of any unauthorised payment which qualifies as a 'scheme chargeable payment' (*FA 2004, ss 239–241*).

Potentially the scheme administrator could have to pay up to 40 per cent of the amount of the unauthorised payment that counts as a 'scheme chargeable payment'. However, there is a complicated formula which allows the scheme administrator to reduce its liability by part of any tax paid by the member or recipient to meet the unauthorised payments charge. As long as the 40 per cent tax is paid by the member or recipient, this should result in the scheme only being liable for payment of an extra 15 per cent (*FA 2004, s 240*).

Tax consequences of deregistration – deregistration charge

16.28 If the registration of the scheme is withdrawn, a deregistration charge is payable of 40 per cent of the value of any sums held by the pension scheme immediately before deregistration and the market value of any assets held at that time for the purposes of the pension scheme (*FA 2004, s 242*).

The Pension Rules (*FA 2004, s 165*)

Normal minimum pension age

16.29 Under Pension Rule 1, broadly benefits cannot be paid before the 'normal minimum pension age,' other than where the ill-health condition is met. The normal minimum pension age is age 50 but will increase to age 55 from 6 April 2010. Members who immediately prior to A-Day had an existing actual or prospective right under the rules of the pension scheme (as they stood at 10 December 2003) to draw any benefit before age 55 may, on and after 6 April 2010, retain those rights and have a 'protected pension age' (*FA 2004, Sch 36, paras 21, 22*).

The right to a protected pension age under an occupational pension scheme is lost if all the member's benefits payable under arrangements under the pension scheme are not paid at the same time. The protection may also be lost in certain circumstances where the member continues in employment or is re-employed (*FA 2004, Sch 36, para 22(7)–(7J)*). This issue needs to be considered if flexible benefit commencement provisions are introduced post A-Day. The right to a protected pension age can be preserved in certain circumstances on block transfers (*FA 2004, Sch 36, para 22(6)*).

Where, prior to A-Day, an individual had an actual or prospective right under a scheme to the payment of benefits before age 50 (because of a prescribed occupation), that right is also protected, subject to satisfying certain conditions (*FA 2004, Sch 36, paras 21, 23*; *Registered Pension Schemes (Prescribed Schemes and Occupations) Regulations 2005 (SI 2005/3451)*).

If a pension is paid to a member before the normal minimum pension age (or protected pension age) other than when the 'ill-health condition' is met (see **16.30** below), the instalments of pension paid prior to that age will be unauthorised member payments.

Ill-health retirement

16.30 The ill-health condition is met if:

(*a*) the scheme administrator has received evidence from a registered medical practitioner that the member is (and will continue to be) incapable of carrying on the member's occupation because of physical or mental impairment; and

(*b*) the member has in fact ceased to carry on the member's occupation (*FA 2004, Sch 28, Part 1, para 1*).

HMRC expects the medical evidence to be in writing and appropriate records should be kept to demonstrate that it has been received.

It is permissible (as was the case before A-Day) to reduce or stop an ill-health pension if the member recovers (*FA 2004, Sch 28, Part 1, para 2(3), (4)*).

The new ill-health condition is similar, but not identical, to the pre A-Day definition of 'Incapacity' in IR12 (2001) (see **16.111** below). Care should be taken to ensure that operation of pre A-Day ill-health retirement rules do not result in the making of unauthorised member payments.

Flexible retirement

16.31 Under the pre A-Day taxation regime, it was a requirement in most cases that, to take benefits from a tax approved occupational pension scheme, a member must retire from service. Benefits could not generally be taken in tranches unless the member transferred out his benefits to a personal pension scheme or, if the scheme rules permitted, took advantage of the opportunity to delay taking his AVC fund until a later date.

Under the *FA 2004* regime, there is nothing to prevent the member taking benefits from any type of registered pension scheme in tranches (whether still in employment or not) if the scheme rules permit it. In certain circumstances, however, this can lead to the loss of transitional relief. For example, if a member has a protected pension age below age 55 this protected minimum pension age may be lost (see **16.29** above). Additionally, any protection relating to the maximum amount of tax-free lump sum relating to pre A-Day rights where this exceeds the normal 25 per cent limit (see **16.42** below) can be lost if not all pensions are taken at the same time. Care should be taken not to breach the age discrimination legislation when designing any flexible retirement arrangements (see CHAPTER 9).

Pensions payable by defined benefits arrangements

16.32 Defined benefits arrangements can only pay 'scheme pensions' (Pension Rule 3). Scheme pensions are either pensions paid directly by the scheme out of its own resources or by an insurance company selected by the scheme administrator (*FA 2004, Sch 28, Part 1, para 2*).

Generally, scheme pensions must be payable (at least annually) until the date of the member's death or until the later of the member's death and the end of a fixed term of up to ten years.

FA 2004 does permit the pension to be reduced in certain circumstances. These circumstances include the situation when all scheme pensions payable to or in respect of the members are reduced or in relation to the payment of bridging pensions.

If a scheme pension is reduced in circumstances other than those permitted under the Pension Rules this will result in all subsequent pension payments being treated as unauthorised payments with the tax consequences discussed above.

Pensions payable by defined contributions arrangements

16.33 Money purchase arrangements may pay a 'scheme pension', a 'lifetime annuity' or an 'unsecured pension' to a member who has not yet reached age 75. However, a scheme pension can only be paid if the member has first been given the opportunity to select a lifetime annuity (Pension Rule 4 – *FA 2004, s 165*).

'Unsecured pension fund'

16.34 An 'unsecured pension fund' broadly means any sums or assets held for the purposes of the arrangement as member designated funds. Sums or assets will be member designated funds if they:

(*a*) have been designated at any time under the arrangement as available for the payment of unsecured pension, and

(*b*) arise or (directly or indirectly) derive, from sums or assets which have been so designated or which so arise or derive, and

(*c*) have not been applied towards the provision of a scheme pension (*FA 2004, Sch 28, Part 1, para 8*).

In practice this means any funds that the member is entitled to after he has crystallised his entitlement to benefits under the scheme and is in income draw-down but which have not yet been applied to secure a pension or annuity. If a member reaches age 75 and still has any relevant uncrystallised funds, such funds are then treated as having been designated under the arrangement for the payment of unsecured pension.

'Lifetime annuity'

16.35 A 'lifetime annuity' is an annuity payable by an insurance company which meets certain specified requirements. Broadly:

(*a*) the member has to have an opportunity to select the insurance company;

(*b*) it is payable until the member's death or, if later, until the expiry of any guarantee period under the contract not exceeding ten years;

(*c*) its amount either cannot decrease or falls to be determined in a manner prescribed in regulations made by the Board of the Inland Revenue (*FA 2004, Sch 28, para 3*).

'Unsecured pension'

16.36 An 'unsecured pension' is broadly either a short-term annuity or income withdrawal (*FA 2004, Sch 28, para 4*).

'Short-term annuity'

16.37 An annuity is a 'short-term annuity' if:

(*a*) it is purchased using sums or assets representing the whole or part of the member's unsecured pension fund in respect of an arrangement;

(*b*) it is payable by an insurance company;

(*c*) the member has an opportunity to select the insurance company;

(*d*) it is payable for a term that does not exceed five years and ends before the member reaches the age of 75; and

(*e*) its amount either cannot decrease or falls to be determined in any manner prescribed by regulations made by HMRC (*FA 2004, Sch 28, Part 1, para 6*).

The idea of short-term annuities was thought up by the Treasury when it was under pressure to relax the requirement that pension funds had to be applied at age 75 to purchase an annuity. It is designed to give members greater flexibility as to how they apply assets in retirement.

Alternatively secured pension

16.38 Once a member of a money purchase arrangement reaches age 75, a scheme pension, a lifetime annuity or alternatively secured pension must be provided.

The alternatively secured pension is a type of income draw-down which can continue on and after age 75 where the amount withdrawn each year cannot exceed 90 per cent of the basic amount for the alternatively secured pension year (Pension Rule 7 – *FA 2004, s 165*). There are complicated rules relating to the calculation of the amount that can be withdrawn (*FA 2004, Sch 28, Part 1, para 12*). The reason why members may wish to take advantage of this option is that it avoids having to purchase an annuity at 75. On the death of a member prior to 6 April 2007, it was possible, where the member left no dependants, for any remaining assets to be applied for the benefit of other members of the scheme by paying a 'transfer lump sum death benefit'. However, where the member dies on or after 6 April 2007 leaving no dependants, the only benefit that may be paid which is an authorised member payment is a charity lump sum death benefit (see **16.59** below).

Ten-year guarantee

16.39 If the member dies before the end of the period of ten years beginning with the day on which he became entitled to a scheme pension or an annuity payment may continue to be made (to any person) until the end of that period (Pension Rule 2 – *FA 2004, s 165*).

It is permissible for a scheme pension or a lifetime annuity with a ten-year guarantee to cease after the date of the member's death and before the end of the ten-year term if the annuitant marries, enters a civil partnership, reaches the age of 18 or ceases to be in full-time education (*FA 2004, Sch 28, paras 2(6), 3(2)*).

The lump sum rule (*FA 2004, s 166*)

16.40 Under the lump sum rule, no lump sum may be paid other than:

(*a*) a pension commencement lump sum;

(*b*) a serious ill-health lump sum;

(*c*) a short service refund lump sum;

(*d*) a trivial commutation lump sum;

(*e*) a winding-up lump sum; or

(*f*) a lifetime allowance excess lump sum (*FA 2004, s 166*).

If any other lump sum is paid, it will count as an unauthorised payment unless it is covered by any of the transitional saving provisions.

Pension commencement lump sums

16.41 A person becomes entitled to a pension commencement lump sum immediately before he becomes entitled to a pension in connection with which it is paid (or, if the person dies before becoming entitled to the pension in connection with which it was anticipated it would be paid, immediately before death) (*FA 2004, s 166(2)*).

A person is entitled to a pension commencement lump sum if:

(*a*) the member becomes entitled to it before reaching age 75;

(*b*) the member becomes entitled to it in connection with becoming entitled to a relevant pension (or dies after becoming entitled to it but before becoming entitled to the relevant pension in connection with which it was anticipated that the member would become entitled to it);

(*c*) it is paid when all or part of the member's lifetime allowance is available;

(*d*) it is paid within the period beginning six months before, and ending one year after, the day on which the member becomes entitled to it;

(*e*) it is paid when the member has reached normal minimum pension age (or the ill-health condition is satisfied); and

(*f*) it is not an excluded lump sum (*FA 2004, Sch 29, Part 1, para 1*).

Generally, when a member becomes entitled to a scheme pension, a pension commencement lump sum can be paid of up to one-quarter of the value of the benefits that are crystallised for lifetime allowance purposes. Any lump sum paid in excess of the permitted maximum lump sum will count as an unauthorised payment.

The pension commencement lump sum is paid tax free (*ITEPA 2003, s 636A(1)(a)*, as inserted by *FA 2004, Sch 31, para 11*).

The pension entitlement giving rise to the pension commencement lump sum does not have to arise under the same arrangement paying the lump sum but may be calculated on a scheme wide basis. For example, as long as all benefits are taken at the same time as the scheme pension comes into payment, in a defined benefits scheme the member's additional voluntary contribution fund could be applied to provide all the lump sum rather than commuting scheme pension to provide the lump sum. Pre A-Day restrictions preventing additional voluntary contributions from being used to provide a lump sum where the additional voluntary contributions commenced on or after 8 April 1987 no longer apply.

Pension commencement lump sum – transitional relief

16.42 A pension commencement lump sum in excess of the normal 25 per cent limit may be paid in certain circumstances where the member was entitled or prospectively entitled to a higher lump sum benefit on 5 April 2006.

In the case of a member who has primary protection and lump sum rights of more than £375,000 on 5 April 2006, the permitted maximum lump sum will be replaced by a different higher figure. The manner in which this works is complicated and is set out in the *Registered Pension Schemes (Enhanced Lifetime Allowance) Regulations 2006 (SI 2006/131)* and explained in RPSM03105140.

In the case of a member with enhanced protection and lump sum rights of more than £375,000 on 5 April 2006, the permitted maximum will broadly be the proportion of the fund which could have been taken as a lump sum benefit on 5 April 2006.

Members who do not have primary or enhanced protection and whose uncrystallised lump sum is less than £375,000 on 5 April 2006 may also be able to take a larger lump sum if the percentage of their benefits that could be taken as a lump sum as at 5 April 2006 under pre A-Day HMRC requirements exceeded 25 per cent (*FA 2004, Sch 36, para 31*). There is no need to register with HMRC to benefit for this protection, but scheme administrators will need to keep a record of the maximum permitted percentage tax-free cash that could be taken immediately before A-Day.

Pension commencement lump sums – recycling of lump sums

16.43 The Government announced in its 'Pension Tax Simplification – Pre Budget Report Technical Note' that it would take action to stop potential abuse of the pension tax simplification rules by boosting the amount in the pension scheme through artificially generated tax reliefs. In particular, where the member withdraws a tax-free lump sum and then reinvests it back into a registered pension scheme, generating further tax relief on the amount reinvested. Anti-avoidance provisions were inserted into *FA 2004* (*Sch 29, para 3A*) by *FA 2006* to target cases where lump sums are taken with the sole or main purpose of reinvesting them through the pension scheme.

Serious ill-health lump sum

16.44 A serious ill-health lump sum can be paid if:

(*a*) the scheme administrator has received evidence from a registered medical practitioner that the member is expected to live for less than one year;

(*b*) all or part of the member's lifetime allowance is available;

(*c*) it is paid in respect of an uncrystallised arrangement;

(*d*) it extinguishes the member's entitlement to benefits under the arrangement, and

(*e*) the member has not reached the age of 75 (*FA 2004, Sch 29, Part 1, para 4*).

An uncrystallised arrangement is an arrangement in respect of which there has been no previous benefit crystallisation event (*FA 2004, Sch 29, Part 1, para 4(2)*).

There is no liability to income tax on a serious ill-health lump sum (*ITEPA 2003, s 636A(1)(b)*, as inserted by *FA 2004, Sch 31, para 11*).

If a member's pension is commuted on serious ill-health grounds, any GMP which has accrued must still be provided for the spouse. HMRC take the view that, in order to extinguish that entitlement, any attaching spouse's pension required by the contracting out legislation must be provided following the member's death under a separate arrangement.

Short service refund lump sum

16.45 A short service refund lump sum allows for the return of a member's contributions in relation to an individual who is a member of an occupational pension scheme and whose pensionable service is terminated in circumstances where he is not entitled to short-service benefit under the scheme (*FA 2004, Sch 29, Part 1, para 5*). In broad terms, such a lump sum may become payable where a leaver has completed less than two years' qualifying service under the scheme and has not either been provided with deferred benefits under the scheme or elected for a transfer payment to be made to another scheme or arrangement (see CHAPTER 6).

The scheme administrator is liable to tax on the short-service refund lump sum at the rate of 20 per cent on sums up to £10,800 and 40 per cent on any excess above this amount (*FA 2004, s 205*). The Treasury has power, by order, to increase or decrease these rates, or the £10,800 limit. Tax should be deducted from any payment by the administrator where the rules of the scheme so permit.

Where interest is paid on a short service refund lump sum it is treated as a scheme administration member payment. Payments must be made on an arm's length commercial basis. If the interest paid exceeds a reasonable commercial rate of return, any excess will be treated as an unauthorised member payment and will be taxed in the manner described above (RPSM09104740). We understand that, in order to avoid making an unauthorised payment, HMRC require refunds to be treated as two distinct and separate elements:

(*a*) the amount of the contributions actually paid by the member (tax deductible and payable by the scheme administrator); and

(*b*) the amount of any interest/investment growth (payable gross to the member, who must account for the tax on a self-assessment tax return).

Refund of excess contributions lump sum

16.46 A refund of excess contributions can be made where the member has paid relievable pension contributions in any tax year which are more than the annual allowance (*FA 2004, Sch 29, Part 1, para 6*). The rules of a registered scheme would need to make provision for this payment to be made. Any repayment must be made before the end of six years following the end of the tax year in which the excess contributions lump sum is paid. A refund of excess contributions lump sum is not subject to income tax (*ITEPA 2003, s 636A(1)(c)*, as inserted by *FA 2004, Sch 31, para 11*). If interest is paid, it will count as a scheme administration member payment and, if the interest is not calculated at a reasonable commercial rate, the excess may be treated as an unauthorised member payment, with the resulting tax consequences discussed above.

Trivial commutation lump sum

16.47 A lump sum is a trivial commutation lump sum if:

(*a*) no trivial commutation lump sum has previously been paid to the member (by any registered pension scheme) or, if such a lump sum has previously been paid, before the end of the commutation period;

(*b*) on the nominated date, the value of the member's pension rights does not exceed the commutation limit;

(*c*) all or part of the member's lifetime allowance is available;

(*d*) it extinguishes the member's entitlement to benefits under the pension scheme;

(*e*) the member has reached the age of 60 but has not reached the age of 75 (*FA 2004, Sch 29, Part 1, paras 7–9*).

The commutation limit is 1 per cent of the standard lifetime allowance on the nominated date. The member's pension rights on the nominated date are all the member's crystallised and uncrystallised pension rights on that date under all registered arrangements. The benefits from the registered pension schemes that are going to be commuted have to be commuted within the trivial commutation period, which is the 12-month period beginning with the day on which a trivial lump sum is first paid to the member.

If a member receives a trivial commutation lump sum, he is treated as having taxable pension income for the tax year in which the payment is made equal to the amount of the lump sum. However, if the member has not become entitled to any benefits under the pension scheme, the taxable pension income is 75 per cent of the lump sum (*ITEPA 2003, s 636B*, as inserted by *FA 2004, Sch 31, para 11*).

RPSM09104920 makes it clear that, when valuing the member's entitlement, the value of any spouse's or dependant's pensions should be taken into account. RPSM09104930 goes on to say that, 'Where specifically identifiable contingent dependant benefits/rights exist, these too must be commuted with the member's benefits. They must be included when valuing the member's pension rights'. Any trivial commutation lump sum must be paid to the member not the spouse (see *FA 2004, s 166(1)*). Changes to the contracting-out legislation allow GMP and *s 9(2B)* rights to be commuted on the grounds of triviality.

Winding-up lump sum

16.48 A lump sum is a winding-up lump sum if:

(*a*) the pension scheme is an occupational pension scheme;

(*b*) the pension scheme is being wound up;

(*c*) the member's employment meets certain conditions;

(*d*) all or part of a member's lifetime allowance is available;

(*e*) it extinguishes the member's entitlement to benefits under the pension scheme; and

(*f*) the member has not reached age 75 (*FA 2004, Sch 29, Part 1, para 10*, as modified by *FA 2007*).

There is no lower age limit for payment of the benefit and again the commutation limit is 1 per cent of the standard lifetime allowance when the lump sum is paid.

The employment conditions are that any employer of the member at the time the lump sum is paid who has made contributions under that scheme in the last five years in respect of the member:

(i) is not making contributions under any registered pension scheme in respect of the member; and

(ii) undertakes to HMRC not to make such contributions during the period of one year beginning with the day on which the lump sum is paid (*FA 2004, Sch 29, Part 1, para 10(3)*).

If a member receives a winding-up lump sum, he is treated as having taxable pension income for the tax year in which the payment is made equal to the amount of the lump sum. However, if the member has not become entitled to any benefits under the pension scheme, the taxable pension income is 75 per cent of the lump sum (*ITEPA 2003, s 636B*, as inserted by *FA 2004, Sch 31, para 11*).

Lifetime allowance excess lump sum

16.49 This is the lump sum which is paid when none of the member's lifetime allowance is available. A lifetime allowance excess lump sum is subject to the 55 per cent lifetime allowance tax charge. It cannot be paid before the member reaches normal minimum pension age (unless the ill-health condition is met) (*FA 2004, Sch 29, Part 1, para 11*). The payment has to be made before age 75 or it will count as an unauthorised payment.

It will be necessary for scheme rules to contain express provision for payment of a lifetime allowance excess lump sum.

Pension death benefit rules (*FA 2004, s 167*)

Dependants' and children's pensions

16.50 Under the pension death benefit rules, pension death benefits can only be made to 'dependants' (Pension Death Benefit Rule 1 – *FA 2004, s 167*).

The following persons qualify as 'dependants':

(i) A person who was married to, or the civil partner of, the member at the date of the member's death.

(ii) If the rules of the scheme so provide, a person who was married to, or the civil partner of, the member when the member first became entitled to a pension under the scheme.

(iii) A child of the member is a dependant if the child:

- has not reached the age of 23; or
- has reached that age and, in the opinion of the scheme administrator, was at the date of the member's death dependent on the member because of physical or mental impairment.

(iv) A person who was not married to, or the civil partner of, the member at the date of the member's death and is not a child of the member who, in the opinion of the scheme's administrator, at the date of the member's death:

- was financially dependent on the member;
- was in a financial relationship with the member of mutual dependence; or
- was dependent on the member because of physical or mental impairment (*FA 2004, Sch 28, para 15*).

In certain respects, the new definition is more restrictive than that which applied under the pre A-Day regime (as set out in IR12 (2001)), in particular the requirement that a child's pension must cease by age 23, whether or not the child is in full-time education. This means that if, under the *FA 2004* regime, a pension continues to be paid after the child has reached age 23, it is potentially an unauthorised payment with the tax consequences that entails. There are transitional provisions which, in limited circumstances, enable certain children's pensions to continue beyond age 23.

Dependants' pensions under defined benefits arrangements

16.51 The only type of dependants' pensions that can be paid in respect of a defined benefits arrangement is a 'dependants' scheme pension' (Pension

Death Benefit Rule 2 – *FA 2004, s 167*). A dependants' scheme pension is either a pension paid directly by the scheme out of its own resources or by an insurance company selected by the scheme administrator (*FA 2004, Sch 28, Part 2, para 16*).

Dependants' pensions under money purchase arrangements

16.52 The types of dependants' pensions that can be paid under money purchase arrangements to a dependant who has not reached age 75 are a 'dependants' scheme pension' (see **16.51** above), a 'dependants' annuity' or a 'dependants' unsecured pension'. However, a dependants' scheme pension can only be paid if the member or the dependant has first been given the opportunity to select a dependant's lifetime annuity (Pension Death Benefit Rule 3 – *FA 2004, s 167*).

A dependants' unsecured pension means:

(*a*) a dependants' short-term annuity; or

(*b*) a dependants' income withdrawal.

A dependants' short-term annuity is similar to a member's short-term annuity so is secured with an annuity using unsecured funds and can last for a period of up to five years.

Income withdrawal is also possible up to age 75 and again the total amount of dependants' unsecured pension paid to a dependant in respect of a defined contributions arrangement must not exceed 120 per cent of the basis amount for the unsecured pension year (Pension Death Benefit Rule 4 – *FA 2004, s 167*).

Once the dependant reaches age 75, it is possible to have a dependant's alternatively secured pension fund (Pension Death Benefit Rule 6 – *FA 2004, s 167*).

Lump sum death benefit rule (*FA 2004, s 168*)

Death benefits (before and after benefit crystallisation)

16.53 Under the lump sum death benefit rule, no lump sum death benefits can be paid other than:

(*a*) a defined benefits lump sum death benefit;

(*b*) a pension protection lump sum death benefit;

(*c*) an uncrystallised funds lump sum death benefit;

(*d*) an annuity protection lump sum death benefit;

(*e*) an unsecured pension fund lump sum death benefit;

(*f*) a charity lump sum death benefit;

(g) a trivial commutation lump sum death benefit; or

(*h*) a winding-up lump sum death benefit.

For this purpose 'lump sum death benefit' means a lump sum payable on the death of the member.

A defined benefits lump sum death benefit

16.54 A lump sum death benefit is a 'defined benefits lump sum death benefit' if:

(*a*) the member has not reached the age of 75 at the date of the member's death;

(*b*) it is paid in respect of a defined benefits arrangement;

(*c*) it is paid before the end of the period of two years beginning with the earlier of the day on which the scheme administrator first knew of the member's death and the day on which the scheme administrator could first reasonably be expected to have known of it; and

(*d*) it is not a pension protection lump sum death benefit, a trivial commutation lump sum death benefit or a winding-up lump sum death benefit (*FA 2004, Sch 29, Part 2, para 13*, as modified by *FA 2007*).

The pre A-Day restriction, limiting the maximum tax-free lump sum death benefit payable under a retirement benefits scheme approved under *ICTA 1988, Part XIV, Chapter I* to (normally) four times final remuneration plus a return of employee contributions (see **16.115** below), no longer applies. Post A-Day, all of the member's benefits can be paid out as a lump sum benefit on death in service or death in deferment, up to the available lifetime allowance applicable to the member.

A defined benefits lump sum death benefit is free of income tax (*ITEPA 2003, s 636A(1)(d)*, as inserted by *FA 2004, Sch 31, para 11*).

A pension protection lump sum death benefit

16.55 This benefit can be paid on death before age 75 in respect of a scheme pension under a defined benefits arrangement where the member has specified that it is to be treated as a pension protection lump sum death benefit (instead of a defined benefits lump sum death benefit).

A lump sum death benefit is a pension protection lump sum death benefit if:

(*a*) the member has not reached the age of 75 at the date of the member's death;

(*b*) it is paid in respect of a defined benefits arrangement;

(*c*) it is paid in respect of a scheme pension to which the member was entitled at the date of the member's death; and

(*d*) the member has specified that it is to be treated as a pension protection lump sum death benefit (instead of a defined benefits lump sum death benefit).

The maximum lump sum that can be paid is broadly the amount crystallised by reason of the member becoming entitled to a pension, less the amount of pension paid before the date of death and less the amount of pension protection lump sum death benefit previously paid in respect of the pension (*FA 2004, Sch 29, Part 2, para 14*).

An administrator is subject to tax on the payment of a pension protection lump sum death benefit at the rate of 35 per cent (*FA 2004, s 206*; *ITEPA 2003, s 636A(4)(b)*, as inserted by *FA 2004, Sch 31, para 11*).

In the run up to A-Day, there was considerable uncertainty about whether an existing five-year guarantee lump sum payable on death after retirement under a defined benefits arrangement would be an unauthorised payment, a defined benefit lump sum death benefit or a pension protection fund lump sum death benefit. It would appear that, in most cases, the payment will be treated as a 'defined benefit lump sum death benefit' and can still be paid tax free as long as the member is below age 75 at the date of death has not specified that the payment should be treated as a pension protection lump sum death benefit, in relation to a defined benefits arrangement. The position in relation to defined contribution arrangements is set out at **16.57** below. There is transitional protection for five-year guarantee payments where the pension is in payment before A-Day and the member dies after age 75 where the member has specified that the payment should be treated as a pension protection lump sum death benefit (*FA 2004, Sch 36, para 36*). There will, however, be a 35 per cent tax charge.

Uncrystallised funds lump sum death benefit

16.56 An uncrystallised funds lump sum death benefit is a lump sum death benefit paid from a money purchase arrangement out of relevant uncrystallised funds before the end of a period of two years beginning on the day the member died (*FA 2004, Sch 29, para 15*). It cannot exceed the sums and market value of the assets that constitute the relevant uncrystallised funds immediately before the payment is made.

An uncrystallised funds lump sum death benefit is free of income tax (*ITEPA 2003, s 636A*, as inserted by *FA 2004, Sch 31, para 11*).

Annuity protection lump sum death benefit

16.57 This is the equivalent of the pension protection lump sum death benefit but paid from a money purchase arrangement in respect of a scheme pension or lifetime annuity to which the member was entitled at the date of the member's death if the member has not reached the age of 75 at the date of death (*FA 2004, Sch 29, Part 2, para 16*).

A scheme administrator is subject to tax on the payment of an annuity pension protection lump sum death benefit at the rate of 35 per cent (*FA 2004, s 206*; *ITEPA 2003, s 636A(4)(b)*, as inserted by *FA 2004, Sch 31, para 11*).

It would appear that a payment under a five-year guarantee paid from a money purchase arrangement will count as an annuity protection lump sum death benefit and be subject to a 35 per cent tax charge.

There may be inheritance tax consequences on the payment of an annuity protection lump sum death benefit (see **16.79** below).

Unsecured pension fund lump sum death benefit

16.58 If a member is below age 75 and is entitled to income withdrawal from the arrangement at the date of death, or if a dependant is below age 75 and is entitled to income withdrawal at the date of death, the member's or dependant's unsecured pension fund can be used to provide an unsecured pension fund lump sum death benefit (*FA 2004, Sch 29, Part 2, para 17*).

An administrator is subject to tax on the payment of an unsecured pension fund lump sum death benefit at the rate of 35 per cent (*FA 2004, s 206*; *ITEPA 2003, s 636A(4)(c)*, as inserted by *FA 2004, Sch 31, para 11*).

There may be inheritance tax consequences on the payment of an unsecured pension fund lump sum death benefit (see **16.79** below).

A charity lump sum death benefit

16.59 A charity lump sum death benefit can be paid from a money purchase arrangement if:

(*a*) the member had reached the age of 75 at the date of death;

(*b*) there are no dependants of the member;

(*c*) it is paid in respect of a member's alternatively secured pension fund; and

(*d*) it is paid to a charity nominated by the member (or, if the member made no nomination, selected by the scheme administrator) (*FA 2004, Sch 29, Part 2, para 18,* as modified by *FA 2007*).

A charity lump sum death benefit can also be paid on the death of a dependant of a member in similar circumstances.

The charity lump sum death benefit cannot exceed the amount of the member's or dependant's alternatively secured pension fund before the payment is made. There does not appear to be any tax charge in relation to this type of payment.

Trivial commutation lump sum death benefit

16.60 Where a member dies before reaching age 75, a trivial commutation lump sum death benefit can be paid to a dependant to extinguish the dependant's entitlement to a dependant's pension. The amount of the lump sum cannot exceed 1 per cent of the standard lifetime allowance on the date the lump sum is paid (*FA 2004, Sch 29, Part 2, para 20*).

If a trivial commutation lump sum death benefit is paid, the person who receives it is treated as having taxable income for the tax year in which the payment is made equal to the amount of the lump sum (*ITEPA 2003, s 636C,* as inserted by *FA 2004, Sch 31, para 11*).

Winding-up lump sum death benefit

16.61 On the winding up of a pension scheme, a winding-up lump sum death benefit can be paid to a dependant to extinguish the dependant's entitlement to pension death benefit and lump sum death benefit in respect of the member. Again, the amount of the lump sum paid cannot exceed 1 per cent of the standard lifetime allowance on the date the lump sum is paid (*FA 2004, Sch 29, Part 2, para 21*).

If a winding-up lump sum death benefit is paid, the person who receives it is treated as having taxable income for the tax year in which the payment is made equal to the amount of the lump sum (*ITEPA 2003, s 636C*, as inserted by *FA 2004, Sch 31, para 11*).

Life assurance only members in occupational pension schemes

16.62 In most cases it is possible to retain life assurance only members in occupational pension schemes. As explained in **16.21** above, the trustees or managers of occupational pension schemes with their main administration in the UK have an obligation to secure that the activities of the scheme are restricted to 'retirement benefit activities' (*PA 2004, s 255*). Broadly, 'retirement benefit activities' are operations *related to* retirement benefits and activities *arising from* operations *related to* retirement benefits.

There is uncertainty whether the provision of life assurance benefits for members who are included in a scheme solely for such benefits fall within the definition of 'retirement benefits'. This will depend on what is meant by 'related to', as highlighted above. It would appear from the parliamentary debates that the relevant provisions in *PA 2004* were inserted to mirror the EU *Directive 2003/41/EC on the Activities and Supervision of Institutions for Occupational Retirement Provisions* ('*IORP Directive*') and were not intended to restrict existing activities of occupational pension schemes. However, on a narrow interpretation of *PA 2004* provisions, only members with full scheme benefits could have death benefits 'arising from' or 'supplementary to' them. But, on a wider view, the death benefits would be sufficiently 'related to' the retirement benefits provided to other members to be allowed. The Regulator's view is that, as long as there is a concrete and identifiable link between an individual's life assurance benefits and 'main' pension benefits, then there will be no breach of this requirement. This may require the scheme providing the life assurance benefits to include an express clause that those members entitled to those benefits are also entitled to pension benefits in another scheme made available by the employer.

Transfers

Transfers out

16.63 If the rules of the scheme permit, or there is a statutory right to transfer, a member will, generally, be able to transfer his benefits under the *FA 2004* regime without adverse tax consequences, subject to certain conditions (see RPSM, Chapter 14). Broadly, a transfer can be made without adverse tax consequences if it counts as a 'recognised transfer' – a type of authorised payment (*FA 2004, ss 164(c), 169*). A 'recognised transfer' is a transfer of sums or assets held for the purposes of, or representing accrued rights under, a registered pension scheme so as to be held for the purposes of, or to represent rights under:

(*a*) another registered pension scheme; or

(*b*) a qualifying recognised overseas pension scheme (see below),

in connection with a member of that pension scheme (*FA 2004, s 169*). Transfers from a registered pension scheme to an insurance company will also generally count as recognised transfers if the sums transferred are applied to provide a scheme pension or dependant's scheme pension (*FA 2004, s 169(1A)–(1C)*).

A recognised transfer will not be treated as a contribution (*FA 2004, s 188(5)*).

For lifetime allowance purposes:

(*a*) a transfer to another registered pension scheme will not be a benefit crystallisation event; and

(*b*) a transfer to a qualifying recognised overseas pension scheme will be tested under benefit crystallisation event 8 (see **16.14** above).

With regard to the annual allowance test, for defined benefits arrangements and cash balance arrangements, the test is performed by comparing the value of rights between the opening value and closing value in a pension input period. Any increase in the rights between the two will produce the pension input amount to be tested (see **16.17** above). Where a recognised transfer is made, it is necessary to make certain adjustments to the closing values of the arrangements under both the transferring and receiving schemes, so as to compare like with like. Therefore, the market value of the assets transferred out of an arrangement during a pension input period are included in the member's closing value in the arrangement (ie they are added back) and, where there has been a transfer in, they are subtracted from the member's closing value in the pension input period in the receiving scheme (*FA 2004, s 236(4)–(7)*).

In the case of a transfer made from a registered pension scheme to a qualifying recognised overseas pension scheme, both a transfer and benefit crystallisation event 8 will take place. HMRC has confirmed in guidance that, although the amount crystallised is also added to the closing value of the pension input amount of the arrangement under the transferring scheme, as there is only one transaction, the effect of the legislation is that there is only one 'add back' in these situations. If a transfer is made which is not a recognised transfer, it will count as an unauthorised payment with the tax consequences discussed previously.

The administrator of the transferring scheme should ensure that any transfer is made directly to the administrator or the insurance company which issues policies under the receiving scheme. Failure to do so can result in a fine of up to £3,000 (see *FA 2004, s 266* and the commentary in RPSM14107010).

Care also needs to be taken to avoid any loss of transitional protection on making a transfer (see *FA 2004, Sch 36, para 12*, as amended by *FA 2005*).

Partial transfers

16.64 Under the *FA 2004* regime, it is possible to make a partial transfer from any type of registered pension scheme as long as the rights under the arrangement being transferred are uncrystallised. Any transfer is also subject to relevant contracting-out transfer requirements and the cash equivalent transfer ('CETV') requirements under *PSA 1993* (see CHAPTER 6).

If a partial transfer is to be made from an occupational pension scheme, a specific power will need to be inserted in the scheme's rules (independently of any CETV transfer right) together with provision for an appropriate discharge for trustees when a partial transfer is made.

Transfers to qualifying recognised overseas pension schemes

16.65 A transfer out can also be made without adverse tax consequences to a qualifying recognised overseas pension scheme. A qualifying recognised overseas pension scheme is a pension scheme which:

(*a*) meets the conditions enabling it to be treated as an "overseas pension scheme' under *FA 2004, s 150(7)*;

(*b*) meets the additional conditions enabling it to be treated as a 'recognised overseas pension scheme' under *FA 2004, s 150(8)*; and

(*c*) meets other conditions laid down in *FA 2004, s 169*.

An overseas pension scheme is broadly a pension scheme (other than a registered scheme) which:

(*a*) is established in a country or territory outside the UK; and

(*b*) is regulated as a pension scheme in the country in which it is established or, if there is no body by which it could be regulated, then certain conditions must be met;

(*c*) is 'recognised for tax purposes' by the country or territory in which it is established; and (*d*) must satisfy certain conditions set out in HMRC regulations relating to the regulation and tax recognition of the scheme (*Pension Schemes (Categories of Country and Requirements for Overseas Pension Schemes and Recognised Overseas Pension Schemes) Regulations 2006 (SI 2006/206), reg* 2, and see also RPSM14101030).

An overseas pension scheme will count as a recognised overseas pension scheme broadly if it is established:

(*a*) in a Member State of the European Union, Norway, Liechtenstein or Iceland; or

(*b*) in a country or territory with which the UK has a double taxation agreement that contains exchange of information and non-discrimination provisions; or

(*c*) any other country or territory if, at the time of the recognised transfer, the rules of the scheme provide that:

   (i) at least 70 per cent of the funds transferred will be designated by the scheme manager for the purpose of providing the member with an income for life;

   (ii) the pension benefits (and any associated lump sum) payable to the member under the scheme, to the extent that they relate to the transfer, are payable no earlier than would be permitted under a UK registered pension scheme (see **16.29** above); and

   (iii) membership of the scheme is open to persons resident in the country or territory in which it is established (*FA 2004, s 150(8)*; *Pension Schemes (Categories of Country and Requirements for Overseas Pension Schemes and Recognised Overseas Pension Schemes) Regulations 2006, reg 3*).

For a recognised overseas pension scheme to count as a 'qualifying recognised overseas pension scheme', the scheme manager of the scheme to which the transfer will be made must:

(*a*) have notified HMRC that the scheme is a recognised overseas pension scheme and have provided any such evidence that it is an overseas pension scheme as HMRC may require;

(*b*) have informed HMRC of the name of the country or territory in which the scheme is established, providing evidence, if the scheme is not a scheme established in an EU Member State, Norway, Liechtenstein, Iceland or in a country or territory with which the UK has a Double Taxation Agreement which contains exchange of information and non-discrimination provisions, that the scheme meets the other requirements for a recognised overseas pension scheme (see above);

(*c*) have provided any other evidence required by HMRC;

(*d*) have undertaken to notify HMRC if the scheme ceases to be a recognised overseas pension scheme; and

(*e*) have undertaken to provide HMRC with certain information on making payments in respect of certain scheme members (*FA 2004, s 169(2)*; *Pension Schemes (Information Requirements – Qualifying Overseas Pension Schemes, Qualifying Recognised Overseas Pensions Schemes and Corresponding Relief) Regulations 2006 (SI 2006/208), reg 3*; and RPSM14101050).

HMRC has power to exclude a scheme from being a qualifying recognised overseas pension scheme in certain circumstances where there has been a failure to comply with the prescribed information requirements and, broadly, by reason of the failure, it is inappropriate that a transfer from a registered scheme should be a recognised transfer (see *FA 2004, s 169(5)* and RPSM14101050 for commentary). There is an appeal procedure against such a decision under *FA 2004, s 170*.

HMRC maintains a list of qualifying recognised overseas pension schemes that have consented to their details being published – not all qualifying recognised overseas pension schemes will necessarily feature within it.

If a transfer is made to a qualifying recognised overseas pension scheme, the transfer will be a benefit crystallisation event for the purposes of the member's lifetime allowance (Benefit Crystallisation Event 8 – *FA 2004, s 216* and see RPSM14101060). Accordingly, if the amount crystallised exceeds the individual's remaining lifetime allowance, tax is chargeable at 25 per cent not the 55 per cent lump sum rate. The administrator will also have to report to HMRC that a transfer has been made to a qualifying recognised overseas pension scheme (*Registered Pension Schemes (Provision of Information) Regulations 2006 (SI 2006/567), reg 3* – Reportable Event 9).

Retention of pre A-Day rights – transitional protection post transfer

16.66 If a member is entitled to a protected low pension age of less than 50, they may be able to retain their protected low pension age following the transfer if certain conditions are met (*FA 2004, Sch 36, paras 21, 23(5)*).

If a member is entitled to a 'protected pension age' of below 55 (see **16.29** above), they may still be able to retain that 'protected pension age' following a transfer if they meet certain conditions (*FA 2004, Sch 36, paras 21, 22(5)*).

The requirements for the continued application of:

(*a*) primary protection;

(*b*) enhanced protection (*FA 2004, Sch 36, para 12*);

(*c*) lump sum protection in transferring a scheme where the member has primary protection;

(*d*) lump sum protection where the member is entitled to a lump sum of more than 25 per cent of rights;

(*e*) a protected low pension age (*FA 2004, Sch 36, paras 21, 23*); and

(*f*) a low normal minimum pension age (*FA 2004, Sch 36, paras 21, 22*);

following a transfer are described in RPSM14105000. Careful consideration needs to be given before making a transfer as to whether any of these protections could be lost as a result.

Transfers of pensions in payment or rights where there is already an entitlement to benefits

16.67 Generally under the pre A-Day tax regimes, transfers could not be made once the member had reached normal retirement age (see, for example, paragraph 10.22 of IR12 (2001)). *FA 2004* permits the transfer of pensions in payment or rights where there is an entitlement to benefits (for example, income withdrawal or drawdown) subject to certain conditions being met.

The conditions relating to such transfers are described in RPSM14106000. Failure to meet the required conditions will result in the payment being an unauthorised payment with the tax consequences discussed previously. The rules or governing documentation of the registered scheme will generally need to make express provision for the making of such transfers.

Transfers in

16.68 A transfer in can be accepted from:

(*a*) a registered scheme; or

(*b*) a recognised overseas pension scheme; or

(*c*) an unregistered pension scheme which does not count as a recognised overseas pension scheme (for example, an employer financed retirement benefits scheme or a non-UK pension scheme that does not satisfy the requirements to count as a recognised overseas pension scheme).

A transfer in from any of these sources will not count as an unauthorised payment. Under the pre A-Day regime, the only transfers permitted were between tax-approved arrangements (see paragraph 10.21 of IR12 (2001)). Transfers in do not count as a contribution to the scheme so are not tax relievable (see *FA 2004. s 188(5)*). There will also be no benefit crystallisation event on a transfer in.

Contracting-out requirements relating to transfers in also have to be complied with (see CHAPTER 4).

As, generally, no UK tax relief will have been received on benefits transferred in from a recognised overseas pension scheme, special treatment is given in relation to the lifetime allowance. The individual's lifetime allowance can be enhanced by the amount of the transfer in if an application is made to HMRC (see *FA 2004, ss 224–226* and RPSM14103020 onwards). The enhancement will not apply in relation to any part of the transfer payment which is derived from tax relieved contributions to a qualifying overseas pension scheme.

On a transfer from a non-registered scheme that is not a recognised overseas pension scheme, again there is no tax relief on the transfer in, but the investment funds derived from the transfer will be free of income and capital gains tax (see RPSM14104010). There will again be no benefit crystallisation event on the transfer in but, when the member takes their benefits, the amount crystallised that is derived from the transfer in will count towards the lifetime allowance.

Investment and scheme borrowing

16.69 It was originally proposed that, from A-Day, there would be a single investment regime for all types of registered pension schemes. Under the original proposals, registered pension schemes were to be given the right to invest in residential property and other tangible assets. This rule was to extend to self-directed pension schemes which were, under the pre A-Day rules, prohibited from investing in certain assets. A summary of the pre A-Day rules is set out in SECTION B of this chapter from **16.94** below.

It was announced in the 'Pensions Tax Simplification – Pre-Budget Report Technical Note' published in December 2005 that, to prevent abuse of the proposed new investment rules by people directing the scheme to acquire assets from which a personal benefit is derived, rather than acquiring assets for the purpose of building a fund for retirement, the Government had decided to tighten the rules governing allowable investments by certain types of registered pension schemes, notably those where investment could be member directed. Those changes were introduced into *FA 2004* (as *Sch 29A*) by *FA 2006* in relation to 'investment-regulated pension schemes'. These are schemes where a member, or person related to a member, is or has been able, directly or indirectly, to direct, influence or advise on scheme investment. The legislation applies to direct and indirect investment in residential property and most forms of tangible moveable property which are collectively referred to as 'taxable property' (see CHAPTER 13 for a more detailed discussion of this subject). Broadly if an investment-regulated pension scheme, directly or indirectly, purchases taxable property, the purchase will be subject to an unauthorised payment charge with the various tax consequences discussed above.

Scheme borrowing is limited to 50 per cent of scheme assets at the time the loan is taken out. Any borrowing above that limit will count as an unauthorised payment with the tax consequences discussed above (*FA 2004, s 189, Sch 30*). In practice, only trust based occupational schemes with fewer than 100 members or certain categories of 'small schemes' will be able to take advantage of this flexibility as, generally, trust based schemes are not permitted to borrow money or act as a guarantor, other than for the purpose of providing temporary liquidity for the scheme and on a temporary basis (*Occupational Pension Scheme (Investment) Regulations 2005 (SI 2005/3378), reg 5* – see CHAPTER 10).

Restrictions on investment in the sponsoring employer and associated employers are limited to 5 per cent of the fund value (see CHAPTER 10).

Fund income

General

16.70 Investment income derived from investments or deposits held for the purposes of a registered pension scheme is exempt from income tax (*FA 2004, s 186*). This exemption does not apply, however, to investments or deposits held as a member of a property investment LLP (*FA 2004, s 186(2)*) or in relation to taxable property held by an investment-regulated pension scheme (*FA 2004, ss 185A–185H*).

Income from a trading activity of a registered pension scheme does not fall within the above exemption (see **16.71** below and CHAPTER 10 for a discussion of what is meant by 'trading').

Underwriting fees are included within the definition of 'investments' under the above exemption, so will qualify for tax relief in relation to investments held by a registered pension scheme (*FA 2004, s 186(1)(b)*). Stock lending fees received by a registered pension scheme from any investment held by a registered pension scheme will, generally, also be exempt unless they derive from investments in a property investment LLP (*FA 2004, s 186*; *ICTA 1988, s 129B*).

Underwriting commissions applied for the purposes of a registered pension scheme which are not relevant foreign income and which would otherwise be chargeable to income tax under *ITTOIA 2005, Part 5, Chapter 8* (income not otherwise charged) are also exempt from income tax (*FA 2004, s 186(1)(b)*).

Futures and options contracts involving registered pension schemes are also defined as falling within the definition of investments and therefore fall within the exemption for income tax (*FA 2004, s 186(3)*).

Any gains realised by a person on a disposal of investments held for the purposes of a registered pension scheme are not chargeable to capital gains tax (*TCGA 1992, s 271*, as amended by *FA 2004, s 187*). However, a gain arising from the acquisition or disposal of assets held as a member of a property investment LLP will be a chargeable gain liable to capital gains tax (*TCGA 1992, s 271(12)*, as amended by *FA 2004, s 187(7)*).

Capital gains derived from dealing in financial futures or options are also exempt from capital gains tax (*TCGA 1992, s 271(10)*)).

If a registered pension scheme invests directly in assets, the income and gain from that investment will benefit from tax relief. Registered pension schemes can also pay premiums to invest indirectly in assets through an insurance policy where the underlying assets are owned by the insurance company. These underlying investments do not benefit from the same tax exemptions.

An insurance company can, however, apply the premiums it receives from registered pension schemes to its 'pension business' fund, which will enable them to benefit from a similar tax treatment to that which would apply if they were directly invested. The tax treatment of an insurance company's pension business fund is set out in *ICTA 1988, Part XII, Chapter I*. The definition of 'pension business' in *ICTA 1988, s 413B* has been amended to remove the pre A-Day 'correspondence' requirements that used to apply for investments made by occupational pension schemes approved under *ICTA 1988, Part XIV, Chapter I* (*FA 2004, Sch 35, para 20*). Under the new definition, broadly, 'pension business' is so much of a company's life assurance business as is referable to contracts entered into for the purposes of a registered pension scheme or the reinsurance of that business. If, immediately before A-Day, an annuity policy was treated as falling within the definition of pension business, it is, for the purposes of the definition of 'pension business', treated as having been entered into for the purposes of a registered pension scheme (*ICTA 1988, s 431B(3)*, as amended). When a pension scheme ceases to be a registered scheme, any of the insurance company's business that was pension business when the registered scheme ceased to be a registered scheme ceases to be pension business (*ICTA 1988, s 431B(2)*, as amended).

Trading

16.71 Certain activities undertaken by pension scheme trustees may be classed as trading by HMRC. This does not prevent a pension scheme from being a registered pension scheme. However, tax is payable on the income derived from such activities. This is discussed in CHAPTER 10.

Tax treatment of payments to employers

Authorised surplus payments

16.72 If a repayment of surplus is made to an employer, this must be in accordance with the requirements of *PA 1995, s 37* (see CHAPTER 11). An authorised surplus payment will be an authorised employer payment if it meets the requirements prescribed under *FA 2004, s 177* (*Registered Pension Schemes (Authorised Surplus Payments) Regulations 2006, SI 2006/574*), which include compliance with *PA 1995, s 37*. There will be a 35 per cent tax charge on any authorised surplus payments to the employer. The scheme administrator is liable to pay the tax and should account for it by using the accounting for tax return (see **16.84** below and RPSM04102030).

Tax treatment of benefits paid out to members

Pension benefits

16.73 Pensions paid under a registered pension scheme (other than any pension which gives rise to an unauthorised payments charge) will be taxable as pension income (*ITEPA 2003, ss 566(4), 579A* and *579B*). The taxable pension income for the year is the full amount of the pension under the registered pension scheme that accrues in the year irrespective of when any amount is actually paid (*ITEPA 2003, s 579B*). The person liable for the income tax is the person receiving or entitled to the pension under the registered pension scheme (*ITEPA 2003, s 579C*). This applies to all types of pensions paid under a registered scheme including:

(*a*) an annuity under, or purchased with sums or assets held for the purposes of, or representing acquired rights under, a registered pension scheme; and

(*b*) income withdrawal or dependant's income withdrawal under a registered pension scheme (*ITEPA 2003, s 579D*).

Any unauthorised pension paid under a registered pension scheme will also be chargeable to income tax as pension income unless the unauthorised pension has been assessed to income tax as an unauthorised payment.

PAYE will apply to all pensions from registered pension schemes. The payer of the pension must deduct PAYE in accordance with PAYE rules before paying the pension. There are transitional provisions for:

(i) retirement annuity contracts;

(ii) pensions that were taxed before 6 April 2006 but accrued after 6 April 2006; and

(iii) annuities that were paid from a scheme that was formerly an approved scheme that does not become a registered scheme (see RPSM04101020 for details).

Lump sums free of income tax

16.74 No liability to income tax arises on a lump sum paid under a registered pension scheme if the lump sum is:

(*a*) a pension commencement lump sum;

(*b*) a serious ill-health lump sum;

(*c*) a refund of excess contributions lump sum;

(*d*) a defined benefits lump sum death benefit;

(*e*) an uncrystallised funds lump sum death benefit (*ITEPA 2003, s 636A*).

A lifetime allowance charge can still arise, however, if the benefits crystallised on a benefit crystallisation exceed the remaining available lifetime allowance.

Lump sums subject to tax

16.75 A lump sum under a registered pension scheme which is:

(*a*) a pension protection lump sum death benefit;

(*b*) an annuity protection lump sum death benefit; or

(*c*) an unsecured pension fund lump sum death benefit,

is subject to income tax under *FA 2004, s 206*. The rate of tax is 35 per cent in respect of the lump sum death benefit, but the rate of tax charged may be decreased or increased by Treasury order. The person liable to the tax is the scheme administrator. Tax is charged on the amount of lump sum paid, or, if the rules of the scheme permit the scheme administrator to deduct the tax before payment, the amount of the lump sum before deduction of tax (*FA 2004, s 206*).

The accounting for tax return is used to account for the special lump sum death benefit charge (see **16.84** below).

Tax treatment of short service refund lump sums

16.76 A short service refund lump sum under a registered pension scheme (see **16.45** above) is subject to income tax in accordance with *FA 2004, s 205* (charge to tax on scheme administrator in respect of such a lump sum) but not otherwise.

Tax treatment of trivial commutation and winding-up lump sums

16.77 If a trivial commutation lump or winding-up lump sum is paid to a member of a registered pension scheme, they are treated as if they have received taxable pension income for the tax year in which the payment is made equal to the amount of the lump sum.

If a trivial commutation lump sum death benefit or a winding-up lump sum death benefit is paid to a person under a registered pension scheme, the person is treated as having taxable pension income for the tax year in which the payment is made equal to the amount of the lump sum.

Scheme administration member payment

16.78 A scheme administration member payment is a payment by a registered pension scheme to or in respect of a member, or former member, of a pension scheme that is made for the purposes of the administration or management of the pension scheme (*FA 2004, s 171*). This might include payment of wages to a person administering the scheme or payments made to purchase a pension scheme asset or a payment representing interest on a short service refund lump sum payment (see **16.76** above). If a scheme administration payment is made, normal tax rules would apply to each type of payment (see RPSM04101150).

Inheritance tax

16.79 There is no general inheritance tax exemption for registered pension schemes (see RPSM04100060).

Most occupational pension schemes that are registered pension schemes will be set up under trust. Trusts are a kind of settled property for inheritance tax ('IHT'). There are, however, a number of specific exemptions which take registered pension schemes outside the usual charges on this type of settlement for IHT purposes. As explained in RPSM04100060, this means that:

(*a*) contributions by individuals under registered pension schemes are not treated as chargeable transfers and not subject to IHT (*Inheritance Tax Act 1984, s 12(2)* ('*IHTA 1984*'));

(*b*) property held for the purposes of a registered pension scheme is not subject to an IHT charge which would otherwise be levied on a discretionary trust every ten years (*IHTA 1984, s 58(1)(d)*);

(*c*) IHT charges do not generally arise on a distribution of capital from a registered pension scheme such as a payment of a lump sum on death or retirement; and

(*d*) the value of the IHT estate on death will not generally include any value representing a pension or annuity, but see below in relation to provisions introduced by *FA 2006* (*IHTA 1984, s 151*).

HMRC is concerned that pension planning should not be used to avoid IHT. A discussion paper on IHT was issued by HMRC on 21 July 2005. This resulted in amendments being made to *IHTA 1984* by *FA 2006, Sch 22*. The rules apply differently, depending on whether the member dies before age 75 or on or after his 75th birthday.

Where a scheme member dies before age 75, the previous IHT rules will continue to apply. These rules were, until *FA 2006,* concessionary practice but can now be found in *IHTA 1984, s 12*. An IHT charge can arise under *IHTA 1984, s 3(3)* if a scheme member does not exercise his right to take pension benefits. The charge applies at the latest time when the right could be exercised (ie immediately before death). For example, if a member did not take his pension when he was seriously ill and this resulted in an enhanced death benefit, then IHT might apply. Under *IHTA 1984, s 12*, IHT is not charged in respect of those enhanced benefits where the beneficiary is a spouse, civil partner or financial dependant of the member or a charity. Neither is IHT applied where a member chooses not to exercise a right at a time when this choice does not trigger a charge (for example, choosing not to take a pension when he is in good health) and does not subsequently vary that choice when in poor health.

Different rules apply where the member dies on or after age 75 and the member has an alternatively secured pension. These were inserted by *FA 2006* as *IHTA 1984, ss 151A–151C*. Any funds used to make a payment to an employer or provide benefits for anyone other than a spouse, civil partner or financial dependant, or transferred to a charity, will be subject to an IHT charge as if the funds were part of the deceased member's estate. Any left-over funds not used to provide benefits for a spouse, civil partner or financial dependant, or transferred to a charity will also be treated as former part of the original member's estate for IHT purposes. An IHT charge may also fall on the estate of a dependant where the dependant himself opts for an alternatively secured pension derived from benefits inherited from the original member.

In addition, *FA 2008* includes provisions to close a loophole which allowed tax relieved pension savings to be 'diverted' into inheritance instead of being used to buy an annuity at age 75. Such surrenders, if made on or after 10 October 2007 in relation to deaths on or after 6 April 2008, will be subject to unauthorised payments charges as well as IHT, where applicable:

(*a*) an unauthorised payments charge when a member surrenders rights to payments under a lifetime or dependant's annuity;

(*b*) an unauthorised payments charge when a member dies and a 'connected person' becomes entitled to increase his or her rights under the scheme as a result of that death (essentially this prevents members of 'family' SIPPs or SSASs from receiving benefit augmentations as a result of the death of a family member); however, this will not apply on the reallocation of rights after death where the scheme has at least 20 members and the increases are applied at the same rate for each member; and

(*c*) an IHT charge where a member dies aged 75 or over and there is an increase in pension rights attributable to that death or the payment of an unauthorised lump sum.

If a lump sum death benefit is paid under discretionary trusts, where the trustees or employer have discretion to determine who it should be paid to, an IHT charge should not arise. However, if the rules provide for it to be paid automatically to the deceased's personal representatives, it will form part of the deceased's estate and will be subject to IHT. No IHT charge will arise to the extent the estate passes to the deceased member's spouse, civil partner or to a charity.

International benefit issues

The new regime

16.80 The *FA 2004* regime relating to international benefits set out in *FA 2004, Schs 33* and *34* is complicated, and can only be described in outline in this chapter. Reference should be made to RPSM13100000, which contains a detailed description of the *FA 2004* regime. The main elements of the regime are as follows:

(*a*) a member of a registered pension scheme who is a 'relevant overseas individual' can apply to receive an enhancement to their lifetime allowance in respect of non-UK tax relieved contributions;

(*b*) a member of a registered pension scheme who receives a transfer from a recognised overseas pension scheme can apply for an enhancement to their lifetime allowance in respect of the transfer to the extent that it relates to non-UK tax relieved benefits;

(*c*) migrant member tax relief can be obtained from UK tax on contributions to a qualifying overseas pension scheme in certain circumstances;

(*d*) members of a qualifying overseas pension scheme may be subject to UK tax charges in certain circumstances even when they have ceased to be tax resident in the UK; and

(*e*) overseas members of a registered pension scheme receiving payments from a registered pension scheme can be subject to UK income tax unless exempted by virtue of a double tax agreement.

Administration

General

16.81 Detailed guidance on the administration of registered pension schemes is contained in the scheme administrator pages of the RPSM, as most of the obligations to comply with these requirements fall on the administrator, who can be subject to penalties for non-compliance. Members and sponsoring employers of registered pension schemes, qualifying overseas pension schemes and qualifying recognised overseas pension schemes are also obliged to provide information in certain circumstances. Certain information must be submitted electronically and administrators have the option of submitting other information electronically (see *Registered Pension Schemes and Overseas Pension Schemes (Electronic Communication of Returns and Information) Regulations 2006 (SI 2006/570), Schs 1* and *2*).

Administration expenses

16.82 If a pension scheme bears the costs of its administration itself, it will not be able to obtain tax relief on those costs as its income is not taxable (unless it is trading and the costs relate to the trading activity). The employer may obtain tax relief in respect of the costs of establishing and operating a pension scheme if the expenses concerned are wholly and exclusively incurred in running the employer's business (*ICTA 1988, s 74(1)(a)*). However, if the employer pays costs which are attributable to the trustees, for example, a valuer's fees incurred on property valuations, tax relief will not be given.

If the trustees employ someone (as opposed to appointing an agent) to carry out duties in connection with the pension scheme then they will be responsible, as the employer of that person, for deducting income tax via the PAYE system on the remuneration paid.

Value Added Tax ('VAT') incurred by the trustees is an expense of the pension scheme and may be recoverable in certain circumstances. In *JP Morgan Fleming Claverhouse Investment Trust plc and another v The Commissioners of HM Revenue and Customs (Case C-363/05)*, the ECJ held that the management expenses of investment trusts should be exempt from VAT; however, further litigation will probably be needed to confirm that this principle extends to the trustees of occupational pension schemes.

Annual returns by scheme administrator

16.83 A scheme administrator is required to complete and submit an annual return in relation to any tax year if HMRC have served notice on him requiring him to file one (*FA 2004, s 250*). The return must be filed by 31 January next following the end of the tax year to which it relates. The return has to be submitted online (see **16.81** above).

The notice from HMRC will specify the period to be covered by the annual return, which can be the whole or part of any tax year or, where audited accounts have been prepared which end in that tax year, the period or periods covered by those accounts.

Accounting for tax returns

16.84 The scheme administrator of a registered pension scheme must make returns to HMRC of the income tax to which the scheme administrator is liable for each period of three months ending 31 March, 30 June, 30 September or 31 December (*FA 2004, s 254*). A return is only required if tax has been charged on the administrator during this period (RPSM04300020).

An accounting for tax form is provided in electronic format and the return must be delivered electronically (see **16.81** above). The return must be delivered within 45 days of the end of the relevant three-month period. The income tax has to be paid within the same period without the need for an assessment to tax (*FA 2004, s 254(5)*).

Notices requiring production of documents or particulars

16.85 HMRC has wide powers to serve notices requiring any person of a description set out in regulations to produce, or make available for inspection, documents within the person's possession or power which HMRC may reasonably require and to provide HMRC with any particulars which HMRC may reasonably require (*FA 2004, s 252*).

There is an appeals procedure allowing an individual to appeal against any requirement under a *s 252* notice (see *FA 2004, s 253*, as modified by the *Transfer of Tribunal Functions and Revenue and Customs Appeals Order 2009 (SI 2009/56)*).

Events reports to HMRC

16.86 The scheme administrator of a registered pension scheme has to provide specified information to HMRC in respect of any prescribed reportable events that have occurred in the scheme year to which the report relates (*Registered Pension Schemes (Provision of Information) Regulations 2006 (SI 2006/567), reg 3*). Reportable events include benefit crystallisation events, unauthorised payments, pension commencement lump sums, serious ill-health lump sums, suspension of ill-health pensions, transfers to qualifying recognised overseas pension schemes and changes in scheme rules or in the in legal structure of the scheme.

Where a registered pension scheme is wound up, notice that the winding up has been completed must be given to HMRC by the person who, immediately before the scheme was wound up, was the scheme administrator (*Registered Pension Schemes (Provision of Information) Regulations 2006, reg 4*).

A person who has been, or has ceased to be, the scheme administrator must notify HMRC of the termination of his appointment, together with the date the termination took effect, within 30 days (*Registered Pension Schemes (Provision of Information) Regulations 2006, reg 6*).

The information requirements in relation to qualifying overseas pension schemes and qualifying recognised overseas pension schemes (see **16.80** above) are not detailed in this chapter.

16.87 Where a registered pension scheme makes an unauthorised employer payment to a company, that company must provide the following information to HMRC no later than the 31 January following the tax year in which the payment is made:

(*a*) details of the scheme that made the payment;

(*b*) the nature of the payment;

(*c*) the amount of the payment; and

(*d*) the date on which the payment was made (*Registered Pension Schemes (Provision of Information) Regulations 2006, reg 5*).

Information to be provided to the member or his personal representatives by the scheme administrator

16.88 Certain information must also be provided by the scheme administrator to the member or the member's personal representatives, including the information listed below:

(*a*) If a registered pension scheme has made an unauthorised payment to a member of the scheme, the scheme administrator is required to provide to the member who has received the payment details of the nature of the benefit provided; the amount of the unauthorised payment which is treated as being made by the provision of the benefit and the date on which the benefit was provided. This information must be provided no later than the 7 July following the tax year in which the payment was made (*Registered Pension Schemes (Provision of Information) Regulations 2006 (SI 2006/567), reg 13*).

(*b*) Generally, the scheme administrator has to provide to each member:

   (i) who has an actual (as opposed to prospective) entitlement to be paid a pension, at least once in each tax year; or

   (ii) in respect of whom a benefit crystallisation has occurred, within three months of that event,

   a statement of the standard lifetime allowance expended by:

   - benefit crystallisation events in respect of the scheme, to the extent that the sums or assets subject to any such event have not been transferred to another registered pension scheme; and
   - where the first-mentioned scheme has received (whether directly or indirectly) a transfer in respect of the member, any crystallisation event, prior to the transfer in connection with:

      (i) the sums or assets represented by the transfer;

      (ii) sums or assets replaced by the sums or assets mentioned in (i) above.

   In broad terms, the information does not have to be provided if it has already been provided in compliance with certain other requirements of the *Registered Pension Schemes (Provision of Information) Regulations 2006* (*reg 14*).

(*c*) The scheme administrator must also provide the personal representatives of a deceased member of the scheme with information regarding the percentage of the lifetime allowance crystallised by, and the amount and date of payment of a relevant lump sum death benefit in relation to, the member. This information must be provided within three months beginning with the date of the final payment of the benefit. Additionally, the personal representatives may request a statement of the total percentage of standard lifetime allowance expended, at the date of the statement, by:

- any benefit crystallisation event in respect of the deceased member's rights under the scheme to the extent that:

  (i) the sums or assets subject to any such event; and

  (ii) any sums or assets subsequently representing those sums or assets,

  have not been transferred to another registered pension scheme; and

- where sums or assets have been transferred to the scheme from another registered pension scheme (whether directly or indirectly) in respect of the deceased member, any benefit crystallisation event in connection with:

  (i) those sums or assets; and

  (ii) any other sums or assets held prior to the transfer which the sums and assets mentioned in (i) above represented,

  but excluding from that percentage any amount in respect of any relevant lump sum death benefit payment in respect of the deceased member.

Where the personal representatives request this information, the scheme administrator must provide it within two months of the date on which the request is received (*Registered Pension Schemes (Provision of Information) Regulations 2006, reg 8*).

(*d*) If the scheme administrator has made or intends to make a payment on account of his liability to tax in respect of the lifetime allowance charge on a benefit crystallisation event, he must provide the member with a notice giving details of the chargeable amount in respect of the benefit crystallisation event, how the chargeable amount has been calculated and the amount of the resulting tax charge and stating whether the administrator has accounted for the tax or intends to do so. The notice must be provided within three months after the benefit crystallisation event (*Registered Pension Schemes (Provision of Information) Regulations 2006, reg 12*).

Information to be provided by the member and his personal representatives

16.89 If a member of a registered pension scheme wants to rely on entitlement to an enhanced lifetime allowance he must give the scheme administrator the reference number issued by HMRC in respect of that entitlement (*Registered Pension Schemes (Provision of Information) Regulations 2006 (SI 2006/567), reg 11*).

Where a registered pension scheme is treated as making an unauthorised member payment on the grounds that it constitutes a recycled lump sum under *FA 2004, Sch 29, para 3A* (see **16.43** above), the member must notify the scheme administrator, within 30 days of the date on which the unauthorised payment is treated as made of:

(*a*) the date on which the unauthorised payment is treated as made; and

(*b*) the amount of the payment (*Registered Pension Schemes (Provision of Information) Regulations 2006, reg 11A*).

Where a registered pension scheme intends to pay a pension commencement lump sum to a member and *FA 2004, Sch 29, para 2(5A)* applies to determine the permitted maximum, and a benefit crystallisation event has occurred previously in relation to the member in respect of a scheme pension that crystallised under a money purchase arrangement, the member must provide such information as will enable the scheme administrator to calculate the available portion of the member's lump sum allowance (*Registered Pension Schemes (Provision of Information) Regulations 2006, reg 11B*).

If a relevant lump sum death benefit has been paid in respect of a deceased member of a registered pension scheme and the payment, together with any other relevant lump sum death benefits, results in a lifetime allowance charge, the personal representatives of the deceased member (who will be liable for any tax due) have to provide HMRC with certain specified information about the deceased member and the payment (*Registered Pension Schemes (Provision of Information) Regulations 2006, reg 10*).

Information to be provided to and by insurance companies

16.90 If a registered pension scheme has provided an insurance company with funds, otherwise than from an unsecured pension fund, to secure the payment of a scheme pension or a lifetime annuity, the scheme administrator is required to provide the insurance company with a statement of the total percentage of the standard lifetime allowance expended, and any pension commencement lump sum connected with that pension or annuity. This information has to be provided within three months of the date on which the recipient becomes entitled to the pension or annuity. The insurance company must then provide to each pensioner or annuitant, at least once in each tax year, a statement of the percentage of the standard lifetime allowance expended at the date of the statement, by benefit crystallisation events in respect of that pension or annuity and any pension commencement lump sum paid in connection with that pension or annuity (*Registered Pension Schemes (Provision of Information) Regulations 2006 (SI 2006/567), reg 16*).

Similar requirements apply where a registered pension scheme has, for the same purpose, provided an insurance company with funds from an unsecured pension fund (*Registered Pension Schemes (Provision of Information) Regulations 2006, reg 17*).

Where an insurance company or other person has paid to a member of a registered pension scheme an annuity and the member to whom the annuity is paid has died, the insurance company is required, within two months of a request, to provide to the personal representatives of the deceased member details of the cumulative total percentage of the standard lifetime allowance crystallised, at the date of the statement, by benefit crystallisation events in respect of the deceased member under the scheme or any scheme from which assets have been transferred to the scheme in respect of the deceased member's pension rights (*Registered Pension Schemes (Provision of Information) Regulations 2006, reg 9*).

Retention of records

16.91 Any of the following documents that are in the possession or control of the persons listed below relating to any of the following matters have to be preserved in relation to a registered pension scheme, namely:

(*a*) any monies received by or owing to the scheme;

(*b*) any investments or assets held by the scheme;

(*c*) any payments made by the scheme;

(*d*) any contracts to purchase a lifetime annuity in respect of a member of the scheme; and

(*e*) the administration of the scheme.

(*Registered Pension Schemes (Provision of Information) Regulations 2006 (SI 2006/567), reg 18(1)*.)

The persons subject to this record keeping obligation are:

(i) any person who is or has been the scheme administrator;

(ii) any person who is or has been a trustee of the scheme;

(iii) any person who provides or has provided administrative services to the scheme; and

(iv) if the scheme is an occupational pension scheme, any person who is or has been a sponsoring employer or a director of an employing company.

(*Registered Pension Schemes (Provision of Information) Regulations 2006, reg 18(2)*.)

The obligation to preserve the documents does not apply to a person who has ceased to act in relation to a scheme or ceased to provide administrative services in relation to a scheme if he has transferred all documents to another person who has succeeded him in acting in relation to the scheme or providing administrative services to the scheme (*Registered Pension Schemes (Provision of Information) Regulations 2006, reg 18(3)*).

The obligation to preserve the documents applies for the tax year to which they relate and the following six tax years (*Registered Pension Schemes (Provision of Information) Regulations 2006, reg 18(4)*).

Information to be provided between scheme administrators

16.92 If a member's crystallised rights under one registered pension scheme ('Scheme A'), are transferred to another registered scheme ('Scheme B'), the scheme administrator of Scheme A must provide to the administrator of Scheme B, within three months of the transfer, a statement of the total percentage of the standard lifetime allowance expended, at the date of the statement, by benefit crystallisation events in respect of Scheme A (and in respect of any scheme from which Scheme A had previously received a transfer) in connection with the sums and assets represented by the transfer (*Registered Pension Schemes (Provision of Information) Regulations 2006 (SI 2006/567), reg 15*).

Penalties

16.93 Penalties that can be levied include the following:

(*a*) Failure to provide the registered pension scheme return in relation to any tax year where notice has been served requiring one to be submitted can give rise to a penalty of £100 on the scheme administrator. A further penalty not exceeding £60 a day for each day on which the failure continues can also be levied (*FA 2004, ss 250, 257(1)*).

(*b*) If the scheme administrator of a registered pension scheme fraudulently or negligently makes an incorrect registered scheme return in response to a notice from HMRC to provide one or delivers any incorrect accounts, statements or other documents with such a return the scheme administrator is liable to a penalty not exceeding £3,000 (*FA 2004, s 257(4)*).

(*c*) Failure by the administrator of a registered pension scheme to provide an accounting return can give rise to a fine of £100 for each quarter or part quarter for which the failure continues up to the fourth quarter where the number of people covered by the return is ten or less. Where the number of persons whose particulars should have been included in the return is more than ten the penalty rises to £100 for each ten persons or part thereof (so for 25 persons there will be a £300 penalty) for each quarter or part quarter from which failure continues up to and including the fourth (see *FA 2004, s 260*).

(*d*) If the scheme administrator fraudulently or negligently makes an incorrect accounting return the scheme administrator is liable to a penalty not exceeding the difference in the amount of tax shown in the form and the amount that should have been due (*FA 2004, s 260(6)*).

(*e*) Any person who fraudulently or negligently makes a false statement or representation is liable to a penalty not exceeding £3,000 if as a result the person or any person obtains relief from or repayment of tax chargeable under *FA 2004, Part 4* or a registered scheme makes a payment which is an unauthorised payment (*FA 2004, s 264(1)*).

(*f*) Any person who assists in or induces the preparation of any document which the person knows is incorrect and will or is likely to cause a registered pension scheme to make an unauthorised payment is liable to a penalty not exceeding £3,000 (*FA 2004, s 264(2)*).

(*g*) A failure to produce a document required by a notice served under *FA 2004, s 252* can give rise to a penalty not exceeding £300. Where the failure continues, a further penalty not exceeding £60 a day can be levied (*FA 2004, s 259(1), (2)*).

(*h*) A person who fraudulently or negligently produces or makes available for inspection any incorrect documents or provides incorrect particulars in response to a notice under *FA 2004, s 252* can be liable to a penalty not exceeding £3,000 (*FA 2004, s 259(4)*).

(*i*) Failure to provide or make available any document or information required under the enhanced lifetime allowance regulations can result on a penalty not exceeding £3,000 on the individual (*FA 2004, s 262*).

(*j*) Where an individual has claimed enhanced protection, failure to notify HMRC that relevant benefit accrual has occurred resulting in loss of protection within 90 days of its occurring can result in a penalty on the individual of up to £3,000 (*FA 2004, s 263*).

(*k*) If HMRC considers that a scheme is being wound up wholly or mainly to facilitate the payment of winding-up lump sums or winding-up lump sum death benefits (or both) the scheme administrator is liable to a penalty of up to £3,000 in respect of each member to or in respect of whom such payments are made (*FA 2004, s 265*).

Section B

Pre A-Day Revenue limits

16.94 As mentioned at the beginning of this chapter (see **16.1** above), many occupational pension schemes which before A-Day were tax approved may choose not to disapply all or some of the existing pre A-Day Revenue limits, or will write similar requirements into their rules as scheme limits. Consequently, for a number of occupational pension schemes, the limits (or some of them) will have continued application. For reference purposes, this part of the chapter outlines the key features of pre A-Day Revenue limits on benefits provided under tax-approved occupational pension schemes.

Transitional arrangements

16.95 Under *FA 2004, Sch 36, para 3*, the Commissioners of HMRC have the power, by regulations, to modify the rules of pension schemes if such modifications appear to be appropriate as a consequence of the introduction of the new taxation regime. This power is exercised by means of the *Registered Pension Schemes (Modification of the Rules of Existing Schemes) Regulations 2006 (SI 2006/364)* (the '*Modification Regulations*'). Their main effect is to provide schemes with a transitional period of five years from A-Day in which to modify their scheme rules to comply with the requirements of the new legislation.

During the transitional period, the Regulations are intended to have the following effects:

(*a*) any rule *requiring* trustees to make an unauthorised payment (see **16.24** above) will be construed as conferring a *discretion* to make that payment;

(*b*) if the scheme rules limit any benefit by reference to the permitted maximum (see **16.98** below), the permitted maximum will continue to apply;

(*c*) if the scheme rules provide for the payment of a specified sum or rate of pension and refer to the possibility of that sum or rate of pension being such greater amount as would not prejudice approval of the scheme by HMRC, the rules will be construed as authorising the trustees to make only those payments they could have made prior to A-Day;

(*d*) if the scheme rules provide for benefits to be limited to those which would not prejudice approval of the scheme by HMRC, the rules will be construed as prohibiting the trustees from making payments that they would not have been authorised to make prior to A-Day;

(*e*) scheme rules are modified to permit the trustees to reduce a member's benefits in respect of the administrator's liability for the lifetime allowance charge (see **16.1** and **16.49** above).

With regard to limits on benefits provided by occupational pension schemes, the net effect of the *Modification Regulations* is that, until the scheme rules are amended (and the provisions of the Regulations are expressly disapplied), no additional liabilities are imposed on schemes as a result of the introduction of the A-Day taxation regime. In particular, the limits imposed on benefits in order for a scheme to obtain tax -approved status under the pre A-Day regime continue to apply to a registered pension scheme during the transitional period. This is, of course, of most relevance to defined benefit occupational pension schemes. When the amendment is made, the amending deed should make clear which (if any) pre A-Day Revenue limits are retained.

Limits applicable to exempt approved schemes

16.96 Prior to A-Day, HMRC exercised its discretion under *ICTA 1988, s 591* to approve schemes in accordance with guidelines set out in an office manual which was summarised in Practice Notes, the last version of which was IR12 (2001). The requirements which a scheme had to meet in order to obtain approval related primarily to the maximum benefits which could be paid from the scheme. There were also limits on the contributions members could pay to the scheme. Further details of the pre A-Day limits on benefits are summarised in **16.101** to **16.119** below.

It is important to note that HMRC's Practice Notes set out the maximum benefits that could be paid. Pension schemes were not obliged to pay maximum benefits and, in the vast majority of final salary schemes, the rules effectively limited the benefits payable to lesser amounts.

Remuneration and final remuneration

16.97 The maximum benefits a member could receive from an exempt approved occupational pension scheme and the maximum contributions he could make to such a scheme were calculated by reference to his 'final remuneration'. As the expression suggests, final remuneration was itself calculated by reference to 'remuneration'.

Remuneration

16.98 Remuneration included any emoluments chargeable to tax under *ITEPA 2003, s 15* or *21*, except:

(*a*) sums arising from the acquisition or disposal of shares or from a right to acquire shares; and

(*b*) payments on the termination of office (for example, redundancy payments and golden handshakes).

(*ITEPA 2003, Part 6, Chapter 3*; Glossary to IR12 (2001); *ICTA 1988, s 612*)

Remuneration was limited in certain circumstances by legislation.

For members joining pension schemes on or after 17 March 1987, but before 1 June 1989, generally known as 'high earners', the amount of remuneration which could be used to determine cash lump sum benefits could not exceed £105,600 (previously £100,000 but increased from 6 April 2005) (*ICTA 1988, Sch 23, para 6(2)*, *Pensions Update 153*).

The level of remuneration which may be taken into account for the purposes of determining the maximum benefits payable was restricted to the 'permitted maximum' or, as it is colloquially known, the 'earnings cap' imposed by *ICTA 1988, s 590C*.

The earnings cap was first introduced in 1989 and was set at £60,000 per annum for the tax year 1989/90. The legislation contained provision for the earnings cap to be increased annually in line with the retail prices index rounded up to the nearest multiple of £600 (*ICTA 1988, s 590C(5)*), and the amount was prescribed annually by Treasury order. The earnings cap for the tax year 2005/06 was £105,600. HMRC now publishes annually the amount which, but for the repeal of *ICTA 1988, s 590C* on 6 April 2006, would have been the permitted maximum figure. For the tax year 2009/10, this would have been £123,600.

The earnings cap generally applied to all members of schemes established on or after 14 March 1989. It also applied to members of schemes established before 14 March 1989 who became members on or after 1 June 1989. However, it did not apply where employees were considered to have continuity of membership from before 1 June 1989 (*Retirement Benefits Schemes (Continuation of Rights of Members of Approved Schemes) Regulations 1990 (SI 1990/2101)*).

For example, if a member moved from one pension scheme of an employer to another scheme of the same employer, he could be treated as if he had always been a member of the second scheme and so would not necessarily become subject to the earnings cap.

Final remuneration

16.99 The definition of final remuneration is set out in HMRC's IR12 (2001) Appendix I. There are two basic definitions of final remuneration, depending upon the category of member involved. Broadly, these definitions are:

(*a*) the highest remuneration liable to income tax under *ITEPA 2003, s 15* or *21* for any one of the five years preceding a member's date of retirement, leaving pensionable service or death (whichever is earlier), being the total of:

  (i) the basic pay for the year in question ('the basic pay year'); and

  (ii) the yearly average over three or more consecutive years ending with the expiry of the corresponding basic pay year of any fluctuating emoluments; or

(*b*) the yearly average of the total remuneration liable to income tax under *ITEPA 2003, s 15* or *21* for any three or more consecutive years ending not earlier than ten years before the date of retirement, leaving pensionable service or death (whichever is earlier).

Whichever formula gave the best results could be used for most members but only the second formula could be used for controlling directors or other members whose remuneration after 5 April 1987 exceeded £100,000 per annum (subsequently £105,600 from 5 April 2005: see **16.98** above). The restriction was introduced because the directors of private companies are able to control the remuneration paid to them. Their ability to increase their remuneration just before they retire was therefore restricted by the imposition of the three-year averaging.

Fluctuating emoluments included any remuneration other than basic salary which fluctuated from year to year, for example, bonuses (IR12 (2001) Appendix I). Again, the three-year averaging requirement aimed to prevent 'back-end loading'. Fluctuating emoluments paid in a single year could be used in the calculation of final remuneration only with the prior consent of HMRC.

The 'basic pay year' used for calculating final remuneration had to fall in the relevant period prior to the date of retirement, leaving service or death but did not have to end on that date. It could be several years before then, with remuneration paid in earlier years being increased in line with the Retail Prices Index. Any convenient year could be used, eg the company's accounting year, the tax year, or the year ending on retirement.

Normal retirement date

16.100 There was a requirement that the normal retirement date of any member must be specified in the rules of the scheme (IR12 (2001) PN 6.5 to 6.11). It could differ for different categories of member but had to be between the ages of 60 to 75. Lower ages were permitted in some employments, for example, for sportsmen or those with hazardous occupations. Female members of occupational pension schemes who joined before 1 June 1989 were permitted to have a normal retirement date of 55. This HMRC distinction did not, however, override the requirements for equal treatment of men and women.

Maximum benefits

The three regimes

16.101 The maximum benefits in respect of a member were partly governed by his date of admission to membership of the pension scheme. As noted in **16.98**, there were three regimes in this respect:

(*a*) admission to membership before 17 March 1987;

(*b*) admission to membership of a scheme established before 14 March 1989, between 17 March 1987 and 31 May 1989 (inclusive); and

(*c*) admission to membership from 1 June 1989.

In some circumstances, a member who would otherwise have fallen within categories (*b*) and (*c*) could be treated for these purposes as if he had joined the scheme on an earlier date, eg where a member moved between schemes following the sale of his employer.

Members who fell within categories (*a*) and (*b*) were said to have 'continued rights' (IR12 (2001) Appendix III). Such a member could elect to be treated as if he had been admitted to membership on or after 1 June 1989. An election could be made at any time before benefits commenced, were bought out or transferred, or attainment of age 75, whichever occurred first. Following such an election, the member's benefits would be based on HMRC's permitted maxima for members joining pension schemes on or after 1 June 1989, but they became subject to the earnings cap (see **16.98** above).

Pension at normal retirement date

Maximum total benefits

16.102 The maximum total benefits that could be provided on retirement under an approved scheme were calculated by reference to an employee's length of service with the employer and his final remuneration. Total benefits were measured in terms of an annual pension for the member payable for life, being the aggregate of any pension payable (including, where the member did not fall within the administrative easement described in **16.103** below (IR12 (2001) PN 7.7), any pension debit) and the pension equivalent of any non-pension benefits (IR12 (2001) PN 7.2). The maximum aggregate benefit payable without taking account of 'retained benefits' (see **16.119** below) was a pension (of which part could be taken in lump sum form as described in **16.106** below) of 1/60th of final remuneration for each year of service (up to 40 years) (IR12 (2001) PN 7.3). However, this was subject to special provisions relating to controlling directors (IR12 (2001) PN 7.10) and the aggregation of benefits with other approved schemes (IR12 (2001) PN 7.25 and 7.26).

Pension sharing easement

16.103 Under an administrative easement, pension debits could be ignored in calculating the member's maximum permissible total benefits, both pension and lump sum, under IR12 (2001) PN 7.2. With two important exceptions, the easement applied to members of schemes other than simplified defined contribution schemes. The first exception was a controlling director (within the meaning in *Retirement Benefits Schemes (Sharing* of *Pensions on Divorce or Annulment) Regulations 2000 (SI 2000/1085), reg 5(5))*. The second exception related to members whose earnings exceeded one quarter of the permitted maximum determined at its level for the year of assessment in which the marriage was dissolved. For this purpose, earnings meant those in respect of pensionable service to which the scheme related, and which were received during the year of assessment immediately preceding the year of assessment in which the dissolution or annulment of the marriage occurred, and from which tax was deducted under PAYE.

The test was applied as at the date of divorce and once it was satisfied, the pension debit could be permanently ignored, that is irrespective of subsequent employment changes (IR12 (2001) PN 7.7).

Pre-17 March 1987 member

16.104 For a member who became, or was treated as having become, a member prior to 17 March 1987, the maximum permissible pension of two-thirds of final remuneration could be accrued over a period of ten years' service, in accordance with the following table:

Years of service to normal retirement date	**Maximum pension (before any commutation and including the annuity value of any lump sum entitlement) expressed as 60ths of final remuneration**
1–5	1 for each year
6	8
7	16
8	24
9	32
10 or more	40

Regardless of the date on which the member joined the scheme, the pension (unless it did not exceed 1/60th of final remuneration for each year of service) could not, when aggregated with any 'retained benefits' (see **16.119** below), exceed two-thirds of final remuneration.

Post-17 March 1987 member

16.105 The maximum pension payable to a member on retirement at normal retirement date was, as indicated in **16.102** above, two-thirds of his final remuneration (IR12 (2001) Part 7). For a person who became, or was treated as having become, a member on or after 17 March 1987 (that is a person who was within either category (*b*) or (*c*) as described in **16.101** above), this was restricted to 1/30th of final remuneration for each year of service, subject to a maximum of 20 years.

Cash lump sum at normal retirement date

16.106 Members were allowed to commute some or all of their pension for a tax-free cash lump sum (IR12 (2001) Part 8). *Pensions Update 135* (December 2002) clarified how the Inland Revenue expected approved schemes to administer tax-free lump sum retirement benefits. The lump sum was limited to no more than 3/80ths of final remuneration for each year of service, up to a maximum of 40 years. This allowed a cash lump sum of one and a half times final remuneration to be paid after 40 years of service. A higher accrual rate was permitted if the member had continued rights (see **16.101** above).

The actual accrual rate depended on when the member was treated as having joined the scheme, and was calculated in accordance with **16.107** to **16.109** below, as appropriate.

Pre-17 March 1987 member

16.107 If the member was treated as having joined the scheme before 17 March 1987, the following table applied:

Years of service to normal retirement date	**Maximum lump sum expressed as 80ths of final remuneration**
1–8	3 for each year
9	30
10	36
11	42
12	48
13	54
14	63
15	72
16	81
17	90
18	99
19	108
20 or more	120

The limits described in this paragraph did not apply where a member's benefit entitlement in a scheme was permanently reduced following a pension sharing order and the member did not fall within the pension sharing administrative easement described in **16.103** above. The calculation of the maximum lump sum benefit in these circumstances depended on whether the lump sum was obtained by commutation of pension or whether the scheme rules provided for a pension and a separate lump sum rather than a commutable pension. In the former case the maximum lump sum benefit was the greater of:

(*a*) 2.25 times the initial annual rate of pension after reduction to take account of the pension debit; or

(*b*) an amount determined in accordance with the scheme rules as if there had been no pension share, then reduced by 2.25 times the amount of pension from the pension debit calculated at the member's normal retirement date.

Where scheme rules provided for a pension and a separate lump sum as opposed to a commutable pension, the maximum lump sum benefit was the greater of:

(*a*) three times the initial annual rate of the separate pension after reduction to take account of the pension debit; or

(*b*) an amount determined in accordance with the scheme rules as if there had been no pension share, but then reduced by three times the amount of pension from the pension debit calculated at the member's normal retirement date (IR12 (2001) PN 8.26).

Post-16 March 1987 but pre-1 June 1989 member

16.108 If the member was treated as having joined the scheme during the period from 17 March 1987 to 31 May 1989 (inclusive), then (except for schemes commencing on or after 14 March 1989 (see **16.109** below)) a more complex formula applied. The member could use the higher accrual rate set out in the table in **16.107** above, but only to the same proportionate extent that his pension from the scheme (before any part of it had been exchanged for a lump sum or given up to provide further pensions for dependants) fell within the range between 1/60th and 1/80th of final remuneration for each year.

These limits did not apply where a member's benefit entitlement in a scheme had been permanently reduced following a pension sharing order and the member did not fall within the administrative easement. In such circumstances, the maximum lump sum benefit was calculated in accordance with **16.107** above.

Post-31 May 1989 member

16.109 If the member was treated as having joined the scheme on or after 1 June 1989 (or before then if the scheme itself commenced on or after 14 March 1989), and his pension (before any part of it had been exchanged for a lump sum or given up to provide further pensions for dependants) exceeded 1/60th of final remuneration for each year of service, his lump sum could be increased to 2.25 times the annual amount of that pension.

However, in any of the above cases, the lump sum plus any 'retained benefits' (see **16.119** below) could not exceed one and a half times final remuneration.

For the purpose of calculating Revenue limits, commutation factors were set by the Inland Revenue to determine the cash value provided for each £1.00 of pension given up (IR12 (2001) Part 7). A commutation factor of 12:1 had to be used irrespective of age, sex or escalation rate for current members and those members with continued rights who opted for the post-31 May 1989 regime. For members with continued rights, commutation factors differed according to age. At age 60 a commutation factor of between 10.2 and 11.0 could be used; at age 65 the range was 9.0 to 9.8 (IR12 (2001) PN 7.59). It was possible to agree enhanced commutation factors with HMRC outside these ranges.

Early retirement and leaving service before normal retirement date

16.110 The rules of approved occupational pension schemes could permit members to draw early retirement benefits at any age after 50 (or earlier on grounds of incapacity), provided they actually retired or ceased pensionable service with the employer concerned (IR12 (2001) PN 10.8). A female member with continued rights could receive early retirement benefits from age 45 if she retired within ten years of her normal retirement date as such members were permitted to have a normal retirement date of 55.

The receipt of an early retirement pension did not preclude a member from taking up employment elsewhere although the early retirement benefits may have had to be taken into account as 'retained benefits' (see **16.119** below) if the member joined the subsequent employer's pension scheme. If a member was subsequently re-employed by the employer from whose scheme early retirement benefits had been, or were being, paid the rules of the scheme could permit the suspension of the early retirement pension (IR12 (2001) PN 7.32); if the member was to accrue further benefits under the scheme the early retirement benefits had to be suspended (IR12 (2001) Appendix IV).

Early retirement on grounds of incapacity

16.111 If a member retired early at any age on grounds of incapacity, his benefits could be calculated in the same manner as if he had retired at normal retirement date. Both his actual service and potential service (ie the service he would have completed had he remained a member up to his normal retirement date) could count towards the calculation. Final remuneration was calculated as at his date of actual retirement.

'Incapacity' was defined in the Glossary to IR12 (2001) as 'physical or mental deterioration which is sufficiently serious to prevent the individual from following his or her normal employment, or which seriously impairs his or her earning capacity. It does not mean simply a decline in energy or ability'.

Early retirement other than on grounds of incapacity

16.112 The maximum pension payable from an approved scheme on early retirement, other than on grounds of incapacity (IR12 (2001) PN 10.9 to 10.14), for a member without continued rights was the greater of:

(*a*) 1/60th of final remuneration for each year of service up to a maximum of 40 years; and (*b*) the lesser of:

(i) 1/30th of final remuneration for each year of service up to a maximum of 20 years; and

(ii) 2/3rds of final remuneration less 'retained benefits' (see **16.119** below).

Where the member had a pension debit in relation to the scheme and did not fall within the administrative easement described in **16.103** above, the maximum benefits were calculated in accordance with the requirements set out above but had to be reduced by the pension debit.

The maximum cash lump sum payable in such circumstances (IR12 (2001) PN 10.15 to 10.18) was 3/80ths of final remuneration for each year of service up to a maximum of 40 years or, if greater, an amount equal to 2.25 times the initial annual rate of pension to be paid (before any part of that pension had been commuted for the lump sum or given up to provide further pensions for dependants). However, (unless the lump sum did not exceed 3/80th of final remuneration for each year of service) the lump sum could not, when aggregated with any 'retained benefits' (see **16.119** below), exceed one and a half times final remuneration.

For members with continued rights (see **16.101** above), the maximum pension on early retirement was either 1/60th of final remuneration for each year of service up to a maximum of 40 years or, if more favourable, the amount calculated by the formula:

$$\frac{N}{NS} \times P;$$

where:

N is the number of actual years of service up to a maximum of 40 years;

NS is the number of actual years of service plus years of potential service to normal retirement date; and

P is the maximum pension the member could have received had he remained in service until normal retirement date calculated by reference to final remuneration as at the date of termination of pensionable service.

For members with continued rights (see **16.101** above) the maximum cash lump sum available on early retirement was either 3/80ths of final remuneration for each year of service up to a maximum of 40 years or, if more favourable, the amount calculated by the formula:

$$\frac{N}{NS} \times LS;$$

where:

N is the number of actual years of service with a maximum of 40 years;

NS is the number of actual years of service plus years of potential service to normal retirement date; and

LS is the maximum lump sum the member could have received had he remained in pensionable service until normal retirement date calculated by reference to final remuneration at the date of termination of pensionable service.

Leaving service benefits

16.113 If a member left service before reaching normal retirement date, several options were available regarding his accrued benefits (IR12 (2001) Part 10). If the member was at least age 50, retirement benefits could be paid immediately if the scheme's rules permitted it. If the member had not reached age 50, benefits could be left in the scheme and paid either after age 50 as early retirement benefits or at normal retirement date. The maximum benefits payable on leaving service in respect of pensions and cash lump sums were, broadly, the same as those payable on early retirement.

Alternatively, a deferred annuity could be purchased or a transfer value paid to another occupational or personal pension scheme. In these circumstances, it is important to remember that the amount used to purchase the annuity or the amount of the transfer value could not exceed HMRC's maximum amount for early retirement benefits. In particular, there were limitations on making transfer payments to personal pension schemes for controlling directors and other members whose remuneration exceeded the earnings cap (*Personal Pension Schemes (Transfer Payments) Regulations 2001 (SI 2001/119)*).

Retirement after normal retirement date

16.114 In certain circumstances, a member could be permitted to postpone receipt of his benefits until after normal retirement date (IR12 (2001) PN 7.43 to 7.46). The calculation of the maximum pension permissible by HMRC on late retirement depended on whether the member had continued rights.

If the member had continued rights (see **16.101** above), his maximum pension was the greatest of:

(*a*) his maximum pension at normal retirement date, but substituting the date of actual retirement for normal retirement date;

(*b*) his maximum pension at normal retirement date plus 1/60th (up to a maximum of 5/60th) for each further year of service over 40 years after normal retirement date; and (*c*) his maximum pension at normal retirement date increased by increases in the Retail Price Index or by actuarial increases (whichever produces the greater result) since normal retirement date,

except that the first two options were not available to controlling directors other than in respect of service after age 70.

If the member did not have continued rights (see **16.101** above), the maximum pension was the maximum pension he could have received if his date of actual retirement had been substituted for his normal retirement date.

Death benefits

Lump sums payable on death in service before normal retirement date

16.115 On a member's death in service before reaching normal retirement date (IR12 (2001) Part 11), a lump sum could be paid equal to the greater of:

(*a*) £5,000; and

(*b*) four times final remuneration less 'retained benefits' (see **16.119** below).

In addition, a refund of the member's own contributions could be paid with or without interest. As a member's death cannot be foreseen, the definition of final remuneration was more generous than at normal retirement date. Final remuneration on death could be:

(i) the annual basic salary immediately before death; or

(ii) the annual basic salary immediately before death plus the average of fluctuating emoluments during the three years up to the date of death; or

(iii) the total remuneration, fixed and fluctuating, paid during any period of 12 months falling within the three years prior to death.

If a scheme's rules provided for a lump sum benefit on death that did not exceed twice the member's final remuneration, 'retained benefits' (see **16.119** below) did not need to be taken into account.

Spouses' and dependants' benefits

16.116 Following the death of a member in service or after retirement, a spouse's and/or dependant's pension could be provided. The maximum level of all such pensions could not exceed two-thirds of the maximum pension that could have been provided for the deceased member had he retired due to incapacity immediately before death, calculated as though there had been no lump sum commutation at retirement and as if the deceased had no 'retained benefits' (see **16.119** below) from earlier occupations.

Death of an early leaver

16.117 If a former active member died before age 50, having deferred benefits in the scheme, a cash lump sum could be paid. Spouse's and dependants' pensions could also be provided, calculated by reference to the deceased member's maximum approvable deferred pension.

Death in service after normal retirement date

16.118 Where a member died in service after normal retirement date, maximum benefits could be provided on the basis of death in service (see **16.115** and **16.116** above). In the case of a member with continued rights, benefits could be provided on the basis that the member died in retirement having retired the day before the date of death.

Retained benefits

16.119 Retained benefits (IR12 (2001) Appendix I) generally were retained rights to relevant benefits and, where appropriate, pension debits built up in previous employments or periods of self-employment from schemes or contractual arrangements which had benefited from tax privileges.

Section C

Non-registered pension schemes

16.120 From 6 April 2006, pension schemes which are not registered pension schemes are employer-financed retirement benefit schemes ('EFRBS'). Essentially, all existing pre A-Day unapproved pension schemes come under the tax regime applicable to EFRBS.

Former unapproved arrangements

16.121 Prior to A-Day, unapproved pension schemes were established by employers to top up benefits for employees whose benefits were limited by legislation. This applied, in particular, to employees subject to the so-called 'earnings cap' (see **16.98** above). There were two types of unapproved schemes: funded unapproved retirement benefit schemes ('FURBS'), and unfunded unapproved retirement benefit schemes ('UURBS').

FURBS

16.122 In broad terms, the pre A-Day tax treatment of a FURBS can be summarised as set out below.

(*a*) Contributions by the employer were allowable against corporation tax as soon as they were made.

(*b*) The employee was taxed on the employer's contributions as a benefit in kind.

(*c*) National Insurance contributions ('NICs') were payable on the contributions made.

(*d*) Investment returns were subject to tax at the basic rate on income (provided the FURBS was established for the sole purpose of providing 'relevant benefits', as defined in *ICTA 1988, s 612*, as applicable prior to 6 April 2006), and capital gains were subject to capital gains tax (with tapering relief available).

(*e*) Benefits payable to the employee were subject to income tax when paid as a pension; however, there was no liability to income tax if the benefits were paid as a lump sum (as long as the employer's contributions had been taxed on the employee as a benefit in kind when they were paid in). In practice, all benefits paid from FURBS on an employee's retirement have been paid as a tax-free lump sum in order to avoid the double tax charge. No NICs were payable on the lump sum.

(*f*) Lump sum benefits on the death of an employee were free from liability to income tax and also free from inheritance tax, provided that the benefits were paid under a discretionary trust and the FURBS qualified as a 'sponsored superannuation scheme' (as defined in *ICTA 1988, s 624*, as applicable prior to 6 April 1988).

UURBS

16.123 The pre A-Day tax treatment of an UURBS is considerably more straightforward than that of a FURBS, and can be summarised as set out below:

(*a*) Payments of benefit made to an employee were deductible for corporation tax when made.

(*b*) The employee was subject to income tax on payment of the benefit (whether paid as a lump sum or a pension).

(*c*) Lump sum benefits on the death of an employee were free from inheritance tax if they were provided from a 'sponsored superannuation scheme' under a discretionary trust; however, income tax was payable on the benefit (unless it was insured – ie 'funded').

EFRBS from A-Day

16.124 As EFRBS are not registered pension schemes, they are not subject to the *FA 2004* regime.

In view of the flexibility of the *FA 2004* regime to allow for (potentially) unlimited pensions within registered schemes, the only limit being on how much tax relief is given, the need for top-up schemes like the pre A-Day unapproved schemes has largely fallen away (unless the aim is to provide benefits that would not be allowed under a registered scheme). Non-registered pension schemes are allowed to continue but they do not receive any particular tax-favoured status. In particular, it should be noted that the exemptions from inheritance tax previously afforded to 'sponsored superannuation schemes' no longer apply (see **16.127** below).

A summary of the tax treatment of EFRBS from 6 April 2006 is set out below:

(*a*) The value of the individual's benefits is not taken into account for the purpose of testing against the lifetime allowance (see **16.7** above).

(*b*) Contributions are not subject to the annual allowance charge (see **16.17** above).

(*c*) All contributions paid after 5 April 2006 are treated as if made to an employee benefit trust. This means that, when contributions are made, no income tax or NICs are payable, and no corporation tax relief is available to the employer on those contributions. When the benefits are paid, income tax will be charged and relief from corporation tax given.

(*d*) So long as the employment relationship between employer and employee has ceased, there is no National Insurance charge on the benefits paid from an EFRBS, provided that the benefits are within the limits of benefits that can be paid under a registered scheme. As registered pension schemes may only pay a lump sum retirement benefit of up to a maximum of (broadly) 25 per cent of the value of the scheme benefits (see **16.41** above), this means that, in order to avoid any National Insurance charge, the lump sum must not exceed 25 per cent of the fund.

(*e*) The taxation of investment income has been aligned with the rates paid by higher rate taxpayers. Investment returns, whether income or capital gains, are taxed at 40 per cent (dividends at 32.5 per cent). Tapering relief continues to be available on capital gains tax.

(*f*) There is no automatic relief from inheritance tax (see **16.127** below).

Unfunded EFRBS

16.125 It can be seen from the above summary that the tax treatment of EFRBS is similar to the tax regime to which UURBS were subject prior to A-Day. Consequently, there continues to be a place for unfunded EFRBS under the new regime. Indeed, if an employee already has, or is likely by retirement to have, benefits that exceed the lifetime allowance, an unfunded EFRBS could be a viable option for providing retirement benefits in excess of this amount. The rate of tax on benefits payable under the EFRBS (currently 40 per cent) is less than the penal 55 per cent applied to lump sums in excess of the lifetime allowance payable from a registered scheme.

How attractive an employee finds an unfunded EFRBS will depend upon his view as to security. An unfunded benefit promise is only of value to the extent that the employer remains in existence and is able to pay the benefit. One way of addressing this concern is to provide some form of security for the promise, such as a charge over certain assets. Pre A-Day there were concerns that such a security would give rise to a tax charge if HMRC considered it to constitute funding. Under the post-A-Day regime this is immaterial, as employees will now be taxed on receipt of benefits from an EFRBS whether the scheme is funded or unfunded.

For many employees who had pre A-Day UURBS arrangements in place at 6 April 2006 and whose retirement benefits were not likely to exceed the lifetime allowance, it was sensible to consolidate their benefits under the UURBS and roll them into the employer's registered scheme, though, if this was done after 5 July 2006, the benefits would count against the individual's annual allowance in the tax year in which benefits are included in the registered scheme (other than in the tax year in which the individual becomes entitled to the benefits). Of course, rolling unfunded benefits into a registered pension scheme may not be advisable if there are concerns that the registered pension scheme might enter into the Pension Protection Fund, in view of the cap on PPF benefits (see CHAPTER 5). In those circumstances, a secured unfunded EFRBS, as referred to above, might be a more attractive option.

Funded EFRBS

16.126 The absence of any tax relief on contributions paid by an employer after 5 April 2006 to an EFRBS makes funded EFRBS an unattractive option (at least for employers). Transitional protections allow benefits under an EFRBS that were accrued before 6 April 2006 to be paid as a tax-free lump sum, provided that the employee was taxed on the employer's contributions paid into the arrangement (see **16.122**(*b*) and (*e*) above). However, any part of a lump sum attributable to contributions paid into an EFRBS after 5 April 2006 is taxable, so most employers will have ceased paying contributions into former FURBS (now EFRBS) after 5 April 2006 and investigated other options for compensating the employee.

Inheritance tax

16.127 Pension schemes established under trust are settled property for inheritance tax ('IHT') purposes. A number of specific exemptions take registered pension schemes outside the usual charges on this type of settlement for IHT purposes (see **16.79** above). Prior to 6 April 2006, most FURBS were also able to obtain these exemptions by virtue of being 'sponsored superannuation schemes' (*IHTA 1984, s 151(1)*). In practice, this required the payment of a separately identifiable administration charge by the employer. However, the exemption for sponsored superannuation schemes has, from 6 April 2006, been repealed (by *FA 2004, s 203(4)*). This means that EFRBS will be subject to the periodic charge and exit charge applicable to settlements without interest in possession (referred to in **16.79** above). Transitional IHT protection is available for pre-6 April 2006 funds.

Appendix I

Penalties under the Pensions Act 1995, Pensions Act 2004 and other legislation

Types of penalty

General

The *Pensions Act 1995* (*PA 1995*) carries a number of sanctions for non-compliance, ranging from fines to, in extreme cases, imprisonment. Many failures to comply with the requirements of the *Pensions Act 2004* (*PA 2004*) also give rise to penalties, but these are mostly confined to fines.

Civil penalties

The Regulator may require a person to pay a penalty in respect of an act or omission in contravention of various requirements of *PA 1995* and *PA 2004* (*PA 1995, s 10*). The maximum amount of the penalty varies from £5,000 in the case of an individual and £50,000 in any other case or such lower amount as may be prescribed. The time limit for payment is usually 28 days.

Where a penalty is recoverable from a corporate body, and the act or omission was done with the connivance or consent of an officer (or, in some cases, a managing shareholder) of the company, the Regulator may instead impose a penalty on that person.

Prohibition from acting as a trustee

The Regulator has the power to prohibit an individual from being a trustee (or director of a trustee company). The effect of a prohibition order is that the individual is removed as a trustee (*PA 1995, s 3*). The Regulator also has the power to suspend a trustee (*PA 1995, s 4*). The effect of the suspension order is to prohibit the trustee from exercising his functions in respect of the scheme(s) in question.

Criminal penalties

Certain transgressions carry criminal sanctions. Penalties for conviction of an offence are:

(*a*) on summary conviction – a fine not exceeding the statutory maximum; and

(*b*) on conviction on indictment – a fine or imprisonment or both.

Where an offence committed by a corporate body is proved to have been committed with the consent or connivance of an officer or purported officer of the company, that person is guilty of an offence and subject to the same punishment.

Appeals

The powers of the Regulator to impose penalties and prohibit trustees are 'reserved regulatory functions' exercisable by the Determinations Panel (*PA 2004, s 10*). Appeals against decisions of the Determinations Panel may be referred to the Pensions Regulator Tribunal (*PA 2004, s 103*). The Tribunal must determine any reference to it and then must remit the matter to the Determinations Panel with appropriate directions (which may include a direction to vary or revoke the original decision). A party to a determination of the Tribunal may, with permission, appeal to the court on a point of law.

Summary of penalties

A brief summary of the main transgressions for which penalties may be imposed is set out in the table below. This is not an exhaustive list.

Pensions Act 1995, s 10	
CIVIL SANCTIONS IMPOSED ON:	**HOW THE PENALTY ARISES:**
TRUSTEE/MANAGER	
	Failure to comply with a direction of the Regulator to make payments to members, include a statement in the annual report and send a statement to members (*PA 1995, s 15*)

	Failure to give notice to the Regulator that a trustee appointed under *PA 1995, s 23* is no longer an independent person (*PA 1995, s 25*, amended by *PA 2004, s 36*)
	Failure to give notice (required under *Scheme Administration Regulations 1996 (SI 1996/1715), reg 9*) of trustee meetings where decisions taken by majority (*PA 1995, s 32*)
	Failure to prepare or maintain a statement of investment principles or failure to obtain and consider advice before preparing the statement (*PA 1995, s 35*)
	Failure to obtain and consider proper advice before making an investment or failure to comply with the *Investment Regulations* (*PA 1995, s 36*)
	Failure to comply with requirements in relation to the payment of surplus to an employer (*PA 1995, s 37*)
	Investing in employer-related investments in excess of statutory limit (*PA 1995, s 40*)
	Failure to disclose documentation and information when required to do so (*Disclosure Regulations (SI 1996/1655)* made under *PA 1995, s 41*)
	Placing reliance on the skill and judgment of legal or other specified professional advisers (as to which, see *Scheme Administration Regulations 1996 (SI 1996/1715), reg 2*) not appointed by the trustees (*PA 1995, s 47*)
	Failure to appoint a scheme auditor, scheme actuary or fund manager when required to do so or failure to comply with requirements prescribed regarding the appointment of professional advisers (*PA 1995, s 47*)
	Failure to keep money in a separate account and failure to maintain adequate records relating to trustee meetings and certain transactions as required by regulations (see, in particular, the *Scheme Administration Regulations 1996 (SI 1996/1715)*) (*PA 1995, s 49*)
	Failure to give notice to the Regulator and the member of the failure of the employer to pay deductions from the employee's earnings to the trustees within the prescribed time (*PA 1995, s 49*)

	Failure to comply with the statutory requirements to keep written records of any determinations or decisions in relation to the winding up of the scheme (*PA 1995, s 49A*)
	Failure to make and/or implement arrangements for the resolution of disputes (*PA 1995, s 50*)
	Failure to take all reasonable steps to ensure that a modification is not voidable (*PA 1995, ss 67(2) and 67I(2)*)
	Failure to comply with any requirement imposed by the Regulator under *PA 1995, s 67G(5)* (*PA 1995, s 67I(4)*)
	Exercising a power to make a regulated modification in contravention of an order under *PA 1995, s 67H(2)(a)*
	Failure to comply with any requirement specified in an order under *PA 1995, s 67H(2)(b)*
	Failure to comply with the statutory order on a winding up (*PA 1995, s 73B*)
	Exercising a power to distribute excess assets on a winding up to an employer without having complied with the statutory requirements (*PA 1995, s 76*)
	Failure to prepare a schedule of payments for a defined contributions scheme (*PA 1995, s 87*)
	Failure to notify the Regulator and members within the required time where payments have not been made in accordance with the schedule of payments (*PA 1995, s 88*)
	Failure to provide a statement of guaranteed cash equivalent when required to do so or failure to comply with a transfer notice given by an eligible member (*PA 1995, s 153*; *PSA 1993, ss 93A, 99* and *101*) (includes statements/transfers in respect of pension credit benefits)
	Failure to make a report regarding a scheme's winding up where required to do so (*PA 1995, s 72A*)
	Failure to comply with a direction given by the Regulator to facilitate winding up (*PA 1995, s 72C*)
	Failure to comply with an improvement notice issued by the Regulator (*PA 2004, s 13*)
	Failure to comply with the terms of a freezing order issued by the Regulator (*PA 2004, s 24*)

	Failure to comply with a winding-up order or a freezing order issued by the Regulator (*PA 2004, s 28*)
	Failure to comply with directions where the Regulator revokes a freezing order (*PA 2004, s 30*)
	Failure to comply with a requirement from the Regulator to make a contribution on the revocation of a freezing order (*PA 2004, s 30*) applies to any trustee or manager who fails to take all reasonable steps to report the failure of the employer to pay
	Failure to comply with a notification order issued by the Regulator in relation to a freezing order (*PA 2004, s 31*)
	Failure to comply with a direction from the Regulator to suspend recovery of a *s 75* debt (*PA 2004, ss 41 and 50*)
	Failure to provide the Regulator with information in relation to the register (*PA 2004, s 62*)
	Failure to provide a scheme return to the Regulator (*PA 2004, s 64*)
	Failure to notify the Regulator of 'notifiable events' (*PA 2004, s 69*)
	Failure to comply with a report notice issued by the Regulator (*PA 2004, s 71*)
	Failure to comply with statutory requirements during an assessment period (*PA 2004, s 133*)
	Failure to comply with directions of the PPF Board during an assessment period (*PA 2004, s 134*)
	Failure to comply with statutory restrictions on winding up during an assessment period (*PA 2004, s 135*)
	Payment of benefits at PPF level during an assessment period (*PA 2004, s 138*)
	Deciding applications for ill-health pensions within six months of the assessment date (*PA 2004, s 140*)
	Failure to comply with directions of the PPF Board to wind up the scheme (*PA 2004, s 154*)
	Failure to comply with directions of the Regulator in relation to backdating the winding up of a scheme (*PA 2004, s 219*)

	Failure to prepare and review statement of funding principles (*PA 2004, s 223*)
	Failure to comply with requirements for winding up procedure (*PA 2004, s 231A*)
	Failure to obtain, receive and make available to the employer, an actuarial valuation or report (*PA 2004, s 224*)
	Failure to comply with the requirements in relation to a recovery plan (*PA 2004, s 226*)
	Failure to comply with the requirements in relation to a schedule of contributions (*PA 2004, s 227*)
	Failure to report failure to pay contributions where reasonable grounds to believe it may be of material significance to the Regulator (*PA 2004, s 228*)
	Failure to secure the agreement of the employer where required (*PA 2004, s 229*)
	Failure to report failure to agree to the Regulator (*PA 2004, s 229*)
	Failure to obtain the advice of the actuary where required (*PA 2004, s 230*)
	Failure to make arrangements for member-nominated trustees or member-nominated directors or failure to implement arrangements or appropriate rules (*PA 2004, s 241*)
	Failure to comply with requirements for member-nominated directors of corporate trustees (*PA 2004, s 242*)
	Accepting a funding payment if the scheme is not established under trust or does not have written benefit rules (*PA 2004, s 252*)
	A UK-based occupational pension scheme has activities which are not 'retirement based' (*PA 2004, s 255*)
	No amount may be paid out of scheme assets for the purpose of reimbursing any trustee or manager in relation to fines or civil penalties imposed under *PA 1995, PA 2004* or *PSA 1993* (*PA 2004, s 256*)
	Accepting or permitting reimbursement for fines or civil penalties imposed under *PA 1995, PA 2004* or *PSA 1993* (*PA 2004, s 256*)

	Failure to secure that the conditions for registration of a stakeholders' scheme are fulfilled while the scheme is registered (*WRPA 1999, s 2*)
	Failure to discharge liability in respect of a pension credit within the implementation period (*WRPA 1999, s 33*)
	Failure to notify the Regulator of a failure to discharge liability for a pension credit within the implementation period (*WRPA 1999, s 33*)
	Failure to notify the Regulator of the failure to comply with the transfer notice in respect of a pension credit benefit (*WRPA 1999, s 33*)
	Failure to provide a statement of entitlement to members when applied for by a member (*PSA 1993, s 93A*)
	Failure to carry out what a member of the scheme requires within six months of the necessary date as regards the exercise of the option conferred by *PSA 1993, s 95* (*PSA 1993, s 99*)
	Failure to notify a member of his right to a cash transfer sum within a reasonable period (*PSA 1993, s 101AC*)
	Failure to carry out early leaver's request for a cash transfer sum (*PSA 1993, s 101AG*)
	Failure on application of an eligible member of a salary related occupational pension scheme, to provide him with a written statement of the amount of cash equivalent of his pension credit benefit under the scheme (*PSA 1993, s 101H*)
	Failure to notify the Regulator of the failure to comply with transfer notice before the end of the period for compliance (*PSA 1993, s 101J*)
	Failure to notify the Regulator and/or the employee where contributions shown on the record of the direct payment arrangements had not been paid before the due date or failure to provide information to employee at specified intervals (*PSA 1993, s 111A*)
EMPLOYER	
	Failure to keep adequate records, as required by regulations (*PA 1995, s 49*)

	Deducting contributions from employees' earnings and failing to pay them to the trustees within required time with no reasonable excuse for doing so (*PA 1995, s 49*) (unless it is required to pay a penalty under *WRPA 1999, s 3(7)* for failures in respect of stakeholder schemes)
	Failure to make payments to a defined contributions scheme in accordance with the schedule of payments (*PA 1995, s 88*)
	Failure to comply with the terms of a freezing order issued by the Regulator (*PA 2004, s 24*) applies to an employer who without reasonable excuse fails to repay contributions required
	Failure to comply with a requirement from the Regulator to make a contribution on the revocation of a freezing order (*PA 2004, s 30*)
	Failure without reasonable excuse to pay contributions in accordance with the schedule of contributions or debt arising (*PA 2004, s 228*)
	Failure to comply with requirements regarding contribution payments to scheme with main administration outside the EEA states (*PA 2004, s 253*)
	Failure to comply with duty to facilitate access to stakeholders' pension scheme (*WRPA 1999, s 3*)
	Failure to prepare/maintain a record for direct payment arrangements regarding contributions to personal pension schemes or to send a copy of the record to the trustees or managers (*PSA 1993, s 111A*) (unless it is required to pay a penalty under *WRPA 1999, s 3(7)* for failures in respect of stakeholder pensions)
	Failure to pay the contribution payable under direct payment arrangements to the trustee/managers of the scheme on or before its due date (*PSA 1993, s 111A*)
MISCELLANEOUS	
Person purporting to exercise power	Non-trustee purporting to exercise a power in relation to the payment of surplus to the employer (*PA 1995, s 37*)
Prescribed person	Failure to keep adequate records, as required by regulations (*PA 1995, s 49*)

Any person other than trustees	Without reasonable excuse, exercising a power to modify a scheme without trustee consent or in breach of the timing requirement (*PA 1995, s 67I(3)*)
Any other person	Exercising a power to make a regulated modification in contravention of an order under *PA 1995, s 67H(2)(a)*
Any person	Exercising a power to distribute excess assets on a winding up to an employer without having complied with the statutory requirements (*PA 1995, s 76* of *1995*)
Any person	Failure to comply with a direction given by the Regulator to facilitate winding up (*PA 1995, s 72C*)
Any person to whom a third party notice is issued	Failure without reasonable excuse to comply with a third party notice issued by the Regulator (*PA 2004, s 14*)
Any deposit taker	Failure without reasonable excuse to comply with a pensions liberation restraining order issued by the Regulator (*PA 2004, s 20*)
Any deposit taker	Failure to take all reasonable steps to comply with a pensions liberation repatriation order issued by the Regulator (*PA 2004, s 21*)
Any other person	Failure to notify the Regulator of 'notifiable events' (*PA 2004, s 69*)
Any person	Failure to report breaches of law to the Regulator (*PA 2004, s 70*)
Any other person issued with a report notice	Failure to comply with a report notice issued by the Regulator (*PA 2004, s 71*)
Any other person	Failure to comply with directions of the PPF Board to wind up the scheme (*PA 2004, s 154*)
Any other person	Failure to comply with directions of the Regulator in relation to backdating the winding up of a scheme (*PA 2004, s 219*)
Any actuary	Failure to report to the Regulator when no certificate of technical provisions can be given (*PA 2004, s 225*)
Any actuary	Failure to report to the Regulator when the schedule of contributions cannot be certified (*PA 2004, s 227*)
Prescribed person	Failure to secure that the conditions for registration of a stakeholders' scheme are fulfilled while the scheme is registered (*WRPA 1999, s 2*)

CRIMINAL SANCTIONS IMPOSED ON:	**HOW THE PENALTY ARISES:**
TRUSTEE/MANAGER	
	Investing in employer-related investments in excess of statutory limit (*PA 1995, s 40*)
MISCELLANEOUS	
Any person purporting to so act	Purporting to act as a trustee whilst disqualified (*PA 1995, s 30*)
Any actuary or auditor so acting	Acting as an auditor or actuary whilst ineligible (*PA 1995, s 28*)
Any person	Being knowingly concerned in the fraudulent evasion of the obligation to pay deductions from employees' earnings to the trustees within the prescribed time (*PA 1995, s 49*)
Pensions Act 1995, s 3	
PROHIBITION ORDER IMPOSED ON:	**HOW THE PENALTY ARISES:**
TRUSTEE/MANAGER	
	Failure to give notice (required under *Scheme Administration Regulations 1996 (SI 1996/1715), reg 9*) of trustee meetings where decisions taken by majority (*PA 1995, s 32*)
	Failure to prepare or maintain a statement of investment principles or failure to obtain and consider advice before preparing the statement (*PA 1995, s 35*)
	Failure to obtain and consider proper advice before making an investment or failure to comply with the *Investment Regulations* (*PA 1995, s 36*)
	Failure to comply with requirements in relation to the payment of surplus to an employer (*PA 1995, s 37*)
	Failure to make arrangements for member-nominated trustees or member-nominated directors or failure to implement arrangements or appropriate rules (*PA 2004, s 241*)
	Placing reliance on the skill and judgment of legal or other specified professional advisers (as to which, see *Scheme Administration Regulations 1996 (SI 1996/1715), reg 2*) not appointed by the trustees (*PA 1995, s 47*)

MISCELLANEOUS	
Person purporting to exercise power	Non-trustee purporting to exercise a power in relation to the payment of surplus to the employer (*PA 1995, s 37*)
Pensions Act 2004	
CRIMINAL SANCTIONS IMPOSED ON:	**HOW THE PENALTY ARISES:**
TRUSTEE/MANAGER	
	Accepting or permitting reimbursement for fines or civil penalties imposed under *PA 1995, PA 2004* or *PSA 1993* (*PA 2004, s 256*)
MISCELLANEOUS	
Any person	Failure to provide information or produce a document when required under *PA 2004, s 72* (*PA 2004, s 77(1)*)
Any person	Delaying or obstructing an inspector exercising any power under *PA 2004, s 73, 74* or *75,* neglecting or refusing to produce any document under *PA 2004, s 75* or neglecting or refusing to answer questions or provide information when required by the Regulator (*PA 2004, s 77(2)*)
Any person	Intentionally and without reasonable excuse altering, suppressing, concealing or destroying a document required by the Regulator (*PA 2004, s 77(5)*)
Any person	Knowingly or recklessly providing false or misleading information to the Regulator (*PA 2004, s 80*)
Any person	Disclosing restricted information received from the Regulator without authority (*PA 2004, s 82*)
Any person	Failure to provide information or produce a document when required under *PA 2004, s 191* (*PA 2004, s 193(1)*)
Any person	Delaying or obstructing a person appointed by the PPF Board exercising any power under *PA 2004, s 192,* neglecting or refusing to produce any document under *PA 2004, s 192* or neglecting or refusing to answer questions or provide information when required (*PA 2004, s 193(2)*)
Any person	Intentionally and without reasonable excuse altering, suppressing, concealing or destroying a document required by the Board of the PPF (*PA 2004, s 193(6)*)

Any person	Knowingly or recklessly providing false or misleading information to the Board of the PPF (*PA 2004, s 195*)
Any person	Disclosing restricted information received from the Board of the PPF without authority (*PA 2004, s 197*)
Pensions Act 2008 – relevant provisions expected to be in force from October 2012	
CIVIL SANCTIONS IMPOSED ON:	***HOW THE PENALTY ARISES:***
ANY (TRUSTEE / MANAGER / EMPLOYER)	
Employer	*Failure to provide a personal accounts scheme (PA 2008, s 35)* *(Compliance Notice or Unpaid Contribution Notice)*
Employer	*Where a scheme is in place, failure to adhere to auto-enrolment provisions (including re-enrolment). Failure to allow a qualifying employee to opt in or out of the scheme and/or provide information to the qualifying employees or Pensions Regulator.* *(PA 2008, s 35) (Compliance Notice or Unpaid Contribution Notice)*
Employer	*Failure to comply with a compliance notice, contribution notice (see above) or notice under PA 2004, s 72. (PA 2008, s 40) (a fixed penalty notice can be imposed)*
Employer	*Contravention of automatic-enrolment, the right to opt-in or refund of contributions following an opt-out, or contravention of information requirements to workers. (PA 2008, s 40) (a fixed penalty notice can be imposed)*
Employer	*Failure to comply with a compliance notice, contribution notice (see above) or notice under PA 2004, s 72 before a specified date (where no review or referral has been made). (PA 2008, s 41) (an escalating fixed penalty notice can be imposed)*

Regulations	
Occupational Pensions Schemes (Requirement to Obtain Audited Accounts and a Statement from the Auditor) Regulations 1996 (SI 1996/1975)	
CIVIL SANCTIONS IMPOSED ON:	**HOW THE PENALTY ARISES:**
Trustee or Manager	Failure without reasonable excuse to obtain audited accounts or an auditor's contribution statement within seven months of end of scheme year (*reg 3*)
Occupational Pension Schemes (Preservation of Benefit) Regulations 1991 (SI 1991/167)	
CIVIL PENALTY IMPOSED ON:	**HOW THE PENALTY ARISES:**
Any person	Failure to provide information regarding transfer of accrued rights without consent (*reg 27B*)
Disclosure Regulations (SI 1996/1655)	
CIVIL PENALTY IMPOSED ON:	**HOW THE PENALTY ARISES:**
Any person	Failure to comply with any requirement of the *Disclosure Regulations* (*reg 11*)
Pensions on Divorce etc (Provision of Information) Regulations 2000 (SI 2000/1048)	
CIVIL PENALTY IMPOSED ON:	**HOW THE PENALTY ARISES:**
Trustee or Manager	Failure to provide specified information regarding pension sharing (*reg 9*)

Occupational Pension Scheme (Winding Up) Regulations 1996 (SI 1996/3126), reg 11 made under PA 1995, s 38	
CIVIL PENALTY IMPOSED ON:	**HOW THE PENALTY ARISES:**
Any person	Failure to issue appropriate notice within one month following determination to defer winding up of scheme or as to when liabilities are to be determined
Finance Act 2004	
CIVIL SANCTIONS IMPOSED ON:	**HOW THE PENALTY ARISES:**
SCHEME ADMINISTRATOR (usually the trustees)	
	Failure to provide scheme return (*FA 2004, s 257*)
	Failure to make an accounting return (*FA 2004, s 260*) This can result in a civil penalty *and* scheme sanction charge.
	Winding up wholly or mainly to facilitate the payment of lump sums (*FA 2004, s 265*)
	Transferring sums to insured schemes unless payment is made to the scheme administrator or relevant insurance company (*FA 2004, s 266*)
MISCELLANEOUS	
Person who fails to comply	Failure to provide information required by regulations (*FA 2004, s 258*)
Person who fails to comply	Failure to comply with notice to provide documents or particulars (*FA 2004, s 259*)
The individual member	Providing false or fraudulent information in relation to enhanced lifetime allowance or failing to provide information (*FA 2004, ss 261* and *262*)
The individual member	Failure to notify the HMRC within 90 days of relevant benefit accrual in relation to enhanced protection of lifetime allowance (*FA 2004, s 263*)
Person making the statement	Fraudulently or negligently making a false statement (*FA 2004, s 264*)

FSMA 2000	
CIVIL SANCTIONS IMPOSED ON:	**HOW THE PENALTY ARISES:**
Any approved person issued with a statement of principle	Failure to comply with a statement of principle issued by the FSA (*FSMA 2000, s 66*) (A civil penalty or statement of misconduct can be imposed)
Any approved person	Knowing concern in a contravention, by a relevant authorised person, of a requirement imposed on that authorised person by, or under, *FSMA 2000* (*FSMA 2000, s 66*) (A civil penalty or statement of misconduct can be imposed)
Any person or persons privy to unpublished price sensitive information	Engaging in, or by act or omission encouraging or requiring another to engage in, market abuse (*FSMA 2000, s 123*) (A civil penalty or statement indicating engagement in market abuse can be imposed)
Any person subject to a notice of objection	Failure to abide by a restriction notice issued by the FSA (*FSMA 2000, s 191B*) (punishable by restrictions on voting powers and/or use of shares)
Any authorised person	Contravention of a requirement relating to authorised persons under *FSMA 2000* (*FSMA 2000, ss 205* and *206*) (Civil penalty or statement of contravention issued by the FSA)
Any authorised person	Communicating an invitation or inducement to participate in an unauthorised collective investment scheme (*FSMA 2000, ss 238 & 241*) (Civil action by a private person – *see FSMA 2000, s 150*)
Any person	On application to the FSA or the Secretary of State there is a reasonable likelihood or actual case of a potential or continuing relevant requirement under the Act being contravened (*FSMA 2000, s 380*) (An Injunction can be imposed)
Any person	Accruing profit or causing loss as a result of a contravention or knowing involvement in a contravention of a relevant requirement (*FSMA 2000, s 382*) (a Restitution order can be imposed)
CRIMINAL SANCTIONS IMPOSED ON:	**HOW THE PENALTY ARISES**
Any person acting in the course of business	Carrying on a regulated activity while unauthorised, or not exempt from the general prohibition (*FSMA 2000, s 23*)

Any person acting in the course of business	Communicating an invitation or inducement to engage in investment activity (*FSMA 2000, s 25*)
Any person who is deemed to be unfit and improper by the FSA	An unfit and improper individual carrying out functions in relation to a regulated activity for an authorised person (*FSMA 2000, s 56*) (Prohibition order can be imposed)
Any person under a duty to notify	Failure to notify the FSA of a step which would result in the acquiring or increase in of control over a UK authorised person (*FSMA 2000, s 178*) (Criminal offence punishable by fine only) (see *FSMA 2000, s 191F*)
Any person who is in possession of confidential information	Disclosure or use of confidential information by, or obtained from, a primary recipient without the relevant consent (*FSMA 2000, s 352*)
Any person	Accruing or making a profit or causing loss as a result of a contravention or knowing involvement in a contravention of a relevant requirement (*FSMA 2000, s 382*)
Any person	Making a statement, promise or forecast which is known to be misleading, false or deceptive in a material particular (*FSMA 2000, s 397*)
Any person	Dishonestly concealing any material facts whether in connection with a statement, promise or forecast made by the offender or otherwise (*FSMA 2000, s 397*)
Any person	Recklessly making (dishonestly or otherwise) a statement, promise or forecast which is misleading, false or deceptive in a material particular (*FSMA 2000, s 397*)
Any person	Knowingly or recklessly giving the FSA information which is false or misleading in a material particular in purported compliance with any requirement imposed by or under the *Act* (*FSMA 2000, s 398*) (Criminal offence (punishable by fine only))

Appendix II

Summary of the application of the Occupational Pension Schemes (Disclosure of Information) Regulations 1996 (SI 1996/1655) (the 'Disclosure Regulations'), and other requirements to disclose information

NOTE: In July 2007, as part of the DWP's Deregulatory Review of private pensions, the Government established a working group to consider a principles-based approach to the disclosure requirements.

In March 2009, the DWP issued a consultation on amendments to the disclosure regime, concluding that an entirely principles-based approach is not appropriate. The DWP is now of the view that it is necessary to specify disclosure requirements in certain circumstances, such as when the information is concerning member benefits. The DWP consultation paper also contained proposals to simplify the disclosure regime into a single set of regulations.

The consultation ended on May 2009 and the DWP issued draft regulations for consultation in January 2010. The idea of principles-based disclosure has been abandoned and the consolidation of the disclosure regime into a single set of regulations postponed. It is intended that the amending regulations, which introduce provisions dealing with electronic disclosure to members, will come into force in October 2010.

To be disclosed	Disclosure to	Form of disclosure	When
CONSTITUTION OF THE SCHEME (***Disclosure Regulations, reg 3***) **(all schemes)**			
The contents of: ● the trust deed or other document constituting the scheme; ● the rules (if not in above document); ● any documents amending, supplementing or superseding any of the above; ● a document setting out the names and addresses of participating employers, if not in the above documents. Reference to (or text of) relevant provisions of Acts or statutory instruments set out or referred to in the above documents. English translation if necessary.	● Members, prospective members and their spouses or civil partners. ● Beneficiaries. ● Recognised trade unions. *Only information relevant to an individual need be disclosed to him or to his trade union.*	● Copy for inspection, free of charge at a place which is reasonable; or ● Personal copy at a reasonable charge (ie cost of copying, postage & packaging) or, if publicly available, notice of where a copy may be obtained from.	On request, within two months of the request being made.
BASIC INFORMATION ABOUT THE SCHEME (***Disclosure Regulations, reg 4, Sch 1***) **(all schemes)**			
Membership Categories of people who are eligible to be members and whether they are admitted: ● only on their own application; or ● automatically unless they request not to be admitted; or ● subject to the consent of their employer.	● Members, prospective members and their spouses or civil partners. ● Beneficiaries. ● Recognised trade unions.	No specified form but must include a written statement that further information is available, giving address to which inquiries should be sent.	As of course, to every prospective member or, if not practicable to do so, within two months of his becoming a member.

To be disclosed	Disclosure to	Form of disclosure	When
The conditions of eligibility for membership. The period of notice (if any) which a member must give to terminate his pensionable service. Whether and on what conditions (if any) a member may re-enter pensionable service before normal pension age.	*Only information relevant to an individual need be disclosed to him or to his trade union.*		To the extent that any information has not been given to a person who was an active member or pensioner on 5 April 1997, it must have been given to that person by 5 April 1998 (or, in the case of a deferred member, within two months of him becoming a pensioner, if later).
Contributions How employers' contributions are determined. How members' normal contributions are determined. What arrangements are made for members to pay additional voluntary contributions.			Otherwise, on request, (unless the same information was provided in the 12 months prior to the request being made), as soon as practicable and in any event, within two months of the date of receipt of request.
Scheme details Whether the scheme is a tax-approved scheme and, if not, whether an application for tax approval has been made.[1]			Details of material changes must be drawn to attention of members and beneficiaries (but not excluded persons) before the change if practicable, but in any event, within three months after the change.

1 The Disclosure Regulations should have been amended to take account of FA 2004 and this paragraph ought to require information on whether the scheme is registered, not approved. No such amendments have been made as yet.

To be disclosed	Disclosure to	Form of disclosure	When
Which of the relevant employments are, and which are not, contracted out. Whether the scheme is contracted out for these employments by virtue of the *Pension Schemes Act 1993* (*PSA 1993*) or by being one to which regulations made under *Pensions Act 1995* (*PA 1995*), *s 149* apply (mixed benefit contracted-out schemes). The short title of the enactment (if any) which provides for: ● the setting up of the scheme; and ● the determination of the rate or amount of the benefits. **Benefits** Normal pension age under the scheme (except simplified defined contribution schemes). What benefits are payable and how they are calculated (including how pensionable earnings are defined and the rate at which benefits accrue and including, in a contracted-out money purchase or hybrid scheme, that the amount of assets allocated for the provision of protected rights benefits are increased, how they are increased and why that method is used).			

To be disclosed	Disclosure to	Form of disclosure	When
The conditions on which benefits are paid. Whether and, if so, when and on what conditions, survivors' benefits are payable. Which benefits, if any, are payable only at some person's discretion. Whether there is a power under the scheme to increase pensions after they have become payable, and, if so, who may exercise it, and to what extent it is discretionary. Where the scheme is a hybrid scheme for contracting-out purposes, the circumstances in which the nature of a member's accrued rights may alter and a statement that the trustees will notify the member if his rights are affected. **Administration** What arrangements are made, and in what circumstances, for estimates or statements of a guaranteed cash equivalent, for the refund of contributions and the preservation or transfer of the accrued rights of early leavers.			

To be disclosed	Disclosure to	Form of disclosure	When
Whether, and the circumstances in which, the trustees will accept cash equivalents and provide transfer credits and whether this is discretionary. If applicable, a statement to the effect that the trustees have directed that any cash equivalent shall not take into account discretionary benefits. A statement summarising the way in which transfer values are calculated. A statement that an annual report is available on request (except public sector schemes). A statement that the following information is available on request: ● Unless the scheme is exempt, what procedures it has for the internal resolution of disputes, including the address and job title of the person to be contacted. ● A statement that the Pensions Advisory Service is available to assist in connection with queries and unresolved disputes and the address at which it may be contacted.			

To be disclosed	Disclosure to	Form of disclosure	When
• A statement that the Pensions Ombudsman may investigate and determine any complaint or dispute of fact or law in relation to an occupational pension scheme and the address at which he may be contacted. • A statement that the Pensions Regulator is able to intervene in the running of schemes where trustees, employers or other professional advisers have failed in their duties, and in certain other circumstances, and the address at which it may be contacted. • The address to which inquiries about the scheme generally or about an individual's entitlement to benefit should be sent.			

To be disclosed	Disclosure to	Form of disclosure	When
INFORMATION TO BE MADE AVAILABLE TO INDIVIDUALS (*Disclosure Regulations, reg 5, Sch 2*) **(all schemes)**			
Pensions (all schemes)			
The amount of benefit which is payable and if a benefit is payable periodically: ● the conditions (if any) subject to which payment will be continued; and ● the provisions (if any) under which the amount payable may be altered. The rights and options (if any) available on the death of a member or beneficiary, and the procedures for exercising them.	Any person to whom a benefit has become, or is about to become, payable.	Information plus written statement that further information is available, giving address to which inquiries should be sent.	As of course, before or within one month (two months where the person is retiring before normal pension age) after the date on which benefit becomes payable.
If the amount of benefit is to be altered (other than under a provision already notified to the person concerned): ● the amount of benefit which is payable to the person; and ● the rights and options (if any) available on the person's death and the procedures for exercising them.	Any person in receipt of a benefit.	Information plus written statement that further information is available, giving address to which inquiries should be sent.	As of course, before or within one month after the later of the date of the decision to make the alteration and the effective date of the alteration.

To be disclosed	Disclosure to	Form of disclosure	When
Active members, deferred members and pension credit members: all schemes except money purchase schemes			
● in the case of an active member: – the amounts of the member's and his survivors' benefits which would be payable (ignoring future salary increases) from normal pension age or death if his pensionable service were to terminate either (at the trustees' discretion) within one month of the date on which the information is given or on his normal pension age; and – the amount of any death in service benefits which would be payable if he died within one month of the date on which the information is given, with details of how those benefits are calculated (except simplified deferred contributions schemes).	Any member.	Information plus written statement that further information is available, giving the address to which inquiries should be sent.	On request (unless within 12 months of information being given following a similar request), as soon as practicable, and in any event within two months of the request.

To be disclosed	Disclosure to	Form of disclosure	When
• In the case of a deferred member, the date pensionable service ceased and the amounts of his own and his survivors' benefits payable from normal pension age or death. • In either case the information must include: – date on which the member's pensionable service commenced; – the accrual rate or formula for calculating the member's own benefits and any survivors' benefits; – the amount of the member's pensionable remuneration on the relevant date (ie for an active member the date when the information is given or a date within a month thereof and for a deferred member, the date pensionable service ceased); and – details of how any deduction from benefits is calculated.			

To be disclosed	Disclosure to	Form of disclosure	When
● In the case of a pension credit member, the amounts of his own benefits and of any survivors' benefits payable from normal pension age or death. The information in respect of a pension credit member must include: – the method or formula for calculating the member's own benefits and any survivors' benefits; and – details of how any deduction from benefits is calculated.			
All members: money purchase schemes In the case of a scheme which provides money purchase benefits (excluding stakeholder schemes): ● the amount of contributions (before the making of any deductions) credited to the member during the preceding scheme year and, where the scheme is contracted out, the contributions attributable to: – the minimum payments required to be made in respect of the member by his employer during the preceding year;	Each member who is eligible for money purchase benefits (except excluded persons).	Information plus written statement that further information is available, giving address to which inquiries should be sent.	As of course, within 12 months of the end of each scheme year.

To be disclosed	Disclosure to	Form of disclosure	When
– any rebate payments made by the DWP; – the age-related payments (if any) made by the DWP; and – the date of birth used in determining the appropriate age-related percentage and name and address of whom to contact should the date of birth be incorrect. • in the case of a simplified defined contribution scheme, the amount or fraction of contributions applied to insure death benefits; • the value of: – the member's protected rights as at a specified date; – the member's accrued rights (other than protected rights) at the same or another specified date; and – the cash equivalent of the member's rights, if different. • in the case of a pension credit member: – the value of his accrued rights under the scheme at a specified date; and – his cash equivalent if different.			

To be disclosed	Disclosure to	Form of disclosure	When
• an illustration of the amount of the pension which would be likely to accrue to a member, or be capable of being secured by him at retirement in respect of his money purchase benefits that may arise under the scheme. The following statements must accompany the illustration: – that the information is provided only for the purposes of illustration; – that its provision is required by law; – how to obtain further information from the trustees that the information has been prepared by reference to the assumptions; – that certain general assumptions have been made about the nature of the investments and their likely performance; – that the amount referred to is expressed in today's prices; – that the actual amount of any pension under the scheme will depend on considerations which may differ from the assumptions made for the purpose of providing the illustration;			

To be disclosed	Disclosure to	Form of disclosure	When
– specifying any assumptions made in relation to future contributions to the scheme; – of the assumptions; – of the member's retirement date; and – of the illustration date used for the purpose of calculating the amount referred to in the illustration.			
Hybrid schemes Where a hybrid scheme is contracted-out and under the rules of the scheme an earner's service is contracted-out, employment will cease to qualify him for benefits under one part of the scheme but begin to qualify him for benefits under another part of the scheme: ● the date he begins to qualify for different benefits; and ● the basis on which his rights accrued after that date will be contracted-out.	Each member who ceases to qualify under one part of the scheme and begins to qualify for benefits under the other part of the scheme.	Information plus written statement that further information is available, giving address to which inquiries should be sent.	Within two months after the date on which his service begins to qualify him for different benefits.

To be disclosed	Disclosure to	Form of disclosure	When
Money purchase schemes Where a scheme is, or has been a money purchase scheme or provides money purchase benefits, the options available to the member within the scheme rules.	Each member and pension credit member who is eligible for money purchase benefits.	Information plus written statement that further information is available, giving address to which inquiries should be sent.	As of course, at least six months prior to normal pension age or date of retirement (or within seven days if less than six months until retirement).
Money purchase schemes ceasing to contract out Where a scheme ceases to be a contracted-out money purchase scheme: In the case of a member other than a pension credit member: ● the amount of contributions (before any deductions) credited to the member during the immediately preceding scheme year including contributions attributable to: – the minimum payments required to be made in respect of the member by his employer during the preceding year; – any rebate payments made by the DWP; – the age-related payments (if any) made by the DWP; and	Each member who has ceased to be contracted-out.	Information plus written statement that further information is available, giving address to which inquiries should be sent.	In respect of the notification that the scheme has ceased to be contracted-out, as soon as practicable but in any event within one month of the scheme ceasing to contract out. In respect of the other information, as soon as practicable and in any event within four months of the scheme ceasing to contract out.

To be disclosed	Disclosure to	Form of disclosure	When
– the date of birth used in determining the appropriate age-related percentage and the name of whom to contact and their address should the date of birth be incorrect. In the case of a simplified defined contribution scheme, the amount or fraction of contributions applied to insure death benefits: ● the value of: – the member's protected rights as at a specified date; – the member's accrued rights (excluding protected rights) as at the same or another specified date; – the cash equivalent of the member's rights, if different; ● the date on which the scheme ceased to be such a scheme; ● the options available in respect of protected rights; and			

To be disclosed	Disclosure to	Form of disclosure	When
Where a scheme ceases to be a contracted-out money purchase scheme: ● if the scheme is not able to meet its liabilities in full, an account of the amount by which protected rights and accrued rights other than protected rights have been reduced, and of the action taken by the scheme, or which is open to the member to take, to restore their value. In the case of a pension credit member: ● the value of the pension credit member's safeguarded rights under the scheme as at a specified date; and ● the value of the pension credit member's accrued rights (other than his safeguarded rights under the scheme at the same or another specified date); and ● his cash equivalent if different.			

To be disclosed	Disclosure to	Form of disclosure	When
Contingent beneficiaries (all schemes)			
Where a member or beneficiary has died: • the rights and options (if any) available to the contingent beneficiary, and the procedures for exercising them; and • the provisions under which any contingent pension may or will be increased, and the extent to which such increases are discretionary or a statement that there are no such provisions.	Any contingent beneficiary who is at least 18 and whose address is known to the trustees. Personal representative of the deceased or any person entitled to act on behalf of the contingent beneficiary.	Information plus written statement that further information is available, giving address to which inquiries should be sent.	As of course, as soon as practicable and in any event within two months of trustees receiving notification of the death. On request (unless within three years of information being given to same person in same capacity), as soon as practicable and in any event within two months of request being made.
Transfers (all schemes)			
Whether the member or prospective member is entitled to acquire transfer credits in exchange for a cash equivalent or other transfer payment provided by another scheme, and if so, a statement of those transfer credits.	Any member or prospective member.	Information plus written statement that further information is available, giving address to which inquiries should be sent.	On request (unless within 12 months of information being given following a similar request) within two months of request.

To be disclosed	Disclosure to	Form of disclosure	When
Winding-up (all schemes)			
Where trustees have commenced winding-up the scheme or a section of a multi-employer scheme which is to be treated as a separate scheme: • notification of the winding-up and the reasons for it and the name and address of a person to whom any further inquiries about the scheme should be sent; • notification of whether death benefits will continue to be payable; • if the independent trustee requirements apply, notification that at least one of the trustees is required to be an independent person; • what action is being taken to establish the scheme's liabilities and to recover any assets; when it is anticipated final details will be known; and (where the trustees have sufficient information) an indication of the extent to which, the actuarial value of accrued rights are likely to be reduced.	All members, all persons entitled to a pension credit and beneficiaries (except excluded persons) (but only active members in relation to the second point).	Information plus written statement that further information is available, giving address to which inquiries should be sent.	As of course, as soon as practicable and in any event within one month of the winding-up trigger. In addition, in the case of the final point, at least once in every successive 12-month period until the completion of the winding-up.

To be disclosed	Disclosure to	Form of disclosure	When
Where, before 6 April 1997, trustees have commenced winding-up the scheme or a section of a multi-employer scheme which is to be treated as a separate scheme: ● what action is being taken to establish the scheme's liabilities and to recover any assets; ● when it is anticipated final details will be known; and ● (when the trustees have sufficient information) an indication of the extent to which the actuarial value of accrued rights is likely to be reduced.	All members and beneficiaries (except excluded persons).	Information plus written statement that further information is available giving address to which inquiries should be sent.	At least once in every successive 12-month period beginning with the date of commencement of the winding-up and ending with the date of the completion of the winding-up.
Where trustees are engaged in winding-up the scheme or a section of a multi-employer scheme which is to be treated as a separate scheme: ● the amount of benefit which is payable to the person; ● if a benefit is payable periodically: – the provisions (if any) under which the amount payable may be altered; – the conditions (if any) subject to which payment will be continued;	Every beneficiary and every member who is entitled to payment of benefits (except excluded persons).	Information plus written statement that further information is available, giving address to which inquiries should be sent.	As soon as practicable and in any event within three months the trustees having discharged their liabilities.

To be disclosed	Disclosure to	Form of disclosure	When
● (except in the case of money purchase schemes) if the member is not entitled to payment of benefits an estimate of amount of the member's own benefits and of his survivors' benefits which are expected to be payable from normal pension age or death; ● notification of: – whether, and if so by how much, the benefits are reduced because of insufficient scheme resources; – who has or will become liable to pay benefits after scheme is wound up.			
Where a report has been made by the trustees or managers of the scheme to the Regulator under *PA 1995, s 72A*, a copy of the report must contain the following: ● name of scheme; ● date on which winding-up commenced; ● scheme registration number; ● statement as to the nature of the benefits provided by the scheme; ● statement as to whether an independent trustee has been appointed;	Any member or beneficiary who requests a copy.	Written report.	Within two months of the request.

To be disclosed	Disclosure to	Form of disclosure	When
● name and address of scheme actuary (if relevant); ● name and address of any third party administrator; ● estimate of when winding-up will be completed; ● statement as to what steps have been taken in the winding-up, what steps remain and when each step is estimated to be completed; ● a statement as to whether any particular difficulties are hindering the winding-up.			
Stakeholder pensions Where stakeholder scheme is removed from the register of such schemes: ● notification of that fact and of the fact that it is required to commence winding-up under the rules.	Every member (except excluded persons).	Information plus written statement that further information is available giving address to which inquiries should be sent.	Within two weeks of being notified of the removal from the register.

To be disclosed	Disclosure to	Form of disclosure	When
Scheme funding			
Where the scheme is one to which *Pensions Act 2004, Part 3* (*PA 2004*) applies and a valuation under *s 224* has been obtained: ● summary funding statement.	All members and beneficiaries (except excluded persons).		On, or before, or within a reasonable period after, the date by which the trustees are required to ensure that the valuation or report is received by them. A reasonable period is usually deemed to be three months – see *Pensions Regulator Code of Practice No.3, para 144*.
Where the scheme is one to which *PA 2004, Part 3* applies, has at least 100 members and a valuation under *s 224* has not yet been obtained: ● summary funding statement.	All members and beneficiaries (except excluded persons).		By 22 September 2006 and in each subsequent year.
Where a scheme has been modified as regards the future accrual of benefits by the Regulator under *PA 2004, s 231(2)(a)*: ● notification of that fact.	All active members.		Within one month of the modification taking effect.

To be disclosed	Disclosure to	Form of disclosure	When
AVAILABILITY AND CONTENT OF ANNUAL REPORT (*Disclosure Regulations, reg 6, Sch 3*) **(all schemes except certain public sector schemes (*reg 6(2)*))**			
A document which contains: ● the audited accounts and the auditor's statement required under *PA 1995, s 41* for the scheme year to which the document relates; ● the latest actuarial statement given under *PA 1995, s 41*; ● the latest actuarial certificate obtained in accordance with *PA 2004, s 227*; ● the names of the persons, including the directors of any sole trustee company, who were trustees during the relevant year; ● the provisions of the scheme (or articles of association in the case of a sole trustee company) in relation to appointing and removing trustees (or directors of the sole trustee company); ● the names of the professional advisers and others who have acted for the trustees during the year, with an indication of any change since the previous year;	● Members and prospective members and their spouses or civil partners. ● Beneficiaries. ● Recognised trade unions.	● Personal copy of latest report/information free of charge (on first request) plus written statement that further information is available, giving address to which inquiries should be sent; ● Copies of reports/ information for previous five years available: – for inspection (free of charge) at a place that is reasonable; or – personal copy (at a reasonable charge), plus written statement that further information is available, giving address to which inquiries should be sent.	To be available within seven months of end of each scheme year which ends after 6 April 1997 and to be provided within two months of request.

To be disclosed	Disclosure to	Form of disclosure	When
• the address to which inquiries about the scheme generally or about an individual's entitlement to benefit should be sent; • the number of active, deferred and pensioner members and beneficiaries as at any one date during the scheme year; • except in a money purchase scheme, the percentage increases made during the year to pensions in payment and deferred pensions and a statement of the extent to which they are discretionary (if variable for different individuals, state the maximum, minimum and average); • (except in the case of an insured money purchase scheme) a statement, where applicable, explaining: – why any cash equivalents paid during the year were not calculated and verified in accordance with legislative requirements; – why cash equivalents paid during the year were less than the amount for which legislation provides and when full values were or will be available; and			

To be disclosed	Disclosure to	Form of disclosure	When
– whether, and if so how, discretionary benefits are included in the calculation of transfer values; ● a statement as to whether the accounts have been prepared and audited in accordance with *PA 1995, s 41* (unless exempt), and if not, the reasons why not, and a statement as to how the situation has been or is likely to be resolved; ● details of who has managed the investments during the year and the extent of any delegation by the trustees; ● confirmation of whether the trustees have produced a statement of investment principles in accordance with *PA 1995, s 35* (unless exempt), advising that a copy is available on request; ● a statement as to the trustees' policy on the custody of the scheme's assets (except in relation to a wholly insured scheme);			

To be disclosed	Disclosure to	Form of disclosure	When
● unless exempt from the requirement to produce a statement of investment principles, an investment report containing: – a statement by the trustees, or fund manager, providing details of any investments which were not made in accordance with the statement of investment principles, giving the reasons why and explaining what action, if any, has been or will be taken to resolve the position; – a review of the investment performance during the year and a period of between three and five years ending with the year, including an assessment of the nature, disposition, marketability, security and valuation of the scheme's assets; ● a copy of any statement made on the resignation or removal of the auditor or actuary; ● where the scheme has employer-related investments a statement: – as to a percentage of the scheme's resources so invested;			

To be disclosed	Disclosure to	Form of disclosure	When
– if that percentage exceeds 5%, as to the percentage of the scheme's resources which are not subject to the statutory restrictions; and – if the statutory restriction on employer-related investments is exceeded, the steps taken (or to be taken) to secure compliance, and when those steps will be taken.			
AVAILABILITY OF OTHER DOCUMENTS (***Disclosure Regulations, reg 7***) **(Public service schemes are exempt)**			
Statement of funding principles where required under *PA 2004, s 223.* Where *PA 2004, Part 3* applies to the scheme, the latest actuarial valuation under *PA 2004, s 224* received by the trustees and an actuarial report received by them under that section if more recent. Any recovery plan prepared under *PA 2004, s 226* which is currently in force. Payment schedule where required under *PA 1995, s 87* or schedule of contributions where required under *PA 2004, s 227.*	● Members, prospective members and their spouses or civil partners. ● Beneficiaries. ● Recognised trade unions.	● Copy for inspection, free of charge at a place which is reasonable. ● Personal copy at reasonable charge. Document must be accompanied by a written statement that further information is available, giving address to which inquiries should be sent.	On request, within two months of the request being made.

To be disclosed	Disclosure to	Form of disclosure	When
Latest statement of principles governing decisions about investments where required under *PA 1995, s 35*. An outline of the winding up procedure prepared or revised under *PA 2004, s 231A*.			
LIMITED DISCLOSURE IN RELATION TO UNAPPROVED SCHEMES[2] (***Disclosure Regulations, reg 8, Sch 1***) **(all schemes other than public sector schemes)**			
• What benefits are payable under the scheme and how they are calculated (including how pensionable earnings are defined and the rate at which benefits accrue). • What arrangements are made and in what circumstances for estimates of cash equivalents, statements of entitlement to guaranteed cash equivalents, refunds to contributions and preservation or transfer of accrued rights in relation to early leavers. • What procedures the scheme has for the internal resolution of disputes (unless it is an exempt scheme under *PA 1995, s 50(8)*) and the address and job title of the person to be contacted in order to have recourse to these.	• Members. • Prospective members. • Recognised trade unions. *Only information relevant to an individual need be disclosed to his trade union.*	Written statement that further information is available, giving address to which inquiries should be sent.	As of course, to every prospective member and, where not practical, to a person within two months of his becoming a member.

2 The Disclosure Regulations should have been amended to take account of FA 2004 and this section ought to relate to schemes which are unregistered.

To be disclosed	Disclosure to	Form of disclosure	When
• A statement that the Pensions Advisory Service is available at any time to assist members and beneficiaries of the scheme in connection with pension queries and the resolution of disputes and the address at which TPAS may be contacted. • A statement that the Pensions Ombudsman may investigate and determine any complaint of fact or law in relation to an occupational pension scheme and the address at which he may be contacted. • A statement that the Regulator is able to intervene in the running of schemes where trustees, employers or professional advisers have failed in their duties and the address at which it may be contacted. • The address to which inquiries about the scheme generally or about an individual's entitlement to benefit should be sent. • A statement as to which of the benefits are and which are not funded and, where benefits are funded, the manner in which they are secured.			

To be disclosed	Disclosure to	Form of disclosure	When
• A statement that the provisions of *PA 1995* are not applicable to the scheme (subject to certain exceptions).			
INFORMATION TO BE FURNISHED TO EARLY LEAVERS (***Occupational Pension Schemes (Preservation of Benefit) Regulations 1991 (SI 1991/167), reg 27A***) **(all schemes)**			
Any information relating to the rights and options available to a member whose pensionable service terminates before he attains normal pension age.	Any member or prospective member.	To be furnished in writing.	As soon as practicable and, in any event, within two months of the request being made (unless within 12 months of information being given following a similar request).
	Any deferred member.	To be furnished in writing.	As of course, as soon as practicable and, in any event, within two months of notification of termination of pensionable service.
Information whether a refund of contributions is, or would be, available in any circumstances together with an estimate of the amount of the refund and an explanation of the method of calculation.	Any person who has paid contributions to the scheme (which have not already been refunded).	To be furnished in writing.	As soon as practicable and, in any event, within two months after request (unless he has already been told that there will be no refund or the request is within 12 months of information being given following a similar request).

To be disclosed	Disclosure to	Form of disclosure	When
TRANSFER OF MEMBER'S ACCRUED RIGHTS WITHOUT CONSENT (***Occupational Pension Schemes (Preservation of Benefit) Regulations 1991 (SI 1991/167), reg 12(4B)***) **(all schemes)**			
Information about the proposed transfer and details of the value of the rights to be transferred including rights in respect of death in service benefits and survivors' benefits.	Those members being transferred.	In writing.	Not less than one month before the proposed transfer is due to take place.
CASH EQUIVALENTS AND TRANSFER VALUES (***Occupational Pension Schemes (Transfer Values) Regulations 1996 (SI 1996/1847), reg 11, Sch 1***) **(all schemes)**			
The '*Sch 1* Information', ie: Whether a cash equivalent is available or would be available if pensionable service were to terminate and, if so: ● an estimate of the amount calculated in accordance with *reg 7* or *7E* on the basis that the members' pensionable service terminated on a particular date; ● the accrued rights to which it relates; ● whether any part of the estimated part of the cash equivalent is attributable to additional benefits awarded at the discretion of the trustees or which will be awarded if their established custom continues unaltered;	Active members of any scheme. Deferred members of a money purchase scheme.	To be provided by the trustees in writing.	As soon as reasonably practicable and, in any event, within three months of the member's request (such request not being one made less than 12 months since the last occasion when the information was provided).

To be disclosed	Disclosure to	Form of disclosure	When
● if the estimated amount of the cash equivalent included a reduction of the initial cash equivalent: – a statement of that fact; – a statement of the amount of the reduction; – an explanation of the reason for the reduction which must refer to the paragraph of *Sch 1A* relied upon; – an estimate of the date (if any) by which an unreduced cash equivalent will be available; – a statement of the member's right to obtain further estimates. Whether any transfer value is available or would be so available if the member's pensionable service were to terminate and if so: ● an estimate of its amount; ● the accrued rights to which it relates; ● whether any part of the estimated amount of the transfer value is attributable to additional benefits (wholly or only to part) which have been or will be awarded at the discretion of the trustees:			

To be disclosed	Disclosure to	Form of disclosure	When
– if the estimated amount of the transfer value has been reduced to an amount which is less than it otherwise would be because of an actuary's opinion that the scheme's assets are insufficient to meet its liabilities in full, then a statement of that fact and an explanation and an estimate of the date (if any) by which it will be possible to make available a transfer value the amount of which is not so reduced, and a statement of the member's rights to obtain further estimates. Where information is made available under *Sch 1* to a member of a salary related scheme, the information also includes: – a statement that the Financial Services Authority, the Pensions Regulator and the Pensions Advisory Service provide information about transfers that may assist the member in deciding whether to transfer;			

To be disclosed	Disclosure to	Form of disclosure	When
– if the scheme is an eligible scheme as defined in *PA 2004, s 126*, confirmation that the Scheme is so eligible and that the Board of the Pension Protection Fund exists; – a recommendation that the member should take financial advice before making decisions about transfers.			
The statement of entitlement to a guaranteed cash equivalent shall be accompanied by: ● '*Sch 1* information' in relation to any cash equivalent of or transfer value in relation to the member's money purchase benefits (if any) under the scheme calculated by reference to the guarantee date; ● A statement as to: – whether, for what reasons and by what amount the member's initial cash equivalent has been reduced as well as the paragraph of *Sch 1A* which has been relied upon, together with an estimate of the date by which it will be possible to make available a guaranteed cash equivalent which is not so reduced;	An active or deferred member whose membership has terminated at least one year before normal retirement age.	Statement/report in writing.	Within a period of ten working days after the 'guarantee date' (which must be within a period of three months beginning with the date of the member's application).

To be disclosed	Disclosure to	Form of disclosure	When
– the terms and effect of *reg 6(3)* (no right to make an application for a guaranteed statement of entitlement within 12 months of the last application); – an explanation of the member's right to take the guaranteed cash equivalent and the need for that member to submit a written application to do so within three months beginning on the guarantee date; – an explanation that in exceptional circumstances the guaranteed cash equivalent may be reduced and that member will be so informed if that is the case. – where the scheme has begun to wind up, an explanation that the value of the member's guaranteed cash equivalent may be affected by the winding up and that a decision to take a guaranteed cash equivalent should be given careful consideration.			

To be disclosed	Disclosure to	Form of disclosure	When
● Notification of any member's reduction or increase in guaranteed cash equivalent under *regulation 9* including: – the reasons for and the amount of the reduction/increase; – *[an estimate of the date (if any) by which an unreduced guaranteed cash equivalent will be available;]* – indication of the paragraph of *regulation 9* which has been relied upon; – a statement explaining that the member has a further three months from the date on which the member was informed of the reduction/increase to make a written application to take the guaranteed cash equivalent as reduced/increased.	Relevant member.	In writing.	Within ten days of reduction/increase (excluding weekends, Christmas Day, New Year's Day and Good Friday).

To be disclosed	Disclosure to	Form of disclosure	When
WINDING-UP (*Occupational Pension Schemes (Winding Up) Regulations 1996 (SI 1996/3126), reg 11*) **(all schemes)**			
Details of any determination made: ● to defer winding-up the scheme; ● as to the time when the priorities into which the liability in respect of any person falls under *PA 1995, s 73(4)* is fixed; or ● as to the time when the amounts or descriptions of liabilities of the scheme are to be determined for the purposes of any rule of the scheme setting out the scheme's winding-up priorities.	The members of the scheme. Any other person whose entitlement to payment of a pension or any other benefit under the scheme has arisen.	In writing.	Within one month of the date that the determination is made.
MODIFICATION ON WINDING-UP (*PA 1995, s 71A*; ***Occupational Pension Schemes (Winding Up Notices and Reports etc) Regulations 2002 (SI 2002/459), reg 8***)			
Where the trustees or managers make an application to the Pensions Regulator to modify the scheme in accordance with *PA 1995, 71A*, a notice setting out: For all recipients: (a) the modification requested; (b) the effects, if any, which the modification would or might have: (i) on benefits under the scheme that are in payment at the time of the application, and	Members for whom they have a current address. The insolvency practitioner (if the modification would reduce the value of the assets which might otherwise be distributed to the employer on the winding-up) or, as the case may be, the official receivers.	In writing.	Before the trustees or manager make the application to the Pensions Regulator.

To be disclosed	Disclosure to	Form of disclosure	When
(ii) on benefits under it which are or may be payable at a later time; (c) the reason for requesting the modification; (d) whether the modification would reduce the value of the assets which might otherwise be distributed to that employer on winding up; (e) the date of the notice; (f) an explanation that a member may make representations to the Regulator about the modification within one month from the date of the notice; In addition, for the insolvency practitioner: (g) whether any previous application has been made to the court or to the Pensions Regulator for an order to make the modification requested by the application or any similar modification (only to be included in notice to insolvency practitioner).			

To be disclosed	Disclosure to	Form of disclosure	When
BASIC INFORMATION ABOUT PENSIONS AND DIVORCE (***Pensions on Divorce etc (Provision of Information) Regulations 2000 (SI 2000/1048), reg 2***)			
• A valuation of pension rights or benefits accrued under the member's pension arrangement not available to the spouse or civil partner of the member. • A statement that on the member's request or pursuant to a court order a valuation of pension rights or benefits will be provided to the member or the court. • A statement summarising the way in which the valuation is calculated. • The pension benefits which are included in the valuation. • Whether the trustees offer membership to a person entitled to a pension credit and, if so, the types of benefit available. • Whether the trustees intend to discharge their liability for a pension credit other than by offering membership. • A schedule of charges which will apply.	Member. Member's spouse or civil partner. Court.		• On request within three months beginning with the date the trustees receive the request or order for the provision of information; or • Within six weeks if the member has notified the trustees on the date of the request or order that the information is needed in connection with proceedings commenced under any of the provisions referred to in *WRPA 1999, s 23(1)(a)*; or • Within such shorter period as the court may specify; or • If the request does not include a request for a valuation or if the member's spouse or civil partner requests the information under *Pensions on Divorce etc (Provision of Information) Regulations 2000, reg 2(3)*, within one month of the date of receipt of the request or court order.

To be disclosed	Disclosure to	Form of disclosure	When
• Any other information relevant to any power relating to matters specified in *Welfare Reform and Pensions Act 1999* (*WRPA 1999*), *s 23(1)(a)* and which is not specified in *Occupational Pension Schemes (Disclosure of Information) Regulations 1996 (SI 1996/1655), Sch 1* or 2, or *Personal Pension Schemes (Disclosure of Information) Regulations 1987 (SI 1987/1110), Sch 1* or 2 (available to the court only). At the same time as providing the information set out above, the trustees may supply information specified in *Pensions on Divorce etc (Provision of Information) Regulations 2000, reg 4*.			
DIVORCE (***Pensions on Divorce etc (Provision of Information) Regulations 2000 (SI 2000/1048), reg 4***) **(all schemes)**			
• The full name of the pension arrangement and address to which any order or provision should be sent. • In the case of an occupational pension scheme whether the scheme is winding-up and, if so, the date of commencement of the winding-up and the name and address of the trustees who are dealing with the winding-up.	To the member or the court.		Within 21 days of the date when the trustees received notification that a Pension Sharing Order or provision may be made or if later a date set by the court or, if the court has specified a date which is more than 21 days, by that date.

To be disclosed	Disclosure to	Form of disclosure	When
• In the case of an occupational pension scheme whether a cash equivalent of the member's rights would be reduced if calculated on the date the trustees received notification that a pension sharing order or provision may be made. • Whether the person responsible for the pension arrangement is aware of the member's rights being subject to any of the following and, if so, to specify which: – any order or provision specified in *WRPA 1999, s 28(1)*; – an order under *Matrimonial Causes Act 1973, s 23* (so far as it includes provision made by virtue of *s 25B* or *25C* of that Act); – an order under *Family Law (Scotland) Act 1985, s 12A(2)* or *(3)* which relates to benefits or future benefits to which the member is entitled under the pension arrangement; – an order under *Matrimonial Causes (Northern Ireland) Order 1978, art 25* so far as it includes provision made by virtue of art *27B* or *27C* of that order;			

To be disclosed	Disclosure to	Form of disclosure	When
– a forfeiture order; – a bankruptcy order; – An order of sequestration on a member's estate or the making of an appointment on his estate of a judicial factor under *Solicitors (Scotland) Act 1980, s 41.* ● Whether the member's rights under the pension arrangement include any rights which are not shareable. ● If not provided previously, whether the trustees require any charges to be paid and, if so, whether prior to the commencement of the implementation period those are required to be paid in full, or the proportion which is required. ● Whether the trustees may levy additional charges and, if so, the scale which is likely to be charged. ● Whether the member is a trustee of the pension arrangement. ● Whether the trustees may request information about the member's state of health if a pension sharing order or provision were made.			

To be disclosed	Disclosure to	Form of disclosure	When
• Whether the trustees require information in addition to that specified in *Pensions on Divorce etc (Provision of Information) Regulations 2000, reg 5* in order to implement the pension sharing order or provision.			
PROVISION OF INFORMATION AFTER THE DEATH OF THE PERSON ENTITLED TO THE PENSION CREDIT (*Pensions on Divorce etc (Provision of Information) Regulations 2000 (SI 2000/1048), reg 6*)			
Where the person entitled to the pension credit dies before the trustees have discharged their liability, the trustees must notify relevant persons: • how the trustees intend to discharge their liability; • whether the trustees intend to recover charges and, if so, a schedule of those charges; • a list of any further information required in order to discharge their liability.	Any person whom the trustees consider should be notified.	In writing.	Within 21 days of receipt of the notification of death.

To be disclosed	Disclosure to	Form of disclosure	When
PROVISION OF INFORMATION AFTER RECEIVING A PENSION SHARING ORDER (***Pensions on Divorce etc (Provision of Information) Regulations 2000 (SI 2000/1048), reg 7***)			
On receipt of a pension sharing order or a provision: ● a notice of charges; ● a list of information relating to the transferor or the transferee or (where *Pensions on Divorce etc (Provision of Information) Regulations 2000. reg 6(1)* applies a person other than the person entitled to the pension credit, which has been requested already, which the trustees need or which remains outstanding); ● a notice of implementation; or ● a statement of why the trustees are unable to implement the pension sharing order or agreement.	The transferor or transferee or where *Pensions on Divorce etc (Provision of Information) Regulations 2000, reg 6(1)* applies to the person other than the person entitled to the pension credit (referred to in *Pension Sharing (Implementation and Discharge of Liability) Regulations 2000 (SI 2000/1053), reg 6*).	In writing.	Within 21 days of receipt of the pension sharing order or provision or, in the case of a notice of implementation, the later of the days specified in *WRPA 1999, s 34(1)(a)* and *(b)*.
PROVISION OF INFORMATION AFTER IIMPLEMENTATION OF AN ORDER (***Pensions on Divorce etc (Provision of Information) Regulations 2000 (SI 2000/1048), reg 8***)			
Notice of discharge of liability including: *(where the transferor's pension is not in payment)* ● the value of the transferor's accrued rights on a cash equivalent basis;	Transferor or transferee or the person entitled to the pension credit by virtue of *Pension Sharing (Implementation and Discharge of Liability) Regulations 2000 (SI 2000/1053), reg 6.*		Within 21 days of the date of discharge of the pension credit.

To be disclosed	Disclosure to	Form of disclosure	When
• the value of the pension debit; • any amount deducted by way of charges; • the value of the transferor's rights after the deductions of the pension debit and charges; • the transfer day; **OR** *(where the transferor's pension is in payment)* • the value of the transferor's benefits on a cash equivalent basis; • the value of the pension debit; • the amount of the pension which was in payment before the pension credit liability was discharged; • the amount of pension payable following the deduction of the pension debit; • the transfer day; • the amount of any unpaid charges; • how those charges will be recovered; **OR** *(in the case of a transferee whose pension is not in payment and who will become a member)* • the value of the pension credit; • the amount deducted by way of charges;			

To be disclosed	Disclosure to	Form of disclosure	When
• the value of the pension credit after deduction of charges; • the transfer day; • any periodical charges to be made including when and how those charges will be recovered; • information concerning membership of the pension arrangement which is relevant to the transferee; **OR** *(in the case of the transferee who is transferring his pension credit rights out of the pension arrangement from which those rights were derived)* • the value of the pension credit; • the amount of any charges deducted; • the value of the pension credit after the deduction; • the transfer day; • details of the pension arrangement including its name, address, reference number, telephone number and where available the business facsimile number and e-mail address to which the pension credit has been transferred: **OR**			

To be disclosed	**Disclosure to**	**Form of disclosure**	**When**
(in the case of a transferee who has reached normal benefit age on the transfer day and whose pension credit liability has been discharged) ● the amount of pension credit benefit to be paid to the transferee; ● the date when the pension credit benefit is to be paid to the transferee; ● the transfer date; ● details of any unpaid charges and how those charges will be recovered; **OR** *(in the case of a person entitled to the pension credit by virtue of Pension Sharing (Implementation and Discharge of Liability) Regulations 2000 (SI 2000/1053), reg 6)* ● the value of the pension credit rights; ● any amount deducted by way of charges; ● the value of the pension credit after deduction of charges; ● the transfer day; ● details of any unpaid charges, including how and when those charges will be recovered.			

To be disclosed	Disclosure to	Form of disclosure	When
PROVISION OF INFORMATION AFTER RECEPT OF AN EARMARKING ORDER (***Pensions on Divorce etc (Provision of Information) Regulations 2000 (SI 2000/1048), reg 10***) (***all schemes***)			
● If a member's pension is not in payment, a list of circumstances in respect of any changes which the member or spouse or civil partner must notify to the trustees. ● (except in Scotland) If the order is made in respect of a member whose pension is in payment the notice will include: – the value of the pension rights or benefit of the member; – the amount of the member's pension after implementation of the order; – the first date when a pension pursuant to the order is to be made; – a list of the circumstances which the member and spouse or civil partner must notify to the trustees; – (to member only) the amount of the member's pension currently in payment and the amount of the member's pension after the order has been implemented.	● Member. ● Spouse or civil partner.	Notice in writing.	Within 21 days of receipt of the order.

To be disclosed	Disclosure to	Form of disclosure	When
• In any event: – the amount of any charges not yet paid by the member or spouse or civil partner in respect of the provision of information and how those charges will be recovered including the date when payment is required in whole or in part, the sums payable by the member and spouse or civil partner respectively and whether the sum will be deducted from payments of pension to the member or from payments for the spouse or civil partner.			
INFORMATION ABOUT PENSIONS AND DIVORCE AND DISSOLUTION OF A CIVIL PARTNERSHIP: VALUATION OF PENSION BENEFITS (***Pensions on Divorce etc (Provision of Information) Regulations 2000 (SI 2000/1048), reg 3***)			
Information set out in *Occupational Pension Schemes (Transfer Values) Regulations 1996 (SI 1996/1847), reg 11, Sch 1.*	Any member.	In writing.	As soon as practicable and always within three months of the request.

To be disclosed	Disclosure to	Form of disclosure	When
DISCLOSURE OF INFORMATION TO MEMBERS (*Stakeholder Pension Schemes Regulations 2000 (SI 2000/1403), reg 18*) **(all schemes)**			
For as far as that information relates to that statement year or to the part of that statement year beginning with the first day of that statement year (whether or not that day is earlier than the day on which he becomes a member) and ending with the time at which he so ceases: ● the value of the member's rights under the scheme on the day before the first day of the statement year, being an amount which is not less than the cash equivalent of those rights on that date; ● the value of the member's rights on the last day of the statement year, being an amount which is not less than the cash equivalent of those rights on that day or where he ceases during the statement year to be a member, at the time immediately prior to the time at which he so ceases, being an amount which is not less than the cash equivalent of those rights at the time immediately prior to the time at which he so ceases (and the amount of the value that is attributable to investment gains or losses made or sustained);	Member for all or part of a statement year.	In writing.	Within three months of the end of that statement year or where he ceases during that statement year to be a member, or from the time he ceases to be a member to within three months of the end of that statement year.

To be disclosed	Disclosure to	Form of disclosure	When
• the amount of each contribution made by or on behalf of the member and the date on which it was received; • the amount of each contribution made by any employer and the date on which it was received; • except where contributions referred to in sub-paragraphs (d) and (e) are increased by the trustees or manager in anticipation of a payment to the scheme by the Inland Revenue by way of tax relief in respect of the member, the amount of each such payment by the Inland Revenue and the date on which it was received; • the amount of each payment to the scheme by way of minimum contributions in respect of the member and the date on which it was received; • the amount of each payment made to the scheme by way of minimum payments in respect of the member and the date on which it was received;			

To be disclosed	Disclosure to	Form of disclosure	When
• the amount of each payment made to the scheme under *PSA 1993, s 42A(3)* in respect of the member and the date on which it was received; • the amount of any transfer payment made to the scheme in respect of the member, the name of the scheme or arrangement from which the payment was made and the date on which it was made; • any amount credited to the member's account in respect of a credit within the meaning of *s 29* (pension sharing: creation of pension debits and credits); • any reduction under *s 31* (pension sharing: reduction of benefit), or any enactment in force in Northern Ireland corresponding to that section, in the benefits or future benefits to which the member is entitled under the scheme; • any contributions refunded under the provisions of *Income and Corporation Taxes Act 1988, Part XIV, Chapter IV* (pension schemes, social security benefits, life annuities etc);			

To be disclosed	Disclosure to	Form of disclosure	When
● any amount paid to the member in accordance with *Finance Act 2004, Sch 28, para 7* or *21* (as the case may be); ● any other amount deducted from the member's account, the nature of the deduction and the date on which it was made; ● the total amount of any part of any of the contributions and payments which has not been credited to the member's account and the manner in which that amount has been used; ● the member's date of birth used in determining the appropriate age-related percentage for the purposes of *PSA 1993, s 42A* and the name and address of whom to contact should that date be incorrect; ● where the whole or any part of the member's rights under the scheme is represented by rights in a with-profits fund;			

To be disclosed	Disclosure to	Form of disclosure	When
• the principles adopted in allocating rights under that fund, including the extent of any smoothing of investment returns and the levels of any guarantees; • the principles which will be adopted in allocating such rights if the member's rights under the scheme cease to be represented by rights in that fund; • in relation to any reduction relating to the reduction of members' rights, the rate, expressed as an annual percentage rate, at which, and the period in relation to which, deductions giving rise to that reduction were made, or where such deductions were made in relation to different periods at different rates; • each rate, expressed as an annual percentage rate, at which those deductions were made; and • the period in relation to which they were made at that rate.			

To be disclosed	Disclosure to	Form of disclosure	When
DISCLOSURE REQUIREMENTS AND PENALTIES (*Occupational Pension Schemes (Independent Trustee) Regulations 2005 (SI 2005/703), reg 13*)			
The trustee and the independent trustee must provide: ● their name and address; ● the scale of fees chargeable; ● details of amounts charged to the scheme by the trustees in the past 12 months.	Every member and or relevant trade union (in relation to the first point, as of course, within a reasonable period of appointment). Every member, prospective member or relevant trade union (in relation to all three points).	In writing.	As of course, within a reasonable period of appointment. Within a reasonable period following the request (unless the same information was provided to the same person or trade union in the 12 months prior to the request being made).
NOTIFICATION OF RIGHT TO CASH TRANSFER SUM OR CONTRIBUTION REFUND (*PA 2004, s 264*, **inserting** *s 101AC* **into** *PSA 1993*)			
Information adequate to explain the nature of the right acquired by him and how he may exercise the right and such other information as may be prescribed. The statement must specify, in particular in relation to the cash transfer sum to which the member acquires a right, its amount and the permitted ways in which the member can use it, the amount of the contribution refund to which the member so acquires a right, and the last day on which the member may exercise the right.	A member whose pensionable service has terminated.	A statement in writing.	Within a reasonable period after the termination. This should usually be within three months.

To be disclosed	Disclosure to	Form of disclosure	When
INFORMATION AND CONSULTATION OF EMPLOYEES (***Information and Consultation of Employees Regulations 2004 (SI 2004/3426)***)			
Provision of information on: ● decisions likely to lead to substantial changes in work organisation or in contractual relations, eg introduction of, or a change to, compulsory retirement age or changes to an occupational pension scheme but only where there was a contractual right to participate in the scheme; ● recent development of the undertakings' activities and economic situation; ● the situation, structure and probable development of employment within the undertaking. *Regulation 17A* excludes certain consultation where it is required under the *Occupational and Personal Pension Schemes (Consultation by Employers and Miscellaneous Amendment) Regulations 2006* (see below).	Information and consultation representatives in organisations with 150 or more from 6 April 2005, with 100 or more from 6 April 2007 and with 50 or more from 6 April 2008.	Ensure that the method and content of the consultation are appropriate. Consult on the basis of the information supplied to the information and consultation representatives and in such a way as to enable the information and consultation representatives to meet the employer at the relevant level of management depending on the subject under discussion and to obtain a reasoned response from the employer to any such opinion. The employer must notify the information and consultation representatives in writing that it is complying with its duty under the legislation.	Either in line with any existing information or consultation agreements, or a negotiated information and consultation agreements or, in default, with appropriate timing. Must be given at such time, in such fashion and with such content as are appropriate to enable, in particular, the information and consultation representatives to conduct an adequate study and, where necessary, to prepare for consultation.

To be disclosed	Disclosure to	Form of disclosure	When
CONSULTATION BY EMPLOYERS REQUIREMENT (***Occupational and Personal Pension Schemes (Consultation by Employers and Miscellaneous Amendment) Regulations 2006 (SI 2006/349)***)			
For employers with occupational pension schemes, the listed changes caught by the consultation requirement include: ● increasing the normal retirement age; ● closing to new members; ● stopping accrual of all benefits; ● removing an employer's liability to make contributions; ● introducing member contributions or increasing them; ● changing any final salary benefits to money purchase benefits; ● changing the basis for determining the rate of future accrual of final salary benefits; ● reducing any other future accruals in a final salary scheme; ● reducing employer contributions for money purchase benefits.	The employer must embark on a consultation process with one or more of the following: ● a trade union representative recognised for collective bargaining purposes; ● an elected information and consultation representative (elected under the *Information and Consultation of Employees Regulations 2004 (SI 2004/3426)*; or In the absence of the appointment of one of the above, the employer must consult with representatives elected under the pension consultation requirement specifically in relation to the proposed pension changes.	Consultation but employer must provide written information about the proposed changes.	At least two months before the change takes effect.

To be disclosed	Disclosure to	Form of disclosure	When
For employers with personal pension schemes where the contributions are payable under direct payment arrangements, the changes which are caught include: ● ceasing employer contributions to a scheme; ● reducing employer contributions; ● increasing member contributions.	The employer must consult directly with affected members of the pension scheme (which includes employees who are not yet members of the scheme but who are or will become eligible to join) where there are no representatives in place for direct consultation. All employees affected by the proposed changes must be consulted except those in: ● public service pension schemes; ● small occupational pension schemes, ie a scheme with fewer than 12 members where all the members are trustees of the scheme and either the rules of the scheme provide that all decisions are made only by the trustees who are members of the scheme by unanimous agreement or the scheme has a trustee who is independent in relation to the scheme for the purposes of *PA 1995, s 23* and is registered in the register maintained by the Authority in accordance with regulations;		

To be disclosed	Disclosure to	Form of disclosure	When
	• an occupational pension scheme with fewer than two members; and • an occupational pension scheme which is an employer-financed retirement benefits scheme. • In employment where the employer has a maximum of at least 150 employees from 6 April 2006, 100 from 6 April 2007 and 50 from 6 April 2008.		
ENROLMENT INFORMATION PROVIDED FOR THE PURPOSES OF AUTOMATIC ENROLMENT (draft *Occupational and Personal Pension Schemes (Automatic Enrolment) Regulations 2010, regs 2, 8*)			
The enrolment information, being: • a statement in the following terms 'You have been or will be automatically enrolled into a pension scheme to help you save for your retirement'; • the jobholder's automatic enrolment date; • the name, telephone number, physical and electronic contact details of the scheme into which the jobholder is to be enrolled; • the value of contributions that will be deducted from the jobholder's remuneration and made to the scheme;	Any jobholder being automatically enrolled into an occupational pension scheme or a personal pension scheme.	In writing	Within one month beginning on the jobholders automatic enrolment date.

To be disclosed	Disclosure to	Form of disclosure	When
● confirmation as to whether tax relief will be through net pay arrangements or relief at source arrangements; ● a statement that the jobholder may remain an active member of the scheme without employer interference unless the jobholder is or becomes an active member of another qualifying scheme; ● that the jobholder has a right to opt out of the scheme during the opt-out period; ● the start and end date of the opt-out period under *reg 11* or *12* applicable to the jobholder; ● that opting out can only occur through the completion of the opt-out notice and its submission to the employer; ● the source from which the opt-out notice must be obtained; ● that opting out means that the jobholder will be considered not to have become an active member of the scheme on that occasion;			

To be disclosed	Disclosure to	Form of disclosure	When
• that, after a completed opt out notice is received by the employer, any contributions paid by the jobholder will be refunded to the jobholder by the employer; • that the jobholder who opts out may opt in, in which case the employer will be required to arrange for the jobholder to become an active member of an automatic enrolment scheme once in any 12-month period; • a statement that, after the opt-out period, the jobholder may cease to make contributions towards their pension in accordance with scheme rules; • that a jobholder who opts out or who ceases active membership of an automatic enrolment scheme will be automatically re-enrolled into such a scheme by the employer in accordance with regulations made under *Pensions Act 2008, s 5*; and • details of where to obtain further information about pension and saving retirement.			

To be disclosed	Disclosure to	Form of disclosure	When
INFORMATION ON THE RIGHT TO OPT IN TO PENSION SAVING (draft ***Occupational and Personal Pension Schemes (Automatic Enrolment) Regulations 2010, reg 18***)			
● A statement that the jobholder may, by notice, require the employer to make arrangements for the jobholder to join an automatic enrolment scheme. ● A statement that the opt in notice must be in writing and be signed by the worker and where the notice is in an electronic format, include a statement confirming that the jobholder personally submitted the notice. ● A statement that the opt in notice must be given to the employer. ● Where the jobholder may become an active member of a money purchase scheme or a personal pension scheme: – a statement that the jobholder may receive a contribution from the employer and the value of that contribution in any pay reference period, and – the value of contributions which the jobholder will be required to make in any relevant pay reference period.			

To be disclosed	Disclosure to	Form of disclosure	When
• Details of where to obtain further information about pensions and saving for retirement.			
INFORMATION ON THE RIGHT TO OPT IN TO PENSION SAVING (draft *Occupational and Personal Pension Schemes (Automatic Enrolment) Regulations 2010, reg 22*)			
• A statement that the worker may, by notice, require the employer to make arrangements for the worker to join a pension scheme; • A statement that a joining notice must be in writing and be signed by the worker and where the notice is in an electronic format, include a statement confirming that the worker personally submitted the notice; • A statement that the worker may, in accordance with the scheme rules choose how much to contribute to a pension scheme; and • Details of where to obtain further information about pensions and saving for retirement.	Workers without qualifying earnings, ie less than £5,035 over the relevant pay reference period *(Pensions Act 2008, s 9)*	In writing.	Within one month of the worker first qualifying for the right to opt in under *Pensions Act 2008, s 9*.

To be disclosed	Disclosure to	Form of disclosure	When
DETAILS OF QUALIFYING SCHEME (draft ***Occupational and Personal Pension Schemes (Automatic Enrolment) Regulations 2010, reg 25*****)**			
• The name, physical location and electronic contact details of the scheme in which the jobholder is an active member. • Confirmation that the scheme of which the jobholder is an active member is a qualifying scheme. • A statement that the jobholder may remain an active member of that qualifying scheme without employer interference unless the jobholder is or becomes an active member of another qualifying scheme.	Jobholders who are active members of a qualifying scheme on the automatic enrolment date.	In writing.	Within two months after the jobholder's automatic enrolment date.
DETAILS OF JOBHOLDERS AFFECTED BY POSTPONEMENT (draft ***Occupational and Personal Pension Schemes (Automatic Enrolment) Regulations 2010, reg 39*****)**			
• Reasons for the postponement of automatic enrolment. • A statement that during the period prior to the automatic enrolment date the jobholder has no entitlement to become an active member of an automatic enrolment scheme under the Act. • The date on which automatic enrolment will commence. • Details of where to obtain further information about pensions and saving for retirement.	All jobholders whose automatic enrolment date has been postponed.	In writing.	Within one month after the postponed automatic enrolment date which applies to the jobholder.

Index

[*all references are to paragraph number*]